International Handbook of Internet Research

T0189392

Jeremy Hunsinger · Lisbeth Klastrup ·
Matthew Allen
Editors

International Handbook
of Internet Research

 Springer

Editors
Jeremy Hunsinger
Virginia Tech
Dept. Political Science
531 Major Williams Hall
Blacksburg VA 24061
USA
jhuns@vt.edu

Lisbeth Klastrup
Digital Culture and Mobile Communication
  Research Group
IT University of Copenhagen
Rued Langgaardsvej 7
DK-2300 Copenhagen S
Denmark
klastrup@itu.dk

Matthew Allen
Department of Internet Studies
School of Media, Culture and Creative Arts
Curtin University of Technology
CRICOS 00301J
Bentley WA 6102
Australia
m.allen@curtin.edu.au

ISBN 978-94-007-9395-8   ISBN 978-1-4020-9789-8 (eBook)
DOI 10.1007/978-1-4020-9789-8
Springer Dordrecht Heidelberg London New York

© Springer Science+Business Media B.V. 2010
Softcover re-print of the Hardcover 1st edition 2010
No part of this work may be reproduced, stored in a retrieval system, or transmitted in any form or by
any means, electronic, mechanical, photocopying, microfilming, recording or otherwise, without written
permission from the Publisher, with the exception of any material supplied specifically for the purpose
of being entered and executed on a computer system, for exclusive use by the purchaser of the work.

Printed on acid-free paper

Springer is part of Springer Science+Business Media (www.springer.com)

Acknowledgements

The editors would like to thank the contributors to the volumes for all their effort that they put into bringing it to completion. We would like to thank Marie, Harmen, and Maria at Springer for aiding us and being extremely patient with us.

Acknowledgements

Contents

Contributors

Barbara Adkins Queensland University of Technology, Brisbane, Queensland, Australia, b.adkins@qut.edu.au

Meredith Anderson Department of Sociology, Louisiana State University, Baton Rouge, Louisiana, USA, mande15@lsu.edu

Karen Baker Integrative Oceanography Division, SIO University of California at San Diego, La Jolla, California, USA

Naomi S. Baron Department of Language and Foreign Studies, American University, Washington, District of Columbia, USA, nbaron@american.edu

Richard A. Bartle School of Computer Science and Electronic Engineering, University of Essex, UK, rabartle@essex.ac.uk; richard@MUD.CO.UK

Hillary Bays Modyco CNRS-UMR 7114, Celith-EHESS, University Paris X & University of Cergy-Pontoise; UCP, Department de Langues, Cergy-Pontoise, hillary.bays@u-cergy.fr, hdbays@free.fr

Evangelia Berdou Research Fellow in Knowledge, Information and Communication and Social Change, Institute for Development Studies, University of Sussex, Brighton, BN1 9RE, UK, e.berdou@sussex.ac.uk

Matthijs den Besten Pôle de Recherche en Economie et Gestion, Ecole Polytechnique, Paris, France, matthijs.den-besten@polytechnique.edu

Geoffrey C. Bowker School of Information Sciences, University of Pittsburg, Pittsburgh, Pennsylvania, USA, gbowker@pitt.edu

Axel Bruns Creative Industries Faculty, Queensland University of Technology, Brisbane, Queensland, Australia, a.bruns@qut.edu.au

Dan L. Burk University of California, Irvine, California, USA, dburk@uci.edu

Julie-Anne Carroll Queensland University of Technology, Brisbane, Queensland, Australia, jm.carroll@qut.edu.au

Sean Cubitt Media and Communications Program, The University of Melbourne, Victoria, Australia, scubitt@unimelb.edu.au

Paul A. David Stanford University, Stanford, California, USA; United Nations University (UNU-MERIT), Maastricht, The Netherlands; Ecole Polytechnique & Telecom ParisTech, Paris, France, pad@stanford.edu

Nicola Döring Ilmenau University of Technology/Technische Universitaet Ilmenau Media Design and Media Psychology/Medienkonzeption und Medienpsychologie Ehrenbergstr. 29 (EAZ 2217), D-98693 Ilmenau, Germany, nicola.doering@tu-ilmenau.de

Ricardo Duque Professor of Social Studies of Science, Department of Social Studies of Science, University of Vienna, Vienna, Austria, rick.duque@univie.ac.at

Dan-Bright S. Dzorgbo Department of Sociology, University of Ghana, Legon, Accra, Ghana, ddzorgbo@yahoo.co.uk

Anders Fagerjord førsteamanuensis, Dr. Art. Undervisningsleder, Institutt for Medier og Kommunikasjon, University of Oslo, Oslo, anders.fagerjord@media.uio.no

Marcus Foth Queensland University of Technology, Brisbane, Queensland, Australia, m.foth@qut.edu.au

Suely Fragoso Universidade do Vale do Rio do Sinos (Unisinos), São Leopoldo, Rio Grande do Sul, Brazil, suely.fragoso@ymail.com

Kevin Gillan School of Social Sciences, The University of Manchester, Manchester, UK, kevin.gillan@manchester.ac.uk

Justin Harris Temple University, Philadelphia, Pennsylvania, USA, hjustin@temple.edu

Susan C. Herring School of Library and Information Science, Bloomington, Indiana, USA, herring@indiana.edu

Janine S. Hiller School of Business, Virginia Tech, Blacksburg, Virginia, USA, jhiller@vt.edu

Jeremy Hunsinger Center for Digital Discourse and Culture, Virginia Tech, Blacksburg, Virginia, USA, jhuns@vt.edu

Steve Jones Department of Communication, University of Illinois, Chicago, Illinois, USA, sjones@uic.edu

Andrea Kavanaugh Senior Research Scientist, Associate Director Center for Human Computer Interaction, Department of Computer Science, Virginia Tech, Blacksburg, Virginia, USA, kavan@vt.edu

Marjorie D. Kibby School of Humanities and Social Science, The University of Newcastle, Callaghan, Australia, marj.kibby@newcastle.edu.au

Lisbeth Klastrup Innovative Communication Research Group, IT University of Copenhagen, Copenhagen S, Denmark, klastrup@itu.dk

Arne H. Krumsvik Department of Media and Communication, University of Oslo, Oslo, Norway, a.h.krumsvik@media.uio.no

Alberto Efendy Maldonado Universidade do Vale do Rio do Sinos (Unisinos), São Leopoldo, Rio Grande do Sul, Brazil, alefma2@yahoo.com.br

Robin Mansell Department of Media and Communications, London School of Economics and Political Science, London, UK, r.e.mansell@lse.ac.uk

Rochelle Mazar Emerging Technologies Librarian, University of Toronto, Mississauga, Ontario, Canada, rochelle.mazar@utoronto.ca

Paul N. Mbatia Department of Sociology, University of Nairobi, Nairobi, Kenya, pmbatia2002@yahoo.com

Graham Meikle Department of Film, Media & Journalism, University of Stirling, Stirling, FK9 4LA, Scotland, graham.meikle@stir.ac.uk

B. Paige Miller University of Wisconsin, River Falls, Wisconsin, USA, paige.miller@uwrf.edu

Florence Millerand Professeure, Département de communication sociale et publique, Faculté de communication, Université du Québec à Montréal, Case postale 8888, succursale Centre-ville, Montréal, Quebec, Canada, millerand.florence@uqam.ca

Bonnie Nardi Department of Informatics, University of California, Irvine, UK, nardi@ics.uci.edu

Susanna Paasonen Helsinki Collegium for Advanced Studies, University of Helsinki, Helsinki, Finland, susanna.paasonen@helsinki.fi

Antony Palackal Loyola College of Social Sciences, Thiruvananthapuram, India, antonypalackal@yahoo.com

Manuel A. Perez-Quinones Department of Communication, Virginia Tech, Blacksburg, Virginia, USA, perez@cs.vt.edu

Jenny Pickerill Department of Geography, University of Leicester, Leicester, UK, j.pickerill@leicester.ac.uk

Jill Walker Rettberg Department of Linguistic, Literary and Aesthetic Studies, University of Bergen, Bergen, Norway, jill.walker.rettberg@uib.no

David Ribes Communication, Culture and Technology, Georgetown University, Washington, District of Columbia, USA, dr273@georgetown.edu

William Sanders Director, Arts Initiative and Blacksburg Electronic Village, Communications Network Services, Suite 312, Blacksburg, Virginia, USA

David Savat Humanities and Social Sciences, The University of Western Australia, Perth, Australia, Savat@cyllene.uwa.edu.au

Ralph Schroeder Oxford Internet Institute, University of Oxford, Oxford, UK, ralph.schroeder@oii.ox.ac.uk

Wesley Shrum Department of Sociology, Louisiana State University, Baton Rouge, Louisiana, USA, wshrum@vt.edu

Malin Sveningsson Elm Department of Media and Communication studies, Karlstad University, Karlstad, Sweden, malin.sveningsson@kau.se

John C. Tedesco Department of Communication, Virginia Tech, Blacksburg, Virginia, USA, tedesco@vt.edu

Lisbeth Thorlacius Institute of Communication, University of Roskilde, Roskilde, Denmark, lisbetht@ruc.dk

Frank Webster Department of Sociology, City University, London, UK, F.Webster@city.ac.uk

Michele Willson Department of Internet Studies, School of Media, Culture and Creative Arts, Curtin University of Technology, Perth, Western Australia, m.willson@curtin.edu.au

Marcus Antonius Ynalvez Department of Behavioral Sciences, Texas A&M International University, Laredo, Texas, USA, mynalvez@tamiu.edu

Michael Zimmer School of Information Studies, University of Wisconsin-Milwaukee, Milwaukee, Wisconsin, USA, zimmerm@uwm.edu

The New Media, the New Meanwhile, and the Same Old Stories

Steve Jones

We make some of the same claims for the internet that we had made for media that preceded it. It will improve education; it will supplant learning. It will aid terrorism; it will encourage mutual understanding; it will bring people together; it will isolate us. The internet has been pigeonholed into the same discourse that has surrounded media moral panics since movies and comic books were blamed for the decline of America's youth.

But no matter how much one tries, as a medium the internet refuses to be pigeonholed. The adage that the internet is "a medium of mediums" is now more than ever true, as it is used to broadcast video, radio, news, voice, and indeed most all of the communication that had once been given its own place in the panoply of electronic media. Why not, therefore, study video online as we had studied it before the internet's spread? Why not study online news just as print news has been studied?

While there may be some reasons to do so, particularly for comparative purposes and because there is much that is valuable about existing methods and theories, I think we rightly sense there is something special about these uses of media when they occur via the internet, computer and, increasingly, mobile devices, rather than via the media that had once delivered them. Just the mind-boggling scale of the internet makes the media experience different. Never have so many, near and far, had access to so much information, and to so many others, and so quickly.

It is along those dimensions (information, people, distance, time) that we undertake, unsurprisingly, most of our studies of internet phenomena. But is there anything particular about the internet that the study of it will give us new or improved insight into human matters? Or is it another means of telling the same stories about people, places, and events that humanists and social scientists have told for years, decades, centuries?

Not long before his death in 2006, James Carey wrote a couple of essays that took the internet seriously (even if they did not take it as their starting point). In one essay he noted that the internet "has never arrested my imagination as some

S. Jones (✉)
Department of Communication, University of Illinois. Chicago, Illinois, USA
e-mail: sjones@uic.edu

older technologies have" (2005, p. 444). Perhaps we should not be surprised. By the time the internet became widespread the magic of the media had disappeared. Older technologies' introductions were often attended by wonder, amazement, even awe. Electricity, perhaps the first "medium of mediums," though harnessed for commercial and consumer use, continued to draw rapturous attention from poets, pundits, and ordinary individuals. Occasionally during the early years of what are now considered "old" media, some technologies were accorded magical or mystical powers (for a fascinating discussion of these phenomena see *Haunted Media* (2000) by Jeffrey Sconce). But Carey was always one to decenter the object of study, and his decentering of the internet is what gives his observations of its consequences a depth of context lacking in more mundane efforts to think about the internet. In the case of Carey's efforts it is clear he is less thinking about the internet and more thinking through it, to ascertain its presence in the social, cultural, political, and economic contexts of its time.

The main context within which Carey situated the internet's ascendance was its growth at a time of rising nationalism. At the end of an essay titled "The internet and the End of the National Communication System," Carey noted that

> The internet is at the center of the integration of a new media ecology which transforms the structural relations among older media such (as) print and broadcast and integrates them to a new center around the defining technologies of computer and satellite. The economic struggle among firms attempting to control and dominate this complex is the outer and visible edge of deeper transformations in the structure of nations and other forms of social relations. This new media ecology develops in relation to new physical ecology among peoples represented by world-wide migrations over national borders, the formation of diasporic groups and what we might call the diaspora of the internet itself wherein new social groupings are formed and organized. In turn, and at the cultural level, there is a struggle over new patterns and forms of identity, new representations of nations and transnational associations, and the eruption of "identity politics." The end point of all of these changes is quite uncertain. . . .We should remind ourselves that the culminating event of the communications revolution of the 1890s came when the guns of August sounded in 1914 and the twentieth century really began. (1998, p. 34).

Obviously there is a lot packed into this single (abridged) summary paragraph. The most interesting element is the somewhat understated notion of a "diaspora of the internet." Perhaps the ongoing processes of forming, coming, and going that characterize online communities are less like the mythic community-building so often claimed for them and more like processes of migration and immigration, but without the usual risks attendant to moving one's self, family, and/or possessions. To put it another way, the internet may provide a reconception of mobility that on the one hand can be understood better by re-examining what we know about migration, immigration, and the processes of moving (whether across town or across the globe) and on the other hand those processes of mobility may be better understood in contemporary times if we take into consideration the internet's role in them. How has diaspora changed among those who have internet access? How has immigration changed with internet access (and with other new media now available, such as mobile phones and inexpensive long distance calling)?

Carey's last essays were more forcefully concerned with questions of borders going up and coming down, and of border crossings, than any of his previous essays. Carey found the rhetoric of convergence remarkably similar to the rhetoric of the "electrical sublime" he critiqued two decades previously (1970a, 1970b):

> The global village created by communications technology has turned out to be a rather peculiar place. It is not a place of convergence where the cultures of the world arrive at some omega point of agreement and identity. Everything has risen: Communications and transportation have uprooted human cultures and set them in motion once again. Yet nothing has converged: These cultures are in motion in their infinite variety and painful diversity. There are days when we wish for the dangerous certitude of squared-off countries pitted against one another – the United States versus the Soviet Union. However, today we encounter collage societies barely hanging together, where host and migrant cultures leak into one another. The very technology that is bringing us together physically and imaginatively is just as assuredly driving us apart. (1993, pp. 182–183)

It is not hard to show a clear trajectory from this 1993 text (from a speech given in 1992) to Carey's last published work that shows a preoccupation with but one question: How do we get along with one another? One way is by telling stories we wish to be true. That is not to say that there is anything delusional about discourse. Rather, it is that discourse is a means by which negotiation of social relations occurs, and as such is on the one hand fluid and on the other hand occurring in anticipation and through imagination of a desired goal (which itself may be fluid).

In his book *Imagined Communities*, Benedict Anderson noted that in the eighteenth century two new "forms of imagining" arose, the newspaper and the novel, that enabled the ascendance of national identities. These two forms are particularly interesting for their blending of fact and fiction. Subsequent media reiterated national identity through form and substance, medium and message, but relied ultimately on the telling of a story. The internet shares this reliance on storytelling. It is in some sense a storytelling machine. It is a means by which we create and share our stories, our selves, our hopes, our desires. And, as Anderson noted of the novel, even more so the internet, as a storytelling machine, relies on a "complex gloss upon the word 'meanwhile'" (1983, p. 30). The newspaper brought the novel's sense of simultaneity out of fiction and into fact. It brought to daily consciousness the omnipresent sense that there were things happening elsewhere, beyond the horizon, which might have consequences for us and to which we might pay attention. It brought, in other words, an early (and imaginary) version of what is now known as "multitasking," communicating via multiple media with multiple people at the same time.

While most thinking about the internet has focused on its scale in relation to space and distance, little has been said about its scale in relation to time. The sense an internet user has of simultaneity and interconnection is akin to that of the reader of a novel who presumes connections between characters, places, and events or that of the newspaper reader who takes for granted that the news stories reported in the day's edition all took place at about the same time. It is not the conception of time electronic mass media, particularly television, had fostered, when one had the sense that "the whole world was watching" meant something not about surveillance but about viewing an event on TV at the same time as millions of others. For the reader of a novel action occurs during "novel time," an indeterminate and infinitely "pause-able" time marked by reading. For an internet user, however, action occurs during real time, but it is never quite clear how the user's time synchronizes with that of another user. In cases of synchronous communication such as when using IM it is still not clear to what degree one has the other user's attention. Most internet users' experience of others is asynchronous (anecdotally evident by the surprise one often feels when the passing back and forth of e-mail messages seems synchronous). It is this asynchronous passage of time that most strongly marks internet use. Every choice about attending to an e-mail, web page, blog, IM, etc., is a choice to not attend to another message and thus to not attend to another person (with obvious exceptions noted, such as automated e-mail). Multitasking can only go so far to alleviate the sense that as one reads or composes an e-mail message there is, meanwhile, another message or posting or site that might be missed. The strongest feeling an internet user has is not one of overcoming space (perhaps we now take it for granted that the internet has made distance merely a physical concern?) but of being unable to overcome time. It seems as if the speed of internet communication has enabled the temporal compression of communication in a way that allows one to do more in the present, to get more into the moment, into "now." But now is a very short time, one quickly senses, and the greater the effort to maximize it, the shorter it seems, and the greater the sense of its passing, usually unnoticed.

It is worth emphasizing that every decision about how to spend one's time and about where to turn one's attention is also a decision about not paying attention to something or someone else and not spending time on or with something or someone else. The internet has accelerated the rate at which such decisions are made and gave practical form to the concept of "networked individualism" (Wellman et al., 2003) by emphasizing linking, connection, as the instrumentality of choice. But as Carey wrote about the new forms of communication in the late nineteenth century, we do not yet know the consequences of our newfound instrumentality:

> The 1890s appears to be a moment when people actively shed their past, shed ways of being and belonging, and created a society in motion that lacked a clear sense of where it was going or what it would be when it got there. These were moments organized by media, defined by media, commented upon by media, formed within media or at least as responses to new conditions of social life brought about in part by new media.

> The 1890s also involved kicking over the narrative structures of the past, of searching for a new metanarrative within which to tell the story of the modern. (1998, p. 33)

It would be simple and somewhat satisfying (and quite possibly accurate) to note that 100 years later, due to the quick and widespread adoption of the internet and the world wide web in the 1990s, that a similar process was under way.

However, it is too soon to know just what narrative structures are being kicked over and to know what new metanarrative is being crafted. One dimension of the new narrative is most likely about community and the individual, about how we get along with one another. The general sense we have of community is still that it's "a good thing," which elides the reality that every community is at once inclusive and exclusive. By making community the focus of concerns (if not making it an object of study) one is set on a path that takes focus away from the individual, and there is no particularly good way to understand internet users in an aggregate form. Our efforts to categorize users, whether quantitative or qualitative, avoid the reality of a medium that permits an individuality greater than other electronic media and puts people together in groups of our own making who would in all likelihood never consider themselves able to be conjoined. Behavior is one thing, a sense of belonging is another. We can witness and possibly measure the former; the latter remains ephemeral and difficult to express, much less measure.

Another dimension of the new metanarrative being crafted is one of narrative itself. As I mentioned, the internet is a storytelling machine. With old media those who told stories were set apart in society, as poets, journalists, singers, artists. With new media anyone can tell a story. The locus of creation and control of new narratives has thus shifted. As Carey contended in a passage I quoted earlier, the "new media ecology develops in relation to new physical ecology among peoples represented by world-wide migrations over national borders, the formation of diasporic groups and by what we might call the diaspora of the internet itself wherein new social groupings are formed and organized" (1998, p. 34). Despite having had over 100 years to observe and learn since the last communications revolution, when the merger of media and electricity formed the foundation for modern media, we seem to be no better prepared to make sense of the present one. It is crucial that we find ways to understand the shared and multiple realities of those immersed in this new media ecology, difficult as it may be to do so since we as researchers are also always already immersed in it. We must listen to the new stories being told in a new medium of mediums. If we do not we will not comprehend or understand the shifting power relations that are already making themselves visible in new political formations and discourse at local and global levels that may be a harbinger of the guns of an August yet to come.

References

Anderson, B. (1983). *Imagined communities*. London: Verso.

Carey, J. W. (1993). Everything that rises must diverge: Notes on communications, technology and the symbolic construction of the social. In P. Guant (Ed.), *Beyond agendas* (pp. 171–184). Westport, CO: Greenwood Press.

Carey, J.W. (1998). The internet and the end of the national communication system: Uncertain predictions of an uncertain future. *Journalism & Mass Communication Quarterly*, 75(1), 28–34.

Carey, J. W. (2005). Historical pragmatism and the internet. *New Media & Society*, 7(4), 443–455.

Carey, J. W., & Quirk, J. J. (1970a). The mythos of the electronic revolution – Part I. *American Scholar*, 39(1), 219–241.

Carey, J. W., & Quirk, J. J. (1970b). The mythos of the electronic revolution – Part II. *American Scholar*, 39(2), 395–424.

Sconce, J. (2000). *Haunted media: Electronic presence from telegraphy to television*. Durham, NC: Duke University Press.

Wellman, B., Quan-Haase, A., Boase, J., Chen, W., Hampton, K., Isla de Diaz, I., et al. (2003). The social affordances of the internet for networked individualism. *Journal of Computer-Mediated Communication*, *8*(3). Available online at http://jcmc.indiana.edu/vol8/issue3/wellman.html. Last accessed April 20, 2008.

Introduction

Internet research spans many disciplines. From the computer or information sciences, through engineering, and to social sciences, humanities and the arts, almost all of our disciplines have made contributions to internet research, whether in the effort to understand the effect of the internet on their area of study, or to investigate the social and political changes related to the internet, or to design and develop software and hardware for the network. The possibility and extent of contributions of internet research vary across disciplines, as do the purposes, methods, and outcomes. Even the epistemological underpinnings differ widely. The internet, then, does not have a discipline of study for itself: It is a field for research (Baym, 2005), an open environment that simultaneously supports many approaches and techniques not otherwise commensurable with each other. There are, of course, some inhibitions that limit explorations in this field: research ethics, disciplinary conventions, local and national norms, customs, laws, borders, and so on. Yet these limits on the internet as a field for research have not prevented the rapid expansion and exploration of the internet. After nearly two decades of research and scholarship, the limits are a positive contribution, providing bases for discussion and interrogation of the contexts of our research, making internet research better for all. These 'limits,' challenges that constrain the theoretically limitless space for internet research, create boundaries that give definition to the field and provide us with a particular topography that enables research and investigation.

The effects of the internet on the research environment for all the disciplines is hard to ignore. From the production of research to its publishing, the internet has become intertwined with research practices. Massive cyberinfrastructures connecting supercomputers, personal computers, and smaller devices, such as phones, personal digital assistants and netbooks, are in everyday use in research and writing. These technologies have changed the practices of knowledge work, from the way scholars access, review and understand information, through note-taking and bibliographic work, the way they collect, analyse and share data, through the way they share and collectively use commonplaces and ideas, to the way they publish research and responses to it. With these changes progressing through all researchers' current careers, it is important to be aware of internet research and its implications for our disciplines, our research, and our everyday lives.

Given the plurality of lives and technologies involved in the internet and therefore in internet research, one cannot help but realise that researching issues, investigating problems and developing new knowledge require a sort of radical contextualism as Steve Jones, one of the leading contributors to this field, would have it (Jones, 2005). As researchers we need to be explicitly aware of and reflexively situated within the contexts of our research objects. As Jones discusses, this awareness and situatedness require researchers to develop an understanding of the history and culture of the internet, and through that understanding, a knowledge of the operations of power (Jones, 2005, p. 231). The history is multiple. We must move beyond telling the history of the successes of the technologies (for example, Hafner & Lyon, 1996), and of the significant figures, and instead write stories of the construction of internet technologies, treating the successes *and* failures, inclusions and exclusions, as part of the same overall history that brought about the state of affairs that we are researching. Notably, we need to also be able to reflexively tell the story of what choices we made that brought us to this study and the broader history of the story itself within and outside of the disciplines in which we work. A similar awareness is necessary when accounting for cultures, our place in them, the place of our research in them and how we treat them. The only way to pursue a radical contextualism is with a radical reflexivity. The reflexivity of researchers transforms the facts and narratives we tell, from subjective experiences to shared models, and makes them into a science (Bourdieu, 2004).

When people research the internet, this investigation confronts the mediations of a broad range of technologies and their situatedness within the plurality of human endeavours. The internet is a network of networks, with the networks comprised of wires, fiber-optic cables and wireless transmission and all manner of intermediary enabling technologies from the modem to the satellite. These networks transfer information as fragments encapsulated within a set of protocols that define the way this information creates relations between sender and receiver, through metadata that permits the decomposition and recomposition of the information and the addressing necessary for its transmission, transit and receipt. This system gives technical effect to 'internetworking.' Key to these protocols is the transfer control protocol/internet protocol stack that allows routers, switches and hubs to direct packets of information to their final destination, routing around broken connections, finding efficient pathways and all but invisibly linking innumerable host computers, serving as both clients and servers.

However, the networks themselves, while interesting in their mediations (such as management, filtering, prioritisation), are not the core issue for internet research. Internet research tends to focus on the *ends* of the networks: the computers, telephones, and related devices and the humans who use them, or – it often seems – are used by those devices. It is through these interfaces that people access and create content, receive and send communications and perform computer-enabled informatic transactions that, altogether, generate the phenomenon that is the internet for most humans. Our actions through these networks generate new forms of social and technical interaction that have enabled new social, cultural, political or

legal constructs within which many of us now live and that affect almost everyone on the planet, even if by their digital exclusion from them. This internet is a
re/mediator and re/constructor of human lives, communities, and interests in all of
their diversity; the alternatives that it provides for are as extensive as imaginations,
competence, and freedom to explore permit.

As media converge in the internet age, television, radio, and even paper-based
media are available via the internet or are being reshaped by the internet into new
forms. The transition from broadcast and mass media to networked media in the last
40 years has moved from mass consumption of media to an individualised pattern
of consumption, and with that there has been an increasing tendency towards decentralisation and disintermediation, and even, in recent years, significant increases
in co-participatory production. From blogging, Wikipedia, MySpace, YouTube,
Facebook, to the truly distributed Bittorrent system, the channels of distribution are
absorbing the time of a population of producers, and in some interpretations we are
developing towards an economy of 'produsers' (Bruns, 2006). Since the late 1960s it
has been clear that there is labour not only in production but also in consumption and
usage (Baudrillard, 1981; Luke, 1990). This labour is distributed through our lives
as consumers, across mental, communal, and environmental ecologies (Guattari,
2000). As our labours are embedded in the world and distributed across the global
internet through our production and consumption of media, communities and cultures develop around them. Over time, these communities tend to move beyond their
transactional origins and develop identities, norms and convention that then begin
to define them. These communities and cultures are part of the larger phenomena
that constitute the internet.

The Association of Internet Researchers is one of these communities, within
which is fused all of the particular and profound impacts of the internet as a means of
knowledge work, an object of study, and as the medium through which community
bonds can be forged and sustained. The association, whose history is discussed elsewhere in more detail (Consalvo et al., 2004), is in many places: an email list of 1600
people, an academic association with several hundred members, an annual conference, and several publishing activities; it has many purposes – friendship, debate,
inquiry, support and contention. Most of all the association is interdisciplinary, internationally oriented, collegial and in its diversity reflects the extraordinary breadth
and complexity of the field of internet research. This volume is intended to serve
that community.

The contributions to the *International Handbook of Internet Research* are expansive, though by the nature of the limitation of space, they cannot cover the whole
range of possible contributions. We have focussed on covering the social nature of
the internet and tried to include materials that cover many of the aspects of our lived
lives using the internet. We have materials on chat, on games, on critical thought, on
politics, on social experience, and others. On another level, we tried to be inclusive
by publishing materials that deal with the various ecologies of our lived experience. We have papers discussing mental and individual experiences, papers that
describe our social lives and immediate shared spheres, and papers that deal with

the global and environmental aspects of the internet in relation to our lives. These papers represent what we think is an expansive and representative sample of research across the field of internet research. In their publishing, we hope to contribute to the field of internet research and provide foundations for future research.

References

Baudrillard, J. (1981). *For a critique of the political economy of the sign.* St. Louis, MO: Telos Press.

Baym, N. K. (2005). Introduction: Internet research as it isn't, is, could be, and should be. *The Information Society, 21*(4), 229–232.

Bourdieu, P. (2004). *Science of science and reflexivity.* Chicago: University of Chicago Press.

Bruns, A. (2006). Towards produsage: Futures for user-led content production. *Proceedings: Cultural attitudes towards communication and technology*, Brisbane, Australia.

Consalvo, M., Baym, N., Hunsinger, J., Jensen, K. B., Logie, J., Murero, M., et al. (2004). *Internet research annual: Selected papers from the association of internet researchers conferences 2000–2002 (digital formations, 19).* New York: Peter Lang Publishing.

Guattari, F. (2000). *The three ecologies* (G. Genosko, Trans.). London: Athlone Press.

Hafner, K. & Lyon, M. (1996). *Where wizards stay up late: The origins of the Internet.* New York: Simon and Schuster.

Jones, S. (2005). Fizz in the field: Toward a basis for an emergent Internet Studies. *The Information Society, 21*(4), 233–237.

Luke, T. W. (1990). *Screens of power: Ideology, domination, and resistance in informational society.* Champaign: University of Illinois Press.

Are Instant Messages Speech?

Naomi S. Baron

Since the emergence of popular instant messaging platforms such as ICQ, AOL, Yahoo! Messenger, and MSN Messenger, it has been common to refer to IM exchanges as "conversations" and to allude to "speaking" on IM. But to what extent does IM actually resemble spoken language?[1]

Much of the early research on IM focused on social issues, such as who uses it, how often, and for what purposes (e.g., Boneva, Quinn, Kraut, Kiesler, & Shklovski, 2006; Grinter & Palen, 2002; Isaacs, Walendowski, Whittaker, Schiano, & Kamm, 2002; Lenhart, Rainie, & Lewis, 2001; Nardi, Whittaker, & Bradner, 2000; Schiano et al., 2002). With the exception of Jacobs (2003), Hård af Segerstad (2002), and now Tagliamonte and Denis (2008), very little research examined the linguistic guts of IM. Therefore, in 2003, my students and I undertook a pilot study of how American college students linguistically craft their IM conversations, with specific interest in the speech-versus-writing question. We also wondered whether gender played a role in the answer.[2]

Speech versus Writing

Writing is not merely a transcription of spoken language. While the differences between speech and writing lie along a continuum rather than being absolutes (Tannen, 1982a, 1982b; Chafe & Tannen, 1987), there are a number of conventional differences between the two media, as we see in Fig. 1.[3]

N.S. Baron (✉)
Department of Language and Foreign Studies, American University,
Washington, District of Columbia, USA
e-mail: nbaron@american.edu

[1]Portions of the analysis is this article appear in Baron (2004, 2008a, In Press).

[2]I am grateful to Lauren Squires, Sara Tench, and Marshall Thompson for assistance in designing the study and gathering IM conversations and to Lauren Squires and Juliette Sligar for help in analyzing the data.

[3]This list draws upon my own previous work (Baron, 2000, 2003), along with studies by Chafe and Danielewicz (1987) and Crystal (2001).

J. Hunsinger et al. (eds.), *International Handbook of Internet Research*,
DOI 10.1007/978-1-4020-9789-8_1, © Springer Science+Business Media B.V. 2010

	Speech	Writing
STRUCTURAL PROPERTIES		
▪ number of participants	dialogue	monologue
▪ durability	ephemeral (real-time)	durable (time-independent)
▪ level of specificity	more vague	more precise
▪ structural accoutrements	prosodic & kinesic cues	document formatting
SENTENCE CHARACTERISTICS		
▪ sentence length	shorter units of expression	longer units of expression
▪ one-word sentences	very common	very few
▪ sentence-initial coordinate conjunctions	frequent	generally avoided
▪ structural complexity	simpler	more complex
▪ verb tense	present tense	varied (esp. past & future)
VOCABULARY CHARACTERISTICS		
▪ use of contractions	common	less common
▪ abbreviations, acronyms	infrequent	common
▪ scope of vocabulary	more concrete more colloquial narrower lexical choices more slang & obscenity	more abstract more literary wider lexical choices less slang or obscenity
▪ pronouns	many 1st & 2nd person	fewer 1st or 2nd person (except in letters)
▪ deictics (e.g., *here*, *now*)	use (since have situational context)	avoid (since have no situational context)

Fig. 1 Conventional differences between speech and writing

Since the early 1990s, internet scholars have explored whether computer-mediated communication (CMC) is a form of speech or writing.[4] In a literature survey involving e-mail, bulletin boards, and computer conferencing, I concluded that as of the late 1990s, CMC resembled speech in that it was largely unedited, it contained many first- and second-person pronouns, it commonly used present

---

[4]See Baron (2008a) for discussion of the linguistic nature of CMC, along with implications for traditional written language.

tense and contractions, it was generally informal, and CMC language could be rude or obscene. At the same time, CMC looked like writing in that the medium was durable, and participants commonly used a wide range of vocabulary choices and complex syntax (Baron, 1998). A few years later, Crystal (2001) investigated many types of CMC, including the web, e-mail, chat, and virtual worlds such as MUDs and MOOs. Coining the term "Netspeak" to refer to language used in CMC as a whole, Crystal concluded that "Netspeak has far more properties linking it to writing than to speech" (2001, p. 47). However, neither Crystal nor I had looked at IM.

Speech as Discourse: Introducing Intonation Units

To understand what it means to "talk on IM," we need to consider give and take between speakers in face-to-face (or telephone) encounters. Obvious issues involve the length of the conversation – in words, in turns (a "turn" being the language a speaker uses while he or she holds the floor before ceding it or being interrupted), and in time on the clock. Another consideration is how conversations are opened or closed.[5]

There is also the issue of dividing turns into smaller units. Within a single turn, a speaker might utter a sequence of smaller chunks, such as

chunk 1: I was wondering
chunk 2: whether you're coming to dinner tonight
chunk 3: or you need to work.

Chafe (1994) refers to these spoken chunks as "intonation units." The primary linguistic indicators demarcating a spoken intonation unit are

- a rising or falling pitch at the end of a clause (i.e., a string of language having a subject and a predicate)
- a brief pause at the beginning of an intonation unit
- a conjunction (typically *and*, though alternatively *but* or *so*) at the beginning of an intonation unit

Grammatically, the intonation unit is likely to be a clause, though some clauses extend over several intonation units.

What is the connection between spoken intonation units and IM? In IM conversations, participants frequently break their written messages into chunks. Consider this IM sequence, which is a single sentence broken into five transmissions:

---

[5]Research by Sacks and Schegloff (e.g., Sacks, Schegloff, & Jefferson, 1974; Schegloff & Sacks, 1973) laid the groundwork for contemporary conversational analysis.

transmission 1:   that must feel nice
transmission 2:   to be in love
transmission 3:   in the spring
transmission 4:   with birds chirping
transmission 5:   and frogs leaping

Are sequences of IM transmissions analogous to sequential intonation units in spoken face-to-face conversation? If so, the analogy would support the argument that IM is a speech-like form of communication.[6]

Gender and Language

Speech versus writing is one yardstick against which to measure IM. A second is gender.

The topic of gender differences in language has a long history (see, e.g., Cameron, 1998; Eckert, 1989; Holmes & Meyerhoff, 2003). Most studies have considered spoken language, though a small body of research has examined written style. Internet researchers have also begun exploring gender-based correlates of online behavior. Nearly all of this work has drawn upon one-to-many data sources such as chat, listservs, or computer conferencing. With a few exceptions (e.g., Boneva & Kraut, 2002; Thomson, Murachver, & Green, 2001), we know little about gender differences in one-to-one CMC such as e-mail and IM.

How might gender affect language? Most simply, languages may restrict particular words, sounds, or grammatical patterns to males or females. In Japanese, for example, only males are supposed to refer to themselves using the first-person pronoun *boku*. Sometimes a whole language is reserved for one gender, as in Australia, where Warlpiri women use a sign language that males are forbidden to learn (Kendon, 1980). Other gender differences result from subtle acculturation. For instance, females are commonly described as using more politeness indicators than males, while men more frequently interrupt women (Coates, 1993). Many of these differences have been documented cross-culturally (Chambers, 1992; Holmes, 1993).

---

[6]The fit between Chafe's notion of a (spoken) intonation unit and transmission units in IM is not precise. In IM, distinct transmissions are easy to count: You can always tell when the sender hits "Enter." With speech, dividing up a conversational turn into intonation units leaves more room for ambiguity. Nonetheless, Chafe's intonation units give us a place to start in analyzing IM as spoken or written language.

Speech and Gender

Other gender distinctions are more functional. Linguists have argued that women tend to use conversation predominantly to facilitate social interaction, while males are more prone to convey information (Cameron, 1998; Coates, 1993; Eckert & McConnell-Ginet, 2003; Holmes, 1993; Romaine, 2003; Tannen, 1994). Women are more likely to use affective markers ("I know how you feel"), diminutives ("little bitty insect"), hedge words (*perhaps, sort of*), politeness markers ("I hate to bother you"), and tag questions ("We're leaving at 8:00 pm, aren't we?") than men. By contrast, men more commonly use referential language ("The stock market took a nosedive today") and profanity and employ fewer first-person pronouns.

Another aspect of speech that often breaks along gender lines is adherence to normative language standards. On average, women's speech reflects more standard pronunciation, vocabulary, and grammar (Chambers, 1992; Holmes, 1993; James, 1996; Labov, 1991).

Writing and Gender

A handful of studies have looked at gender differences in written language. Biber and his colleagues (Biber, 1988; Biber, Conrad, & Reppen, 1998; Biber & Finegan, 1997) have studied the historical relationship between speech and writing by analyzing large collections of spoken and written data. One of Biber's measures is what he calls "involved" (as opposed to "informational"). This metric includes use of present-tense verbs, first- and second-person pronouns, contractions, and so-called private verbs such as *think* or *feel*. Nearly all of these characteristics are associated with speech rather than writing. The distinction between "involved" versus "informational" roughly parallels the "social" versus "informative" dichotomy we have already talked about for speech.

Mulac and Lundell (1994) studied impromptu descriptive essays written by college students. Assignments were coded with respect to "male language variables" (such as judgmental adjectives, elliptical sentences, and sentence-initial conjunctions or filler words) versus "female language variables" (e.g., references to emotion, sentence-initial adverbials, uncertainty verbs, or hedge words). Using these variables, the authors correctly identified the writer's gender almost three-quarters of the time. Similarly, using a language-based algorithm, a team of computer scientists claims approximately 80% accuracy in identifying a writer's gender (Koppel, Argamon, & Shimoni, 2002; Argamon, Koppel, Fine, & Shimoni, 2003).

A third way of assessing gender differences in written language is standardized achievement tests, such as described in *The Nation's Report Card* (National Center for Educational Statistics, 2002). Over the years, girls have consistently outpaced boys on the writing component of the test.

Gender and CMC

Herring (2000, 2003) has demonstrated that online dynamics often replicate offline gender patterns. On asynchronous discussion lists and newsgroups, males typically dominate conversation (posting longer messages, asserting opinions as "facts") whereas females are more likely to qualify and justify their assertions, apologize, and "in general, manifest an 'aligned' orientation toward their interlocutors" (2003, p. 207). In one-to-many synchronous CMC forums, while levels of male and female participation seem to be more balanced in the number of messages and message length, males remain more aggressive, while females typed three times as many representations of smiles or laughter, and their conversational style was more aligned and supportive (Herring, 2003).

Unlike the CMC platforms Herring studied, IM is one-to-one communication, in which conversational partners nearly always know each other, often quite well. (In one-to-many forums, users often participate anonymously or with a camouflaged identity, and interlocutors may be strangers.) It is also easy to gather samples from same-sex IM conversational pairs, facilitating the study of gender issues.

The IM Study

In the Spring of 2003, we gathered IM conversations between undergraduates (or recent graduates) at American University, Washington, DC. The version of IM we selected was America Online's freely downloadable program AIM (AOL Instant Messenger), which nearly all students at the university used. A group of student experimenters initiated IM conversations with peers on their AIM buddy lists. Participants were allowed to edit out any words or turns they wished to delete (an option rarely taken), and user screen names were anonymized. Student experimenters then electronically forwarded the IM conversation files to a project website.

Essential Terminology

Some terminology proved useful in analyzing the IM conversations:[7]

> **Transmission Unit**: an instant message that has been sent
> e.g., Max: hey man
>
> **Utterance**: a sentence or sentence fragment in IM
> e.g., Susan: Somebody shoot me! [sentence]
> e.g., Zach: if the walls could talk [sentence fragment]

---

[7] Student names in examples throughout the article are pseudonyms.

Sequence: one or more IM transmissions sent seriatim by the same person

    e.g., Max: hey man

    Max: whassup

    [this sequence equals two IM transmission units]

Closing: a series of transmissions (between IM partners) at the end of an IM conversation, beginning with one party initiating closure and ending with termination of the IM connection

    e.g., Sam: Hey, I gotta go [first indication that Sam will terminate the conversation]

                    ...[subsequent conversational transmissions]

    Sam: I'm outta here [final transmission in conversation]

Utterance Chunking: breaking a single IM utterance ("sentence") into two or more transmissions

    e.g., Joan: that must feel nice

    Joan: to be in love

    Joan: in the spring

  Note: Each of the transmission units making up the utterance is an utterance chunk.

Utterance Break Pair: two sequential transmissions that are grammatically part of the same utterance

    e.g., Allyson: what are you bringing to the dorm party

    Allyson: on Saturday?

The most fundamental notion here is the IM **transmission unit**. Some transmission units correspond to a full sentence, as in Susan's "Somebody shoot me!" Other times, the transmission may be just a piece of a sentence, as with Zach's "if the walls could talk." Transmissions may also contain more than one sentence. Jill, for example, wrote "and the prof left – he forgot something in his office."

An **utterance** is essentially a sentence – or a piece of a sentence. Some utterances are fully contained within a single transmission unit (as with "Somebody shoot me!"). Other times, the utterance is broken up ("chunked") into multiple turns. For example, Max's **sequence** of two transmissions comprises a single utterance:

transmission unit 1: hey man

transmission unit 2: whassup

A **closing** is a kind of long goodbye.

Utterance chunking is the process of breaking an IM utterance into multiple transmissions. Each transmission is an utterance chunk. But where in the utterance does the chunking occur? If the total utterance is "hey man, whassup," does the break into two transmissions always take place between "man" and "whassup"? Why not between "hey" and "man"?

This "where" question is important. We saw that Chafe's intonation units (for analyzing speech) can be recognized either prosodically (by rising or falling pitch or by beginning with a brief pause) or grammatically (beginning with a conjunction such as *and* or constituting a single clause, such as "Somebody shoot me!"). Are IM utterances broken into sequential transmissions at the same grammatical points as spoken utterances?

Our final term enables us to describe the relationship between two chunks within an utterance. An **utterance break pair** is two sequential transmissions that are part of the same utterance, as in

> transmission unit 1: what are you bringing to the dorm party
> transmission unit 2: on Saturday?

Of interest is the grammatical relationship between "what are you bringing to the dorm party" and "on Saturday."

Questions About IM

Our research questions regarding the linguistic makeup of IM clustered into three categories: conversational scaffolding, lexical issues, and utterance breaks.

Conversational scaffolding deals with how a conversation is put together. We began by evaluating individual IM transmissions: How long were they? How many consisted of just one word? How many transmissions were there per minute? Next, we considered how transmissions were combined to form sequences: What was the longest sequence in each conversation? How many transmissions were there per sequence? And how common were sequences in the corpus? Finally, we looked at conversation length: How many transmissions were there per conversation? How long did conversations take? And how long did it take to say goodbye?

The second broad category of analysis was the **lexicon**. We focused on various types of shortenings (abbreviations, acronyms, and contractions) along with emoticons. We also tracked the level of accuracy: How often were words misspelled, and how frequently did people correct the error in an immediately following transmission?

The third set of questions involved **utterance breaks**. Where in a sentence did the breaks occur, and how did these IM break points compare with breaks in face-to-face spoken language?

General Findings

We collected 23 IM conversations, containing 2,185 transmissions, made up of 11,718 words. There were nine conversations between females, nine between males, and five involving male–female pairs.[8] Some analyses were performed on the entire set of IM conversations whereas others were restricted to comparing female–female and male–male conversations (together totaling 1,861 transmissions).

Conversational Scaffolding

We first looked at conversational scaffolding: a profile of the IM transmissions; sequences and utterance chunking; and conversation length and closings.

Transmissions

The mean length of transmission was 5.4 words. While the longest transmission was 44 words, others were quite short. One out of every five transmissions was a single word.

Is 5.4 words long or short? In their contrastive analysis of spoken and written language, Chafe and Danielewicz (1987, p. 96) reported that informal spoken conversational intonation units averaged 6.2 words, while academic lectures averaged 7.3 words. For writing (which they divided into "punctuation units"), traditional letters averaged 8.4 words, and written academic papers averaged 9.3 words. At 5.4 words, our IM transmissions more closely resembled informal face-to-face speech than letters or academic works.

We next calculated how many transmissions were sent per minute. The mean: barely four transmissions a minute. Elsewhere (Baron, 2008b) I have suggested that students probably typed so few words per minute in a conversation because they were multitasking with other offline and online activities, including additional IM conversations.

Sequences and Utterance Chunking

Another reason IM transmissions were, on average, relatively short is because so many IMs are written seriatim, together making up the equivalent of a sentence. Nearly half the sample consisted of sequences of two or more transmissions. The longest sequence was 18 successive transmissions.

---

[8]Our original study design was scaled back due to slippage in subject participation. However, many of our results have been corroborated by other investigators' research (e.g., Squires, 2007; Tagliamonte & Denis, 2008).

A total of 16 females and 6 males participated in the conversations. In the female sample, the same student experimenters engaged in conversations with multiple interlocutors. In the male sample, more than one conversation between the same interlocutor pair was sometimes included in the sample.

We looked more closely at the transmission sequences to see which ones contained distinct utterances, such as

> transmission 1: i'm sorry [utterance 1]
> transmission 2: if it makes you feel any better, i'm being held
> captive by two of Julie's papers [utterance 2]

and which constituted pieces of larger sentences, as in

> transmission 1: in the past
> transmission 2: people have found stuff under the cushions
> [together, a single utterance]

Eliminating the one-word transmissions (which were rarely part of multi-transmission sequences), roughly one-sixth of the remaining transmissions in the data were part of an utterance break pair (that is, two sequential transmissions that are components of the same larger sentence).

Conversation Length and Closings

IM conversations averaged more than 93 transmissions apiece and almost 24 minutes long. However, IM conversations showed enormous variety, ranging from quick three-or-four-transmission volleys to sessions stretching over more than 200 transmissions and exceeding an hour.

We also examined how people ended their conversations. From the first indication that one partner intended to sign off up until actual closure, people took an average of 7 transmissions and roughly 40 seconds. Much as in face-to-face spoken encounters, terminating an IM conversation can be a drawn-out process. For example:

Gale:	**hey, I gotta run**
Sally:	Okay.
Sally:	I'll ttyl?
Gale:	**gotta do errands.**
Gale:	**yep!**
Sally:	Okay.
Sally:	:)
Gale:	**talk to you soon**
Sally:	Alrighty.

Lexical Issues

Abbreviations

In tallying IM abbreviations, we included only what we might call CMC abbreviations – abbreviations that appear to be distinctive to CMC. Excluded were forms that commonly appear in offline writing (such as *hrs = hours*) or represent spoken usage (*cuz = because*).[9]

Abbreviations proved sparse. Out of 11,718 words, only 31 were CMC abbreviations:

bc (also *b/c*) = *because*	5
bf = boyfriend	2
cya = see you	7
k = OK	16
y? = why	1

Acronyms

Again, we tabulated acronyms that appear to be distinctive to CMC.[10] Only 90 CMC acronyms appeared:

brb = be right back	3
btw = by the way	2
g/g (also *g2g*) = *got to go*	2
LMAO = laughing my __ off	1
lol (also *LOL*) = *laughing out loud*	76
OMG = oh my god	1
ttyl = talk to you later	5

LOL was the most prevalent acronym, but the term did not always indicate the humorous response suggested by the words "laughing out loud." Rather, *LOL,* along with *heehee* or *haha* (both also common in IM), were sometimes used as phatic fillers, the equivalent of *OK, cool,* or *yeah.*

Contractions

Out of 763 cases in which participants could have chosen a contraction, they only did so 65% of the time. Compare this situation with casual speech. For a class project, my students tallied how often contractions were used in a sample of college students' informal conversation. The answer: roughly 95% of the time.

---

[9]The line is sometimes difficult to draw. For instance, *b/c* for *because* was included as a CMC abbreviation, whereas *prob* for *problem* or *convo* for *conversation* was not.

[10]Excluded were acronyms such as *US = United States* or *TA = teaching assistant.*

The appearance of uncontracted forms in IM brings messages a more formal (and written) tone than we usually associate with IM.

Emoticons

There were also very few emoticons – a total of 49:

:-) = smiley	31
:-(= frowny	5
O:-) = angel	4
:-P = sticking out tongue, with nose	3
;-) = winking	2
:-\ = undecided	1
:-[= embarrassed	1
:P = sticking out tongue, without nose	1
:- = [probably a typographical error]	1

The most common emoticon was the smiley (31 out of the 49). Not everyone used emoticons, and just 3 subjects accounted for 33 of the tokens.

Spelling and Self-Correction

Only 171 words were misspelled or lacked necessary punctuation (averaging one error every 12.8 transmissions). More than one-third of the errors came from omitting an apostrophe in a contraction (such as *thats*) or a possessive form (*Sams*). Another third were garden-variety spelling mistakes – adding or omitting letters, or using the wrong letter. Some mistakes probably came from sloppy typing, including the 21% of errors involving metathesis (switching letter order, as in *somethign* for *something*).

In 9% of the cases, the person noticed the problem and fixed it (or tried to) in the next transmission. For instance, when a subject had typed *awway* (and sent off the IM), he corrected it to *away* in the following transmission. Self-corrections did not follow a clear pattern. Changing *awway* to *away* probably wasn't necessary for the recipient to interpret the original message. Other errors that were not corrected did challenge intelligibility (such as not correcting *feidls* to *fields*). Out of the 15 self-corrections, none involved adding in a missing apostrophe.

Utterance Breaks

For the utterance break analysis, we looked at nine conversations between females and nine between males. Males were significantly more likely to break their utterances into chunks (i.e., sending each chunk as a separate transmission). Table 1 summarizes the findings:[11]

Table 1 Total utterance breaks, by gender

	Total break pairs	Total transmissions in corpus	Break pairs as % of total transmissions
Females	84	1097	13
Males	105	767	23
Total	189	1864	17

Grammatical Makeup of Break Pairs

We next coded each of the 189 break pairs by analyzing the grammatical relationship between the first transmission and the second. Take the break pair sequence

transmission 1: what are you bringing to the dorm party
transmission 2: on Saturday?

"On Saturday" is an adverbial prepositional phrase, modifying the sentence in the first transmission, "what are you bringing to the dorm party." The coding scheme looked at the grammatical structure of the *second* member of the break pair, in relationship to the first member (here, at the grammatical function of "on Saturday").[12]

Grammatical Analysis of Utterance Break Points

Table 2 summarizes the grammatical analysis of break pairs.

Conjunctions are the primary device for breaking utterances into multiple transmissions. Out of 189 break pair sets, 112 (nearly 60%) began the second transmission with a conjunction. Of these 112 cases, 89 used a coordinating or subordinating conjunction to introduce a sentence (such as "*and* she never talks about him" or "*if* I paid my own airfare"). The remaining 23 were conjunctions introducing a noun phrase ("*or* circleville") or verb phrase ("*and* had to pay back the bank"). Separating coordinating conjunctions (e.g., *and* or *but*) from subordinating conjunctions (e.g., *because* and *although*), we find that more than four out of five IM transmissions that appeared as the second member of an utterance break pair (and that began with a conjunction) used a coordinating conjunction.

---

[11]For statistical details on the analysis of IM conversations described in this article, see Baron (2004, in press).

[12]For the full coding scheme see Baron (in press).

Table 2 Grammatical analysis of break pairs

Grammatical type	Females (%)	Males (%)	Total (%)
Conjunctions and sentences or phrases introduced by conjunctions	48	69	59
Independent clauses	23	10	15
Adjectives and adjectival phrases	7	9	8
Adverbs and adverbial phrases	12	6	9
Noun phrases	10	6	7
Verb phrases	1	2	2

The next most prevalent grammatical type for beginning the second transmission in a break pair was independent (sometimes called "main") clauses (for example, *"that's all I'm saying"*). Of the 189 break pairs, 15% constituted independent clauses. Grammatically, independent clauses are also sentences (or sentence fragments). If we combine conjunctions introducing sentences with the independent clause category, we account for roughly 62% of the total 189 utterance breaks.

The remaining cases of second transmissions in a break pair were largely adjectives ("completely harmless"), adverbs ("on Saturday"), or nouns ("radio station"). Then there were a couple of stragglers, plus one lone example in which the second element was a verb phrase – that is, in which the break appeared between the subject and the predicate:

transmission unit 1: and then Pat McGee Band
transmission unit 2: perform like 7

Intuitively, an utterance break between the two main constituents of a sentence – the noun phrase subject and verb phrase predicate – seems a natural place to anticipate finding chunking in IM conversations. Oddly, this pattern occurred only once in all the IM conversations.

The Gender Question

What happens when we re-examine the conversations by gender? We only consider features where gender seems to make a difference.

Conversational Scaffolding

Transmissions

The longest transmission, 44 words, was by a female. (The longest male transmission was 34 words.) Averaging the longest transmissions in each of the nine female–female and the nine male–male conversations, female "longest transmissions" averaged almost 28 words, while males averaged not quite 20.

Sequences and Utterance Chunking

Females used considerably more multi-transmission sequences than did males. However, examining only sequences that chunk sentences into multiple transmissions, the balance shifts. Males were almost twice as likely to carve up sentences into sequential transmissions as were females.

Conversation Length and Closings

Female–female conversations were roughly a third longer (in both number of transmissions and time on the clock) than male–male conversations. Females averaged almost 122 transmissions per conversation, lasting an average of 31 minutes. Males averaged 85 transmissions per conversation, with conversations averaging only 19 minutes.

Lexical Issues

Contractions

We reported that participants used contractions 65% of the time they had the option. But usage differed significantly by gender. While males used contracted forms 77% of the times possible, females did so only 57% of the time.

Emoticons

Females were the prime users of emoticons. Three-quarters of the 16 females used one or more emoticons. Of the 6 males, only 1 used emoticons.

Utterance Breaks

Males were significantly more likely than females (69 versus 48%) to begin the second transmission in a break pair with a conjunction. Females were significantly more likely than males (23 versus 10%) to chain together related sentences.

IM as Speech or Writing

How does IM compare linguistically with face-to-face speech or conventional writing? Figure 2 summarizes our findings thus far.

Besides a few lexical issues, plus utterance breaks involving independent clauses, Fig. 2 suggests that IM more closely resembles speech than writing. However, we need a closer look at the relationship between IM utterance breaks and the way spoken discourse works.

On a number of points, the IM data and Chafe's findings for speech seem strongly congruent. Average lengths for both IM transmission units and Chafe's intonation units are relatively short (IM: 5.4 words; intonation units for informal

	Similar to face-to-face speech	Similar to conventional writing
GENERAL DISCOURSE SCAFFOLDING		
• average turn length	Yes	No
• one-word utterances	Yes	No
• conversational closings	Yes	No
LEXICAL ISSUES		
• use of contractions	Somewhat[13]	Somewhat
• CMC abbreviations, acronyms	No[14]	Somewhat
• emoticons	Yes[15]	No
UTTERANCE BREAKS (UB)		
• frequency of chunking utterances into multiple sequential transmissions	Yes	No
• Second member of UB pair begins with conjunction	Yes	No
• Second member of UB pair begins with coordinating conjunction	Yes	No
• Second member of UB pair begins with independent clause	Somewhat[16]	Yes

Fig. 2 Comparison of IM with face-to-face speech and conventional writing

speech: roughly 6 words) (Chafe, 1980, p. 14). In both cases, coordinating conjunctions commonly initiate a new transmission or intonation unit. Moreover, in both instances, new units are sometimes made up of independent clauses (Chafe, 1980, p. 15).

On other measures, the comparison fails. In IM, grammatical breaks between adjectives and nouns were infrequent (5 examples out of 189), and breaks between

---

[13]While contractions appeared in the corpus, there were fewer than anticipated.

[14]Some CMC abbreviations and acronyms appeared in the corpus, though fewer than anticipated.

[15]Emoticons are sometimes used in lieu of (spoken) prosodic or kinesic cues available in face-to-face communication.

[16]Speech is often characterized by run-on sentences whose components are chained together with coordinating conjunctions. Whole sentences in formal writing generally do not begin with conjunctions.

noun phrases and verb phrases were rare (only one case). Chafe, however, reports multiple instances in spoken language in which a pause occurred between a modifier and a noun, or falling intonation separated a noun phrase and a verb phrase (e.g., (1980, p. 20, 46)).

The Significance of Gender in IM

Earlier, we saw that female language (both spoken and written) is more likely to have an involved or social function, while male communication is more informational. Similarly, female language is commonly more standard than that of males. How do these findings about traditional speech and writing compare with IM data?

In IM, females were more "talkative" than males. Women had the longest individual transmissions, had longer overall conversations, and took longer to say goodbye. Mulac and Lundell found that females used longer sentences in written essays than did males. Possibly our IM findings reflect a female writing style rather than a female speech style. The finding that females used fewer contracted forms than males also suggests that women have a greater tendency to treat IM as a written medium.

Another measure of the social function of CMC is use of emoticons. In our data, females were far more likely to use emoticons than males. Herring reported a similar finding in her study of one-to-many synchronous communication. Since emoticons can be interpreted as visual cues substituting for prosody or kinesics, their use in IM suggests a more spoken than written cast.

The utterance-break data shed yet more light on how gender shapes IM as spoken or written discourse. Males were significantly more likely to chunk sentences into multiple IM transmissions than were females. Males were also significantly more apt than females to begin the second member of an utterance break pair with a conjunction, while females were significantly more likely to begin the second member of such a break pair with an independent clause. The conjunction pattern is more commonly found in speech; the independent clause pattern is more characteristic of writing. While the intonation units Chafe and Danielewicz analyzed in face-to-face speech began with a coordinating conjunction 34% of the time, only 4% of the punctuation units in their academic writing sample began this way (1987, p. 103).

Taking gender into account, the comparison of IM with face-to-face speech versus conventional writing undergoes a shift, as shown in Fig. 3.

Are Instant Messages Speech?

The simple answer: "no," though there are enough speech-like elements (especially in male IM conversations) to explain why it seems so natural to talk about IM "conversations" and not IM "letters." Just as we commonly speak face to face while engaging in additional activities (walking down the street, doing the dishes), young

	Similar to face-to-face speech		Similar to conventional writing	
	Males	Females	Males	Females
GENERAL DISCOURSE SCAFFOLDING				
▪ conversational closings		Longer	Shorter	
LEXICAL ISSUES				
▪ use of contractions	More frequent			Less frequent
▪ emoticons		More frequent[17]	Less frequent	
UTTERANCE BREAKS (UB)				
▪ frequency of chunking utterances into multiple sequential transmissions	More frequent			Less frequent
▪ Second member of UB pair begins with conjunction	More frequent			Less frequent
▪ Second member of UB pair begins with independent clause	Less frequent			More frequent

Fig. 3 Gender-based comparison of IM with face-to-face speech and conventional writing

people are typically doing something else (online, offline, or both) while conducting IM conversations. As with speaking (and unlike writing), IM conversations are not generally targets of someone's normative eye or red pen. The goal of an IM conversation is nearly always to get your message across, not to produce an entry for an essay contest.

While male IM conversations have a great deal in common with face-to-face speech, female IM conversations more closely approximate conventional writing patterns. The two exceptions to this generalization are conversational closings and use of emoticons, both of which were more pronounced among females and both of which are more analogous with traditional spoken than written communication.

Why, then, does an informal medium like IM assume some dimensions of more formal, written language? The answer reflects what the philosopher John Dewey called "habit strength." Today's college students (at least in the United States) have often been typing on a computer keyboard for more than a decade. Much of this typing is for school work, which is apt to be subjected to academic scrutiny. Acronyms, abbreviations, and contractions are no more welcome than poor spelling. School children learn what is required. With years of repeated practice, their fingers tend to go on automatic pilot.

---

[17] However, as with CMC abbreviations and acronyms, there were relatively few emoticons in the data.

It is not, therefore, surprising to see school-appropriate writing habits crop up in IM, which is produced on the same keyboard as those formal school assignments – and sometimes, at the same time. Since girls, on average, produce better writing than boys in the K-12 years, it makes sense to expect that female IM conversations will reveal heightened standards, including fewer contractions, fewer sentences chunked into multiple transmissions, and fewer sentence breaks involving a conjunction, in comparison with males.

Speech or writing? Some of both, but not as much speech as we have tended to assume. What is more, gender matters.

References

Argamon, S., M. Koppel, J. Fine, and A. R. Shimoni (2003), "Gender, Genre, and Writing Style in Formal Written Texts," *Text* 23:321–346.

Baron, N. S. (1998), "Letters by Phone or Speech by Other Means: The Linguistics of Email," *Language and Communication* 18:133–170.

Baron, N. S. (2000), *Alphabet to Email: How Written English Evolved and Where It's Heading.* London: Routledge.

Baron, N. S. (2003), "Why Email Looks Like Speech: Proofreading, Pedagogy, and Public Face," in J. Aitchison and D. Lewis, eds., *New Media Language.* London: Routledge, pp. 102–113.

Baron, N. S. (2004), "'See You Online': Gender Issues in College Student Use of Instant Messaging," *Journal of Language and Social Psychology* 23(4):397–423.

Baron, N. S. (2008a), *Always On: Language in an Online and Mobile World.* New York: Oxford University Press.

Baron, N. S. (2008b), "Adjusting the Volume: Technology and Multitasking in Discourse Control," in J. Katz, ed., *Handbook of Mobile Communication Studies.* Cambridge, MA: MIT Press, pp. 177–193.

Baron, N. S. (In Press), "Discourse Structures in Instant Messaging: The Case of Utterance Breaks," to appear in S. Herring, ed., *Computer-Mediated Conversation.* Cresskill, NJ: Hampton Press.

Biber, D. (1988), *Variation across Speech and Writing.* Cambridge: Cambridge University Press.

Biber, D., S. Conrad, and R. Reppen (1998), *Corpus Linguistics: Investigating Language Structure and Use.* Cambridge: Cambridge University Press.

Biber, D. and E. Finegan (1997), "Diachronic Relations among Speech-Based and Written Registers in English," in T. Nevalainen and L. Kahlas-Tarkka, eds., *To Explain the Present: Studies in the Changing English Language in Honour of Matti Rissanen.* Helsinki: Modern Language Society, pp. 253–275.

Boneva, B. and R. Kraut (2002), "Email, Gender, and Personal Relations," in B. Wellman and C. Haythornthwaite, eds., *The Internet in Everyday Life.* Oxford: Blackwell, pp. 372–403.

Boneva, B., A. Quinn, R. Kraut, S. Kiesler, and I. Shklovski (2006), "Teenage Communication in the Instant Messaging Era," in R. Kraut, M. Brynin, and S. Kiesler, eds., *Computer, Phones, and the Internet.* Oxford: Oxford University Press, pp. 201–218.

Cameron, D. (1998), "Gender, Language, and Discourse: A Review Essay," *Signs: Journal of Women in Culture and Society* 23:945–973.

Chafe, W. (1980), "The Deployment of Consciousness in the Production of a Narrative," in W. Chafe, ed., *The Pear Stories: Cognitive, Cultural, and Linguistic Aspects of Narrative Production.* Norwood, NJ: Ablex, pp. 9–50.

Chafe, W. (1994), *Discourse, Consciousness, and Time: The Flow and Displacement of Conscious Experience in Speaking and Writing.* Chicago: University of Chicago Press.

Chafe, W. and J. Danielewicz (1987), "Properties of Spoken and Written Language," in R. Horowitz and S. J. Samuels, eds., *Comprehending Oral and Written Language*. San Diego: Academic Press, pp. 83–113.

Chafe, W. and D. Tannen (1987), "The Relation between Written and Spoken Language," *Annual Review of Anthropology* 16:383–407.

Chambers, J. K. (1992), "Linguistic Correlates of Gender and Sex," *English World-Wide* 13: 173–218.

Coates, J. (1993), *Women, Men, and Language*, 2nd edition. London: Longman.

Crystal, D. (2001), *Language and the Internet*. Cambridge: Cambridge University Press.

Eckert, P. (1989), *Jocks and Burnouts: Social Categories and Identities in High School*. New York: Teachers College Press.

Eckert, P. and S. McConnell-Ginet (2003), *Language and Gender*. New York: Cambridge University Press.

Grinter, R. and L. Palen (2002), "Instant Messaging in Teen Life," *Proceedings of the ACM Conference on Computer Supported Cooperative Work* (CSCW '02). New Orleans, LA, November 16–20. New York: ACM Press, pp. 21–30.

Hård af Segerstad, Y. (2002), *Use and Adaptation of Written language to the Conditions of Computer-Mediated Communication*. Department of Linguistics, Göteborg: Göteborg University.

Herring, S. (2000), "Gender Differences in CMC: Findings and Implications," *The CPSR Newsletter*, Winter. Available at http://www.cpsr.org/publications/newsletters/issues/2000/Winter2000/herring.html.

Herring, S. (2003), "Gender and Power in Online Communication," in J. Holmes and M. Meyerhoff, ed., *The Handbook of Language and Gender*. Oxford: Blackwell, pp. 202–228.

Holmes, J. (1993), "Women's Talk: The Question of Sociolinguistic Universals," *Australian Journal of Communication* 20:125–149.

Holmes, J. and M. Meyerhoff, eds. (2003). *The Handbook of Language and Gender*. Malden, MA: Blackwell.

Isaacs, E., A. Walendowski, S. Whittaker, D. Schiano, and C. Kamm (2002), "The Character, Functions, and Styles of Instant Messaging in the Workplace," *Proceedings of the ACM Conference on Computer Supported Cooperative Work* (CSCW '02). New Orleans, LA. New York: ACM Press, pp. 11–20.

Jacobs, G. (2003), "Breaking Down Virtual Walls: Understanding the Real Space/Cyberspace Connections of Language and Literacy in Adolescents' Use of Instant Messaging," Paper presented at the American Educational Research Association, Chicago, IL, April.

James, D. (1996), "Women, Men, and Prestige Speech Forms: A Critical Review," in V.L. Bergvall, J.M. Bing, and A.F. Freed, eds., *Rethinking Language and Gender Research*. London: Longman, pp. 98–125.

Kendon, A. (1980), "The Sign Language of the Women of Yuendumu: A Preliminary Report on the Structure of Warlpiri Sign Language. *Sign Language Studies* 27:101–112.

Koppel, M., S. Argamon, and A. R. Shimoni (2002), "Automatically Categorizing Written Texts by Author Gender," *Literary and Linguistic Computing* 17:401–412.

Labov, W. (1991), "The Intersection of Sex and Social Class in the Course of Linguistic Change," *Language Variation and Change* 2:205–254.

Lenhart, A., L. Rainie, and O. Lewis (2001), "Teenage Life Online: The Rise of the Instant-Message Generation and the Internet's Impact on Friendships and Family Relationships," *Pew Internet & American Life Project*. Available at http://www.pewinternet.org/pdfs/PIP_Teens_Report.pdf.

Mulac, A. and T. L. Lundell (1994), "Effects of Gender-Linked Language Differences in Adults' Written Discourse: Multivariate Tests of Language Effects," *Language and Communication* 14:299–309.

Nardi, B., S. Whittaker, and E. Bradner (2000), "Interaction and Outeraction: Instant Messaging in Action," *Proceedings of the ACM Conference on Computer Supported Cooperative Work* (CSCW '00). Philadelphia, PA. New York: ACM Press, pp. 79–88.

National Center for Educational Statistics (2002), *The Nation's Report Card: Writing 2002*. National Assessment of Educational Progress. Washington, DC: US Department of Education, Institute of Educational Sciences.

Romaine, S. (2003), "Variation in Language and Gender," in J. Holmes and M. Meyerhoff, eds., *The Handbook of Language and Gender*. Malden, MA: Blackwell, pp. 98–118.

Sacks, H., E. Schegloff, and G. Jefferson (1974) "A Simplest Systematics for the Organization of Turn-Taking in Conversation," *Language* 50:696–735.

Schegloff, E. and H. Sacks (1973), "Opening up Closings," *Semiotica* 7:289–327.

Schiano, D., C. Chen, J. Ginsberg, U. Gretarsdottir, M. Huddleston, and E. Isaacs (2002), "Teen Use of Messaging Media," *Proceedings of the ACM Conference on Human Factors in Computing Systems* (CHI '02). Minneapolis, MN. New York: ACM Press, pp. 594–595.

Squires, L. (2007), "Whats the Use of Apostrophes? Gender Differences and Linguistic Variation in Instant Messaging," *American University TESOL Working Papers* Number 4. Available at http://www.american.edu/tesol/CMCSquiresFinal.pdf .

Tagliamonte, S. and D. Denis (2008), "Linguistic Ruin? LOL! Instant Messaging and Teen Language," *American Speech* 83(1):3–34.

Tannen, D. (1982a), "Oral and Written Strategies in Spoken and Written Narratives," *Language* 58:1–21.

Tannen, D. (1982b), "The Oral/Literate Continuum in Discourse," in D. Tannen, ed., *Spoken and Written Language: Exploring Orality and Literacy*. Norwood, NJ: Ablex, pp. 1–16.

Tannen, D. (1994), *Gender and Discourse*. New York: Oxford University Press.

Thomson, R., T. Murachver, and J. Green (2001), "Where is the Gender in Gendered Language?" *Psychological Science* 12:171–175.

From MUDs to MMORPGs: The History of Virtual Worlds

Richard A. Bartle

Introduction

Golf was invented in China (Ling, 1991). There is evidence from the *Dongxuan Records* (Wei, Song dynasty) that a game called *chuiwan* ("hitting ball") was played as early as the year 945. A silk scroll, *The Autumn Banquet* (unknown, Ming dynasty), depicts a man swinging something with the appearance of a golf club at something with the appearance of a golf ball, having the apparent aim of conveying it into something with the appearance of a golf hole.

Golf was also invented in France (Flannery & Leech, 2003), where it was known as *palle mail*. Tax records from 1292 show that makers of clubs and balls had to pay a toll to sell their goods to nobles outside Paris. A book of prayers, *Les Heures de la Duchesse de Bourgogne* (unknown, c1500), contains illustrations of men swinging something with the appearance of a golf club at something with the appearance of a golf ball, having the apparent aim of conveying it into something with the appearance of a golf hole.

Golf was also invented variously in Middle Egypt, ancient Greece, ancient Rome (*paganica*), England (*cambuca*), Ireland (*camanachd*) and the Netherlands (*kolf*) (*golf*, 2008).

Nevertheless, despite these assorted claims as to the invention of golf, it is indisputable that the modern game is the product of Scotland.[1] The golf played today is the direct descendent only of the version that the Scots developed. Follow the audit trail from the US Masters back in time, and Scotland is where it ends.

So it is with virtual worlds.

R.A. Bartle (✉)
School of Computer Science and Electronic Engineering, University of Essex, UK
e-mail: rabartle@essex.ac.uk

[1]Even though it was banned there by the parliament of James II in 1457. They banned football (soccer) at the same time.

J. Hunsinger et al. (eds.), *International Handbook of Internet Research*,
DOI 10.1007/978-1-4020-9789-8_2, © Springer Science+Business Media B.V. 2010

Hitting a ball into a hole with a stick is a fairly obvious idea, so it's unsurprising that what we now know as golf had been conceived as a game many times throughout history. Likewise, creating a virtual world doesn't qualify as an act of genius – it was always going to happen. In fact, as we shall see, the concept has been invented independently at least six times and probably more. Most of these worlds had little or no impact on the future development of the concept, however. Therefore, when it comes to understanding their history, the important question is not so much which one came *first* as which one is the *primogenitor* of today's virtual worlds.

As it happens, depending on your view of what counts as a virtual world, the one that appeared first chronologically is also the beginning of the audit trail. Before getting into details, though, we should first consider what exactly we mean by the term *virtual world*.

Essentially, a virtual world is an automated, shared, persistent environment with and through which people can interact in real time by means of a virtual self. Let's look at those qualifiers one by one:

- Automated: the virtual world implements a coherent set of rules (its *physics*) that entirely define what changes its real-life visitors (termed *players*) can make to that world.
- Shared: more than one player can be in the exact same virtual world at once.
- Persistent: if you stop playing then come back later, the virtual world will have continued to exist in your absence.
- Environment: the virtual world manifests surroundings in which the player activities take place.
- Interact *with*: players can perform actions within the virtual world which produce results that are relayed back to them.
- Interact *through*: players can communicate with one another under the auspices of the virtual world.
- Real time: the virtual world generates feedback for events pretty well the moment they occur.
- Virtual self: each player identifies with a unique entity within the virtual world (their *character*) through which all their in-world activity is channelled.

In other words, a virtual world is a pretend place that several people can visit at once whenever they like, using their computers.

Under this definition, the first virtual world was probably *MUD*.

The First Age: 1978–1985

MUD ("Multi-User Dungeon") was written by computer science undergraduates Roy Trubshaw and Richard Bartle[2] at the University of Essex, England, in the

---

[2]Conflict of interests warning: this is me.

autumn of 1978. The first, proof-of-concept version took Trubshaw only a few hours to complete, but established the basic software foundation upon which a full virtual world could be constructed. Work immediately began on version 2, which had reached a playable state by December when Bartle became involved (initially, to design content).[3] This second version satisfied all the criteria listed above, and it would be recognisable as a virtual world by players of such games today.

MUD was text based, meaning that everything the characters did, saw, heard or otherwise experienced was reported in words. In this regard, it could be argued that *MUD* was merely a multi-player development of the early adventure games such as *Colossal Cave Adventure* (Crowther & Woods, 1976) and *Zork* (Anderson, Blank, Daniels, & Lebling, 1977). This is a fair point, as Trubshaw did indeed draw on his understanding of those games when designing *MUD*.[4]

However, *MUD* was as radical a departure from *Zork* as *Zork* was from *Dungeons and Dragons* (Gygax & Arneson, 1974). The puzzle-based, narratively constrained format of adventure games couldn't work in the setting of a multi-player game: the *world* had to assume dominance, not the problem-solving. Half-hearted attempts elsewhere to create multi-player versions of *Zork* and *Colossal Cave Adventure* foundered on this point. What Trubshaw and Bartle realised was that they had to make *MUD* open-ended, a notion that accorded well with their philosophy of promoting personal freedom.[5] Bartle in particular saw the need to create a new form of gameplay for *MUD* as a means of giving people freedom to be – and become – their real selves (Bartle, 2003).

Version 2 of *MUD* was written in assembly language, and it gradually became more and more unwieldy as features were added. In the fall of 1979, Trubshaw decided to rewrite it from scratch, and began work on version 3 (using BCPL, a fore-runner of C). He had its core working by Easter 1980, but it only did perhaps 25% of what he envisaged. With his finals looming, he handed control of the code over to Bartle (who is a year younger). Bartle finished the engine and wrote almost all the content to complete what, despite its being version 3, was to become known as *MUD1*.

Local players were able to use the *MUD* system to write their own virtual worlds.[6] Non-local players were able to access *MUD* through packet-switching

---

[3]My oldest extant program listings for *MUD*, along with original design artefacts, are deposited in the archives of Stanford University Libraries and Academic Information Resources. They asked first. http://library.stanford.edu/.

[4]He acknowledged this in *MUD*'s very name: the *D*, while chosen primarily to complete a memorable acronym, formally stands for *Dungeon* (a Fortran port of *Zork* that Trubshaw had encountered).

[5]This "personal freedom allows people to do good" world view was common among those who worked with computers at the time, probably because only those holding to that particular set of values could function as programmers in those experimental, tool-free days (Levy, 1984).

[6]The best-known of these were *ROCK* (Fox, 1983) and *MIST* (Barham et al., 1987).

networks[7] and dial-up lines, and it was inevitable that in time they, too, would be inspired to write their own virtual worlds – but on their own computers.

Bartle put the concept into the public domain in 1985.

The Second Age: 1985–1989

The first *MUD1*-inspired virtual worlds to appear that weren't native to Essex University were *Shades* (Newell, 1985), *Gods* (Laurie, 1985) and *AMP* (Blandford, 1985). They were swiftly joined by the progressive *MirrorWorld* (Cordrey, Rogers, Wood, & Billington, 1986) and others. Because these games were all derived from *MUD*, they were referred to as MUDs; this is why *MUD* itself was redubbed *MUD1*.

Although most of these games began as free services, it soon became clear that there was money to be made from operating them. In 1985, *MUD1* launched on CompuNet in the UK and, a year later, on CompuServe in the USA. *Shades* was taken up by Micronet800, which operated independently in an area of British Telecom's nationwide Prestel viewdata network. *Gods* and *MirrorWorld* set up their own servers and hosted several virtual worlds on them. While some of these were *MUD1*inspired, others were derivatives of *MUD1*'s own "children". *MUD* itself was rewritten for the final time as *MUD2*.

All in all, scores of virtual worlds were written in the UK during the Second Age, mainly by enthusiasts of one or more of the "big four" (*MUD1*, *Shades*, *Gods* and *MirrorWorld*) who worked alone or in very small groups. The period is remembered as one of great excitement and experimentation. By 1987, almost all the key coding matters and gameplay tropes had been identified and nailed down; by 1989, so had the social and management procedures, including the protocols and tools for dealing with player problems (what would today be called "customer service issues").

Some degree of commercial success came to *MUD1*, *Shades*, *Gods*, *Avalon* (Simmons, James, Baber, & Evans, 1989) and *Federation II* [8] (Lenton, 1989). However, the expensive nature of telephone calls in the UK at the time meant that access to virtual worlds was effectively a luxury. The university sector did produce some new free games, but few escaped the confines of their host institution.

---

[7]As part of a joint project with the Post Office (now British Telecom), Essex University had an X.25 connection to the ARPAnet, the network which later evolved into the internet.

[8]There was no *Federation I*: the game began life in 1985 as a CompuNet project called *Multi-User Galaxy Game*, in an attempt to create a home-grown alternative to *MUD1*. It is notable for being the first virtual world to use a Science Fiction setting, although few (if any) other SF virtual worlds directly descend from it. Its de-emphasising of combat did influence other early virtual worlds, however.

There was one exception: *AberMUD*, so named because it originated at the University of Wales, Aberystwyth. Written by Alan Cox[9] in 1987, it wasn't particularly noteworthy in terms of its design (it relied rather heavily on combat), but it was fun to play and newbies liked it. The first version was coded in B (a stripped-down BCPL); after a year, though, Cox ported it to C. This was to prove a defining moment in virtual world history: being written in C meant that *AberMUD* could run under Unix – an operating system adopted by many computer science departments across the globe, connected by what was coming to be known as "the internet".

The Third Age: 1989–1995

AberMUD rampaged across university computer science departments, with local copies appearing on thousands of machines. It was the first virtual world most players had seen, and they wanted more. Duly inspired or frustrated by *AberMUD*, some of them began writing their own such virtual worlds, the most important results being *TinyMUD*, *LPMUD* and *DikuMUD*. Their differing views on what virtual worlds were "about" led to a schism that persists to this day.

TinyMUD was written by Jim Aspnes at Carnegie Mellon University in 1989. It had two "parent" worlds: *AberMUD* and a world called *Monster*. *Monster* had been developed in 1988 by Rich Skrenta of Northwestern University without his having any awareness of the existence of other virtual worlds. Its main difference from the *MUD1* tree was that it allowed players to create new content from within the virtual world itself; this had been the standard in *MUD* version 2, but had been dropped in the switch to version 3 and hadn't been picked up by any of its descendents.

TinyMUD was a deliberate de-gaming of *AberMUD*. Player activity centred on creating locations and populating them with objects; there was no formal gameplay whatsoever. This gave the virtual world a decidedly more communal feel. Although not quite the first such "social" virtual world (it was marginally predated by a *Shades* descendent, *Void* (Lindus, 1989)), it is the progenitor from which almost all subsequent ones descend.

TinyMUD itself lasted barely a year. Ultimately, its problem was that there was little substance to it. You could build things, but you couldn't make what you built do a lot. In 1990, Stephen White wrote *TinyMUCK* to extend the basic functionality.[10] He swiftly followed this up with *MOO* ("MUD, Object-Oriented"), which featured a fully functioning scripting language for object creation. *MOO* subsequently gave birth to *LambdaMOO* (Curtis, 1990), which became *the* social virtual world of the 1990s. *TinyMUCK*, meanwhile, sprouted Larry Foard's 1990 *TinyMUSH*.[11] This

---

[9]He is also well known for his pioneering work on the Linux operating system, in 2005 receiving a *LinuxWorld* lifetime achievement award in recognition of his efforts.

[10]*TinyMUCK* came with its own language, TinyMUF ("Multi-User Forth") embedded within.

[11]As with the MUCK in TinyMUCK, the MUSH in TinyMUSH wasn't intended to be an acronym.

introduced several innovative features, such as event triggering and programmable non-player characters.

From *TinyMUD*, then, there are three main sub-branches, or *codebases*: MOOs, which have found a niche in education; MUSHes, which are popular among narrative-driven role players; MUCKs, which are used mainly for social interaction. None of these have any meaningful game-like component, and their developers tend to distance them from the other direct descendents of *AberMUD*, which do.

LPMUD took its name from its author, Lars Pensjö, of the University of Gothenburg, Sweden. Pensjö had played *AberMUD* and *TinyMUD*, and wanted the gameplay of the former with the flexibility of the latter (in part, because he felt that other people were better at game design than he[12]). To this end, he devised a user-friendly, object-oriented language called LPC for creating game worlds. Because of LPC's expressive power, every LPMUD that was made was individual.

This is not something that could be said of *DikuMUD*. Created in 1990 by a group of friends[13] at the Department of Computer Science at the University of Copenhagen,[14] Denmark, it took the opposite approach to *TinyMUD* and focused on intensifying the game aspects of *AberMUD*, drawing heavily on concepts from *Advanced Dungeons and Dragons* such as character classes. The developers also eschewed the *TinyMUD* and *LPMUD* trend towards empowering players, hard-coding everything in C. This might have been a bad move, but they coded it *very* well. The gameplay of *DikuMUD* was deep and compelling, and its "runs out of the box" ease of installation ensured that lots of people got to experience it. Players of social worlds and the cerebral *LPMUD*s were speedily outnumbered by devotees of *DikuMUD* and its numerous progeny.

The Third Age of virtual world design can thus be characterised as a period of expansion. Indeed, a 1993 study of internet traffic showed that 10% of all the bits on the NSFnet backbone belonged to MUDs. However, with expansion came division: the tensions between people who played virtual worlds for social reasons and those who played for the gameplay came to a head, leading to a social/game world split that's still with us today.

Although the Third Age was dominated by virtual worlds played for free on university-run computers, professional virtual world developers had not been idle. They had the better products, but attracting new players was proving difficult.

If only they could find a way to reach a larger audience. . . ..

The Fourth Age: 1995–1997

The first commercial virtual world was probably *Sceptre of Goth*.

---

[12]"I didn't think I would be able to design a good adventure. By allowing wizards coding rights, I thought others could help me with this." Lars Pensjö, quoted in (Reese, 1996).

[13]Katja Nyboe, Tom Madsen, Hans Henrik Staerfeldt, Michael Seifert and Sebastian Hammer.

[14]Datalogisk Institut ved Københavns Universitet.

Around the same time that Roy Trubshaw wrote *MUD*, Alan Klietz wrote a game called *Milieu* on a computer operated by the Minnesota Educational Computer Consortium. It was inspired mainly by *Colossal Cave Adventure* and *Dungeons and Dragons*, and during its development acquired the necessary features that would today categorise it as a MUD (although it was developed completely independently of *MUD*). In 1983, Klietz ported it to an IBM XT, renaming it *Sceptre of Goth*. He formed a company, GamBit, to franchise the game to others, and it launched successfully as a commercial product in six US cities.

GamBit sold its software to a company called InterPlay, which promptly (and for unrelated reasons) went bankrupt. *Sceptre of Goth* disappeared with it. It was not without influence, however: it inspired *GemStone*, of which more anon.

Although early virtual worlds flowered in the UK, the cost of accessing them (over telephone lines) was prohibitive. In contrast, phone calls in the USA cost pretty well nothing, so large online service providers such as CompuServe emerged there. Games were actually very profitable for CompuServe, but were seldom promoted for fear of putting off business users and parents.

The first online service to embrace games was GEnie, set up in 1985 by Bill Louden (the former head of games at CompuServe). The strategy had mixed results: by the early 1990s games accounted for 40% of GEnie's revenue,[15] but it had far fewer subscribers than CompuServe[16] because business users and parents were indeed put off by a games-first attitude.

GEnie's games product manager at the time was Jessica Mulligan, who had arrived from another 1985 start-up, QuantumLink (later to become AOL). QuantumLink featured a popular early graphical chat-oriented world, *Habitat* (Morningstar & Farmer, 1985), and Mulligan had recommended acquiring the *Advanced Dungeons and Dragons* licence for an online game (eventually realised as *Never Winter Nights*[17] (Daglow & Mataga, 1991)). At GEnie, she oversaw a product line that came to include some of the finest online games of the day. The year 1990 saw the introduction of old UK favourite, *Federation II*, followed by two important newcomers: *GemStone* and *Dragon's Gate*.

David Whatley's original *GemStone* was a hard-coded prototype which would not readily run on GEnie's mainframes. Whatley formed a company, Simutronics, to develop *GemStone*, hiring (among others) five ex-*Sceptre of Goth* people to create content for its new game engine. Following *Gemstone*'s launch, Simutronics started on *GemStone III*, which was even better suited to GEnie's system.

Adventures Unlimited Software, Inc. ("AUSI") had been set up 5 years earlier by programmer Mark Jacobs to run a virtual world called *Aradath* that he had created (independently of *MUD*). *Aradath* had adopted the (at the time) innovative

---

[15]The usual figure quoted is 70%, but according to Neil Harris, who was Director, Marketing at GEnie, it peaked at 40%.

[16]CompuServe had well over a million around this time; GEnie claimed 400,000 but the reality was somewhere between 100,000 and 125,000.

[17]Note that although this shares the *Forgotten Realms* setting of the 2002 BioWare game of the same name, there's no formal connection between the two.

approach of charging users a flat fee to play, rather than using per-hour rates. One of Simutronics' lead programmers, Darrin Hyrup, was sufficiently impressed by AUSI's potential that he signed up with Jacobs to write *Dragon's Gate*. The result was a compelling, well-engineered game world.

In 1993, the online market was dominated by five US providers: CompuServe, Prodigy, AOL, Delphi and GEnie. Smaller, sector-specific services existed, which for games included MPG-Net and The Sierra Network.[18] Those commercial virtual world developers who could get their games on one or more of these systems were in reasonable shape; times were lean for those that couldn't.

Then came the roller-coaster ride.

With the arrival of the world wide web in 1994, people became excited by "online". They flocked to those companies that could offer internet access. Some service providers, led by AOL, readily accepted their business; others, most notably CompuServe, remained aloof (much to their cost). By 1995, hordes of internet new-bies were signed up to AOL, looking for interesting content. Naturally, a good many of them wanted to play games.

So began the short but remarkable Fourth Age of virtual worlds. With *NeverWinter Nights* only able to accommodate 500 simultaneous users, AOL swooped on *GemStone III*, *Dragon's Gate* and *Federation II*, offering them a fair royalty on its hourly fees. The result was that developers found themselves taking in over a million dollars a month. It was a tremendous time to be in the industry *if* your game was on AOL; if it wasn't, it was somewhat frustrating.

It couldn't last. When small bulletin-board systems began to offer internet access for a flat, monthly fee, AOL had to follow suit. In December, 1996, it changed its $2.95 hourly charge to $19.99 per month all-in, and by the middle of 1997 the money machine had stopped.

Thus, the Fourth Age of virtual worlds ended. Despite its short duration, though, it had made a significant point: virtual worlds could be lucrative. The wider games industry began to take notice: although handling 3,000 players at once for a flat monthly fee was not profitable, suppose some way of attracting, say, ten times this number could be found? Yet would that many people really play a text game in the late 1990s?

Fortunately, virtual worlds don't have to be textual.

The Fifth Age: 1995–Present

Graphical virtual worlds were not a new idea.

PLATO ("Programmed Logic for Automated Teaching Operation") started life as an innovative computer-aided learning system at the University of Illinois in 1960. The fourth version, which began operation in 1972, featured an integrated graphics-capable plasma display and excellent network connectivity; it was way ahead of

---

[18]Renamed the *ImagiNation Network* in 1994.

its time, and trail-blazed many ideas which have since become mainstream. Some of the games developed on it set out principles which would greatly influence the design of later games on other systems.

Naturally, it had virtual worlds.

It's actually quite difficult to pin down which of several PLATO IV games was its first virtual world; even PLATO enthusiasts seem unable to agree. It's generally recognised that *Avatar*[19] (Maggs, Shapira, & Sides, 1979) probably qualifies: it features high degrees of player interaction and contains all of the features expected of a virtual world. Its only failing is in its poor persistence, but then *MUD1* was only marginally better in that regard. However, *Avatar* was created to beat *Oubliette* (Schwaiger et al., 1977). Was *Oubliette* a virtual world? Well, its player interaction was extremely limited and it was not truly persistent, but does that completely rule it out? *Oubliette* in turn drew from *Mines of Moria* (Miller et al., 1976), which had even less interaction, and *Mines of Moria* was itself ultimately inspired by *Orthanc* (Resch, Kemp, & Hagstrom, 1973). *Orthanc* was not a shared *world*, but it allowed shared *communication* between players across games. Does that make it a virtual world?

In the end, it's moot: although PLATO left a great legacy in many areas of hardware, software, interface and game design, its influence on the development of virtual worlds is practically zero.[20] There's no audit trail from today's virtual worlds back to those of PLATO. Golf was invented in China.

This is true of several other graphical virtual worlds. For example, although *Habitat* was a fair success, it didn't inspire any successful imitators; its main influence has come through the authors' must-read post-mortem (Morningstar & Farmer, 1991).

One graphical virtual world from which others did flow was *Islands of Kesmai*, written by Kelton Flinn and John Taylor in 1981 at the University of Virginia. It was an early signing by Bill Louden at CompuServe,[21] where it went live in December 1985. The term "graphics" is used fairly loosely here, as *IOK* used groups of ASCII characters to display its virtual world: [ ] represented a wall, for example. These groups were arranged as a flat tessellation of squares to present a bird's eye view. Later game worlds, particularly AOL's *NeverWinter Nights* and MPG-net's *Kingdom of Drakkar* (Lineberger, 1992), copied the idea but replaced the ASCII with 2D images.

Despite these pictorial advances, today's Fifth Age graphical worlds owe very little to *NWN* or *KoD*: their roots lie almost entirely in the Third Age with DikuMUDs. The idea of graphical MUDs was an old and obvious one – it wasn't as if anyone had to see *IOK* to get the idea of them – and although their interfaces are different,

---

[19]*Avatar* was the most successful ever PLATO game, accounting for 6% of all PLATO usage during its tenure.

[20]It would be completely zero, but a few influential people in the virtual world industry did cut their teeth on PLATO. In particular, producer Gordon Walton, lawyer Andy Zaffron and designer David Shapiro ("Dr Cat") played a lot of *Avatar*.

[21]It was also offered to The Source, but was not received favourably even though it already ran on the same type of mainframe (Prime Computer) it used.

the engineering behind a graphical world is much the same as that behind a textual one. There were thousands of people who had experience playing, developing and designing textual worlds, as opposed to a few dozen at most who had worked on graphical worlds; therefore, when companies were looking for people to hire to work on new graphical worlds, they found a huge supply of talented people from a textual-world background and almost none from a graphical-world background. As a result, today's graphical worlds are not the descendents of earlier graphical worlds, but of textual worlds. Furthermore, this leap from text to graphics happened the same way twice: in the Far East and in the West.

MUDs had arrived in Oriental universities in the early 1990s, and rapidly gained popularity among students in China, Taiwan and South Korea. As elsewhere, the players were keen to write their own games, and some went on to do so.

The South Korean government's decision to promote investment in internet infrastructure prompted two companies to develop graphical virtual worlds. Perhaps surprisingly, both worlds were designed by the same person, Jake Song.[22] Song had written a MUD called *Baramue Nara* while a student at the Korea Advanced Institute of Science and Technology in 1994. His first graphical world was Nexon's *The Kingdom of the Winds*, launched in 1996; NCSoft's *Lineage* followed in 1997. Both games were enormous successes: *KotW* picked up a million subscribers, and *Lineage*, at its peak, around four times as many. Both games opted for a third-person, isometric viewpoint which has the same tessellated-squares base of the *IOK* derivatives but places the camera at an angle so as to give the impression of a 3D landscape (technically, this is known as a $2\frac{1}{2}D$ approach – it looks 3D but you can't have caves or bridges).

Meanwhile, back in the West, there were four companies working on (what were at the time called) graphical MUDs. Each had a different approach, and, as they all knew about each other, there was something of a race to become the "first" such game.

The winner was *Meridian 59*, designed by Mike Sellers and Damion Schubert, which went live in 1996.[23] It was also $2\frac{1}{2}D$, but presented a first-person viewpoint with proper perspective. Unfortunately, although its design was sound, it launched prematurely: it didn't have enough content; its graphics didn't compare well with those of single-player games of the era; too few potential players had internet connections[24]; its publisher (3DO) didn't market it well. If it hadn't tried to be first, it could have become the paradigm; instead, it became the pioneer.

Second out, in 1997, was *Ultima Online*, and it is with this game that the tide really turned. Its lead designer, Raph Koster, had co-created the very much admired *LegendMUD*[25] (Delashmit, Koster, & Koster, 1994), and he set out to build

---

[22]Perhaps unsurprisingly, he's now regarded as one of Korea's most esteemed game designers.

[23]Indeed, it went live exactly 10 years ago to the day that I'm writing this: 27 September, 1996.

[24]It garnered around 12,000 players, with each instantiation of the world capable of holding around 250 players – about the same as for contemporary textual worlds.

[25]It was an offshoot of the 1992 *World of Carnage* (where the Koster met *Meridian 59*'s Damion Schubert), and although ultimately derived from *DikuMUD* was – and remains – an incredibly

something which was a *world* rather than a *game*. With the name and setting of the much-loved *Ultima* (Garriott, 1980) series[26] behind it, the *UO* team believed they may be able to attract large numbers of players – perhaps, in their dreams, as many as 40,000! When they hit 100,000 within a year of launch, suddenly what had been regarded as something of a backwater by mainstream games companies was treated seriously. Those 100,000 players were paying $9.95 a month *having already bought the game*, and none of that money was going to retailers. *UO* was no longer simply an online role-playing game, it was a *massively multiplayer online role-playing game* – an MMORPG.

UO was the breakthrough world, but it fell victim to its own success. The flood of players who swept through it rapidly overwhelmed the content and caused severe technical difficulties.[27] There was pressure to deal with problems expediently, papering over cracks that should really have been replastered. Even so, *UO* was to peak at around 250,000 players during the period 2001–2003, and today still has numbers that most start-ups would be overjoyed to obtain.

Ultima Online had an isometric viewpoint, like *Lineage*, so again was 2½D. The first fully 3D virtual world was *EverQuest* (McQuaid, Clover, & Trost, 1999).

EverQuest was basically a DikuMUD with a graphical front-end bolted on.[28] Its look was similar but superior to *M59*'s, filling more of the screen and so increasing the sense of immersion engendered. It launched just as *UO* was getting some bad press and was publicised very well. Its DikuMUD heritage gave it compelling gameplay, and within 6 months it had overtaken *UO* as the #1 virtual world in the West. In its 2001–2004 heyday, its 425,000+ player base was regarded with envy by every other developer, and over a hundred new worlds were announced that aimed to take its crown (mainly by mimicking it). In terms of today's graphical worlds, it is *EQ* rather than *UO* or *M59* that most deserves to be called the progenitor.

The fourth major virtual world to go live was *Asheron's Call* (Ragaini, 1999), which came out 9 months after *EQ* but was itself a year late. Also fully 3D, had it beaten EQ to the punch it could have done exceptionally well; as it was, it barely managed to break the 100,000 benchmark in *EQ*'s wake.

It was almost two years before the next notable game world appeared – *Anarchy Online* (Godager, 2001). *AO* was Europe's first foray into the marketplace, being a joint Norwegian/Irish venture with a Science Fiction premise. Unfortunately, its launch was a disaster from which it never fully recovered.

---

detailed fantasy world, with deep, hand-crafted quests. Delashmit, its programmer, left in 1995 to become lead programmer for *Ultima Online*, and it was he who recommended the Kosters to Origin Systems (*UO*'s publisher).

[26] The Ultima series of role-playing games was famed for combining open-ended gameplay with a strong narrative. For a list of the full series, see http://www.mobygames.com/game-group/ultima-series.

[27] At one point, the internet bandwidth used by *UO* was greater than that used by New York.

[28] So close are the similarities that *EverQuest*'s programmers were obliged to sign a sworn statement to confirm that they didn't use any *DikuMUD* code in the game. http://www.dikumud.com/img/server.gif.

The same could not be said of *Dark Age of Camelot*, which materialised four months later. The reason was experience: *DAoC* was developed by Mythic Entertainment, a reinvention of AUSI – the developers of *Dragon's Gate*.[29] Its well-prepared, smooth launch[30] remains to this day a model of exactly how to do things right, and Mark Jacobs' carefully targeted design ensured that it picked up the players to match. Within a year it had 200,000 subscribers, supplanting *AC* in the "big three" (with *EQ* and *UO*).[31] These virtual worlds remained pre-eminent until 2004.

With many upcoming virtual worlds in development, promising better graphics and more advanced gameplay, the leading developers decided to bring out new products themselves. These came in two basic flavours: existing virtual worlds with the number 2 after their name; new virtual worlds based on popular franchises.

The first two franchised virtual worlds to gain a head of publicity were *The Sims Online* and *Star Wars Galaxies*. *The Sims* (Wright, 2000) is a hugely successful series of single-player games, and it was natural that executives would consider it a prime candidate for making into a virtual world. Virtual world designers, however, were perplexed: *The Sims* is, in essence, a virtual dollhouse; people play *with* dolls, not *as* them. Sure enough, it shot up to over 100,000 players within a year of its December 2002 launch, but then shed them almost as rapidly to reach a plateau of around 30,000.

Star Wars Galaxies had an excellent pedigree: a much-loved movie series and, in Raph Koster, a virtual world designer of proven ability. It was regarded as a serious contender to become the first Western virtual world to rack up a million players – and had it launched to Koster's design it could indeed have done so. However, it ran into production delays, and went live in June 2003 missing several important features. Although it reached an impressive 300,000 players almost immediately, and maintained that figure for nearly 18 months, it then slid badly as the promised content still failed to appear. The "Combat Upgrade" of April 2005 and the "New Game Enhancements" that followed in December changed *SWG*'s character entirely, losing it tens of thousands of players (although successfully stabilising around those who remained).

Other new virtual worlds set in existing imaginary universes have fared even less well than *SWG*. *The Matrix Online* (Ragaini, 2005), despite being designed by Toby Ragaini (who was also responsible for *Asheron's Call*), didn't even reach 50,000 subscribers after launching in March 2005. Only Turbine Inc.'s *The Lord of the*

---

[29]This is why I said Fifth-Age virtual worlds were *almost* entirely descended from Third-Age worlds. Mythic products *DAoC* and *Warhammer: Age of Reckoning* came from a Fourth-Age world and are currently the only major MMORPGs not to be a direct descendent of *MUD1* (although Simutronics' *Hero's Journey*, a derivative of *Gemstone IV*, will shortly join them).

[30]A launch is said to be smooth if the players can buy and install the software without problem; they can access the servers without problem; there are neither too many nor too few servers available; the servers don't crash; the clients don't crash; there are no horrendous bugs that render the world unplayable. All this is well known to virtual world developers, yet products are still launched which manage to fail in every one of these respects...

[31]Alternatively, for those with a soft spot for *AC*, expanding the "big three" to the "big four".

Rings Online can be regarded as a success – but it followed at least three failed attempts by other companies to fit the licence.

Most of the "add a 2" worlds were not great triumphs either. Electronic Arts canned several follow-ups to *Ultima Online*, one after the other, before any were even launched. *Asheron's Call 2* removed all the gameplay elements that players complained about and was left with a boring, empty husk.

There were attempts by console manufacturers to crack the virtual world market, beginning with SEGA's 2000 offering, *Phantasy Star Online* (Sonic Team, 2000) for the Dreamcast, but the lack of a keyboard as standard with most consoles undermined this effort. To date, the only real success has been Sony's 2002 *Final Fantasy XI* (Square Co., 2002) for the Playstation 2, helped largely by its additional provision of a PC client.

In practice, the cost of creating graphical worlds was so high that most of the new games announced never made it to beta-testing. Some, however, did. Furthermore, the ones that survived tended not to be the *EverQuest* clones that comprised the bulk of the announcements. Of particular note are the following, all of which went live in 2003: *A Tale in the Desert* (Tepper, 2003), *Toontown* (Walt Disney Imagineering, 2003), *Yohoho! Puzzle Pirates* (James, 2003),[32] *Project Entropia* (Timkrans et al., 2003) and *EVE Online* (Emilsson, 2003).

With dozens of new virtual worlds appearing every year both in the West and in the Far East, it would be fruitless to list them all here.[33] To bring us up to date, there are two, however, that merit special mention: *Second Life* and *World of Warcraft*.

Second Life is not a game, because it has no embedded gameplay. It's a social world, the latter-day successor to *LambdaMOO*. Developed by Linden Labs in 2003, all its content is created by its players, who buy and sell their wares for "Linden dollars" – an internal currency that can be purchased with real currency. Its player-empowerment innovations are ground-breaking, and it leads the way in establishing virtual worlds' relationship to society at large. It is the automatic first point of call for non-gamer journalists and academics who want to find out more about virtual worlds, and its precedents are marking out the real/virtual boundary in ways that game worlds are reluctant to consider. There are other free-to-play social worlds that have a larger user base (in particular *Habbo Hotel*, which has over 4 million unique visitors per month[34] compared to *Second Life*'s 1 million[35]); however, it is *Second Life* that is the more likely to affect real-world social policy.

By all rights, the other virtual world I should be talking about is *EverQuest II* (Cao, 2004). Unlike its fellow sequels, *EQ2* did very well: it had a superb launch, was critically acclaimed by players of *EverQuest* and had over 300,000 players

---

[32] Daniel James has long experience in virtual world design: he was a player of *MUD1* (for which he wrote the wizards' guide in 1984) and was one of the designers of *Avalon* in 1989.

[33] For a reasonable list, see http://www.mmorpg.com/gamelist.cfm/gameId/0.

[34] http://www.sulake.com/pressroom_releases_01122005.html.

[35] Daily updated figures are shown at https://secondlife.com/currency/economy.php (free registration required).

within three months. It had a solid design, proven gameplay, quality graphics, stable hardware, experienced customer service representatives, excellent publicity *and* the *EverQuest* name. It couldn't fail, and indeed it didn't: by all previous metrics, it was a success. So why does it now barely rate a mention?

The answer is that a few weeks after *EQ2* launched, *World of Warcraft* arrived. *WoW* has some 11 million players at the time of writing, and those numbers are still rising.

There are several factors that contributed to *WoW*'s success – the *Warcraft* name, its huge development budget[36] – but what it really comes down to is *craftsmanship* and *design*. The developers, Blizzard Entertainment, had some experience of running a large-scale online game in *Diablo II* (Hedlund, 2000), the success of which had been marred by their making a number of classic mistakes. They learned from these, put all the necessary infrastructure in place and polished the software until it shone. It was unquestionably going to be a quality product in terms of its implementation.

WoW's designers were Rob Pardo, Jeffrey Kaplan and Tom Chilton. Pardo and Kaplan had been heavy players of *EverQuest*, and Chilton was lead designer of the fifth *Ultima Online* expansion, *Age of Shadows*. They gave *WoW* a more whimsical look than its competitors (which were heading towards photorealism) and made it easy to play solo (instead of always in groups). There were many reasons to play and few reasons not to, and while *WoW*'s design elements are not all particularly original, the way they are fitted together is done *very* cleverly. Crucially, the different forms of gameplay that coexist alongside each other make *WoW* just as popular in the Far East as in the West: around half its players live in China (Schiesel, 2006).

The state of play at the moment is the following:

- *World of Warcraft* rules virtual worlds as games.
- *Second Life* has the most influence over policy-makers and opinion-formers, at least in the West.
- Large populations of players frequent social spaces that may be regarded as virtual worlds, such as *Habbo Hotel*,[37] *Active Worlds*[38] and *Virtual Magic Kingdom*.[39]
- Browser-situated games, which can be played through office or school firewalls, are an emerging category. The leader here is Java-based *RuneScape* (Gower, 2002), which has 800,000 paying customers and over 9 million playing for free (Radd, 2006).

---

[36] The amount spent to develop *World of Warcraft* is variously quoted at between $30m and $60m, both with and without the promotional costs.

[37] http://www.habbohotel.com/habbo/en/.

[38] http://www.activeworlds.com/.

[39] http://vmk.disney.go.com/vmk/en_US/index?name=VMKHomePage.

- There is a renaissance of virtual world design, with developers seeking new angles and genres rather than trying to compete on the centre ground. They're going with micropayment business models, rather than subscriptions.
- Games that use licensed IP still have potential.
- The Far East, particularly South Korea, is way ahead of the West when it comes to integrating virtual worlds into mainstream culture.

So where will virtual worlds go next?

Conclusion

We've been here before.

Graphical virtual worlds have pretty well followed the same historical path as their textual predecessors. We're currently at about 1992. We had an original paradigm which gave rise to three or four early successes that ruled the roost for a period, a sudden flourishing of different designs and a split between social and game-like worlds. The current market is dominated by a handful of large operators that make it increasingly difficult for others to compete for players.

If graphical worlds follow the textual precedent, we can therefore expect to see the following:

- The introduction of some equivalent of codebases – free or inexpensive game engines that allow the creation of new virtual worlds without major programming effort. This is already starting to happen with projects such as *Multiverse*,[40] *Realmcrafter*[41] and *Worldforge*.[42]
- Serious use of virtual worlds as tools for education and training.
- The proliferation of virtual worlds created by and for groups of friends, perhaps even down to the granularity of a personal *Facebook* page. *Metaplace*[43] looks to be the model here.
- The continued existence of large-scale commercial worlds, albeit with less of a grip on more experienced players.
- Increased understanding of design issues.
- Some major paradigm shift which will start the cycle all over again.

Virtual worlds have been invented on at least six separate occasions: *MUD*, *Sceptre of Goth*, *Avatar*, *Islands of Kesmai*, *Aradath* and *Monster*. They were always going to happen, and they were always going to go graphical. Today's extravaganzas are the latest in what promises to be a long chain of developments. Although some

---

[40] http://www.multiverse.net/.

[41] http://www.realmcrafter.com/.

[42] http://www.worldforge.org/.

[43] https://www.metaplace.com/.

of what we can expect in the next decade is foreseeable, much is not. Will there be some kind of world wide web of worlds, or will society move on? Is *World of Warcraft* the zenith of large-population worlds, or will something appear that is to *WoW* as *WoW* is to the once-dominant *EQ*? Will the real world welcome the virtual, or seek to weaken them through regulation?

Whatever happens, we can be sure of one thing: the history of virtual worlds does not end here.

References

Anderson, T., Blank, M., Daniels, B., & Lebling, D. (1977). *Zork*. Cambridge, MA: Massachusetts Institute of Technology.

Barham, D., Goodjohn, P., Medhurst, J., Morris, D., Plumb, S., Friday, P., et al. (1987). *MIST*. Essex: University of Essex.

Bartle, R. (2003). *Designing virtual worlds*. Indianapolis, IN: New Riders.

Blandford, M. (1985). *AMP: Adventure for multiple players*.

Cao, C. (2004). *EverQuest 2*. San Diego, CA: Sony Online Entertainment.

Cordrey, P., Rogers, T., Wood, L., & Billington, N. (1986). *MirrorWorld*. Input/Output World of Adventure.

Crowther, W., & Woods, D. (1976). *Colossal cave adventure*. Cambridge, MA: Bolt, Beranek and Newman.

Curtis, P. (1990). *LambdaMOO*.

Daglow, D., & Mataga, C. (1991). *NeverWinter nights*. Stormfront Studios.

Delashmit, R., Koster, K., & Koster, R. (1994). *LegendMUD*.

Emilsson, K. (2003). *EVE online*. CCP Games.

Flannery, M., & Leech, R. (2003). *Golf through the ages: 600 years of golfing art*. Fairfield, IA: Golf Links Press. Retrieved from http://www.golfspast.com/golfthroughtheages/

Fox, P. (1983). *ROCK*. Essex: University of Essex.

Garriott, R. (1980). *Akalabeth: World of doom*. California Pacific Computer.

Godager, G. (2001). *Anarchy online*. Funcom.

golf (2008). *Encyclopaedia Britannica online*. Retrieved from http://www.britannica.com/eb/article-222217

Gower, A. (2002). *RuneScape*. Cambridge: Jagex.

Gygax, G., & Arneson, D. (1974). *Dungeons and dragons*. Lake Geneva, WI: Tactical Studies Rules.

Hedlund, S. (2000). *Diablo II*. Irvine, California: Blizzard Entertainment.

James, D. (2003). *Yohoho! Puzzle pirates*. San Francisco, CA: Three Rings.

Laurie, B. (1985). *Gods*. Lap of the Gods.

Lenton, A. (1989). *Federation II*. Barking: CompuNet.

Levy, S. (1984). *Hackers: Heroes of the computer revolution*. Garden City, NY: Anchor Press.

Lindus, C. (1989). *Void*.

Lineberger, B. (1992). *The Kingdom of Drakkar*. Cary, NC: MPG-net.

Ling H. (1991). Verification of the fact that golf originated from Chuiwan. *Bulletin for the Australian Society for Sports History, 14*, 12–23. Retrieved from http://www.aafla.org/SportsLibrary/ASSH%20Bulletins/No%2014/ASSHBulletin14c.pdf#search=%22dongxuan%20records%22

Maggs, B., Shapira, A., Sides, D. (1979). *Avatar*. Urbana, IL: University of Illinois.

McQuaid, B., Clover, S., & Trost, B. (1999). *EverQuest*. San Diego, CA: Verant Interactive/Sony Online Entertainment

Miller, C., et al. (1976). *Mines of moria*. Urbana, IL: University of Illinois

Morningstar, C., & Randall Farmer, F. (1985). *Habitat*. San Francisco, CA: Lucasfilms

Morningstar, C., & Randall Farmer, F. (1991). The lessons of Lucasfilm's habitat. In M. Benedickt (Ed.), *Cyberspace: First steps*. Cambridge, MA: MIT Press. Retrieved from http://www.fudco.com/chip/lessons.html

Newell, N. (1985). *Shades*. London: Micronet800.

Radd, D. (2006, July 17). *WildTangent explores RuneScape. GameDaily Biz*. Retrieved from http://biz.gamedaily.com/industry/adwatch/?id=13256&page=1

Ragaini, T. (1999). *Asheron's Call*. Westwood, MA: Turbine.

Ragaini, T. (2005). *The Matrix Online*. San Francisco, CA: Sega.

Reese, G. (1996). *The LPC Timeline v1.6*. Excerpted: http://www.coremud.org/dragon/mudos_docs/about/history.html. Archived: http://web.archive.org/web/20041011031443/http://www.imaginary.com/LPMud/timeline.html

Resch, P., Kemp, L., & Hagstrom, E. (1973). *Orthanc*. Urbana, IL: University of Illinois.

Schiesel, S. (2006, September 5). Online game, made in U.S., seizes the globe. *New York Times*. Retrieved from http://www.nytimes.com/2006/09/05/technology/05wow.html (free registration required).

Schwaiger, J., et al. (1977). *Oubliette*. Urbana, IL: University of Illinois.

Simmons, Y., James, D., Baber, J., & Evans, P. (1989). *Avalon*. Input/Output World of Adventure.

Sonic Team (2000). *Phantasy Star Online*. San Francisco, CA: Sega.

Square Co. (2002). *Final Fantasy XI*. Tokyo: Sony/Square Enix.

Tepper, A. (2003). *A Tale in the Desert*. Pittsburgh, PA: eGenesis.

Timkrans, J. W., et al. (2003). *Project Entropia*. Gothenburg: MindArk.

unknown: *The autumn banquet*. Ming Dynasty (1368–1644). Retrieved from http://www.heritagemuseum.gov.hk/english/exhibition_highlight_file/ex38_5.htm

unknown: *Les heures de la Duchesse de Bourgogne*, September. France. circa 1500. Retrieved from http://www.moleiro.com/images/164/en/f._27r,_calendar,_September.html

Walt Disney Imagineering (2003). *Toontown*. Burbank, CA: The Walt Disney Company.

Wei, T. *Dongxuan Records* v12. Song Dynasty (960–1279).

Wright, W. (2000). *The Sims*. Redwood City, CA: Electronic Arts.

Visual Iconic Patterns of Instant Messaging: Steps Towards Understanding Visual Conversations

Hillary Bays

Text, emoticons, short animations and sound are among the different media which are the tools to communicate in instant messaging (IM). Add that to the screen which is segmented into distinctive zones, and further subdivided according to the number and disposition of conversations or other parallel activities, and then combine that with the user's surrounding physical environment to constitute the whole IM experience. With colourful screens and a particular lingo, this type of expression can be likened to "visual art" (Danet, 2001) or the "virtual" replication of an audible phonology with several input (Stevenson, 1999). Instead, it should be viewed as an interactive platform for communication. The configuration of visual cues allows us to approach this subject as a *gestalt* founded on visual perception and eventually to postulate a visual phonology to describe it linguistically.

This article will deal with three main issues. First, since recording synchronous, textual interaction has been problematic within the research community, we will describe a new in situ method of data collection. Our aim is to expose the particularity of an IM corpus using recording techniques (including text, video and screen capture) which highlight not only the micro-phenomenal level of the recorded conversation, but the macro-socio level of synchronous interaction. We will focus in particular on the use and function of visual markers – smileys, emoticons, animations – in instant messaging conversations. Therefore, using an interactional linguistics approach we can study the importance of iconic markers and physical behaviour emergent in synchronous CMC. Second, we will briefly outline a taxonomy of these visual markers which serve as an iconic sublanguage in the interactions. Finally, we identify patterns of use for these visual conversational cues. Our goal is to propose a kind of visual phonology as a means of interpreting their function within the larger context of other visual conversation codes and co-produced, physical behaviour.

By concentrating on the visual markers of instant messaging, we hope to demonstrate in a more systematic way that *the use of smileys in conversation is not*

H. Bays (✉)
Modyco CNRS-UMR 7114, University Paris X & University of Cergy-Pontoise Departement de Langues, 33 bd du Port, 95011 Cergy-Pontoise 33-1-34-25-60-00
e-mail: hillary.bays@u-cergy.fr

J. Hunsinger et al. (eds.), *International Handbook of Internet Research*,
DOI 10.1007/978-1-4020-9789-8_3, © Springer Science+Business Media B.V. 2010

arbitrary but an organized interactional, situated and structured practice.[1] As such, smileys may be understood as a kind of visual prosody and having a pragmatic function. *The use of emoticons constitutes a kind of meta-language, like a visual prosody used to frame discourse and aid understanding* relying on a culturally identifiable and persistent visual form. More broadly, this study aims at understanding the cognitive and interactional role of smileys within a holistic conversation which emerges in and around IM and are parallel and in addition to webcam and text modes.

Literature Review

Given the popularity of instant messaging especially among teens, researchers, educators, journalists and parents have become interested in understanding its use. As such, we find more and more literature about instant messaging in the general press and in some circles of academic CMC research as well. These papers talk about the social aspects of IM (Blum, 2004; Gross, 2004; Lenhart, Rainie, & Lewis, 2001; Wellman, 2001, 2007; Yahoo! Survey, 2007), in higher education (Blum, 2004; Farmer, 2003), using IM as a collaborative tool in the workplace (Delalande, 2007; Quan-Hasse, Cothrel, & Wellman, 2005; Shiu & Lenhart, 2004) and the consequences of IM on writing practices such as spelling and sentence construction (O'Connor, 2006). Several studies by the Pew Research Center (Lenhart et al., 2001; Shiu & Lenhart, 2004) have looked into instant messaging in the American population in general as with American teens. While not oriented to linguistics in particular, Randall (2002) provides insight as to how people in Canada construct IM language with emoticons and abbreviations.

Linguists Baron (2003, 2005a, 2005b, 2005c, 2007), Tagliamonte and Denis (2006) and Schieffelin and Jones (2008) have published empirical analyses of IM language including statistics on structural and lexical features. Related studies include linguistic analyses of asynchronous CMC such as those by Anis (1988, 1998, 1999), Herring (1996), Yates (1996) and synchronous CMC by Isabelle Pierozak (Pierosak, ed., *Glottopol*, 2007) covering research on chat in French and Creole contexts.[2]

These previous studies of what many call the mixed oral and textual mode of IM have measured quantitative factors, e.g. spelling, length of turn, number of smileys used and gender differences (Baron, 2005a, 2005b, 2005c), by relying on the text printout of these conversations. Quantitative factors should be taken into consideration when examining the structure of IM conversations. However, they are insufficient for understanding the whole conversational practice. This is because

---

[1] For more on situated and shared practice of language organisation, cf. Harold Garfinkel, *Studies in Ethnomethodology*, Englewood Cliffs, NJ, Prentice Hall, 1967.

[2] Another article in this volume of particular interest to studying visual cues is by Marcoccia and Gauducheau (2007) dealing with the oral-written dimension of smileys in discussion groups and emails.

IM conversations are dynamic, and it is important to see the whole gestalt by including the environment and surroundings of the interaction. This means that everything from the onscreen activity with its colours and mosaic of windows to the physical environment of the user who may be listening to music, talking on the phone or engaged in exogenous conversations[3] are also important to forming the whole IM experience. Thus, secondary methods of recording data are essential to the study of visual cues in these situations as they are in the study of face-to-face conversation with gestures, gaze and body position playing interactional roles. Phenomenologically, it is the whole process that the participants consider as the "conversation".

Compiling the Data: Multimodal Recording

The data for this article were drawn from a linguistic study of instant messaging and chat called *Rythmes et temporalités de la communication électronique – RYTE* (Bays, de Fornel, & Verdier, 2006). This research observed the function of temporalities created and rhythm in electronic synchronic conversations as well as in the context of language production itself. Today's research is an offshoot of this first project, aimed at more fully understanding one aspect of the rhythmic processes of synchronous CMC.

To capture the subject, screen and the surrounding environment, we used simultaneous multi-modal synchronous recording methods including two or three angles of video (frontal, profile and subjective views) and automatic screen capture using CamStudio (recording documents into AVI format) during the IM session.[4] Time-tagged logs of the event were also recorded for each session of chat. Then, these inputs were synchronized making possible a more complete analysis of the whole process of communication including body position, gesture, gaze and hand movements co-produced with the online activity (Fig. 1). With this type of recording technique we could then measure the temporality of the activity with its punctuated moments of activity followed by periods of waiting.

The data included 17 subjects aged 15 to 38, recorded over a period of about 9 months mostly in one Parisian cybercafé, but also at home, and for one data session in a language laboratory at the University of Cergy-Pontoise. The duration of the recordings lasts from five minutes to a little more than an hour.[5] The samples represent nine different language groups including Creole from Guadaloupe, French (8 subjects) and Malagasy. The subjects were chosen mainly from the network

---

[3]Cf: Baron, N. (2008). "Adjusting the Volume: Technology and Multitasking in Discourse Control".

[4]Each session consists of multiple conversations. In a typical scenario, the user had three to ten different conversations for each session and therefore multiple XML log files.

[5]The duration was also influenced by the length of the video cassettes and the fact that the participants were in a cybercafé.

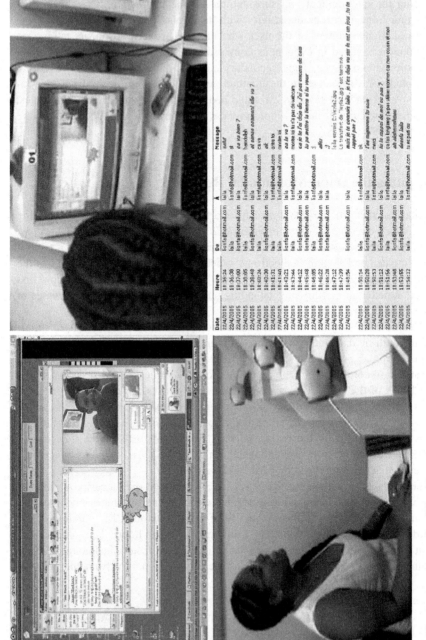

Fig. 1 Four simultaneous views of an IM session

of relations known to the researchers.[6] Others were found "on site" because the cybercafé was located in close proximity to a youth hostel.

Authenticity of Data: Images, ASCII and Physical Movements

An essential reason for using the visual capture of the activity hinges on authenticity. The printout logs of these conversations do not show the reality of the screen activity because icons, animated text and other visual cues do not appear in the transcripts as images, but are recorded as ASCII-coded elements. It is therefore impossible to distinguish from the logs whether a participant used an image or actually used the ASCII punctuation to express a smiley (resulting in very different interpretations of the socio-identification practices) or how the duration of an animation influenced the flow of text production.

It is also impossible with the text printout to show the participants' physical reactions to the screen. The multimodality of our method allows us to observe physical co-production such as hand movements or gaze, which may demonstrate different modes and involvement in conversation and activity, and may mark sequences of temporalities in the IM conversation. Each phase of the exchange – composing, sending, waiting for the reply, reading the response, and performing other intermittent tasks (Fig. 2) – is accompanied by physical movement: looking down at the keyboard to type, checking the screen for new information, erasing and rewriting, etc., whereby the loop continues. Variation in the time attributed to the message loop exists primarily according to the number of dyadic conversations or external activities the user is engaged in.

We observed in our video data that the subjects physically approach the screen and computer during the composition of the message (the keyboard is often placed close to the screen). This distance was larger or smaller depending first on the space available in the immediate surroundings (in the cybercafé or at home), then on the user's engagement in the conversation and his typing competence. Users who are proficient typists and who can visually verify their message on the screen as they type before it is sent to the conversation are more distant from the screen. Those who are less adept mostly bend over the keyboard watching the placement of their fingers. The visual verification of their typed message happens after they have finished typing and is generally closer to the screen.

Before the message is sent, the person also quickly checks for any new information on the screen which might change the relevance of what he was writing – which

---

[6]In the search for subjects, we discovered that IM is considered a very private activity, and many people were unwilling to participate. Other subjects curtailed some of their more intimate exchanges first by announcing to their conversation partners that they were in a study and being recorded and by avoiding embarrassing subjects that may have arisen.

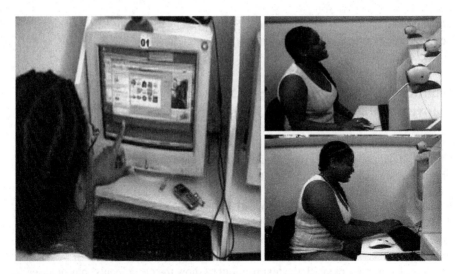

Fig. 2 Reacting to the screen: pointing, laughing, plunging into the keyboard

might require rewriting – and then verifies the message which is still in his composition window. At this stage, the fingers of the user are suspended over the keyboard
in a holding position. After the message is validated visually, several examples in
our corpus show the sender adding a particular physical emphasis when pressing
the return button to send, as if to speed up the transmission of the message or to add
more force to what was "said".

Once the message is sent, the person goes into a waiting mode, his gaze is on the
screen and his hand returns to rest on the mouse, either waiting for the next message
to appear on the screen or ready to click on a blinking tab which will open another
conversation window or rather to change activities such as reading a blog or email.
In this waiting period, each participant has his own idiosyncrasies such as stroking
facial hair, playing with hair, scratching or pulling on his own clothing, etc.

When the new message appears, there is an immediate often physical reaction.
Among others, we found laughs, shaking heads, pointing fingers at the screen, having a dumbfounded expression and moving lips to read the new message. Generally,
these are the same physical attitudes that can be found in other conversational
settings from face-to-face interaction to talking on the telephone, whereas this
behaviour is rare (at most) for email or reading a blog.

Finally, the cycle of interaction resumes. Curiously, at the end of the entire IM
session, the user often pushes the keyboard back towards the screen, away from
himself, signifying as well that he is physically distancing himself from the activity,
that he is no longer present.

Physical reactions are, therefore, one mark of synchronous communication and
suggest that despite the technological barrier participants behave similarly to a
face-to-face conversation. Therefore, this recording technique was necessary to
capture the entire conversational event.

A "True" IM Conversation: Smileys, Images and Animation

Despite the richness of IM conversations, we would like to focus our analysis on one salient feature of the conversations in order to understand how this element functions within the whole process. So, here we will discuss the recurrent use of non-text markers and visual additions to the text messages because of the large variety and preponderance of icons, animations and colourful visual cues in the conversational activity. We did not consider other visually oriented features such as the voluntary exchange of photos or using shared tools such as a white board or playing games in IM.

Background/History of Smiley Icon/Evolution of the Icon

Of all the visual cues in IM, the smiley – which celebrated its 25th anniversary in September 2007 – is the most ubiquitous. What was created in 1982 by Scott Fahlman to "convey a sense that an expression was not to be taken seriously" (Randall, 2002) has become an iconic addition to electronic communication which represents the interpersonal and conversational world of CMC, particularly in email, chat and IM.

Originally, the image of the smiley face derives from the 1960s "happy face", which was then translated into punctuation to become the emoticon. Since then, variations on the simple ASCII happy face have been added to represent many other expressions and forms from a winking face, to a happy face with a hat, Uncle Sam, a face looking left or right, or a frontal view.[7] In the early days of chat, multiple iconic forms were imagined that subsequently became so codified that they were no longer understood as punctuation. Later, by converting the punctuation back into the yellow happy face form (a reversal from the symbolic to iconic), Yahoo! and MSN added these features directly into their instant messaging software, and today they are widely used by the majority of instant messaging users (82% according to a Yahoo! Emoticons survey, 2007). Today using a smiley is less of a creative endeavour and more of a referential act as most smileys come from the provided repertoires or depositories on the internet. Throughout their diverse manifestations, smileys have retained their original light-hearted meaning and function.

Ironically, despite their contemporary popularity, for most users, this standard element of the IM repertoire is no longer directly associated with the happy face of the 1960s or to the punctuation smileys. However, the shortcuts to produce these symbols as well as the XML text file that records the log still use punctuation to

---

[7] In Japanese chat, ASCII smileys have a "frontal" point of view and are read vertically instead of horizontally.

convey the smiley. The smiley face is represented in the logs as the original :). Nonetheless, this historic reference is not systematic: the *flower* smiley is represented as [F] instead of @>-,–. To choose an emoticon it is more common for the user to select an image from the provided repertoire. But, though the use of shortcuts is possible, the aim is usually to produce the visual cue, not the punctuation. And, with the exception of one subject in our study who wanted to identify his discourse with a more historical internet use, all of the other subjects used the repertoire exclusively to select their smileys. So, emoticons have followed a general trend of internet evolution (as identified by Neil Stephenson in his 1993 article), of transforming "hard to formulate" text into more image-based communication (e.g. from telnet to WWW, from MUDs to Second Life, from Usenet to Youtube).

In today's IM, the basic smiley is a well-known and recognizable picture. Also called emoticons, their terminology gives them their function, to be "smiley" or emotional; they are "abbreviations for expressions of mood, tone of voice or instructions to the reader" (Randall, 2002). They have so often been described as markers to express emotion that people have adopted this definition associating the use of these icons to what they believe is internet sociability and the stereotype of internet behaviour; and successive users of IM are socialized into this interactional behaviour. Additionally, when a new smiley is invented and used, its interpretation relies on this larger convention associated with CMC, which then includes variations on the original smiley. So, seeing the punctuation, or seeing the yellow faced smileys, etc., on the screen of the chat window, participants immediately recognize these as conversational markers, turns and additions to the exchange.

Perceptual Cues

But, smileys are more than just references to emotion. Within the interaction they also provide the reader perceptual cues for understanding the interaction. First, the colour of the smileys or animations contrasts with the background giving a clear sign of activity. In addition, using colored text helps the reader to know immediately in which conversation he is discussing as each of the windows looks slightly different. The collective effect helps to distinguish forms and functions in the multicoloured and multilayered environment.

Importance of Smileys to Conversationalists

Smileys are part of the interaction. Image-based contributions to the conversation are integral to IM exchanges. About 82% of the 40,000 people surveyed in the Yahoo! Emoticon survey said they use them regularly in their messages. Today, there are more than 50 different forms of these emoticons pre-programmed into the system (Fig. 3), and it is also possible to download supplementary icons from

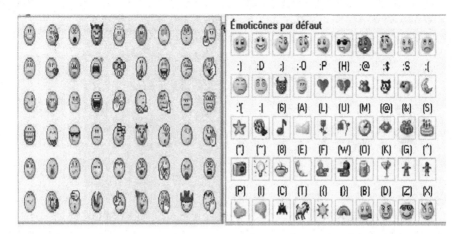

Fig. 3 Smileys from Yahoo! IM and MSN repertoires

internet depositories in order to enrich the panoply of smileys and symbols in a personalized, individual repertoire.

The use of personalized smileys is significant in interaction, as the following example demonstrates (Fig. 4). In this passage the user <une second> declares to his conversational partner <Yutichou-ö> that he is not in his usual physical environment – he is in a cybercafé.

His conversational environment is thus affected by this change in location in the fact that he does not have his usual repertoire of smileys. So, in the conversation, he asks his friend to send him some smileys, which she does in abundance.

Subsequently, he adds some of them to the repertoire that he has in the cybercafé making corresponding keystroke shortcuts to get to them, an added sign of familiarity with the IM system (Fig. 5).[8] Note also that he responds to her sending the smileys by communicating three times by way of a smiley.

| 10/03/2006 | 21:59:47 | Une seconde ! | Yutichou-ö | Au fait, étant dans un cybercafé, je n'ai plus mles smileys ^^" tu pourrais me les renvoyer, toi qui en as tant ? ^^ |
| 10/03/2006 | 22:01:29 | Yutichou-ö | Une seconde ! | Pas de problème :P |

Fig. 4 Franck/Cecile *("By the way, since I am in a cybercafé I don't have my smileys ^^ can you who have so many, send me some^^" "No problem :P")*

[8]In a recent survey of instant messaging, Yahoo! found that 66% of the 40,000 IM users surveyed have memorized at least 3 text-character shortcuts for using emoticons, while 19% have memorized 10 or more, cf. http://blog.messenger.yahoo.com/blog/2007/07/10/emoticon-survey-results/ (accessed 28 October 2007).

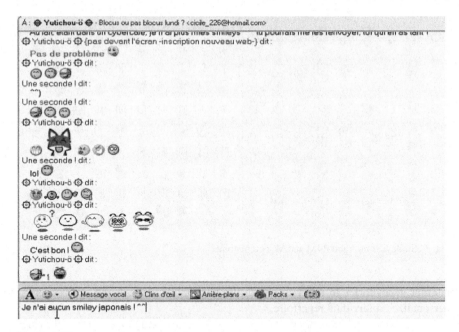

Fig. 5 Adding new smileys to repertoire

Classifying Images and Smileys

To study these smileys in our corpus, we sought to establish a basic taxonomy of smileys and their *use* in IM conversation which looks at which smileys were actually used by participants in the conversation, including their selection processes, frequency or incidence of use, placement and their role as turns in interaction.

For a brief sample of this study, we manually coded 3 of the 17 XML sessions of the text logs that were recorded in the previous study and a hierarchical, classification system similar to the Linnean system used in the life sciences was developed. Non-text interaction was divided under categories such as standard/iconic smiley, symbolic smiley or animation, adjusting to the potentially wide variety of symbols available to IM users.[9]

In our small sample, we found a total of 17 different smileys: 7 standard and 10 symbolic smileys. The most recurrent were the *Happy Face*, *Wink* and *Tongue Out* iconic smileys followed by *Flower* and *Lips* symbolic smileys. There were also three text-based images, which we call idiosyncratic, and one recurrent text-punctuation

---

[9] We opted against using a more "morphological" approach, in which the stem symbol is the base form of a round, yellow circle because identifying prefixes, infixes or suffixes proved more problematic, in particular, for smileys that are not based on the smiley face such as the rainbow or lips.

smiley (^^). There were also a total of six different animations, which accounts for nearly all of the animations available in the limited MSN repertoire found at the cybercafé.

Interaction and Visual Cues

Observing placement and frequency in the emergent exchange, we can identify which smileys or which category of smileys is used "appropriately" (in a Gricean pragmatic sense) in the turn. Though we have only had the means to produce a preliminary result and further samples and quantitative studies are needed, we hypothesize that further investigation will confirm the regularity of certain smileys and types of smileys at particular spots in the conversation, thus demonstrating that the selection of which smiley to use where is not arbitrary.

In terms of frequency, it is important to establish how many and which smileys are used on average in a conversation and the demographics of these, for example, based on the age, sex or origins of the subject (Baron, 2005a, 2005b, 2005c). Though our sample is too small to make conclusive remarks here, empirical evidence shows that our findings corroborate with the Yahoo! Emoticons survey that older users use less smileys, but the overall majority of users do use them. In our corpus, the older subjects – for example, the doctoral students or those who work – use less smileys and animations than the younger high school students or undergraduates. For example, in a 1-hour session of chat, Thomas, a recent graduate from an engineering school in his mid-twenties uses only five smileys, of which four are the *standard winking* and one is the *standard astonished* smiley with its mouth open. In contrast, the three 15-year-old subjects and their conversation partners use a smiley in nearly half of their contributions. This frequency not only demonstrates a familiarity with the IM software and the potential of its expressive features but also reveals an adherence to a particular identity group.

Another essential aspect to studying IM from an interactional point of view is to identify the placement of the smiley within the sentence and then within the conversation, such as at the opening, closing or at a topic transition. We have identified three major types: those in a regular or static position, those used in the emergent chat activity and those used as the turn itself. We found that iconic smileys are included in the turn whereas symbolic smiley were more "stand-alone" elements.

Stable Smileys: Header and Nickname

We begin with smileys that remain principally stable throughout the conversation. These are found in the header of the conversation with the nickname and *away message* (Baron, 2003) of the participant. Though technically modifiable, a person does not change his nickname often, not least because it is his mark of identity on his correspondents' contact lists allowing him to enter into a conversation with them.

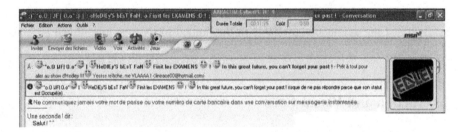

Fig. 6 Nickname with text and smileys

However, the away message can change from one session to the next depending on the person's mood, location or if there is a break in the session (e.g. to eat or answer the phone[10]).

Establishing a certain personal look is very important to IM conversations, and these static symbols are part of the user's visual stamp. The nickname is the first aspect which gives the text a personal quality or "voice". The user will personalize this space using a mix of punctuation, numbers, capital and lower case letters as well as smileys and font colours. In the first of these two examples (Fig. 6) the nickname is composed of an alteration of upper and lower case text and three standard smileys. In the second example (Fig. 7), the nickname is surrounded by ASCII-based images including a Japanese smiley using a light blue font.

Despite its unchanging nature, the nickname constitutes a partially dynamic element in the conversation because it is posted on the screen each time the user sends a message.

In the case where a nickname is long and takes the interactional form of having several sentence fractions or clauses, as in Fig. 6, smileys are used to divide these different propositions. In effect, the smileys inserted help to visually break up the screen into not only the horizontal division as prescribed by the addition of new

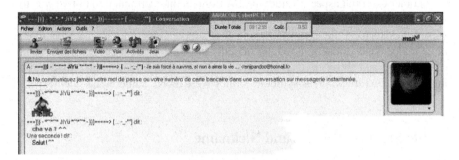

Fig. 7 Nickname made of ASCII symbols and Japanese smiley

---

[10]The long breaks described by other researchers of IM did not occur in our sample study due to the fact that the participants were connecting from a cybercafé.

sentences but a vertical division with the smileys aligning themselves into regular patterns as consecutive contributions are sent to the screen.

Smileys in Interaction

Now, let us turn to the placement of smileys within the conversation where their use is more dynamic and they fulfil an active role in the ensuing interaction, for example, to denote a pause (or breath) or to mark affect. We have identified the most common placement of smileys within the conversations, notably at the end of a line or sentence or in the middle of a contribution to break up different propositions. Less commonly, they are found at the beginning of a sentence. Another common use of the smiley is as the whole message, or the turn itself.

Smileys as End-Focus and Prosody

English has a syntax which is highly governed by word position. The final position in a clause or sentence is often the most important place for conveying information. We tend to place previous or assumed information at the beginning of a sentence while the second part of the sentence is reserved for the new or most important information. As such, a smiley placed at the end of the sentence retroactively stresses the meaning of a particular written message whether to add irony or an affective dimension, giving iconic or "face-to-face" (Marcoccia & Gaulducheau, 2007) emphasis or acting as an interpretive marker.

Each smiley loosely represents an expression that adds an extra dimension to the semantics, for example, the jocularity of a sexual reference (Fig. 8) or the shocked confusion of a negative discovery of bad news (Fig. 9). There is also the representation of anger in a steaming red face or suspicion with eyes scanning back and forth (Fig. 10).

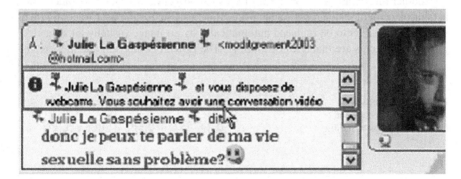

Fig. 8 Jocularity *("So, I can talk to you openly about my sexual life? :P")*

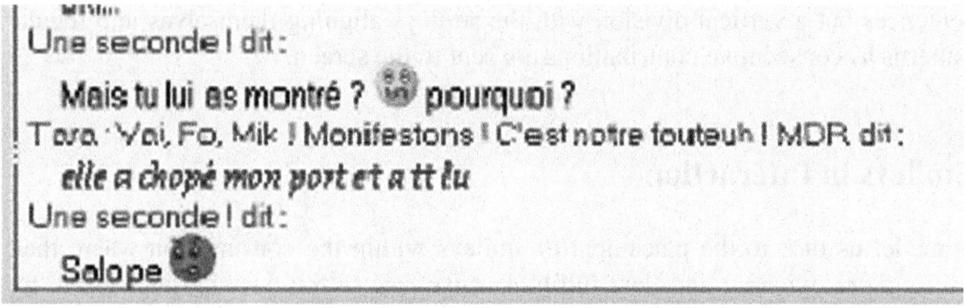

Fig. 9 Confusion and anger ("You showed her? `:$ Why?") ("Bitch >:(")

These variations act as a kind of visual prosody, adding emphasis and a key to understanding the sentence much like rising tone or strong intonation and facial expressions might on the spoken word. In addition, they clearly mark the end of the proposition or the *Turn Relevance Place* (Sacks, Schegloff, & Jefferson, 1974), indicating that the turn is finished. Accordingly, we found no instances of a smiley being used at the end of a syntaxically fractured sentence where the turn continued in the next line.

But, visual prosody does not correlate directly with physical prosody. For example, onset/pre-turn prosody is uncommon (if not impossible) in spoken language. Though less common, a smiley can be placed at the beginning of the line preceding a sentence in order to model the interpretation of the coming contribution as in three of the messages below (in particular, the final line translated as ":) *I miss you*" (Fig. 11).

In terms of rhythm,[11] smileys constitute a beat at the beginning of the sentence to launch a rhythm; within the sentence to maintain cadence and accentuate a point; and at the end to mark prosodic variation. The gaze of the reader marks a short pause before continuing to read the contribution. This phenomenon is more obvious in the spatial division created by the interjection of smileys in the away message or in multi-clause contributions.

Another more idiosyncratic use of images in conversation which is unique to IM is their placement inside a particular word. It is possible for the user to configure a string of characters to be replaced automatically by an image (usually an animated gif), like shortcuts are made to use smileys. The flow of composing the message is

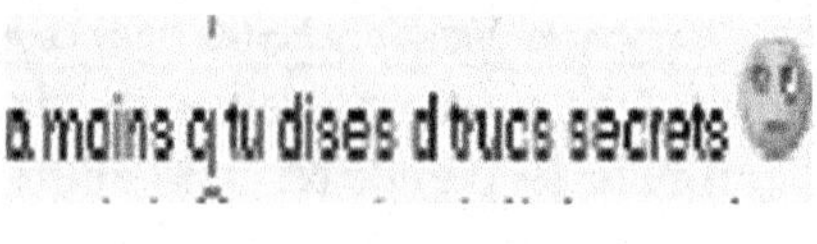

Fig. 10 Suspicious eyes, animated to scan back and forth ("*Unless you're telling secrets* ;|")

---

[11]Cf. Bays (2001, 2003, 2005), Bays et al. (2006).

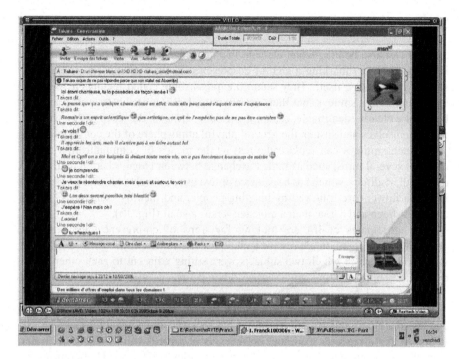

Fig. 11 Interphrasal and pre-turn smileys

not disturbed because the fingers do not leave the keyboard for the mouse to choose the image desired. In this case (Fig. 12), <Sdifer> replaces the word "non" with an image of Yoda shaking his head. The result is a curious mix of text and image for the word "sinon" (*otherwise*). The resulting rebus adds colour and dynamism to the screen, though it may hinder comprehension of the sentence. This dynamic shows that IM is more than a "phoneticized" written language (Anis, 1998).

Fig. 12 Rebus, intertextual smiley

Smileys as Whole Turns

Smileys can also be the pivotal element in a sequence of turns serving a primarily interactive role by marking a sign of co-presence in the activity. The smileys are sent as the message itself. They seem to express some coded feelings as with the hearts and kisses smileys, but they are often used in a more abstract way and are bereft of a clearly identifiable, semantic meaning. Instead, the users parlay with the icons themselves and sustain the general playful atmosphere of the conversation.

As such, smileys can replace the text as the means of communication over a series of several turns, such as in this exchange between Hugo, <hac 'n natif>, and dldldldldl, <sdifer>, which has a sequence of five turns entirely composed of smileys in which flowers are followed by hugging people, and then by "sentences" which oppose a sheep and a goat then a monster versus a snail (Fig. 13).

The participants of IM are looking for signs of co-presence and common ground through common expressive techniques. This phenomenon was observable in our video data in which two subjects were sitting adjacent to each other in the cybercafé[12] both chatting with several other people as well as with each other (Fig. 14).

The scene is as follows: after having sent the *piece of pizza* smiley to his partner – and friend – Hugo looks to see if Antoine has received and noticed his message. He is hoping for a reaction. Antoine, however, is occupied with selecting an avatar from the repertoire and does not see the pizza smiley right away. Hugo repeatedly glances over at the screen of his neighbour whose conversation windows are filled with signs, images and special characters. Finally, when Antoine clicks over to the conversation window he has with Hugo, Hugo sees that Antoine has received and seen the pizza symbol sent earlier. Hugo smiles and begins selecting another smiley to send to Antoine even before he receives Antoine's response of the rainbow smiley although this appears nearly instantaneously. Throughout the exchange of smileys,

Fig. 13 Exchange of
symbolic smileys

---

[12]The video and screen capture data were recorded in a Parisian cybercafé (Bays et al., 2006, Avi4. 00 :23 :10).

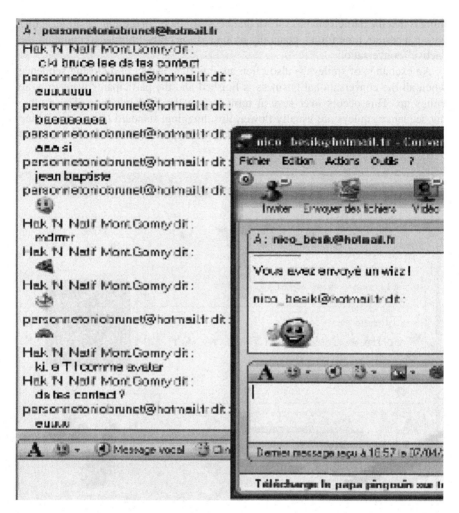

Fig. 14 Creating a bond through symbolic smileys

Hugo continues to look back and forth from his own screen over onto Antoine's, verifying that his contribution has been received and observing the reaction of his friend and interlocutor.

Smileys help manage the juggling of multiple chat windows by simply marking co-presence in an "active" conversation. That is, to show continual presence in front of the screen and in a particular conversation, the participant can simply send a smiley as his turn, as a kind of conversation filler. This accords him time to scroll back up the conversation window to see what the topic was and how it evolved while he was away in order to answer the adjacent pair or contribute a relevant message to the topic. The ambiguity of its semantic meaning allows the smiley to be relevant in many situations and to retain the general tone of the conversation. The important thing is that the participant has shown that he is still there, in the conversation, acting within a certain time frame, generally around 20 seconds, in order to maintain the "active" conversation.

An exchange of smileys is also often an important aspect of a closing sequence when all the conversational business is finished and the participants want to wrap things up. This occurs over several turns before the final goodbye. These closing sequence smileys are usually flower, lips, hugging, standard happy or winking and, less often, moon or clock. In addition, this sequence often takes the form of

Fig. 15 Closing sequence with smileys

several echo turns in which the interlocutor sends the same smiley – usually flowers, hearts or lips – back to the subject, thereby creating a bond of common ground. Participants choose the smileys that might represent the feeling that they want to give at the end of the conversation (hugs, "it's late", etc.). In the example (Fig. 15), we see that the interlocutor has already said "bonne soirée" (*good night*), and our subject has already sent the lips smiley, he is now selecting a second smiley to send in the closing sequence.

Animations as Interaction

Animations, like smileys, are integral to the IM register. There are two basic types of animations in IM. The smaller types (usually animated .gif) are used in the message and serve the same function as a smiley or replace text. The larger types, *winks*, do not appear in the composition window; rather they are displayed across the entire conversation window. The placement of animated *winks* gives them a central role in the conversation because all other activity stops while the user focuses on the event. They expand across the screen and interrupt the textual exchange by momentarily monopolizing the whole space and reorienting the conversation into an iconic or symbolic form of interaction.

They are complex conversational tools because they are dynamic and their abstract character – evocative or humorous – also makes it difficult to ascribe to them a clear semantic definition. Similarly to smileys, some of these animations are easily understood as signs of affect, such as the heart or the red lips. Since both connote affection they often fit into a coherent sequence of adjacent pairs, sent consecutively. Other animations are more complex because the visual message can be interpreted in different ways by mobilizing different cognitive categories or fields of experience. For example, sending *musical notes* could be an invitation to change to a lighter subject, an invitation to exchange music or simply to represent the relaxing feeling that the sender feels. Their meaning can only be understood when placed in the context of the preceding dialogue and the previous turns, and even so, this meaning may neither be precise nor stable, particularly from one user to the next. In sum, they are interactive rather than content conveying devices.

In the following sequence (Fig. 16), consisting of five different screen animations back to back, we see how the subjects select their winks from a repertoire and add them to the ongoing exchange. The onset begins with the user who is vexed by what her partner has said; so, she writes her feelings in text and then reinforces her disapproval by way of a crying smiley. She continues with a second turn by sending the *wink* of a boy throwing a water balloon at him (perhaps meaning retaliation).

In between these animations we also find text contributions which punctuate the surprise or give a little bit of detail. During the course of the animation, however, there are no other immediate contributions either in this conversation or in the parallel one (the second conversation window). Each participant waits to see what will transpire and then responds. The animation of the boy throwing a water balloon

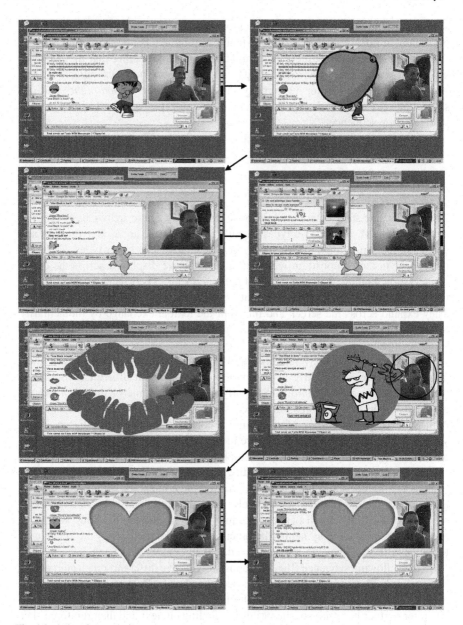

Fig. 16 Animation as topic

is answered by a dancing pig icon, followed by lips, then a character that smashes an amplifier and finally a heart.

At the end of these series of exchanges, the interlocutor sends a concluding emoticon of a blushing face and thanks her for the kiss, simultaneously ceasing the aggressive mood and finding common ground. With this, she forgives him for the earlier aggression, accepts his thanks and concludes the sequence with "you're welcome" (de rien) as the animation finishes its course on her screen.

In this one segment of the interaction, the participants mobilize a good number of the *winks* at their disposal in the IM repertoire. We could say that in this exchange animation is the visual *topic* which is developed over several turns.

An animated topic demonstrates a partially endogenous passage within the IM session, like suspended time, because it focalizes the interaction wholly on the event, the series of animations. Nevertheless, the above example also shows that this type of visual parlance does not eliminate the need for the textual exchange as the participants continue to insert brief textual excerpts between the animations. This implies that these animated exchanges have a limited function within the global activity and that the central activity of chat is the exchange of content (here in the textual form, but also more and more through webcam and voice).

Note also that our multimodal recording technique has captured the expressions of the subject in the webcam image of Fig. 16 in photos six and seven.[13] In screen shot six, he reacts to his screen with an expression of recognizing the animation. In the next screen shot (7) he dives back down to the keyboard and is busy replying. Finally we see him leaning towards the screen, waiting for a sign that his reply has appeared on the screen or waiting for a reaction in picture eight. This is a good example of how co-presence is established and maintained in the distant conversation through webcam and how the physical reaction of the participant may also influence the choice of winks or the response.

Conclusion

In this study, we have shown that multimodal recording techniques are necessary to capture a more holistic approach to CMC interaction. In particular this shows the production of physical movement accompanying each segment of the interaction, which can be associated to meaningful physical behaviour. Then we discussed the origins and use of different smileys (standard or symbolic) and animations (intertextual and interactional) which may merit a classification system for further analysis. More importantly, we looked at smileys and animation on a structural level due to their placement and frequency, constituting sometimes whole turns and sequences of turns as well as managing the space of the conversation.

An IM conversation is visual, making it a unique linguistic register. To understand it better, its analysis may be informed by sign language studies. For example, the physical rhythm of the visual IM conversation may have parallels in sign language where distinct physical movements are associated to each part of the conversation. Furthermore, the parameters of a sign consist in its configuration,

---

[13]Figures 1 and 2, above, show video stills of our subject reacting to this same exchange of animations. Likewise, she points at the screen selecting, laughs and then types her reply.

movement, orientation, place and the facial gestures that accompany the sign. We can draw similarities between the creation of a sign and the establishment of codified visual cues for smileys (text/non-text, static/animated, pre- mid- or post sentence...) which correspond to a particular semantic context and interactional environment. There is a need for further research in this direction in order to test the validity of a taxonomy of smileys and visual markers that will examine the role they play in modulating and accentuating the electronic conversation. It would be an exaggeration, however, to place sign language and the use of visual markers in IM on the same plane of communicability. Rather, we can see that this iconic and symbolic level of language co-exists with the textual exchange. Perhaps further study of these iconic structures in a computer-mediated, synchronous environment will give us insight to the workings of rhythm in language and perception, also in sign language.

In studying the linguistics of synchronous CMC, we hope to see how iconic, physical and rhythmic patterns in IM conversations constitute a sort of visual prosody or extra-semantic element that aids comprehension and overall conversation management. We might suggest that there is a cognitive separation of the emotional/affective through images (smileys and animation) and the cerebral/logical content (text or voice) and that these parallel registers can play out in different rhythms. This leads us to the broader questions about the analysis of visual language (sign or CMC) taking into consideration such multimodality, concurrent codes as well as the overriding question of rhythm in the underpinnings of all conversational activity. Systemizing this analysis could lead to establishing a phonology with which users – and researchers – interpret and manipulate textual, iconic and physical visual cues.

Acknowledgments The corpus used for this article was made possible by a grant from the French CNRS for the previous research project on *Rhythm and Temporalities of Electronic Communication* by Michel de Fornel, Maud Verdier and Hillary Bays. Special thanks go to Maud Verdier who diligently worked collecting a good portion of the data and on assembling the final report, to Michel de Fornel for some insight on recording electronic conversation using methods generally reserved for interaction studies and to Mickaëlle Lantin for digitalizing and organizing the video data.

References

Anis, J. (1988). *L'écriture, théories et descriptions*. Bruxelles: De Boeck-Université.
Anis, J. (1998). *Texte et ordinateur: l'écriture réinventée*. Bruxelles: De Boeck Université.
Anis, J. (1999). *Internet communication et langue francaise*. Paris: Hermes Science Publications.
Auer, P., Cooper-Kuhlen, E., Müller, F. (1999). *Language in time, the rhythm and tempo of spoken interaction*. Oxford: Oxford University Press.
Baron, N. (2003). Language of the internet. In A. Farghali (Ed.), *The Stanford handbook for language engineers* (pp. 59–127). Stanford, CA: CSLI Publications.
Baron, N. (2005a, February 17–21). *Instant messaging by American college students: A case study in computer mediated communication*. American Association for the Advancement of Science annual meeting.
Baron, N. (2005b). Tethered or mobile? Use of away messages in instant messaging by American college students (with Lauren Squires, Sara Tench, and Marshall Thompson). In R. Ling &

P. Pederson (Eds.) *Mobile communications: Re-negotiation of the social sphere* (pp. 293–311). London: Springer-Verlag.

Baron, N. (2005c). Instant messaging and the future of language. *Communications of the ACM, 48*(7), 29–31.

Baron, N. (2007). The mechanics of text messaging and instant messaging among American college students (with Rich Ling). *Journal of Language and Social Psychology, 26*, 291–298.

Baron, N. (2008). Adjusting the volume: Technology and multitasking in discourse control. In J. E. Katz (Ed.), *Handbook of mobile communication studies* (pp. 177–193). Cambridge, MA: MIT Press.

Bays, H. (2001). *Interaction conversationnelle en internet relay chat*. Doctoral dissertation in Linguistics, directed by Professor Pierre Encreve at the Ecole des Hautes Etudes en Sciences Sociales, Paris, defended 21 décembre 2001.

Bays, H. (2003, March). *Temporalité en internet relay chat: Le rythme du discours électronique*. Communication électronique, conference at the Ecole des Hautes Etudes en Sciences Sociales, Paris.

Bays, H. (2005, October 6–9). *Visio-verbal constructions of rhythm in IM & IRC: A cross-linguistic study*. Internet research 6.0: Generations, Proceedings of the 6th Annual Conference of the Association of Internet Researchers, Chicago, IL, USA.

Bays, H., de Fornel, M., & Verdier, M. (2006). *Rythmes et temporalités de la conversation Electronique (RYTE)*. Research report for the CNRS program PI-TCAN.

Blum, S. (2004). Instant messaging: Functions of a new communicative tool. *Anthropology 427*: Doing things with words.

Bunn, J. (2002). *Wave forms: A natural syntax for rhythmic language*. Palo Alto, CA: Stanford University Press.

Chen, L., & Gaines, B. (1998). Modeling and supporting virtual cooperative interaction through the world wide web. In F. Sudweeks, M. McLaughlin, & S. Rafaeli (Eds.), *Network and netplay, virtual groups on the internet* (pp. 221–242). Cambridge, MA: MIT Press.

Cuxac, C. (2000). *La LSF, les voies de l'iconicité*. Paris: Ophrys.

Cuxac, C., Fusellier-Souza, I., & Sallandre, M.-A. (1999). Iconicité et catégorisations dans les langues des signes. *Sémiotiques, 16*, 143–166.

Danet, B. (2001). *Cyberpl@y: Communicating online*. Oxford: Berg Publishers. Companion web site, URL http://pluto.mscc.huji.ac.il/~msdanet/cyberpl@y/

Delalande, M.-A. (2007). La messagerie instantanée freine la productivité des enterprises. *Le Monde Informatique*, Edition du 12/10/2007.

Derks, D., Bos, A. E. R., & Von Grumkow, J. (2007). Emoticons and social interaction on the internet: The importance of social context. *Computers in Human Behavior, 23*, 842–849.

Farmer, R. (2003). Instant messaging – Collaborative tool or educator's nightmare! *NA Web 2003*, http://www.unb.ca/naweb/proceedings/2003/PaperFarmer.html [29 October 2007].

Finn, A. (1999). Temporality and technology convergence. *Information, Communication & Society, 2*(2), 174–200.

Gross, E. F. (2004). Adolescent internet use: What we expect, what teens report. *Applied Developmental Psychology, 25*, 633–649.

Haiman, J. (1985). *Natural syntax: Iconicity and erosion*. Cambridge: Cambridge University Press.

Herring, S., (Ed.). (1996). *Computer-mediated communication: Linguistic, social and cross-cultural perspectives*. Pragmatics and Beyond series. Amsterdam: John Benjamins.

Kharif, O. (2001, April 23). The man who brought a :-) to your dcreen. *Business Week Online*. Retrieved from http://www.businessweek.com/bwdaily/dnflash/apr2001/nf20010423_785.htm [29 October 2007].

Lenhart, A., Rainie, L., & Lewis, O. (2001). *Teenage life online: The rise of the instant-message generation and the internet's impact on friendships and family relationships*. Retrieved from http://www.pewinternet.org/pdfs/PIP_Teens_Report.pdf [29 October 2007].

Marcoccia, M., & Gaducheau, N. (2007). L'analyse du rôle des smileys en production et en réception: Un retour sur la question de l'oralité des écrits numériques. In I. Pierozak

(Ed.), *Glottopol, revue sociologique en ligne*. Retrieved from http://www.univ-rouen.fr/dyalang/glottopol/numero_10.html#sommaire [29 October 2007].

Metzger, M. (2001). Discourse analysis. In C. Lucas (Ed.), *The sociolinguistics of sign languages* (pp. 112–144). Cambridge: Cambridge University Press.

Milford, M. (2007, September 17). It began with smiley. *Delaware Online*. Retrieved from http://delawareonline.com/apps/pbcs.dll/article?AID=/20070917/BUSINESS/70917002/1003 [29 October 2007].

O'Connor, A. (2006). Instant messaging: Friend or foe of student writing? *New Horizons for Learning*, March 2005 Retrieved from http://www.newhorizons.org/strategies/literacy/oconnor.htm [29 October 2007].

Pierozak, I. (Ed.). (2007, July). Regards sur l'internet, dans ses dimensions langagières. Penser les continuités et discontinuities En hommage à Jacques Anis. *Glottopol: revue sociologique en ligne* (10). Retrieved from http://www.univ-rouen.fr/dyalang/glottopol/numero_10.html [29 October 2007].

Pinolosacco, G. (2007, January). La sociologie visuelle. *Sociétés*.

Quan-Hasse, A., Cothrel, J., & Wellman, B. (2005). Instant messaging for collaboration: A case study of a high-tech firm. *Journal of Computer-Mediated Communication, 10*(4), article 13. Retrieved from http://jcmc.indiana.edu/vol10/issue4/quan-haase.html

Randall, N. (2002). Lingo online: A report on the language of the keyboard generation. California: MSN publications. Retrieved from http://arts.uwaterloo.ca/~nrandall/LingoOnline-finalreport.pdf [29 October 2007].

Sacks, H., Schegloff, E. A., & Jefferson, G. (1974). A simplest systematics for the organization of turn-taking for conversation. *Language, 50*, 696–735.

Schieffelin, B., & Jones, G. (2008). Enquoting voices, accomplishing talk: Uses of *be + like* in instant messaging. *Language & Communication, 29*(1), 77–113.

Shiu, E., & Lenhart, A. (2004). How Americans use instant messaging. Washington, DC: Pew Internet and American Life Project. Retrieved from http://www.pewinternet.org [October 29, 2007].

Stephenson, N. (1993, September 13). Smiley's people. *The New Republic*, 52. Retrieved from http://www.spesh.com/lee/ns/smiley.html

Stevenson, J. (1999). The language of internet chat rooms. *Language Data Investigation*. Retrieved from http://www.demo.inty.net/Units/IRC.htm [29 October 2007].

Tagliamonte, S., & Denis, D. (2006, Aug 2). *OMG, will txting and IM lead 2 bad grammar?* Linguistics Society of Canada and the United States annual meeting.

Walther, J. B., & D'Addario, K. P. (2001). The impact of emoticons on message interpretation in computer-mediated communication. *Social Science Computer Review, 19*(3), 324–347.

Wellman, B. (2001). Computer networks as social networks. *Science, 293*, 2031–2034.

Wellman, B. (2007). Emoticons panel interview on *The Current*, Canadian Broadcasting Corporation. Retrieved from http://www.cbc.ca/thecurrent/2007/200709/20070926.html [29 October 2007].

Yahoo! Emoticon Survey Results (2007, July 10). Retrieved from http://blog.messenger.yahoo.com/blog/2007/07/10/emoticon-survey-results/ [29 October 2007].

Yates, S. J. (1996). Oral and written linguistic aspects of computer conferencing: A corpus based study. In S. C. Herring (Ed.), *Computer-mediated communication. linguistic, social and cross-cultural perspectives* (pp. 29–46). Amsterdam/Philadelphia: John Benjamins.

Yechi, L. (1996). *The geometry of visual phonology*. Stanford, CA: Center for the Study of Language and Information (CSLI) Publications.

Research in e-Science and Open Access to Data and Information

Matthijs den Besten, Paul A. David, and Ralph Schroeder

Introduction

Anyone enquiring about "e-science" is bound to be led to a quotation from John Taylor's (2001) introductory description of this movement's essence as being "about global collaboration in key areas of science and the next generation of infrastructure that will enable it." Although much that has been written about e-science is occupied with the engineering and application of an enhanced technological infrastructure for the transmission, processing, and storing of digital data and information (Hey, 2005), this article steps back to consider other, non-technological requirements for attaining the ostensible goal of e-science programs – augmenting the scale and effectiveness of global collaboration in scientific research.

Global scientific collaboration takes many forms, but from the various initiatives around the world a consensus is emerging that collaboration should aim to be "open" – or at least that there should be a substantial measure of "open access" to the data and information underlying published research and to communication tools. For example, the Atkins Committee, in a seminal NSF report that set the stage for research on "cyber-infrastructure" in the natural sciences and engineering in the United States, advocated "open platforms" and referred to the grid as an "infrastructure for open scientific research" (Atkins et al., 2003, pp. 4, 38). In a follow-up report expanding that vision to include the social sciences, Berman and Brady (2005, p. 19) likewise stress the need for a "shared cyber-infrastructure." In the UK, the e-Science Core Program has required that the middleware being developed by its projects be released under open source software licenses and established an Open Middleware Infrastructure Institute (OMII). The e-Infrastructure Reflection Group (a high-level European body formed in 2003 to monitor and advise on policy and administrative frameworks for easy and cost-effective shared use of grid computing, data storage, and networking resources) has gone further, issuing an

M. den Besten (✉)
Pôle de Recherche en Economie et Gestion, Ecole Polytechnique, Paris, France
e-mail: matthijs.den-besten@polytechnique.edu

J. Hunsinger et al. (eds.), *International Handbook of Internet Research*,
DOI 10.1007/978-1-4020-9789-8_4, © Springer Science+Business Media B.V. 2010

"e-infrastructure roadmap" (Leenaars, 2005, pp. 15–17, 22, 27). The e-IRG roadmap calls for open standard grid protocol stacks, open source middleware, "transparent access to relevant [grid] data sources, and sharing of run-time software and interaction data including medical imagery, high-resolution video and haptic and tactile information" and for public funding of scientific software development because "current Intellectual Property Right solutions are not in the interest of science" (p. 16).

Provision of enhanced technical means of accessing distributed research resources is neither a necessary nor a sufficient condition for achieving open scientific collaboration (David, 2006; David & Spence, 2008). Collaboration technologies – both infrastructures and specific application tools and instruments – may be used to facilitate the work of distributed members of "closed clubs," including government labs engaged in secret defense projects and corporate R&D teams that work with proprietary data and materials, guarding their findings as trade secrets until they obtain the legal protections granted by intellectual property rights. Nor do researchers' tools *as such* define the organizational character of collaboration. This is evident from the fact that many academic researchers who fully and frequently disclose their findings, and collaborate freely with colleagues on an informal, non-contractual basis, nonetheless employ proprietary software and patented instruments and publish in commercial scientific journals that charge high subscription fees.

At the same time, it should be acknowledged that the availability of certain classes of tools, and the ease with which they may be used by researchers within and across scientific domains, is quite likely to affect organizational decisions and shape the ethos and actions of the work groups that adopt those tools. Some basic collaboration technologies – notably e-network infrastructure such as grid services and middleware platforms – are particularly potent enablers of distributed multi-participant collaborations; they may significantly augment the data, information, and computational resources that can be mobilized by more loosely organized, "bottom-up" networks of researchers engaging in "open science." The availability of access to those resources on "share-and-share alike" terms can induce researchers' participation in passive as well as active collaboration arrangements, acquainting them with benefits of cooperation and thereby reinforcing the ethos of open science.

The sections that follow present our understanding of the term "open science," its significance for epistemologists, sociologists, and economists studying the relationships between institutional structures, working procedures, and the formation of scientific knowledge and discuss ways that this concept may be applied to assess the "open-ness" of certain structural features and organizational practices observable in programmatic e-science initiatives and particular projects. We then consider some results from preliminary empirical enquiries, intended primarily to illustrate the empirical implementation of our proposed conceptual framework. Although only a limited sample of U.K. e-science projects (to date) have been selected for study from this perspective, the recent findings based on structured interviews and responses to a targeted e-mail survey of research project directors display noteworthy consistencies and support our contention that further investigation along the conceptual and methodological lines explored will prove to be both feasible and illuminating.

Open Science

Many of the key formal institutions of modern science are quite familiar not only to specialists concerned with the economics and the sociology of science, technology, and innovation, but equally to academic researchers of all disciplinary stripes. It is a striking phenomenon, well noted in the sociology of science, that there is high degree of mimetic professional organization and behavior across the diverse cognitive domains of academic endeavor. Whether in the mathematical and natural sciences or the social sciences or the humanities, each discipline has its professional academies and learned societies, journal refereeing procedures, public and private foundation grant programs, peer-panels for merit review of funding applications, organized competitions, prizes, and public awards. The outward forms are strikingly similar, even if the details of the internal arrangements may differ.

Ethos, Norms, and Institutions

The norms of "the Republic of Science" that were so famously articulated by Merton (1942, 1973) are summarized compactly by the mnemonic device "CUDOS": communalism, universalism, disinterestedness, originality, and skepticism.[1] These five key norms constitute a clearly delineated ethos to which members of the academic research community generally subscribe, even though their individual behaviors may not always conform to its strictures. It is important to appreciate both their separate and systemic effects as being conducive to the functional allocation of resources in an idealized research system, and they can be set out briefly, as in the following paragraphs.

Communalism emphasizes the cooperative character of enquiry, stressing that the accumulation of scientific understanding emerges through the interactions among individual contributors; however much each may strive to contribute solely to the advancement of science, production of "reliable knowledge" cannot proceed far in isolation and so remains a fundamentally collective pursuit. Therefore, research agendas as well as findings ought to be under the control of personally (or corporately) *disinterested* agents: the specific nature and import of the new knowledge that is being sought should not be of such significant personal interest to the

---

[1]The nmenonic *Cudos* was introduced by Merton's 1942 essay on the normative structure of science, but the association of the "O" with originality was a subsequent modification that has become conventional (see Ziman, 1994).

researchers involved that it risks skewing their methods or their reporting of "findings," and thereby rendering the results useless, or, worse, potentially detrimental to the research work of others.

Full disclosure of data and information about the methods by which new findings were obtained is another aspect of communal cooperation, vital both to maintain the effectiveness of new entrants to particular research domains and to speed validation of the results produced. The force of the norm of *universalism*, in turn, is required in order to keep entry into scientific work and discourse open for all persons of "competence," regardless of their personal and ascriptive attributes; equity aside, this preserves access to human talent and mitigates social pressures for conformity of opinion. Ultimately, *originality* of intellectual contributions is the touchstone of acceptance of priority claims, and the source of collegiate reputations upon which material and non-pecuniary rewards are based. Since s*kepticism* is the appropriate attitude toward all priority claims, those who seek recognition and peer esteem for their contribution should take no offence when scientific peers subject their work to close scrutiny, and, instead cooperate with the process of establishing the validity of their research conclusions and the merits of their assertion of priority.

A Functionalist Rationale for the Norms of "Open Science"

It is thus possible to elaborate a functionalist explanation for the "open" part of the institutional complex of modern science, by focusing on its economic and social efficiency properties in the pursuit of knowledge, and the supportive role played by norms that tend to reinforce cooperative behaviors among scientists (Dasgupta & David, 1987, 1994; David, 1998a, 2003). This rationale highlights the "incentive compatibility" of the key norm of disclosure within a collegiate reputation-based reward system grounded upon validated claims to priority in discovery or invention. In brief, rapid disclosures abet rapid validation of findings, reduce excess duplication of research effort, enlarge the domain of complementarities, and yield beneficial "spill-overs" among research programs. Without delving deeper into the details of this analysis, it may be noted that it is the difficulty of monitoring research effort that makes it necessary for both the open science system and the intellectual property regime to tie researchers' rewards in one way or another to priority in the production of observable "research outputs" that can be submitted to "validity testing and valorization" – whether directly by peer assessment or indirectly through their application in the markets for goods and services.

The specific functionality of the information-disclosure norms and social organization of open science rests upon the greater efficacy of data and information-sharing as a basis for the cooperative, cumulative generation of eventually reliable additions to the stock of knowledge. Treating new findings as tantamount to being in the public domain fully exploits the "public goods" properties that permit data and information to be concurrently shared in use and re-used indefinitely, and thus promotes faster growth of the stock of knowledge. This contrasts with the information control and access restrictions that generally are required in order to appropriate private material benefits from the possession of (scientific and technological) knowledge. In the proprietary research regime, discoveries and inventions must either be held secret or be "protected" by gaining monopoly rights to their commercial exploitation. Otherwise, the unlimited entry of competing users could destroy the private profitability of investing in research and development.

One may then say, somewhat baldly, that the regime of proprietary technology (*qua* social organization) is conducive to the maximization of private wealth stocks that reflect current and expected future flows of economic rents (extra-normal profits). While the prospective award of exclusive "exploitation rights" have this effect by strengthening incentives for private investments in R&D and innovative commercialization based on the new information, the restrictions that IP monopolies impose on the use of that knowledge perversely curtail the social benefits that it will yield. By contrast, because open science (*qua* social organization) calls for liberal dissemination of new information, it is more conducive to both the maximization of the rate of growth of society's stocks of reliable knowledge and to raising the marginal social rate of return from research expenditures. But it, too, is a flawed institutional mechanism: rivalries for priority in the revelation of discoveries and inventions induce the withholding of information ("temporary suspension of cooperation") among close competitors in specific areas of ongoing research. Moreover, adherents to open science's disclosure norms cannot become economically self-sustaining: being obliged to quickly disclose what they learn and thereby to relinquish control over its economic exploitation, their research requires the support of charitable patrons or public funding agencies.

The two distinctive organizational regimes thus serve quite different purposes that are complementary and highly fruitful when they co-exist at the macro-institutional level. This functional juxtaposition suggests a logical explanation for their co-existence, and the perpetuation of institutional and cultural separations between the communities of researchers forming "the Republic of Science" and those who are engaged in commercially oriented R&D conducted under proprietary rules. Yet, these alternative resource allocation mechanisms are not entirely compatible within a common institutional setting; *a fortiori,* within same project organization there will be an unstable competitive tension between the two and the tendency is for the more fragile, cooperative micro-level arrangements and incentives to be undermined.

"Open Science" Norms, Social Communications, and Collective Cognitive Performance

The relationship between the norms that Merton (1942) perceived as underlying the institutionalized organization and stratified social structure of scientific communities, and the way the scientific research process proceeds when viewed from the epistemological perspective, forms a question with which sociologists and philosophers of science have wrestled and about which there has been not a little internal disciplinary struggle.[2] With a few notable exceptions, philosophers and epistemologists of science shared a primary interest in *normative* questions concerned with the nature of the beliefs that people *ought* to hold about their surroundings.[3] While the classical approach in such endeavors sought to settle questions on an *aprioristic* basis, through solely conceptual arguments, a significant departure from that tradition took shape in the movement to "naturalize" epistemology and the philosophy of science. Following the work of the philosopher W.V.O. Quine (1953), this development sought to inject into such accounts some facts about the actual epistemic situations with which human must contend. Quine (1969) coined the term "naturalized epistemology," arguing that the positivist distinction between contexts of "discovery" and "justification" could be "naturalistically" translated into questions of perceptual psychology and sociology of knowledge, respectively. The former involves studying people's behavioral dispositions to associate words with situations, whereas the latter is studied by examining the communication patterns by which such dispositions become stabilized for a community.

In a broad sense it may be said that this latter branch of the "naturalized epistemology" program has been carried forward by the research movement associated with the "new economics of science." This emerged in the 1990s among social scientists informed by the analytical perspectives of modern micro-economic theory, which they undertook to apply to the study of patterns of resource allocation that would arise from the social communication behaviors among communities of researchers whose conduct conformed in varying degrees with the institutionalized norms and ethos of "open science."[4] To understand how this latter point of departure was arrived at, one must refer back to the second of the two domains into which the study of scientific activities was formerly divided. That comprised the territory in which sociologists of science following the leadership of Robert K. Merton sought to understand the social context of modern science, its characteristic institutionalized modes of organization, and the associated behavioral norms and cultural ethos which guided the participants' transactions and permitted them to succeed collectively, if not always individually, in their pursuit of knowledge about the external world.[5] There were influential contributors to the history of science and technology who pointed to the role of external, material conditions affecting the physical

---

[2]See, e.g., Popper (1959, 1963), Quine (1962), Kuhn (1962/1970), Lakatos (1970).

[3]For a sketch of the classical philosophy of science as a domain of concerns completely disjoint from the sociology and history of science, which is deliberately overdrawn for effect, see David (1998b). A more nuanced, but nonetheless compact account is provided by Fuller (1994).

[4]Papers following Dasgupta and David (1987, 1994) in this genre include David, Mowery, and Steinmueller (1992), Trajtenberg, Henderson, and Jaffe (1992), Arora and Gambardella (1994, 1997); David (1994, 1996); Gambardella (1994), David and Foray (1995), Arora, David, and Gambardella (1998), Geuna (1999). Some of the foregoing are noticed in the wider survey of the economics of science by Stephan (1996).

[5]See, particularly, Merton (1942, 1968) among the writings assembled in Merton (1973); see also, among the many works of Merton's students, Crane (1965, 1972), Cole and Cole (1967), Cole and Cole (1973), Cole (1978), Zuckerman and Merton (1971).

phenomena that scientists undertook to study and the ways in which they some-times went about it. But, the canonical investigations in the sociology of science focused upon generic behavioral and organizational problems that were represented to be largely independent of the specific substantive concerns of the scientific dis-cipline in question and orthogonal to its cognitive contents and claims at particular historical junctures.

While adherents to these philosophical and sociological approaches to the study of science, therefore, appear (from today's perspective) to have been collectively hesitant to assert any claims to the territory staked out by the other disciplines,[6] dur-ing the 1970s a new generation of sociologists took up the sociology of scientific knowledge – "SSK," as it came to be styled. They insisted that the cognitive and the social dimensions of science should no longer remain compartmentalized as distinct, specialized fields of inquiry.[7] Instead, the subject matter had to be seen in reality to be inseparable, because in "discourse" – within whose terms it was held possible to analyze everything – social and cognitive contexts are thoroughly inter-penetrating and mutually interactive. For those within the SSK movement it appeared that there was little substance to the old sociology of science's preoccupation with macro-institutional structures, institutionalized reward systems, the social norms, and the relationship of these to the organization of resource allocation within scientific com-munities. Encouraged to examine the practices of individual scientists and particular workgroups in academic research domains, they found that the pictures constructed by the Mertonian "normative structure" of science were highly idealized, and so could not readily account for many recurring micro-level realities that presented themselves to outside observers of "laboratory life" (Latour & Woolgar, 1979); worse, the idealized normative account was held by critics to be an apologetic for "the scientific establishment" in that it accorded salience to institutionalize practices that were "functional" while glossing over dysfunctional aspects of the conduct of organized research. Criticism of its predecessors aside, the positive aspiration of this post-Mertonian generation of "sociologists of scientific knowledge" was to end the separation between epistemology and the sociology knowledge – by showing how societal forces translated into social processes that shaped the ways that scientists worked, the questions on which they chose to work, and the manner in which those questions were satisfactorily resolved (or left unresolved) by scientific communities.

Economists for the most part have been quite content to study the efficiency of resource allocation in the production of goods and services without stopping to inquire even superficially into the specific natures and concrete shapes of those commodities, much less entering into serious discussion of how they come to be

---

[6]In consequence, only occasionally, and rather tenuously, did their studies attempt to draw links between the ways in which communities of scientists were organized and rewarded, and the ways in which scientific statements were created and accepted within those communities. This is a gloss on a very extensive literature, for fuller discussion of which see Ben-David (1991), Callon (1995), and Leydesdorff (1995).

[7]See Barnes (1974, 1977), Bloor (1976), Mulkay (1979), Latour & Woolgar (1979), Knorr-Cetina (1981).

differentiated in design and human perception.[8] Considered from that angle, it is perhaps not too surprising that contributors to the "new economics of science" (following Dasgupta & David, 1994) found it attractive to begin by reworking the terrain of organizational analysis already ploughed to good effect by sociologists in the Mertonian tradition. From that point of departure it was natural (being economists) to proceed to analyze how the structure of incentives created in a community whose members subscribed to the norms of open science would affect the efficiency of resource allocation in the production of generic information to which a significant measure of reliability could be attached; and then to compare the workings of an academic, open science research regime with the alternative system commercially oriented R&D grounded on the legal protections afforded to owners of trade secrets and intellectual property rights.[9]

This line of enquiry initially did not trouble itself too much about the nature of "scientific reliability," nor over the details of the ways in which that ("trustworthy") quality of information might be acquired, nor any of the other issues of socio-cognitive interaction that have occupied the sociology of scientific knowledge. But it was soon recognized that continuing to proceed in that fashion, which essentially ignored the foundation-level connections between the social organization of research and the nature of its information-products, was a mistake that was likely (sooner or later) to cause difficulties for an enterprise that aimed eventually to provide useful guidance for public policies affecting science.[10] Instead of continuing to focus exclusively upon the behavior of the individual researcher viewed in isolation, sociologists and economists have lately been giving greater attention to the systematic gathering and analysis of empirical evidence about role differentiation, specialization, and cooperative patterns of resource allocation within and between teams, consortia, and institutionalized research networks.

As a consequence of these developments, contributions in the social sciences – from quantitative sociology, from the bibliometrics of science (van Raan, 1988) and "scientometics" Leydesdorff (1995, 2006), as well as from the "new economics of science" – have become more closely aligned with the promising departure from older traditions in both epistemology and sociology that has marked the work of Kitcher (1993) on "social epistemology." The latter philosophical development

---

[8]See Bacharach, Gambetta et al. (1994) for an exceptional departure from this tradition in economics.

[9]See, in addition to works cited above (fn. 4), e.g., David (1996, 1998a, 2003, 2004), Turner and Mairesse (2002), Carayol (2003), Carayol and Dalle (2003), Carayol and Matt (2004, 2006).

[10]See, e.g., Brock and Durlauf (1999), David (1998b, 2002). Apart from the policy-relevant considerations noted in the following text, it may be argued that the cumulative, incremental development of propositions on which quasi-stable consensuses are formed among scientists do constitute grounds for insisting on the validity of drawing a cognitive distinction between the scientific and the other cultural pursuits. Because such resistance to "relativism" remains strongly contested in some quarters of contemporary "science studies," David develops an argument defending it on "evolutionary epistemological" grounds. For a defense of "objectivism" and criticism of "social constructivism" in science studies, see Schroeder (2007a).

explores the connections between the collective cognitive performance of scientific researchers and the organization and conduct of social communications among them – by identifying the conditions under which groups of individuals operating in conformity with various recognized procedures for modifying their individual research practices and informational transactions are able, through their interactions, to generate "a progressive sequence of consensus practices."[11]

This is indeed a most welcome trend, because the accompanying movement away from empirical research conducted with the atomistic agent framework therefore may redirect the attention of science policy toward considering the ways in which research communities' collective epistemological performance over that long run could be improved by the provision of more adequate technical infrastructures and the reinforcement of norms and informal practices conductive to efficient resource-sharing and collaborative interactions. If one asks whether social science research really can be informative on those matters, some signs of an affirmative answer are to be found in the recent quantitative work that is building upon the foundations of previous bibliometric studies. Such studies measure and explain patterns in the intensity of scientific co-publications not only involving authors affiliated with different academic host institutions, but with different laboratories within the same institute or university.[12] Micro-level research on science in this vein has successfully identified factors that are significant in promoting collaboration among scientists that lead to co-publications, and some that inhibit it.[13] Nevertheless, as promising as this is, the data sources on which such research have had to rely largely preclude one from saying anything very concrete about the effects upon productive collaboration of variations in incentive structures, institutional policies, and laboratory-level practices concerning dataflow controls, external releases of results, and the conditions for sharing access to materials and specialized facilities – institutional details that have remained sparsely observed and far from adequately documented.

---

[11] See Kitcher (1993, Ch. 8). This article, on "The Organization of Cognitive Labor," opens by asking whether, in an "epistemically well-designed social system," it is possible that "the individual ways of responding to nature matter far less than the coordination, cooperation, and competition that go on among the individuals?" (p. 303)

[12] See Blau (1973), Beaver and Rosen (1979), Katz (1994) for studies of scientific collaboration in the sociological and bibliometric tradition using co-publications. While economists have followed Jaffe, Trajtenberg, and Henderson (1993) who used patent co-citations, and cross-citations between scientific publications and patents to try to gauge the extent of knowledge flows and inferred collaboration between academic and university scientists, Mairesse and Turner (2006) recently have broken new ground in measuring and econometrically explaining variations in the intensity of co-publication among the members of the large community of physicists in the condensed matter section of the CNRS.

[13] The statistically significant positive factors include both characteristics of the individual researchers (e.g., age, professional status, publication history) and their structural or institutional situations (e.g., department or laboratory size and disciplinary specialization, institutional reputation, ease of face-to-face interactions gauged by spatial proximity to other laboratories with specialization in the same or complementary research field).

Empirical Questions About the Degrees of "Openness" of the Organization of Research

The major point underscored by the preceding review of the treatment of scientific communication and collaboration in the evolving literature on the philosophy and social science of scientific research is the emergence of a generally shared recognition of the reciprocal interdependence between the ethos and normative structures of research communities, on the one hand, and, on the other hand, the informal arrangements and institutionally reinforced conditions of access to research findings, underlying data and methodologies. Together, the norms and rules affecting communications through personal networks and broadcast channels, and the interchange of personnel among scientific workgroups, shape the possibilities of coordination and effective collaboration.[14] They thereby impinge upon the efficiency of scientific projects internal use of resources, and of resource allocation among the members of separate projects who constitute "invisible colleges" that are distributed across academic departments, institutes, universities, transcending national and regional boundaries – extending even into research laboratories of business corporations and government agencies.

The foregoing considerations have given us strong reason to regard the formal and informal *institutional* arrangements governing access to scientific and technical data and information, no less than to physical research facilities, instruments, materials, as critically influential among the factors determining how fully e-science will be able to realize the potentials for the advancement of reliable knowledge that are being created by advances in digital information technologies.

Questions concerning the actual extent of "openness" of research processes identified with contemporary e-science therefore ought to address at least two main sets of issues pertaining to the conduct of "open science." The first set concerns the terms on which individuals may enter and leave research projects. Who is permitted to join the collaboration? Are all of the participating researchers able to gain full access to the project's databases and other key research resources? How easy or hard is it for members and new entrants to develop distinct agendas of enquiry within the context of the ongoing project, and how much control do they retain over the communication of their findings? What restrictions are placed (formally or informally) on the uses they may make of data, information, and knowledge in their possession after they exit from the research collaboration?

The second set of questions concerns the norms and rules governing disclosure of data and information about research methods and results. How fully and quickly is information about research procedures and data released by the project? How completely is it documented and annotated – so as to be not only accessible but useable by those outside the immediate research group? On what terms and

---

[14]See Fry, Schroeder, and den Besten (2009), Schroeder (2008), and den Besten, David, and Schroeder (2009) for further discussions of the distinction between generic research technologies and narrowly defined research tools and its bearing on the potential for openness in e-science.

with what delays are external researchers able to access materials, data, and project results? Are findings held back, rather than being disclosed in order to first obtain intellectual property rights on a scientific project's research results, and if so, then for how long is it usual for publication to be delayed (whether by the members or their respective host institutions)? Can research partners in university–business collaborations require that some findings or data not be made public? And when intellectual property rights to the use of research results have been obtained, will its use be lincenced to outsiders on an exclusive or a non-exclusive basis? Do material transfer agreements among university-based projects impose charges (for cell lines, reagents, specimens) that require external researchers to pay substantially more than the costs of making the actual transfers? In the case of publicly funded research groups, are the rights to use such legally "protected" information and data conditional on payment of patent fees, copyright royalties such that the members of the research group have discretionary control, or is control exercised by external parties (in their host institution, or the funding sources)?

Ideally, these and still other questions might be formulated as a simple checklist, such as the one devised by Stanford University (1996) to provide guidelines for faculty compliance with its "openness in research" policy. The Stanford checklist, however, having initially been designed primarily to implement rules against secrecy in sponsored research, actually is too limited in its scope for our present purposes, and a fuller, more specific set of questions (inspired by this source) has been designed for gathering data in the context of contemporary UK research projects. This empirical framework has been "field tested" both in a small number of structured interviews and a subsequent more extensive e-mail-targeted survey of e-science project leaders.[15] It is not intended to be comprehensive, and, instead, focuses on salient aspects of "openness and collaboration in academic science research" that could be illuminated by implementing systematic surveys of this kind on a much wider scale.

Of course, to pursue a substantially expanded program of inquiry into evolving e-science practices along these lines would necessitate some substantive modifications of the questionnaire in order to appropriately "customize" the interview protocols and the survey template, which has been designed for exploratory, "proof-of-concept" investigations. Conducting research of this kind across a widened international survey field certainly would require adjustments to allow for the greater diversity of institutional and organizational forms, research cultures, languages, and technical nomenclatures. Furthermore, practical considerations might call also for abridging the questionnaires, so as to reduce the burden upon respondents and obtain

---

[15]For a report on the structured interviews, see Fry et al. (2008). David, den Besten, and Schroeder (2006) present a preliminary version of the framework of questions from which were developed both the structured interview protocol and subsequent online survey questionnaire, the result of which is reported by den Besten and David (2008). The complete set of survey questions may be consulted in den Besten et al. (2009) and is also available online as the Oxford eScience Information Access Survey at http://www.oii.ox.ac.uk/microsites/oess/oesias; see Q. 8 for questions directly inspired by the Stanford checklist.

reasonably high response rates from an internationally administered survey – while avoiding costly individual e-mail-targeting and follow-up requests for cooperation from potential respondents.

e-Science as Open Science

Researchers in public sector science and engineering organizations historically have been at the forefront of many basic technological advances underlying new paradigms of digital information creation and dissemination. Their pressing needs for more powerful information processing and communication tools have led to many of the key enabling technologies of the "Information Society," including its mainframe computers, packet-switched data networks, the TPC/IP protocols of the internet and the world wide web, its proliferation of markup languages, the Semantic Web, and many more recent advances that facilitate distributed conduct of collaborative research.

Collaboration Infrastructures, Tools and Materials, and Open Access Dissemination

For essentially the same reasons, scientific and engineering research communities throughout the world now are active in developing not only technical infrastructure tools like grid and middleware platforms, but also a new array of shareable digital data and information dissemination resources, including public-domain digital data archives and federated open data networks, open institutional repositories, "open access" electronic journals, and open-source software applications.[16]

Peer-to-peer sharing of computing facilities – from SETI@Home to the International Virtual Observatory Alliance – focus on cooperative arrangements for distributed support of long-term exploratory research projects. Collaborative community-based open source software engineering projects – which, like the "free encyclopedia" Wikipedia, makes use of voluntary collective efforts to produce and maintain new information artifacts that, being produced by and for expert researchers, can constitute critical resources for those in specialized scientific fields. Repositories such as MIT's D-Space and OpenCourseWare, Southampton University's "*e*Prints," the physics arXiv pre-print repository, and GenBank are emblematic products of academic pro-activity in providing "open access" to research data and information. They complement the major scientific database development work of public institutes, such as the US NCBI and the Europe's EBI in bioinformatics.

---

[16] See David (2005); Dalle, David, Ghosh, and Steinmueller (2005); David and Uhlir (2005, 2006); Uhlir and Schröder (2007); Schroeder (2007b).

But the availability of this expanding array of facilities for scientific cooperation and coordination does not substitute for public and private agency actions to support the open science conduct of research; nor can it transform the incentive and "reward systems" affecting the behaviors of researchers and research managers. Moreover, policies that involve disclosure of research findings can be consonant with the pursuit of goals quite removed from those traditional open science communities. Business corporations may encourage publication of employees' R&D results in peer-reviewed "open access" journals and conference proceedings for various strategic reasons: greater freedom to publish their results may prove effective in recruiting talented young scientists and engineers; disclosing results also can be a way to pre-empt a "frontier" research area that might otherwise be contested by rival firms. Yet, because the corporate research lab's ultimate purpose is to improve the "bottom line" of a profit-seeking business, R&D managers must be discriminating when setting the research agendas that employees are allowed to pursue and when deciding which results may be disclosed to whom, when, and with what degree of completeness.

The goals of the organization conducting the research, rather than its selection of supporting tools and managerial techniques, thus set the balance of the configuration of its project's policies and practices; that overall configuration is what must be assessed in order to distinguish "open science" conduct from other institutional arrangements that may be found in contemporary e-science programs and projects.

e-Science Infrastructure Engineering

To examine the realities of e-science practices regarding "openness" it is both appropriate and feasible to focus on the undertakings initiated in 2001 by the UK's e-Science Core Program for the development of middleware platforms. Most of the university-based projects funded by this program were exploratory tool-building activities and would seem to be good candidates for "open science practice" in addition to having been the earliest of the programs to be launched in the present century under the banner of "e-science."[17] According to the program's Director, Tony Hey, a basic policy decision was taken at the outset to make these projects' results available as open source software. Implementation of this policy was pursued subsequently by the founding of the Open Middleware Infrastructure Institute (OMII), the stated purpose of which is to "leverage the wider development community through open source software development" (http://www.omii.ac.uk). That would appear to meet basic disclosure norms of open science, because a peculiar property of the output of software engineering research is that the artifacts produced (i.e., the code) also reveal the method of their construction.

---

[17]See David and Spence (2003, 2008) for descriptions of the pilot projects and discussion of their relationship to the US "collaboratories" projects of the 1990s, and the more recent NSF "Cyberinfrastructure" Program. The discussion in this section draws upon David et al. (2006).

The OMII's description of its mission, however, points to a strategic purpose behind the open source release policy. To become "the source for reliable, interoperable and open-source Grid middleware, ensuring the continued success of Grid-enabled e-Science in the UK," the institute is promoting adoption of an open web services standard adopted widely among UK-funded e-science projects (http://www.omii.ac.uk/about/index.jsp; Atkinson et al., 2005). Provision of an open source reference implementation thus is seen as a means of making the institute's web services standard more attractive to a broader array of potential users, including those in the industrial sector. OMII's mission statement supports this view:

> "Key members of the OMII have specific experience in industrial software development. We will also leverage the wider development community through open source software development. The OMII intends to lead the evolution of Grid Middleware through an open consultative process with major software vendors and major UK, EU and US projects."[18]

In some significant respects the development of OMII into OMII-UK, like the web services standard that the institute now is promoting, appears to parallel the course of evolution of the GlobusToolkit grid service protocols that were developed by a joint public–private project of the Distributed Systems Laboratory (US Argonne National Laboratory). The initial goal of the Globus project, similarly, was to enable scientific research organizations to share enhanced computing resources; it too released code under an open source software license.[19] But, in December 2004, the leaders of the Globus project launched the Univa Corporation as a provider of commercial software, technical support, and professional services for the construction of grids based on Globus open source software. A number of the major hardware and software systems companies presently are aligned with this venture in the Globus Alliance (http://www.univa.com/pdf/Univa-Launch_Release.pdf).

Manifestly, the dissemination of software engineering products as open source code has been quite compatible with both projects' evolution into "e-science" infrastructure and grid/web services providers whose activities are diverging from the traditional open science conduct of science and engineering research. OMII-UK now describes itself in business terms as creating an integrated "e-Science value chain" by providing infrastructure, components, and solutions for "the e-science end user" (De Roure, 2006). Being neither a multi-site research collaboration nor a public entity supporting exploratory ("blue-sky") software engineering, it focuses on (a) "forming partnerships with targeted user communities," (b) sourcing code provided

---

[18]See http://www.omii.ac.uk/about/index.jsp, emphasis added. The foregoing, however, is a rather different rationale than the one offered previously by Program Director Hey's statement at the September 2004 e-Science All Hands Meeting (http://www.allhands.org.uk/proceedings/proceedings/introduction.pdf):"...WebServicesstill are 'work in progress' so we must adopt conservative strategies to safeguard our UK investments and ensure that we converge on the standards that eventually emerge...."

[19]The idiosyncratic features of the Globus license are discussed by David and Spence (2003, pp. 32–33, and Appendix 4).

by other grid service and middleware developers, (c) coordinating the "quality-assured software engineering" carried out by OMII-UK partners and its "managed program," (d) "tracking and engagement with the standards processes," and, (e) building a "sustainable business" by attracting "partnerships and new investors."

As an organization intermediating between university researchers and business clients, the institute maintains a repository that can "ingest" code contributions from external sources – if these match the OMII criteria. In practice, such donations come from UK academic research groups and especially from the coordinated software "production pipelines" operating at three partner institutions – Southampton, Manchester, and Edinburgh. Getting software into the OMII repository is one thing, however, and accessing the "quality-assured" middleware code is something else again. Given OMII-UK's "sustainable business" goal, it is perhaps not surprising that unauthorized outsiders are not allowed to download the evaluation version of OMII client/server code; only the older stable versions can be accessed from the website. But, the terms on which even those versions are available from the Institute's repository disappoint expectations of easy "open access."[20]

Lastly, it should be remarked that the web service standardization efforts of IBM and Microsoft– the big contenders for that potentially important business market – have been moving toward OASIS and therefore away from the W3C's open standards approach. Since the OMII-UK and the Globus Alliance appear to be aligning themselves and thereby reinforcing this shift, they may be creating a serious impediment to the future emergence of open web service standards. The source of this threat is OASIS's policy of allowing publication of standards that require payments of licensing fees to patent holders (see Wikipedia (2008) entry for "OASIS"). Aside from the drawbacks of proprietary standards, this could well have the added effect of foreclosing a volunteer-based open source implementation of web service standards.

The UK's OMII initiative thus appears to have "morphed" into something other than a conventional academic research program to build an enhanced open science infrastructure. By transforming "research-level" code created by e-science projects into tested and well-documented "production-level" middleware and grid software solutions, it is likely that the institute will have contributed substantially to facilitate the work of future e-science researchers. Whether it will prove to have promoted global expansion of "open science" e-collaborations, as much as proprietary R&D and e-business, however, remains much less clear.

---

[20]Non-client researchers, after registering and obtaining a login name and password, may proceed to download software packages, but they will not necessarily obtain the underlying source code. David et al. (2006) reported that an attempt to download version 1.0 of OMII's certificate management tool yielded a tar-ball within which was a jar-file containing java byte-code; procedures for extracting the corresponding java source code from that file are far from straightforward. Since May 2007, OMII has made the source code available (Chang, personal communication). Chang, Mills, and Newhouse (2007) provide reflections on open source and sustainability from the perspective of OMII.

e-Science Research Projects

We turn now to examine current collaborations that have emerged in several key domains of research that the infrastructure is intended to enable: (1) e-DiaMoND, a grid-enabled prototype system intended to support breast cancer screening, mammography training, and epidemiological research; (2) MiMeG, which currently aims to produce software for the collaborative analysis and annotation of video data of human interactions; and (3) Combe-chem, an e-science test-bed that integrates existing sources of chemical structure and properties data and augments them within a grid-based information and knowledge environment. Although none of these quite different projects have developed income-generating activities that might conflict directly with their adherence to open science norms, it is striking that all three have confronted other difficult issues related to "control rights" over data and information.

For e-DiaMoND the problem of control of mammography images remained unresolved when this "proof of concept" project reached its scheduled end. The researchers' original intentions to distribute standardized images for research and diagnostic purposes over electronic networks clashed with the clinicians' concerns about their professional responsibilities to patients, protecting patient privacy, and assuring ethical uses of the data. Convincing clinical practitioners to trust the researchers and engineering a comprehensive, adequately flexible security system proved to be less straightforward than had been expected (Jirotka et al., 2005). Even "to develop a clear legal framework that fairly accounts for the needs of patients, clinicians, researchers and those in commerce" – one that the project's diverse partners would be able to work with – has been surprisingly difficult (Hinds et al., 2005).

MiMeG, an ESRC-funded e-social science project, encountered similar problems: the researchers who employed the tool for collaborative analysis of video streams felt that the trust of the persons whose images they were studying would be violated by archiving the collaboration's data and making it available for re-use by other researchers, possibly for purposes other than the one for which consent originally had been obtained. It remains to be seen whether or not the ethical *desiderata* of privacy and informed consent of experimental subjects can be satisfied in future projects of this kind that plan sharing research data via the grid.

For the present, however, MiMeG has abandoned the project's initial intention to analyze video collaboratively via e-networks and is focusing on the development of video analysis tools that other researchers can use. In that connection it is significant that the research software created by MiMeG is being released under the GNU GPL license (and hence distributed at minimal cost for non-commercial use). This policy resulted at least in part from the use of some GPL components (such as the MySQL relational database) to build the project's software tools. In addition, however, MiMeG is encouraging external users to participate in further developing its recently released video analysis software tools. In these respects, the project has been able to go forward in the collaborative "open science" mode.

The Combe-chem project at Southampton University is funded under the EPRSC's e-science program and includes several departments and related projects. Only a few organizational features of this complex collaboration can be considered here, but several important aspects of its activities clearly are "open." One utilizes the pre-existing EPSRC National Crystallographic Service, which has allowed remote "users" from UK universities to submit samples of chemical compounds to the laboratory at Southampton for x-ray analysis. Combe-chem accepts submitted samples and returns them via a Globus-based grid and web services infrastructure (see Coles, Frey, Hursthouse, Light, Meacham, et al., 2005, appendix B). At present this service has some 150 subscribers who submit more than 1000 samples per annum (Frey, 2004, 1031).

In addition to demonstrating and developing this grid implementation, a major project goal is to increase the archiving of analyzed samples, thereby averting the loss of un-archived information and the consequently wasteful repetition of crystallographic analyses. Formerly, chemical analysis results yielded by these techniques were "archived" by virtue of their publication in research journals, most of which were available on a "subscription only" basis. Now it is possible to make results available in open access repositories via the open archive initiative (OAI) and deposited in e-Bank UK archives and ePrints publications (Coles, Frey, Hursthouse, Light, Carr, et al., 2005). Because they are put into RDF (Resource Description Framework) and other standard metadata formats, the archived results are searchable via the Semantic Web. With only 20% of data generated in crystallographic work currently reaching the public domain (Allen, 2004) and not all of it being readily searchable, this service extension is an important open science advance. Combe-chem's interrelated e-science activities thus illustrate four facets of open science practice: (a) using the Globus and web services open source grid software, (b) providing web access to shared resources for a diverse research community, (c) open access archiving and dissemination of results through an open repository, and (d) formatting of information using open standards. Like other publicly funded academic research, the project interacts easily with the world of commercial scientific publishing: fee charging journals that adhere to "subscriber only access" policies provide readers with links to the Combe-chem data archive. Moreover, as is the case in other collaborative projects that fit the traditional open science model quite closely, Combe-chem has been able nonetheless to draw some sponsorship support from industry – IBM having been interested in this deployment of a grid service [Interview with J. Frey, P.I., Combe-chem: 29.11.2005].

Structured Interviews and Online Survey Findings

The questions about degrees of openness that we outlined in the section "Open Science Norms, Social Communications, and Collective Cognitive Performance" could be answered, at least in some part by the people involved in the research and development projects associated with the e-Science program in the UK. Fry et al.

(2009) have carried out a series of structured interviews with a small group of the principal investigators of U.K. e-science projects, designed to assess perceptions and practices relating to aspects of "openness" of the projects for which they had leadership responsibilities. A related questionnaire, suitable for implementation in an on-line internet survey was developed on the basis of this experience and implemented in an e-mail targeted survey of a larger population of U.K. e-science projects P.I.s. The results obtained from the latter survey by den Besten and David (2008) are broadly congruent with the detailed and more nuanced impressions drawn from the structured interviews.

Open Science in e-Science – Policy or Contingency? Insights from In-Depth Interviews

Fry et al. (2009) report the findings from their use of a structured interview in conducting in-depth interviews about the relationships between collaboration in "e-science" and "open science," with 12 individuals who had roles as principal investigators, project managers and developers engaged in UK e-Science projects during 2006.[21] The interview questions focused on research inputs, software development processes, access to resources, project documentation, dissemination of outputs and by-products, licensing issues, and institutional contracts. A focal interest of the approach in this study was the authors' juxtaposition of research project leaders' perceptions and views concerning research governance policies at the institutional level, with the responses describing local practices at the project level. As a detailed discussion of the responses (along with related documentary evidence drawn from the respective project's websites) is available elsewhere, it will be sufficient here to summarize briefly the main thrust of Fry et al.'s (2009) findings.

Their interviews suggest that the desirability of maintaining conditions of "openness" in "doing (academic) science" is part of a generally shared research ethos among this sample of university-based project leaders. More specifically, the latter were not only cognizant of but receptive to the U.K. e-science Pilot Program's strong policy stance favoring open source software tools and sharing of informational resources. Nevertheless, there were many uncertainties and yet-to-be resolved issues surrounding the practical implementation of both the informal norms and formal policies supporting open science practices. Making software tools and data available to external users might mean simply putting these research outputs online, but that need not be the same thing as making them sufficiently robust and well documented to be widely utilized.[22] It seems that for those with leadership responsibilities at

---

[21] Fry et al.'s (2009) structured interview protocol elaborated and modified the extended questionnaire proposed by David et al. (2006).

[22] As Fry et al. (2009) point out, "The effort to make the tools or data suitable or robust enough to make them into a commonly used resource may be considerable, and thus represents a Catch-22 situation for researchers: a large effort can be made, which may not be useful, but if it

the project level, the most salient and fundamental challenges in resolving issues of openness in practice and operating policies, and thereby moving toward coherent institutional infrastructures for e-science research, involve the coordination and integration of goals across the diverse array of e-science efforts.[23]

By comparison, much less concern is voiced about the resolution of tensions between IPR (intellectual property rights) protections and the provision of timely common-use access to research tools, data, and results. This is not really surprising when the context is considered, even though these issues have been very much at the center of public discussions and debates about the effects of the growth of "academic patenting" on the "openness" of publicly funded research.[24] The programmatic focus of U.K. e-science has not been on biomedical research and biotechnology, life science fields in which patenting is especially important for subsequent commercial innovation. Furthermore, EU policy has circumscribed the patenting of software (without eliminating the patenting of embedded algorithms and a wider class of so-called computer implemented inventions), and in the UK itself, government agencies funding e-science projects have explicitly prohibited university grant and contract recipients from filing software patents that would vitiate the open source licensing of their outputs of middleware and applications software.

Most of the foregoing observations, although drawn from structured interviews conducted with a only a very small and non-random sample of project leaders, turn out to be quite informative – in that these impressions are reinforced by the findings of a subsequent online survey that sought responses from the entire population of principal investigators on U.K. e-science projects.

---

is not attempted, then it cannot be useful in the first place. Nevertheless, all projects expressed the aspiration to contribute to a common resource, even if this was sometimes expressed as a hope rather than a certainty or foregone conclusion."

[23]Coordination and integration problems calling for solutions that take the form of interoperability standards posed particularly difficult challenges for on-going projects in the UK e-Science Pilot Programme, according to Fry et al. (2009), whereas some new software tools required compatibility with existing tools (for example, tools from the CQeSS project which developed e-social Science tools for large quantitative datasets needed to be interoperable with Stata) and this might be technically difficult to implement. Achieving integration with other tools that are currently under development confronts more fundamental uncertainties about the requirements for compatibility or interoperability. The same applies to complying with standards, ontologies, and metadata that are still in the process of development.

[24]See, e.g., David and Hall (2006); David (2007). Much of that discussion, however, has focused on the implications of the patenting of research tools, and *sui generis* legal protection of database rights (in the EU) in the areas of genomics, biogenetics, and proteinomics, the patenting of computer software (in the US) and computer-implemented inventions (in the EU), and extensive patenting of nanotechnology research tools. While those have been very active fields of academic science research, and growing university ownership of patents, they are not represented in the UK's e-Science core program and so do not appear among the projects included in either the structured interview or the survey samples discussed here.

Contract Terms and "Openness in Research": Survey Findings on e-Science Projects

Systematic and detailed data at the individual project level about the openness of information and data resources remain quite limited, both as regards actual practices and the priority assigned to these issues among project leaders' concerns. A glimpse of what the larger landscape might be like in this regard, however, is provided by the responses to a recent online survey of issues in U.K. e-science that was conducted among the principal investigators that could be identified and contacted by e-mail on the basis of National e-Science Centre (NeSC) data about the projects and their principal investigators (see den Besten & David, 2008; den Besten et al., 2009).[25] Out of the 122 P.I.s that were contacted, 30 responded with detailed information for an equal number of projects. [26] A comparison of the distribution of the projects for which responses were obtained with the distribution of the whole population of NeSC projects showed remarkable similarities along the several dimensions on which quantitative comparisons could be made – including project grant size, number of consortium members and project start dates. This correspondence is reassuring, providing a measure of confidence in the representativeness of the picture that can be formed from this admittedly very restricted survey sample.

Formal agreements governing the conduct of publicly funded university research projects may, and sometimes do, involve explicit terms concerned with the locus and nature of control over data and publications, and the assignment of intellectual property rights based upon research results, especially when there are several collaborating institutions and the parties include business organizations. The survey sought to elicit information about project leaders' understandings of these matters and the importance they attached to such bearing as the terms of their respective project's agreement might have upon information access issues. It did so by posing various questions intended to probe the extent of participant's knowledge of the circumstances of the contractual agreement governing their project,

---

[25]This questionnaire instrument, the Oxford e-Science Information Access Survey (OeSIAS) which was posted on SurveyMonkey (www.surveymonkey.com), is reproduced in den Besten and David (2009). Particular questions among the 19 in the survey's substantive portion (many of which were comprised of several sub-items) are referred to in the following text and footnotes by their number in source, thus [OeSIAS, Q.1].

[26]This number represented just over 10% of the projects listed by NeSC, implying a "project response rate" of 25%. The number of individual responses to this survey was larger, because P.I.s receiving the e-mail request were asked also to send it on to non-P.I. members of their project (which yielded an additional 21 responses that are not discussed here; also, in three cases more than one P.I. for a single project returned the questionnaire). The present analysis used only the one with the lowest frequency of "don't know" responses. The low apparent response rate from P.I.s and projects may be due in some part to the relatively short time interval allowed for those who submitted survey replies to be eligible to receive a book-token gift. The existence of projects that appear more than once in the NeSC database and had multiple (co-) P.I.s also would contribute to reducing the apparent rate of "project" responses.

namely, the identities of the parties responsible for its initial drafting and subsequent modifications (if any), as well as some of the contract's specific terms.[27]

The overall impression one draws from these survey responses is, once again, quite broadly congruent with the impressions that Fry et al. (2009) report on the basis of their 12 in-depth interviews. That applies also in regard to their vagueness as to the way that their project's governing agreement(s) had been arrived at. More than one-third of the projects' P.I. and non-P.I. members either could not or would not say whether it was the lead scientists, or university administrative and service offices, or funding agency staff that had framed the initial project agreement; nor could they say who – if anyone – subsequently had sought contract modifications, whether before or after the funding contract(s) had been signed and the project was launched officially. The latter aspect of the results predominantly reflect the reality that in many instances a university-based project's scientific activities already are underway well before the completion of the initial template of a legal agreement, let alone the signing of a contract. Furthermore, the responsibility for producing an agreement that will fund and govern the collaboration typically will be in the hands of actors that are not directly engaged in the project or involved in any way with its scientific work: staff in the host universities' research services offices (sometimes their legal counsel's offices), or officers of public funding agencies, or both. When multiple partners are involved, the role of the funding agency in the formal framing of the project – and hence in the framing much of its governing agreement, tends to be augmented vis-à-vis that of both the academic host institutions and sponsoring business companies.[28]

With a few notable exceptions, involving restrictions on the uses of proprietary data and publication of findings (where a collaboration had industrial partners), the terms of the agreement governing their project to which respondent P.I.s could respond were not such as would breach "openness in research" guidelines modeled on those of the Stanford University guidelines (1996). Excluding the respondents who either found the question "not applicable" to their project or "did not know" the answer, between 96 and 98% of the replies reported that the terms of the agreement governing their project neither restricted research participation on the basis of country of origin or citizenship, nor required participation in EU-citizens-only research

---

[27]Unlike other survey findings discussed in sections "contract terms and openness in research" and "provision of information access in e-science projects", the results obtained from the seven items in Survey Question 8 are based on the complete tabulation of the answers from all 54 survey respondents – including both the three cases of reports on multiple projects by a single P.I., and the 21 non-P.I.s.

[28]Funding bodies sometimes seek to form larger joint projects by bringing together academics that have submitted separate (competing) proposals, especially where there are opportunities to exploit differences in the applicants' respective areas of special expertise. For further discussion of the formal legal context of collaborative e-science, see David and Spence (2008, Sect. 2.3) and Fitzgerald (2008, Chs. 6, 11, 12).

meetings, nor prohibited the involvement of research personnel from outside the EU.[29]

When asked whether their project agreement gave a sponsor the right of pre-publication review for purposes other than the preparation of a patent application, or the exclusion of proprietary data – i.e., the right to suppress findings that (presumably) were simply deemed "commercially sensitive" – 92% among those replying definitively said "No." Although approximately one-quarter of all the respondents did not give a definitive reply because this was not applicable to their project (one may suppose there was no sponsor that would have such interest), 19% of those who accepted the question as relevant did not know whether to give a "yes", or a "no" answer. Almost as high a proportion (87%) among the definitive (yes or no) responses reported that their project placed no restrictions on access to proprietary data that would have the effect of significantly blocking the work of a participating researcher. But, in the latter case, there was a considerable lower fraction of "don't know" responses (11%) among all those who accepted the question as pertinent for their respective projects.

The highest proportions of "don't know" responses were elicited by the questionnaire items concerning the existence of project contract terms and sponsorship agreements that were to be kept confidential, or provision that mandated project compliance with government regulations restricting the export of material or software (deemed sensitive for national "defense" purposes). The latter represented between 26 and 28% of those respondents who did not dismiss these specific issues as irrelevant to the circumstances of their project. Of course, it is to be expected that quite a few participants would not be uninformed about contract provisions that were supposed to be confidential, *a fortiori* when a substantial share of them were not project P.I.s. Nonetheless, among those who thought they could give a definitive answer to the question declared that their project's agreement contained no such restrictive provisions.

The survey results just reviewed suggest that these e-science projects generally are free from positive, contractually imposed restrictions on the participation of qualified researchers and significant restraints upon participants' access to critical data resources and ability eventually to make public their research results. That a substantial fraction of project members appear not to be informed about the specifics of the project agreements under whose terms they are working is not very surprising, as many scientists express disinterest if not impatience with such matters, wishing to get on with their work without such distractions, and therefore leaving it to others – including some among their fellow P.I.s – to deal with legal aspects of governance if and when problems of that nature intrude into the scientific conduct of the project. That between 20–30% of participants remain uninformed about the details

---

[29] Among all the respondents who found these three questionnaire items (in Q 8) applicable to the circumstances of their respective projects, approximately 11% said they did not know the answer to the question.

of contract terms that appear germane to the conduct of their research projects therefore could be taken as a healthy indication, namely, that issues involving restrictive provisions projects' contractual terms intrude upon the researchers' work only very infrequently and so have remained little discussed among them.

Encouraging as that would be, the absence of formal, contractually imposed restraints on disclosure and access to scientific information and data resources leaves a substantial margin of uncertainty as to how closely the norms of "open science" are approximated by the operating practices and informal arrangements that are typically found within these projects. To probe into those important areas of "local" policy and practice, it is possible to examine the results obtained from a different set of the survey's questions.

Provision of Information Access in e-Science Projects: Practices and Policy Concerns

The survey respondents were asked (see [OeSIAS, Q.6]) to classify their respective projects with regard to two taxonomic principles. First, with which of the following functional scientific tasks was the project mainly engaged? (1) generic tool development, (2) application development, or (3) end-use application. Second, toward which among the main collaborative e-science forms was their project's work principally oriented to furthering? (i) grid access to distributed computing capacity, (ii) access to remote hardware instruments, (iii) access to specialized software, (iv) access to linked datasets or federated databases, (v) collaborative research with non-co-located teams. Although with these 2 axes and the resulting 15 taxonomic combinations a more elaborate taxonomy may be constructed (den Besten & David, 2008), for purposes of empirical analysis of the present small survey, the project classifications were collapsed into 3 broader purpose-engagement categories: (I) developing generic middleware tools for access to distributed computing resources and instruments (8 projects), (II) combining application development with database resources (11 projects), and (III) combining end-use for collaborative research (7 projects). A residual category absorbed 4 projects characterized by mixed purposes and activities that resisted simple summary description. In the following, we therefore focus on findings relating to the project-purpose clusters that can be concisely labeled as (I) *middleware-*, (II) *database-*, and (III) *end-user community* oriented.[30]

From responses to survey question about measures actually undertaken to provide access to data and information relating to project results to researchers within the project and to outside researchers (specifically from [OeSIAS, Q.10;, Q.13, and, Q.13]) it is possible to form some sense of the relative importance of these goals

---

[30]Considering only the "classifiable" group of projects, their percentage distribution among the broad "purpose-engagement" clusters is seen to be 31% with *middleware* (I), 42% with *database applications* (II), and 27% with *end-user communities* (III).

among the projects. What emerges is that when projects are grouped by main purpose category (I, II, or III), the distribution of responses differs noticeably from group to group. One simple measure of relative importance is the ratio for the group between "yes" (Y) responses, signifying that specific access-enhancing facilities were being provided, and "no"(N) responses.[31]

The overall pattern in this (Y/N) response ratio displays systematic variation along two axes. Along the first axis, there is rather wider attention to providing external researchers with information access, compared with concerns about within-project access provision by means of working paper and publication repositories, databases, and regular data-stream access. Thus, the external-vs-internal access differences in the Y/N ratio holds within each of the main project-purpose categories: for the 3.0 vs 1.0 for projects in the *database* group, 0.91 vs. 0.44 for those in the *end-user community* group, and 0.35 vs. 0 in the *middleware* group. These figures also display the second axis along which there is systematic variation: attention to providing information access (both to outside and to inside researchers) is relatively more widespread among the database projects, less so among the end-user community projects, and least evident among the middleware development projects.

The existence of a separate institution created by the U.K. e-science project that is dedicated to improving robustness and distributing open middleware, namely the OMII (discussed previously), may well account for the latter feature of the pattern. That comparatively lower priorities appear to be attached to the internal provision of formal information access facilities among all three project-purpose categories may well reflect the fact that only two-fifths of the survey responses pertain to projects that involved more than two consortium members, and another two-fifths of them had no other participating team. The management of inter-team information flows and data exchanges therefore may not be perceived among these projects as presenting major challenges.

Looking at the project start dates for the surveyed projects, one may group them into three cohorts whose relative sizes in the aggregate reflect the marked recent deceleration in the funding dynamics of the UK's e-science program as a whole: the pre-2003 cohort accounts for about 40% of the survey sample, the 2003–2004 cohort another 40%, leaving 20% in the post-2004 cohort. Within that temporal framework, something further may be said in regard to the specific information access repositories that have been provided to members of these projects, the extent to which the latter are required to deposit materials therein, and also about the trends in the diffusion of these particular information management practices. The survey inquired about two main types of depositories: "common repositories" – for project-generated working papers and memos, for software code, and for data; "open access" repositories for project publications (department or university wide), for

---

[31]In compiling the results reported in the text, counts of instances where respondents said the particular question was not applicable, or that they did not know, have been omitted.

project preprints, project-generated software (we can distinguish version-controlled code, middleware, and applications software), and project-generated datasets.[32]

Common repositories for projects' research outputs in the form of working papers and software code appear to have been established quite widely from the early days of the UK e-science program: at least, those for working papers and memos are reported by 77% of the projects among the pre-2003 cohort, and almost as large a proportion of the post-2004 cohort; whereas 69% of the projects forming the early cohort provide common repositories for software code, and they are universally present among the most recent cohort. Comparison of the pre-2003 and post-2004 cohorts shows a rise also in the proportion of projects that are requiring the deposit of software code in these common repositories. In the case of data, however, common repositories are found only about half as frequently, and there is no evident secular movement on the part of projects that do provide them to also require that participants deposit their data.

It should be clear that the access to the "common" repositories that these e-science projects maintain may be restricted in many ways, and it is therefore of particular interest to turn to the available data about "open access" repositories. One finds in the case of data that there are essentially no "open-access" repositories in the sense in which that term is understood currently. On the other hand, the spread of institutionally maintained (department- or university-wide) repositories for "OA publications" is noticeably strong, although the proportion of cases in which participants are required to deposit material has not increased. The opposite pattern of change appears for pre-print repositories – their ubiquity has risen less markedly, but where these facilities have been set up, deposit requirements have become universal.

With regard to the various types of repositories for software, it seems clear that the proportion of open access repositories has approached the 30% share of middleware development projects in the total, and the relative frequency of adoption of version-control systems (with their archives) has more-or-less matched the relative share of middleware projects in the total – at least among the initial and most recent cohorts. Open access repositories for applications software have been established less frequently among the projects in the survey sample, but, where they do exist among the more recent product cohorts, the requirement mandating deposit of project-created computer code is widespread as it is in the case among projects engaged in developing middleware.

What stands out most clearly from the findings reviewed in this section is that high-level policy guidelines, set by the funding agency, can exert a potent influence on the pattern of adoption of open access archiving of scientific research products. In this instance there was an important early policy commitment by the U.K. e-science core program that middleware "deliverables" from its pilot projects would be made available as open source code, and this requirement for the research projects has been maintained (as has been noted above, in the section "e-Science Infrastructure

---

[32]See den Besten et al. (2009, Table 2), for fuller presentation of the survey results reviewed here than the survey questions in [OeSIAS, Q. 10 and Q. 11].

Engineering") – even though there has been an evolution away from the original expectations of open source release of these outputs under GNU General Public Licenses once they had passed through the OMII's enhancement and repacking process.

The extent to which the provision of access to data and information is perceived *at the project level* to be a matter of explicit policy concern varies with the projects' roles in e-Research. This is only to be expected, particularly in view of the varied nature of these projects' "deliverables" and the existence of higher level policy regarding the software that is being created. A clear pattern of co-variation is evident in the responses to the question "Was the provision of access to data and information to members of the project a matter of particular concern and discussion in your project?"; and a parallel question referring to "external researchers" (see OeSIAS, Questions 16,17).[33] Among the projects engaged in *middleware development*, none expressed a concern for access within the project – presumably because the organization of the project and the ubiquity of open access code repositories meant that the matter had largely been settled. In contrast, however, the issue of external access was seen to be an important project concern by a third of the respondent P.I.s from the projects developing *middleware*. That concern was expressed also by one-third respondents from projects involved with *user-communities* and *database resources,*especially the latter group.[34]

The responses concerning "obstacles encountered by the project in achieving openness" (see OeSIAS, Question 18) are consistent with the survey finding regarding actual practices and policy concerns at the project level, for they indicate that providing access to information to people *within* the project was not found to be a problem deserving mention. All but two of the P.I.s indicated at least one type of common repository to which participants were given access. Open access repositories are almost only provided where access for external research is seen as a concern within the project, which is the case for about one-third of the projects for which survey data are available. Project participants are not always instructed to contribute to the repositories when the latter are provided, and it appears to be generally assumed that they will do so. On the other hand, none of the respondents indicated that their project was paying fees for the maintenance of an institutional or external repository to which their researchers would be given access.[35] Among the respondents who stated that the provision of access to outsiders was an important project goal, almost two-thirds listed one or more obstacles that had been encountered in achieving it; whereas among those who stated that such provision was not a project concern,

---

[33] Over half of the projects having more diffuse purposes – that is, purposes not preponderantly oriented toward either construction of middleware, research community usage, or applications and database resources – failed to provide clear answers to questions 16 and 17. Responses from the "other purposes" group are not included in the analysis whose results are described in the text.

[34] Specifically, providing access to researchers outside the project was a significant concern for almost two-thirds of the *data*-centric projects and a third of *community*-centric projects.

[35] Perhaps this question should have been phrased differently, e.g., "Would the project be willing to pay repository charges, and for the inclusion of open access journals?"

almost half volunteered that they had encountered practical obstacles to external dissemination of their research outputs.[36]

Conclusion

We have described both the rationale and key identifying characteristics of collaborative "open science," and have begun to explore ways to map the regions of practice where e-science and open science coincide. Although there are many e-science tools that could support distributed projects that conduct research in ways that accord more or less closely to open science norms, this does not assure that such is or will be the case wherever collaborative research is pursued under the name of "e-science." Even academic e-science projects whose leaders subscribe to the ethos of "openness in research" and institute some concrete "open access" practices fall short of those norms in one or more respects, especially in regard to effective sharing of data resources and timely external disclosure of research findings. But, as has been shown, e-science projects are far from homogeneous, and in order to understand the variations in their information sharing policies and practices it is necessary to take into account the diversity of their scientific purposes, the technical nature of their tasks, and the details of their organizational structures. The review presented here of the empirical evidence pertaining to U.K.-funded e-science projects has been able to draw upon recent studies that carried out a small number of in-depth (highly insightful) interviews with selected P.I.s and obtained quantitative data from the responses to an online survey of e-science project leaders and other participants. These efforts in data collection and analysis represent only a trial step in what is envisaged as a far broader and longer term program of systematic inquiries into the evolving global conduct of e-science.

Acknowledgments Most of the authors' research on the underlying data has been supported by ESRC grant RES-149-25-1022 for the Oxford e-Social Science (OeSS) Project on Ethical, Legal and Institutional Dynamics of Grid-enabled e-Sciences. Our thanks go first to Jenny Fry, Jeremy Frey and Mike Fraser for their contributions in connection with the structured interviews, and to Anne Trefethen for her help in the fielding of the online survey of UK e-Science P.I.s. We also are grateful for the institutional support received from several quarters during the research planning stage and the preparation of this essay: the Oxford internet Institute (David, and Schroeder) and the Oxford e-Research Centre (den Besten). David also acknowledges with gratitude the support of the Stanford Institute for Economic Policy Research's Program on Knowledge, Networks and Institutions for Innovation (KNIIP), for his research and writing on open science which the present work has drawn upon. Responsibility for the judgments expressed, as well as any mistakes and misinterpretations that may be found herein, remains solely ours.

---

[36]Eleven respondents listed external access among their project goals, nine said it was not an important concern, and another nine respondents left this question unanswered.

References

Allen, F. H. (2004). High-throughput crystallography: The challenge of publishing, storing and using the results. *Crystallography Reviews, 10,* 3–15.

Arora, A., David, P. A., & Gambardella, A. (1998). Reputation and competence in publicly funded science: estimating the effects on research group productivity. *Annales d' Economie et de Statistique, 49/50,* 163–198 (Numero Exceptionelle, J. Mairesse, Ed.).

Arora, A., & Gambardella, A. (1994). The changing technology of technological change: General and abstract knowledge and the division of innovative labour. *Research Policy, 23,* 523–532.

Arora, A., & Gambardella, A. (1997). Public policy towards science: picking stars or spreading the wealth? *Revue d'economie industrielle, 79,* 63–75.

Atkins, D. E., Droegmaier, K. K., Felman, S. I., Garcia-Molin, H., Klein, M.L., Messerschmitt, D.G., et al. (2003). Revolutionizing science and engineering through cyberinfrastructure. Technical report, *National Science Foundation Blue-Ribbon Advisory Panel on Cyberinfrastructure.* Washington, DC: NSF.

Atkinson, M., DeRoure, D., Dunlop, A., Fox, G., Henderson, P., Hey, T., et al. (2005). Web service grids: An evolutionary approach. *Concurrency and Computation: Practice and Experience, 17*(2), 377–390.

Bacharach, M., Gambetta, D., et al. (1994). The economics of salience: A research proposal. Unpublished paper, Oxford Institute of Economics and Statistics.

Barnes, B. (1974). *Scientific knowledge and sociological theory.* London: Routledge and Kegan Paul

Barnes, B. (1977). *Interests and the growth of knowledge.* London: Routledge and Kegan Paul.

Beaver, D., & Rosen, R. (1979). Studies in scientific collaboration, Part 2: Scientific co-authorship, research productivity and visibility in the French scientific elite. *Scientometrics, 1,* 133–149.

Ben-David, J. (1991). *Scientific growth: Essays on the social organization and ethos of science.* In G. Freudenthal (Ed.), Berkeley, CA: University of California Press.

Berman, F., & Brady, H. (2005). NSF SBE-CISE workshop on cyber-infrastructure and the social sciences. Final report, San Diego Supercomputing Centre.

Blau, J. (1973). Patterns of communication among theoretical high energy physicists. *Sociometry, 37,* 391–406.

Bloor, D. (1976). *Knowledge and social imagery.* London: Routledge and Kegan Paul.

Brock, W. A., & Durlauf, S. N. (1999). A formal model of theory choice in science. *Economic Theory, 14*(1), 13–130.

Callon, M. (1995). Four models for the dynamics of science. In S. Jasanoff, G. E. Markle, J. C. Petersen, & T. Pinch, (Eds.), *Handbook of science and technology studies* (pp. 29–63). London: Sage Publications.

Carayol, N. (2003). The incentive properties of the Matthew effect in academic competition. Working Papers of BETA 2003-11 ULP, Strasbourg.

Carayol, N., & Dalle, J.-M. (2007). Sequential problem choice and the reward system in open science, BETA Working Papers of BETA 2003-12, ULP Strasbourg, 2003. Revised and published in *Structural Change and Economic Dynamics, 18*(2), 167–191.

Carayol, N., & Matt, M. (2004). Does research organization influence academic production? Laboratory level evidence from a large European university. *Research Policy, 33*(8), 1081–1102.

Carayol, N., & Matt, M. (2006). Individual and collective determinants of academic scientists' productivity. *Information Economics and Policy, 18*(1), 55–72.

Chang, V., Mills, H., & Newhouse, S. (2007, September10–13). From open source to long-term sustainability: Review of business models and case studies. In *All Hands Meeting 2007, OMII-UK Workshop,* Nottingham, UK.

Cole, J., & Cole, S. (1973). *Social stratification in science.* Chicago: Chicago University Press.

Cole, S. (1978). Scientific reward systems: A comparative analysis. In R.A. Jones (Ed.), *Research in sociology of knowledge, sciences and art* (pp. 167–190). Greenwich, CT: JAI Press.

Cole, S., & Cole, J. (1967). Scientific output and recognition. *American Sociological Review, 32*, 377–390.

Coles, S. J., Frey, J. G., Hursthouse, M. B., Light, M., Carr, L., DeRoure, D., et al. (2005). The end-to-end crystallographic experiment in an e-science environment: From conception to publication. *Proceedings of the Fourth UK e-Science All Hands Meeting*, Nottingham, UK.

Coles, S. J., Frey, J. G., Hursthouse, M. B., Light, M. E., Meacham, K. E., Marvin, D. J., et al. (2005). ECSES – Examining crystal structures using "e-science": A demonstrator employing web and grid services to enhance user participation in crystallographic experiments. *Journal of Applied Crystallography, 38*, 819–826.

Crane, D. (1972). *Invisible colleges: Diffusion of knowledge in scientific communities*. Chicago: The University of Chicago Press.

Crane, D. (1965). Scientists at major and minor universities: A study in productivity and recognition. *American Sociological Review, 30*, 699–714.

Dalle, J.-M., David, P. A., Ghosh, R. A., & Steinmueller, W. E. (2005). Advancing economic research on the free and open source software mode of production. In M. Wynants & J. Cornelis (Eds.), *How open will the future be? Social and cultural scenarios based on open standards and open-source software*. Brussels: VUB Press. Preprint available at http://siepr.stanford.edu/papers/pdf/04-03.html

Dasgupta, P., & David, P. A. (1987). Information disclosure and the economics of science and technology. In G. Feiwel (Ed.), Chapter 16 in *Arrow and the ascent of modern economic theory* (pp. 519–542). New York: New York University Press .

Dasgupta, P., & David, P. A. (1994). Toward a new economics of science. *Research Policy, 23*, 487–521

David, P. (1994). Positive feedbacks and research productivity in science: Reopening another black box. In O. Grandstrand (Ed.), *Economics and technology* (pp. 65–85). Amsterdam: Elsevier.

David, P. A. (1996). Science reorganized? Post-modern visions of research and the curse of success. *Proceedings of the 2nd International Symposium on Research Funding*, Ottawa.

David, P. A. (1998a). Common agency contracting and the emergence of "open science" institutions. *American Economic Review, 88*(2), 15–21.

David, P. A. (1998b). Communication norms and the collective cognitive performance of "invisible colleges". In G. Barba Navaretti, P. Dasgupta, K.-G. Maler, & D. Siniscalco (Eds.), *Creation and the transfer of knowledge: Institutions and incentives*. New York: Springer.

David, P. A. (2002, December). *Cooperation, creativity and closure in scientific research networks: Modelling the simpler dynamics of epistemic communities*. SIEPR-CREEG Seminar Paper in Technology & Social Science. Paris: Bibliothque Albin Michel (Économie). Revision available at http://siepr.stanford.edu/programs/SST_Seminars/David_All.pdf

David, P. A. (2003). The economic logic of "open science" and the balance between private property rights and the public domain in scientific data and information. In J. Esanu & P.F. Uhlir (Eds.), *The role of scientific and technical data and information in the public domain: Proceedings of a symposium* (pp. 19–34). Washington, DC: Academy Press.

David, P. A. (2004). Can "open science" be protected from the evolving regime of intellectual property rights protections. *Journal of Theoretical and Institutional Economics, 160*, 1–26. Available at: http://siepr.stanford.edu/papers/pdf/02-42.html.

David, P. A. (2006). Toward a cyberinfrastructure for enhanced scientific collaboration: providing its "soft" foundations may be the hardest part. In B. Kahin (Ed.), *Advancing knowledge and the knowledge economy* (pp. 431–454). Cambridge: MIT Press Preprint available at http://www.oii.ox.ac.uk/resources/publications/RR4.pdf

David, P. A. (2007). Innovation and Europe's universities: Second thoughts about embracing the Bayh-Dole regime. In F. Malerba & S. Brusoni (Eds.), *Perspectives on innovation*. Cambridge: Cambridge University Press Preprint available at http://siepr.stanford.edu/papers/pdf/04-27.html

David, P. A., den Besten, M., & Schroeder, R. (2006, December). How "open" is e-science? *e-Science '06: Proceedings of the IEEE 2nd International Conference on eScience and Grid*

Computing, Amsterdam, v. Iss, 33 ff. Available at http://ieeexplore.ieee.org/iel5/4030972/ 4030973/04031006.pdf?isnumber=4030973â=STD&arnumber=4031006&arnumber= 4031006&arSt=33&ared=33&arAuthor=David%2C+P.A.%3B+den+Besten%2C+M.%3B+ Schroeder%2C+R.

David, P. A., & Foray, D. (1995). Accessing and expanding the knowledge-base in science and technology. *STI*-Review, *16*, 13–38.

David, P. A., & Hall, B. H. (2006). Property and the pursuit of knowledge: an introduction. *Research Policy, 35*(June–July) [Special Issue, Guest-edited by P. A. David & B. H. Hall].

David, P. A., Mowery, D. R., & Steinmueller, W. E. (1992). Analyzing the payoffs from basic research. *Economics of Innovation and New Technology, 2*(4), 73–90.

David, P. A., & Spence, M. (2003). Toward institutional infrastructures for e-science. *Oxford Internet Institute Research Report 2*, Oxford. Available at http://www.oii.ox.ac.uk/ research/project.cfm?id=26

David, P. A., & Spence, M. (2008). Designing institutional infrastructures for e-science, Ch. 5. In B. Fitzgerald (Ed.), *Legal and policy framework for e-research: Realizing the potential*. Sydney: University of Sydney Press.

David, P. A., & Uhlir, P. F. (2005, September 1–2). Creating the global information commons for e-science: Workshop rationale and plan. UNESCO, Paris. Available at http://www.codataweb.org/UNESCOmtg/workshopplan.html

David, P. A., & Uhlir, P. F. (2006, April 17). Creating global information commons for science: An international initiative of the committee on data for science and technology (CODATA). Unpublished prospectus..

De Roure, D. (2006, April 10–12). The OMII experience. Presentation to the OSSWatch Conference on *Sustainability and Open Source*, Said Business School, Oxford. Available at http://www.oss-watch.ac.uk/events/2006-04-10-12/presentations/davidderoure.pdf

den Besten, M., & David, P. A. (2009, January). Data and information access in e-research: Results from a 2008 survey among UK e-science project participants. Report 18, Oxford Internet Institute. Retrieved from http://ssrn.com/abstract=1323812

den Besten, M., & David, P. A. (2008, September 11–13). Mapping e-science's path in the collaboration space. Paper presented to the conference on Oxford e-Research Conference 2008. Retrieved from http://www.oii.ox.ac.uk/microsites/eresearch08/

den Besten, M., David, P. A., & Schroeder, R. (2009). Will e-science be open science? In W. H. Dutton & P. Jeffreys (Eds.), *World wide research*.Cambridge, MA: MIT Press.

Fitzgerald, B. (Ed.). (2008). *Legal and policy framework for e-research: Realizing the potential*. Sydney: University of Sydney Press.

Frey, J. G. (2004). Dark lab or smart lab: The challenges for the 21st century laboratory software. *Organic Research and Development, 8*(6), 1024–1035.

Fry, J., Schroeder, R., & den Besten, M. (2009). Open science in e-science: Contingency or policy? *Journal of Documentation, 65*(1), 6–32.

Fuller, S. (1994). A guide to the philosophy and sociology of science for social psychology of science, Ch. 17. In W. Shadish & S. Fuller (Eds.), *The social psychology of science*. New York: The Guilford Press.

Gambardella, A. (1994). *Science and innovation*. Cambridge: Cambridge University Press.

Geuna, A. (1999). *The economics of knowledge production: Funding and the structure of university research*. Cheltenham: Edward Elgar.

Hey, T. (2005). e-Science and open access. *Berlin 3 Open Access: Progress in Implementing the Berlin Declaration on Open Access to Knowledge in the Sciences and Humanities*. University of Southampton, UK.

Hinds, C., Jirotka, M., Rahman, M., D'Agostino, G., Meyer, C., Piper, T., et al. (2005). Ownership of intellectual property rights in medical data in collaborative computing environments. *First International Conference on e-Social Science*.

Jaffe, A. B., Trajtenberg, M., & Henderson, R. (1993). Geographic localization of knowledge spillovers as evidenced by patent citations. *Quarterly Journal of Economics, 108*(3), 557–598.

Jirotka, M., Procter, R., Hartswood, M., Slack, R., Simpson, A., Coopmans, C., et al. (2005). Collaboration and trust in healthcare innovation: The eDiaMoND case study. *Computer Supported Cooperative Work, 14*(4), 369–398.

Katz, J. S. (1994). Geographical proximity and scientific collaboration. *Scientometrics, 31*(1), 31–43.

Kitcher, P. (1993). *The advancement of science: Science without legend, objectivity without Illusions*. Chicago: University of Chicago Press.

Knorr-Cetina, K. (1981). *The manufacture of knowledge: An essay on the constructivist and contextual nature of science*. Oxford: Pergamon Press.

Kuhn, T. S. (1962/1970). *The structure of scientific revolutions*. 1st/2nd ed. Chicago: University of Chicago Press.

Lakatos, I. (1970). Falsification and the methodology of scientific research programs. In I. Lakatos & A. Musgrave (Eds.), *Criticism and the growth of knowledge*. Cambridge: Cambridge University Press.

Latour, B., & Woolgar, S. (1979). *Laboratory life*. Beverly Hills: Sage Publications.

Leenaars, M. (2005). e-Infrastructures roadmap. *e-Infrastructure Reflection Group Technical Report*. Available at http://www.e-irg.org/roadmap/eIRG-roadmap.pdf

Leydesdorff, L. (1995). *The challenge of scientometrics: The development, measurement, and self-organization of scientific communities*. 2nd ed. Leiden: DSWO Press, Universal Publishers: uPUBLIS.com. Available at http://www.upublish.com/books/leydesdorff.htm

Leydesdorff, L. (2006). *The knowledge-based economy: Modeled, measured, simulated*. Boca Raton, LA: Universal Publishers.

Mairesse, J., & Turner, L. (2006). Measurement and explanation of the intensity of co-publication in scientific research: an analysis at the laboratory level, Ch. 10. In C. Antonelli, D. Foray, B. Hall, & W. E. Steinmueller (Eds.), *New frontiers in the economics of innovation and new technology: Essays in honour of Paul A. David*. Cheltenham: Edward. Elgar.

Merton, R. K. (1942). The normative structure of science. In N. W. Storer (Ed.), *The sociology of science: Theoretical and empirical investigations* (pp. 267–278). Chicago: University of Chicago Press, 1973.

Merton, R. K. (1968). The Matthew effect in science. *Science, 159*(3810), 56–63.

Merton, R. K. (1973). *The sociology of science: Theoretical and empirical investigations*. N. W. Storer (Ed.), Chicago: University of Chicago Press.

Mulkay, M. (1979). *Science and the sociology of knowledge*. London: George Allen and Unwin.

Popper, K. R. (1959). *Logic of scientific discovery,* London: Hutchinson.

Popper, K. R. (1963). *Conjectures and refutations*. London: Routledge & Kegan Paul.

Quine, W. V. O. (Ed.). (1953). Two dogmas of empiricism. *From a logical point of view*. Cambridge, MA: Harvard University Press.

Quine, W. V. O. (Ed.). (1962). Carnap and logical truth. *Logic and language: Studies dedicated to professor Rudolf Carnap on the occasion of his seventieth birthday* (pp. 350–374). Dordrecht: Reidel.

Quine, W. V. O. (Ed.). (1969). Epistemology naturalized. *Ontological relativity and other essays*. New York: Columbia University PressSchroeder, R. (2007a). *Rethinking science, technology and social change*. Stanford: Stanford University Press.

Schroeder, R. (2007b). e-Research infrastructures and open science: Towards a new system of knowledge production? *Prometheus, 25*(1), 1–17.

Schroeder, R. (2008). e-Sciences as research technologies: Reconfiguring disciplines, globalizing knowledge. *Social Science Information, 47*(2), 131–157.

Stanford University (1996). Openness in research. *Stanford University Research Policy Handbook,* Ch. 2.6, Stanford, CA. Openness in research checklist at: http://www.stanford.edu/dept/DoR/C-Res/ITARlist.html

Stephan, P. (1996). The Economics of science. *Journal of Economic Literature, 34*(3), 1199–1262.

Taylor, J. (2001). Presentation at e-science meeting by the Director of the Research Councils, Office of Science and Technology, UK. Available at: http://www.e-science.clrc.ac.uk.

Trajtenberg, M., Henderson, R., & Jaffe, A. B. (1992). Ivory tower versus corporate lab: An empirical study of basic research and appropriability, National Bureau of Economic Research Working Paper No. 4146 (August).

Turner, L., & Mairesse, J. (2002). Explaining individual productivity differences in public research: How important are non-individual determinants? An econometric analysis of French Physiciists (1986–1997). Working Paper-Cahiers de la MSE 2002-66. Université Paris-I.

Uhlir, P. F., & Schroder, P. (2007). Open date for global science. *Data Science Journal*, 6. (Special Issue, Part 2: Analysis of Policy Issues), OD36–OD53.

van Raan, A. F. J. (Ed.). (1988). *Handbook of quantitative studies of science and technology.* Amsterdam: Elsevier.

Wikipedia (2008). Entry for "OASIS." Available at http://en.wikipedia.org/wiki/OASIS_ (organization). Last accessed on November 14, 2008.

Ziman, J. M. (1994). *Prometheus bound.* Cambridge: Cambridge University Press.

Zuckerman, H., & Merton, R. K. (1971). Institutionalization and patterns of evaluation in science, reprinted in R. K. Merton. In N. W. Storer (Ed.), *The sociology of science: Theoretical and empirical investigations* (pp. 460–496). Chicago: University of Chicago Press, 1973.

Toward Information Infrastructure Studies: Ways of Knowing in a Networked Environment

Geoffrey C. Bowker, Karen Baker, Florence Millerand, and David Ribes

Introduction

It is rare enough in human history that fundamentally new ways of working are developed, which changed the way in which information was gathered, processed, stored, and reused. When we developed speech, writing, and printing, new forms of action at a distance over time became possible (Clanchy, 1993; Goody, 1987). It now seems natural to update this triad by adding the internet. It is clear that each new work mode has accompanied – rather than preceded or followed – social, economic, and organizational upheavals.

In this article we explore the current change accompanying the development of the internet in terms of its relationship with the nature and production of knowledge. We move from a definition of infrastructure to the exploration of a historical context for its development. We continue with the organizational, political, and finally onto-logical dimensions of its development. Many of our examples will be drawn from scientific cyberinfrastructure; however, where appropriate, links to knowledge work in the arts and humanities and in business will be made.

PART 1: THE WHAT OF INFORMATION INFRASTRUCTURE

What Is Infrastructure?

The term "infrastructure" evokes vast sets of collective equipment necessary to human activities, such as buildings, roads, bridges, rail tracks, channels, ports, and communications networks. Beyond bricks, mortar, pipes or wires, infrastructure also encompasses more abstract entities, such as protocols (human and computer), standards, and memory.

G.C. Bowker (✉)
School of Information Sciences, University of Pittsburg, Pittsburgh, Pennsylvania, USA
e-mail: gbowker@pitt.edu

J. Hunsinger et al. (eds.), *International Handbook of Internet Research*,
DOI 10.1007/978-1-4020-9789-8_5, © Springer Science+Business Media B.V. 2010

Superadded to the term "information," infrastructure refers loosely to digital facilities and services usually associated with the internet: computational services, help desks, and data repositories to name a few. In the same vein but in a broader sweep, the Global Information Infrastructure (GII) refers to worldwide information and communication systems that process and transport data inside and outside national boundaries.

The field of science and technology studies (STS) explores the phenomenon of "infrastructuring" (Hughes, 1983, 1989; Scott, 1998). Infrastructure typically exists in the background, it is invisible, and it is frequently taken for granted (Star & Ruhleder, 1994). The work of infrastructure and its maintenance is itself often that of undervalued or invisible workers (Shapin, 1989; Star, 1991). In such a marginalized state its consequences become difficult to trace and politics are easily buried in technical encodings (Hanseth, Monteiro, & Hatling, 1996; Monteiro & Hanseth, 1997). The design of infrastructure itself can make its effects more or less visible (Bowker, Timmermans, & Star, 1995). Calls to study infrastructure in STS have engendered methods for making it and associated, emergent roles visible (Edwards, 2003; Karasti & Baker, 2004; Ribes & Baker, 2007): practical methods such as observing during moments of breakdown (Star, 1999) or conceptual methods such as "infrastructural inversion" (Bowker, 1994).

Here we take infrastructure as a broad category referring to *pervasive enabling resources in network form*, and we argue that a theoretical understanding of infrastructure is crucial to its design, use, and maintenance. This understanding plays a critical role in associated fields such as informatics, library science, and new media – all fields that underpin communication in large-scale and long-term collaborative science. In our analysis we extend conventional understandings of infrastructure as "tubes and wires" to the technologies and organizations which enable knowledge work: supercolliders, orbiting telescopes, supercomputer centers, polar research stations, national laboratories, and other research instruments of "big" science. In addition our image would be incomplete without the variety of scientific organizations, such as funding agencies, professional societies, libraries and databases, scientific publishing houses, review systems, and so on, that are inherent to the functioning of science. As Leigh Star has noted, infrastructure is relational: the daily work of one person is the infrastructure of another (Star & Ruhleder, 1996). Finally, we further open the conceptual umbrella of infrastructure to include the individuals – designers and developers, users and mediators, managers and administrators – in existing and emergent roles associated with information infrastructure.

Large-scale information infrastructures (or in today's language of large-scale scientific projects, cyberinfrastructure and e-Science) aim at supporting research practices through a vast array of community digital services and resources (collaboratories and centers, data and code repositories, best practices and standards development, visualization tools and high performance computing, and so on). Two main issues are associated with such projects: first, the idea of a shared infrastructure in the sense of a public good; second, the idea of sustainability, of supporting research over the long term. What we understand by the concept of infrastructure has significant consequences in terms of how we design the support environments for scientific research. For instance, concerns about infrastructure in everyday scientific practices tend to follow a reactive pattern such as when scientific imperatives require updated infrastructure components. When a new instrument comes available, there is frequently a lot more data or a new type of data to process and manage than existing resources can afford (basically "more resources are needed for the work to get done"). Traditional vision tends to favor immediate responses, usually in terms of additional human resources or new technological tools.

An alternative vision of infrastructure may better take into account the social and organizational dimensions of infrastructure. This vision requires adopting a long term rather than immediate timeframe and thinking about infrastructure not only in terms of human versus technological components but in terms of a set of interrelated social, organizational, and technical components or systems (whether the data will be shared, systems interoperable, standards proprietary, or maintenance and redesign factored in).

Thinking of infrastructure this way requires a major shift in thinking. It involves changing common views and metaphors on infrastructure: from transparency to visibility, from substrate to substance, from short term to long term (Karasti, Baker, & Halkola, 2006; Star & Ruhleder, 1996). Usually perceived as something "just there," ready-at-hand, completely transparent, something upon which something else "runs" or "operates" (a system of railroad tracks upon which rail cars run; a computer network upon which a research lab operates or disseminates data like the WWW), any infrastructure that has been the target topic of activities has probably also been the object of passionate debates – for the engineers in charge of building the railroad system or for the scientists and technologists in charge of developing the network. Related to this taken-for-granted aspect of infrastructure, STS speaks of invisible work, complex problems, and the challenges of alignment in the face of breakdowns. Understanding the nature of infrastructural work involves unfolding the political, ethical, and social choices that have been made throughout its development. Analytically, this exercise consists in "going backstage" (Goffman, 1956; Star, 1999), looking for the infrastructure in the making and practicing "infrastructural inversion" (Bowker, 1994) that is shifting the emphasis from changes in infrastructural components to changes in infrastructural relations. Infrastructure is indeed a fundamentally relational concept; it emerges for people in practice, connected to activities and structures. It consists of both static and dynamic elements, each equally important to ensure a functional system.

Defining Information Infrastructure

Most often, information infrastructure is defined by jotting down a laundry list of characteristics. Instead of discussing the technologies, or even the particular affordances, of infrastructure, we focus on capturing the underlying concept and placing this within a historical lineage. We ask, beyond the immediacy of introducing high-end technologies to the sciences, what is information infrastructure really about? Early National Science Foundation reports focused on digital libraries and global environmental system science (Futrell & the AC-ERE, 2003; Hedstrom et al., 2002). The Atkins NSF report (Atkins et al., 2003) focuses on cyberinfrastructure, defining cyberinfrastructure as those layers that sit between base technology (a computer science concern) and discipline-specific science. The central concentration is on value-added systems and services that can be widely shared across scientific domains, both supporting and enabling large increases in multi-disciplinary science while reducing duplication of effort and resources. According to the Atkins Report, cyberinfrastructure consists of ". . .hardware, software, personnel, services and organizations" (Atkins et al., 2003, p.13). This list recognizes from the outset that information infrastructure is about more than just wires and machines. A more recent cyberinfrastructure vision document is similarly diffuse, though it regrettably somewhat sidelines the social and organizational in the definition[1]:

> Cyberinfrastructure integrates hardware for computing, data and networks, digitally enabled sensors, observatories and experimental facilities, and an interoperable suite of software and middleware services and tools. Investments in interdisciplinary teams and cyberinfrastructure professionals with expertise in algorithm development, system operations, and applications development are also essential to exploit the full power of cyberinfrastructure to create, disseminate, and preserve scientific data, information, and knowledge. (*NSF CI Council, 2006*, p. 6)

Both these definitions do, however, draw attention to the complex if not dynamic nature of cyberinfrastructure development. A recent report to NSF (Edwards, Jackson, Bowker, & Knobel, 2007) presents the history and theory of infrastructure as one approach to understanding the dynamics, tension, and the design of infrastructure.

Cyberinfrastructure projects come in many forms but they often seek to bring together, under a single umbrella, various domain sciences with novel information technologies. For example, GEON "the geosciences network" seeks to provide computing resources such as visualization and data integration to the broader earth sciences. Here, a single information infrastructure is to become the clearinghouse for data in paleobotany, geophysics, and metamorphic petrology (http://geongrid.org; Ribes, 2006). Similarly, LEAD "Linked Environments for Atmospheric Discovery" seeks to enable real-time analysis of weather data for meteorologists and atmospheric scientists (http://leadproject.org). Both projects are ambitious and have encountered problems in working across disciplinary boundaries (Lawrence, 2006; Ribes & Bowker, 2008). Challenges exist across temporal boundaries as well. With concern for long-term data and information rather than information infrastructure per se, the LTER since 1980 has focused on creating long-term scientific understandings of biomes (http://lternet.edu). In building information infrastructures,

---

[1] This reminds us that while social and organizational theory have made inroads into the technically dominated fields of information infrastructure design, maintaining such accomplishments will require continuous and active engagement by practicing social scientists in the field of cyberinfrastructure.

always a long-term venture, programs and communities are faced with developing technologies that look farther ahead than immediate research concerns.

While accepting this broad characterization, the long-term perspective such as that of the Atkin's report and of long-term scientific endeavors incorporated today as part of a temporal continuum (i.e., the "long-now," Brand, 1999; the "invisible present," Magnuson, 1990) invites a discussion of first principles. For this we return to Star & Ruhleder's now classic definition of infrastructure (Star & Ruhleder, 1996) originally composed for a paper on one of the early scientific collaboratories, the Worm Community System. We show in Fig. 1 how their definitions can be ordered along two axes, one explicitly non-spatial and the other spatial: the social/technical and the individual/group or local/global. As Star and Ruhleder put it, the "configuration of these dimensions forms "an infrastructure", which is without absolute boundary or *a priori* definition" (p. 113). We think of infrastructures and their construction as distributions along these axes rather than as tensions between polar opposites. Our argument is an ecological one; it calls for investigating infrastructure building a set of distributed activities – technical, social and institutional.

Everyday decisions in terms of infrastructure design, development, or enactment involve such distributions. What needs a technical fix? What needs a social

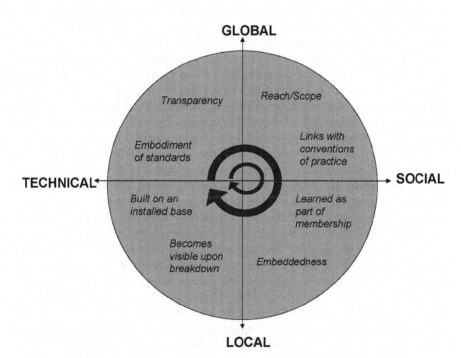

Cyberinfrastructure as *distributions* along technical/social & global/local axes

Fig. 1 Information infrastructure as distributions along technical/social and global/local axes

fix? Critical technical, social, and organizational path dependencies established in the present will have long-term consequences – with each new lock-in an aura of inevitability about technical and organizational choices builds (Arthur, 1994). Looking at the distribution of qualities between the social and the technical allows us to investigate the discontinuity within the (apparent) continuity of technological development that usually tends to mask decision points, thus allowing for writing stories in new forms (MacKenzie, 1993). We cannot do the history of software without doing the history of their surrounding organizations.

In building cyberinfrastructure, the key question is not whether a problem is a "social" problem or a "technical" one. That is putting it the wrong way around. The question is whether we choose, for any given problem, a primarily social or a technical solution, or some combination. It is the *distribution* of solutions that is of concern as the object of study and as a series of elements that support infrastructure in different ways at different moments.

An everyday example comes from the problem of e-mail security. How do I distribute my trust? I can delegate it to my machine, and deploy firewalls, password protection, and version controls. Or I can work socially and organizationally to make certain that members of my scientific community understand and police norms about data usage.

Similarly within cyberinfrastructures, metadata generation can be automatic (frequently problematic), the role of an *in situ* data manager or the role of a receiving archive. Generally it sits unhappily between the three. In general, perspectives, standards and conventions get distributed.

An example in scientific efforts comes from the challenge of data issues in the sciences, i.e., data access and sharing across various disciplines, institutions, technical platforms, and across long periods of time. What interoperability strategy best suits the design of shared databases with highly distributed and heterogeneous data sets? How to distribute work and responsibilities between databases, users, and institutions? One can think of an ontology that would allow requests in natural language from a variety of interdisciplinary scientist users – in this case the work of drawing equivalences between discipline terminologies is delegated to the machine (who's in charge of crafting the ontology remains at stake). One can also think of a standardized metadata language that would leave the competence to the scientists – who would have to appropriate first the syntax of the metadata language to be able to then discover the data (rewarding mechanisms for that remain to be defined).

Let us suppose the metadata standard approach was selected. Now how to distribute between the local and the global, or between individual versus community needs? "An infrastructure occurs when the tension between local and global is resolved" (Star & Ruhleder, 1996, p. 114). While occurring, how are an infrastructure's qualities being distributed between the local and the global? For instance, to what extent is a metadata standard designed generic enough to represent a domain ("reach or scope") while aiming at fitting local structures, social arrangements, and technologies ("embeddedness")?

For our purposes, cyberinfrastructure is the set of organizational practices, technical infrastructure, and social norms that collectively provide for the smooth operation of scientific work at a distance (Latour, 1992; NSF CI Council, 2006).

Being all three subjects to contingent distributive actions, these are objects of design and engineering; a cyberinfrastructure will fail if any one is ignored. Key to any new infrastructure is its ability to permit the distribution of action over space and time.

The Long Now of Information Infrastructure

Stewart Brand's "clock of the long now" will chime once every millennium: a cuckoo will pop out (Brand, 1999). Accustomed as we are to the "information revolution," the accelerating pace of the 24/7 lifestyle, and the multi-connectivity provided by the world wide web, we rarely step back and ask what changes have been occurring at a slower pace, in the background. For the development of cyberinfrastructure, the long now is about 200 years. This is when two sets of changes began to occur in the organization of knowledge and the academies that have accompanied – slowly – the rise of an information infrastructure to support them. On the one hand is the exponential increase in information gathering activities by the state (statistics) and on the other is the emergence of knowledge workers (the encyclopedists) and the accompanying development of technologies and organizational practices to sort, sift, and store information.

When dealing with information infrastructures, we need to look to the whole array of organizational forms, practices, and institutions that accompany, make possible, and inflect the development of new technology, their related practices, and their distributions. JoAnne Yates made this point beautifully in describing the first commercial use of punch card data tabulators in the insurance industry. She demonstrates that use became possible because of *organizational* changes within the industry. Without new forms of information management, heralded by such low status technologies as the manila folder or carbon paper and accompanied by new organizational forms, there would have been no niche for punch card readers to occupy (Yates, 1989). Similarly, Manuel Castells argued that the roots of contemporary "network society" are new organizational forms created in support of large corporate organizations, which long predate the arrival of computerization (Castells, 1996). James Beniger described the entire period from the first Industrial Revolution to the present as an ongoing "control revolution" in which societies responded to mass production, distribution, and consumption with both technological and organizational changes, designed to manage ever-increasing flows of goods, services, and information (Beniger, 1986). In general there is more continuity than cleavage in the relationship of contemporary "information society" to the past (Chandler & Cortada, 2003).

The lesson of all these studies is that organizations are (in part) information processors (Stinchcombe, 1990). People, routines, forms, and classification systems are as integral to information handling as computers, ethernet cables, and web protocols. The boundary between technological and organizational means of information processing is both diffuse and mobile. It can be shifted in either direction and technological mechanisms can only substitute for human and organizational ones when the latter are prepared to support such a substitution.

The impacts of contemporary infrastructure are pervasive. In the "long now," two key facets of scientific information infrastructures stand out. One clusters around the nature of work in the social and natural sciences. Scientific disciplines were formed in the early 1800s, a time Michel Serres describes as the era of x-ology, where "x" was "geo," "socio," "bio," and so forth (Serres, 1990). Auguste Comte classified the division of labor in the sciences, placing mathematics and physics as the most developed and best models and sociology as the most complex and least developed – more or less where Norbert Wiener placed them 130 years later in *Cybernetics and Society* (Weiner, 1951). This was also the period during which the object we now call the database came to be the lynchpin of the natural and social sciences. Statistics etymologically refers to "state-istics," or the quantitative study of societies (states); it arose along with censuses, medical records, climatology, and other increasingly powerful techniques for monitoring population composition and health (Porter, 1986). Equally, the natural sciences – moved by the spirit of the encyclopedists – began creating vast repositories of data. Such repositories were housed in individual laboratories or in institutions, such as botanical gardens and museums of natural history. Today they are increasingly held in electronic form, and this is fast becoming the norm rather than the exception. Indeed, a researcher publishing a protein sequence must also publish his or her data in the (now worldwide) Protein Data Bank (http://www.wwpdb.org). A somewhat analogous publishing effort by the Ecological Society of America was initiated in 1998 for digital supplements, including databases and source code for simulation models (http://www.esapubs.org/archive/). The use of this forum has developed differently as one might expect, given the significant cultural and data differences between the fields of ecology and bioinformatics.

The second facet clusters around scientists' communication patterns. In the 17th and 18th centuries scientists were largely "men of letters" created an information infrastructure to exchange both public and private correspondence, such as the famous Leibniz/Clarke exchange (Desmond & Moore, 1991; Leibniz, Clarke, & Alexander, 1998). From the early nineteenth century a complex structure of national and international conferences and publishing practices developed, including in particular the peer-reviewed scientific journal – at the same time as personal communication networks continued to develop (Desmond & Moore, 1991). Communication among an ever-broader scientific community was no longer two-way, but *n*-way. New forms of transportation further undergirded the development of a truly international scientific community aided also by *linguae francae*, principally English and French.

Similarly, today's scientific infrastructures must be understood as an outgrowth of these developments rather than ahistorically as "revolutionary" or "radical."[2]

---

[2]The claims of revolutionary change about our information infrastructure are somewhat akin to the millennialism of every generation since the industrial revolution. We are living the epoch of the database founded in the era of governmentality (late eighteenth century) – and all the claims that we see today about speed, time, and distribution have been with us since that epoch.

Databases and *n*-way communication among scientists have developed as organizationally and institutionally embedded practices and norms. There is far more continuity than many recognize precisely due to the 'always invented here' claims of much computer and information science. However, as scientific infrastructure goes digital, we can also identify a genuine discontinuity. The social and natural sciences evolved together with communication and data-processing technology. Changes in data handling and communications have profound ripple effects throughout the complex web of relations that constitutes natural and social scientific activity; infrastructures thus grow slowly.

PART 2: DESIGNING COMMUNITIES, TECHNOLOGIES AND KNOWLEDGE

In the context of the internet, Infrastructure Studies spans the set of information and communication technology and services that secure and underlie much of modern work and play. It explores the ways in which

- *new forms of sociality* are being enabled/shaped by and shaping Information and Communication Technologies (ICT). Objects of study here will typically be communities of scientists (e.g., cyberinfrastructure, e-science, collaboratories); new kinds of intentional community (e.g., support groups for sufferers of a particular rare disease), and studies of distributed collective practice (e.g., scientific networks, communities of practice, transnational businesses). This is the social dimension of the new infrastructure.
- *social, ethical and political values* are being built into these self-effacing, self-perpetuating infrastructures.
- the nature of *knowledge work* is changing with the introduction of new information technologies, modes of representation, and the accompanying shifts in work practice and systems for the accreditation of knowledge. This is the ontological dimension of the new infrastructure.

We shall examine some core concepts from each of these themes in turn, referring in each to aspects of the definition of infrastructure.

New Forms of Sociality: Organizational and Community Issues

Mediation

In contrast to large-scale physical infrastructures that may be viewed as the responsibility of a business, city, or government, the internet transitioned from a research environment into an open-bazaar, committee-run entity and today is being re-defined in a marketplace of policies and regulations. The internet and its associated information infrastructure is reaching beyond the immediacy of the physical and technical, extending to individual and community realms as well as into organizational and cultural structures and expectations. The scope and ramifications of "information" – from access, quality, and distribution to exchange – is vast, bringing with it responsibilities and exposing needs. Mediation appears an appropriately ambiguous term to suggest the multiple new dimensions to be developed and interfaces to be tended. With its whole-culture, whole-earth reach, there is aligning, weaving, and arbitrating to be carried out between systems and networks, people and organizations, habits and cultures. Infrastructure studies is best considered as "process building," involving both community building and system building. An infrastructure studies "process-building" framework must take account of both the use of technology for automation and effective disintermediation as well as the increased need for support, for tending by growing numbers and varieties of mediation professionals. New types of mediation are required for managing information, new forms such as that represented by activity theory or by ethnographic work (Engestrom, 1990; Nardi & O'Day, 1996).

Process Building

Because of the broad implications for information infrastructures, the sweep of information systems compares to that of governance systems. The pooling of information within infrastructures provides a distribution of relations such as group identity, makes available community findings, and provides a mechanism for staying in touch by sharing information and files – the coin of the realm. The need for participation holds the same import for information infrastructures as for democratic systems. Engaged participation of diverse participants ensures that issues such as standards formation and continued maintenance and update are addressed (Hanseth et al., 1996). If participants have been active in the formation of infrastructure elements, they are more likely to have a deeper awareness of alternatives and have had a voice in mediating choices inherent to issues such as standards formation and community goals (Millerand & Bowker, 2009). This then calls for a forum where multiple perspectives are considered and where the timeless tensions between local and general, between short term and long term are addressed. Once in place, information procedures and standards become a general requirement or driver that facilitate development for some, that misrepresent or perhaps ignore some, and that potentially alienate others (Berg & Timmermans, 2000). One aspect of infrastructure studies inquiry is consideration of new types of roles evolving with the process of building information infrastructure – roles such as digital librarians, information managers, and network specialists. These represent new strategies – and new attitudes – that are organizationally situated to support an internet generation of participants.

System Sustaining

Just as power and energy today underpin the functioning of automated services, so the information infrastructure has evolved to be regarded as an essential, ubiquitous service for delivery, access, and exchange of information. With technology-related resources, issues of change, redesign, and support arise with respect to hardware, software, networks, and human resources and relations as we gain experience with technology, its mediation, and its interfaces. Here, mediation encompasses relations between people, between machines, or between communities as well as a vast variety of human–technology interfaces. Through new roles explicitly incorporating mediation, there are opportunities for sensitivity to silences and absences that may be organizationally instantiated – a layer of professionals trained to notice who is not represented or who is misrepresented. Articulation work is well recognized in STS (Strauss, 1988, 1993), in the literature of design (Bratteteig, 2003; Schmidt & Bannon, 1992) and in ethnographic studies (Baker & Millerand, 2007; Sawyer & Tapia, 2006) though not always as an integral part of the information infrastructure process building– local, community, national, or international. We note that infrastructure work frequently entails frequent and ongoing articulation work in order to enable continued functionality.

Infrastructure in Time

Infrastructure building involves alignment work involving different time scales. The Long-Term Ecological Research program provides an interesting example with its mission to further understanding of environmental change through interdisciplinary collaboration and long-term research projects (LTER: http://lternet.edu; Hobbie, Carpenter, Grimm, Gosz, & Seastedt, 2003). In addition to the LTER moving beyond the "plot" of traditional ecoscience to analyze change at the scale of a continent, one of the chief challenges is to move beyond a 1–6 year funding cycle of projects or a 30-year career cycle of the scientist to create baselines of data spanning multiple decades. While the preservation of data over time, and their storage in conditions appropriate to their present and future use, has always been a priority within the LTER network, a new urgency arises with the development of scientific cyberinfrastructure projects aiming to support long-term and large-scale ecological research. Aligning what is naturally misaligned (funding cycles, scientists career trajectories, ecosystem cycles) is fundamentally an issue of distribution between technologies, communities, organizations, institutions, and participating individuals.

Lemke presents the important principle of heterochrony, variations in the parameters of temporal change associated with different parts of a system (Lemke, 2000). Understanding cyberinfrastructure building requires understanding the timescales for operation of its different components and how they are articulated so that processes have an apparent continuity across time. Ecological systems consist of different components with various change rates and scales of size. Indeed these differences are why they can absorb shocks and survive:

> Some parts respond quickly to the shock, allowing slower parts to ignore the shock and maintain their steady duties of system continuity. The combination of fast and slow components makes the system resilient, along with the way the differently paced parts affected each other. [. . .] All durable dynamic systems have this sort of structure; it is what makes them adaptable and robust. (Brand, 1999, p. 34)

Heterochrony in cyberinfrastructure development is a major issue. It is a statement of the obvious to say that given the extremely rapid developments in information technology, parts of a technological system are frequently outdated before the whole system can be assembled, thus requiring development of ad hoc, last minute arrangements. It is also common to find that when a new technology is released and becomes of high interest for user communities, it ceases to be of interest to its developers who are already working on another state-of-the-art technological project – thus leaving critical issues such as maintenance and redevelopment over time largely unaddressed. Other examples are drawn-out collaboration processes when disparate groups try to collaborate but work within differing time frames, resulting in different rates of interest, uptake, and/or learning.

A system – whatever the blend of technical, organizational, social – consists of multiple layers and dimensions at differing stages of maturity. In addition, the designers, developers, deployers, enactors, and users of data and information are at different phases of technological interest, awareness, and/or skills (Millerand and Bowker, forthcoming). Thus an individual's interface with others about technology or with the system itself at any one time presents a scenario of differing local arrangements, conceptual development, and individual understandings. Even with here-and-now, small-scale expectations and interactions, participants confront what can be called differing "readiness factors" (Olson & Olson, 2000). The introduction of technology is discussed in the champion literature with leadership depending upon different types of goals, champions (e.g., project, technical, and user champions), and innovators (e.g., gatekeepers focused on products in particular and conceptualists focused on approaches) (Howell & Higgins, 1990; Schon, 1963). In planning for the internet, there is a shifting baseline of understanding as the user/designer base of experience grows. In terms of the growing user/design literature, two points were developed early on: (1) for planning and learning to be effective, it needs to be based on the learner's experience (Dewey, 1902); (2) individuals have perceptual as well as information processing limits (Weick, 1979). As an example, consider the pervasiveness of electronic spreadsheets as an organizing tool. Experience with numbers stored in columns or matrix form was a territory and an approach over which accountants reigned for decades. Even after initial development of the electronic spreadsheet concept, the tool and the public matured together over time. In a sense, for those who are part of the digital culture, availability and familiarity with spreadsheet use has likely raised their readiness for work with say Data Grids.

Social and Political Values

What kind of a thing is the internet? We do not do it justice when we see it as wires and modems, bells and whistles. Conceptually, let us for a moment imagine it as a very large database, an outcome of the late eighteenth-century encyclopedist impulse to record all of the world's knowledge and make it freely accessible. It was rendered possible by not only the development of electricity but also by the development across the nineteenth century of large-scale classification systems in any of a number of domains, of library classifications above all (the MARC record turns electronic and then morphs into the Dublin Core). Today, one can find both widely held standards such as the ISO standards (International Organization for Standardization, http://www.iso.org) as well as an emergent set of working standards in community arenas. Now it is clear that how we arrange information in encyclopedias has social and political dimensions (do we look under "t" for "terrorist," "f" for freedom fighter, or "i" for "insurgent," for example?) cite. The art and science of classification plays an underappreciated but recurring role in the organization of information (Bowker & Star, 1999; Epstein, 2007).

It is a database that constantly needs updating. Indeed, looking back to the 1911 edition of the Encyclopedia Britannica – considered by many the finest edition – one finds a number of categories which did not stand the test of time and do not hold today – aether, phrenology, and poltergeist, for example (http://www.1911encyclopedia.org/). So how do you design a database, for the ages, which reflects the values that we as a society want to develop – be these the very abstract value of pluralism or specific ones, such as carbon neutrality or producing green technology. Looking forward from 2000, there are new topics to include – from blogging to dataspaces and infrastructure – as well as new data types to incorporate – from metadata to pervasive sensors and streamed data. Indeed, to date, the internet is inclusive. It is a "dataspace" into which we can add a growing variety of artifacts (Franklin, Halevy, & Maier, 2005).

These design issues are playing out across the board in information infrastructure development as the problem of deciding what kind of objects to people your world with, how to describe data with metadata and how to build ontologies (Sowa, 2000). Building ontologies involves gathering domain knowledge, formalizing this knowledge into a machine computable format, and encoding it into machine language. This is the stripped down technical understanding of knowledge acquisition. But in the work of building ontologies as undertaken today, ontology-building specialists typically find that domain practitioners are not readily prepared for ontology building. Ontology work is a quintessential act of distribution – taking knowledge out of a closed community of practice and allowing for its reuse and reshaping by others in different fields. First there is the enrollment of the domain. To bring experts on board is to inform them of the technology of ontology, its strengths in the face of other interoperability strategies, and the particular work it will require. Enrolling practitioners is securing an investment in technological direction by a domain community. Second is the work of knowledge acquisition. Written sources such as textbooks and technical treatises are often not precise enough for transformation into description logics: there may be competing accounts of the same phenomena, overlapping taxonomies and standards, or outright contradictions (Bowker, 2000). Similarly in consulting authorities in a domain, a programmer may find that these experts are not immediately able to state domain knowledge in the terms necessary for ontology building. In short, the ontology specialist often finds that what participants in a domain consider their validated and structured knowledge is not readily compatible with ontology building. So third is understanding that ontologies are not static. Though frequently viewed as a product to finish, it is dynamic ontologies with associated process-building activities designed, developed, and deployed locally that will allow ontologies to grow and to change. And finally, the technical activity of ontology building is always coupled with the background work of identifying and informing a broader community of future ontology users.

Social and political choices are evidently being made in the building of large interoperable databases and ontologies in the social sciences and the humanities – one needs only look at controversies around ethnic classification in the US census, debates around Wikipedia content and editing, or the classification system of the Library of Congress. However, they are also present across the range of natural sciences. As drug companies create databases of plants that may have medicinal value, they frequently relegate indigenous understanding of those plants to free text fields that are essentially useless – the political decision not to use local knowledge is enforced by a simple technical fix (Hayden, 2003; Latour, 1993). If a dominant subgroup within a given discipline gets to define the ontology of the database, they can reinforce their power – a simple example here is the neurophysiological approach to mental illness at the heart of DSM, the Diagnostic and Statistical Manual (Kirk & Kutchins, 1992): this classification system, used in both research and medical reimbursement, renders it extremely difficult for Freudian therapists to present their diagnoses.

Knowledge Work

Let us now anathematize techno hubris. Much technological infrastructure development has been motivated by the belief that if we build it they will come. Little was learned from the experience of supercomputer centers (built, they didn't come) or collaboratories (built, they left early). It is not enough to put out a new technical infrastructure – it needs to be woven into the daily practices of knowledge workers. It has emerged from the last ten years of information infrastructure development that a wide range of cultural and organizational changes need to be made if the new infrastructure is going to bear fruit.

We are dealing with a massively entrenched set of institutions, built around the last information age and fighting for its life. The rationale for publishing journals shifts (just as music producers are finding less purchase for the album) when single papers can be issued to a mass audience at the push of a button. This then leads to questioning the reasons to work with the publishing industry, since the work of peer review is done on a volunteer basis by the scientific community, with the journals contributing only to the expense and hence unavailability of the final product. However, one does not just click one's heels together and make a multi-billion dollar enterprise go away – as Chandler has shown there is remarkable historical continuity among major corporations (Chandler & Hikino, 1994). And yet the very nature of publishing is changing and will potentially change more. Similarly, universities grew up in previous eras of communication technology – one traveled to campuses in order to study with particular learned professors and to become immersed in a learning environment. There seems little reason to restrict universities to campuses (or libraries to buildings) when you have the ability to share information easily across the internet.

And yet there is inevitably a cultural dimension as well. People love libraries and campuses; they don't tend to feel so fond of their computer screens. Take the issue of publishing for example. Over the past 30 years, the Missouri Botanical Gardens has twice failed to move the Flora of North America into the electronic realm. The problem has not been technical capability. To view it in broadest perspective, it is that botany grew up with the printed book. Some of first incunabalae were botanical field guides. Works in botany stand the test of time – it is one of the few scientific fields where work from the eighteenth and nineteenth centuries is still regarded as valid and interesting. It has proven very difficult to get botanists trained in this tradition to move to the sharing of uncertain results in ephemeral form: their whole scientific tradition is devoted to provenance and finality.

Within the field of science studies, ethnographic work has described scientific knowledge production as a specialized form of work. By focusing on the hands-on processes of how knowledge, or at an even finer granularity, how "a fact" is constructed these ethnographic "laboratory studies" have contributed greatly to a body of empirical evidence complicating notions of a scientific method; knowledge and fact production; scientific rationalities; data sharing and interpretation (Knorr-Cetina, 1981; Latour & Woolgar, 1979; Lynch, 1985). In conjunction with a "turn to practice," lab studies were also crucial in a "turn to the material" by shifting analytic focus to instrumentation, data (including "second- and third-order" representations such as derived data sets, visualizations, photographs, charts, and graphs), and the movements of these "traces" across the physical site of the laboratory itself. By making a combination of the "practical and material" accessible to the sociological analyst another avenue was opened for the study of "scientific content." The methodological imperative, then, becomes to treat "technical" dimensions of activity no differently than any other sociological object of interest: with appropriate access and determination of the researcher, human activity is fundamentally observable whether "scientific," "lay," or "technical."

Thus rather than the rhetoric of revolutionary fervor that permeates cyberinfrastructure circles, infrastructure studies take as its object change at a much more mundane scale: as forms of practice, routine, or distributed cognition associated with knowledge work. Is this position against a possibility of "revolution?" Not at all. It is, rather, a research sensibility which seeks to make transformations of infrastructure visible relative to the everyday work of scientists, information technologists, or information managers.

As we have argued, the new information infrastructure is fundamentally about distribution. Consider the long history of European development over the past 1500 years. When trade was difficult and scarce, community centers were built up close to resource reserves: coal, water, arable land. With the first industrial revolution of the eleventh century, the use of water power (windmills) and the plough created conditions where cities could grow away from this cluster of resources. With the second industrial revolution (the eighteenth and nineteenth centuries), global resource distribution became possible through new communication and transportation infrastructures. Now, over the past 200 years, our emergent information society has (gradually) moved to a further form of distribution where complex social, organizational, and knowledge work can be practiced on a global scale, which leads to the question of how we study it.

PART 3: TOWARDS A SCIENCE OF INFORMATION INFRASTRUCTURE

The internet is changing what we know and how we know it; accordingly the study of information infrastructure studies is a field with an emerging research agenda. We need new images and mindsets. The classic argument here is from Paul David (David, 1985): computers were very bad typewriters; electrical dynamos were very bad steam generators – leading to the classic productivity paradox where their respective introductions led to 30 year drops in productivity. Only when we truly think the new technology can we use it to its fullest. The internet opens an array of information infrastructure issues whose resolution will frame the future of the digital realm, issues of data sharing and database query, community standards and data spaces, domain repositories and ontologies, grid portals and resource sharing: "Infrastructure is an idea, a vision or an ideal, but it is also a practice, a commitment and a long term endeavor" (Ribes, 2006, p. 299).

The fields which have contributed to this new science include, but are not limited to, computer science, information science, communication, organization theory, cognitive science, and science and technology studies. Teams of researchers have emerged from their disciplinary silos to claim special expertise on information infrastructure – often in the process denying the expertise of others, as is normal in attempts to professionalize (Abbott, 1988). We have argued in this article that we cannot simply fragment the parts of such studies into separate fields. As with transdisciplinary science in general (Gibbons et al., 1994), there is a fundamental scope and unity to the field that reflects the very nature of the new infrastructure – one in which the global and the local, the social and the technical are in flux in new and interesting ways for the first time in 500 years. The decisions we make over the next 50 years will have very long-term consequences.

We have looked so far at the nature of information infrastructure and some emergent themes in its study. We conclude with a few themes native to this emerging field that must be addressed in order to move the field to the next level.

The first theme is research organization. Following an infrastructure is not an easy task for the qualitative social scientist, who typically has been immersed in a particular tribe, project, group and has been able to interview key players and observe them at work. As some have complained in Hollywood, there is little to catch the eye in watching someone typing on a keyboard – and those who are spending a lot of time online are immersed in a community to which the researcher does not have physical access. There are two responses here. First, we need new models for scalable qualitative research: is the appropriate sized research team more of the order of 15–20 rather than the 0–2 typical of many programs? One way to look at this is in terms of Ross Ashby's Law of Requisite Variety (Ashby, 1956): we need as much span in our research teams as there is in the phenomena we are studying.

Further, we need better forms of multi-modal research – there is no one methodology which is going to prevail – the phenomena themselves evoke a range each with strengths and weaknesses. For example, from social network analysis we have a semi-quantitative approach that brings together a great deal of data but which typically ignores domain content, meanings, and practice. We also have the hermeneutic tradition of readings of scientific texts and more recently databases; this is a method that provides rich situated detail but it typically ignores organization. Infrastructure is "large" spanning time and space, but it is also "small" coming in contact with routine and everyday practice. Thus, infrastructure studies require drawing together methods that are equal to the ambitions of its phenomenon.

This leads directly into our second theme, an integrative view. In order to understand the new information infrastructure we need to move beyond seeing the social, organizational, and cognitive sitting somehow on top of or beside the wires and gateways of the physical infrastructure. Each layer is riven through with each of these dimensions – and we need to train social scientists and information scientists to move freely between all of them. This is not just a good idea – it is something of a law if we want to fully understand emergent phenomena in the development of new ways of knowing.

Our third theme is a direct consequence: we need to be sensitive to the development and spread of new ways of knowing across information infrastructures. Consider the issues of classification systems, ontologies, and metadata that subtend so much work on the web. Patrick Tort has written a marvelous book about the development of classification systems in the nineteenth century (Tort, 1989). In this book he charts the rise and eventual dominance of genetic classification systems, which sort things into piles by their origin points (the origin of species, for example) in a whole range of different fields. Now there was at this point no "science" of classification, no set of conferences that everyone was going to – the new systems spread virally among many different populations. The development of information infrastructures facilitates the viral spread of ontologies and classifications – indeed when you look under the hood of various cyberinfrastructure projects you often find the same underlying architecture and design philosophy being promoted by a small set of actors. To the extent that we train social scientists to look *within* particular fields or projects, we are missing one of the most interesting features of information infrastructures: their ability to promote combined (if uneven) development across a very broad range of work practices.

We are convinced that we are in the midst of developing fundamentally new ways of knowing – though we would put this in a 200 year span rather than a machine-centered 50 year frame. Understanding these in order to rethink the nature of knowledge on the one hand and improve design on the other entails developing fundamental new ways of working in natural and social science. We need to move beyond the "endless frontier" model of building information infrastructure and start to look at just what homesteading means in this new landscape. Information infrastructure is a great tool for distribution of knowledge, culture, and practice. Homesteading the space it has slowly opened out over the past two centuries involves building new kinds of community, new kinds of disciplinary homes, and new understandings of ourselves.

References

Abbott, A. (1988). *The system of professions: An essay on the division of expert labor.* Chicago: University of Chicago Press.

Arthur, B. (1994). *Increasing returns and path dependence in the economy.* Ann Arbor: University of Michigan Press.

Ashby, W. R. (1956). *Introduction to cybernetics.* London: Chapman & Hall.

Atkins, D. E., Droegemeier, K. K., Feldman, S. I., Garcia-Molina, H., Klein, M. L., Messerschmitt, D. G., et al. (2003). *Revolutionizing science and engineering through cyberinfrastructure.* Report of the National Science Foundation Blue-Ribbon Advisory Panel on Cyberinfrastructure.

Baker, K. S., & Millerand, F. (2007, January 3–6). *Articulation work supporting information infrastructure design: Coordination, categorization, and assessment in practice.* Proceedings of the 40th Hawaii International Conference on System Sciences (HICSS), Big Island, Hawaii, IEEE Computer Society, New Brunswick, NJ.

Beniger, J. R. (1986). *The control revolution: Technological and economic origins of the information society.* Cambridge, MA: Harvard University Press.

Berg, M., & Timmermans, S. (2000). Orders and their others: On the constitution of universalities in medical work. *Configurations, 8,* 31–61.

Bowker, G. C. (1994). *Science on the run: Information management and industrial geophysics at schlumberger, 1920–1940.* Cambridge, MA: MIT Press.

Bowker, G. C. (2000). Biodiversity datadiversity. *Social Studies of Science, 30*(5), 643–683.

Bowker, G. C., & Star, S. L. (1999). *Sorting things out: Classification and its consequences.* Cambridge, MA: MIT Press.

Bowker, G. C., Timmermans, S., & Star, S. L. (1995). Infrastructure and organizational transformation: Classifying nurses' work. In W. Orlikowski, G. Walsham, M. R. Jones, & J. I. DeGross (Eds.), *Information technology and changes in organizational work* (pp. 344–370). London: Chapman and Hall.

Brand, S. (1999). *The clock of the long now: Time and responsibility: The ideas behind the world's slowest computer.* New York: Basic Books.

Bratteteig, T. (2003). *Making change: Dealing with relations between design and use.* PhD Thesis, University of Oslo, Norway.

Castells, M. (1996). *The rise of the network society.* Cambridge, MA: Blackwell Publishers.

Chandler, A. D., Jr., & Cortada, J. W. (2003). *A nation transformed by information: How information has shaped the United States from Colonial times to the present* (pp. 185–226). New York, NY: Oxford University Press.

Chandler, A. D., & Hikino, T. (1994). *Scale and scope: The dynamics of industrial capitalism.* Cambridge, MA: Belknap Press.

Clanchy, M. T. (1993). *From memory to written record, England 1066–1307* (2nd ed.). Oxford, Cambridge: Blackwell.

David, P. (1985). *Computer and dynamo: The modern productivity paradox in a not-too-distant mirror*. Stanford: Center for Economic Policy Research, Stanford University.

Desmond, A. J., & Moore, J. R. (1991). *Darwin*. New York: Warner Books.

Dewey, J. (1902). *The child and the curriculum*. Chicago: University of Chicago Press.

Edwards, P. (2003). Infrastructure and modernity: Force, time, and social organization. In T. J. Misa, P. Brey, & A. Feenberg (Eds.), *The history of sociotechnical systems. Modernity and technology* (pp. 185–226). Cambridge, MA: The MIT Press.

Edwards, P. N., Jackson, S. J., Bowker, G. C., & Knobel, C. (2007). *Understanding infrastructure: Dynamics, tensions, and design*. NSF Report of a Workshop on "History & Theory of Infrastructure: Lessons for New Scientific Cyberinfrastructures". Retrieved from http://hdl.handle.net/2027.42/49353.

Engestrom, Y. (1990). *Learning, working, and imagining*. Helsinki: Orienta-Konsutit Og.

Epstein, S. (2007). *Inclusion: The politics of difference in medical research*. Chicago: University of Chicago Press.

Franklin, M., Halevy, A., & Maier, D. (2005). From databases to dataspaces: A new abstraction for information management. *SIGMOD Record, 34*(4), 27–33.

Futrell, J., & the AC-ERE (2003, May). *Environmental cyberinfrastructure (ECI): Tools for the study of complex environmental systems*. http://catalog.rcls.org/ipac20/ipac.jsp?session= 12746364037TU.158230&profile=mid&uri=link=3100007~!974625~!3100001~!3100002 &aspect=subtab111&menu=search&ri=1&source=~!anser&term=Environmental+cyberin-frastructure+%28ECI%29+tools+for+the+study+of+complex+environmental+systems.&index =PALLTI

Gibbons, M., Limoges, C., Nowotny, H., Schwartzman, S., Scott, P., & Trow, M. (1994). *The new production of knowledge: The dynamics of science and research in contemporary societies*. London: Thousand Oaks, CA: Sage Publications.

Goffman, E. (1956). *The presentation of self in everyday life*. New York: Doubleday.

Goody, J. (1987). *The interface between the written and the oral*. Cambridge: Cambridge University Press.

Hanseth, O., Monteiro, E., & Hatling, M. (1996). Developing information infrastructure: The tension between standardization and flexibility. *Science, Technology & Human Values, 21*(4), 407–426.

Hayden, C. (2003). *When nature goes public: The making and unmaking of bioprospecting in Mexico*. Princeton: Princeton University Press.

Hedstrom, M., Dawes, S., Fleischhauer, C., Gray, J., Lynch, C., McCrary, V., et al. (2002). It's about time: Research challenges in digital archiving and long-term preservation committee: NSF-DGO Report on NSF Workshop on research challenges in digital archiving. Digital Gov Program, NSF Div of Info and Intelligent Systems.

Hobbie, J. E., Carpenter, S. R., Grimm, N. B., Gosz, J. R., & Seastedt, T. R. (2003). The US long term ecological research program. *BioScience, 53*(2), 21–32.

Howell, J. M., & Higgins, C. A. (1990). Champions of technological innovation. *Administrative Science Quarterly, 35*(2), 317–341.

Hughes, T. P. (1983). *Networks of power: Electrification in western society, 1880–1930*. Baltimore: John Hopkins University Press.

Hughes, T. P. (1989). Evolution of large technological systems. In W. E. Bijker, T. P. Hughes, & T. J. Pinch (Eds.), *The social construction of technological systems: New directions in the sociology and history of technology* (pp. 51–82). Cambridge, MA; London: The MIT Press.

Karasti, H., & Baker, K. (2004, January). *Infrastructuring for the long-term: Ecological information management*. Proceedings of the 37th Hawaii International Conference on System Sciences. HICSS38, IEEE Computer Society, Big Island, Hawaii.

Karasti, H., Baker, K. S., & Halkola, E. (2006). Enriching the notion of data curation in eScience: Data managing and information infrastructuring in the long term ecological research (LTER) network. In M. Jirotka, R. Procter, T. Rodden, & G. Bowker (Eds.), *Computer Supported*

Cooperative Work: An International Journal. Special Issue: Collaboration in e-Research, *15*(4), 321–358.

Kirk, S. A., & Kutchins, H. (1992). *The selling of the DSM: The rhetoric of science in psychiatry.* New York: Aldine de Gruyter.

Knorr-Cetina, K. (1981). *The manufacture of knowledge: An essay on the constructivist and contextual nature of science.* Oxford: Pergamon Press.

Latour, B. (1992). Where are the missing masses? The sociology of a few mundane artifacts. In W. E. Bijker & J. Law (Eds.), *Shaping technology, building society: Studies in sociotechnical change* (pp. 225–258). Cambridge: MIT Press.

Latour, B. (1993). *La Clef de Berlin et Autres Leçons d'un Amateur de Sciences.* Paris: La Decouverte.

Latour, B., & Woolgar, S. (1979). *Laboratory life: The construction of scientific facts.* Beverly Hills: Sage Publications.

Lawrence, K. A. (2006). Walking the tightrope: The balancing acts of a large e-Research project. *Computer Supported Cooperative Work, 15*(4), 385–411.

Leibniz, G. W., Clarke, S., & Alexander, H. G. (1998). *The Leibniz-Clarke correspondence.* New York: Manchester University Press.

Lemke, J. L. (2000). Across the scales of time: Artifacts, activities, and meanings in ecosocial systems. *Mind, Culture, and Activity, 7*(4), 273–290.

Lynch, M. (1985). *Art and artifact in laboratory science.* Boston, MA: Routledge and Kegan Paul.

MacKenzie, D. (1993). *Inventing accuracy: A historical sociology of nuclear missile guidance.* Cambridge, MA: The MIT Press.

Magnuson, J. J. (1990). Long-term ecological research and the invisible present. *BioScience, 40*(7), 495–501.

Millerand, F., & Bowker, G. C. (2009). Metadata standards, trajectories and enactment in the life of an ontology. In S. L. Star & M. Lampland (Eds.), *Formalizing practices: Reckoning with standards, numbers and models in science and everyday life* (pp. 149–167). Ithaca, NY: Cornell University Press.

Monteiro, E., & Hanseth, O. (1997). Inscribing behaviour in information infrastructure standards. *Science, Technology & Human Values, 21*(4), 407–426.

Nardi, B., & O'Day, V. (1996). Intelligent agents: What we learned at the library. *Libri, 46*, 59–88.

NSF Cyberinfrastructure Council (2006). NSF's cyberinfrastructure vision for 21st century discovery (Version 7.1). Retrieved from http://www.nsf.gov/od/oci/ci-v7.pdf

Olson, G. M., & Olson, J. S. (2000). Distance matters. *Human-Computer Interaction, 15*, 139–178.

Porter, T. M. (1986). *The rise of statistical thinking, 1820–1900.* Princeton, NJ: Princeton University Press.

Ribes, D. (2006). *Universal informatics: Building cyberinfrastructure, interoperating the geosciences.* Unpublished Ph.D. dissertation, Department of Sociology (Science Studies), University of California, San Diego.

Ribes, D., & Baker, K. S. (2007). *Modes of social science engagement in community infrastructure design.* Proceedings of Third International Conference on Communities and Technology, Springer, London, pp. 107–130.

Ribes, D., & Bowker, G. C. (2008). GEON: Organizing for interdisciplinary collaboration. In G. M. Olson, J. S. Olson, & A. Zimmerman (Eds.), *Science on the internet* (pp. 311–330). Cambridge: MIT Press.

Sawyer, S., & Tapia, A. (2006). Always articulating: Theorizing on mobile and wireless technologies. *The Information Society, 22*(5), 311–323.

Schmidt, K., & Bannon, L. (1992). Taking CSCW seriously: Supporting articulation work. *Computer Supported Cooperative Work, 1*(1), 7–40.

Schon, D. A. (1963). Champions for radical new inventions. *Harvard Business Review, 41*, 77–86.

Scott, J. C. (1998). *Seeing like a state: How certain schemes to improve the human condition have failed.* New Haven: Yale University Press.

Serres, M. (1990). *Le Contrat Naturel*. Paris: Editions Françous Bourin.

Shapin, A. P. (1989). The invisible technician. *American Scientist, 77*, 554–563.

Sowa, J. (2000). *Knowledge representation: Logical, hilosophical, and computational foundations*. Pacific Grove, CA: Brooks/Cole.

Star, S. L. (1991). The sociology of the invisible: The primacy of work in the writings of Anselm Strauss. In D. Maines (Ed.), *Social organization and social process: Essays in honor of Anselm Strauss* (pp. 265–283). Hawthorne, NY: Aldine de Gruyter.

Star, S. L. (1999). The ethnography of infrastructure. *American Behavioral Scientist, 43*(3), 377–391.

Star, S. L., & Ruhleder, K. (1994, October 22–26). Steps towards an ecology of infrastructure: Complex problems in design and access for large-scale collaborative systems. Proceedings of the Conference on Computer Supported Cooperative Work (CSCW 94 – Transcending Boundaries), Chapel Hill, NC. ACM Press, New York, pp. 253–264.

Star, S. L., & Ruhleder, K. (1996). Steps toward an ecology of infrastructure: Design and access for large information spaces. *Information Systems Research, 7*(1), 111–134.

Stinchcombe, A. (1990). *Information and organizations*. Berkeley: University of California Press.

Strauss, A. (1988). The articulation of project work: An organizational process. *The Sociological Quarterly, 29*(2), 163–178.

Strauss, A. L. (1993). *Continual permutations of action*. New York: Aldine De Gruyter.

Tort, P. (1989). *La Raison Classificatoire: Les complexes Discursifs – Quinze Etudes*. Paris: Aubier.

Weick, K. E. (1979). *The social psychology of organizing*. Reading, MA: Addison-Wesley Publishing Company.

Weiner, N. (1951). *Cybernetics and society*. New York, NY: Executive Techniques.

Yates, J. (1989). *Control through communication: The rise of system in American management*. Baltimore, MD: Johns Hopkins University Press.

From Reader to Writer: Citizen Journalism as News Produsage

Axel Bruns

> *Over the past few years, the outlines of a new form of journalism have begun to emerge. Call it participatory journalism or one of its kindred names – open-source journalism, personal media, grassroots reporting – but everyone from individuals to online newspapers has begun to take notice.*
> (Lasica, 2003a, n.pag.)

Today, participatory or citizen journalism – journalism which enables readers to become writers – exists online and offline in a variety of forms and formats, operates under a number of editorial schemes, and focuses on a wide range of topics from the specialist to the generic and the micro-local to the global. Key models in this phenomenon include veteran sites *Slashdot* and *Indymedia*, as well as news-related weblogs; more recent additions into the mix have been the South Korean *OhmyNews*, which in 2003 was "the most influential online news site in that country, attracting an estimated 2 million readers a day" (Gillmor, 2003a, p. 7), with its new Japanese and international offshoots, as well as the *Wikipedia* with its highly up-to-date news and current events section and its more recent offshoot *Wikinews*, and even citizen-produced video news as it is found in sites such as *YouTube* and *Current.tv*.

Such sites emerged alongside the "new" social software and Web 2.0 environments, or indeed (like *Slashdot*'s content management system Slash) inspired and spurred on the development of such advanced web publishing tools even before those terms were first introduced into the debate. The newer generations of citizen journalism are built on the groundwork by these early developers.

A key cultural factor driving the emergence of citizen journalism, on the other hand, were (and continue to be) the shortcomings of mainstream media – whether these are caused by a limited understanding of complex specialist topics (which led to the development of technology news site *Slashdot*) or a systemic and deliberate avoidance of controversial themes for political or economic reasons (which inspired

A. Bruns (✉)
Creative Industries Faculty, Queensland University of Technology, Brisbane, Queensland, Australia
e-mail: a.bruns@qut.edu.au

J. Hunsinger et al. (eds.), *International Handbook of Internet Research*,
DOI 10.1007/978-1-4020-9789-8_6, © Springer Science+Business Media B.V. 2010

the setup of the Independent Media Centres that form the *Indymedia* network, as well as of *OhmyNews*). "As the mainstream mediaspace, particularly in the United States, becomes increasingly centralised and profit-driven, its ability to offer a multiplicity of perspectives on affairs of global importance is diminished" (Rushkoff, 2003, p. 17) – citizen journalism's intention is to fill the spaces abandoned by the mainstream.

The Citizen Journalism Process

Citizen journalism's practices differ markedly from those of the mainstream news industry, however. For the most part, its proponents have realised that, as Bardoel and Deuze put it, "with the explosive increase of information on a worldwide scale, the necessity of offering information about information has become a crucial addition to journalism's skills and tasks . . . . This redefines the journalist's role as an annotational or orientational one, a shift from the watchdog to the 'guidedog'" (2001, p. 94). Further, citizen journalism places "average" citizens rather than salaried journalists in that "guidedog" role, writing and submitting stories which are less frequently the outcome of direct investigative reporting, and more often collect and collate available information on certain newsworthy topics. The practice here is similar most of all to that of industry journalists compiling stories from a variety of news agency feeds and combining it with further evaluation and commentary.

Rather than as a perpetuation of traditional gatekeeping practices, then, which are no longer effective in a world where source information is directly available to journalists and news users alike (that is, where the "gates" to keep have multiplied beyond all control), the underlying principle of citizen journalism is one of gate*watching*: citizen journalists engage in the continued observation of the output gates of key institutions and organisations as well as of news outlets, and the gathering and compilation of those items of information which are relevant to the story at hand (for a detailed description of this process, see Bruns, 2005). In their reports, citizen journalists – as gatewatchers and information "guidedogs" – focus more on publicising the availability of important information than on publishing new stories, in other words, and rely on their readers to draw their own conclusions from such reports as well as the source information they link to.

Editorial oversight of this process remains limited (or indeed is absent altogether, in some cases), for a variety of reasons. On the one hand, the gatewatching/publicising process could be seen as requiring less policing as it builds on information available elsewhere; "bad" stories are thus easily identified by editors and readers as they often quite obviously misrepresent the sources they use (this is not the case in traditional, industrial journalism, where the veracity of a journalist's appropriation of news agency reports in developing their story is difficult to confirm for readers unless they have direct access to the source reports). On the other hand, and more importantly, citizen journalism usually relies on its users as participants in the process at the output (story publication) and response (commentary) stages as much as it does at the input (story submission) stage – rather than installing site owners and editors as the final arbiters of story quality, in other words, citizen journalism usually relies on its users to evaluate submitted stories.

This takes place differently in different citizen journalism sites. While some sites (such as *Slashdot* or *OhmyNews*) retain the role of traditional content editors, if in a strictly limited fashion, some (such as *Kuro5hin* or *Plastic*) allow all registered users to comment and/or vote on submitted stories before they are "officially" published, while others (such as most *Indymedia* sites) publish all submitted stories automatically, leaving it to their users to debate and evaluate the quality and veracity of news stories through commentary and discussion functions attached to each story. Further, especially in wiki-based sites like *Wikipedia* and *Wikinews* it also becomes possible for users to continue to edit and improve stories *after* publication; this approaches what Matthew Arnison, developer of the first *Indymedia* content management system, describes as "open editing", and as a desirable further development beyond the "open publishing" already practiced in many Independent Media Centre sites (2002).

Such post-publication filtering and editing is by necessity a collaborative effort and today takes place predominantly through comments and discussion – users may provide further information and references which extend, support, or contradict details of the original story, they may comment on the summary of information provided in the article, or they may provide alternative points of view to those espoused in the story itself. Frequently, such discussion and debate is significantly more detailed than the story which sparked it, showing that in citizen journalism the primary focus is on such discursive engagement more than on the mere provision of facts; as Chan describes it in her study of *Slashdot*, "highlighting the expertise of users and the value of their participation, news reading shifts from an act centred on the reports and analyses of news professionals and designated experts, to one often equally focussed on the assessment and opinions of fellow users on the network" (2002, Chap. 2, n.pag.).

News production in such environments, in other words, is community-based; it "proceeds from a logic of engagement founded upon notions of production and involvement rather than consumption and spectacle" (Gibson & Kelly, 2000, p. 11) and therefore deserves the description as participatory, citizen journalism. Users in such environments are always also invited to be producers of content; indeed, the boundaries between the two roles are increasingly blurred and irrelevant. As we will see soon, it becomes more useful to describe their role as that of a hybrid user-producer, or *produser* (Bruns, 2008).

This supports Gillmor's observation that "if contemporary American journalism is a lecture, what it is evolving into is something that incorporates a conversation and seminar" (2003b, p. 79). At its best, such discursive citizen journalism – found in dedicated citizen journalism websites as much as in the even further decentralised, distributed discussions of the news blogosphere – approaches what Heikkilä and Kunelius postulate as deliberative journalism: "deliberative journalism would underscore the variety of ways to frame an issue. It would assume that opinions – not to mention majorities and minorities – do not precede public deliberation, that thoughts and opinions do not precede their articulation in public, but that they start to emerge when the frames are publicly shared" (2002, n.pag.). Further, it realises a challenge for journalism which was first set by scholar Herbert Gans in 1980:

> Ideally, . . . the news should be omniperspectival; it should present and represent all perspectives in and on America. This idea, however, is unachievable . . . . It is possible to suggest, however, that the news, and the news media, be multiperspectival, presenting and representing as many perspectives as possible – and at the very least, more than today. (1980, pp. 312–313)

Today, the stories and debates of citizen journalism can be seen as a form of multiperspectival news.

A further implication of this discursive, deliberative, multiperspectival mode of news coverage, however, is also that the stories of citizen journalism remain by necessity always unfinished; as Hiler puts it, "the Blogosphere is pioneering a new form of iterative journalism" (2002, n.pag.), and this applies also for citizen journalism more generally. In a collaborative, commentary- and discussion-based citizen journalism model it always remains possible for new and insightful comments and distributions to be added to a story even well after its time of publication; further, in an open editing model (perhaps especially in wiki-based environments) there always remains the possibility of new revelations which require a fundamental revision of the existing piece. As *Kuro5hin* operator Rusty Foster puts it, "the story is a process, now, instead of a product, like the news industry has taught us to think. It's never done, and the story is always evolving. Collaborative media gives [*sic*] us the power to contribute to that evolution, to all be part of the reporting of news, just like we're all part of the making of it" (2001, n.pag.).

Such comments begin to point to what is perhaps one of the most enduring misconceptions introduced through industrial journalism, one which might stem from the prevailing paradigms of the industrial age itself: that news or other products (especially of an information nature) can be neatly divided into finalised versions, editions, and issues. *Kuro5hin*'s Rusty Foster summarises the traditional perspective: "the way journalism right now works in the mainstream media is an industrial process: . . . You collect raw material from sources, and then you package it into a product and you deliver it to eyeballs. It's a very neat, very simple, very 19th century way of thinking about doing things" (Foster qtd. in *New Forms of Journalism*, 2001, n.pag.). As an alternative to this package-and-deliver metaphor, artist Brian Eno suggests that

> the right word is "unfinished." Think of cultural products, or art works, or the people who use them even, as being unfinished. Permanently unfinished. We come from a cultural heritage that says things have a "nature," and that this nature is fixed and describable. We find more and more that this idea is insupportable – the "nature" of something is not by any means singular, and depends on where and when you find it, and what you want it for. (Qtd. in Kelly, 1995, n.pag.)

Open News and Open Source

If citizen journalism in its various forms and "new media technologies and trends in civil society force us to rethink journalism's role at the start of the new millennium, in particular its traditional definition as a top-down profession" (Bardoel &

Deuze, 2001, p. 92), then, this points to parallels with other challenges to traditional industrial-style information production models – most obviously perhaps the open source software development model. As Meikle notes for the Independent Media Centre network, "the IMC philosophy of open publishing is ... entirely consistent with its technical foundations in the open source movement. Both essentially argue that anyone can and should be trusted to be both creative and responsible. ... In yielding editorial control in favour of relying on participants to be responsible in their contributions, the IMCs trust that a self-selection process will keep the projects on track" (2002, p. 108); this applies similarly also for many or most other participatory, citizen journalism projects, which we could therefore also describe as "open news" (see Bruns, 2003, 2005).

Indeed, open news projects translate what Stalder and Hirsh have described as "open source intelligence", or "OS-INT", to the production of news content: "OS-INT means the application of collaborative principles developed by the Open Source Software movement to the gathering and analysis of information. These principles include: peer review, reputation- rather than sanctions-based authority, the free sharing of products, and flexible levels of involvement and responsibility" (2002, n.pag.).

In addition to these principles, it is possible to draw further parallels: for example, where in open source development the source code to software is always also available so that potential users can check for bugs and verify the absence of malicious hidden code, in open news there are links to source reports embedded in articles so that users can check for misrepresentations or malicious misinformation. Both models also accept content as inherently incomplete, in line with Brian Eno's observations: open source as well as open news explicitly invite further user contributions in aid of a continual, iterative, and evolutionary development process. It should be noted that such continuous collaborative improvement, which requires the reappropriation and redevelopment of existing content, also relies on the use of alternative copyright licences – but to date, only open source has effectively and widely deployed a solid set of free/libre/open source software (FLOSS) licences, while on average open news sites so far only dabble in the use of creative commons or GNU PDL licences, and in many cases could be seen as operating with open disregard for existing copyright legislation (especially in their practices of citation or outright republication of copyright source materials).

In further similarity to open source, open news proponents also support a "power of eyeballs" argument, which relies on the collective insights of a broad userbase rather than on a small number of professional editors for quality assurance. As Rusty Foster puts it, "collaborative media relies [*sic*] on the simple fact that people like to argue. I don't care how many people CNN runs any given report by, we run it by more. More people, in most cases, equals more accountability, equals better quality" (2001, n.pag.).

However, crucial differences with open source software production also emerge at this point. Compared to open source, where sophisticated models are now in place for facilitating and coordinating distributed collaborative development efforts, the administrative structures for open news publishing still remain in their infancy. To date, it is possible to trace four broad models, which further exist in a number of local variations:

1. *Supervised or editor-assisted gatewatching:*
   This model emerged with *Slashdot*, where site editors retain the right to make a selection from all submitted news stories, and publish only those stories they deem relevant to the site. However, there is no further policing of subsequent commentary and debates. *OhmyNews* has further extended this model by partnering citizen and professional journalists – here, "all stories are fact checked and edited by professional editors" (2003, n.pag.).

2. *Gatewatching and community-based administration:*
   Sites such as *Kuro5hin* and *Plastic* responded to what they regarded as shortcomings in the *Slashdot* model by further opening the editorial process and removing the special privileges of dedicated site editors. Here, all submitted stories are made available to registered users for editorial commentary and subsequent voting – only stories which undergo this process and receive a sufficient amount of votes are ultimately published to the general public. Thus, "the audience acts as editor before and after publishing" (Bowman & Willis, 2003, p. 28).

3. *Open publishing:*
   As Meikle describes it, "open publishing is the key idea behind the IMC. There are no staff reporters as such – instead, the content is generated by anyone who decides to take part. There is no gatekeeping and no editorial selection process – participants are free to upload whatever they choose, from articles and reports to announcements and appeals for equipment or advice" (2002, p. 89). While this ensures total freedom from editorial intervention, it also provides a wide opening for abuse by vandals or political extremists and has become an increasing problem for *Indymedia* sites – to the point that some sites have introduced limitations to the open publishing model (such as a more traditionally edited front page). For Arnison, this is an unavoidable development: "as Indymedia grows it is drifting away from open publishing" (2002, n.pag.). In addition to *Indymedia*, the publishing approaches found in the blogosphere could generally also be described as a (decentralised) form of open publishing; however, individual blog sites may institute their own editorial principles and processes.

4. *Open editing:*
   Arnison suggests that "open publishing is about more than just open posting. It's also about open editing" (2002, n.pag.). However, to date wiki-based publications, rather than extensions of traditional open news content management systems, provide the most successful model for open editing approaches. Such sites again appeal to a "power of eyeballs" argument and invite all users to contribute by adding information and fixing errors; additionally – and in distinction from other open news sites – *Wikipedia* and *Wikinews* have also instituted a "Neutral Point of View" (NPOV) doctrine for their content, which at first glance could be seen to support a Gansian multiperspectivality model. Actual applications of such policies differ markedly across both sites, however; as discussed elsewhere (Bruns, 2006), *Wikinews* contributors' interpretation of NPOV

is overly literal to the point of squeezing "the life out of their stories, reducing lively news coverage to dull regurgitation of facts" (Yeomans, 2005, n.pag.), while by comparison *Wikipedia* also benefits from its significantly larger contributor base and can thus provide more effective and up-to-date coverage of news and current events.

Citizen Journalism as News Produsage

Overall, while similarities to open source are strong for open news, there are also some crucial differences between the two fields of content production. It becomes important, then, to develop broader, overarching models of collaborative content production in post-industrial, informational contexts. In this approach, open news (along with open source and other forms) is "an example of how the internet can be used as a democratic medium or innovation commons where its users share control over the creation, publication and usage of content" (Platon & Deuze, 2003, p. 339), pointing to what Rushkoff has described as "new metaphors for cooperation, new faith in the power of networked activity and new evidence of our ability to participate actively in the authorship of our collective destiny" (2003, p. 18).

In pursuing such new metaphors, it is important to fundamentally question the models of cooperation and content production which we have inherited from the industrial age – indeed, as audiences have become users and industrially produced products have become collaboratively authored content, we need to question the very language of production itself. As noted previously, in collaborative content creation environments it is becoming difficult if not impossible to tell mere users from producers; a sliding scale of user engagement rather than traditional distinctions between producers, distributors, and consumers now applies. We are entering an environment where users are always already also producers of content, or indeed have become hybrid *produsers*. Their practices of *produsage*, then, whether taking place in open source software development, open news publishing, or other fields, exhibit four fundamental characteristics (see Bruns, 2008), described below.

Open Participation, Communal Evaluation

Produsage is based on a principle of inclusivity, not exclusivity, and is therefore open to all comers. Produsage therefore draws on as broad a range of available knowledge, skills, talents, and ideas as is available and encourages its participants to apply these diverse capacities to the project at hand. Their contributions are in turn evaluated by other participants as they make their own contributions to the shared effort: those contributions deemed useful and relevant will be further improved upon, while those which are not will remain unused.

Fluid Heterarchy, Ad Hoc Meritocracy

Produsage necessarily proceeds from a principle of equipotentiality: the assumption that while the skills and abilities of all participants in the produsage project are not equal, they have an equal ability to make a worthy contribution to the project. Leadership is determined through the continuous communal evaluation of participants and their ideas and through the degree of community merit they are able to accumulate in the process; in this sense, then, produsage communities are ad hoc meritocracies.

Unfinished Artefacts, Continuing Process

The process of produsage must necessarily remain continually unfinished and infinitely continuing. Produsage does not work towards the completion of products (for distribution to end users or consumers); instead, it is engaged in an iterative, evolutionary process aimed at the gradual improvement of the community's shared content. The content found in a produsage community always represents only a temporary artefact of the ongoing process, a snapshot in time which is likely to be different again the next minute, the next hour, or the next day.

Common Property, Individual Rewards

The communal produsage of content necessarily builds on the assumption that content created in this process will continue to be available to all future participants just as it was available to those participants who have already made contributions. Participation in produsage projects is generally motivated mainly by the ability of produsers to contribute to a shared, communal purpose. But although content is held communally, produsers are able to gain personal merit from their individual contributions – and in some cases this has been converted into tangible outcomes for dedicated produsers.

Described in such terms, then, produsage can be shown to exist in a wide variety of domains – in open source and open news, but also in the collaborative narrative and content development which takes place in massively multi-user online games, in the collaborative creative processes of sites ranging from *Flickr* and *ccMixter* through to *YouTube* and *Current.tv*, and in the multiperspectival knowledge spaces of *del.icio.us*, *Wikipedia*, and *Google Earth*. It is also harnessed by commercial operators such as Amazon (for example, through its recommendation systems) or Google (amongst others through its PageRank algorithm and *Google News* content aggregator). Indeed, web 2.0 and social software can be seen as projects built on broad trends towards produsage as a paradigm replacing traditional, industrial production, and many commercial operators are taking note (see, for example, *Trendwatching.com*'s 2005 coverage of "customer-made" products).

Especially as far as informational content is concerned, produsage is distinctly different from industrial production – and this has important implications for news and journalism. Taken to its logical conclusion, informational produsage ends the traditional product cycle; its outcomes are no longer discrete versions of products – in the case of journalistic produsage, individual stories representing all that is known about a given event at the time of publication – but a diffuse sequence of ongoing and potentially never-ending revisions; as news content, this would resemble an up-to-date wiki entry much more than it would replicate traditional journalistic writing.

Similarly, informational produsage fundamentally alters producer/distributor/consumer relations, eradicating any inherent systemic differences between them; as Shirky puts it,

> in changing the relations between media and individuals, the internet does not herald the rise of a powerful consumer. The internet heralds the disappearance of the consumer altogether, because the internet destroys the noisy advertiser/silent consumer relationship that the mass media relies [sic] upon. The rise of the internet undermines the existence of the consumer because it undermines the role of mass media. In the age of the internet, no one is a passive consumer anymore because everyone is a media outlet. (2000, n.pag.)

Finally, and perhaps most problematically, this eradication of differences through the rise of the produser and the free availability of content as part of collaborative produsage projects also necessitates a fundamental shift in commercial practices. While such a shift is yet to occur in many domains, open source provides an early template for this: here, the core business of commercial operators lies no longer in the sale of products, but in the provision of services. As Dafermos points out, "making money out of open source/free software is not evil – as some people wrongly believe – as long as the community rules are strictly adhered to" (2003, n.pag.), and indeed companies such as Red Hat are highly successful in this environment even though they engage in a field where content is freely available.

Questions for News Produsage

If we apply produsage theory systematically to participatory citizen journalism, then, a number of key questions emerge – questions which also apply across the different domains of produsage overall.

Content Ownership

First, as Thake points out,

> one of the fundamental issues at stake in the open source debate is ownership of the text. There are media projects currently at work that completely destabilise concepts of ownership and copyright, projects that have the chance to point toward an altogether new, non-proprietary future. (2004, b. 2)

However, the answer cannot be simply to ignore copyright and, by implication, content ownership altogether. Open source today has found mature and sophisticated tools for addressing the shared ownership of content and permitting continuing collaborative produsage while preventing unauthorised commercial exploitation. Beyond defining what further use is acceptable for the outcomes of their own produsage processes, however, open news participants must also become more aware of the implications of their use of source materials. While some of the uses made of existing materials may be covered under applicable fair use, news commentary, or even parody exceptions to existing copyright laws, at a time of increasingly restrictive and pro-corporate revisions to copyright legislation such protections are by no means guaranteed to survive. This means that on the one hand, news produsers need to show more awareness of what is permitted under applicable laws, but on the other they also need to join the struggle to keep their practices legal.

Trust

A second key question for citizen journalism is one of trust. Again, strong parallels between open source and open news can be found here – for some time, open source has battled against perceptions which held that a community-produced, non-commercial software package could not possibly meet the standards set by proprietary competitors. It is evident from its widespread use especially in mission-critical environments – from web servers to spacecraft – that the open source community has won that battle and has demonstrated the quality of its outcomes as equivalent to, or better than, comparable commercial solutions; indeed, it is commercial operators who have been forced to some extent to reveal their source code in order to prove that no bugs or malicious code were hidden within it.

In this context, open source also profits from its ability to make available both thoroughly tested and slightly older "stable" versions of its software, *and* bleeding-edge, just-released beta versions; users can therefore choose the level of collaborative quality assurance they are comfortable with. The same, however, does not apply in open news: here, too, "the working parts of journalism are exposed. Open publishing assumes the reader is smart and might want to be a writer and an editor ... . Open publishing assumes that the reader can tell a crappy story from a good one. That the reader can find what they're after, and might help other readers looking for the same trail" (Arnison, 2003, n.pag.), but at the same time, most of the content of open news exists by necessity in a "perpetual beta" (or even alpha) version.

On the other hand, of course, this perpetual beta state is perhaps unavoidable if we adopt Eno's model of informational content as always necessarily unfinished – even in sites like *Kuro5hin* which institute elaborate communal editing processes. The unfinished nature of content, in this view, serves as a call for users both to critically approach any content they encounter and to become active produsers and further improve its quality. This is in line with the overall "power of eyeballs" argument, which holds that even in spite of brief temporary aberrations, the quality of collaborative authored content will generally show a steady improvement, and it also points to a different form of trust – one based not in traditional editorial processes but in a community of peers: "when the audience owns the medium, and owns the power to equitably compete in the same space, the medium and its forms carry a level of trust not found in any other media to date" (Bowman & Willis, 2003, p. 44).

Similar to open source, the performance of traditional content production industries may prove to be helpful here – in much the same way that perceptions of poor production quality and customer service for commercial software have driven sizeable numbers of users towards open source software, perceptions of systemic bias and commercial and political agendas in the mainstream news industry have strengthened the role of citizen journalism. As Walsh describes the developments of recent years, "once the 'news,' which journalism traditionally presents as the objective truth, was revealed to be a manufactured product – a product manufactured, moreover, by methods that seemed cynical and manipulative to many outsiders – the knowledge hegemony of journalism began to show cracks" (2003, p. 369).

The full implications of this still continuing shift remain yet to be established – but we can take *Kuro5hin*'s Rusty Foster as speaking on behalf of a large community of citizen journalists when he notes that "we may be biased, but at least we're obviously biased. And K5 has so many different points of view, that a fairer process can emerge from a balance of biases" (2001, n.pag.). The growing realisation that industrial journalism has severely compromised its professional ideals should not relieve citizen journalism from its own obligations to ethical conduct, however. As Lasica notes, those "who dabble in the journalistic process would do well to study the ethics guidelines and conflict of interest policies of news organisations that have formulated a set of standards derived from decades of trial and error" (2003b, n.pag.) – even if the enforcement of such guidelines is sometimes unacceptably lax in mainstream journalism itself.

In particular, the question of liability remains largely untested for open source, open news, and other communally prodused content. While "use at your own risk" disclaimers are more or less explicitly in place, their effectiveness in fending off potential legal action is as yet unclear – as is the question of who (in a massively co-produced project that may not require contributors to provide personal identification details) would be held responsible for any errors: operators of produsage environments may be at risk from the actions of their contributors here. Additionally, in comparison to open source, where new revisions can fix the bugs overlooked in previous iterations and are likely to be downloaded by virtually all existing users of the software, the clientele of citizen journalism news sites is more fleeting – the reach of corrections to misinformation in news stories is likely to be far more limited.

Economic Model

A third question arising from the conceptualisation of citizen journalism as a form of produsage concerns its economic models. As Shirky argues, blogs and other forms of citizen journalism cannot be commercial enterprises in themselves:

"They are such an efficient tool for distributing the written word that they make publishing a financially worthless activity. It's intuitively appealing to believe that by making the connection between writer and reader more direct, Weblogs will improve the environment for direct payments as well, but the opposite is true. By removing the barriers to publishing, Weblogs ensure that the few people who earn anything from their Weblogs will make their money indirectly" (2002, n.pag.).

This phenomenon is hardly restricted to citizen journalism, however: industrial journalism, too, has yet to develop sustainable models for online publishing – and additionally, activities such as classified advertising, which have traditionally underwritten the publication of print newspapers, are increasingly moving to stand-alone websites which are profitable in themselves, but no longer cross-subsidise news journalism. This has already led to a reduction in journalism staff in many news organisations around the world.

If sustaining themselves through selling the news is no longer a viable business model for most news organisations, let alone for citizen journalists, then citizen journalism may need to look elsewhere to ensure its sustainability. Some ideas may again be gleaned from the open source community in this context – key opportunities may be developed around what can be described as the following:

- **Harvesting the hive** – the systematic gathering of relevant content from quality citizen (and mainstream) journalism sites in order to republish it in other formats. We see beginnings of this model already in major content aggregator sites such as *Google News*, but also many smaller, more specialised aggregators. Citizen journalists may be able to build on their strengths as gatewatchers in this context and offer this gatewatching service to the general public (funded by donations, subscriptions, or advertising) or to paying clients wishing to keep track of current views in the extended mediasphere.
- **Harbouring the hive** – the commercial provision of spaces for produser communities. While not a commercial entity in its own right, the Wikimedia Foundation, as well as the loosely related wiki hosting service Wikia provide useful models here, as does *Sourceforge* in the open source field, or *Flickr* (which offers fee-paying "pro" accounts in addition to its basic free option) for creative produsage. The viability of such services depends on the willingness of produser communities to pay for commercial hosting, however – and while numerous commercial blog providers exist, the same may not be the case for hosting solutions for collaborative citizen journalism sites (see Bruns, 2008).

If neither of these models offers a great deal of sustainable economic support for citizen journalism, then this should cause significant concern for proponents of such activities. However, in open source itself, individual contributors often make a living in paid employment and have part of their work time set aside to contribute to open source projects as this is seen to benefit the employer in turn, or they cross-subsidise their open source development activities from income generated through making available their expertise in installing, developing, and maintaining open source software packages. In either case, in other words, they contribute freely to content development but sell ancillary services related to the content they have been involved in developing.

It is interesting to consider how such models could translate to citizen journalism. On the one hand, an argument could be established that employers (especially perhaps in the public sector) should permit their staff to participate in citizen journalism activities, as this would benefit society overall. The participation of professionally employed journalists in bona fide citizen journalism projects (that is, engagement beyond the pseudo-blogs currently operated by many mainstream news websites) could also boost their own and their news organisation's standing in the wider community. On the other hand, individual citizen journalists might also be able to commercialise the skills gained in their engagement in citizen journalism, for example, by becoming paid media pundits or by advising commercial clients on the dynamics of online communities. However, such citizen journalism consultancy models, ranging from for-pay blogging schemes which encourage bloggers to spread positive messages about specific products to persistent politically biased interference in *Wikipedia* content, can generate significant community backlash, too.

Conclusion

The twin questions of how to finance citizen journalism sites and citizen journalists' participation in them therefore remain of paramount importance for the overall collaborative open news project. Even in spite of such serious questions of sustainability, and in spite of the continuing ambivalent response to citizen journalism from the traditional journalism industry, however, citizen journalism has already shown a strong impact on journalism itself, and some journalists and journalism organisations, at least, look at these new models "through the professional lens of a "competitor-colleague" journalism which may yet prove to be the crucible for new ways of reconnecting journalism, news and media professionals with ideals of sharing access and participatory storytelling in journalism" (Platon & Deuze, 2003, p. 352).

Perhaps a more fundamental task is to ensure a broad societal basis for participation in the project. As Bardoel and Deuze warn, "in general, the new opportunities will, as always, favour the privileged, while people on the other side of the "digital divide" will continue to rely on public service-orientated mediators" (2001, p. 99), but such divisions are not acceptable for citizen journalism in the longer term. Heikkilä and Kunelius similarly note that "public participation requires certain cultural and social competences that are not evenly distributed in societies. It may be that criteria set for what is reasonable and constructive discussion suit the educated, and relatively well paid journalists and their peers, but probably not all the citizens" (2002, n.pag.), but if this divide cannot be overcome, citizen journalism itself may be doomed to fail.

On the other hand, if broad societal involvement in citizen journalism can be established – if a critical mass can be found – then even dubious financial sustainability will not be able to undermine the overall citizen journalism project. As in open source, and as in so many other produsage models, in that case a lack of steady financial support could force a further decentralisation of citizen journalism across a wide range of networked websites, wikis, and blogs, but it could not diminish citizens' enthusiasm for participating in such collaborative produsage-based environments.

If this is indeed the case, then, as Rushkoff has put it, "in an era when crass perversions of populism, and exaggerated calls for national security, threaten the very premises of representational democracy and free discourse, interactive technologies offer us a ray of hope for a renewed spirit of genuine civic engagement" (2003, p. 16). If this hope can be realised, then the *Slashdot*s, *Indymedia*s, and *Wikipedia*s of citizen journalism might come and go, but the overall paradigm shift in informational content creation from production to produsage continues on. "The best evidence we have that something truly new is going on is our mainstream media's inability to understand it" (Rushkoff, 2003, pp. 53–4).

References

Arnison, M. (2002). *Open editing: A crucial part of open publishing.* Accessed December 11, 2003, from http://www.cat.org.au/maffew/cat/openedit.html

Arnison, M. (2003). *Open publishing is the same as free software.* Accessed December 11, 2003, from http://www.cat.org.au/maffew/cat/openpub.html

Bardoel, J., & Deuze, M. (2001). 'Network journalism': Converging competencies of old and new media professionals. *Australian Journalism Review, 23*(3), 91–103.

Bowman, S., & Willis, C. (2003). *We media: How audiences are shaping the future of news and information.* Reston, VA: The Media Center at the American Press Institute. Accessed May 21, 2004, from http://www.hypergene.net/wemedia/download/we_media.pdf

Bruns, A. (2003). *From blogs to open news: Notes towards a taxonomy of P2P publications.* Paper presented at ANZCA 2003 conference in Brisbane, July 9–11, 2003. Accessed November 20, 2004, from http://www.bgsb.qut.edu.au/conferences/ANZCA03/Proceedings/papers/bruns_full.pdf

Bruns, A. (2005). *Gatewatching: Collaborative online news production.* New York: Peter Lang.

Bruns, A. (2006). Wikinews: The next generation of online news? *Scan Journal, 3*(1). Accessed October 31, 2006, from http://scan.net.au/scan/journal/display.php?journal_id=69

Bruns, A. (2008). *Blogs, Wikipedia, second life, and beyond: From production to produsage.* New York: Peter Lang.

Chan, A. J. (2002). *Collaborative news networks: Distributed editing, collective action, and the construction of online news on Slashdot.org.* M.Sc. thesis, MIT. Accessed February 6, 2003, from http://web.mit.edu/anita1/www/thesis/Index.html

Dafermos, G. (2003). The search for community and profit: Slashdot and OpenFlows. *George Dafermos' radio weblog.* Accessed September 6, 2004, from http://radio.weblogs.com/0117128/stories/2003/04/03/theSearchForCommunityAndProfitSlashdotAndOpenflows.html

Foster, R. (2001). The utter failure of weblogs as journalism. *Kuro5hin.* Accessed September 27, 2004, from http://www.kuro5hin.org/story/2001/10/11/232538/32

Gans, H. J. (1980). *Deciding what's news: A study of CBS Evening News, NBC Nightly News, Newsweek, and Time.* New York: Vintage.

Gibson, J., & Kelly, A. (2000). Become the media. *Arena Magazine, 49,* 10–1.

Gillmor, D. (2003a). Foreword. In S. Bowman & C. Willis (Eds.), *We media: How audiences are shaping the future of news and information.* Reston, VA: The Media Center at the American Press Institute. Accessed May 21, 2004, from http://www.hypergene.net/wemedia/download/we_media.pdf

Gillmor, D. (2003b). Moving toward participatory journalism. *Nieman Reports*, pp. 79–80.

Heikkilä, H., & Kunelius, R. (2002). Access, dialogue, deliberation: Experimenting with three concepts of journalism criticism. *The international media and democracy project.* Accessed February 20, 2004, from http://www.imdp.org/artman/publish/article_27.shtml

Hiler, J. (2002). Blogosphere: The emerging media ecosystem: How weblogs and journalists work together to report, filter and break the news. *Microcontent news: The online magazine for weblogs, webzines, and personal publishing.* Accessed May 31, 2004, from http://www.microcontentnews.com/articles/blogosphere.htm

Kelly, K. (1995), *Gossip is philosophy.* Interview with Brian Eno, *Wired* 3.05. Accessed September 27, 2004, http://www.wired.com/wired/archive/3.05/eno.html

Lasica, J. D. (2003a). Participatory journalism puts the reader in the driver's seat. *Online Journalism Review.* Accessed February 20, 2004, from http://www.ojr.org/ojr/workplace/1060218311.php

Lasica, J. D. (2003b). Random acts of journalism: Beyond 'is it or isn't it journalism?': How blogs and journalism need each other0. *JD's blog: New media musings.* Accessed September 27, 2004, from http://www.jdlasica.com/blog/archives/2003_03_12.html

Meikle, G. (2002). *Future active: Media activism and the internet.* New York: Routledge.

New Forms of Journalism: Weblogs, Community News, Self-Publishing and More (2001). Panel on 'journalism's new life forms,' second annual conference of the Online News Association, University of California, Berkeley, CA. Accessed May 31, 2004, from http://www.jdlasica.com/articles/ONApanel.html

Platon, S., & Deuze, M. (2003). Indymedia journalism: A radical way of making, selecting and sharing news? *Journalism, 4*(3), 336–55.

Rushkoff, D. (2003). *Open source democracy: How online communication is changing offline politics.* London: Demos. Accessed April 22, 2004, from http://www.demos.co.uk/opensourcedemocracy_pdf_media_public.aspx

Shirky, C. (2000). RIP the consumer, 1900–1999. *Clay Shirky's Writings about the Internet: Economics & Culture, Media & Community, Open Source.* Accessed May 31, 2004, from http://www.shirky.com/writings/consumer.html

Shirky, C. (2002). Weblogs and the mass amateurization of publishing. *Clay shirky's writings about the internet: Economics & culture, media & community, open source.* Accessed February 20, 2004, from http://www.shirky.com/writings/weblogs_publishing.html

Stalder, F., & Hirsh, J. (2002). Open source intelligence. *First Monday, 7*(6). Accessed April 22, 2004, from http://www.firstmonday.org/issues/issue7_6/stalder/

Thake, W. (2004). Editing and the crisis of open source. *M/C Journal, 7*(3). Accessed October 1, 2004, from http://journal.media-culture.org.au/0406/04_Thake.php

Trendwatching.com (2005). *Customer-made.* Accessed October 31, 2005, from http://www.trendwatching.com/trends/CUSTOMERMADE.htm

Walsh, P. (2003). That withered paradigm: The web, the expert, and the information hegemony. In H. Jenkins & D. Thorburn (Eds.), *Democracy and new media* (pp. 365–72). Cambridge, MA: MIT Press.

Yeomans, M. (2005). The birth of Wikinews. *Citizen's Kane.* Accessed September 19, 2005, from http://citizenskane.blogspot.com/

The Mereology of Digital Copyright

Dan L. Burk

Introduction

The development of the internet has facilitated widespread access to a vast array of digitized works in a variety of electronic formats. Increased access to such digitized works has heightened the need for robust systems that can identify and index online resources, in order to allow users to locate and access the new wealth of digitized materials in what amounts to a global virtual library (Goldman, 2006). Cataloging and indexing has always been critical to library functions, but never more so than in the decentralized, emergent library that constitutes the internet. Consequently, search engines such as the Google database have developed as key tools for facilitating access to online resources; if the resource is not indexed via such a database, it effectively ceases to exist (Introna & Nissenbaum, 2000).

Such control over access to digital resources implicates control over the use and disposition of those resources. Information cannot be used until it is found. In the physical world, control of information has been incident to physical or legal ownership that determines access or exclusion. Works of creative authorship have long been subject to ownership under the rubric of copyright law, which offers defined exclusive rights as an incentive for creation and publication of expressive works. However, the copyright system that developed in a world of hardcopy print is challenged both by the technology of digitization and by the construction of metadata indexes for digitized works. Rules of ownership developed to control access to atoms apply only uncertainly when used to control access to bits.

The troubled interplay between copyright and digital expression is nowhere more apparent than in the controversial Google Book Search project, where search engine technology intersects with indexed databases scanned into electronic format from hardcopy materials. In this article, I analyze the copyright status of this project, using it as a vehicle to develop certain themes that are emerging as fundamental issues in the copyright of digitized texts. Specifically, I look at copyright's treatment

D.L. Burk (✉)
University of California, Irvine, California, USA
e-mail: dburk@uci.edu

J. Hunsinger et al. (eds.), *International Handbook of Internet Research*,
DOI 10.1007/978-1-4020-9789-8_7, © Springer Science+Business Media B.V. 2010

of the relationship of parts of digital texts to the whole: copyright's mereology of digital texts.

I begin by describing the Google Book Search project, touching briefly on the legal rationale relied upon by Google for scanning copyrighted works into its database without permission of the copyright holders. I then move to the issue that has received less attention: the copyright status of the metadata relational database that is the core of the project. This database, I argue, is emblematic of the broader issues facing copyright in an age of digitization, and I discuss several cases that bear upon the legal status of such a meta-database. I conclude by sketching the challenges that copyright law will need to encompass as works of authorship move from fixation as atoms to recordation as bits.

The Google Book Project

The Google Book Search project is an ambitious – even audacious – attempt to make available via the internet a searchable database of texts previously available only as bound, printed matter (Band, 2005). The project uses Google search engine technology to achieve indexing and retrieval of texts that have been scanned from printed format to digital format. But the scanning process requires access to the physical printed texts. This has been accomplished via two complementary initiatives. The first of these initiatives is the uncontroversial "publisher program" in which publishers provide copies of books to be scanned, or if available, provide electronic files of book text, under terms specified by the publisher. The second portion of the Google effort has been more controversial. Google has entered into agreements with several libraries, including those of Harvard University, the University of Michigan, the New York Public Library, and Oxford University, to gain access to and scan all or part of the library's holdings. The exact terms of the agreements are undisclosed, but it is clear that at least some of these agreements will result in scanning of books for which the library owns the physical volume, but does not have the right to make or authorize making of copies, including scanned digital copies.

In both portions of the project book pages are scanned to produce high-quality, but not archival quality images. The scanned images are then parsed by Google search technology. At present, Google is keeping the original images stored and has agreed to provide copies of the original images back to the library from which the book was scanned. But the images are not the database which users search or from which results are returned. Rather, a relational database built up from the scanned images is the core of the project. An index is built of each word in the scanned text and its relationship to nearby words. This relational database is made available via the Google website. When a user searches the database using keywords, a snippet of the text is returned, comprising the keyword sought and a certain number of surrounding words. If a book is deemed to be in the public domain, the full text may be made available; if the book is still in copyright, the availability of text is restricted.

Although access to the re-constructed text is parsimonious, the mere scanning of the books to produce the relational database has created a firestorm of controversy. But Google has argued that obtaining permission to scan the books would be prohibitive – even determining whether permission is needed would be prohibitive. Prior to 1978, copyright in the United States was granted for a term of years, with renewable extension. Some authors may have failed to renew the copyright for the extended term, in which case the work may have fallen into the public domain and may be copied freely – but it will often be difficult to determine whether a work was renewed. Additionally, since the early 1990s, US copyright law has not required that a copyright notice be placed on published works. Prior to that time, publication of a work without notice automatically placed it into the public domain, so that lack of a notice signaled that the work could be freely copied. This is no longer a requirement for published works, so more recently published works that are protected by copyright may have no indication of who held the copyright when the work was published.

And the complexity of book determining a book's copyright status does not end there. Copyright may have been transferred to an entity other than the author or publisher; publishers may have gone out of business; authors may be deceased; the heirs of authors, who may or may not have inherited the copyright to the work, may be difficult or impossible to locate. Consequently, the cost of simply locating the copyright holders of many books, in order to obtain permission for their works to be scanned into the database, is potentially enormous. Naturally, if copyright holders for the books can be located, some may decline permission to scan the book, diminishing the usefulness of the resultant database with each permission denied. But such refusals are a relatively simple and straightforward problem; it is equally likely that copyright owners, once located, could demand idiosyncratic fees or place restrictions on the use of the scanned work – the cost of such fees, as well as the cost of negotiating such permissions, would further add to the expense of creating the database.

This scenario appears to threaten the creation of an "anti-commons" that might stifle the development of a comprehensive book database, whether compiled by Google or by anyone else. Typically, property rights are allocated to prevent the so-called tragedy of the commons, where resources are misallocated because no one is motivated by ownership interests to maintain the resource (Boyle, 2003). But an "anti-commons" can potentially occur in situations where permissions from multiple property holders are necessary to complete a project and where the transactions cost of obtaining such permissions becomes prohibitive – that is, where there are too many property rights and rights holders, rather than too few (Heller, 1998).

Google has attempted to solve this problem by moving ahead with the scanning of books, but giving publishers and authors the option of requesting that their work not be scanned into the database. This approach effectively shifts the burden of asserting exclusive rights to copyright holders, requiring them to come forward and "opt out" of the project. Copyright holders have complained that this approach impermissibly inverts the basic exclusivity premise of intellectual property: that copying is prohibited unless authorized. However, the Google "opt-out" procedure operates from the premise that Google has the right to copy the works, but as a courtesy will refrain from doing so if asked. Much of the legal controversy to date over the Google "opt-out" assertion has focused upon determining how Google could claim to be in a position to make copies without obtaining advance copyright permission.

The legal justification for Google's opt-out position rests largely on the American doctrine of fair use, a highly flexible, fact-specific exception to the rights of copyright holders. This American exception to the exclusive rights of copyright holders has been explained by some commentators as a solution to the problem of high transaction costs (Gordon, 1982; Loren, 1997). This theory of "fair use as market failure" argues that fair use is necessary when the transaction costs of reaching agreement on authorized use is too high – when the copyright owner cannot be easily found, or demands a fee in excess of the value of the use, or the negotiations are protracted and cumbersome, and so on. In such cases the law permits the user to circumvent the negotiation process and move ahead with the use, effectively taking a compulsory license at a zero royalty (Burk, 1999). Often this will occur in the case of minor, de minimis uses, where the value of the use is relatively low relative to the costs of search, negotiation, and so on. But it could also occur when the value of the use is high and aggregate search costs are prohibitive, as in the anti-commons scenario.

Several US cases have held that producing a temporary or intermediate copy, which is produced in the process of developing a product different than the copyrighted work, is a fair use. For example, courts have repeatedly held that a copy of software made in the process of decompiling the software for reverse engineering, in order to produce an interoperable complimentary product or even a competing product, is fair (Samuelson, 1993). The copy made is temporary, it is made in order to extract unprotected information about functionality, the result is a different product altogether, and the intermediate copy is not part of the product marketed to the public. A similar rationale might be applied to the Google Book Search database. The scanned images are unnecessary to the final product; although images are being provided to the partner libraries, they can be discarded. They are not the end product that is to be offered to the public; rather, they are a mechanism or vehicle for creating the end product, which is the searchable database. These considerations make Google's fair use position at least tenable and perhaps even decisive in the United States – but reliance on this US doctrine has prompted Google to restrict book search access to internet users in the United States.

Such aspects of the Google project are fascinating and critically important. But they have already received treatment elsewhere and are likely to be the subject of further analysis and critique (Band, 2005). For this article, they are necessary primarily as a backdrop to a different set of issues that are foregrounded in the Google project, but which are endemic to digital copyright. Here I wish to focus on the more fundamental and potentially far-reaching problem, of ownership over metadata in digitized works. This analysis centers on the database that Google is building from the scanned texts, rather than the act of scanning images. The database appears to consist of words and of metadata defining the relationship between those words. As a matter of black-letter copyright law, words are not protected by copyright, so no book publisher or author can claim copyright infringement of individual words. But more troubling is the status of the meta-database that records the relationship between those words. The question I consider there, then, is whether Google has created an infringing copy of copyrighted books by building a database that allows disaggregated words to be re-assembled into the text of those books.

Defining Digital Copies

The first question in determining whether Google's database infringes the copyright in the scanned book texts is whether Google has made a *copy* for purposes of the copyright statute. Somewhat surprisingly, the first answer to this question dates back to the beginning of the 20th century, to the advent of automated player pianos, which played popular songs from paper rolls in which the music was coded as punched holes. Music composers objected that such piano rolls – precursors to the punch cards on which computer data were later stored – when made without their permission infringed the copyright in their musical compositions. But the US Supreme Court held that such piano rolls did not fall under the copyright statute, but were rather a piece of a machine that produced music, akin to a cog or toothed wheel in a music box. Machines and other functional devices are not covered by copyright; if covered by intellectual property law at all, they belong to the patent system. Consequently, the encoding of copyrighted music as punched holes was held not to constitute a violation of the copyright. (*White-Smith Music Publishing Co.*, 1907).

Congress responded to this decision, and to the ensuing distress of music composers, by creating a new category of copyrightable work, the phonorecord, intended to bring sound recordings within the Copyright Act. Soon the category of phonorecords also encompassed the phonograph record in which sounds were recorded as grooves in vinyl discs – a critically important format for the distribution of popular music. In fact, this category of copyrightable fixation would eventually extend to encoding of music in a series of successive technological media: the magnetic flux of reel to reel, eight-track, and cassette tapes, as well as the optical pits of compact discs. Since each of these formats, as well as other new media such as videotape, could be considered parts of a machine in the same sense as a player piano roll, Congress also amended the statutory definition of copies to include both those media "now known or later developed" from which the work could be perceived by a human being unaided, and from which perception of a work required the aid of a machine.

The media "later developed" to instantiate copyrightable works of course came to include digital media, perceived with the aid of a computer – the logical successors to the player piano roll (Burk, 2000). Coin-operated video arcade games were among the earliest digitized works considered under this provision. The popularity of these games during the 1970s and 1980s led to unauthorized "knock-offs" of the most popular games and to copyright suits against the copyists. Game developers had registered videotapes of the game displays with the federal Copyright Office, but copyists argued that such game displays did not satisfy the requirements for copyright because the game output was not fixed in the circuits that generated the display – what was fixed was a computer program that produced the output. As evidence that the display was unfixed, the copyists pointed out that the game display changed each time the game was played, in response to player input. In a related argument, the copyists pointed out that no copy of the work was contained in the chips; rather, the work was generated from instructions programmed into the chip. A variety of instructions or programs might produce the same output, and registration of the display should not entitle the copyright holder to every set of instructions producing such a display.

In cases such as *Stern Electronics v. Kaufmann* and *Williams Electronics v. Artic International*, the courts rejected such arguments on the basis of the statutory definition, holding that if the work could be perceived with the aid of a machine, then it must be fixed in the game's semiconductor chip. But under this holding, "perceive" must implicitly include *generation* or re-assembly of a work. The pattern of voltages in a chip and the pattern of magnetic flux on a disc are both profoundly and subtly different than the grooves of a vinyl phonograph record. Such analog recordings use one physical quantity to represent another. Consequently, analog media maintain some relationship within the record of a work corresponding to the relationships within the work itself. Digital records need not maintain such analogous relationships, but are instead series of sequences of bits that can be read to re-construct the work. While the digital version of the work is in some sense a record of the work, it is not a *recording* of the work as found in previous media.

Thus, unlike a microform reader which simply amplifies human perception, computer code constitutes a set of instructions for generating the work perceived – but the courts held that perception of output implied existence of a digital copy. As a corollary, these cases also skirted the contested definitional lines between "data" and "software" – a sequence of bits containing the *instructions* to generate music or text and a sequence of bits constituting the *record* of digitized music or text appear to be treated identically under these opinions. The *Stern* and *Williams* courts were likely less concerned with the technicalities of digital processing than they were with the end product of the process – an audiovisual work that, to all appearances, fell within copyright's statutory subject matter – and with developing a plausible social policy for such end products. Consequently, these early gaming cases proved pivotal to establishing the copyrightability of computer programs, but their implications for storage of digital copies may not be consistent with more recent decisions.

New York Times v. Tasini

The relationship between the arrangement of text in hardcopy materials and arrangement of digitized texts within a database was central to the decision of the US Supreme Court in *New York Times v. Tasini*. The *Tasini* case involved an infringement claims by independently contracted or freelance writers who had licensed stories to a wide variety of periodical publications: newspapers and magazines including the New York Times, Time magazine, and Newsday. Many of these hardcopy periodicals had, since licensing or purchasing the freelance stories, begun making their contents available in searchable full-text electronic format. Some periodicals developed online databases, others provided their contents on CD-ROM or similar electronic formats. Because the licenses or copyright transfers from the authors were executed before electronic versions of periodicals became common, the transfers did not address publication of the stories in databases or other electronic formats. Consequently, the authors claimed that inclusion of their stories in electronic formats was an unauthorized re-publication of their work, for which no rights had been granted to the periodical publishers.

In defense, the publishers relied upon section 201 of the copyright statute, which both establishes copyright in collective works and distinguishes such copyright from that in the individual contributions to a collective work. Under this section of the statute, copyright may subsist in the original selection and arrangement of copyrighted works in a collective work, such as an anthology. This copyright in the collective work is separate and distinct from the copyright in any given work included in the collective work – copyright in the constituent works need not be transferred to the author or compiler of a collective work. The holder of the collective work copyright is limited in the subsequent uses to which she may put the individual works comprising the collective work. Absent transfer of the copyright in the constituent works, the holder of the collective work copyright may use the constituent works only in a revision or re-issue of the initial collective work.

The publishers argued that the databases constituted a "revision" of the hardcopy periodical issues in which articles originally appeared, and therefore the publishers had the right to include the articles in the database collections. But this defense was rejected by the Supreme Court, which held that the periodical databases or electronic versions of the periodicals were not equivalent to the print versions. The Court reasoned that the articles in the databases had been disaggregated from their sequence and relationship in the print edition. Because the articles were no longer in the context of their original publication, but rather divorced of their print media relationships, the section 201 revisioning privilege did not apply.

The Court rejected the contention that the electronic and CD databases contained the original periodicals despite the fact that articles retrieved in searches would display the pagination and publication markings of the periodical in which they were originally published. The Court held that such indicia were indicative of the article having previously appeared in the periodical, but were not indicative of the article as retrieved being part of the periodical. Rather, the articles were better thought of as components of a super-compendium or library consisting of all the disaggregated articles, and such a super-compendium was not equivalent to the original periodical. The Court specifically rejected an analogy to microform records, as microforms, unlike electronic databases, recorded the original sequence of the periodicals. The court also rejected the argument that because the users of the databases could re-assemble the articles into the original sequence, that database was a revision to the original periodicals, anymore than a hardcopy library from which a patron could retrieve and re-assemble a periodical sequence would be a "revision" of those periodicals.

Matthew Bender v. West Publishing Co.

A similar set of issues is found in copyright cases considering the protectability of relationships within the compiled text of volumes of judicial opinions. The development of legal research databases from these opinions occasioned the disputes in such cases, when West Publishing Company attempted to prevent rival database publishers from adopting a standardized case citation format. West Publishing was and remains the major publisher of bound, hardcopy volumes of judicial reports, collecting the judicial opinions from essentially every jurisdiction in the United States. While some jurisdictions published their own reporters, in many instances, the West reporter volumes were the only judicial reporters for certain jurisdictions.

Consequently, citation to the West reporter volumes became effectively an industry standard: anyone practicing in the legal profession used citations to the West bound hardcopy reports, not only in office documents and memoranda but in official documents filed with the court system. Law students across the United States were trained to use West citations as an essential component of their professional preparation. Judicial opinions routinely used West citations. Indeed, many courts required attorneys practicing before them to use West citations in motions and briefs and allowed the use of no other system, because the West reporter volumes were most commonly available to judges searching for and citing to judicial precedent.

With the advent of electronic storage and retrieval systems containing searchable, full-text versions of judicial opinions, West transferred its reporter volume text to electronic format. West's subscription database, Westlaw, used the "star pagination" system, which inserted into the electronic text of opinions numerical markers corresponding to the location of pages in the bound hardcopy reporter volumes. A rival legal publisher provided a competing product made up of judicial opinions on CD-ROM discs that could be accessed by a purchaser's own machine rather than via online database access. The text of these opinions on CD-ROM included "star pagination" markers relating judicial opinion text to the published West reporter volumes – without such citations to the West volumes, the electronic databases would be essentially useless to lawyers and other legal professionals.

However, West sued to prevent its competitors from using such pagination markers, arguing that appropriation of the star pagination citations was essentially appropriation of their published volumes – arguing, in other words, that such markers, indicating the position of text in the published volumes, mapped onto the published volume in such a way as to effectively constitute a copy of the hardcopy book. According to West the CD-ROM discs comprised "copies" of the West reporter volumes because the selection and arrangement of cases in the West reporters could be perceived with the aid of a machine by use of the star pagination markers. In other words, by following the star pagination markers, a user could employ the automated functions of the CD-ROM to view or print cases in the same order found in the bound West reporter volumes, and this meant that the CD-ROMs contained copies of the West volumes.

The court rejected this argument, holding that offering the capability to regenerate the West volumes was not equivalent to offering copies of the West volumes. The sequence of page breaks signified by star pagination was not itself original, as it was created by a mechanical typesetting process and not by any creative selection and arrangement of West's. Moreover, even though star pagination markers might reveal to a reader how the West arrangement could be recreated, that arrangement was not fixed in the CD-ROM disc. Only manipulation of the data by a user would produce the West volume case sequence, and the products of user manipulation were copies fixed in the discs. Distinguishing the video game cases such as *Stern Electronics*, the court reasoned that adopting West's argument regarding fixation would effectively extend West's copyright to all arrangements or re-arrangements that could be generated by a user, and West was not entitled to control user-generated arrangements.

Copyright and Metadata

Although the Google project is novel is scope and vision, digitized works have been the subject of copyright controversy for well over a quarter century, so that previous cases offer some suggestion as to how Google's meta-database should be regarded. The precedent that seems most relevant to the status of the Google database may appear to point in different directions. Taken on their own, the early videogame cases seem to suggest that the form of digital fixation is itself irrelevant; so long as the copyrighted work can be re-generated as output from the circuits of a machine, it does not matter what kind of coding or instructions one would find at the machine level. This in turn seems to indicate that the set of instructions, or meta-data, necessary to re-construct a copyrighted work itself constitutes an infringing copy of the work – that the metadata describing a work reproduces the originality in the work.

But it is not clear that this result is sensible, that instructions leading to a particular selection and arrangement are necessarily equivalent to selection and arrangement itself. Certainly this would not be the result if considering written instructions to a human, rather than coded instructions to a machine – if, for example, an art expert meticulously examined a famous painting and then wrote out detailed instructions for re-creating the painting, brush stroke by brush stroke, it seems fairly clear that such instructions would not be considered to constitute a copy of the initial painting. The same would surely be true if the instructions were implemented by a machine; if a copyist developed a mechanical painting arm and programmed it to reproduce in fine detail the brush strokes of a painting, even if the product of the mechanical arm constituted a copy of the initial painting, the program instructing the movements of the mechanical arm would not be a copy. Such instructions might themselves warrant copyright protection, although that protection would likely be minimal, since the underlying process is excluded from copyright protection, and only whatever creativity might be found in the expression of the instructions could be covered by copyright. But the copyright in the instructions would clearly not cover the result of following the instructions.

Later cases dealing with digitized hardcopy works suggest that when individual uncopyrightable elements of a copyrighted work are stored electronically so as to disrupt the relationship found between them in the original work, no copy has been made. Although decided in the context of a very specific statutory provision – section 201 – the reasoning in *Tasini* suggests that digital versions of hardcopy materials do not infringe copyright in the hardcopy text, due to the disaggregation that occurs in digital storage and retrieval. Neither did the Supreme Court view user initiated re-assembly of the hardcopy sequence as infringement, due to the disaggregated nature of the database from which the user was working. The presence of metadata sufficient to re-assemble the original texts did not change this view. This tends to suggest that neither the Google database of disaggregated book text nor the meta-database of book text relationships should be viewed as infringing copies of the books.

Much as in the *Tasini* decision, the analysis in *West* suggests that neither disaggregated digitized text nor relational metadata regarding that text constitute a copy of the original text for purposes of the copyright statute. But the reasoning in the *West* decision bears even more directly upon the Google situation, as this analysis is not seen through the lens of section 201 republication. Unlike the databases in *Tasini* and *West*, the Google Book Search database does not maintain the works scanned into it as discrete retrievable works, but atomizes them to the level of individual words. The largest retrievable chunk is a snippet of a few dozen words. Thus the Google database resembles its original texts even less than did the databases in *Tasini* and *West* and seems even less likely to constitute and infringing copy.

The analysis in these cases demarcates a general set of concerns not only for the Google project but for digital copyright generally. Although the law of copyright was developed in an analog world, creative works of all kinds are now captured as series of sequences of bits rather than as analog records. This change in the fixation of works has several consequences that are problematic for the basic doctrines of copyright. Most of these consequences flow from the fungible nature of bits. Previous analog media typically encoded different types of works in different formats – motion pictures were not recorded as grooves in vinyl; musical compositions were not recorded as grains of silver nitrate on celluloid. But digitized music or software or text are all just sequences of bits, not anything that can as encoded be differentiated as pictures or music or text. Data processors make no distinction between bits that represent a photograph or painting or a piece of music or a piece of text, or for that matter between bits representing a copyrightable work and bits representing something uncopyrightable, such as a Fourier transform series.

Because digital records use this common building block of the bit, it is possible to arrange that common building block into all kinds of copyrightable works. In this sense, digital media turns everything – all kinds of copyrightable works – into databases, into compilations of fungible elements (Burk, 2005). Everything is reduceable to discrete elements, none of which is individually original. This in turn means that there must necessarily be some type of metadata, some type of organizational instruction, as to the manner in which the bits are to be reassembled. And it is at this level that the original expression necessary for copyright protection must reside, in the manner in which the bits have been arranged to encode music or text or graphics. There is nothing original in any of the individual bits that can be read to constitute a photograph or text or musical composition. The originality lies not in the components, the bits of information, but in the way that the bits of information are arranged.

Such atomistic reduction of copyrighted works to fungible units may not necessarily be the product of digital technologies; previous media show the same characteristics to some degree. For example, it is possible to view print media as an arrangement of individual letters from the alphabet into words, and at the next level of organization, as an arrangement of individual words into a novel, play, or poem. This reductionist view presents the same doctrinal problem: surely the letter "A" is not of itself protectable in copyright, nor is the letter "B," nor are individual words. The only original aspect of the work must be the author's selection and arrangement of the words and letters. The same is true in the case of other copyrightable works, such as a musical composition or an Impressionist painting. No individual dab of paint or musical note will entail the requisite originality for copyright. Rather, the arrangement of the dabs of paint and the arrangement of individual notes, structured to communicate a particular idea, are original.

Thus, the essence of copyright seems to lie in original selection and arrangement of fungible elements (Burk, 2005). Digitization makes this result more apparent, because it facilitates the disaggregation of individual elements. Although this principle could be applied to previous analog or physical types of media, it was largely a matter of academic or philosophical speculation – an exercise in determining how many works of original authorship could dance on the head of a pin. But the issue is now unavoidable, and therein lies the paradox for copyright doctrine: copyrightable selection and arrangement cannot exist in a vacuum, there must be selection and arrangement of *something*. This seems to be the message of the *Tasini* and *West* decisions. Relational metadata, as generated in *Tasini* or *West* or in the Google Book Search database, is a description of the selection and arrangement of atomistic elements in the work described, but cannot itself be a copy of the work, because the metadata does not incorporate the atomized elements of the work.

This is presumably good news for the Google project, as it argues powerfully against their disaggregated textual database constituting an infringing copy, quite apart from an analysis of fair use. But this reductionist conclusion also in some sense places copyright doctrine on a collision course with itself. If no individual bit of data warrants copyright protection, and the metadata used to arrange such bits also fails the criteria for copyright, then it is unclear what in digital content might warrant copyright protection. Indeed, this outcome implies that the Google meta-database itself, for all the investment that has gone into it, is no more eligible for copyright protection than any other digital work in the database of databases that comprises the emerging global information structure. The ongoing challenge to encourage such investments will be to strike a balance between holism and reductionism in the mereology of digital copyright.

References

17 U.S.C. § 101 (2000).
17 U.S.C. § 102 (2000).
17 U.S.C. § 106 (2000).
17 U.S.C. § 107 (2000).
17 U.S.C. § 201 (2000).
Band, J. (2005). The Google print library project: Fair or foul? *Journal of Internet Law, 9*, 1–4.
Boyle, J. (2003). The second enclosure movement and the construction of the public domain. *Law & Contemporary Problems, 66*, 33–74.
Burk, D. (1999). Muddy rules for cyberspace. *Cardozo Law Review, 21*, 121–179.
Burk, D. (2000). Patenting speech. *Texas Law Review, 79*, 99–162.
Burk, D. (2005). Expression, selection, abstraction: Copyright's golden braid. *Syracuse Law Review, 55*, 593–618.
Goldman, E. (2006). Search engine bias and the demise of search engine utopianism. *Yale Journal of Law and Technology, 8*, 188–199.
Gordon, W. J. (1982). Fair use as market failure: A structural and economic analysis of the Betamax case and its predecessors. *Columbia Law Review, 82*, 1600–1657.
Heller, M. (1998). The tragedy of the anticommons: Property in the transition from Marx to markets. *Harvard Law Review, 11*, 621–688.
Introna, L., & Nissenbaum, H. (2000). Shaping the web: Why the politics of search engines matters. *The Information Society, 16*, 1–17.
Loren, L. P. (1997). Redefining the market failure approach to fair use in an era of copyright permission systems. *Journal of Intellectual Property Law, 5*, 1–58.
Matthew Bender & Co. v. West Publishing. Co., 158 F.3d 693 (2d Cir. 1998).
New York Times Co., Inc., v. Tasini, 533 U.S. 483 (2001).
Samuelson, P. (1993). Fair use for computer programs and other copyrightable works in digital form: The implications of *Sony, Galoob* and *Sega. Journal of Intellectual Property Law, 1*, 49–118.
Stern Electronics Co. v. Kaufmann, 669 F.2d 852 (2d Cir. 1982).
White-Smith Music Publishing Company v. Apollo Company, 209 U.S. 1 (1907).
Williams Electronics, Inc. v. Artic International, Inc., 685 F.2d 870 (3d Cir. 1982).

Traversing Urban Social Spaces: How Online Research Helps Unveil Offline Practice

Julie-Anne Carroll, Marcus Foth, and Barbara Adkins

Introduction

The internet has advanced to become the prime communication medium that connects many threads across the fabric of everyday life. The increasing ubiquity of internet services and applications has led many scholars to question the dichotomy between cyberspace and real space. New media and information and communication technology afford an increasingly seamless transition between mediated and unmediated forms of interaction (Boase, Horrigan, Wellman, & Rainie, 2006; Foth & Hearn, 2007; Mesch & Levanon, 2003; Wellman & Haythornthwaite, 2002). Emails are sent to friends at work to organise a night at the movies. Responses are received via email. After work on the way home, SMS (short message service) texts are exchanged to agree on the genre, film and venue. At home, friends might communicate last minute change of plans via instant messengers. And at the venue, they find each other without the need for a dedicated meeting place – a mobile phone call typically starts with the question: "Hey, where are you?"

The majority of emails, SMS texts and phone calls connect people who are proximate to each other (Wellman, 2001). Communication partners are most often collocated in the same physical area which is large enough to allow for socio-cultural diversity but small enough to be traversed easily by means of public or private transport. Additionally, the density of urban space increases. In 2006, the global share of people living in cities has grown larger than the share of people living outside cities in rural and remote areas. The continuing influx of residents into urban, peri-urban and metropolitan areas results in ecological and socio-cultural challenges. Governments at all levels are aware that the continuation of a low-density urban sprawl is not sustainable and are looking at information and communication technology (ICT), and specifically the internet as the nervous system of the city (Townsend, 2009), for answers. Urbanisation has global economic relevance

J.-A. Carroll (✉)
Queensland University of Technology, Creative Industries Precinct, Brisbane,
Queensland, Australia
e-mail: jm.carroll@qut.edu.au

J. Hunsinger et al. (eds.), *International Handbook of Internet Research*,
DOI 10.1007/978-1-4020-9789-8_8, © Springer Science+Business Media B.V. 2010

and compact city policies are being developed and implemented in capitals around the world to deal with population pressures and urban expansion.

Urban informatics is an emerging cluster of people interested in research and development at this intersection of people, place and technology with a focus on cities, locative media and mobile technology. The research approach discussed in this article is designed to produce empirical evidence to help us analyse and better understand the impact of the digital and physical design of the built environment on the health and well-being of urban residents. In this article we describe how we expand the conventional toolbox of research methods (such as surveys, focus groups and interviews) to now also include internet research methods. We highlight how the results of the analysis of data collected via a blog allowed us to understand and traverse urban social spaces.

Internet Research Methods

With the growing popularity of the internet and associated new media applications, scholars such as Jones (1999) – the Founding President of the Association of Internet Researchers (AoIR) – came up with research methods for studying internet use and online behaviour. Miller and Slater (2000) present how an ethnographic approach helped them understand the political economy of the internet in Trinidad and Tobago. And similarly, Hine (2000) proposes "virtual ethnography" as a way to study the social aspects of information provision and consumption on the internet. She later followed up with a volume which presents a set of virtual methods to examine social science research on the internet (Hine, 2005) which echoes the efforts of Jankowski & Van Selm (2008, in press) in the context of new media research. Ethnography is also the underpinning principal method of choice for Howard (2002) in his attempt to explore organisational forms built around new media and the internet.

These examples have in common that they are concerned with researching the internet per se. And similarly, newer new media such as mobile phones have also sparked creative re-appropriations of research methods to understand their use and embeddedness in work and lifestyle contexts (Hagen, Robertson, Kan, & Sadler, 2005). However, only relatively recently have internet-enabled or internet-supported research methods been receiving a wider level of attention and acceptance by academia beyond the core group of "internet researchers". Internet research methods run on the internet but an increasing number of scholars appreciate that they are not limited to the internet as a subject or an epistemological field of study. They can in fact be employed to elicit responses from any study participants who prefer to interact and engage with the study online. Yet, the research questions are not necessarily about the internet. Dillman (2007), for example, has translated and further refined the traditional survey instrument into an online delivery mode. Dutton, Carusi, & Peltu (2006) discuss their experience of conducting social research with participants who co-exist in digital worlds and consider the challenges and opportunities that require a multidisciplinary engagement of research expertise and tools.

The use of blogs – short for web logs – for the collection of research data from study participants has only recently been discovered although journals and diaries have long been used to store field notes and participant observations. Blogs enable a more participatory and real-time means to write up notes and research responses. Their use has been described in health and education as well as business contexts (Boulos, Maramba, & Wheeler, 2006; Bruns & Jacobs, 2006; Lee, Hwang, & Lee, 2006). Here we discuss the use of a blog for the purpose of encouraging urban residents of a master-planned community site to talk about their lifestyle choices and the impact these choices have on their health and well-being. Before we delve into the main discussion, we present our case study site.

The Case of an Urban Village Development

The Kelvin Grove Urban Village (KGUV) is the Queensland Government's flagship urban renewal project. Through its Department of Housing, and in partnership with Queensland University of Technology, this 16 hectare master-planned community (see Fig. 1) seeks to demonstrate best practice in sustainable, mixed-use urban development. By "linking learning with enterprise and creative industry with community", the KGUV (www.kgurbanvillage.com.au) is designed to evolve as a diverse city fringe neighbourhood. Situated 2 km from Brisbane's CBD, it is based

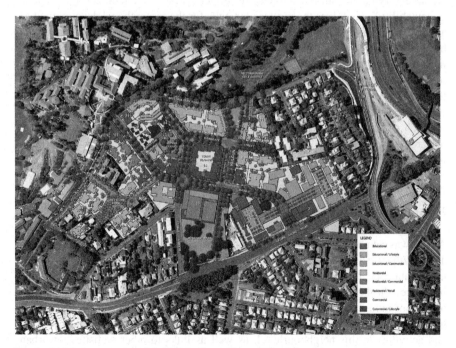

Fig. 1 Aerial shot courtesy of the Kelvin Grove Urban Village development team

on a traditional village design, with a town centre and shops on the main streets. Since planning for the Village started in 2000 and construction started in 2002, AUD 1 billion have already been committed to deliver a heterogeneous design that brings together infrastructure with educational, cultural, residential, health, retail, recreational and business facilities within one precinct.

The following numbers and statistics illustrate the progress and development trajectory of the KGUV:

- When completed, there will be over 8,000 sqm (GFA) of retail space and in excess of 82,000 sqm (GFA) of commercial space located throughout KGUV.
- In 2007, there were 375 residential units (including 7 townhouses and 155 affordable housing units) in the KGUV. This is anticipated to exceed 1,000 two-bedroom equivalent units once the Village is complete (including student and senior accommodation).
- In 2007, there were 10,800 students and 1,800 staff based at the Kelvin Grove campus of QUT, and a total of 1,663 students and approx. 150 staff at Kelvin Grove State College.

Our diverse research interests are positioned under the collective umbrella of "New Media in the Urban Village". The Department of Housing acknowledges that the strategic design of the built environment and access to the ICT infrastructure are necessary but not sufficient to ensure "effective use" (Gurstein, 2003) or "social sustainability". Therefore the master plan calls for the research and development of appropriate interventions, measures and systems which can provide mechanisms to help link the people and businesses that "live, learn, work and play" at the KGUV, including residents of the KGUV and nearby areas (including affordable housing residents, seniors and students); university staff and students living or studying in the KGUV and nearby areas; businesses and their customers; and visitors. Our suite of research projects are aimed at responding to this call. We now introduce the main research methodology of one of these studies that forms part of this program of research – a study to produce insights into the impact of urban living contexts on lifestyle, health and well-being.

Data Collection with a Blog

A blog was set up entitled "The Effects of a New Urban Context on Health" (located at http://theeffectsofanewurbancontextonhealth.blogspot.com/) as an online, qualitative data collection mechanism for gathering information about the everyday, local influences on the amount of physical activity residents achieve in this new urban neighbourhood. It contained five posts by the researchers which were comprised of photographs of the Village, questions for participants to answer about their lifestyles and activities in this neighbourhood, as well as links to other websites on urban life and physical activity. One of the key goals of the research was to tap into the everyday lives and situations of the Brisbane Housing Company (BHC) residents, a lower socio-economic demographic living within the village. It is well documented in the public health research that lower socio-economic living contexts, such as households and neighbourhoods, appear to exert a powerful influence on the types of health-related behaviours that can be observed there (Dunn & Cummins, 2007; Monden, van Lenthe, & Mackenbach, 2006; Parkes & Kearns, 2006) with lower socio-economic environments being significantly connected with lower amounts of physical activity and poorer health (Galea et al., 2007; Giles-Corti & Donovan, 2002; Kavanagh et al., 2005; Wright, Kessler, & Barrett, 2007).

The Blog as an Internet Research Tool

A blog is a form of website that is typically used as a personal diary or log, with entries and postings made primarily by the author of the blog. The appeal of the blog is said to be due to the creation of a space where people can "express their opinions and views on different topics without fear of censorship" (Bachnik, Szymczyk, Leszcznks, & Podaidlo, 2005, p. 3179) and have been found to "generate a sense of community" amongst people with shared interests (Nardi, Schiano, Gumbrecht, & Swartz, 2004). Some of the many reasons for blogging include documenting one's life, a commentary, catharsis, a muse and as a community forum. Blogs have been used amongst academic and research communities to share experiences and processes, or to share knowledge or resources, such as the case of a blog created for learning and sharing knowledge about research methods (Giarre & Jaccheri, 2005, p. 2716), or to investigate how a blog aided collaboration in learning about health impact assessments amongst practitioners and researchers (Harris-Roxas, Harris, Kemp, & Harris, 2006). However, little has been written about the potential for blogs to provide an online location for the collection and storage of qualitative data. While the blog is a recognised, valid way of communicating in business, art and research contexts (Bruns & Jacobs, 2006; Fischer, 2001; Herring, Scheidt, Bonus, & Wright, 2004), we found no examples of research that used a blog as a *data collection tool* in our review of the literature. In noting the rarity of blogs in research generally, it is widely established that email is now recognised as a useful digital mechanism for gaining in-depth information on various research topics (Meho, 2006).

The "Effects of a New Urban Context on Health' blog was set up to act as an interface between the real-time, everyday lived experiences in the Kelvin Grove Urban Village, and the reflective contemplations and insights created by the residents about their neighbourhood. This online communication mechanism provided a way to collate individual, online contributions to our research questions within an open, visually accessible, community-centred forum. It gave participants an opportunity to write their own stories, opinions and answers in a shared, virtual space where they were able to view anonymous input from other residents; and from where we could view and study their answers as a collective. Further, this gave the participants a quiet and reflective space in which to scribe accounts of physical activity in the urban environment without the often complicated dimension of group dynamics and social or communicative noise present in face-to-face communication. It offered a unique opportunity to create a cyber-communal response to everyday life in the Kelvin Grove Urban Village by bringing people together online to generate a rich descriptive profile of the neighbourhood from different residential perspectives.

Study Participants

Only KGUV residents who occupied the Brisbane Housing Company (BHC) units were selected for participation in the study. Earning less than AUD 25,000 per year, BHC residents live in government-supported, 'affordable housing' buildings in KGUV. The BHC residents were categorised as 'lower socio-economic' via both housing type and income. BHC residents who had indicated their willingness to participate in further research on the surveys mailed out for the quantitative phase of this research project were contacted by telephone, with 16 BHC residents accepting our invitation to participate in the research.

Access and Ability to Use the Internet to Generate Data

Due to the lower socio-economic demographic being studied in this internet research project, we anticipated a lack of access amongst participants to the technologies required to run the blog. The majority of participants did not have a computer in their own homes due to their poor financial situations and were provided with laptops from the nearby university library. Participants were given assistance to set up the laptops and connect to the internet using the university's dial-up mechanism to avoid access fees by the local internet service provider. Brief instructions were given on how to post comments in response to the photographs and questions on the blog, and participants were encouraged to write as much, and as openly and candidly as possible. It was explained to participants that their answers were confidential, as they were assigned numbers as usernames on the blog that did not identify them in any way.

Procedure

Participants contributed to the blog over a six month period (July to December 2006) by addressing questions posted by the researchers about their relationship between their living context and their physical activity levels. The blog was divided up by posts into the following four themes:

1. *Moving into a New Urban Environment*
2. *Depth of Engagement with Neighbourhood Resources*
3. *The Social and Psychological Aspects of Physical Activity*
4. *Self, Health and Space: What moves you?*

While themes one to three focused on questions about how the built environment and social and communicative processes influence their physical activity levels, the fourth post offered a space for free comments, opinions, incidence reports and networking opportunities within the neighbourhood. For example, residents suggested activities that they were interested in pursuing to see if others responded and to form walking groups and social gatherings offline. While the questions on each post were specific, they were designed to be open and to act as a catalyst for broader responses to their use of the resources and infrastructure in the community, and to generate insights into the attitudes of this socio-economic demographic towards health more generally. Further, we were interested in the networks that formed on the blog and whether these were pursued and maintained between neighbours following their online contributions. Figure 2 shows how one of the posts appeared on-screen.

For this post, I am interested in finding out the degree to which you are aware of what is available in your neighbourhood, and which resources you are most interested in using or accessing for physical activity.

Q1. Are you aware of the public transport options available to you from the Village, and do you use them? If so, which ones to you use and why?

Q2. Do you ever use the parks or BBQ areas to socialise, rest, play sport, care for children, exercise or any other reason? If so, how often? What is your opinion of the local KGUV parks and green spaces? How could they be improved to make you use them more?

Q3. Do you use any of the pathways or bikeways? If so, what do you use them for, and do you find that they help you to walk or exercise more than you could where you were living previously?

Q.4 Are you aware of any other health-related resources that are near to the Village or that will be available to you soon, eg health clinic, GP, gymnasium, pool etc. Do you think you are likely to use these kinds of resources? Why/why not?

Q5. Overall, would you say that KGUV is a place that promotes or allows physical activity for residents? If so, in what ways does it achieve this or not achieve this?

posted by Julie-Anne @ 6:47 PM 80 comments

Fig. 2 Depth of engagement with neighbourhood resources for physical activity

Analysis: From Data to Insights

As described in the previous section, the blog data were collected by a series of posts, each of which involved a discussion topic under which specific questions were arranged. The responses to the blog questions provide an example of the way they enable collective sharing of personal stories. The responses accumulated on the website provided an opportunity to examine the ways in which participants related their housing choices to specific aspects of their biography in a shared space. The work of Lefebvre, a social theorist concerned with human practices in urban spaces, was used as an analytical framework for understanding the utterances in terms of the relationships identified by him as central to the conceptualisation of the production of space. A central differentiation in his model is between "representations of space" and "representational spaces". "Representations of space" refers to "conceptualised space: the space of scientists, planners, urbanists, technocratic subdividers and social engineers. . .all of whom identify what is lived and what is perceived with what is conceived". "Representational spaces" on the other hand refers to "space as directly *lived* through its associated images and symbols", and hence the space of the "inhabitants" and "users" (Lefebvre, 1991, p. 38). In terms of this conceptual distinction the object of knowledge in the study of urban space . . .

> . . . *is precisely the fragmented and uncertain connection between elaborated representations of space on the one hand and representational spaces. . .on the other; and this object implies (and explains) a subject – that subject in whom lived, perceived and conceived (known) come together in a spatial practice.* (Lefebvre, 1991, p. 230)

The analytical model thus provides a context in which urban experience can be understood in terms of differential levels and kinds of power and constraint in the production of space and the relationships between them. Inequities in fields such as health and, specifically, the role of local uses of space can then be understood as involving different configurations of these relationships. Through this analytical framework, the 214 contributions to the blog 'The Effects of a New Urban Context on Health' revealed a subjective portrait by residents of both *representational spaces* and *representations of space.* That is, it illuminated the relationship between what their expectations were of this new urban neighbourhood in light of the media and promotional material describing what their lifestyles might look like there versus their everyday lived experiences and interactions with the physical and social aspects of design there.

The data provided insights about the social connections that had already formed in the community, as well as varying degrees of participation by residents in the events and services available with implications for health. The blog gave a chronological portrayal of residents' choices and intentions regarding their health and lifestyles as they moved in and adjusted to a new environment, their current activities and their future intentions for their lives at KGUV. It also highlighted the ways in which they engaged with the marketing rhetoric around the concept of a 'new urban' environment, such as discourses around co-location with other services, and how this shaped their expectations of what life would be like moving to the KGUV. The following quote from the blog illustrates how their expectations of the place were shaped around the marketing rhetoric that accompanied this new urban development:

'I think the Village will promote physical activity as it is a new concept in living so I am looking forward to new ideas'
'The Village appears to promote a healthier lifestyle through its advertising promotions.'

Their comments about physical activity reflect both the degree to which they feel encompassed in a community that promotes or comes 'pre-packaged' with incentives for more active lifestyles, and an assessment of their own ability to achieve this, given their individual constraints and circumstances. The data generated in response to the questions posted on the blog produced relatively pointed and focused responses, and this has been attributed to the lack of prompting or encouragement ordinarily given in face-to-face communication, and the amount of time participants had to reflect upon and edit their answers. These data were delivered in a 'clean' and somewhat manicured form and would require additional qualitative methods to further unpack the answers given in this online forum or obtain more in-depth responses.

However, the data produced in the fourth post *'Self, Health and Space: What moves you'?* gave rise to more open and uninhibited communication and interactions, wherein residents were vocal about some of the challenges they faced living in government-supported housing, and their desires to create a more grass-roots community response of groups that met the needs and interests of different sub-groups within the BHC demographic. Social networks were inspired and established and pursued offline following contributions to this post, including a walking group, and a series of morning-teas and community barbecues. The way in which the participants embraced the technology and used it to suggest ideas for a better quality of life there, and to connect with other residents, indicates the potential for ICT to be used in future action research concerned with the health and well-being of target demographics.

The key findings included an illustration of some of the individual and household barriers to pursuing a more active and healthy lifestyle, such as caring-roles, disability, illness and fear of living alone.

'I have arthritis in both knees and find movement is restricted at times but feel better after exercise.'
'I am unable to leave Ted unattended even to take a quick walk around our pathways.'
'I would exercise, but I am too scared of what will happen to me out walking by myself.'

A general hostility and cynicism towards mass-media health promotion on physical activity was exposed, with residents expressing a preference for community interventions and opportunities that matched their circumstances and their neighbourhood resources.

'No. TV does not sell me on anything. I think there is too much said about diets and exercise.'

'I am not usually prone to just accept because TV or papers tell me this or that will benefit my health wise or physically.'

Aspects of the design principles inherent within *New Urbanism* were praised by participants, who expressed an appreciation for being close to a number of desirable destinations, including Brisbane CBD, having access to green spaces, and wide path and bikeways, and being in close proximity to what they referred to as 'respectable' venues such as the local theatre and university.

'The difference in living in a university area at the Village is the educational value.'

'I use the BBQ area to socialise with my neighbours. I love the Victoria park, if you walk there at night is it wonderful sightseeing, you can see the beautiful city.'

'I like the parks surrounding the area because they are so gorgeous and I feel comfortable and satisfied with the air. I just walk around and sit down and with the other people resting there.'

All of these factors contributed to increased confidence in the neighbourhood and a greater propensity to walk in local areas. However, the blog also revealed the complex social challenges living amongst other poorer people with similar difficulties and constraints, and this aspect of the data has implications for both urban designers and health promotion experts.

'Our neighbour next door – you couldn't wish to meet a nicer couple. And the lass with the baby she is fine now that the baby has a cot, but before she was crying alot. The smokers drive us mad, because they are chain smokers. And we had to call the police because a man was throwing shoes at our louvres at 4am in the morning. Most of our neighbours are good.'

What the blog revealed was an ongoing response to the physical and social aspects of a neighbourhood by a poorer demographic with implications for health and well-being. The data from the blog contain a collective narrative that is useful for a range of disciplines interested in the complex and highly inter-connected relationships between people and their urban living environments.

Conclusion

The use of a 'blog' as an online mechanism for the collection of qualitative data in a new urban setting was an effective means for gaining insight into the everyday responses of residents to their living environment in ways that affect their lifestyles and health. The different ways in which residents engaged with the resources in their neighbourhood and interacted with neighbours, as well as their responses to a master-planned community with specific lifestyles pre-packaged in the marketing rhetoric profiling the Village were captured and revealed in the comments and discussions posted on the blog. Uninterrupted logs and stories were scribed by participants, while still being able to 'hear' the views and insights of other residents regarding their everyday lived experiences in the Village since moving there. The shared virtual space gave a rich profile of different perspectives from residents about the kinds of interactions, social processes and engagements with resources such as health services, retail outlets, artistic venues and public spaces they had undertaken in the time they had lived in the Village. In this sense, the blog as a specific kind of online forum provided access to the offline worlds of these residents offering crucial insights into their experiences and perspectives in relation to the represented space of KGUV. Further research is needed that employs data collection instruments on the internet both as a means for gaining in-depth insights into social contexts and urban settings, and as a type of action research wherein one can observe the networks and connections that form online in ways that both unveil and influence offline practice.

Acknowledgements This research was supported under the Australian Research Council's Discovery Projects funding scheme, project number DP0663854, *New Media in the Urban Village: Mapping Communicative Ecologies and Socio-Economic Innovation in Emerging Inner-City Residential Developments.* Dr. Marcus Foth was the recipient of an Australian Postdoctoral Fellowship. The authors would like to thank Dr. Helen Klaebe for her valuable assistance with this study. We would also like to thank the residents for sharing their stories with us in this online forum.

References

Bachnik, W., Szymczyk, S., Leszcznks, P., & Podaidlo, R. (2005). Quantitative and sociological analysis of blog networks. *Acta Physical Polonica B, 36*(10), 3179–3191.

Boase, J., Horrigan, J. B., Wellman, B., & Rainie, L. (2006). *The strength of internet ties.* Washington, DC: Pew Internet & American Life Project.

Boulos, M. N. K., Maramba, I., & Wheeler, S. (2006). Wikis, blogs and podcasts: A new generation of web-based tools for virtual collaborative clinical practice and education. *BMC Medical Education, 6*(41), 1–8.

Bruns, A., & Jacobs, J. (Eds.). (2006). *Uses of blogs.* New York: Peter Lang.

Dillman, D. A. (2007). *Mail and internet surveys: The tailored design method* (3rd ed.). Hoboken, NJ: Wiley.

Dunn, J. R., & Cummins, S. (2007). Placing health in context. *Social Science & Medicine, 65*(9), 1821–1824.

Dutton, W. H., Carusi, A., & Peltu, M. (2006). Fostering multidisciplinary engagement: Communication challenges for social research on emerging digital technologies. *Prometheus, 24*(2), 129–149.

Fischer, G. (2001). *Communities of interest: Learning through the interaction of multiple knowledge systems.* Paper presented at the 24th Annual Information Systems Research Seminar (IRIS'24), Norway.

Foth, M., & Hearn, G. (2007). Networked individualism of urban residents: Discovering the communicative ecology in inner-city apartment buildings. *Information, Communication & Society, 10*(5), 749–772.

Galea, S., Ahern, J., Nandi, A., Tracy, M., Beard, J., & Vlahov, D. (2007). Urban neighbourhood poverty and the incidence of depression in a population-based cohort study. *AEP, 17*(3), 171–179.

Giarre, L., & Jaccheri, L. (2005). Learning research methods and processes via sharing experience in a BLOG. *Decision and Control, 12*(15), 2716–2720.

Giles-Corti, B., & Donovan, R. J. (2002). Socioeconomic status differences in recreational physical activity levels and real and perceived access to a supportive physical. *Preventive Medicine, 35*(6), 601–611.

Gurstein, M. (2003). Effective use: A community informatics strategy beyond the digital divide. *First Monday, 8*(12).

Hagen, P., Robertson, T., Kan, M., & Sadler, K. (2005). *Emerging research methods for understanding mobile technology use.* Paper presented at the OZCHI Conference, November 23–25, 2005, Canberra, ACT, Australia.

Harris-Roxas, B., Harris, P., Kemp, L., & Harris, E. (2006). *Facilitating practioner networks: Do weblogs have a role in promoting collaborative learning in HIA?* Paper presented at the 7th international health impact assessment conference, April 5–6, Cardiff, Wales, UK.

Herring, S., Scheidt, L., Bonus, S., & Wright, E. (2004). *Bridging the gap: A genre analysis of weblogs.* Paper presented at the 37th Annual HICSS Conference, Big Island, Hawaii.

Hine, C. (2000). *Virtual ethnography.* London: Sage.

Hine, C. (Ed.). (2005). *Virtual methods: Issues in social research on the internet.* Oxford: Berg.

Howard, P. N. (2002). Network ethnography and the hypermedia organization: New media, new organizations, new methods. *New Media & Society, 4*(4), 550–574.

Jankowski, N. W., & Van Selm, M. (2008, in press). *Researching new media.* London: Sage.

Jones, S. G. (Ed.). (1999). *Doing internet research: Critical issues and methods for examining the net.* Thousand Oaks, CA: Sage.

Kavanagh, A., Goller, J. L., King, T., Jolley, D., Crawford, D., & Turrell, G. (2005). Urban area disadvantage and physical activity: A multilevel study in Melbourne, Australia. *Journal of Epidemiology and Community Health, 11*(59), 934–940.

Lee, S., Hwang, T., & Lee, H.-H. (2006). Corporate blogging strategies of the Fortune 500 companies. *Management Decision, 44*(3), 316–334.

Lefebvre, H. (1991). *The production of space* (D. Nicholson-Smith, Trans.). Oxford: Blackwell.

Meho, L. I. (2006). E-mail interviewing in qualitative research: A methodological discussion. *Journal of the American Society for Information Science and Technology, 57*(10), 1284–1295.

Mesch, G. S., & Levanon, Y. (2003). Community networking and locally-based social ties in two suburban localities. *City and Community, 2*(4), 335–351.

Miller, D., & Slater, D. (2000). *The internet: An ethnographic Approach.* Oxford: Berg.

Monden, C. W. S., van Lenthe, F., & Mackenbach, J. P. (2006). A simultaneous analysis of neighbourhood and childhood socio-economic environment with self-assessed health and health-related behaviours. *Health & Place, 12*(4), 394–403.

Nardi, B. A., Schiano, D. J., Gumbrecht, M., & Swartz, M. (2004). Why we blog. *Communications of the ACM, 47*(12), 41–46.

Parkes, A., & Kearns, A. (2006). The multi-dimensional neighbourhood and health. *Health & Place, 12*(1), 1–18.

Townsend, A. (2009). Foreword. In M. Foth (Ed.), *Handbook of research on urban informatics: The practice and promise of the real-time city.* Hershey, PA: Information Science Reference, IGI Global.

Wellman, B. (2001). Physical place and cyberplace: The rise of personalized networking. *International Journal of Urban and Regional Research, 25*(2), 227–252.

Wellman, B., & Haythornthwaite, C. A. (Eds.). (2002). *The internet in everyday life.* Oxford: Blackwell.

Wright, L. E., Kessler, C. L., & Barrett, J. A. (2007). Neighbourhoods matter: Use of hospitals with worse outcomes following total knee replacement by patients from vulnerable populations. *Archives of Internal Medicine, 167*(2), 182–198.

Internet Aesthetics

Sean Cubitt

Archive

In the Canadian Fall of 2005, a group of artists, technologists, curators, activists and scholars met at the Banff Centre's New Media Institute high in the Rockies to debate the history of new media art (http://www.mediarthistory,org/). A convivial but intellectually and technically challenging event, the symposium and its associated summit focussed on shared issues between major centres for digital arts, among them the Fondation Daniel Langlois, the Zentrum für Kunstmedien (ZKM), the San Francisco Exploratorium and the Guggenheim Museum. Central to the discussion was the dawning realisation among curators and artists that digital artworks built a mere decade or two earlier were already falling into disrepair and in many cases were not capable of being restaged in their original forms at all. This was not so much a result of faults in construction as it was a matter of the accelerating reconfiguration of the computing environment.

Take, as a case, Graham Weinbren's *Erl-King*, a landmark interactive installation using a touchscreen interface to provide an interactive audiovisual narrative experience. The equipment that it was designed to run on is now obsolete. The touchscreens no longer work, or work too well, speeding through the interface where once there was a experience of delay, of hiatus between scenes, a slowing down of experience which was integral to the work's aesthetics. Reconstituting the installation for a Guggenheim show, Jon Ippolito designed and built a new platform that emulated the old, placing the original equipment alongside the new device, with its artificially enhanced delays, as a token of the difference between the two artefacts: the original, now all but non-functional, and the remake (http://variablemedia.net/ and Dimitrovsky, 2004).

The problem has parallels in the fine arts. Is a Rembrandt oil encrusted with the patina of age still the Rembrandt that Rembrandt painted? Are the Blake paintings we can see today in the Tate Britain, whose colours are radically altered because

S. Cubitt (✉)
Media and Communications Program, The University of Melbourne, Victoria, Australia
e-mail: scubitt@unimelb.edu.au

J. Hunsinger et al. (eds.), *International Handbook of Internet Research*,
DOI 10.1007/978-1-4020-9789-8_9, © Springer Science+Business Media B.V. 2010

of Blake's ill-fated experiments with egg-tempera, Blake's Blakes or our Blakes? And if we were to reconstitute them, in the manner spectacularly effected in the Sistine Chapel, how are we then to understand the generations for whom the works were muddied and brown, between the original act of making and the reconstituted 'original'? These fraught questions for fine arts are redoubled in the digital media by the rate at which processing and storage media have developed. Where now are the five-inch floppies of yesteryear? Indeed where are the three inch floppies, zip drives, and laserdiscs that once we prized? In the software domain, prior to the web, the democratising of hypermedia arts seemed to depend upon Apple's Hypercard software, but it is a long time since Apple produced a computer capable of running it. What becomes of the art that was produced for that medium?

The early days of art online were not entirely rudimentary. The ASCII signature, for example, remains a significant medium for communication and aesthetic intervention 15 years or so since it first appeared (see Danet, 2001). Shortly after the appearance of the Mosaic browser, the Hugo Boss fashion house was sponsoring a significant poetry site, including both adaptations of existing art practices, like Jenny Holzer's aphorisms, and the beginnings of new forms, like Douglas Davis and Gary Welz's *World's First Collaborative Sentence* (http://ca80.lehman. cuny.edu/davis/Sentence/sentence1.html; see Fletcher, 1999). Is this art? Many participants asked the same thing. As an example of distributed creation, it was perhaps as close to the SETI project, which still deploys unused processing time online to sift through masses of astronomical detail for signs of extra-terrestrial life, as to, say, David Medalla's collaborative physical artwork *Eskimo Carver* or Joseph Beuys' oak-planting projects of the 1960s. Projects which are clearly not presented as art, like Tom Ray's *Tierra* internet wildlife preserve, now jostle with others like *confluence.org*, a collaborative project to take a photograph at every integer crossing of lines of longitude and latitude. Is this art? It seems as conceptual and as purposeless. The term 'art' does not appear on the *confluence*site, which is about incongruity, about adventure, and about the pleasing absurdity of joining a project whose members will rarely if ever meet, but who share, for some hours at least, a common goal and a common space, a kind of conviviality which, however, has become significant to contemporary art beyond the net (see Bourriaud, 2002; Kester, 2004).

Meanwhile Mark Amerika's *Grammatron* (http://www.grammatron.com/) and the online presentation of fragments from the Eastgate Systems stable of hyper-novelists (http://www.eastgate.com/) promised a revolution in the literary arts, extending the notion of the 'open text' that Eco (1962) had first described in Joyce's *Finnegans Wake*. It was however Adaweb, which eked out a remarkable posthumous existence courtesy of the Walker Art Gallery for a number of years, that first raised the question of what a web archive might confidently achieve for the emergent art forms of the web and what it could not. The Walker archive carefully framed the Adaweb content with an identifying set of logos marking it as a 'property' of the Walker website. It was clear enough to any user that the works onscreen were no longer live: that they were in fact museumised, exhibits which, though still capable of breathing, were no longer scampering about seeking attention and feeding from the interactions of their audiences. These were in effect documents, in the same way that video recordings of performances are not performances but documentation, or a tape of an installation is not itself an installation.

For the participants in the Banff Refresh symposium, the choices were stark but complex enough to generate some heated interchanges. Given the vast productivity of the online world, what is to be saved? Paolo Cherchi Usai, in a presentation to the Australia and New Zealand Association for Cinema History on Wellington in 2000, noted that, of the approximately 47 minutes of film exposed in 1896, the world's archives hold approximately 42; but that of something approaching 9 billion hours of exposed film and videotape recorded in 1999, the world's film and television archives hold considerably less than 1%. On the figures produced by the Berkeley team exploring the question *How Much Information* (http://www2.sims.berkeley.edu/research/projects/how-much-info-2003/), the total amount of digital, photographic and print information produced in 2003 – 92% of it stored on hard drives – came close to 5 exabytes, with the quantity increasing by 30% year on year since their first survey of 1999. The chance of preserving more than a tiny proportion is minimal, and yet for an archivist the question of what to record is vital. How are we to know which episode of what soap opera will feature the first appearance of some future president? What sporting event will be marked by a protester throwing herself under the king's horse, an event accidentally recorded at the Derby in 1913? Will future researchers want our art or our blogs, and what qualities will they be looking for, in a 100, or 500, or a 1000 years – the kinds of horizon an archivist must confront economically, efficiently, ethically and aesthetically.

For the art community, the traditional answer has been that canon formation is the requisite and dependable model. Though we know both that tastes change and that today we are far more interested in women and colonised or enslaved artists than was the case a mere generation ago, canon formation seems to occur of its own accord in the internet world as much as in the traditional galleries and museums. Skimming the literature that has begun to emerge on the first decade of internet art, some names recur regularly, while others are already marginal, and still others have slipped away into darkness already. Artists, curators and archivists are part of this equation, but so too are reviewers, scholars, catalogue essayists and participants in online and e-mail fora like rhizome and fibre:culture. What we write about today, or more specifically who we write about, is likely to have an impact on who makes it onto the hard-drives of history, when the tale of our transitional times is told. Ironically, it is the old media of galleries and the written word that have the longevity, while digital media are all too susceptible to 'the gnawing criticism of the mice'.

Besides the accidental or deliberate construction of canons (plural, and 'deliberate', because many if not most archives are funded in part if not in whole to collect national artists), there lies the technical feasibility of storing, maintaining and reviving works. Discussants on the CRUMB new media curation mailing list in 2006 spent a substantial amount of time checking examples of long-lived installations, among them a number which incorporate their own power sources. This works for certain kinds of installation, notably those that do not require hard-drives, screens or projectors, all of which are subject to the ravages of time. Two possible solutions suggested themselves to the Banff group: to store code rather than works and to ensure the most accurate possible description of the look and feel of artworks when first presented. The second is more intriguing and challenging than it looks. Few new media art critics (and there are pitifully few of those in any case) spend much time describing in detail issues such as colour gamuts, the refresh rates of screens, the angle and throw of projectors, the degree of light-trapping desired or achieved, the levels of volume and the acoustic properties of the spaces involved. Training ourselves to do so is a significant task for those of us who do undertake this kind of work. The former, the issue of code storage, raises the related question of what constitutes a work of digital art.

Theoretically, code is more or less absolute: it is the nature of the digital beast. But code, as we have already noted, is itself mutable. Even a transcription of an artwork into machine code is not necessarily going to allow the artwork to compile and execute in the manner in which it was intended, while attempts to run software coding rely on the maintenance of operating systems and software platforms apart from their normal commercial or open-source evolution. As Sandy Baldwin (2002–2003) notes, procedural art, like the Fluxus practice of issuing instructions for the execution of an art experience or Oulipo or Mac Low's procedural poetics, are in a certain sense codeworks, but lack the autonomy of running code on a computer. In any case, the eventual phenomena that appear as, for example, text, video or audio outputs will depend on the end user's peripherals, peripherals which are themselves in constant evolution. Formats that we believe to be resilient such as pdf, mp3 and html have a tendency to change. With their changes goes, in certain instance such as jodi's notorious *Error Code 404*, the references that make the artwork work as art.

Many partial or temporary solutions suggest themselves: migration from platform to platform, for example, though that is so time consuming that it implies abandoning new projects in favour of recycling old ones. This solution might have tempted i/o/d as a way of keeping their WebStalker alternative browser available; but the WebStalker lies mouldering, its last platform the Mac OS 9 now itself an emulation on the current generation of machines, while archive boxes, one by one, get the dead pixel, the blue screen of death, and find their way to the recycler. The open source code is there; and the program is apparently not too hard to rewrite, but somehow there are always better things to be doing. The work has served its purpose, and lives on in screen grabs and in texts like Matt Fuller's (2003, 2005). This latter is an alternative strategy: to recognise the difficulty of keeping digital artworks alive, at least in the form in which they first appeared, and to amass as much documentation as possible in the most robust forms we have, which, in general, are the older media of the mechanical era, at least until the arrival of a genuinely universal Turing machine. The terminal solution is to embrace ephemerality. The concept of art as a universal, as a value and a practice which is distinct from the rest of human activity and extracts its value from that distinction, and which is by that token removed from history, proving its value by its ability to survive from generation to generation: this concept of art we may have to abandon. In its place, it is possible that we must grasp that art is just another practice, as valuable but as ephemeral as sex or eating, as worthy of celebration, but as impossible to preserve. The digital arts have, if this is the case, a special relationship to time, one that is especially significant for the development of the internet arts.

Interaction and After

Many hypertext sites open themselves to two criticisms they share with critiques of gaming and critiques of commercial portals. On the one hand, they structure and limit user choices to the selections already engineered for them by the artist; on the other hand, they tend to exclude links outwards from themselves or their preferred enclosed network of mutually supporting IP addresses. Such limitations have been the butt of serious criticisms, such as those of Brian Massumi, for whom

> time and change are added back in as the movement of the subject (cursor) through abstract (cyber) space. The problem is that the backdrop against which that movement takes place remains general . . . . The digital "architecture" framing the movement typically does not itself move. This is the case for example in a closed hypertext environment, where all the possible permutations pre-exist the "change" added by the subject's movement and remain untouched by it'. (2002, p.175)

Mounting a defence is not particularly demanding. Among many artworks that produce a definitive shifting of the 'background' we might include all those that assault the primacy of the browser window, including jodi's various assaults, the WebStalker, and potatoland's Landfill, while the definitional functioning of inter-action as selection among previously designed pathways is given the lie by dozens of applets that, for example, draw in the browser from mouse movements, or that produce different effects from multiple rollovers. Similarly, a number of e-poets, from Loss Pequeño Glazier (http://epc.buffalo.edu/authors/glazier/) to Simon Biggs (http://www.littlepig.org.uk/) use procedural and generative engines, including con-volution algorithms and Markov generators to disrupt the probabilistic flow of message, to emphasise the autonomy of the machine as a partner in communica-tion, to undercut the apparent rationalism of the web, but most of all to generate unforeseen and unforeseeable combinations of language. The demotic form of these modes is flarf, a method for generating text using search engines by enter-ing two unconnected terms and stitching together new texts from the search results, often according to procedural rules. Considered by some the bastard offspring of L=A=N=G=U=A=G=E poetics, it has its revenge in its return to high art via artists like tnwk (the acronym stands for the highly relevant sobriquet *things not worth keeping*), whose *far from silicon fen* online installation (http://www.silicon-fen.net/tnwk/ffsfweb.html) redeploys flarf, with all its connotations of crassness, as an only partly parodic element in a complex portrait of a region of Eastern England caught between the reinvention of heritage and the emergence of sunrise light indus-tries to replace an increasingly industrialised agricultural economy, which no longer supports the working population it did.

In other projects, there is nothing so like a random number generator as a human being, with the sole exception of a cohort of human beings. In Ben Rubin and Mark Hansen's 2002-6 installation *The Listening Post* (http://www. earstudio.com/projects/listeningPost.html), internet relay chat in real time provides the raw material for an installation of hundreds of small LCD screens and audio, powered by a search client that seeks out key terms of discussion, usually the most frequent, and displays them in geometric scrolls across the array, while automated voices recite or sing elements and passages from them according to an electro-acoustic score. This trope, the repurposing of the tidal flows of internet traffic in more or less unrelated audiovisual forms, can be traced to the scientific practices of visualisation and sonification, the practice of treating data so that it can be perceived by human agents. The earliest of these is radar, which converts radio wavelengths and delays into a visual display; equally familiar are the images derived from electron tunnelling microscopy, MRI and PET scans, and from Earth observation and astronomical satellite telemetry.

An exemplary art project which, eschewing interaction, nonetheless meets the strictures of Massumi's critique is r a d i o q u a l i a's *radio astronomy* (http://www.radio-astronomy.net/listen.htm), which serves as live telemetry from the outer planets in the form of a continuous web-radio stream. Such entirely inhuman sources, rendered in humanly perceivable forms, cannot but confound expectations. Far more than that, r a d i o q u a l i a raise questions about the meaning of the term 'remote' as deployed in common parlance and in digital technologies; questions about the meaning of 'real time' when applied to signals that have travelled for light-minutes across space; questions concerning the exclusive claim of human intelligence to the arbitration of what constitutes information; and ultimate questions about the position of humanity in the solar system and the cosmos. Adam Hyde, a founding member of r a d i o q u a l i a, developed with Matthew Biederman and Lotte Meijer another device with an equally profound structure exhibited at isea 2006. *Paper Cup Telephone Network* (http://www.simpel.cc) is a paper cup attached to a string, just like the childhood toy telephones most of us must have constructed. Hyde's cup, however, is connected to a network of other internet-connected paper cups which can answer the caller, who otherwise sees only the string vanishing into a wall, in this case in an anonymous space between the entrances to the symposium washrooms. What is it to be connected without caller ID, without even an address or a trace? Were the responding voices recorded? Synthesised? Co-present? Or remotely connected? What difference does that make to the caller? To what extent is any call always a solipsistic event, a random connection in a chaotic world? What degree of blind trust are we still prepared to give to an anonymous and free network? It is a kind of Turing test, but one whose profundity arises from the possibility that a human might fail it.

It will be clear that many of these examples are not exclusively web based. And yet there are surprisingly few artworks which are exclusively web based, just as there are very few movies, games or commercial product launches that do not also boast some kind of web presence. Matthew Barney's *Cremaster* (http://www.cremaster. net/) and Peter Greenaway's *Tulse Luper Suitcases* (http://www.vtulselupernetwork.

com/) are among the more interesting examples of sites originating externally, but in some sense going native online. Barney's and Greenaway's film cycles are supplemented and to some extent derivatives of physical gallery exhibitions, and in Greenaway's case performances (including VJing), games, books and a sprawling network of online presence that alter the terms of the linear structure of cinema in favour of a navigable interface, partly puzzle-based and to that extent dependent on user memory as well as the architectures of the sites. Both works deploy idiosyncratic systems of reference and something akin to allegory, both rely strongly on both compositional and historical effects of intertextuality that extend well beyond (and before) the web, but both find themselves using the interactive, navigable and spatial orientation of the internet as a model for a kind of memory which is at once personal to the artist, and to some extent at least, like nostalgia, a fictional memory accessible to a wider public to the degree that they engage with the complexity and density of the work on offer. To this extent they match at least one criterion of interactivity: that the interactive work works only to the extent that audiences take on responsibility for the completion of the work, which in previous art forms has always been the responsibility of the artist. The 'becoming' which Massumi so strongly identifies with the aesthetic is then a matter not of an intrinsic quality of the artwork itself, but of its incompletion, its wait for an interactor, and the variety of degrees of completion and incompletion any one user will experience. The crudity of Greenaway's html as opposed to the sophistication of Barney's Flash sites suggests that the two are, however, not commensurable, Greenaway the more ready to expose the artist's own hand as a mode of authenticity, a proximity to hand coding which reveals at least one further aspect of online aesthetics.

The debate over whether digital art requires the ability to write code extends back well before the mass availability of the internet, but with that democratisation the issue has become more urgent. On the one hand lies an argument that off-the-shelf software is reductive, normative and restricting, leading to the proposition that software development is an aesthetic platform of the highest urgency (Broeckmann, 2003). On the other lies the argument that restricting a definition of 'art practice' to those alone who can program is to dismiss the democratic potential of the web, just as the dismissal of snapshooters demeaned the democratic potential of photography before. Certainly projects like RSG's *Carnivore* (http://r-s-g.org/carnivore/) would seem to demonstrate a new way to understand what art is and can do: providing tools, as if in response to Benjamin's slogan in defence of literary modernism against socialist realism, 'An author who teaches writers nothing teaches no-one' (Benjamin, 1999, p. 777). Drawing further on the thesis that digital aesthetics is definitionally interactive, the aesthetic experience would then not be one of contemplating a work, but of working with software, where the art is the software, the experience is using it, and any end products are waste material, sloughed off skins. Rather than simply play a game, then, the invitation would be to use some kind of authoring software to produce your own, and the act of producing would then be the experience of art. There are two critiques to raise here. On the one hand, this experience of interaction approximates the contemporary experience of work. As a number of commentators have indicated, distinguishing work from play in the digital economy is increasingly difficult. Software factories try to provide play-ful environments for their employees, while end-users are invited to play with the product in order to give it its final finish (adding skins to mobile phones for example, or installing personalised ring tones) or indeed to make it function at all (installing the software on a newly purchased computer). Digital play, as in losing yourself in a game or a software environment, belongs to this grey zone between paid employ-ment and recreation and becomes the kind of unpaid work on which the prosumer economy of just-in-time manufacture depends, and the free creative labour which provides beta-testing, or derives new intellectual property from existing packages, without salary (Dyer-Witheford, 1999).

The movement known as net.art depended greatly not only on authored code but on games with, and jokes about, standard coding practices and produced a raft of works of some considerable influence. Many of these, like Olia Lialina's *My Boyfriend Came Back From The War* (http://www.teleportacia.org/war/), were in many respects emotionally satisfying or troubling, and to that extent recognisably developments based on traditional aesthetic interests. Others stand accused by a new generation of artists of elitism, in that they depend on a knowledge of computing and computers which is uncommon. The reaction may perhaps be traced back as far as the early works of young-hae chang heavy industries (http://www.yhchang.com/), vernacular poems in big, bold, rapidly refreshing Flash screens composed of words and phrases in black Monaco on a white background describing aspects of daily life in and around cyberspace accompanied by frenetic free jazz, and in no instances open to interaction. The refusal of interaction marked a specific turning point in the later 1990s, away from the ideals of navigability and towards a non-code based, experientially oriented art that was unembarrassed by its proximity to entertainment. Like the web-comics movement (http://www.thewebcomiclist.com/), such forms relied on wit, speed and word of mouth to win and keep audiences, and while adeptly crafted, do not boast any special programming skills. More recently, in the mid-2000s, a number of artists have turned to Google Earth hacks and similar recycling of existing software as a reliable source of code for conceptual games, especially in the field of interaction between virtual spaces online and the surrounding life of material everyday reality (for example, Julian Bleecker's *Battleship Google Earth*, http://research.techkwondo.com/blog/julian/240).

The argument between democracy and user-friendly technologies, the argument as to whether proprietary software stifles and artisan software opens up possibilities, and the emerging debate over the relative statuses of work and play in the digital economy and in digital aesthetics are by no means clear. The Open Source move-ment, which itself may be considered as a vast collaborative and convivial aesthetic experience, is clearly inspired by democratic ideals, but ideals which have more to do with a democracy of peers on the one hand and on the other hand an appeal to the radical democracy of development agencies like the United Nations Development Program's Asia-Pacific International Open Source Network (http://www.iosn.net/). Between them lie the vast majority of Windows-native internet users, low skilled in terms of code, middle class in the loose usage prevalent in the USA. This is the audience to which a new generation of artists, those who have grown up with the web, want to reach out. The key to the reach, they argue, is the use of cheap, ubiquitous consumer devices like PDAs and cell phones, and the object is to escape from immersion in the virtual world of cyberspace and to rearticulate social and virtual spaces into richly interwoven experiences to which they give the name locative media (Hemment, 2006; Tuters & Varnelis, 2006). A remarkable example of this practice is the project *Urban Tapestries* (http://urbantapestries.net/) established by the London-based art research group Proboscis, an intervention into the urban landscape utilising wireless technologies and internet connectivity to embed narratives, memories, stories, pathways and links into the invisibly networked environment of the city. While some strikingly original programming underlies the project, its goal is to allow easy uploading as well as downloading of users' content as a semantic map overlaid on the otherwise anonymous city streets. There is undoubtedly a nostalgic tinge to this type of locative art, a belief that in some way a mythicised urban community might be brought into being on the basis of a tradition that is not only lost but invented, and that meaningful places might supplant the meaning-free spaces which have become our lot. At the same time, the self-conscious construction of community through technical intermediaries is a continuation by other means of Berners-Lee's founding vision of the web as a place of virtual communion.

Ephemerality

These themes picked from the mass of competing aesthetic activities online touch only the surface, and do so rather deliberately in the ambit of a gallery oriented (post)modernist mode of art making, validated by public discussions which in many respects duplicate the canon-forming activities of traditional art institutions. Net.art as it was practiced in the 1990s by artists like Alexei Shulgin (http://www.easylife.org/), Mongrel (http://www.mongrel.org.uk/) and Vuk Cosic (http://mail.ljudmila.org/~vuk/) – celebrated for example in Rachel Greene's 2004 Thames and Hudson book – was exemplary in that it was work that could exist in no other form than online. A similar purism, with its roots in modernist aesthetics, persists in some avatars of software art. On the other hand, there have been many other works, some by the same artists, which are devotedly hybrid in the media they use, messily involved in suturing together the online and offline worlds. In many instances, these activities become straightforwardly political, as in the case of Indymedia, while in others, like Tuters' own GPS blimp locative project *Fête Mobile* (http://fetemobile.ca/), are more complexly political in using techniques associated with the Minutemen vigilante border patrols. The satirical comedy of RTMark (http://www.rtmark.com/) and the Yes Men (http://www.theyesmen.org/) might in a similar vein be argued to represent what television ought to be like. The 'relational architecture' projects of Rafael Lozano-Hemmer (http://www.lozano-hemmer.com/), likewise, move between the internet, the gallery and the built environment, raising in turn questions concerning the immaterialisation of cityscapes increasingly composed of screens and projections relative to the increasingly material forms of data and financial flows.

Characteristic of both net-native and hybrid forms, however, is a marriage to the concept of space. Radical critics of digital culture like Paul Virilio propose that time is eradicated from a 'landscape of events' (2000) in which the repetitive, unitary steps of digital logic and sampling spatialise the time of perception and history, resulting in the loss of time, or rather its conquest by absolute speed, the quality which, Virilio observes, has always served in the military as the route to mastery of territory. Territorialising cyberspace with metaphors like 'electronic frontier' has as its corollary the re-imagining of the world as map and a reinvention of critical language in a vocabulary of fields, vectors, domains and spaces. It is in this context that the problem of archiving internet art becomes intriguing at a theoretical level.

Take the example of the Davis and Welz *Sentence*. In 1993 or 1994, this was a living entity. Now it is an archive. At some future date, perhaps not far away, the Way Back Machine (http://www.archive.org/) will no longer be able to run it at all – indeed this morning as I checked the url I received an error message apologising for 'technical problems' blocking access. Much of what is being made today will by the nature of things disappear. As one who participated in the early days of the web, and as a scholar of media history, I regret this bitterly, but certainly no more bitterly than I regret mortality in general. I once calculated that the entire population of Australia working 8-hour shifts every day for a year would just about be able to view every foot of exposed film and videotape from that year. This is the kind of discipline required of consumers, to find and attend to the media intended for them. As the competition for leisure time attention intensifies, and as that time is eaten into by the vampiric repetitions of advertising, the time available for aesthetic experience diminishes. On the other hand, we should look forward to an expansion of aesthetic technique to a far wider range of activities, on the model of *confluence.org*, away from the art enclave and into the broadest swathe of human activities. There is after all a utopian dimension to the mixing of both art and life, and of work with play, that should not be forgotten in a critique of the capitalist exploitation of free labour, or the aestheticisation of commerce (to paraphrase Benjamin).

Nor is it entirely remiss to consign the amassed experiences of digital online art to the wastebin: as Benjamin, once again, remarked of history, 'The way in which it is valued as 'heritage' is more insidious than its disappearance could ever be'. Historiography is a cruel art. Though critics of canon formation seek to reconstitute the tradition by including the excluded voices of the past, Benjamin argues that the constitution of the past as canon is itself a snare and a delusion; that historiography's task is as much to erase and destroy as it is to maintain and celebrate. Though there is little in the history of internet art to match the endless disaster of general human history, the principle of destructive justice Benjamin brings to his consideration of the past may serve us here too. A remarkable outcome of the software approach to internet aesthetics is the realisation that code returns, reinvigorated by its fragmentation and rewriting, over again in new generations of software. Neither the bones nor the phenomenological experiences of net.art are forgotten, though it may not be people who remember, and machinic memories may be as partial and as biased as our own.

This suggestion of an aesthetics of disappearance based on the return of the past into the present by way of its perpetual recycling – as Marx described the skills of the peasantry transformed into the mechanisms of the industrial revolution – in turn suggests an aesthetics of a perpetual present. This outcome of the spatialising tendency of network communications would be more depressing, representing as it does the loss of historical process and therefore of the potential for a future other than the present, if the present were not also a victim of the digital. Predictive texting is a small indication of how the present is already being stretched thin between past and future. Based on previous messages, your phone starts to fill in what it believes you want to say using probability algorithms. The problem is that there is so much noise and redundancy in human communications that predictive texting can only be probabilistic, that is, statistically viable. As such it cannot be responsive, as Massumi argues, to singularities, the events that the aesthetic most prizes, those that are richest in information and experience. The math of Viterbi's algorithm, extensively used in voice and other noisy communications systems, is rather elegant and rather complex, but depends upon the finding that the future is only partially dependent on the past; and on a technique of folding the future outcome back into the possible past causes of the present event (Mackenzie, 2007). The microtemporalities of machine time are far from the linear structures of accelerated clock-time imagined by Massumi and Virilio, already reinventing time as a raw material for digital makers.

It is the combination of these factors – of the spatialisation of time and the remaking of the actual–virtual relation in the microtime of machine processing – that the peculiar ephemerality of online arts begins to make some new kind of sense. The archive is no longer an appropriate form or metaphor for the places where old works go. As they assimilate into a geology of the web, comprised of human memories and machinic codes, they begin to form something more like a historical atlas, more like the pathways and legends generated in *Urban Tapestries*. The very leakiness of the web and the internet, their imbrication into everyday life, suggests that we can no longer hope to define digital aesthetics as distinct from any other; and just as digital aesthetics can no longer be spoken in the singular, it can also not be spoken as medium specific. Instead, and in return, it has leaked out into the world and made all aesthetics digital, cognisant of the invisible shadow of data surrounding every poem, every painting, every stone. The gift of the digital to the world it now enters is not then immateriality, nor the end of history, but its redemption in the mortality which, perversely enough, it has taken this planet-spanning network of technology to teach us.

References

Baldwin, S. (2002–2003). Process window: Code work, code aesthetics, code poetics. In *The cybertext yearbook*. Jyväaskylä: Research Centre for Contemporary Culture, University of Jyväaskylä.

Benjamin, W. (1999). The author as producer. In M. W. Jennings, H. Eiland, & G. Smith (Eds.), *Selected writings* (Vol. 2, Part 2, pp. 768–782), 1931–1934. Cambridge MA: Bellknap Press and Harvard University Press.

Bourriaud, N. (2002). *Relational aesthetics* (S. Pleasance & F Woods, Trans.). Paris: Les presses du réel.

Broeckmann, A. (2003). On software as art. *Sarai Reader 03* (pp. 215–218). Delhi: Sarai.

Danet, B. (2001). *Cyberpl@y: Communicating online.* London: Berg.

Dimitrovsky, I. (2004). *Final report, Erl-King project.* Retrieved October 8, 2006, from http://www.variablemedia.net/e/seeingdouble/report.html, April 1.

Dyer-Witheford, N. (1999). *Cyber-Marx: Cycles and circuits of struggle.* Urbana, IL: University of Illinois Press.

Eco, U. (1962). *Opera Apperta: Forma e indeterminazione nelle poetiche contemporanee.* Milano: Bompiani.

Fletcher, G. (1999). *... A cyberculture period.* Paper presented at "Wip-Lash", Department of English, University of Queensland, August. Retrieved October 8, 2006, from http://www.spaceless.com/papers/19.htm

Fuller, M. (2003). *Behind the blip: Essays on software culture,* New York: Autonomedia.

Fuller, M. (2005). *Media ecologies: Materialist energies in art and architecture.* Cambridge, MA: MIT Press.

Greene, R. (2004). *Internet art.* New York: Thames and Hudson.

Hemment, D. (Ed.). (2006). Locative media special issue. *Leonardo Electronic Almanac, 14*(3), June–July. Accessed October 10, 2006, from http://leoalmanac.org/journal/vol_14/lea_v14_n03-04/home.asp

Kester, G. (2004). *Conversation pieces: Community + communication in modern art.* Berkeley, CA: University of California Press.

Mackenzie, A. (2007). Protocols and the irreducible traces of embodiment: The viterbi algorithm and the mosaic of machine time. In R. Hassan & R. Purser (Eds.) *24/7: Time and temporality in the network society.* Stanford, CA: Stanford University Press.

Massumi, B. (2002). *Parables for the virtual: Movement, affect, sensation.* Durham, NC: Duke University Press.

Tuters, M. & Varnelis, K. (2006). Beyond locative media. *Networked publics,* Annenberg Centre for Communication, University of Southern California, January 19. Retrieved August 27, 2006, from http://netpublics.annenberg.edu/trackback/159

Virilio, P. (2000). *A landscape of events* (J. Rose, Trans.). Cambridge, MA: MIT Press.

Internet Sexualities

Nicola Döring

Introduction

The term "internet sexuality" (or OSA, online sexual activities) refers to sexual-related content and activities observable on the internet (cf. Adams, Oye, & Parker, 2003; Cooper, McLoughlin, & Campbell, 2000; Leiblum & Döring, 2002). It designates a variety of sexual phenomena (e.g., pornography, sex education, sexual contacts) related to a wide spectrum of online services and applications (e.g., websites, online chat rooms, peer-to-peer networks). If an even broader range of computer networks – such as the Usenet or bulletin board systems – is included in this extensional definition, one speaks of "online sexuality" or "cybersexuality."

This article presents an overview of the current state of research in internet sexuality. Over 450 relevant academic papers (primarily peer-reviewed journal articles) published between 1993 and 2007 were identified in the databases *PsycInfo* (maintained by the American Psychological Association) and *Web of Science* (maintained by Thomson Scientific). Spanning a period of 15 years, these publications deal with pornography, sex shops, sex work, sex education, sex contacts, and sexual subcultures on the internet (cf. Döring, 2009).

Pornography on the Internet

Explicit, potentially stimulating portrayals of sexual activity exist on the internet in the form of photos and photo series, video clips and films, comics, and texts. Online pornography is provided at websites both free of charge and for a fee. Websites with adult content can be found with the help of pornography search engines (such as www.sextracker.com) and directories (such as www.thehun.com). Pornographic

N. Döring (✉)
Ilmenau University of Technology/Technische Universitaet Ilmenau Media Design
and Media Psychology/Medienkonzeption und Medienpsychologie Ehrenbergstr.
29 (EAZ 2217), D-98693 Ilmenau, Germany
e-mail: nicola.doering@tu-ilmenau.de

J. Hunsinger et al. (eds.), *International Handbook of Internet Research*,
DOI 10.1007/978-1-4020-9789-8_10, © Springer Science+Business Media B.V. 2010

material is also exchanged in peer-to-peer networks, online forums, and chat channels. Alongside erotica/softcore (i.e., portrayals of naked individuals, simulated sex) and hardcore pornography (portrayals of real sexual acts), illegal pornography constitutes a third form of sexually explicit content available online (albeit to a lesser extent). Online child pornography is extremely difficult to find for unsophisticated users, as it is illegal in most countries (cf. Schell, Martin, Hung, & Rueda, 2007). For this reason, child pornography is almost always sold or exchanged in closed circles (publicly accessible depictions of "teen sex" normally involve participants over the age of 18 years; Kuhnen, 2007; Lewandowski, 2003, p. 311). Violent pornography is primarily offered on specialized websites for a fee. Animal pornography, on the other hand, is relatively easy to find free of charge because it is legal in several countries (Lewandowski, 2003, pp. 311–313).

Unique to the internet is the immense quantity and extremely wide range of often free pornographic material accessible anonymously regardless of time or place. These three characteristics of online pornography (anonymity, affordability, and accessibility) are described as a "triple A-engine" that drives its use (Cooper, 1998). The digital format of internet pornography makes it easy for users to search for specific images, archive them in great volume on their home computers, and digitally modify them. The digital format of online pornography also allows users to conveniently produce and distribute their own images. The quantity of cyber pornography in relation to all other content on the internet is estimated at about 1% (Zook, 2007, p. 106). Although small in relative terms, this figure still represents many millions of files.

Production and Content of Online Pornography

At present, very few studies have systematically investigated the types and characteristics of online pornography. Lack of critical attention has also been devoted to providing a differentiated account of the processes and parties involved in its production. The majority of pornography available online was professionally produced (Cronin & Davenport, 2001). In this way, most commercial internet pornography is a stereotypic product of the socio-economic working conditions of the so-called adult industry (Heider & Harp, 2002; Mehta, 2001; Lewandowski, 2003).

Some professional porno actors maintain their own websites in order to gain independent control over the conditions of production (Miller-Young, 2007; Podlas, 2000). Many amateurs also release their self-produced pornography on the internet (e.g., stories: www.asstr.org; photographs: www.altporn.net; videos: www.youporn.com). It is not uncommon for amateur pornography to contain authentic sexual encounters ("reality porn"; Hardy, 2008). In many cases amateur pornography is also marked by a deliberate effort to develop thematic and aesthetic alternatives to mainstream pornography's stereotypes ("alternative porn"). Innovative pornographic depictions (such as pornography made for and by heterosexual and homosexual women) are thus increasingly common on the internet (Attwood, 2007; Schauer, 2005). The emancipatory potential of the internet is contrasted by the greater ease with which illegal online pornography – such as depictions of sexual violence – can be distributed (Gossett & Byrne, 2002).

Usage and Users of Online Pornography

Today, the use of pornography in the Western world is common: A representative study in Norway revealed that the majority of the male and female population between 18 and 49 years of age has used pornographic magazines (men: 96%, women: 73%), video films (m: 96%, w: 76%), or internet content (m: 63%, w: 14%) at least once previously (Træen, Nilsen, & Stigum, 2006, p. 248). In a convenience sample of students in Canada (average age: 20 years), 72% of male and 24% of female participants reported having used online pornography within the last 12 months (Boies, 2002), p. 82). As is the case with offline pornography, online pornography is primarily consumed by individuals in moments of solitude. However, both forms of pornography are also used to a certain extent by couples and groups of friends. The main reasons provided for the voluntary use of pornography are curiosity, sexual stimulation, masturbation, and enhancement of sex life with partners.

Wanted access to online pornography needs to be differentiated from unwanted exposure: A representative sample of adolescent internet users between the ages of 10 and 17 years in the United States revealed that 25% had unintentionally come across online pornography in the last 12 months. One quarter (6%) were very discomforted by the experience (Mitchell, Finkelhor, & Wolak, 2003, p. 9). Few studies have investigated how children and adolescents handle both voluntary and involuntary exposure to pornographic material on a cognitive and emotional level, however. There are various legal provisions, technical solutions (such as filtering software), and educational programs aimed at protecting children and adolescents from online pornography (Dombrowski, Gischlar, & Durst, 2007).

Effects of Online Pornography

In academic studies the discussed effects of online pornography are overwhelmingly negative. It is argued, for example, that certain pathological inclinations can be exacerbated by access to deviant pornographic material: The availability of online child pornography is seen as encouraging the perception that pedosexual behavior is normal, as pedosexuals sometimes use such material to justify their own behavior or sway children to participate in illicit sexual acts (Quayle & Taylor, 2002, cf. section "Sexual Subcultures on the Internet"). The ubiquitous nature of online pornography can also lead to "cyberporn addiction," i.e., compulsive or addictive behavior associated with the use of online pornography (Daneback, Ross, & Månsson, 2006). An intensive preoccupation with online pornography can negatively impact the quality of heterosexual relationships, both sexually and emotionally (Manning, 2006). The use of online pornography in the workplace can impair performance and potentially result in employee dismissal (Cooper, Golden, & Kent-Ferraro, 2002). In addition, the use of online pornography is suspected to encourage negative attitudes toward marriage, family, and monogamy and to foster promiscuous and risky sexual behavior (Lo & Wei, 2005; Lam & Chan, 2007). In any event, studies have been unable to establish the existence of causal relationships to support this final claim. While liberal attitudes toward sexuality may encourage an increased consumption of pornographic material, the body of evidence marshaled to argue that negative consequences result from pornography's use is far from authoritative (Barak, Fisher, Belfry, & Lashambe, 1999). Moreover, claims of negative effects are often based on simple stimulus–response or imitation models. Whether or not and in what manner pornographic images are imitated by its users depends on numerous factors though, particularly on the recipient's evaluation of such practices and interpersonal communication and consent (cf. Fisher & Barak, 2001). An empirical study of such processes has yet to be undertaken.

The potential positive effects of online pornography – such as increased pleasure, self-acceptance, and improved communication between sexual partners, in addition to the widening of traditional sexual roles and scripts – have been the subject of very little academic work to date (cf. Boies, 2002, p. 85; Jacobs, Janssen, & Pasquinelli, 2007; Innala, 2007). When the issue of pornography's effects is broached, the discussion is rarely couched in relative terms with a view to online usage of moderate intensity or other factors which co-determine an individual's sexuality.

Sex Shops on the Internet

There are numerous sex shops on the internet. Sexual products – including toys, sexual aids, lingerie, condoms, aphrodisiacs, and erotica – are sold online by both mass-market retailers (such as www.amazon.com) and specialized sex shops (such as www.adultshop.com). The visibility and easy accessibility of sexual products on the internet might contribute to the increasing normalcy with which the use of such products is viewed, as large segments of the population can now familiarize themselves with and purchase such products discretely (e.g., older adults, Adams et al., 2003). Online sex shops geared toward women (such as www.annsummers.com; www.goodvibrations.com; www.marg.at) present dildos and vibrators as fashionable lifestyle products while communicating new images of female sexuality (Attwood, 2005).

In accordance with the Sexual Behavior Sequence Model, online sex shops can be classified as a sexual stimulus that triggers various physiological, affective, and cognitive reactions in the user depending on his or her predispositions. These reactions can prime the user for sexual activity and also impact the nature of the activities engaged in (Fisher & Barak, 2000, p. 579). There are currently no empirical studies available concerned with investigating the contents and forms of online sex shops (e.g., in contrast to offline sex shops), their clientele, the ways in which they are used, and their effects.

Sex Work on the Internet

While pornography on the internet has been the subject of a large number of studies, very little research has focused on the topic of sex work.

Offline Sex Work

The internet now plays a central role in the marketing of sex tourism, prostitution, and other forms of offline sex work (e.g., strip clubs). Many feminists reject prostitution on the principle that it is a form of sexual exploitation. They argue that the internet encourages sex tourism and prostitution while lending it a patina of normalcy (Hughes, 2000, 2003; Jones, 2001); that online forums concerning prostitutes and the quality of their services impart a cynical view of women (e.g., www.utopiaguide.com; www.theeroticreview.com; Holt & Blevins, 2007); and that online communication with customers constitutes a new form of stress for prostitutes (Davies & Evans, 2007). It is posited that the internet is used in connection with forced prostitution and the sexual trafficking of children and women (Surtees, 2008, p. 56f).

Other feminists who recognize prostitution as a legitimate occupation – on the condition that equitable working conditions are present – have to some extent evaluated the internet in a positive light. The internet offers female and male prostitutes additional opportunities to market their services, work independently, network, or verify the identity of potential clients (Ray, 2007; Uy, Parsons, Bimbi, Koken, & Halkitis, 2004).

Online Sex Work

A new market for sex work has developed online with the advent of live sex shows broadcasted via webcam. A number of professional female sex workers have reported that their activity in online sex shows (which involves responding to customer wishes in front of the camera) is much more comfortable and safe than the prostitution they previously practiced on the street or in brothels (Podlas, 2000; Bernstein, 2007). On the other hand, a potential risk is faced by individuals who chose to enter into the seemingly unproblematic online sex business with excessive haste, overestimating the financial rewards while underestimating the negative psychological and social effects (Ray, 2007). The providers and consumers of online sex services have not been systematically identified, nor have the individual consequences for participants in the online sex business. The effects exercised by the easy accessibility of online sex shows on the social perceptions of women, men, and sexuality also have yet to be explored.

Sex Education on the Internet

Institutions, companies, groups, and individuals use the internet to obtain and provide information about sexuality, as well as to promote changes in attitudes and behavior (e.g., to increase awareness about safe-sex practices).

Access to Online Sex Information

The majority of internet users occasionally search for sex information online (Gray & Klein, 2006). In a convenience sample of 760 Canadian students, 45% of females and 68% of males indicated they had searched for sex information on the internet within the past 12 months (Boies, 2002). The wide variety of content and the confidentiality with which it can be obtained are the main reasons indicated for engaging in such online searches. When assigned the task of finding online information about condom use and sexually transmitted diseases, test participants between the ages of 18 and 21 years in the United States were able to locate an appropriate website within 4 minutes – or five to six clicks – on average (Smith, Gertz, Alvarez, & Lurie, 2000). If an internet-capable computer equipped with filtering software designed to block pornographic content is used (cf. section "Pornography on the Internet"), the most restrictive settings block out 91% of pornographic content, although 24% of sexual information available online is also no longer accessible (Richardson, Resnick, Hansen, Derry, & Rideout, 2002).

Quality of Online Sex Information

Which websites communicate scientific and well-founded medical or psychological sex information? How many websites disseminate questionable or even dangerous advice (e.g., sexual abstinence is an effective method of contraception during adolescence and homosexuality can and should be cured)? Numerous questions such as these have still to be answered. A few studies have dealt with the quality of selected information being offered online for sex education (e.g., in terms of scope, completeness, topicality, factual correctness, web design). Varying informational deficits were discovered in English language websites that presented information on contraception (Weiss & Moore, 2003) and sexually transmitted diseases (Keller, LaBelle, Karimi, & Gupta, 2004), as well as on Chinese websites presenting information on HIV (Li, Lu, Yong, & Zhang, 2006). There have been no systematic comparisons to error rates in other sources of information, though (e.g., print brochures, oral communications of medical personnel). To date, it remains an open question as to which measures best assure quality among suppliers of online sex information (e.g., quality seals) or how one might give online users greater competence as consumers of information in order to help them to evaluate the quality of online content more critically themselves. A collection of links with commentary ("webliographies") – selected by independent experts – could help to orient individuals searching for online sex information (e.g., Millner & Kiser, 2002).

Types of Online Sex Education

In order to ensure sexual well-being and to overcome sexual problems, individuals need to be equipped with sex-related information (I), motivation (M), and behavioral skills (B) (the so-called IMB model of sex education: Barak & Fisher, 2001). For this reason, online sex education covers a broad range of services, including, for example, multimedia training modules for sexual communication skills, regular visits of social workers and sex experts in online sex chats, e-card services designed to warn former sex partners of a possible STD infection (e.g., www.inspot.org), or laboratory results viewable online (Rietmeijer & Shamos, 2007). Control group studies confirm that online interventions lead to an increase in knowledge and changed attitudes (e.g., Lou, Zhao, Gao, & Shah, 2006); to date, changes in behavior have been researched with comparatively less frequency (e.g., Roberto, Zimmerman, Carlyle, & Abner, 2007).

Protected by the anonymity that an online forum provides, it is possible to discuss sexual experiences and to receive information and peer advice from a wide range of different people (Suzuki & Calzo, 2004). This form of online support also includes online self-help groups for sexual topics – with their attendant opportunities (e.g., round-the-clock help, no matter where one is located) and risks (e.g., excessive emotional demands; social conflicts; cf. Waldron, Lavitt, & Kelley, 2000). In scattered instances, the internet is also being used to support sex therapy via e-mail (e.g., www.therelationshipspecialists.com: Hall, 2004).

Sex Contacts on the Internet

There are two forms of sexual contact on the internet: contacts initiated exclusively for computer-mediated exchanges (online sex) and contacts leading to real-world sexual liaisons (offline sex).

Online Sex

When engaging in online sex, partners seek to stimulate one another sexually by exchanging explicit digital texts, images, and/or video – often while masturbating (Daneback, Cooper, & Månsson, 2005; Waskul, 2002). Cybersex partners can be found in various online chat rooms, online communities, online games, or virtual worlds (e.g., Second Life). Fleeting contacts between anonymous strangers are possible, as are more enduring online relationships. As with solo sex, a number of sexual risks are eliminated when engaging in cybersex, including physical violence, unplanned pregnancy, and the transmission of STDs. In contrast to solo sex, however, cybersex offers many of the gratifications associated with partner sex, including sexual and emotional intimacy. Due to its mediated nature and the opportunities it offers for anonymity, cybersex helps to lower inhibitions and also encourages particularly open communication. Sexual inclinations and preferences otherwise concealed in the real world due to the fear of rejection can be acted out on the internet. Participants experience this as liberating, and it often encourages self-acceptance (McKenna, Green, & Smith, 2001).

Online sex provides participants with the opportunity to collect new sexual experiences and engage in sexual activities with a diverse range of partners in a relatively safe and playful setting. Cybersex is not "disembodied" per se. Sexual stimulation is experienced on a bodily level, and physical attributes and carnal reactions are also symbolically portrayed. Cybersex allows participants to present themselves in a much more favorable light than otherwise possible in face-to-face encounters. By projecting a specific persona in an online setting, individuals who are otherwise unexceptional in real-world settings can experience the lust and desire of others: Senior citizens can become young lovers; adolescents can be taken more seriously by portraying themselves as older. While age and skin color are frequently altered in online settings, virtual gender swapping is much less common: Only 1% of people regularly switch gender when going online (Cooper, Scherer, Boies, & Gordon, 1999).

Cybersex should not be classified as a deficient substitute for "real sex," but should instead be understood as a specific form of sexual expression that can play a legitimate role in the sexual and relational life of its participants (Carvalheira & Gomes, 2003; Döring 2000; Ross et al., 2004). The degree to which cybersex is experienced as satisfying and meaningful depends on the participants involved, as well as their behavior and relationships with each other. Women seem to have a stronger preference for cybersex than men (Cooper et al., 1999). In a sample of Swedish internet users who go online for sexual reasons, women in all age groups – aside from those aged 18–24 years – engaged in cybersex more often than men (25–34 years: w: 35%, m: 30%; 35–49 years: w: 37%, m: 25%; 50–65 years: w: 22%, m: 13%; Daneback et al., 2005). Cybersex is also particularly popular among gay and bisexual men (cf. Ross, Rosser, & Stanton, 2004). In a convenience sample of Canadian students (aged 20 years on average), 13% of males and 7% of females responded that they had visited a sex chat room within the past 12 months (Boies, 2002, p. 82).

Aside from its advantages, cybersex is primarily associated with three forms of risk:

1. Extreme usage patterns similar to addictive behavior can result among individuals who suffer from acute psychological afflictions (i.e., cybersex addiction; Schwartz & Southern, 2000). Not infrequently, these behaviors are accompanied by the excessive consumption of other sex-related internet content (online pornography, online sex shops; Daneback et al., 2006).
2. If married persons or individuals with a steady partner secretly engage in cybersex with a third party, this – not infrequently – is registered by the partner as an act of betrayal (so-called online infidelity) and may lead to a crisis or exacerbate existing problems in the relationship (Hertlein & Piercy, 2006; Young, 2006).
3. Cybersex is not always initiated based on mutual consent, which can result in unwanted sexual advances (i.e., "online harassment") among adults and adolescents (Barak, 2005), as well as the online sexual molestation of children: Adults may pose as adolescents in chat rooms intended for teenagers and initiate computer-mediated sexual interactions with under-aged persons. In a US-based random sample of 10- to 17-year-olds, 18% of girls and 8% of boys responded that they had experienced online sexual harassment in 2005; 7% of girls and 2% of boys experienced these contacts as very unpleasant (Mitchell, Wolak, & Finkelhor, 2007, p. 121).

Offline Sex

In two recent surveys conducted in British hospitals, 7 and 5% of heterosexual women, 14 and 10% of heterosexual men, and 47 and 44% of gay men had used the internet to search for offline sex partners within the past 12 months (Malu, Challenor, Theobald, & Barton, 2004; Bolding, Davis, Hart, Sherr, & Elford, 2006). In a Swedish sample of individuals who use the internet for sexual purposes, 35% of men and 40% of women responded that they had had sex at least once with a person met online (Daneback, Månsson, & Ross, 2007). Particularly active were singles, women between 34 and 65 years of age, and homosexual/bisexual men.

Online profiles, photos, and various dating, chat, and social networking sites are used to identify potential sex partners; communication is undertaken by e-mail, chat, webcam, and/or telephone conversations. These means allow relevant criteria such as physical attractiveness, mutual personal interest, matching sexual preferences, and preferred safe-sex practices or HIV status to be clarified in advance. Prior to meeting in the real world, potential partners sometimes engage in online sex (cf. section "Online Sex") and/or telephone sex in order to test their sexual compatibility. Among a large number of potential partners a selection is finally made through this filtering process (Couch & Liamputtong, 2007; Padgett, 2007). The internet expands opportunities for sexual contact among people who live in geographic isolation, as well as among people who seek partners for specific sexual practices, who do not want to be visible on a public stage, or who have little access to typical locations where sexual partners can be met (e.g., people with physical impairments; ethnic minorities).

The online search for offline sexual partners shares the same risks as online sex, as both activities can lead to patterns of addictive behavior. Both of these forms of sexual activity can also be associated with unfaithfulness and relationship problems. Sexual harassment and the sexual abuse of children are further potential risks: Some child molesters, for example, attempt to contact underage children on the internet in order to meet with them in real-world settings (Malesky, 2007). Although some children have been molested by pedosexuals who use the internet to identify and meet their victims, the number of children abused in this manner is exceedingly small in relation to the high number of sexual attacks perpetrated in everyday social settings, despite the intense media attention called to the internet as potential source of abuse (Döring, 2007). All the same, the internet plays a role in sexual crimes against minors by family members and acquaintances (Mitchell, Wolak, & Finkelhor, 2005).

Beyond the aforementioned risks, the online search for offline sex is also presumed to foster the spread of sexually transmitted diseases (particularly HIV). This is because homosexual and heterosexual individuals who seek out sexual partners on the internet tend to be more sexually active, more willing to take risks (i.e., more frequently decline to practice safe sex), and more often affected by STDs (McFarlane, Bull, & Reitmeijer, 2000; McFarlane, Bull, & Reitmeijer, 2002; Liau, Millett, & Marks, 2006). Targeted preventive measures on the internet can help to ameliorate this self-selection effect (Bull, McFarlane, Lloyd, & Rietmeijer, 2004; cf. section

"Types of Online Sex Education"). The possibly increased risk of unplanned preg-
nancies has not yet been investigated. Likewise, there is lack of empirical evidence
as to whether sexual attacks or violations of consent occur with greater frequency
when contact between adults is initiated via the internet as opposed to other means.
Last but not least, there is also a lack of data on the success or failure rates of online
attempts to arrange for offline sex (e.g., problems with no-shows or misleading
online self-descriptions).

On the whole, studies exploring the problems and risks associated with the online
search for offline sex comprise the bulk of scholarship in this area. Virtually no publications describe this type of behavior as largely ordinary and harmless (Daneback
et al., 2007). Even rarer are studies which expressly examine the benefits arising
from this behavior as viewed by its participants – e.g., expanded opportunities for
sexual enjoyment.

Sexual Subcultures on the Internet

When a sexual minority is unfairly discriminated against (e.g., lesbians and gays),
one rightfully welcomes the emancipation and empowerment that internet usage
can bring. By providing an easily accessible platform for the establishment of contacts between individuals of similar creeds and sexual orientations, the internet can
ameliorate social isolation, facilitate social networking, strengthen self-acceptance
and self-identity, help to communicate practical information, and encourage political activism, among other things (e.g., Hillier & Harrison, 2007; McKenna & Bargh,
1998). To some extent, online sexual subcultures have also been subject to processes
of commercialization (as seen with the outgrowth of online sex shops or commercial
dating platform addressing specific sexual minorities). The internet is an important
place of refuge for individuals who do not have access to urban subcultures by
virtue of social restrictions or their place of domicile (such as homosexual youths
in rural areas). The spectrum of sexual subcultures on the internet encompasses
homosexuality and bisexuality (e.g., Heinz, Gu, Inuzuka, & Zender, 2002; Lev
et al., 2005; Nip, 2003), transsexual and transgendered individuals (e.g., Gauthier
& Chaudoir, 2004; Shapiro, 2004), cross-dressers (Hegland & Nelson, 2002), as
well as sadomasochists, practitioners of fetishism and polyamory, or asexuals (e.g.,
www.asexuality.org).

By contrast, the use of the internet by some sexual minorities is often perceived as
a danger, particularly by those viewed as rightfully ostracized for engaging in behavior harmful to themselves or others (Durkin, Forsyth, & Quinn, 2006). It is feared
that the online presence of these deviant minorities could help to justify socially
unacceptable forms of sexual behavior, strengthen the development of pathological
disorders, or even encourage criminal activities. For example, posts which seek to
legitimize the sexual abuse of children are circulated in online forums frequented by
pedophiles, as recent research has shown (Malesky & Ennis, 2004). Online forums
geared toward other varieties of sexual deviation with the potential for grievous
harm (including amputation, cannibalism, and barebacking: Grov, 2004; Tewksbury,

2006) are also seen as a danger. On the other hand, due to the visibility of such sub-cultures on the internet, they can be addressed by research and interventions more easily.

Conclusion

Although the number of studies on internet sexuality increases every year, there are still a number of research gaps: For example, English publications concerning sexual internet use in Islamic countries are missing. Studies on the growing numbers of older users are exceedingly rare. Quantitative data representative of the population at large are lacking for numerous aspects of internet sexuality. There is also a marked deficit of qualitative studies concerned with how online sexual activities are processed cognitively and emotionally by individuals, as well as with how such activities fit into an individual's sexual biography and impact relationships between sexual partners. Conspicuous is that virtually no studies have investigated how adolescents in fact could benefit in their sexual development from various forms of self-determined internet sexuality (e.g., online pornography, online sex). Additional academic work that critically engages with the current state of research in internet sexuality to expose gaps in research, uncover implicit ideological assumptions, and contribute to theory formation would be beneficial.

References

Adams, M. S., Oye, J., & Parker, T. S. (2003). Sexuality of older adults and the internet: From sex education to cybersex. *Sexual and Relationship Therapy, 18*(3), 405–415.

Attwood, F. (2005). Fashion and passion: Marketing sex to women. *Sexualities, 8*(4), 392–406.

Attwood, F. (2007). No money shot? Commerce, pornography and new sex taste cultures. *Sexualities, 10*(4), 441–456.

Barak, A. (2005). Sexual harassment on the Internet. *Social Science Computer Review, 23*(1), 77–92.

Barak, A., & Fisher, W. A. (2001). Toward an Internet-driven, theoretically-based, innovative approach to sex education. *Journal of Sex Research, 38*(4), 324–332.

Barak, A., Fisher, W. A., Belfry, S., & Lashambe, D. R. (1999). Sex, guys, and cyberspace: Effects of internet pornography and individual differences on men's attitudes toward women. *Journal of Psychology & Human Sexuality, 11*(1), 63–91.

Bernstein, E. (2007). Sex work for the middle classes. *Sexualities, 10*(4), 473–488.

Boies, S. C. (2002). University students' uses of and reactions to online sexual information and entertainment: Links to online and offline sexual behaviour. *Canadian Journal of Human Sexuality, 11*(2), 77–89.

Bolding, G., Davis, M., Hart, G., Sherr, L., & Elford, J. (2006). Heterosexual men and women who seek sex through the internet. *International Journal of STD & AIDS, 17*(8), 530–534.

Bull, S. S., McFarlane, M., Lloyd, L., & Rietmeijer, C. (2004). The process of seeking sex partners online and implications for STD/HIV prevention. *AIDS Care, 16*(8), 1012–1020.

Carvalheira, A., & Gomes, F. A. (2003). Cybersex in Portuguese chatrooms: A study of sexual behaviors related to online sex. *Journal of Sex & Marital Therapy, 29*(5), 345–360.

Cooper, A. (1998). Sexuality and the internet: Surfing into the new millennium. *CyberPsychology & Behavior, 1*(2), 187–193.

Cooper, A., Golden, G. H., & Kent-Ferraro, J. (2002). Online sexual behaviors in the workplace: How can human resource departments and employee assistance programs respond effectively? *Sexual Addiction & Compulsivity, 9*(2–3), 149–165.

Cooper, A., McLoughlin, I. P., & Campbell, K. M. (2000). Sexuality in cyberspace: Update for the 21st century. *CyberPsychology & Behavior, 3*(4), 521–536.

Cooper, A., Scherer, C. R., Boies, S. C., & Gordon, B. L. (1999). Sexuality on the Internet: From sexual exploration to pathological expression. *Professional Psychology: Research and Practice, 30*(2), 154–164.

Couch, D., & Liamputtong, P. (2007). Online dating and mating: Perceptions of risk and health among online users. *Health Risk & Society, 9*(3), 275–294.

Cronin, B., & Davenport, E. (2001). E-rogenous zones: Positioning pornography in the digital economy. *Information Society, 17*(1), 33–48.

Daneback, K., Cooper, A., & Månsson, S.-A. (2005). An Internet study of cybersex participants. *Archives of Sexual Behavior, 34*(3), 321–328.

Daneback, K., Månsson, S.-A., & Ross, M. W. (2007). Using the Internet to find offline sex partners. *CyberPsychology & Behavior, 10*(1), 100–107.

Daneback, K., Ross, M. W., & Månsson, S.-A. (2006). Characteristics and behaviors of sexual compulsives who use the Internet for sexual purposes. *Sexual Addiction & Compulsivity, 13*(1), 53–67.

Davies, K., & Evans, L. (2007). A virtual view of managing violence among British escorts. *Deviant Behavior, 28*(6), 525–551.

Dombrowski, S. C., Gischlar, K. L., & Durst, T. (2007). Safeguarding young people from cyber pornography and cyber sexual predation: A major dilemma of the internet. *Child Abuse Review, 16*(3), 153–170.

Döring, N. (2000). Feminist views of cybersex: Victimization, liberation, and empowerment. *Cyberpsychology & Behavior, 3*(5), 863–884.

Döring, N. (2007). Sex, solicitation of on Internet. In J. J. Arnett (Ed.), *Encyclopedia of children, adolescents, and the media* (Vol. 2, pp. 750–753). Thousand Oaks, CA: Sage.

Döring, N. (2009). The internet's impact on sexuality. A critical review of 15 years of research. *Computers in Human Behavior, 25*(5), 1089–1101.

Durkin, K., Forsyth, C. J., & Quinn, J. F. (2006). Pathological Internet communities: A new direction for sexual deviance research in a post-modern era. *Sociological Spectrum, 26*(6), 595–606.

Fisher, W. A., & Barak, A. (2000). Online sex shops: Phenomenological, psychological, and ideological perspectives on Internet sexuality. *CyberPsychology & Behavior, 3*(4), 575–589.

Fisher, W. A., & Barak, A. (2001). Internet pornography: A social psychological perspective on internet sexuality. *Journal of Sex Research, 38*(4), 312–323.

Gauthier, D. K., & Chaudoir, N. K. (2004). Tranny boyz: Cyber community support in negotiating sex and gender mobility among female to male transsexuals. *Deviant Behavior, 25*(4), 375–398.

Gossett, J. L., & Byrne, S. (2002). "CLICK HERE": A content analysis of internet rape sites. *Gender & Society, 16*(5), 689–709.

Gray, N. J., & Klein, J. D. (2006). Adolescents and the internet: Health and sexuality information. *Current Opinion in Obstetrics & Gynecology, 18*(5), 519–524.

Grov, C. (2004). "Make me your death slave": Men who have sex with men and use the internet to intentionally spread HIV. *Deviant Behavior, 25*(4), 329–349.

Hall, P. (2004). Online psychosexual therapy: A summary of pilot study findings. *Sexual and Relationship Therapy, 19*(2), 167–178.

Hardy, S. (2008). The reality of pornography. *Sexualities, 11*(1–2), 60–64.

Hegland, J., & Nelson, N. (2002). Cross-dressers in cyber-space: Exploring the Internet as a tool for expressing gendered identity. *International Journal of Sexuality and Gender Studies, 7*(2–3), 139–161.

Heider, D., & Harp, D. (2002). New hope or old power: Democracy, pornography and the internet. *Howard Journal of Communications, 13*(4), 285–299.

Heinz, B., Gu, L., Inuzuka, A., & Zender, R. (2002). Under the rainbow flag: Webbing global gay identities. *International Journal of Sexuality & Gender Studies, 7*(2–3), 107–124.

Hertlein, K. M., & Piercy, F. P. (2006). Internet infidelity: A critical review of the literature. *The Family Journal, 14*(4), 366–371.

Hillier, L., & Harrison, L. (2007). Building realities less limited than their own: Young people practising same-sex attraction on the internet. *Sexualities, 10*(1), 82–100.

Holt, T. J., & Blevins, K. R. (2007). Examining sex work from the client's perspective: Assessing johns using on-line. *Deviant Behavior, 28*(4), 333–354.

Hughes, D. (2000). "Welcome to rape camp": Sexual exploitation and the Internet in Cambodia. *Journal of Sexual Aggression, 6*(1–2), 29–51.

Hughes, D. (2003). Prostitution online. *Journal of Trauma Practice, 2*(3–4), 115–132.

Innala, S. (2007). Pornography on the net: Same attraction, but new options *Sexologies, 16*(2), 112–120.

Jacobs, K., Janssen, M., & Pasquinelli, M. (Eds.). (2007). *C'lickme. A netporn studies reader.* Amsterdam, NL: Institute of Network Cultures.

Jones, C. (2001). Surfing the crime net: Sex tourism. *Crime Prevention and Community Safety, 3*(3), 53–57.

Keller, S. N., LaBelle, H., Karimi, N., & Gupta, S. (2004). Talking about STD/HIV prevention: A look at communication online. *AIDS Care, 16*(8), 977–992.

Kuhnen, K. (2007). Kinderpornographie und Internet (Child Pornography and Internet). Göttingen: Hogrefe.

Lam, C. B., & Chan, D. K. S. (2007). The use of cyberpornography by young men in Hong Kong: Some psychosocial correlates. *Archives of Sexual Behavior, 36*(4), 588–598.

Leiblum, S., & Döring, N. (2002). Internet sexuality: Known risks and fresh chances for women. In A. Cooper (Ed.), *Sex and the internet: A guidebook for clinicians* (pp. 19–46). Philadelphia, PA: Brunner-Routledge.

Lev, A. I., Dean, G., DeFilippis, L., Evernham, K., McLaughlin, L., & Phillips, C. (2005). Dykes and tykes: A virtual lesbian parenting community. *Journal of Lesbian Studies, 9*(1–2), 81–94.

Lewandowski, S. (2003). Internetpornographie [Internet pornography.]. *Zeitschrift für Sexualforschung, 16*(4), 299–327.

Li, D., Lu, H.-Z., Yong, X., & Zhang, A. (2006). Incomplete information about AIDS on Chinese websites. *AIDS, 20*(18), 2400–2402.

Liau, A., Millett, G., & Marks, G. (2006). Meta-analytic examination of online sex-seeking and sexual risk behavior among men who have sex with men. *Sexually Transmitted Diseases, 33*(9), 576–584.

Lo, V.-H., & Wei, R. (2005). Exposure to Internet pornography and Taiwanese adolescents' sexual attitudes and behavior. *Journal of Broadcasting & Electronic Media, 49*(2), 221–237.

Lou, C., Zhao, Q., Gao, E., & Shah, I. (2006). Can the Internet be used effectively to provide sex education to young people in China? *Journal of Adolescent Health, 39*(5), 720–728.

Malesky, L. A., Jr., (2007). Predatory online behavior: Modus operandi of convicted sex offenders in identifying potential victims and contacting minors over the internet. *Journal of Child Sexual Abuse, 16*(2), 23–32.

Malesky, L. A., Jr., & Ennis, L. (2004). Supportive distortions: An analysis of posts on a pedophile internet message board. *Journal of Addictions & Offender Counseling, 24*(2), 92–100.

Malu, M. K., Challenor, R., Theobald, N., & Barton, S. E. (2004). Seeking and engaging in internet sex: A survey of patients attending genitourinary medicine clinics in Plymouth and in London. *International Journal of STD & AIDS, 15*(11), 720–724.

Manning, J. C. (2006). The impact of Internet pornography on marriage and the family: A review of the research. *Sexual Addiction & Compulsivity, 13*(2–3), 131–165.

McFarlane, M., Bull, S. S., & Reitmeijer, C. A. (2000). The Internet as a newly emerging risk environment for sexually transmitted diseases. *JAMA, 284*(4), 443–446.

McFarlane, M., Bull, S. S., & Rietmeijer, C. A. (2002). Young adults on the internet: Risk behaviors for sexually transmitted diseases and HIV. *Journal of Adolescent Health, 31*(1), 11–16.

McKenna, K. Y. A., & Bargh, J. A. (1998). Coming out in the age of the internet: Identity "demarginalization" through virtual group participation. *Journal of Personality and Social Psychology, 75*(3), 681–694.

McKenna, K. Y. A., Green, A. S., & Smith, P. K. (2001). Demarginalizing the sexual self. *Journal of Sex Research, 38*(4), 302–311.

Mehta, M. D. (2001). Pornography in Usenet: A study of 9,800 randomly selected images. *CyberPsychology & Behavior, 4*(6), 695–703.

Miller-Young, M. (2007). Sexy and smart: Black women and the politics of self-authorship in netporn. In K. Jacobs, M. Janssen, & M. Pasquinelli (Eds.), *C'lickme. A netporn studies reader* (pp. 205–226). Amsterdam, NL: Institute of Network Cultures.

Millner, V. S., & Kiser, J. D. (2002). Sexual information and Internet resources. *The Family Journal, 10*(2), 234–239.

Mitchell, K. J., Finkelhor, D., & Wolak, J. (2003). The exposure of youth to unwanted sexual material on the internet: A national survey of risk, impact, and prevention. *Youth & Society, 34*(3), 330–358.

Mitchell, K. J., Wolak, J., & Finkelhor, D. (2005). Police posing as juveniles online to catch sex offenders: Is it working. *Sexual Abuse: Journal of Research and Treatment, 17*(3), 241–267.

Mitchell, K. J., Wolak, J., & Finkelhor, D. (2007). Trends in youth reports of sexual solicitations, harassment and unwanted exposure to pornography on the internet. *Journal of Adolescent Health, 40*(2), 116–126.

Nip, J. Y. M. (2003). The relationship between online and offline communities: The case of the queer sisters. *Media Culture & Society, 26*(3), 409–428.

Padgett, P. M. (2007). Personal safety and sexual safety for women using online personal ads. *Sexuality Research & Social Policy: A Journal of the NSRC, 4*(2), 27–37.

Podlas, K. (2000). Mistresses of their domain: How female entrepreneurs in cyberporn are initiating a gender power shift. *CyberPsychology & Behavior, 3*(5), 847–854.

Quayle, E., & Taylor, M. (2002). Child pornography and the Internet: Perpetuating a cycle of abuse. *Deviant Behavior, 23*(4), 331–362.

Ray, A. (2007). Sex on the open market: Sex workers harness the power of the Internet. In K. Jacobs, M. Janssen, & M. Pasquinelli (Eds.), *C'lickme. A netporn studies reader* (pp. 45–68). Amsterdam, NL: Institute of Network Cultures.

Richardson, C. R., Resnick, P. J., Hansen, D. L., Derry, H. A., & Rideout, V. J. (2002). Does pornography-blocking software block access to health information on the Internet? *JAMA, 288*(22), 2887–2894.

Rietmeijer, C. A., & Shamos, S. J. (2007). HIV and sexually transmitted infection prevention online: Current state and future prospects. *Sexuality Research & Social Policy: A Journal of the NSRC, 4*(2), 65–73.

Roberto, A. J., Zimmerman, R. S., Carlyle, K. E., & Abner, E. L. (2007). A computer-based approach to preventing pregnancy, STD, and HIV in rural adolescents. *Journal of Health Communication, 12*(1), 53–76.

Ross, M. W., Rosser, B. R. S., & Stanton, J. (2004). Beliefs about cybersex and Internet-mediated sex of Latino men who have Internet sex with men: Relationships with sexual practices in cybersex and in real life. *AIDS Care, 16*(8), 1002–1011.

Schauer, T. (2005). Women's porno: The heterosexual female gaze in porn sites "for women". *Sexuality & Culture: An Interdisciplinary Quarterly, 9*(2), 42–64.

Schell, B. H., Martin, M. V., Hung, P. C. K., & Rueda, L. (2007). Cyber child pornography: A review paper of the social and legal issues and remedies and a proposed technological solution. *Aggression and Violent Behavior, 12*(1), 45–63.

Schwartz, M. F., & Southern, S. (2000). Compulsive cybersex: The new tea room. *Sexual Addiction & Compulsivity, 7*(1–2), 127–144.

Shapiro, E. (2004). "Trans"cending barriers: Transgender organizing on the internet. *Journal of Gay & Lesbian Social Services: Issues in Practice, Policy & Research, 16*(3–4), 165–179.

Smith, M., Gertz, E., Alvarez, S., & Lurie, P. (2000). The content and accessibility of sex education information on the internet. *Health Education & Behavior, 27*(6), 684–694.

Surtees, R. (2008). Traffickers and trafficking in southern and Eastern Europe: Considering the other side of human trafficking. *European Journal of Criminology, 5*(1), 39–68.

Suzuki, L. K., & Calzo, J. P. (2004). The search for peer advice in cyberspace: An examination of online teen bulletin boards about health and sexuality. *Journal of Applied Developmental Psychology, 25*(6), 685–698.

Tewksbury, R. (2006). "Click here for HIV": An analysis of Internet-based bug chasers and bug givers. *Deviant Behavior, 27*(4), 379–395.

Træen, B., Nilsen, T. S., & Stigum, H. (2006). Use of pornography in traditional media and on the internet in Norway. *Journal of Sex Research, 43*(3), 245–254.

Uy, J. M., Parsons, J. T., Bimbi, D. S., Koken, J. A., & Halkitis, P. N. (2004). Gay and bisexual male escorts who advertise on the Internet: Understanding reasons for and effects of involvement in commercial sex. *International Journal of Men's Health, 3*(1), 11–26.

Waldron, V. R., Lavitt, M., & Kelley, D. (2000). The nature and prevention of harm in technology mediated self-help settings: Three exemplars. *Journal of Technology in Human Services, 17*(2–3), 267–293.

Waskul, D. D. (2002). The naked self: Being a body in televideo cybersex. *Symbolic Interaction, 25*(2), 199–227.

Weiss, E., & Moore, K. (2003). An assessment of the quality of information available on the internet about the IUD and the potential impact on contraceptive choices. *Contraception, 68*, 359–364.

Young, K. S. (2006). Online infidelity: Evaluation and treatment implications. *Journal of Couple and Relationship Therapy, 5*(2), 43–56.

Zook, M. (2007). Report on the location of the internet adult industry. In K. Jacobs, M. Janssen, & M. Pasquinelli (Eds.), *C'lickme. A netporn studies reader* (pp. 103–124). Amsterdam, NL: Institute of Network Cultures.

After Convergence: *YouTube* and Remix Culture

Anders Fagerjord

Beyond Convergence

In little more than a year, from November 2005 to the autumn of 2006, *YouTube* became a new media phenomenon. This library of videos uploaded from millions of users is one of the best examples of the complex matrix of new media that are described as *convergence* (Walther, 2005), *convergence culture* (Jenkins, 2006) and *Web 2.0.* (Musser & O'Reilly, 2007). It is complex because the content is unpredictable. On *YouTube*, there are lots of recordings from TV shows and films old and new. Amateur videos of stunts, fiction, parodies and pastiches abound. Professional recordings attempt to market products and artists famous and would-be famous. Regular people put up diary-like recordings of speaking into a camera. Politicians cry for attention in more or less convincing talks, "viral marketing" tries to disguise its commercial message, and fictional diaries pretend to be real. And the declining genre of the music video has found a new life online (Austerlitz, 2007). *YouTube* is not just a web phenomenon; it is in open contest with broadcast TV. TV shows look to *YouTube* for newsworthy or entertaining material. As MediaCentre PCs and AppleTVs occupy the place of the TV set and mobile phones are ready to show you YouTube videos wherever you are, *YouTube* promises to follow you everywhere. *YouTube* seems to me to be a good example to discuss modern online media with, but first, we need to back up a little.

When Nicholas Negroponte resigned from his column in *Wired Magazine* in 1998, he had written for 6 years about new media technology, and his ideas of what the future will bring. Most of Negroponte's influential book *Being Digital* (Negroponte, 1995) originated in the column in *Wired.* But in 1998, it seemed that his crystal ball became clouded. He could no longer write about the changes that would come with the digital future, as the future had arrived. "The digital revolution is over," he wrote in his final column (Negroponte, 1998).

A. Fagerjord (✉)
førsteamanuensis, Dr. Art., Institutt for Medier og Kommunikasjon,
University of Oslo, Oslo
e-mail: anders.fagerjord@media.uio.no

J. Hunsinger et al. (eds.), *International Handbook of Internet Research*,
DOI 10.1007/978-1-4020-9789-8_11, © Springer Science+Business Media B.V. 2010

From the late 1970s, mass media became digital. The effects of this digitization have often been described as *convergence,* the coming together of the media. Media converged in different ways as most media could be represented as numbers on a computer.

Production tools converged. Computers were increasingly used to create and edit text, images, sound, film, and television images. A large array of different media technologies were replaced by software on powerful computers.

Distribution networks converged. All kinds of networks could carry the digital signals representing various media forms. Telephone wires, television cable networks, computer networks, and wireless telephone networks were all able to transmit telephony, television and internet traffic of all kinds.

Business sectors converged. Before digitization, the computer industry, the publishing industry, the telephone industry, the film industry, the music industry and the broadcasting industry were thought of as separate business sectors. Owners of telephone and TV cable networks soon realized, however, that they had become competitors in the business of carrying all kinds of digital signals. News corporations realized that they could also produce radio and television on the computers they had bought for newspaper production. Radical mergers and acquisitions followed, the most spectacular being the combination of Netscape, America Online, Time and Warner culminating in the huge conglomerate AOL Time Warner in 2001.

Genres and services converged. Websites provided stories and information in video and sound as well as writing and images, with links to pages where consumers could shop, reserve tickets, do their banking, or file tax forms.

The technologies used by consumers, such as television sets, telephones, newspapers, video recorders, DVD players, game consoles, and computers converged. As I am writing this, the computer and mobile phone manufacturers are competing in making computers and mobile phones that will replace the last traditional TV sets, radios, and telephones in our homes with computers that are dressed up to look good in the living room, while they basically have the same chips and software inside as the computers used to create the TV and radio shows.

Nicholas Negroponte was one of the first to recognize this development, and he may have been one of the first to use the term *convergence* to describe it.[1] During the 1990s, business leaders, politicians and journalists discovered that *convergence* was a concept that could explain in a very precise manner the huge changes in the media businesses. I will argue, however, that *convergence* is over. The media have already converged. And again, Negroponte may have been one of the first to realize it: "We are now in a digital age" (Negroponte, 1998).

Convergence as a development must logically end at some point either because media cease to converge, or because all media have converged into one, or

---

[1] The *Oxford English Dictionary* has recorded the first use of *convergence* in this sense in 1978, while Stuart Brand reports that Negroponte used it in 1973 (Brand, 1988).

have reached a limit where further convergence is impossible. In theory, it could continue until we only had one kind of technology (a computer), using only one kind of network, to project one combined genre from one single company. It does not seem very likely or desirable, though. Although many have predicted massive merges of media companies, it is likely that markets will consolidate with a number of actors. Most countries' legislators also wish for competition between media houses. There has furthermore become much easier to start up a new media company, as there is no need for large investments in technology for production and distribution. Alongside the market convergence into a small number of media conglomerates, we see an explosion in small niche products, *divergence*.

Perhaps the easiest way to see that convergence is a description with limits is to consider the offering of digital devices. Far from seeing a digital "über-box," a media machine to replace all known media, we are witnessing an explosion of different digital music players, game consoles, video recorders, GPS systems, personal digital assistants, cameras, and mobile phones; and combinations of any number of such devices. In 2007, Apple's iPhone created an enormous buzz. The little black glass and aluminium-convered slab seemed once again to promise to have everything in a small package. A few years earlier, Sony's PlayStation Portable claimed the same. I own both, and as Walther (2005) observes, they have different essential functions. Both are video and music players, but the PSP is a game console, and the iPhone is a phone. After a decade or more of convergence, I certainly do not have any fewer devices now than I had ten years ago, and the owners of my local electronics store are pleased.

The basics of capitalism dictate that technology companies will continue to invent new gadgets for us to buy, and media "content providers" will continue to create messages in many forms.[2] As the idea of total convergence is absurd, we need to ask ourselves when the new developments in the media cannot be explained by the mechanics of convergence anymore. I believe that we are beyond that point. Henry Jenkins, one of those best who understands the mechanics of convergence, admits that "we are not yet ready to cope with its complexities and contradictions" (Jenkins, 2006). My suggestion is to look for other concepts than "convergence" to describe internet phenomena. We can direct our focus in other directions by adopting a new vocabulary.

The concept of convergence is stretched beyond what is meaningful. Several researchers have registered that rather than converging into fewer technologies, companies or genres, we are witnessing a proliferation of media; a *divergence* (cf. Bolter & Grusin, 1999; Fagerjord, 2003b; Liestøl, 2006; Manovich, 2001); Walther, 2005). Some, like Bo Kampmann Walther (2005) or Jenkins (2006) want to subsume *divergence* under *convergence,* as they are part of the same development: the consequences of digitalization. I think, however, that we are able to be more specific, at least in the study of genres and forms of expression. Instead of just noting that their number is increasing, I would like to understand how new forms

---

[2]I have argued this point further in an earlier essay (Fagerjord, 2002).

are developing online. To gain such an understanding, we need to start somewhere, so I will venture a new term to describe what has been going on the last few years: *remix*.

What Comes After Convergence? Remix

My claim, for the time being, is that *remix* is what comes after convergence. Convergence is the process of levelling the differences between the different media. Digital representation has become a *lingua franca;* it has created a shared space where forms from different genres in different media may be combined in new ways, creating new genres. I have characterized this process earlier as a "rhetorical convergence" (Fagerjord, 2003a, 2003b). In the present essay, I will propose the term *remix* to characterize how rhetorical convergence is created. This is only a subtle difference, but by using *remix* I hope to change the focus away from an understanding of media development as convergence, as indicateds above.

As we will see, I am not the first to use this word. Lawrence Lessig (2007) has described modern folk culture as a "remix" culture or a "read/write" culture. Millions of people with inexpensive computers copy and paste elements from digital mass culture and assemble them into new works. (Jenkins (2006) uses the term *Convergence Culture* for the very same phenomenon.) I will use the concept in a similar way, trying to show that it is a fitting description for many phenomena in the age of *YouTube*.

In music, to remix is to create a new version of a recording by altering the mix of the different musical elements, or also to introduce new elements. Some remix artists create completely new pieces by combining elements of different recordings. In what follows, I would like to point out that this is quite parallel to how several new media developments have come about. First, I will describe remix as a way of creating new genres from pieces of earlier genres. Then I will discuss remix as a certain mode of creativity, allowing anyone to become a media *auteur*. Last, I will suggest that the massive file sharing we are witnessing is part of the same development, as a remix culture is a culture of "rip and create".

Remix as Genre Movement

How does a new genre develop? Gunnar Liestøl argues genre development can be described as a process of convergence. Liestøl uses a maelstrom as a metaphor to explain this, referring to Poe's short story "Through the Maelstrom" where a boat is crushed in a maelstrom, and the protagonist only survives by clinging to the debris. When water runs through a narrow sound, strong forces are created, forces that may rip apart a boat that follows the current. The debris – the separate parts of the boat – may be reassembled in new ways afterwards; as a raft in Poe's example (Liestøl, 2007).

In the same way, digitalization makes it possible for us to reassemble parts from earlier media, such as writing and moving images. Or writing and live broadcast. Telephony and photography in the same device. These are developments that have been called examples of convergence. But the figure of convergence breaks down as soon as we realize that there is no end to the creation of new such combinations. This is why I believe *remix* is a better word.

When genres are remixed into new, parts from different media and different technology are often spliced together. This may be difficult to realize, as technologies, media and dominating genres have been so closely knit together that it has been difficult to separate them, even in theory. A medium is more than the technological apparatus that transmits signs from one place from another. In addition to technology, each medium is characterized by a certain form of financing, legal status, social conventions and dominant genres[3] (see Williams, 1975, for discussion of how television became the medium it is today). Genres are families of texts, families that share important aspects such as a certain kind of story, a certain style or a certain subject matter. These three levels are independent. A technology may be used by several media: a printshop can print both books and newspapers. A genre may exist across several media, as detective stories exist in print, film and on television.

These distinctions become blurry on the web. It is possible to film children swimming for 10 minutes and show the film in a cinema theatre, but the cinema institution is built up around a spectacular feature of 90 minutes. Family shots are the domain of video. On the web, on the other hand, family clips, TV news and feature films may be part of the same web page – and sometimes are. And from such mixes, new genres may develop.

Let us look at a popular concept of convergence: the convergence of television and print newspapers. It is a simple idea that has inspired many mergers of television and print companies worldwide. So what does the combination of paper and telly look like? It is immediately clear that it has many different looks already, and more are likely to come. Many online versions of print newspapers offer video as illustrations to their stories; a short video clip is inserted in the page where a photo normally would be. Other web news sites keep the videos in a dedicated window, a "media player", where a selection of video clips are available from a menu, rather independent of the written news of the day. A third way of converging, however, is not to borrow the moving image of television, but rather its *liveness,* the very trait that many theorists consider to be television's most defining characteristic (Eco, 1999; Feuer, 1983; Heath, 1990). A web news site is *live* in the same manner as broadcasting, in that it may distribute its stories as soon they are ready, or even as the events unfold. Sports events are often covered live in writing: A reporter is watching a football match, for example, and typing a written description of the action that is published one line at a time. Some times, these reports are even mirrored on the news site's front page, so it is continually updated: a *live front page.*

---

[3] I am here using 'medium' in the sense of 'mass medium', common in media studies. Within art history, e.g., 'medium' has more the meaning of 'material'.

Genres may form in many ways. Media and genres are combinations of many characteristics that traditionally have occurred in stable combinations: Moving images + address to camera + documentary footage + live broadcast + regular schedule + many short segments presented in a sequence for 20 minutes = television news.

On the web, each of these characteristics, each of the variables in this equation, may be mixed into a new genre in remix culture. For example, moving image + address to camera + documentary footage + recorded broadcast + irregular schedule + many short segments available for selection by user + written comments by viewers = video blog.

I believe the present media developments may effectively be likened to the children's game where cardboard figures of people in different costumes, such as a fireman, a baker, a policeman, a painter, a pirate, Santa Claus, are cut up so the hats, faces, torsos, and legs may be mixed to create new figures. To understand remix culture, we need to understand where the "media figures" are cut, so to speak: We need to isolate the aspects of genres that may be remixed into new genres and media configurations.

What Parts Are Mixed?

In an earlier study of convergence in documentary sites on the web, I identified four variables of texts that may be changed independently in digital genre remix (Fagerjord, 2003a). The four "axes," as I termed them, are:

Sign system: the choice of writing, images, sound, video, etc. Earlier media had choices of sign system; a book cannot contain video. In digital media, the author may use a different sign system or combination of sign systems in every text.

Mode of Acquisition: the "reading" process required of the audience. A movie in a movie theatre is consumed from start to finish without interruptions, while a book may be read in many long or short sittings, and parts may be reread or skipped. Digital media also often offer hyperlinks, allowing each audience member to decide the sequence of the parts. The mode of acquisition is changed radically, for example, when a film is made into a computer game.

Canvas: the size and resolution of the text in time and space. A movie clip on *YouTube* is very different from the viewing experience of the whole feature in a theatre. The *YouTube* clip is shorter, much smaller, and with way inferior sound and image quality. The canvas is limited by technology, as in the *YouTube* example, but also chosen by the author to suit her or his intended audience. It is possible to distribute video in *High Definition* quality on the web (Apple Computers regularly does this), but most web authors consider such a quality to require too much bandwidth. Similarly, most film directors and producers keep movies within 2 hours, or 3 at the most. There is a limit to how long most audience members are willing to stay in the theatre seat. DVD versions of the same films may be longer, however, as they are watched in the comfort of one's home – the *Lord of the Rings* trilogy directed by Peter Jackson is a case in point.

Distribution: the time it takes to create a text, to distribute it to the readers, and how long the text stays available. For a live broadcast, creation and distribution time (or *latency*) are close to zero, and the text is gone when the broadcast is over (zero *permanence*). A regular newspaper may take several days to prepare, a night to print and distribute, and the readers may keep it for as long as they please, for most people a few days. Digital genres may remix these variables. A live video broadcast may be available as a recording for years, for example.

While I believe sign system, acquisition, canvas and distribution are four variables that may be useful in describing any genre, they are the result of a study of the documentary genre. If our ambition is to describe other genres too, we will need additional aspects. If we are to describe the genre conventions and experimenting we can see on *YouTube,* for example, we will need some extra variables in our description.

First of all, the principal distinction that sets the genres of documentary and the feature apart from other genres is the text's relation to *reality.* A documentary film is made primarily from non-fiction photographic footage. News is another genre that rests upon the idea that it is real, relatively objective and true.[4] A genre's relation to reality is another aspect that may be remixed. First, we need to remember that the distinction of fiction/non-fiction is a continuum, not a dichotomy. If we take movies as an example, one can list many fiction films about real events (e.g. *Titanic, JFK, Amadeus*), but also documentaries with elements of fiction[5] (*Roger and Me, Creature Comfort, Thirty-Two Short Films About Glenn Gould*) as well as fiction guised as documentary (*This is Spinal Tap!, The Blair Witch Project*). By paying attention to how a text uses fictional elements, we can often reveal mixing of genres.

The blurring of the border between fiction and non-fiction is, as these examples from cinema show, not necessarily a development that is caused by digitalization. It is quite common online, however, perhaps because the web is a place where anyone can publish at low cost, so it is affordable to experiment. One of the most common forms of genre remix on the web is to use the formal characteristics of news or documentary, but with a different relation to fiction. Blogs are examples of a genre which owns much of its layout to newspaper design, but where the writing has little in common with newspaper reporting. Weblogs are generally written in a personal voice, and many blogs contain fictitious material. Furthermore, on the web, where genres constantly are remixed and redeveloped, much debate is caused from precisely the tension between fact and fiction. Thousands of fans were deeply disappointed when it was revealed that the home schooled teenager Bree in the video blog *Lonelygirl15* (Lonelygirl15, 2007) was a character of fiction, and John Richardson's long piece in

---

[4]The idea of absolute truth is difficult to defend from the attacks of philosophy and poststructuralism, and much of media studies is devoted to demonstrating that news are just one account of many possible of a truth that may never be reachable. I will still argue, however, that what we regard as news is only possible if we believe them to be reasonably true—even for media professors who know that at the end of the day, they may not.

[5]See (Fetveit, 2002)

Esquire of the search for the blogger Isabella V. of *She's a Flight Risk* is a document of the same urge to know whether a story is for real (Richardson, 2003).

Anonymity and posing have been characteristics of digital culture at least since the era of e-mail lists, bulletin board systems and Usenet news groups, long before the commercial internet and the web. Researchers have devoted much interest to members of discussion groups, chat rooms and multiplayer games that have posed online as a different gender and age, as well as robotic characters, computer programs posing as players or discussants (see, among others, Aarseth, 1997; Murray, 1997). The famous cartoon from *The New Yorker* sums it up: a dog is typing at a computer keyboard, noting to another dog: "on the net, nobody knows you're a dog.[6]" Again, the questions of fiction or real is not necessarily caused by, or even a part of, the digital revolution, but in a post-convergence age where remix is the norm, reality and fiction are often both mixed and remixed in new genre developments.

Another important aspect of every genre is purpose, the rationale behind the text's creation and its place in the lives of the audience, what we might call its "social function." Media scholars within the tradition of Cultural Studies have discussed the functions of different media genres for decades (see, e.g. Barthes, 1993; Fiske, 1987; Fiske & Hartley, 1978; Hartley, 1982, 1999; Morley & Brunsdon, 1999; Radway, 1984). We may read the newspaper to be informed, to keep up with the important people in the world (Fiske, 1987 describes news as men's soap opera) and to check that the world still is as we know it. A television sitcom may be a welcome pleasure helping us to relax after a day's work (cf Adorno & Horkheimer, 1999), at the same time confirming our beliefs and ideologies. Charles Cheung is one of many who have noted that the web has allowed ordinary people to publish websites about themselves, thus defining and reworking their identities (Cheung, 2004). Not that it is novel to write to define one's identity, Michel Foucault has noted how people have "written their selves" for centuries (Foucault, 1994), but on the web, this is often a public activity.

It is possible to use formal aspects of some genres and mix with the purpose of another. A blog might, for example, be called a remix of a web news site and a diary. Both news sites and blogs usually have a front page with the most recent items, presented with short leads or excerpts from the full article. The full article is linked from the front page. Articles are posted every week or everyday, which means that the front page is regularly changed. But most blogs differ very much from news sites in terms of topic, tone, and subjectivity. *Lonelygirl15*'s mix of reality and fiction is also a mix of formal aspects from one genre with the social purpose of another. What appeared to be a typical journal-like confessional video blog was shown to be fiction. Instead of being a self-defining exercise, where Bree was taking part in an online social network, it became a narrative, where a story from Bree's life was told in the first person, addressing the camera, affording the pleasures of narrative to its audience.

---

[6] The cartoon is by Peter Steiner, and ran in *The New Yorker* 5 July, 1993.

Although it is customary to speak of weblogs as a somewhat unified genre, it is obvious to anyone that there is enormous variation between blogs. If we speak of blogs as a unified class of websites, what unites them is their publishing technology. Weblogs tend to be served by database-backed systems allowing for quick writing and publishing, archives of older posts, easy linking, systems for user comments, link lists and various other automatic indexing services. This technical apparatus is used to host sites that serve very different purposes. The technology that serves many a teenager's journal is also used to publish the stylish metropolitan news site *Gothamist,* the home page of the Creative Commons movement (working to establish an alternative to copyright), and the home page for the developers of the web browser Apple is using.[7] Many of the genre characteristics of blogs are pre-scribed by the publishing system, so these sites look quite similar, although their aims differ.

Remix as a Mode of Creativity

Remix is not only a helpful concept in understanding how new genres form, it does also seem to be a common technique to create new works. The many videos on *YouTube* demonstrate this.

YouTube is a remix in itself: While it would be a stretch to call *YouTube* an example of convergence, you might call the site a clever remix of a video gallery, a blog-like commenting system, a system of friends and connections as in a social network site such as *LinkedIn* and a file-sharing site or network.The key to the site's success, however, is how easy it is to upload video. Any kind of video is automatically transcoded to Flash, a file format most web browsers can play back without extra installations. Each video is hosted on its own address (URL) that may be bookmarked or e-mailed, and YouTube is also automatically producing HTML code that users can copy and paste to include video in their own web pages. These functions have made it so easy to share video on *YouTube* that in early 2007, 65,000 new videos were uploaded, and 100,000,000 clips viewed each day, according to the company's website (*YouTube*, 2007). Anyone who spends a couple of hours browsing the strange collection will realize that a large proportion of these clips may be characterized as remixes in one way or another.[8]

In his account of computers as a medium for artists, Lev Manovich has called *creativity as selection* and *compositing* two of the "basic operations" of computer software (Manovich, 2001, pp. 120, 123–41). Software applications for design and creativity tend to offer menus of choices for the creator. Manovich's examples include textures and human figures in a 3D animation program, filters in an image editor, libraries of computer code in a programming environment and clip art images

---

[7]<http://gothamist.com>, <http://creativecommons.org>, <http://webkit.org>

[8]At the time of writing, no one has done a statistical analysis of what Youtube's videos are about. I hope future research will give us an overview of what this cornocupia of moving images actually is full of.

in a home page editor on the web. "New media objects are rarely created completely from scratch; usually they are assembled from ready-made parts. Put differently, in computer culture, authentic creation has been replaced by selection from a menu" (p. 124). Whether "authentic creation" has ever been free of combining new elements with copies or pastiches of earlier work is not a discussion I want to open in this article (Manovich does that himself a few pages later) but it certainly has become much faster and easier to combine ready-made parts with computer software and that it often requires no other training than being able to use a computer interface.

Selection goes hand in hand with the other operation, *compositing*, the creation of images from many transparent layers, Manovich notes. The contents of each layers may come from many different sources, and "are fitted together and adjusted in such a way that their separate identities become invisible" (Manovich, 2001, p. 136). Manovich only discusses still images and individual shots in film in his section on compositing. This is less common in amateur videos on *YouTube*, apart from superimposing (written) titles and adding a sound track. Compositing software, and especially effacing the traces of the compositing, is still the work of professionals. What is much more common is to composite in time; to edit together images from different sources to make a clip.[9]

It is not uncommon to find videos on *YouTube* that make an argument, often a political statement.[10] These tend to be collages of television footage, photographs, written documents and explanatory text or voice-over narration. Elements taken from a wide variety of sources are mounted together to a coherent message, trying to get a point through. More often than not, the images and video clips are used against their original purpose; a politician's statement may, for example, be used to show that he is wrong. Imagery, sound and text are remixed into a new whole, following the logics of selection and compositing. Creativity by selection is also apparent in another genre found on *YouTube:* slideshows made of still images, most often images of celebrities taken from magazines. In a typical slideshow, a series of images are selected from a source and then put in a sequence. Using a video editing program, the creator selects different ways of moving the frame over the still images and transitions between them. A soundtrack is created by selecting a piece of music from a collection, and a few lines of text are perhaps added, again by selecting text effects from a menu.[11]

Each user's "channel", that is, the web page with all of his or her *YouTube* videos may be personalized somewhat. Selecting from menus, the user may change colours and some of the elements on the page in an attempt to personalize his or her space.

---

[9]Selection and compositing also has obvious similarities with "mashups", web services that combine services from other websites, such as Google Maps or Amazon book titles with other information. See Musser and O'Reilly (2007) for a discussion of mashups.

[10]For example, see <http://youtube.com/watch?v=J1bm2GpoFfg> or <http://www.youtube.com/watch?v=Sy_8THVO-1w>

[11]See, for example, <http://www.youtube.com/watch?v=_9BTDH2uYuk> or <http://www.youtube.com/watch?v=HApH_HiyK7E>

This use of templates is typical in most of digital creation, especially by amateurs, and is another example of creativity by selection. A template is a "half-baked" work, where some of the elements already are created. The user can fill in his or her detail, and the finished work is created faster, and often better, than it otherwise would be.[12] Media creation by templates is another example of creativity by selection, a kind of creativity that is widespread in digital media. Pre-existing elements are inserted into a pre-existing template, and remixed into a new work, rather like a DJ is mixing music. As Manovich puts it: "The DJ best demonstrates [computer culture's] new logic: selection and combination of preexistent elements. [...] [T]he practice of live electronic music demonstrates that true art lies in the 'mix'" (p. 135).

Rip and Remix Culture

The most popular videos on *YouTube* each day seem to be rips rather than remixes. Clips from television shows, music videos, film trailers, and other short and self-contained scenes from television and film are recorded, digitized, edited in the beginning and end and uploaded to *YouTube*. In short, "ripped". In many cases the copyright holders do this themselves; many record companies, film distributors and television channels have "channels" on *YouTube*. Most television clips seem to be uploaded by regular users, however, even though *YouTube* is trying to weed out infringements of copyright.

Although these clips are not remixed in any visible way, I believe it makes sense to think of them as part of the same remix culture as slideshows and other films made by pre-existing parts.

Why are people ripping and sharing these clips? Certainly not for profit. It is sharing, not selling. In digital media, when convergence has levelled out the differences between media technologies, and copy-and-paste is the most common operation in creation, to isolate a part of a larger text and quote it is normal practice. Moreover, most television and film cannot be linked. Experienced web writers are used to writing hyperlinks to all kinds of interesting material. The web is so enormous that links are some of the most important information; it is the currency of the web. Google's success is based on this: Google's search engine ranks its results based on links to the pages. The logic of the web is that everything should be linkable, and when valuable moving images are not, then *YouTube* is a great way of making them available for linking.

To rip and share a clip without remixing it is in fact to state its value. It is good enough already; it does not need to be enhanced—at least not for the moment. The old maxim holds true on the web: "Plagiarism is the sincerest form of flattery".

A parenthesis may be allowed here: We who work in universities see another form of this rip culture in student papers. Fresh students routinely copy texts from

---

[12]For a further discussion of templates see (Fagerjord, 2005).

the web, especially from *Wikipedia* into their own papers, without quote marks or information about the source. To suspect plagiarism and searching the web for proof has become a routine part of my job. When I point out to my students that this practice will be considered cheating, they often get confused. To copy and paste, rip and remix has become so natural to today's 20-year-olds in Norway that we have to teach them the idea that you might create your own sentences.

I will return to my main argument to point out that the culture of remixing also has made people feel the need for copyright reform. The most marked example of this in recent years has been the Creative Commons, an organization arguing that creators should mark their works with a licence allowing others to use their work to create new works. The Creative Commons has made the text of several such licences available, making it easy for authors to retain their authorial rights while allowing others to cite and remix (see Lessig, 2001 for a legal discussion of these principles).

Remix of Power: Who Gets to the Podium

While there are a lot of rips and remixes, my impression is that most videos on *YouTube* are people filming themselves. They put up a camera and talk to it, or perform in front of it, often in silly ways. Before video sites like *YouTube,* films of this kind were shared among friends and shown in the living room, if they were made at all. *YouTube* has provided a platform for people where they can share these performances with the whole wired world. Everyone can become a broadcaster. The digitalization has brought about a total remix of power relations. Two decades ago, mass media were for the few and wealthy. To create a newspaper or a broadcasting operation required large investments, and for television, you would in most countries also need a licence. Web-based creation services such as blogs and *YouTube* have created the possibility for anyone to run his or her own mass medium (without any guarantees for an audience, though). What has happened when this power was delegated was that most people who take this opportunity use it to perform themselves or their selves, as previously noted.

And this brings us full circle back to the remixing of genres. The digital remix of power relations has opened the gates to people with other purposes than to attract large audiences for public debate or commercials. Elements known from broadcasting and the printing press are remixed with elements of diaries, of private conversations, of local theatre and concerts and many others.

Remix and Creation

This article is about media development in the decades after digitization. I have argued that while *convergence* was a useful term for the first developments, it is no longer helpful in understanding developments in the media. The phase of convergence was the process of introducing digital technologies in all kinds of media production, and thus changing the technological differences between them. Digitalization levelled out the differences, allowing elements earlier known from one medium to be adapted into another.

It is this process of borrowing and adapting between media and genres that I have tried to describe as *remix*. The problem with any term to describe or even explain developments is that it easily may be taken to account for more than what was meant. I do not wish to say that remixing is caused by digitalization. There has of course been remixing going on earlier. We see remixing in music and film before computers entered the editing process. Creative development is often exactly to combine earlier material. *Remix* may be an ill-chosen term for this reason (although not any worse than *convergence*. Could not a 1980s portable cassette radio player be described as a result of the convergence of the radio and the cassette recorder?). I hope to make clear, however, that while remix is one of the oldest forms of creativity, it has become much more widespread in the digital age. What digitalization did was to make this kind of creation much simpler.

Digitalization has levelled the technological differences between media, so remixing of genres is much easier. Any aspects of any genres may constantly be recombined into new genres and services.

Digital data may be copied without loss of quality, so it has become much easier for anyone to remix, recombine and create new dependent works. Template-based tools provide ready-made scaffolding for new works. And as the digital network reaches anyone, the power relations have also been remixed, allowing anyone to be a creator, publisher or broadcaster—or prosumer, as Axel Bruns calls it in his article in this volume.

Novelist William Gibson, the man who coined the term *cyberspace,* put it this way in *Wired* in July 2005:

> Our culture no longer bothers to use words like *appropriation* or *borrowing* to describe those very activities. Today's audience isn't listening at all - it's participating. Indeed, *audience* is as antique a term as *record*, the one archaically passive, the other archaically physical. The record, not the remix, is the anomaly today. The remix is the very nature of the digital. (Gibson, 2005)

References

Aarseth, E. J. (1997). *Cybertext: Perspectives on ergodic literature.* Baltimore, MD: Johns Hopkins University Press.

Adorno, T. W., & Horkheimer, M. (1999). The culture industry: Enlightenment as mass deception (J. Cumming, Trans.). In *Dialectic of the enlightenment* (pp. 120–167). London: Verso.

Austerlitz, S. (2007). *Money for nothing: A history of music video from Beatles to the white stripes.* New York: Continuum.

Barthes, R. (1993). *Mythologies.* London: Vintage.

Bolter, J. D., & Grusin, R. (1999). *Remediation: Understanding new media.* Cambridge, MA: MIT Press.

Brand, S. (1988). *The media lab: Inventing the future at MIT.* New York: Penguin.

Cheung, C. (2004). Identity construction and self-presentation on personal homepages: Emancipatory potentials and reality constraints. In D. Gauntlett & R. Horsley (Eds.), *Web.Studies* (2nd ed., pp. 53–68). London: Arnold.

Eco, U. (1999). *Kant and the platypus: Essays on language and cognition.* London: Secker & Warburg.

Fagerjord, A. (2002). Reading-view(s)ing the Über-box: A critical view on a popular prediction. In M. Eskelinen & R. Koskimaa (Eds.), *Cybertext yearbook 2001* (pp. 99–110). Jyväskylä: Publications of the Research Centre for Contemporary Culture.

Fagerjord, A. (2003a). Four axes of rhetorical convergence. *Dichtung Digital, 4*(30).

Fagerjord, A. (2003b). Rhetorical convergence: Studying web media. In G. Liestøl, A. Morrison, & T. Rasmussen (Eds.), *Digital media revisited* (pp. 293–325). Cambridge: MIT Press.

Fagerjord, A. (2005). Prescripts: Authoring with templates. *Kairos, 10*(1).

Fetveit, A. (2002). *Multiaccentual cinema: Between documentary and fiction.* Oslo: University of Oslo.

Feuer, J. (1983). The concept of 'live television': Ontology as ideology. In E. A. Kaplan (Ed.), *Regarding television* (pp. 12–22). Los Angeles, CA: American Film Institute.

Fiske, J. (1987). *Television culture.* London: Methuen.

Fiske, J., & Hartley, J. (1978). *Reading television.* London: Methuen.

Foucault, M. (1994). Self writing (R. Hurley, Trans.). In P. Rabinow (Ed.), *Ethics* (Vol. 1). London: Penguin.

Gibson, W. (2005). God's little toys. *Wired, 13.7.*

Hartley, J. (1982). *Understanding news.* London: Methuen.

Hartley, J. (1999). *Uses of television.* London: Routledge.

Heath, S. (1990). Representing television. In P. Mellencamp (Ed.), *logics of television.* Bloomington, IN: Indiana University Press.

Jenkins, H. (2006). *Convergence culture: Where old and new media collide.* Cambridge, MA: MIT Press.

Lessig, L. (2001). *The future of ideas.* New York: Vintage.

Lessig, L. (2007). How creativity is being strangled by the law. *TED: Technology, entertainment, design.* Monterey Conference Center, Monterey, TED Conferences. Video recording available at http://www.ted.com/index.php/talks/larry_lessig_says_the_law_is_strangling_creativity.html

Liestøl, G. (2006). Conducting genre convergence for learning. *Continuing Engineering Education and Lifelong Learning, 16*(3/4), 255–270.

Liestøl, G. (2007). The dynamics of convergence and divergence in digital domains. In T. Storsul & D. Stuedahl (Eds.), *The ambivalence of convergence* (pp. 165–178). Gothenburg: Nordicom.

Lonelygirl15. (2007). Lonelygirl15.

Manovich, L. (2001). *The language of new media.* Cambridge: MIT Press.

Morley, D., & Brunsdon, C. (1999). *The nationwide television studies.* London: Routledge.

Murray, J. (1997). *Hamlet on the holodeck: The future of narrative in cyberspace.* Cambridge, MA: MIT Press.

Musser, J., & O'Reilly, T. (2007). *Web 2.0: Principles and best practices.* Sebastopol, CA: O'Reilly.

Negroponte, N. (1995). *Being digital.* London: Hodder and Stoughton.

Negroponte, N. (1998). Beyond digital. *Wired, 6.12.*

Radway, J. A. (1984). *Reading the romance: Women, patriarchy, and popular literature.* Chapel Hill, NC: University of North Carolina Press.

Richardson, J. (2003). *The search for Isabella V. Esquire, 140.4,* http://www.esquire.com/features/ESQ1003-OCT_ISABELLA

Walther, B. K. (2005). *Konvergens og nye medier.* Århus: Academica.

Williams, R. (1975). *Television: Technology and cultural form.* New York: Schocken.

YouTube, I. (2007). YouTube fact sheet.

The Internet in Latin America

Suely Fragoso and Alberto Efendy Maldonado

Despite the unprecedented continued growth in the number of internet users and in the rate of change in this number, as of July 2008 the percentage of the world's population that has access is still only 21.1%. The geographical distribution of internet users is also still very uneven, with high access levels to the internet in North America (73.4%), Oceania (59.5%) and Europe (48.0%). These are followed, in descending order of the percentage of population with access to the internet, by Latin America (22.6%), the Middle East (21.3%), Asia (14.0%) and, in last place, Africa (5.3%) (Table 1) (Miniwatts Marketing Group, 2008). This pattern indicates a potential correlation between the inequalities in access and the economic disparities between continents, but also suggests that other socio-cultural issues, of which language is the most straightforward example, may be important. The fact that 5 years ago Asia was ahead of Latin America (Fragoso, 2003, p. 4) and the Middle East (2006) in penetration also indicates that a complex set of variables is at work.

The general penetration of the internet in Latin America (22.6%) is slightly above the world average (21.1%). The internal inequalities in the Latin American region reflect those of the world in general, with some areas being wealthy and well provided for in infrastructure and services and, in contrast to these, other areas in which living conditions can be described as medieval. Table 2 details the relationship between GNI, the total population and the indices of internet access and technological readiness for several Latin American countries. Taken together these factors indicate once more the insufficiency of economic strength, by itself to define the diverse patterns of internet access, uses and appropriations by different populations in Latin America.

Economic and cultural diversity is not a new factor in the history of Latin America. In fact, "[t]here has never existed one Latin American reality – only hybrid and contingent realities that flow from the historically specific interactions within and between specific social formations and their respective articulations with the world economy" (Sassen & Sanchez, 2005). To visualize the penetration

S. Fragoso (✉)
Universidade do Vale do Rio dos Sinos (Unisinos), São Leopoldo, Rio Grande do sul, Brazil
e-mail: suely.fragoso@ymail.com

J. Hunsinger et al. (eds.), *International Handbook of Internet Research*,
DOI 10.1007/978-1-4020-9789-8_12, © Springer Science+Business Media B.V. 2010

Table 1 World internet usage and population statistics (Miniwatts Marketing Group,[1] 2006)

Regions	Percentage of world population	Percentage of region population with home access to the internet
Africa	14.3	5.3
Asia	56.6	14.0
Europe	12.0	48.0
Middle East	3.0	213
North America	5.1	73.4
Latin America	8.2	22.6
Caribbean	0.4	13.2
Oceania/Australia	0.5	59.5
World total	100.0	21.1

of the internet in Latin America without disregarding its peculiarities it is essential, therefore, to not dilute the specifics of the different localities by overreaching in the generalizations. On the other hand, choosing to take the local idiosyncrasies as the starting point risks losing any view of the internet in the region. Thus we have sought to organize our examination of the internet in Latin America in three parts. Initial considerations, already presented, position Latin America in the global picture. In the next section, we divide the region up into three large blocks, according to the degree of scope of the network and the forms in which it is appropriated in the various areas *vis a vis* fundamentally similar socio-economic conditions. These general profiles guide our discussions based on quantitative data from a variety of sources, which we seek to illustrate using considerations that are focused more strongly on one or other country of the various groups. It is essential to emphasize that these three blocks do not correspond to any pre-existent categories and are proposed solely and exclusively as a form of organizing Latin American countries with respect to internet use at the present moment in time. Above all they are in no manner stale categorizations, given that we are working with highly fluid profiles and a reality that is extremely dynamic. Given that all data used in this section are from external sources, we double and triple checked figures by crossing different sources and took special care not to draw conclusions by comparing data obtained with distinct methodologies. This is of great importance because even the most basic of definitions, such as "internet users", can vary dramatically between sources.

Seeking to capture exactly that which the quantitative generalizations obscure, in the final section we highlight some qualitatively significant examples of forms of appropriation of the internet by nations or groups in Latin America. The cases discussed in this last part lack statistical representativity, but nevertheless are concrete

---

[1] Miniwatts combines the data for Latin America (Central and South America) with those for the Caribbean. We understand that there are fundamental differences in the social, economic and political history of Caribbean countries in comparison to Latin America, with repercussions on the forms and indices of penetration of the internet. For this reason this work does not include the Caribbean nations.

Table 2 Data on internet usage and basic socio-economic indicators for Latin American countries. Total of users and percentage of population with home access compiled from Miniwatts Marketing Group (2008). GNI *per capita* according to *The World Bank* (2008). E-readiness, connectivity and technology infrastructure calculated by EIU and IBM/IBV (2008)

Country	Total of domestic internet users	Percentage of population with home internet access	GNI per capita[2] (2006)	E-readiness[3] Posição (value)	Connectivity and technology infrastructure[4]
Argentina	16,000,000	39.7	5,150.00	44 (5.56)	4.30
Bolivia	580,000	6.4	1,100.00	–	–
Brazil	42,600,000	22.4	4,710.00	42 (5.65)	3.60
Chile	7,035,000	43.2	6,810.00	32 (6.57)	4.50
Colombia	10,097,000	22.8	3,120.00	58 (4.71)	3.40
Costa Rica	1,214,400	29.4	4,980.00	–	–
El Salvador	700,000	10.1	2,680.00	–	–
Ecuador	1,549,000	11.3	2,910.00	63 (4.17)	3.10
Guatemala	1,320,000	10.4	2,590.00	--	–
Honduras	344,100	4.6	1,270.00	–	–
Mexico	23,700,000	21.8	7,830.00	40 (5.88)	3.70
Nicaragua	155,000	2.7	930.00	–	–
Panama	264,316	8.2	5,000.00	–	–
Paraguay	260,000	3.9	1,410.00	–	–
Peru	7,324,300	25,5	2,980.00	51 (5.07)	3.45
Uruguay	1,100,000	31.8	5,310.00	–	–
Venezuela, R.B.	5,297,798	20.4	6,070.00	52 (5.06)	3.7
Latin America	119,540,914	22.6	64,850.00		

examples of the Latin American experience of the internet nowadays. As such they depict the forms of use and appropriation of the internet in the Latin American region in a manner that is at least as consistent, if not more so, as the statistics of the preceding sections.

---

[2]GNI per capita is the gross national income, converted to US dollars using the World Bank *Atlas Method*, divided by the midyear population (The World Bank, 2008).

[3]E-readiness ranking is a weighted collection of nearly 100 quantitative and qualitative criteria, organised into six categories measuring various components of a country's social, political, economic and technological development. The categories are "Connectivity and Technology Infrastructure"; "Business Environment"; "Legal Environment"; "Government Policy and Vision"; "Social and Cultural Environment"; Consumer and business adoption (EIU & IBM/IBV, 2008, pp. 22–23).

[4]Amongst the categories used to derive the e-readiness index is Connectivity and Technology Infrastructure, which "measures the extent to which individuals and businesses can access mobile networks and the internet, and their ability to access digital services through means such as digital identity cards". Penetration and affordability are key metrics, use of secure servers and the commitment of the country to implementing digital identity cards are also taken into account (EIU & IBM/IBV, 2008, p. 22). In 2008, the e-readiness ranking covered 70 countries and did not include Bolivia, Costa Rica, El Salvador, Guatemala, Honduras, Nicaragua, Panama, Paraguay and Uruguay.

The General Picture

Table 2 shows the considerable internal inequalities in the Latin American region. Domestic access to the internet varies between 2.7% in Nicaragua and 43.2% in Chile. The GNI *per capita* is also highly variable, from US $930.00 in Nicaragua to US $7,830.00 in Mexico. The local cultural idiosyncrasies and the peculiarities of the economic systems of each country invalidate the understanding that these averages correspond to the median income of the majority of the population as well as that those generalizations presuppose that internet users are uniformly distributed. The picture is somewhat clearer when the e-readiness ranking and the indices of Connectivity and Technology Infrastructure, where available, are added into the equation. In combination with the percentages of the total population with access to the internet and the indices of GNI per capita, these indicators allow the organization of the presence of the internet in Latin America into three large profiles.

Profile 1

The first profile (P1) is comprised of those countries where 10% or less of the population have home access to the internet: Bolivia, El Salvador, Ecuador, Guatemala, Honduras, Nicaragua, Panama and Paraguay. Their GNI *per capita* varies between US $930.00 (Nicaragua) and US $2,910.00 (Ecuador). Ecuador is the only one of these for which the e-readiness ranking is estimated, appearing in 63rd place (of 70) with Connectivity and Technology Infrastructure index 3.10.

The telecommunications infrastructure tends to be concentrated in the principal cities, but even so are below the world or regional averages. This absence of infrastructure has direct impact on the availability of fixed telephone lines: in Ecuador, for example, only 12.5% of households have a fixed line (Miniwatts Marketing Group, 2008). In Bolivia, fixed telephone lines reach 7% of the households (Miniwatts Marketing Group, 2008), while in Paraguay they reach 18.6% of households. It is necessary to emphasize the unequal distribution of these lines: in the rural areas of Paraguay, for example, only 3.2% of households had a fixed line in 2007, while in the capital, Asuncion, fixed telephone lines were found in 48.7% of the households. The same pattern repeats itself, on a smaller scale, with respect to households with computer and internet access: in 2007 these were 3% nationally, with a notable concentration in Asuncion (29.6%) (DGEEC, 2007), online).

In the small towns and villages of these less established nations of Latin America the population is low density and mostly poor. In the outskirts of the big cities, despite the population density being high, the acquisition power is minimal. In both settings the provision of communications services and access to the internet lack attraction for private suppliers. Thus the internet has only reached the worst-off areas thanks to the provision of subsidized public access points, notably the community telecentres,[5] given that even cybercafes[6] tend to concentrate in the more favourable parts of urban areas.

The first experiments with telecentres in Latin American countries date from 1996. In 1998, there were around 50 telecentres in the region; in 2006 there were already more than 6,500[7] (Delgadillo, Gómez, & Stoll, 2002, pp. 24–26). In contrast to the first projects, typically small scale and undertaken by civil societies, NGOs or local government, the so-called second generation telecentres are born as part of massive connectivity plans, generally with the support of national governments, which have become more aware over the last decade of the importance of connectivity for national economic and political viability in the so-called Information Society.

Mobile telephony has been cited as an important development in overcoming the lack of basic telecommunications infrastructure in Latin America. The total number of mobile connections is already far greater than the number of fixed lines, inclusively in the poorer nations, but the penetration of the mobile phone is much lower in the Latin American region than it is in North America, Europe or Asia. Latin American figures are also low in comparison to other "emergent economies" such as Eastern European countries (GSM, 2005). The cost of calling is high in comparison to the income of the population and the pre-paid system is the most popular.

Profile 2

The intermediate profile (P2) includes countries with domestic internet penetration between 20 and 25%: Brazil, Colombia, Mexico, Peru and Venezuela. Their e-readiness rankings oscillate between 40th (Mexico) and 58th (Colombia). The GNI per capita of three countries of this group is between US $2,980.00 (Peru) and US $4,710.00 (Brazil). Venezuela and Mexico have higher GNI (respectively, US $6,070.00 and US $7,830.00).

The sheer scale of the absolute numbers for Brazil mean that the country is frequently included amongst the richest nations when absolute values for the indicators of access to and use of the internet are considered. This is due, above all, to its large population (the fifth largest in the world, estimated at 187,266,323 in July 2008 (IBGE, 2008)), given that, despite having the largest number of home internet users in Latin America and scoring sixth place in the world in 2007, only 22.4% of Brazilians had home internet access at the time (Miniwatts Marketing Group, 2008).

---

[5]In this text the term "telecentre" is used to designate points of access to computers and the internet that are either free or charged, but are non profit making. Related terms such as *infocentres* and *community digital centres*, are used to refer to telecentres that are so named by a specific project or initiative.

[6]By "cybercafe" we refer to private locations that provide charged public access to the internet to make a profit.

[7]These figures are for non-profit points only.

In the countries of this group there are also concentration and scarcity in the telecommunications infrastructure. In Venezuela the telecommunications infrastructure is highly concentrated in the North, where the majority of the cities are located and most of the population live. Despite this convergence, teledensity is low, with a fraction more than 14 lines per 100 inhabitants (Conatel, 2006a).

The majority of the internet users in the countries with this profile are concentrated in the richest areas of each country, with the penetration being predominantly urban. While, for example, in Colombia as a whole, 11.5% of the population had home access to the internet (Miniwatts Marketing Group, 2006), a sample restricted to the seven principal cities of the country revealed a much higher proportion of home users (54.2%) (Comissión de Regulación de Telecomunicaciones, 2006, s. 2).

The telephony infrastructure in Brazil has developed significantly in recent years, but the conditions vary greatly along the country's 8,544,418 km^2. The comparison of availability data and modes of access to the internet at different resolutions (national, regional, municipal and local) reveal that the disparities occur in a homothetic manner, with similar discrepancies in all places and at all scales of observation. The proportion of individuals with access to the internet varies greatly across Brazil, with the lower rates of inclusion in the North (13%) and Northeast (11%) and the highest indices of home access in the richest urban areas, principally in the South (31%) and Southeast (30%) regions (CGI, 2007a, p. 78).

Access to the internet is proportional to the income of the Brazilians, wherein 82% of the richest versus 2% of the poorest have home access (CGI, 2007a, p. 138). Technological literacy is directly related to educational level in Brazil: 16% of the illiterate and those with basic schooling declared to have already used a computer in 2007, against 94% of graduates (CGI, 2007a, p. 146). The situation is similar in Colombia where the percentage of home users with university education in 2006 was 45%, compared to 9% of users with only primary education (Comissión de Regulación de Telecomunicaciones, 2006, s. 15).

Public internet access points are no less important in P2 countries: usage of paid access points is high in all regions in Brazil, varying between 25% in the Southern Region to 64% in the Northeast, inversely proportional to home access (CGI, 2007a, p. 149). The free public access points are even more popular amongst the lower income population: 53% of users interviewed at *AcessaSP*'s telecentres[8] in August 2006 had family income of less than US $4,000 per year, 45% between US $4,000 and US $12,000 and only 7% above US $12,000 (AcessaSP, 2006), q. 9). Of the telecentre users that answered the same research, 35% had home access to the intenet as well (AcessaSP, 2006, q. 15).

Brazil and Mexico appear in the top 20 countries with the highest number of broadband subscribers in the world in 2007, but in 2008 no Latin American country figured amongst the 20 with highest penetration of broadband (Miniwatts Marketing Group, 2008). In Brazil, while the percentage of connected households where the access is broadband is high (50% of the connected homes in 2007, according to CGI,

---

[8]*AcessaSP* is the São Paulo State Government digital inclusion program.

2007b, p. 5), the proportion of users with connection speeds up to 128 Kbps is also high in all regions (CGI, 2007a, p. 140). The proportion of users with broadband home connection is equally high in other P2 countries as Colombia (around 50% in 2006) and Venezuela (62% in 2006) (Conatel, 2006b, s. 9).

Internet usage in Brazilian companies is 92%, with considerable number of broadband connections. A slight tendency for smaller companies to use the internet less is reflected in the connection bandwidths of these smaller companies. Despite only 48% of the companies with internet access having their own website, they invest heavily in digital security (97% of companies use antivirus software, 73% use anti-spam systems and 67% anti-spyware, 60% have firewalls installed and 49% use secure client–server connections), almost half of Brazilian businesses claimed to have been victims of some form of online attack (CGI, 2007a, pp. 120–124).

Mexico has been a member of NAFTA (North American Free Trade Association) since its inception in the mid-1990s, from which it could be supposed that the country would present internet access patterns and digital inclusion programs with a profile different to those of the rest of Latin America, probably more directed at individual or household access. Nevertheless the average telephone density in Mexico is around 19% and the proportion of home internet users is not much higher: 21.8%. The variation in the availability of telephone infrastructure and services between rural areas and urban ones is significant: while the teledensity in the Federal District is around 41%, in the poorer areas the index is much lower (5% in the state of Chiapas, for example) (Miniwatts Marketing Group, 2008). As other P2 countries, Mexico has nearly as many broadband internet accounts as dial-up (Miniwatts Marketing Group, 2006).

Despite the total number of internet users being constantly on the increase, at least since 2000 the quantity of users that access the internet from public points has increased at a greater rate than those that access from their home (Curry & Kenney, 2006). The installation of telecentres has been particularly successful in Mexico: in 2003 there already existed 3,200 Digital Community Centres in more than 2,400 different Mexican municipalities (Mazatán, 2004) and in 2005 the number of DCCs totalled 7,200 distributed across all of Mexico (e-Mexico, 2006).

The mobile telephone has achieved significant penetration in some P2 countries (Fig. 1), retaining however the pattern of high costs and a customer preference for pre-paid systems. In Venezuela, in contrast to the low density of fixed telephone lines (18.51%), 86.76% of the population had access to a mobile telephone in 2007. The number of users of the pre-paid systems in Venezuela in 2007 was nearly 20 times greater than those using post-paid accounts (Conatel, 2007, online). In 2008, Brazilian teledensity for mobile lines reached 64.50%, being 80.76% pre-paid accounts (Anatel, 2008). The availability of fixed telephone lines increased significantly after the privatization of the telecommunications systems in the 1990s but only 46% of Brazilian residences had a fixed line in 2007, against 74% with mobile phones (CGI, 2007a, p. 133).

In fact, despite the mobile phone being frequently referred to as a solution for connectivity in the less developed nations, it is necessary to place the data in perspective. Few of the phones are of the third generation and many of those that do

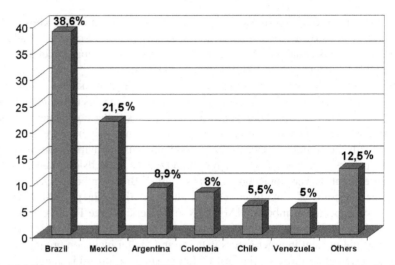

Fig. 1 Mobile telephone market for 2005. The percentages are relative to the totals for Latin America and relate to absolute numbers of users. Data adapted from Comissión de Regulación de Telecomunicaciones, 2005, p. 5

permit access to the internet limit the services to the sending of short text messages and the download of small files for the customization of the phone itself. The availability of high-speed 3G networks and affordability of adequate enabled internet handsets are necessary pre-conditions for the pervasiveness of the mobile internet in Latin America.

Profile 3

The third profile (P3) covers Latin American countries where 30% or more of the population have home access to the internet: Argentina, Chile, Costa Rica and Uruguay. These are countries with GNI per capita between US \$4,980.00 (Costa Rica) and US \$6,810.00 (Chile). Argentina is in 44th place and Chile 32nd in the e-readiness ranking, which is not calculated for Costa Rica or Uruguay.

The case of Argentina, a pioneer in the installation of infrastructure for connection to the internet, is paradigmatic. The access conditions vary widely in the different regions (Scalise, 2005, p. 14), with a clear connection between the level of personal and regional incomes and the access to information and communication technologies (ICTS). The Argentine economic crisis dramatically reduced the rate of penetration of internet access in 2001, but even so the number of connections increased in the order of 50% in comparison to the previous year. In 2002 there was a noticeable return to growth in home access (Gioria, 2004). In 2004, however, half of the internet users in Argentina still connected from public access points (Carrier y Asoc., 2004, p. 1). In 2007, the number of Argentines accessing the internet from public points was estimated at around 5.5 million (Carrier y Asoc., 2007, p. 9). This fact becomes yet more interesting when considering that in 2006 the majority of the 1,350 "Community Technology Centres" that were set up in Argentina between 1999 and 2001 had ceased to operate, and those that still functioned no longer received any public or private support (Coordinadores/as de la Red de CTCs, 2006). What happened is that, despite the pioneering setting up of free internet access points, the high indices of access via public access points in Argentina refers to "kiosks, cybercafes and libraries which provide the client with connections equipped with higher technology than the home connections. This transforms them into an attractive option not only for the lower socio-economic sectors who cannot fund owning a computer and who do not always have a telephone line available [at home], but also for those who have a PC at home which, due to its age, is not equipped to access the Internet" (Gioria, 2004) and those who want broadband access without having to pay the high cost or worry about security matters (viruses, spyware, etc.) (Finquelievich & Finquelievich, 2007; Carrier y Asoc., 2007). Carrier y Asoc. draws attention to the importance of social use of public internet access points, which frequently function as meeting points (Carrier y Asoc., 2004, p. 3). This use is rein-forced by the observation that telecentres are not only popular amongst the less well-off Argentines but also with the younger ones (Carrier y Asoc., 2004, p. 3). To maintain low prices and remain competitive, commercial access points need to reduce installation and maintenance costs, which leads them to function "in pre-carious situations: many working hours, illegal workers, pirate software, minimal updating and maintenance" (Carrier y Asoc., 2007, p. 10). Repeating the pattern seen in the P2 countries, despite the percentage of Argentines with home access being low, penetration of broadband has increased rapidly: from 45% in 2006 to 72% in 2007 and 94% in 2008 (Carrier y Asoc., 2008).

Chile is the country in Latin America with the highest indices of economic and political stability, which positions it as the paradigm of government administration for the region. It is not mere coincidence that it is also the Latin American country with the best telecom infrastructure and regulatory system and the highest internet penetration rates: in 2007, 43.2% of the Chilean population had home access to the internet (Miniwatts Marketing Group, 2008). The fact that 86.6% of the Chilean population already lived in urban áreas in 2002 (86.6% according to the 2002 *census* (Instituto Nacional de Estadísticas, 2005)) influences upwards digital inclusion indicators in Chile given that, as in the other countries examined, the penetration of ICTs into rural areas is notably lower than in the urban zones (Duran, 2004).

The total number of broadband connections in Chile has been growing rapidly, reaching 900,000 lines in 2006 (Vega, 2006, s. 4). This fact becomes more signif-icant when it is placed alongside the equivalent indicators for other countries, as shown in Fig. 2.

The high rate of home internet usage in Chile has not prevented the government from joining forces with the Chilean private sector in an agreement called the *Digital Agenda* signed in 2003. The first stage of the project started with the country already having 1,300 public access points installed and distributed in such a manner that 89.8% of municipalities and 94.2% of the population were within the catchment zone of at least one Infocentre (Duran, 2004, s. 4). Other Chilean projects targeted

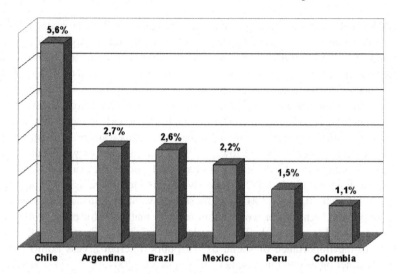

Fig. 2 Broadband internet connection percentages relative to the total population of some Latin American countries (Cisco Systems, 2006a, p. 1)

the provision of access in public libraries, the installation of subsidized telecentres and the installation of public access points specifically for the youth sector. The Chilean *Digital Agenda* also works with the interoperability of public services, with an emphasis on meeting the needs of both the citizenry and the business community (Universia Knowledge@Warthon, 2003).

In 2003, practically 100% of the large and medium companies in Chile and 40% of the small companies were already connected to the internet, with an increasing utilization of broadband (Grupo de Acción Digital, 2004, p. 31). Few of these companies made full use of the facilities that the net provides: only 25% had their own website; 11% used the internet as a sales outlet and 16% used it to make purchases and contact their suppliers (Universia Knowledge@Warthon, 2003). In 2006 the increase in the use of ICTs in general and the internet in particular by Chilean companies was noticeable. While still being lower than those found in the USA or Spain at the time, the indicators of business use of the internet were amongst the highest in Latin America (Godoy, Herrera, Lever, Myrick, & Sepúlveda, 2005, p. 4).

A Closer look

Despite creating a picture of the general internet use in Latin America, the indices presented so far do not capture some peculiarities of the appropriation of the internet in the Latin American region. As much as the fact that the great majority of the Latin American population have no idea what the internet is should be questioned, it is not true that "Latin America's urban elites now have easy access to the internet" and "are as digitized and wired as the urban elite in the U.S." (Angotti, 2005). Everyday experience calls for contextualization of the notion of "home access", given the discrepancies that imply qualitatively different experiences. Even in the wealthy areas of the metropolitan regions of the principal cities in Latin America, telephone line failures are not unusual and fluctuations and interruptions in the electricity supply are relatively frequent. In addition to this consideration has to be given to the far more restricted bandwidth available to Latin America when compared to that available between Northern hemisphere countries, in particular between Europe and the USA, and the direct implications this limitation has for data flow on continental scale (Fig. 3).

Within the continent, it is also necessary to contextualize the meaning of "broadband", given that some studies on Latin America include in this category any permanent connection that functions at a transfer rate of 128 Kbps or more (Cisco Systems, 2006b, s. 3), which is clearly insufficient to avoid data congestion or to permit participation in real time collective activities. Even so, the cost of a broadband subscription is high for the income of many users. One solution for working around the high prices has been to charge for time connected, which prohibits prolonged periods of navigation and significantly changes the experience of the users.

Despite these barriers to full usage of international connectivity the internet has had a positive impact on life in Latin America. Academic work has been considerably strengthened by the penetration of the internet into universities, institutes and research centres. Besides providing access to an enormous body of online international journals, the internet has been fostering a more dynamic research culture. Latin American periodicals, reports, essays, dissertations and theses are increasingly available online.[9]

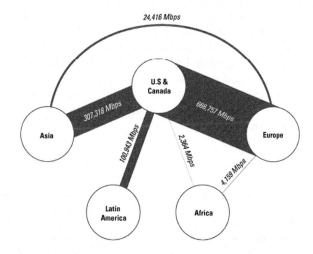

Fig. 3 Intercontinental bandwidth as of mid-2005 (interregional bandwidth below 1,000 Mbps not included) (PriMetrica Inc., 2006)

---

[9]Since 1999, *Plataforma Lattes* (http://lattes.cnpq.br) integrates and makes public the vitae of Brazilian researchers. In 2008, it has been integrated with several other scientific networks. Since 2006, the complete texts of all dissertations and theses defended in Brazil are obligatorily made public (http://www.capes.gov.br).

The internet has also revitalized distance learning, which had been practically at a standstill after more than five decades of widespread attempts in Latin America, led by community radio programs.

The potential of the internet for dissemination has also had a great impact on political practices (in both the strict and wider sense). Contrary to the authoritarian and personal models that have helped Latin American history to be populated by civil wars, dictatorships and institutional failures, the internet has made it possible for the ordinary citizen to access an unparalleled quantity of information concerning public administration. The publication of the names chosen and results of public selection procedures, of the complete text of official documents, judgements, auctions, law proposals, manifestos, and government programmes places in full view – and under scrutiny – the procedures for obtaining, maintaining and exercising power.[10]

Government support has been important for the success of initiatives against digital exclusion. The Latin American experience shows that the mere implementation of telecentres and provision of technological tools or simple "training" to use these have a very low impact, and at times a negative effect[11] on the quality of life of the target communities. Successful projects start from the recognition that the technology is not an exogenic variable and line up the creation and maintenance of the telecentres (in whatever configuration) with wider scope projects, such as poverty relief policies and long-term development programmes (van der Krogt, 2005, p. 4).

Perhaps the most unsettling use of the internet by Latin Americans is in the international finance arena. To understand this one has to bear in mind the high levels of emigration that devastated the region during the 1990s, parallel with the development of the internet. Today, the millions of Latin Americans that left for the Northern hemisphere, principally for the European Union (particularly Spain and Italy) and the USA have found in the net the best (and often only) means by which to communicate with their family and friends that stayed home. They have developed, due to the circumstances, new forms (technologically mediated) of cultivating their family bonds. Conflicts arise and are resolved, emotions run high and low across the net, frequently ending in smiles, tears and laughter in front of the screen.

---

[10]Worth noting are the experiments of making documents and government reports available online in Chile (http://www.gobiernodechile.cl), Brazil (http://www.e.gov.br) and Mexico (http://www.gob.mx/).

[11]Delgadillo, Gómez e Stoll report the existence of power struggles between directors and local leaders, transforming telecentres into a source of personal gain through corruption or theft. They also mention rejection of the telecentre by powerful groups that felt threatened by its role as a meeting point and source of information outside of their control. "In Ecuador, for example, the men of a community forced the closure of the telecentre as a means of ensuring their power and increased the domestic violence practiced against the women of this community" (Delgadillo, Gómez & Stoll, 2002, p. 16).

For millions of Latin Americans the internet is also the most convenient way of sending money earned abroad (often as illegal workers) back to their families. Córdova estimates that approximately US $46 billion are sent back to Latin America and the Caribbean each year by 30 million migrants spread around the globe (Córdova, 2006, p. 1). Large amounts of those remittances avoid legal restraints and taxation flowing through unofficial and informal channels and most of this money is spent on basic family welfare such as food, clothing and education (Zamora, 2006, p. 6). Given the high volume of the transactions that occur in these underground systems it is not surprising that there is interest from the banks and other companies registered as money transferring agencies in "developing and obtaining economies of scale for every link in this financial service, promoting the "bankification" of Latin American emigrants" (Robinson, 2003, p. 3). It has been argued that "the channeling of remittances through the formal financial system is essential in order to harness their potential for development", because this would "open the door for migrants to access financial systems and hence, savings and credit" and because "remittances contribute to the balance of payments and increase reserves of foreign currency" of nations in the receiving end (Ramírez, Domíngue, & Morais, 2005, p. 41). Remittances, as with their destinations and uses, cannot be discussed separately from the causes and effects of migration itself. Stepping outside of the issue, it ought to be possible to examine the capital transfer strategies and the canals set up for these without prejudging them.

It is also fundamental to be predisposed to understand in their context the different modes of use and appropriation of the internet by Latin Americans (from the emerging scientific co-operation networks through to the emotional outbursts in front of a public terminal) so that it will be possible, finally, to start making positive use of the potential of the internet as a powerful "transcultural force through which we allow the view of the other to penetrate and reconfigure ourselves" (Hopenhayn, 2003, p. 21).

References

AcessaSP. (2006). *Ponline 2006, results*. Data supplied by J. Zuquim, research coordinator to S. Fragoso, 2006.

Anatel. (2008). *Telefonia celular cresce 1,5% em janeiro*. Portal de Notícias, published February 2008. Retrieved July 13, 2006, from http://www.anatel.gov.br/Portal/exibirPortalNoticias.do?acao=carregaNoticia&codigo=15485

Angotti, T. (2005). Cities of the Americas in the information age. *Trans Telesymposia*. Issue 2. Moderator V. B. Urban. Information Technology. Retrieved October 20, 2006, from http://www.echonyc.com/~ trans/Telesymposia2/angotti03.html

Carrier y Asoc. (2004). *Documento – Uso de accesos públicos a Internet – 2004*, Retrieved October 10, 2006, from http://www.carrieryasoc.com

Carrier y Asoc. (2007). *Mercado de Acceso Público a internet*, Agosto de 2007. Retrieved July 17, 2008, http://www.carrieryasoc.com

Carrier y Asoc. (2008). *Internet es Banda Ancha, Comentários: informactión, analysis, opinión*, June 27, 2008. Retrieved July 17, 2008, form http://www.comentariosblog.com.ar/?p=132

CGI. (2007a). *Pesquisa sobre o Uso das Tecnologias da Informação e da Comunicação no Brasil – TIC DOMICÍLIOS E TIC EMPRESAS 2007*. Coordenação Mariana Balboni. Retrieved July 7, 2008, from http://www.cgi.br

CGI. (2007b). *Destaques TIC Domicílios 2007 – Uso e Posse de Computador e Internet, Barreiras de Acesso, Uso do Celular, Intenção de aquisição.* Retrieved July 16, 2008, from http://www.cetic.br

Cisco System. (2006a). *Estudio de Banda Ancha en Peru 2005–2010.* Barômetro Cisco de Banda Ancha, IDC. Retrieved October 26, 2006, from http://www.idc.com

Cisco Systems. (2006b). *Estudio de Banda Ancha en Chile 2002–2010,* Barômetro Cisco de Banda Ancha, IDC. Retrieved October 26, 2006, from http://www.idc.com

Comisión de Regulación de Telecomunicaciones. (2005). *Informe Sectorial de Telecomunicaciones.* Deciembre 2005, n. 6. Retrieved October 28, 2006, from http://www.crt.gov.co

Comisión de Regulación de Telecomunicaciones. (2006). *Medición de Factores Multiplicadores para el Cálculo de Usuarios de Internet en Colombia.* Retrieved October 28, 2006, from http://www.crt.gov.co

Conatel. (2006a). *Estadísticas del Setor Telecomunicaciones. Venezuela.* Retrieved October 28, 2006, from http://www.conatel.gov.ve/

Conatel. (2006b). *Socializando las Telecomunicaciones: hacia um novo modelo de desarrollo.* Retrieved July 15, 2008, from http://www.conatel.gov.ve/

Conatel. (2007). *Indicadores Anuales del Setor.* Retrieved July 18, 2008, from http://www.conatel.gov.ve/

Coordinadores/as de la Red de CTCs. (2006). *Carta de los CTCs al presidente Kirchner.* Retrieved October 2, 2006, from EnREDando.org, Comunidads en red, at http://www.enredando.org.ar/index.shtml

Córdova, E. L. (2006). Sending money home: Can remittances reduce poverty? *Id21 Insights* n. 60, January 2006. Retrieved October 31, 2006, from http://www.id21.org

Curry J., & Kenney M. (2006, March). Digital divide or digital development? The internet in Mexico. *First Monday, 11*(3). Retrieved October 3, 2006, from http://firstmonday.org/issues/issue11_3/curry/

Delgadillo, K., Gómez, R., & Stoll, K. (2002). *Telecentros ... ¿Para qué? Lecciones sobre telecentros comunitários em America Latina y el Caribe.* Centro Internacional de Investigaciones para el Desarollo, Canada. Retrieved October 2, 2006, from http://www.idrc.ca/uploads/user-S/11017309191tcparaque.pdf

DGEEC. (2007). *Trípticos con los Principales Resultados de la EPH 2007 – Total País.* Retrieved July 10, 2008, from http://www.dgeec.gov.py/Publicaciones/Biblioteca/EPH2007_Tripticos%20Pricipales%20Resultados/Triptico%20EPH%20total%20pais%202007%20COLOR.pdf

Duran, C. (2004). Acceso a las Tecnologías de Información y Comunicación – Chile. *Global indicators workshop on community access to ICTs.* Mexico City, November 16–19, 2004. Retrieved August 1, 2006, from http://www.itu.int/ITU-D/ict/mexico04/doc/doc/39_chl_s.pdf

EIU & IBM/IBV. (2008). *E-readiness rankings 2008 – Maintaining momentum.* A white paper from the Economist Intelligence Unit. Economist Intelligence Unit e IBM Institute for Business Value. Retrieved July 17, 2008, from http://www-935.ibm.com/services/us/gbs/bus/pdf/ereadiness_rankings_april_2008_final.pdf

e-Mexico. (2006). *Ubica tu Centro Comunitario Digital: Directorio actualizado de los 7,200 CCDs (PDF).* Retrieved October 30, 2006, from http://www.e-mexico.gob.mx/wb2/eMex/eMex_Ubica_tu_CCD

Finquelievich, S., & Finquelievich, D. (2007). Sistemas comunitarios de satisfacción a necesidades de conectividad en la sociedad de la información: el caso de Argentina, *Journal of Community Informatics, 3*(3). Retrieved July 16, 2008, from http://ci-journal.net/index.php/ciej/article/view/413/369

Fragoso, S. (2003). *The multiple facets of the digital divide.* Available at http://www.midiasdigitais.org/

Gioria, B. M. I. (2004). Internet: distribución espacial en Argentina y su relación con factores socioeconómicos. *Scripta Nova – revista electrónica de geografía y ciencias sociales.* Barcelona, Espanha. Retrieved October 2, 2006, from http://www.ub.es/geocrit/nova.htm

Godoy, S., Herrera, S., Lever, G., Myrick, A., & Sepúlveda, M. (2005). *El impacto de las tecnologías de la información en las empresas chilenas respecto a España y Estados Unidos: resultados de la primera encuesta BITChile 2005*. Retrieved October 26 2006, from http://www.wipchile.cl/estudios/informe_final.pdf

Grupo de Acción Digital. (2004). *Agenda digital Chile 2004–2006: te acerca el futuro*. Retrieved October 3, 2006 from http://www.alis-etsi.org/IMG/pdf/AgendaDigital_2004.pdf

GSM. (2005). *Mobile is central to Latin America's economic fortunes*. Press Release published December 8, 2005. Retrieved July 7, 2008, from http://www.gsmworld.com/

Hopenhayn, M. (2003). *Educación, comunicación y cultura en la sociedad de la información: una perspectiva latinoamericana*. Santiago: United Nations. Retrieved June 21, 2003, from http://www.eclac.cl/publicaciones/

IBGE. (2008). *Pop clock*. Retrieved July 10, 2008, from http://www.ibge.gov.br/home/default.php

Instituto Nacional de Estadísticas. (2005). *Chile: Ciudades, Pueblos, Aldeas y Caseríos*. Retrieved July 13, 2008, from http://www.ine.cl/canales/chile_estadistico/demografia_y_vitales/demografia/pdf/cdpubaldcasjunio2005.zip

van der Krogt, S. (2005). *Integración de las Tecnologías de Información y Comunicación en Programas y Políticas de Alivio de la Pobreza – experiencias en América Latina y el Caribe*. Retrieved October 2, 2006, from http://www.ftpiicd.org/files/articles/IntegracionTIC.pdf

Mazatán, J. P. (2004). Taller Mundial de Indicadores para el Acceso Comunitario a las TICs – Experiencia de México. *Global indicators workshop on community access to ICTs*. Mexico City, November 16–19, 2004. Retrieved August 1, 2006, from http://www.itu.int/ITUD/ict/mexico04/doc/doc/46_mex_s.pdf

Miniwatts Marketing Group. (2006). *Internet world stats: Usage and population statistics*. Retrieved October 1, 2006, from http://www.internetworldstats.com/

Miniwatts Marketing Group. (2008). *Internet world stats: Usage and population statistics*. Retrieved July 9, 2008, from http://www.internetworldstats.com/

Primetrica Inc. (2006). *Global internet geography*. Telegeography research. Retrieved July 12, 2008, from http://www.telegeography.com/

Ramírez, C., Domíngue, M. G., & Morais, J. M. (2005). *Crossing borders: Remittances, gender and development*. Santo Domingo, Instraw. Retrieved July 17, 2008, from http://www.uninstraw.org/en/images/stories/remmitances/documents/crossing_borders.pdf

Robinson, S. S. (2003). *Las E-Remesas: Hacia una Política Integral de Remesas para la Región Centroamericana*. Mexico: Instituto para la Conectividad en las Américas.

Sassen, S., & Sanchez, A. (2005). Cities of the Americas in the information age. *Trans Telesymposia*, Issue 2. Moderator V. B. Urban. Conclusions. Retrieved October 20, 2006, from http://www.echonyc.com/~trans/Telesymposia2/sassen05.html

Scalise, J. (2005). *Information and communication technologies (ICTs) in Argentina as measured by the National Institute for Statistics and Census (INDEC)*. Retrieved October 4 2006, from http://www.indec.gov.ar/

Universia Knowledge@Warthon. (2003). *Tecnologías de la información en Chile: un potencial que no despega*. Retrieved July 31, 2006, from Universia Knowledge at Wharton at http://www.wharton.universia.net

Vega, N. (2006). *Estudio de Banda Ancha en Chile 2002–2010*. International Data Corporation, Chile. Retrieved October 26, 2006, from http://www.idc.com

[The] World Bank (2008). *World development indicators database, key development data & statistics*. Data for 2006, published April 2008. Retrieved July 22, 2008, from http://web.worldbank.org/WBSITE/EXTERNAL/DATASTATISTICS/0,,contentMDK:20535285~menuPK:1192694~pagePK:64133150~piPK:64133175~theSitePK:239419,00.html

Zamora, R. G. (2006). A better quality of life? *Id21 insights*, n. 60, Janeiro de 2006. Retrieved July 12, 2008, from http://www.id21.org

Campaigning in a Changing Information Environment: The Anti-war and Peace Movement in Britain

Kevin Gillan, Jenny Pickerill, and Frank Webster

Introduction: the Mediation of War

The experience of war has been in decline for some years. We are left with what John Mueller (2004) appositely calls 'the remnants of war', with decreasing numbers of people victims of armed conflict around the world and obligatory national service much diminished for most young men (*Human Security Report* 2005). In spite of the break up of Yugoslavia in the 1990s, the horrors of Rwanda and the Iraq occupation, most people live far safer lives than their parents and grandparents. The twentieth century was the bloodiest in human history, but mass killing is on the wane. Despite this, huge numbers of people feel anxious, even fearful, that we live in especially dangerous times. Opinion polls record large segments of the populations in the United States and Western Europe putting the risk of war ahead of other public concerns (http://www.angus-reid.com).

Let us underscore this point. Eric Hobsbawm (1994) tells us that the period 1914–1945 may aptly be termed the 'age of catastrophe' since it was characterised by virtually continuous fighting between – and within – fascist, communist and capitalist nations. In many parts of the world, young men aged 18 and over were called to military service as a matter of course, to engage in killing. For lengthy periods nations fought *à outrance*, as total war enveloped them. Describing a 'war of annihilation' in the East and a 'brutal peace' that followed Mark Mazower (1998, p. 216) reminds us of the enormous scale of death and dislocation in Europe between 1939 and 1948: he estimates that 40 million people were killed and many more than that forced from their homes (p. 222). Large-scale conflict continued into the 1980s in wars of national liberation and superpower proxy wars: Algeria, Korea, Congo, Vietnam, Cambodia, Guatemala, Nicaragua. . .

Much of this is within living memory. It stands in marked contrast to the high levels of anxiety and fear expressed about the current situation across age groups. This is not to discount the threat of nuclear proliferation, nor to trivialise the suffering of

F. Webster (✉)
Department of Sociology, City University, London, UK
e-mail: F.Webster@city.ac.uk

J. Hunsinger et al. (eds.), *International Handbook of Internet Research*,
DOI 10.1007/978-1-4020-9789-8_13, © Springer Science+Business Media B.V. 2010

those in Iraq, nor to ignore the atrocities taking place in Darfur. But it is to insist that war, and the threat of war, has *diminished* for most inhabitants of the world over the past two decades.

So how is it that there are such anxieties expressed about war today in spite of the improvements as regards peace? A vital factor has to be the massively increased media coverage. We live now at a time in which we are presented with an unceasing diet of news and comment on the risks of war, of the dangers of terrorism, of reportage of unrest from many parts of the world. This comes to us round the clock, with rolling news, and cable and satellite services ensuring pervasive coverage. It is produced and updated rapidly, it is globalised and it is often in 'real time'. War is dramatic, unquestionably important, a matter of life and death and it can draw literally thousands of journalists to report on it.

There is no direct causal relation between media and fear of war. We prefer to conceive of there being more resources now being available to people who may use these to reflect on a greater range and variety of information about conflict than their forebears. For a good many, perhaps most, these resources generate anxiety and fear. This is a remarkable phenomenon: while our parents and grandparents frequently had direct experience of conflict, today we have much greater knowledge of war, but chiefly at a distance (Seaton, 2005). We are safer from war than ever, yet we witness it, often in appalling detail, as spectators (Ignatieff, 2000). The astonishing informational output lets us know far more about conflict, about campaigns' development and attendant risks, about the consequences of bombing and military clashes than the sailor mobilised to the Atlantic convoys or the 6th Army infantryman encircled at Stalingrad could have imagined. The sailor and infantryman knew well enough what it was to meet the enemy and feel the bitter cold of the Russian winter, but today's media-rich viewer can get instantaneous coverage from many spheres of battle, watch reporters communicating from satellite video phones and then have this digested for its strategic significance by politicians and experts. It is these greater informational resources that enable what Anthony Giddens (1994) calls the 'intensified reflexivity' (p. 24) of life today. Heightened consciousness of war and the threat of war are elements of this.

The Control Paradigm

We would highlight the enormous growth and extension of media today. On one level this is simply a matter of drawing attention to the character of media – lots more channels, 24/7 services, transnational news services such as CNN and BBC World. But what is understood by media must also come to terms with the PC, the world wide web, e-mail, blogs and cognate technologies. Even established media now require reconceptualisation: the *Guardian* newspaper sells less than 400,000 hard copies daily, but its website, *Guardian Unlimited,* achieved between 3 and 4 million hits each day through 2006; the *Times* newspaper makes around 600,000 sales per day, yet the *Times Online* website gets three times that many hits; the BBC News broadcast at 10 PM commands audiences of about 4.5 million, while its website is accessed 20 million times a day (http://www.alexa.com). The internet is the major phenomenon here and it already plays an important role in the ways people become informed about what is happening in their world.

It is not surprising that governments and military forces, being aware that citizens learn about war through media, pay careful attention to managing information. Conscious that public opinion matters enormously when it comes to war, politicians and commanders assiduously practice 'perception management' (Taylor, 1992). They want, as far as they can manage, to have publics receive news and reports that justify their conduct. From this follows much documented practices of 'PsychOps', chaperoning journalists and photo-opportunity events designed by central command.

Those who wage war, yet who seek public legitimacy, endeavour to put the most favourable gloss on their conduct and policies. Media researchers have too readily moved from recognising this aspiration to working with a control model of information about war that presupposes military and government are able to get away with it. Researchers in this mode might undertake, for example, content analysis of newspaper and television reports, demonstrate that there are patterns to reportage and conclude that most of these prioritised government and military spokespeople. The conclusion is easily reached that media are disproportionately influenced by military and government sources.

The most telling criticism of the control paradigm is that it is outmoded. Instead of control, one might better conceive the information environment of war and conflict nowadays as chaotic, certainly more confused and ambiguous than might have been possible even a generation ago (McNair, 2006). Amongst the reasons for this is the resistance of many journalists. It is exceedingly hard for the military and governments to control a diverse group of often hundreds of correspondents who set out from the presumption that all sources are trying to manipulate them (Tumber & Webster, 2006). Not only this, journalists are usually equipped with satellite video phones and laptops that allow them to report more or less immediately with little entourage and without being reliant on official sources, at the same time as they can access huge repositories of alternative information from the internet. Furthermore, the development of satellite and cable television, and transitional news services from BBC World to Al Jazeera, means that audiences have much more differentiated information sources than were possible just a few years ago (Calhoun, 2004). The increased availability of the internet to ordinary citizens, bringing along blogs, e-mails, electronic versions of newspapers and periodicals, video clips and websites, means that any idea of information control being readily achievable from conflict zones must be jettisoned. It is striven for, but the information domain is so febrile, extensive and open that control is at best an aspiration.

It is necessary to conceive of a much more expanded and differentiated information environment than hitherto. The public are receiving their information on war mediated, but this is a mediation that is now considerably more ambiguous. It comes quicker than previous forms, it is less predictable, much denser and more diverse than before. To say this is not to suggest there is a full pluralism operating in the media realm, but it is to insist that space has opened up in a vastly expanded realm. Scholars need to acknowledge that we are 'engaged in the first war in history. . . in an era of e-mails, blogs, cell phones, blackberrys, instant messaging, digital cameras, a global internet with no inhibitions, hand-held video cameras, talk radio, 24-hour news broadcasts, satellite television. There's never been a war fought in this environment before' (Rumsfeld, 2006). This does not deny the mediation of war, but it complicates it to a remarkable degree. Those who wage war have acknowledged the change (Department of Defense, 2003). Then British Prime Minister Blair (2007) appreciated that 'twenty-five years ago, media reports came back from the Falklands [during the 1981-82 war with Argentina] irregularly, heavily controlled', but nowadays internet sites allow 'straight into the living room. . . gruesome images (that are) bypassing the official accounts'. As such, this 'transforms the context within which the military, politics and public opinion interact'. It is time media researchers also recognised this.

An Alternative Information Environment?

When it comes to the mediation of war and the threat of war the information environment might be conceived as one of symbolic struggles between various agencies that compete for time, for news agendas and for interpretations of events. A significant set of players in these symbolic struggles are the anti-war and peace movements. They strive to ensure that their perspective gets access to media in various ways, from organising enormous demonstrations that may be coordinated across the world and be compellingly newsworthy, as in 15 February 2003 where so many people took to the streets of major cities that a *New York Times* writer was moved to describe the action as 'the second superpower' (Tyler, 2003), to presenting journalists with briefing papers setting out well-argued and coherent opposition to those who wage war. They also adopt a panoply of new media – e-mail communications, list serves, websites, discussion groups. . . – in the struggle to ensure that their views get a platform.

We return to the relation of the anti-war and peace movements with established media below, but we would stress here that the changed and changing information environment means that we need to think beyond a settled media in which movements are reported upon. The changed information environment has allowed the anti-war and peace movements to create their own media, even to establish what might be considered an alternative information environment. The web maintainer of Stop the War Coalition (StWC), the main coalition in the UK, described this to us. Like several of his co-activists, he felt that the anti-war movements receive poor coverage in more mainstream media. He complains that 'there are fewer and fewer oppositional voices available in mainstream media; everything seems to be filtered through government and establishment journalists'. He regards StWC's Newsletter (for which he is responsible) that goes out to 20,000 subscribers via a listserve as an important element of an alternative information network for campaigners. It appears fortnightly or so, though in periods of intense activity more frequently, and it offers a digest of key issues, comment on topical matters and hyperlink connections to other sources of information. Given that 'there are fewer and fewer oppositional voices available in mainstream media; everything seems to be filtered through government and establishment journalists'. One suspects that this sentiment is shared by Tom Feeley, the producer of the daily electronic newsletter – Information Clearing House – that circulates from Southern California to subscribers across the world offering 'News you won't find on CNN or FoxNews', the site of which got around 200,000 daily hits through 2006 (http://www.alexa.com).

He told us that 'it's very difficult to get mainstream media to relate to us at all, but I don't care anymore. These people who get livid, 'look we have this demonstration, we have all these people, there's not anything in the paper', I don't expect anything from them (the media) anymore. So if we get something that's just a bonus. And the reason why it doesn't trouble me anymore is because we do definitely have our own networks'. His working day begins around 6 am when he does an online review of 'a whole series of websites that I always look at in terms of information' which he then uses to update StWC's website. He is attuned to what Lance Bennett (2003) calls 'epistemic networks' far and wide which he raids to ensure that information supportive of StWC's priorities is available on its website. This is oppositional information available to anyone checking StWC's website.

He reminded us that this alternative network allows speedy and effective challenges to mainstream accounts. He was being interviewed a few weeks after the arrest in August 2006 of over 20 Muslims in the UK on suspicion of planning terrorist attacks on aircraft by smuggling bomb-making equipment aboard. He pointed out that there has been widespread media coverage of the arrests, but little criticism of the action. He suggested that this could be challenged through the internet resources of StWC: 'there's a whole climate of truth mainstream media has created that we feel we have to counter and... put it on our website. Our treasurer has got a particular interest in the terror plots that we've had... Now he has put together a little pamphlet which actually in a very non political (way), just 'these are the facts of what it was and this is what the result of it was'. You know you get this massive media thing, you get (arrests of suspects)...they're often charged, they go to court, nearly every case so far is thrown out, but when it's thrown out the media doesn't... So initially there's this massive thing like we've got now. Now that type of thing, you respond to those things via the internet and you find the best information is via the internet. From the States there's an article which we got... by an American who found a scientist who'd actually looked at what the...plotters would have to do to actually...' This article raised serious doubts about the technical possibilities of those arrested putting together in-flight the bomb-making constituents that they were alleged to have smuggled aboard.

Mediated Politics

Today's enlarged information domain provides opportunities for dissident views, but it has grown while a traditional informational source has diminished in importance. There has been a perceived decline especially in the public meeting where politicians and activists would come together with interested citizens and discuss matters of the moment. Public meetings still play a vital role in campaigning, but our informant recalls a time when there were many more such occasions where interested parties could be exposed to alternative perspectives. He remembers that, a few years back, 'I would go to a public meeting and it would be brilliant speakers who would give you a context... You could go to meetings all the time, the whole range... but a lot of that's gone'. He reminisced about an older generation of activists who prioritised public meetings and he still recognises the value of this method of getting people involved. But he regards the internet now as key to informing and organising. This is in accord with Manuel Castells (1998) who coined the term 'informational politics' to emphasise that parties and activists must be committed to new media or condemned to 'political marginality' (p. 312). In so far as most people are conscious of war, nowadays this comes through media. Opponents of war must compete in that domain (Castells, 2009).

Information Circuits

All the significant anti-war and peace movements have produced websites that, relatively cheap to set up and maintain, were unknown a decade ago (Pickerill, 2003). The websites contain varying amounts and qualities of information, but typically provide a statement of principles, news and comment as well as links to cognate organisations. They are a first port of call for those wanting to know more, often by-passing secondary information sources such as newspapers. The sites generally offer facilities that allow readers to sign up to a list serve, so that they may receive e-mail messages that will keep them up-to-date direct from the group.

So elements of an alternative information network are in place, but there are complex connections with established media. To better appreciate the current information environment we need to take cognisance of the information circuits that flow between different media, groups and actors. There are several sorts of circuitry that might be distinguished.

1. *Information flows from established media to the anti-war and peace movements.* Interest in a subject makes people eager to seek out information. Anti-war and peace campaigners are hungry for news and comment about conflict and seek it out in a range of media, though quality newspapers on the liberal end of the spectrum, such as the *Guardian* and the anti-Iraq War *Independent,* are disproportionately read. However, this is not simply a matter of activists reading a particular newspaper. StWC's website, for example, presents many articles taken

from mainstream as well as oppositional periodicals, allowing those who wish to access particular pieces – commentaries, features, news items – via hyperlinks from the StWC website. Heavily used in this respect is the *Guardian* newspaper's website, *Guardian Unlimited*, which allows free use of materials. This flow of information to the anti-war and peace sites extends to collating government reports and publications in documents and articles authored by activists. Milan Rai of Justice Not Vengeance produces briefing papers that he distributes to a listmail of around 3000 subscribers. 'All the sources', he explains, 'are completely mainstream', being 'newspapers or government reports or reports from establishment bodies like Chatham House'.

2. *Information flows from anti-war and peace movement activists to mainstream media.* The established media report on the anti-war and peace movements, for example, when it stages a demonstration or rally. In such circumstances the movement adopts various tactics that help get its message across into the mainstream, from cultivating contacts with sympathetic journalists to ensuring high visibility by, for instance, designing eye-catching displays and memorable slogans. For instance, a national demonstration was held in London on 5 August 2006 to protest against the Israeli invasion of Lebanon. StWC had organised the demonstration around the theme of 'Unconditional Ceasefire Now' and to maximise effect it urged members and sympathisers to turn out in large numbers, promoted the support it had from distinguished figures and urged demonstrators to bring along children's shoes to deposit as a symbol of innocent lives being taken by Israel actions. The amount of influence anti-war and peace protesters have is limited, not least because they lack resources as well as expertise in public relations. Lindsey German, convenor of StWC, contrasted the 'very, very slick PR operation' of three wealthy former employees of National Westminster Bank who were facing extradition to America on charges of financial malfeasance during the summer of 2006 with StWC's much more modest endeavours. She admitted that 'it's very hard to punch your weight in that area unless you've got high flying professionals'. Nevertheless, in the current period the fact that two national newspapers (the *Daily Mirror* and the *Independent*) editorially support the anti-war and peace movements does mean that considerable amounts of sympathetic coverage is ensured. Thus on the day of the 5 August 2006 demonstration the *Independent* newspaper supported it with a front page full of mug shot photographs that featured esteemed individuals wearing tee-shirts proclaiming 'Unconditional Ceasefire Now'. Finally, one might note that several anti-war and peace supporters figure regularly in some of the mainstream media – for example, John Pilger, Robert Fisk, Andrew Murray and Gary Younge. These congregate in the pages of the *Guardian, Mirror* and *Independent*, but they are generally then put onto websites where they can be readily accessed by anti-war and peace campaigners.

3. *Websites, Blogs and Interactivity.* These areas of the internet readily service the alternative information networks of the anti-war and peace movements, but some observations on their relationships to established media might be made. As a preliminary, we might remind ourselves of the novelty of cyberspace and

the blogosphere: just a decade ago websites were almost unknown, e-mail just taking off, discussion groups and chat rooms little used. Now websites are prevalent in the anti-war and peace movements, and these often include features that enable readers some interactivity. Blogging has grown rapidly, especially since 2004, so much so that a Harris poll in Britain (*Guardian,* 16 October 2006) reported that 40% of internet users (which amount to about 70% of the population) read a blog. The PEW (Lenhart & Fox, 2006, p. 20) organisation estimates that 90% of bloggers allow readers to respond, hence integrating interactivity into the process. These developments, still inchoate, merit comment in terms of traditional media not least because many journalists are informationally insatiable and avidly seek out sources. As such, we come across materials from websites finding their way into mainstream media. For instance, when Tony Blair admitted on a television talk show that he prayed and would be answerable to God for his Iraq policy, the mother of a soldier killed in that country, Pauline Hickey, wrote a commentary on the StWC website. Later this piece was reprinted in the *Guardian* newspaper (2 March 2006). Such a direct relationship is rare, but it is clear that journalists keep a close eye on the internet and its traffic. As such they are amongst the more avid readers of blogs (and many journalists, especially the commentariat, maintain their own blogs) and this can influence what they write. For instance, during the summer of 2006 when Muslims were arrested in Britain on terrorism charges, Polly Toynbee noted in her *Guardian* column that 'the internet hummed with theories that this was all a plot to deflect attention from Lebanon' (15 August 2006). Regular media such as *The Times* and *Guardian* now also offer reviews and comments on websites and blogs. In addition, some have websites that allow readers to contribute to discussion. For example, the *Comment is Free* section of *Guardian Unlimited* is interactive, featuring articles from the newspaper along with a range of blogs from an extensive list of contributors that are accompanied by often lengthy reader comment; 'The aim is to host an openended space for debate, dispute, argument and agreement and to invite users to comment on everything they read' (http://commentisfree.guardian.co.uk/). Even the BBC, Britain's most used website, enables readers to comment on news items. From a different angle, some blogs can be a form of journalism that is itself newsworthy. For instance, blogs from Baghdad have provided insight into conditions and experiences where journalists cannot easily go. Nor surprisingly, these sites are frequently visited, reported on in traditional media and on occasion produced in book format (Salam Pax, 2003; Riverbend, 2005).

The information environment now instances significant traffic between and across traditional media and the anti-war and peace movements. There is appropriation from the mainstream media, contributions made more or less directly to that media, and, with new media especially, possibilities of amplification, challenge and discussion through interactive features and the growth of the blogosphere. While a good deal of these developments enables an autonomous information network to be constructed, it is also clear that the anti-war and peace movements connect with established media in significant ways. To emphasise, none of this ought to be interpreted as suggesting that we now have a plurality of equal voices – official spokespeople still get the lion's share of attention and it is rare for the anti-war and peace movement actors to set agendas for consideration. It is simply that the information environment is now considerably expanded and possessed of more possibilities of participation than traditional media, and scholars need to acknowledge this fact (Coleman, 2005).

Moving Beyond Mediation

We have emphasised that nowadays war is a mediated experience for most people and that symbolic struggles are a striking feature of today's Information Wars (Tumber & Webster, 2007). But mediation is by no means all there is about war nor is it the whole story of the anti-war and peace movements in Britain. War is about killing and defeating enemies and the anti-war and peace movements want to stop this happening. Exposing people to anti-war and peace perspectives is necessary to effect this, but it is not sufficient. *The New York Times,* in an editorial (31 August 2006), underscored this when it observes that, while a 'majority of Americans now say they oppose the (Iraq) war', it is difficult to find this publicly expressed in marches and vigils. 'Bloggers say there is an anti-war movement online', says the *New York Times,* but 'it takes crowds to get America's attention'. It is cheap to set up a website and it takes little effort to sign an e-mail petition, so not surprisingly electronic campaigns that remain in the realm of the virtual are of limited consequence (Chadwick, 2006, p. 121). It is because this is so that a StWC official criticises 'people who see it [the internet] as the end in itself... There are lots of people actually campaigning who submerge themselves into it completely... I know individuals whose whole life is producing their blogs, but they're not related in any way to anything that goes on, on the ground'.

Acknowledgement of the importance of mediation to contemporary warfare should not lead us into the trap of mediacentrism. In Britain most anti-war and peace campaigners endeavour not just to change consciousnesses, but also to change policies by mobilising opposition to war. It will use new media more or less adroitly, for example, in terms of coordinating members more effectively or marshalling sympathisers more speedily. It may do this in ways that use new media intensively and with ingenuity, as for instance with the Faslane 365 campaign against Trident nuclear missiles that is coordinating a year's series of autonomous peaceful protests of different groups at the Scottish missile site (http://www.faslane365.org/). But the context is one of stopping or preventing war, so more than symbols are involved. David Gee from the Society of Friends, for example, explains that 'if there is an attack on Iraq or on Iran... we instantly have the infrastructure there to mobilise the entire Quaker network, so there'll be somebody in every meeting, in all those 400 odd meetings, that will have access to the internet, at least one person I would have thought, who can quickly look, and it'll be on the home page of the Quaker site, look at the Peace Exchange (website)... There'll be a whole list of things you can do, a briefing, so instantly we can mobilise the whole Quaker community in that case'.

Another way of putting this is to say that to be adequately understood the anti-war and peace movements need to be situated in a wider frame than media. The priority of influencing policy by mobilising opposition is one major dimension of this. Others include campaigning during a period of involvement of US and British military forces in an unpopular war in Iraq, apprehension about international terrorism, concerns about and within Muslim communities regarding Islamism and the distinguishing characteristics of the groups that make up the anti-war and peace movements (Gillan, Pickerill, & Webster 2008).

In arguing for contextualisation, we emphasise two particular matters. One of these would be the limits of the virtual when it comes to understanding the anti-war and peace movements; the other concerns particularities of the British anti-war and peace movements.

Limits of the Virtual

For all the talk about living a mediated existence, of virtual relationships increasing in importance, we need to remember that people also live in situated places and interact, for the most part, face to face with human beings. Their outlooks are not merely formed by virtuality, but also by matters such as biographies, experiences and political circumstances. The significance of this for the anti-war and peace movements in Britain is that, despite their widespread adoption of new media, one is struck by the ways in which places and people root the movements and shape their actions (Taylor, 2007). We may exemplify this with a series of examples:

1. It is striking that the anti-war and peace movements, while they utilise the internet to draw upon transglobal informational sources in putting together their websites and assorted documents, remain emphatically oriented towards the national, and even more local, scenes (Gillan, 2007). Thus while the web officer starts the day by scanning sites around the world to update Stop the War Coalition's website, he stresses that StWC is 'a campaigning organisation' and that this necessarily means materials are oriented to mobilisation of members for demonstrations and protests of one sort or another. Politics remain predominately nationally organised, so campaigners need to focus where they have maximum effect. Kate Hudson, chair of the Campaign for Nuclear Disarmament, observes that 'in Britain, working on a national level, the internet doesn't fundamentally change anything ... communication on certain things can be much easier, and access is quicker. But I don't think it changes how we do things politically, because the most crucial thing is a political approach through forging alliances with different organisations ... so it doesn't fundamentally change our political approach to things'. This is a salutary reminder to those who imagine the anti-war and peace movements to be a global phenomenon.

2. The StWC website is constructed with the needs of local activists to the fore. The web maintainer is conscious that activists need timely and pertinent materials to argue and debate with members of the public. This priority means that, however interesting the articles he finds on his daily trawl, many are rejected because they do not fit with 'giving them (activists) the information that they need . . .in terms of how they're involved in the campaign that we're organising'. This also explains how and why Milan Rai of Justice Not Vengeance creates its widely circulated briefing papers: 'The purpose of the briefing is to give an anti-war activist a set of credible sources with which to argue against current propaganda, both face-to-face with people who they are living with, working with and so on, or if they campaigning in the street, and also if they're writing letters or writing articles and so on. . . . It's supposed to be something that you have on a stall and you could give to someone who is a bit sceptical about what you're saying'.

3. Another factor that fixes anti-war and peace organisations in the locale is their membership base. The degrees of internationalism vary between organisations, with a disparate, middle class and internationally networked group like Women in Black towards one end of the spectrum and decidedly local anti-war groups in a city such as Leicester at the other. However, even an international organisation such as the Society of Friends, with offices on mainland Europe as well as Britain and the USA, was pulled by the local concerns of their membership base which is chiefly in the USA and UK.

4. There may also be a part played here by disposition, as explained to us by Martina Weitsch who works in Brussels for the Quaker Council of European Affairs. Though there were links with North America, she said that 'in terms of coordination, there isn't any because. . . most Quakers see themselves as individuals who happen to come together as a group'. There is a strong ethos in Quaker doctrine of personal responsibility, of bearing witness and following one's conscience. Associated with it is a preference for personal meetings, something one officer at Friends House in the Euston Road explained as Quakers being 'much more about getting together as people. . . .They don't sit in front of the computer, they'd much rather go out and meet people and talk to people. I don't even think five years from now that will have changed a lot. I think probably there will still be that sense of let's get together, physically, and talk about this; why would you do this in cyberspace when you could actually go down the road and see these people?'

5. When one considers the Muslim role in the anti-war movements then the question of the location of actors seems especially important. In Leicester, the Muslim population of approximately 30,000 (dominated by those from an Indian background, but also of Pakistan, Bangladesh and Somali descent) and their 22 mosques are concentrated to the north east of the city, specifically the areas of Highfields and Evington. The majority of Muslims in Leicester are Sunnis (Leicester Council of Faiths, 2002). In such circumstances it is not surprising that anti-war activists, living close by one another and with the mosque as a frequent common meeting point, appear to have little need for internet technologies.

The fact of living proximately means people interact interpersonally rather than virtually.

6. With regard to Muslim participation the anti-war movements it might also be observed that the local mosque and Imams play a key role in organising and motivating. Friday prayers, we were repeatedly told, were crucial in mobilisation of protesters. For instance, Chris Goodwin of the Leicester Campaign to Stop the War said that when her group tried to organise events involving Muslims, then it seemed it happened only when the Muslim leaders gave approval. Appreciation of the engagement of Muslims in anti-war activism has to be aware of the importance of these local, yet faith-based, factors that can be telling.

Uneasy Alliances

The anti-war and peace movements in Britain are often perceived as unified. In truth, the anti-war and peace movements are an uneasy alliance of remarkably diverse groups and individuals. It ranges along several continuums from pacifism to opposition specifically to the American invasion of Iraq, from civil libertarians to anti-imperialists who encourage the defeat of America by Iraqi 'insurgents', from the religiously motivated to the entirely secular, from direct action advocates to those committed to the power of persuasion, from the extra-parliamentary left to peers of the realm, and from right wing fundamentalists, through centrist Liberal Democrats to anarchists (Pickerill & Webster 2006).

While the original Campaign for Nuclear Disarmament (CND) developed in different circumstances, and took as its goal opposition to nuclear weapons, it also aimed to convert the Labour Party to its policy (Parkin, 1968). Today the decline of class politics and of organised labour, plus the fact that it was a Labour Party premier who has played a leading role in the Iraq invasion, means that the present anti-war and peace movements are not only considerably more diverse than its predecessors but also somewhat jaundiced about established political parties. There are lobbies of Parliament, of course, but the anti-war and peace movements have an extra-Parliamentary focus that its predecessors lacked. It is a social movement joined together only by the common concern to oppose the 'war on terror' and pursuit of this goal operates outside party political aegis.

In key respects it is a union of opposites. Feminists march with determinedly patriarchal Muslim elders; orthodox Muslim women wearing hijabs and not infrequently burqas campaign alongside bejeaned students; Jews for Justice marched on 5 August 2006 in London with those who held placards calling for 'Victory to the Resistance' in Lebanon and proclaiming that 'We are all Hezbollah'; and middle aged members of Women in Black quietly walk for peace alongside those, who angrily shout 'George Bush: Terrorist'. Many commentators have made much of these contradictory alliances that are found (Horowitz, 2004), Gita Sahgal of *Women Against Fundamentalists* (2006), for instance, contending that some of the Muslim groups are connected with terrorism and neo-fascist organisations in South East Asia, a view contested by many of the Muslim groups (Bright, 2005; Ware, 2005, 2006).

Despite new media allowing the anti-war and peace movements to switch adeptly their campaigning agendas to include the most topical of issues such as the more recent threats of attack on Iran by American or Israeli forces, it is difficult to envisage the movements remaining united. To be sure, pacifist groups such as the Quakers and anti-nuclear activists like CND will continue, driven by their focus and faith, but the presently most significant formation, Stop the War Coalition, must encompass extraordinarily contradictory constituencies. StWC was driven from the outset by an established Marxist group, the Socialist Workers Party (SWP), which was unprepared for the large ethnic minority involvement. Lindsey German, the convenor of StWC and an SWP stalwart, recalled that in late 2001 the SWP had called a meeting to consider the invasion of Afghanistan and found that 'loads of Muslims came and we didn't know a single Muslim at the time politically'. She describes how people such as her developed relations with Muslim groups: 'the Muslim community really surprised us because we knew nothing about it, and then one of the people who...was of Muslim background himself, he said 'look we should go to the mosques when we were building the demonstration because we knew the first demonstration was about Afghanistan'. So we went to the London mosques'.

However, a price of the coalition has been that the SWP has muted its ideological adherence to socialism and secularism. The website of the SWP (2007) – a group once orthodoxly Leninist – now insists that 'We fight alongside anybody or any organisation that wants to build the movement. The anti-war movement has gained its strength from its unity and breadth. That's why we fight to maintain the principles unity (sic) of all the coalitions and campaigns with which we are involved. We respect people with ideas that are different from ours. So, while we seek to persuade people of our revolutionary ideas, we resist moves to narrow the movement to those who are already part of the radical left'. Some sense of the problems this entails comes from Mike Marqusee, former StWC press officer, who told us that 'the advantage of having the SWP as a national organisation with a . . . printing press and twenty full time workers and a rapid network for the distribution of leaflets. . . was huge in getting the Stop the War Coalition off the ground. . . .And I think they were right, in the sense that they felt that this is a crossroads in global politics. . . It was strong sense that brought people together, and the SWP did have that. They then though took that into meaning that nothing should be allowed to confuse anybody about what was the absolute priority, which meant that the arguments, complex arguments about secularism and religion were not heard. . . . So, for example, pretty early on, those people who. . . questioned the link with MAB (Muslim Association of Britain) were castigated as Islamophobes'. Such tensions are likely ultimately to pull StWC apart.

Conclusion

We began this article by emphasising that people are safer than their predecessors, yet have experience of war and the threat of war through media that is unprecedented in its intensity and range. This must contribute to high levels of anxiety and fear of war recorded in opinion surveys. However, the information environment of which this mediation is composed is shifting, complex and diverse, making adherence to the influential control paradigm in media analysis problematic. Here the anti-war and peace movements find significant space for messages and has even been able to establish elements of an alternative information environment using listserves, websites and related technologies.

However, it would be an egregious mistake to conceive war and its opponents in the anti-war and peace movements solely in terms of media. War is about 'hearts and minds', but it is also about inflicting material damage on people and places. By the same token, anti-war and peace activism is about more than persuasion. When we come to examine the anti-war and peace movements, we have stressed the need to appreciate the wider contexts within which they operate. In particular, we drew attention to the importance of acknowledging that people live in particular places and within particular relationships. This shapes how they organise, respond and campaign against war. Remembering this we may better understand that the anti-war and peace movements in the UK is decidedly national in its focus, that a priority is mobilisation to change policy and that local relationships can be telling. Finally, we drew attention to the diversity and even contradictions found within the anti-war and peace movements. It is a broad coalition united only in that it opposes war.

Acknowledgments The authors would like to thank the ESRC (Economic and Social Research Council) for support of the research included in this article (RES 228-25-0060).

References

Bennett, W. L. (2003). Communicating global activism: Strengths and vulnerabilities of networked politics. *Information, Communication and Society, 6*(2), 143–68.

Blair, T. (2007). *Our nation's future – Defence.* 12 January. Available at http://www/number10. gov.uk/output/Page0735.asp

Bright, M. (2005). Radical links of UK's "moderate" Muslim group. *Observer*, 14 August, p. 8.

Calhoun, C. (2004). Information technology and the international public sphere. In D. Schuler & P. Day (Eds.), *Shaping the network society* (pp. 1–28). Cambridge, MA: MIT Press.

Castells, M. (1998). *The power of identity*. Oxford: Blackwell.

Castells, M. (2009). *Communication power*. Oxford: Oxford University Press.

Chadwick, A. (2006). *Internet politics: States, citizens and new communication technologies.* Oxford: Oxford University Press.

Coleman, S. (2005). Blogs and the new politics of listening. *Political Quarterly, 76*(2), 273–280.

Department of Defense. (2003). *Information operations roadmap*. Washington, DC: Pentagon.

Giddens, A. (1994). Brave new world: The new context of politics. In D. Miliband (Ed.), *Reinventing the left* (pp. 21–38). Cambridge: Polity.

Gillan, K. (2007). The UK anti-war movement online: Uses and limitations of internet technologies for contemporary activism (mimeo).

Gillan, K., Pickerill, J., & Webster, F. (2008). *Anti-war activism: New media and protest in the information age*. London: Palgrave.

Hobsbawm, E. J. (1994). *Age of extremes: The short twentieth century*. London: Michael Joseph.

Horowitz, D. (2004). *Unholy alliance: Radical Islam and the American left*. Washington, DC: Regnery.

Human Security Report 2005: War and Peace in the 21st Century. (2006). New York: Oxford University Press. Available at http://www.humansecurityreport.info/

Ignatieff, M. (2000). *Virtual war: Kosovo and beyond*. London: Chatto and Windus.

Leicester Council of Faiths. (2002). *An overview of the major faiths in the city of Leicester*, Issue 4, www.leicestercounciloffaiths.org.uk

Lenhart, A., & Fox, S. (2006). *Bloggers: A portrait of the internet's new storytellers*. Washington, DC: PEW Internet and American Life Project.

Mazower, M. (1998). *Dark continent: Europe's twentieth century*. Harmondsworth: Penguin.

McNair, B. (2006). *Cultural chaos: Journalism, news and power in a globalised world*. London: Routledge.

Mueller, J. (2004). *The remnants of war* (Cornell Studies in Security Affairs). Ithaca: Cornell University Press.

Parkin, F. (1968). *Middle class radicals*. Manchester: Manchester University Press.

Pax, S. (2003). *The Baghdad blog*. London: Guardian Books.

Pickerill, J. (2003). *Cyberprotest: Environmental activism online*. Manchester: Manchester University Press.

Pickerill, J., & Webster, F. (2006). The anti-war/peace movement in Britain and the conditions of information war. *International Relations, 20*(4), 407–423.

Riverbend. (2005). *Baghdad burning: Girl blog from Iraq*. London: Marion Boyars.

Rumsfeld, D. (2006). *Speech to council on foreign relations*, February 17.

Seaton, J. (2005). *Carnage and the media: The making and breaking of news and violence*. London: Allen Lane.

SWP (Socialist Workers Party). (2007). Accessed January 20, 2007, from http://www.swp.org.uk/about.php

Taylor, I. (2007). Thinking local, acting global. *Peace News*. Accessed February 2, 2007, from http://www.peacenews.info/issues/2480-81/248006.html

Taylor, P. M. (1992). *War and the media: Propaganda and persuasion in the Gulf War*. Manchester: Manchester University Press.

Tumber, H., & Webster, F. (2006). *Journalists under fire: Information war and journalistic practices*. London: Sage.

Tumber, H., & Webster, F. (2007). Globalization and information and communications technologies: The case of war. In G. Ritzer (Ed.), *Blackwell companion to globalization*. Malden, MA: Blackwell.

Tyler, P. (2003). A new power in the streets. *New York Times,* 17 February.

Ware, J. (2005). On Muslim council of Britain. *BBC Today, Radio 4*. Transcript at http://newsvote.bbc.co.uk/mpapps/pagetools/print/news.bbc.co.uk/

Ware, J. (2006). Faith, hate and charity. *BBC Panorama,* 3 August. Transcript at http//news.bbc.co.uk/l/hi/programmes/Panorama/523486.stm

Women Against Fundamentalists. (2006). Hecklers.*BBC Radio 4*, 23 August. Available at http://www.bbc.co.uk/radio4/hecklers/pip/ixhsj

Web Content Analysis: Expanding the Paradigm

Susan C. Herring

Introduction

Since the introduction of the first graphical browser in 1993, the system of inter-linked, hypertext documents known as the World Wide Web (hereafter, "the web") has grown to be the primary multimodal content delivery system on the internet; indeed, today, it is one of the largest content delivery vehicles in the history of the world. Along with this increase in volume, technical web document and website types have also proliferated. From their beginnings as static HTML documents com-prised mainly of text, links, and graphics, web pages have added sound, animations, and video; they have incorporated user interface, user content, and user–user inter-activity features (including, in the latter category, email, discussion forums, chat, and Voice-over-IP); and they have generally converged with other online and offline media to produce hybrid genres such as online news sites, blogs, wikis, photo- and video-sharing sites, and social network sites.

The abundance of web pages and their diversity of form and function (as well as the unprecedented ease with which content can be collected and ana-lyzed using automated tools) provide seemingly endless opportunities for research. At the same time, these characteristics can be daunting to researchers wishing to analyze web content. What methods should one use, and how should they be implemented? Will established methods serve, or should new methods be devised to address new technological phenomena? If new methods are coined, how can their validity and consistency of application across researchers be ensured? This is important if internet research is to be taken seriously and if the results of analy-sis of web content are to be comparable with previous analyses of content in other media.

Content analysis is an established social science methodology concerned broadly with "the objective, systematic, and quantitative description of the content of communication" (Baran, 2002, p. 410; see also Berelson, 1952). As media of

S.C. Herring (✉)
School of Library and Information Science, Bloomington, Indiana, USA
e-mail: herring@indiana.edu

J. Hunsinger et al. (eds.), *International Handbook of Internet Research*,
DOI 10.1007/978-1-4020-9789-8_14, © Springer Science+Business Media B.V. 2010

communication, websites and web pages lend themselves prima facie to content analysis (Weare & Lin, 2000). Indeed, content analysis (henceforth, CA) was one of the first methodologies used in web analysis (e.g., Bates & Lu, 1997), and it has been employed increasingly since, albeit not always in traditional ways (McMillan, 2000).

This article addresses the question of how strictly internet research should embrace traditional CA methods when analyzing web content, as opposed to incorporating methodological innovation, including drawing on methods not traditionally considered CA. Narrow and broad interpretations of the concept of web content analysis are first contrasted and exemplified with relevant scholarship. The utility of a broad interpretation that subsumes the narrow one is then illustrated with reference to research on weblogs (blogs), a popular web format in which features of HTML documents and interactive computer-mediated communication converge (Herring, Scheidt, Bonus, & Wright, 2004, 2005). Examples from the literature are provided of traditional and non-traditional blog content analyses and the methodological challenges they face. It is argued that coming to terms with these challenges can affect the conceptualizations underlying content analysis as a methodological paradigm, in ways that blur the boundaries between CA and other methods, such as discourse analysis and social network analysis. The article concludes by proposing an expanded web content analysis (WebCA) paradigm in which insights from other paradigms are operationalized and implemented within a general CA framework.

Content Analysis

Content analysis is a systematic technique for coding symbolic content (text, images, etc.) found in communication, especially structural features (e.g., message length, distribution of certain text or image components) and semantic themes (Bauer, 2000). While the primary use of CA is to identify and describe patterns in manifest content—what the audience perceives through the senses, rather than what it feels or believes as a result of that content, or what the content producer intended—the technique can also be used for making inferences about intentions and effects (Holsti, 1969; Krippendorff, 1980).

According to Krippendorff (1980), the earliest known application of content analysis was in the 17th century, when the Church conducted a systematic examination of the content of early newspapers. However, it was not until the 1940s and 1950s that content analysis became a well-established paradigm (Berelson, 1952; Berelson & Lazarsfeld, 1948). Its most prototypical uses have been the analysis of written mass media content by scholars of advertising, communication, and journalism. However, in recent decades, CA techniques have also been used increasingly to analyze content on the internet. Perhaps due to its original presentation as a one-to-many broadcast medium, the web has attracted an especially large number of studies that employ content analysis methods.

Web Content Analysis

The phrase "web content analysis" is in fact ambiguous. It can be interpreted in two different senses, the second of which subsumes the first: (1) the application of traditional CA techniques, narrowly construed, to the web [web [content analysis]] and (2) the analysis of web content, broadly construed, using various (traditional and non-traditional) techniques [[web content] analysis]. Both of these senses are represented in the web analysis literature, as discussed below.

A Traditional Approach

The first sense of web content analysis is explicitly argued for by McMillan (2000), who adopts a traditional approach in her discussion of the challenges of applying CA to the web. Drawing on Krippendorff (1980), she notes that CA traditionally involves a set of procedures that can be summarized in five steps:

1) The researcher formulates a research question and/or hypotheses.
2) The researcher selects a sample.
3) Categories are defined for coding.
4) Coders are trained, code the content, and the reliability of their coding is checked.
5) The data collected during the coding process are analyzed and interpreted.

McMillan (2000) advocates adhering to these procedures and their traditional realizations as closely as possible when analyzing web content.

With regard to the first step, *research questions* should be "narrowed" from the many new questions the web raises and a context should be found for them "either in existing or emerging communication theory" (p. 2). Following Krippendorff (1980, p. 66), McMillan states as a requirement for *sampling* that "within the constraints imposed by available knowledge about the phenomena, each unit has the same chance of being represented in the collection of sampling units"—that is, the sample ideally should be random.[1] In defining *coding categories*, she implies that a standard list of categories would be desirable and hints that researchers might apply established categories of content identified in old media studies (e.g., Bush, 1951). Standard units of context are also needed, analogous to those developed in traditional media (cf. the column-inch for newspapers, time measured in seconds for broadcast).

---

[1] While McMillan (2000) acknowledges that "the *size* of the sample depends on factors such as the goals of the study" (p. 2, emphasis added), she does not mention that different research goals/questions might call for different *types* of samples. Rather, she asserts that random samples are required for "rigor" in all CA studies—a claim that many researchers would dispute (see, e.g., note 5).

As regards the fourth step, multiple *coders* should be trained in advance on a portion of a sample, and established methods for calculating intercoder reliability (such as Scott's pi and Holsti's reliability index)[2] should be employed. Finally, although McMillan does not believe that the web poses new challenges as regards the fifth step—*analyzing and interpreting* research findings—she cautions against the "inappropriate" use of statistical tests that assume a random sample (which includes the most frequently used statistical tests), given the difficulty of identifying/constructing a statistically random sample on the web.

While McMillan recognizes and discusses possible ways to overcome specific challenges the web raises to realizing each of these goals, the goals themselves are not fundamentally questioned. She concludes that "new communication tools are not an excuse for ignoring established communication research techniques" (p. 20).

Underlying these recommendations is a concern for rigor and standardization, both of which are undeniably important when seeking to establish the credibility and validity of a new research enterprise. Rather than reinventing the methodological wheel, internet and web researchers can draw upon, and benefit from, well-established traditions. Further, the more similar the methods that are applied to new media are to those used to analyze old media, the easier it is to compare findings in order to attain broader, trans-media understandings.

Problems with the Traditional Approach

At the same time, the narrowness of the above view can be problematic. First, Krippendorff's procedures, as interpreted by McMillan (2000), are rarely followed strictly, even in analyses of old media. Exploratory (rather than theoretically pre-focused) studies are undertaken, non-random samples are used,[3] coding categories are allowed to emerge from data—indeed, this is the cornerstone of the grounded theory approach,[4] which is followed in many content analysis studies—and standard statistical tests are applied to non-random samples in studies of traditional modes of communication. Moreover, these methods are considered legitimate in many circumstances (see Bauer, 2000, for a broader conceptualization of "classical" content analysis).

Such practices are also common in the analysis of new media content, where they may be justified by the nature of the phenomena under investigation. Emergent phenomena require basic description, and phenomena of interest cannot always be identified in advance of establishing a coding scheme—the intermingling of channels of communication on websites may especially require novel coding categories. Moreover, the dynamic nature and sheer number of units of internet analysis

---

[2]For descriptions of these and other classic interrater reliability measures, see Scott (1955), Holsti (1969), and Krippendorff (1980, 2008).

[3]In a review of 25 years of content analyses, Riffe and Freitag (1997; cited in Weare & Lin, 2000) found that most studies were based on convenience or purposive samples; only 22.2% of the studies attempted to be representative of the population of interest.

[4]On grounded theory, see Glaser and Strauss (1967).

makes random sampling infeasible in many cases, as McMillan and others (e.g., Schneider & Foot, 2004; cf. Weare & Lin, 2000) have also noted. Indeed, out of 19 content analysis studies of the web that McMillan (2000) surveyed, most failed to adhere to her strict CA prescriptions. This does not necessarily render the results of such research useless or invalid, however.

Similarly, recent web studies that identify their primary methodology as content analysis also vary in the degree to which they adhere to McMillan's (2000) prescriptions. For example, an informal examination of CA articles published between 2004 and 2007 in the *Journal of Computer-Mediated Communication*, a leading journal for social science research on internet and web communication, reveals studies in which research questions are indeed grounded in traditional theory, multiple coders are used to establish interrater reliability, and coding schemes are adapted from previous communication research (e.g., Singh & Baack, 2004; Waseleski, 2005). However, most of the studies analyze non-random samples (Dimitrova & Neznanski, 2006; Pfeil, Zaphiris, & Ang, 2006; Singh & Baack, 2004; Waseleski, 2005; Young & Foot, 2005), and many invent new coding schemes (e.g., Dimitrova & Neznanski, 2006; Pfeil et al., 2006; Young & Foot, 2005). This suggests the possibility that the 19 articles surveyed by McMillan (2000) do not simply represent an earlier, methodologically less rigorous, phase of web content analysis research, but rather that web content analysis may be following somewhat different norms from those traditionally prescribed for the analysis of communication content by researchers such as Krippendorff and McMillan, or even evolving new norms.

Most challenging to the traditional view, a growing number of web studies analyze types of content that differ from those usually studied in CA—such as textual conversations and hyperlinks—using methodological paradigms other than traditional CA. Although one possibility would be to exclude such studies from consideration in discussions of content analysis, it seems desirable to be able to integrate different methods into the analysis of the content of a multimodal website, rather than stopping the analysis where traditional content analysis methods leave off. For these purposes, a broader methodological perspective is needed.

Non-Traditional Approaches

A number of new media researchers have argued that new communication technologies call for new methods of analysis (e.g., Mitra & Cohen, 1999; Wakeford, 2000). Here it is assumed that any approach to web content analysis that aims to cover a broad range of content should include, at a minimum, methods that allow for the systematic identification of patterns in link and interactive message content, since these types of content are increasingly prevalent on the web. To fulfill this aim, some researchers draw on methodological paradigms from disciplines outside communication. Two non-traditional approaches that claim connections with CA are considered below, one grounded in linguistics and the other in sociology. Computational techniques also increasingly inform the analysis of web content, although they are not usually characterized by their practitioners as CA.

Computer-Mediated Discourse Analysis

One approach to analyzing internet content that extends the traditional notion of what CA is and how it should be applied is computer-mediated discourse analysis (CMDA). The basic methodology of CMDA is described by Herring (2004) as language-focused content analysis supplemented by a toolkit of discourse analysis methods adapted from the study of spoken conversation and written text analysis. As in the more general practice of discourse analysis, the methods employed can be quantitative (involving coding and counting) or qualitative. The former can resemble classical content analysis, but a broader spectrum of approaches is also included. Thus, CMDA is a sub-type of CA (broadly defined), and CA (narrowly defined) is a sub-type of CMDA.

Regarding the implementation of the "coding and counting" approach to CMDA, Herring (2004) lays out a five-step process that resembles that for classical CA:

1) Articulate research question(s)
2) Select computer-mediated data sample
3) Operationalize key concept(s) in terms of discourse features
4) Apply method(s) of analysis to data sample
5) Interpret results

However, in contrast to McMillan's (2000) exhortation that researchers closely follow established practice in order to insure rigor and interpretability, Herring (2004) takes a pragmatic view, recommending paradigm-independent best practices, such as choose a research question that "is empirically answerable from the available data" [p. 346]. She also offers researchers options as regards sample types[5] (e.g., time-based, event-based, participant-based) and coding categories (e.g., pre-existing or emergent from the data), as determined by the research questions and the data under consideration. The greatest challenge in CMDA, and the key to a compelling analysis, lies in operationalizing concepts of theoretical interest (Herring, 2004 elaborates the example of "virtual community") in terms of measurable language behaviors, based on the premise that human behavior in CMC environments is carried out mostly through linguistic means. The importance of qualifying the interpretation of research findings in light of the characteristics of the data sampled is also emphasized.

CMDA has been applied to the analysis of email, discussion forums, chat rooms, and text messaging, all of which are forms of dialogue (or polylogue). It can also be applied to mediated speech (since discourse analysis is originally a spoken language paradigm), as well as to monologue text on web pages (Kutz & Herring, 2005). Finally, it can offer insight into the hypertextual nature of websites, through discourse methods associated with the analysis of intertextuality, or content that refers to content in other texts (Mitra, 1999). Patterns of interconnections

---

[5]Herring (2004, p. 350) notes that "in CMDA, [sampling] is rarely done randomly, since random sampling sacrifices context, and context is important in interpreting discourse analysis results."

formed by hyperlinks are also frequently addressed using methods of social network analysis.

Social Network Analysis

Social network analysis (SNA) could be considered CA in the broad sense of the term, in that it can be used to analyze hyperlinks, which are part of the content of websites—indeed, some would argue that links are the essence of the web (Foot, Schneider, Dougherty, Xenos, & Larsen, 2003). Classical SNA as employed by sociologists is quantitative and statistical; it is used to analyze networks of ties (e.g., as constituted by communication or transaction) between nodes (e.g., people, institutions). SNA is also well suited for analyzing patterns of linking on the web: websites can be considered nodes, links can be considered ties, and the arrangements of links within and across sites can be represented as networks (Jackson, 1997).

While most SNA does not call itself CA, a hybrid approach known as link analysis blurs the boundaries between the two. Links are part of the manifest content of web pages and as such are sometimes included in coding and counting studies of web features (Bates & Lu, 1997; Dimitrova & Neznanski, 2006). The nature of a link in terms of the site it connects to (sometimes called the link destination) has also been coded and analyzed in studies of website credibility (Fogg et al., 2002) and political affiliation (Foot, Schneider, Dougherty, Xenos, & Larsen, 2003). Further, patterns of linking within and across websites have been analyzed as indicators of phenomena ranging from academic quality (Thelwall, 2002) to community formation (Gibson, Kleinberg, & Raghavan, 1998).

Research by Kirsten Foot and Steven Schneider illustrates an approach to link analysis with close affinities to CA. With Park (2003), Foot et al. (2003, n.p.) assert that "hyperlinks are inscriptions of communicative and strategic choices on the part of site producers," similar to other types of web content. Their "mid-range" approach involves "systematic human coding and interpretation of linked-to producer types" in political candidate websites. Multiple, trained coders evaluated links for the presence or absence of connection to certain types of website, and interrater reliability was calculated using Krippendorff's alpha, consistent with standard CA practice.

Schneider and Foot (2004) also analyze networks of links across websites, as in SNA, within constellations that they term "web spheres." A web sphere is "a hyperlinked set of dynamically-defined digital resources that span multiple websites and are deemed relevant, or related, to a central theme or 'object'" (p. 118). An example of a web sphere given by Schneider and Foot is all the sites associated with the 2000 presidential election in the United States.

The above sections suggest that perspectives from other disciplines can be incorporated into traditional CA, while still preserving many of its essential characteristics (e.g., classification and quantification; interrater reliability assessment). The relationships among the approaches summarized above as applied to the analysis of web content are represented in Fig. 1. In the figure, content analysis is listed under Communication (although it is also used in other disciplines) to simplify the

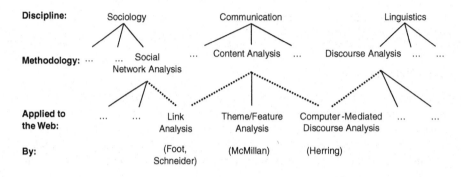

Fig. 1 Some approaches to analyzing web content

presentation, and traditional CA is referred to as Theme/Feature Analysis to indicate the types of content it is typically used to address.

Both narrow and broad CA approaches can be useful in analyzing web content, as illustrated in the next section for the content of one popular web format, the weblog.

Analyzing Blog Content

A weblog (blog, for short) is a type of web document in which dated entries appear in reverse chronological sequence. Blogs started to become popular after the introduction of the first free blogging software in 1999 and entered mainstream awareness after bloggers' commentary on the September 11, 2001, terrorist attacks and the 2003 U.S.-led war on Iraq attracted widespread media attention (Blood, 2002; Herring, Scheidt, Kouper, & Wright, 2006). As of mid-2008, blogs worldwide numbered in the hundreds of millions.[6]

Like other web documents, blogs can be multimodal or purely textual, and variants exist that feature photos, voice recordings (audio blogs), and videos (vlogs). Multimodality poses challenges to content analysis, especially as regards the identification of units of analysis (Weare & Lin, 2000). However, traditional CA has been applied to the analysis of photographs, radio, television, and film content, so these challenges are not new, per se. Of greater interest here are aspects of blogs that enable communication phenomena not found in traditional media.

One aspect of this difference from traditional media is the option for bloggers to allow readers to *comment* on their blog entries, which can give rise to communicative exchanges between bloggers and commenters within a single blog

---

[6]This estimate is based on a report that the number of blogs created at major hosts was 134-144 million in October 2005 (http://www.blogherald.com/2005/10/10/the-blog-herald-blog-count-october-2005/, accessed December 7, 2007). Blog creation, especially in countries outside the U.S., has increased since then, although many blogs have also been abandoned (Wikipedia, June 28, 2008).

and which blur the boundary between static HTML web pages and interactive discussion forums (Herring, Scheidt, et al., 2004, 2005). Another is the option to incorporate *links* into blog sidebars and entries; this is part of the definition of a blog, according to Blood (2002). Links make intertextual connections among blogs and between blogs and other kinds of online media technologically explicit; linking to someone's blog can also function as a turn in a "conversation" between bloggers (Herring, Kouper, et al., 2005). Further, linking from text and images creates integrated, multimodal units in which the contributions of different modalities cannot easily be separated (cf. Weare & Lin, 2000). These features are not unique to blogs, but blogs were among the first types of web document to display them.

In early 2003, when blogs were attracting increasing media coverage in conjunction with the impending US attack on Iraq, rigorous scholarship on blogs was virtually non-existent. At that time, the author, together with several others, formed a research group to study blogs.[7] The original goal of the group was to apply CA methods to randomly selected blogs in order to characterize "typical" blogs, as opposed to the political blogs that were attracting most of the media attention, and thereby to shed light on the blog as an emergent internet genre. However, in order to gain a full picture of the blog genre, the researchers soon realized that it was necessary to extend traditional CA methods, in particular to include methods for the analysis of links and comments.

Traditional Content Analysis of Blogs

Traditional content analysis methods are well suited for analyzing structural features of blog interfaces. Contemporary blogs typically have sidebars containing information about the author(s) and/or the blog, links to other blogs, and sometimes a calendar, photos, advertisements, and icons with links to organizations or products (such as blogging software) with which the blogger is associated. The frequency of these features and how distinguishing each is of the blog genre were analyzed by Herring, Scheidt, et al. (2004, 2005, 2006) using a classical CA approach. Similar general feature analyses have been conducted by Scheidt and Wright (2004), focusing on visual design elements in randomly selected blogs, and by Trammell, Tarkowski, Hofmokl, and Sapp (2006), focusing on blogs on a popular Polish blog-hosting site.

Traditional CA also works well for analyzing themes represented in blog entries and comments. In an analysis of posts in Bush and Kerry's blogs during the 2004 US presidential campaign, Trammell (2006) coded items "for mention of the opponent; attacks, target of the attack (person or record), and the presence of emotional, logical, or source credibility appeals" (p. 403); she found that most posts contained attacks and that Kerry's blog attacked Bush, the incumbent, more than the inverse.

---

[7]The (We)blog Research on Genre (BROG) project. See http://en.wikipedia.org/wiki/BROG, accessed August 26, 2009.

Thematic CA was also employed by Tremayne, Zheng, Lee, and Jeong (2006) in analyzing the political views (e.g., liberal or conservative) and content type (e.g., surveillance, opinion, reporting, personal) expressed in entries posted to "war blogs" during the recent US–Iraq conflict.

However, there are limits to how revealing this approach can be. For example, while the *presence* of links and their manifestation on a blog page (e.g., as text or graphics) can be coded relatively straightforwardly as structural features,[8] this surface approach is unable to capture the *trajectories* of hyperlinks from blogs to other websites or even the nature of link destinations, which is important to understanding the function and meaning of links. Moreover, while the *distribution* of comments can be analyzed with interesting results,[9] the discrete coding and counting approach of traditional CA is ill suited for analyzing patterns of *interaction* via comments, which are inherently relational. Finally, traditional CA is unrevealing about the stylistic or linguistic strategies used to construct entries and comments. These limitations have led blog researchers who favor CA to expand the methodological paradigm in various ways.

Expanded Methods of Blog Content Analysis

A number of blog studies have combined thematic analysis of blog content with link analysis. Williams, Tramell, Postelnicu, Landreville, and Martin (2005) coded the presence of thematic content such as war, economy, and health care in Bush and Kerry's campaign blog entries, but also analyzed the number of hyperlinks, the internal to external hyperlink ratio, and hyperlink destination, to determine if links "led users to media outlets, advocacy groups, within the candidate's own site, political party site, or other external websites" (p. 182). They found that candidate blogs were more likely to provide directives to external links than to direct viewers to content within the blogs, in contrast to the candidates' official websites. Tremayne et al.'s (2006) CA of war blogs also analyzed the distribution of incoming links in relation to other characteristics of blog content and included a social network analysis, which revealed that liberal and conservative war bloggers comprised distinct spheres of interaction with limited connections between them.

In the author's blog research group, the original impetus for moving beyond classical CA was a desire to address empirically a popular perception that the blogosphere, or universe of blogs, was actively "conversational." Sidebar links were analyzed as a manifestation of interaction between blogs: Links from randomly selected blogs were followed from blog to blog to create a snowball sample that was then

---

[8]For example, Herring, Scheidt, et al. (2004, 2005) found that contrary to popular claims that blog entries typically contain links and link often to other blogs, the average number of links in entries in randomly-selected blogs was .65, and most entries contained 0 links. Moreover, the majority of links were to websites created by others, with links to other blogs coming in a distant third.

[9]See, e.g., Herring, Scheidt, et al. (2004, 2005); Mishne and Glance (2006).

plotted as a social network diagram, from which topically focused cliques emerged. Within these cliques, however, even reciprocally linked bloggers blogging on the same topic only rarely left comments in each other's blogs or referred to each other in blog entries (Herring, Kouper, et al., 2005). Ali-Hasan and Adamic (2007) found a similar lack of correspondence between comments or citations in blog entries and contacts linked in the blogrolls of Kuwaiti bloggers. In contrast, Efimova and De Moor (2005) followed links in their study of an extended cross-blog conversation, which they found to be highly interactive, although the conversation itself was their pre-defined unit of analysis, rather than the individual blog.

In all of the above studies of cross-blog "conversation," link analysis was supplemented by analysis of interaction through blog entries and comments. Relatively few studies have as yet focused on interaction in entries and comments, however, in part due to the difficulty of capturing for analysis all parts of conversations that extend across multiple blogs. One computational solution was proposed by Nakajima, Tatemura, Hino, Hara, and Tanaka (2005), who automatically extracted cross-blog "threads," as defined by links in entries to other blogs, in an effort to identify bloggers who take on important conversational roles, such as "agitator" and "summarizer."[10]

Finally, several studies have focused on the language used in expressing blog content. Most of these make use of corpus linguistic methods involving automated counts of word frequencies. For example, Herring and Paolillo (2006) analyzed the frequency of grammatical function words (such as noun determiners and personal pronouns) hypothesized to correspond to male and female writing styles, finding that the two styles better predicted whether the blog was a filter or personal journal than the gender of its author. Huffaker and Calvert (2005) analyzed language style in teenage blogs, using the DICTION analysis software to classify lexical items in relation to assertiveness and emotion. Similarly, Balog, Mishne, and Rijke (2006) analyzed the occurrence of emotion words (such as "excited," "worried," and "sad") in a corpus of blog entries over time, relating spikes in emotional language use to world events.

The last two sections have shown that narrow applications of CA can be revealing about certain types of blog content, but that a broader conception of CA is required in order to capture important features of blogs that the narrow approach does not, including patterns associated with linking, commenting, and language style. Moreover, since the broad conception encompasses the narrow conception (traditional CA can be included in the methodological repertoire of [[web content] analysis]), it is not necessary to adopt both approaches; the broad approach alone is sufficient.

---

[10]This study is an exception to the generalization that most computational web studies do not orient toward content analysis. The stated goal of Nakajima et al. (2005, p. 1) is to capture and analyze "conversational web content" in blogs.

Challenges in Blog Content Analysis

Even when expanded analytical methods are available, challenges to analyzing blog content remain. Data sampling and defining units of analysis still pose challenges similar to those identified by Schneider and Foot (2004) and Weare and Lin (2000) for web analysis in general.

The full extent of the blogosphere is nearly as unmeasurable as that for the web as a whole, given the high rate of churn in blog creation and abandonment, the existence of private blogs, the presumed high number of blogs in other languages hosted by services that are not indexed by English language search engines, and so forth; this makes random sampling of the blogosphere a practical impossibility. Studies that have aimed at broad representation have for the most part had to be satisfied with random sampling from a subset of blogs, accessed from blog hosting services or blog tracking services. Blogs have one advantage over traditional websites, however, in that many preserve archives of earlier content. Still, blog researchers are well advised to download and save versions of the pages they intend to analyze as data, as blogs can and do disappear (Wikipedia, 2008).

With regard to units of analysis, blogs provide a number of natural structural options: Units that have been analyzed in blog content studies include the individual blog, its front page (which presents the most recent entries or posts), the entry + comments, or either the entry or the comment alone. As with websites more generally, however, the interlinked nature of blogs poses problems for delimiting natural groupings of blogs, leading researchers such as Herring, Kouper, et al. (2005) to set arbitrary limits to their snowball samples in terms of degrees of separation and to allow clusters of blogs to emerge from patterns of reciprocal linking.

Finally, the identification and capture of cross-blog exchanges remains a persistent challenge for researchers interested in interactive content, in that "conversations" take place not only through links but also through citations in entries (with or without links), comments left on other blogs, and, in many cases, communication via other media, such as email or instant messaging. The bottom-up and top-down approaches to identifying blog conversations used by Herring, Kouper, et al. (2005) and Efimova and De Moor (2005), respectively, illustrate the types of methodological innovation that blog researchers have made in order to address certain questions about blog content. While traditional CA, CA-related paradigms, and earlier web content analyses all provide useful precedents, most blog researchers have found it necessary to innovate methodologically in some respects.

Toward an Expanded Paradigm

The previous sections have demonstrated the need for a broader construal of web content analysis, one that draws on methods from other disciplines to address characteristic features of the web such as hyperlinks and textual exchanges and that recasts traditional CA notions such as comparable units of analysis, fixed coding schemes, and random sampling to fit the requirements of web research.

This broad construal assumes a more general definition of content than is typically found in traditional CA. In the narrowest sense, "content" in CA refers to the thematic meanings present in text or images and sometimes to the "structures" or "features" of the communicative medium (Schneider & Foot, 2004). In contrast, the approach to content analysis proposed here considers content to be various types of information "contained" in new media documents, including themes, features, links, and exchanges, all of which can communicate meaning. Along with this broader definition comes a broadening of the methodological paradigm; theme and feature analysis methods need to be supplemented with other techniques, in order to capture the contributions of different semiotic systems to the meaning of multimodal, multifunctional web content.

The solution proposed here is a methodologically plural paradigm under the general umbrella of Web Content Analysis (WebCA), which includes the methods discussed in this article, along with other techniques that can address the characteristics of web content (and internet content more generally) as it continues to evolve in new directions. One conceptualization of the proposed paradigm is represented schematically in Fig. 2. Image analysis is included in Fig. 2 as a separate component, because even though image content can be analyzed for its themes and features, the interpretation of visual content can benefit from methods drawn from iconography and semiotics, which are not included in any other component. The ellipses on the right of the figure represent other components not discussed in this article, but that could potentially emerge as important in future research.

The coherence of this approach, and the reason for labeling it "content analysis," is that the methods are informed by the general principles of CA; that is, they must enable "objective, systematic, and quantitative description of the content of [web] communication" (Baran, 2002, p. 410). Thus "exchange analysis," for instance, is not simply a set of methods borrowed from discourse analysis; rather, discourse analysis insights about exchanges are operationalized and implemented as content analysis, following, in as much as possible, a general coding and counting procedure. While the particulars of each WebCA methodological component would need to be specified in future work, one proposed characteristic of the general approach is that classifying and counting phenomena of interest could either be done manually or automated. Although traditional CA has generally relied on manual coding, automated means of identifying phenomena of interest are proving increasingly useful in generating "objective, systematic, and quantitative descriptions" of web content (e.g., Balog et al., 2006; Nakajima et al., 2005).

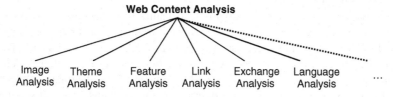

Fig. 2 WebCA: An expanded paradigm

At the highest level, the WebCA umbrella could serve to stimulate articulation of much needed general recommendations regarding data collection and analysis based on the realities of the present-day web and the norms emerging from the growing body of web content research. Moreover, such a pluralistic paradigm could facilitate the generation of principled accounts of, and guidelines for, analyzing content in multiple modes with integrated function (such as links and images or text combined) and single-mode content with multiple functions (such as links that both function as conversational moves and define networks), in order to address the trend toward increasing media convergence on the web (cf. Weare & Lin, 2000).

Conclusion

This article has contrasted a narrow application of traditional content analysis methods to the web with an alternative conceptualization of what content analysis could (and, it has been argued, should) become in response to the challenges raised by new online media. As the review of weblog research illustrated, non-traditional content analyses can benefit scholarly understandings of the web and expand CA as a methodological paradigm. At the same time, any significant expansion of an established paradigm is likely to generate some resistance.

Some might object, for instance, that in opening up the paradigm as suggested above, methodological rigor and interpretability of research results could suffer. Analyses may not be comparable across researchers; some may be ad hoc (cf. McMillan, 2000). It could be difficult to appreciate initially how an analysis involving methodological innovation is representative and reproducible—the criteria for "robust" analysis (Schneider & Foot, 2004). If researchers are permitted to innovate freely, web content analysis could be taken less seriously than other branches of social science.

In response to these concerns, it should be recalled that innovation is a vital process in the evolution of any research paradigm; without it, the paradigm would stagnate. Innovation is especially needed when new phenomena present themselves. This does not mean that web researchers should be allowed to have lax standards; they do, however, need to hold *themselves* to high standards of conceptual clarity, systematicity of sampling and data analysis, and awareness of limitations in interpreting their results, since they cannot depend entirely on traditional CA prescriptions to guide them.

In the meantime, research paradigms tend naturally to become more systematized and formalized over time, as best practices are distilled and refined. As more research on the communicative content of digital media (in its myriad forms) is carried out, the knowledge created will inform future analyses. Coding schemes designed and validated for web content will become available, facilitating comparison of findings across studies. Furthermore, new media themselves will stabilize. As website genres become more conventionalized over time, their sizes and formats will become increasingly standardized, facilitating the selection of units of analysis. More complete indexes and archives of web content will also become available, and better search tools will be developed (e.g., for blog content), facilitating sampling.

As the expanded content analysis paradigm envisioned here advances toward these outcomes, it will not only become more systematic and rigorous; ultimately, it will be more powerful for having integrated innovative responses to new media phenomena during its formative stages.

References

Ali-Hasan, N., & Adamic, L. (2007). *Expressing social relationships on the blog through links and comments*. Paper presented at the international conference for weblogs and social media, Boulder, CO.

Balog, K., Mishne, G., & Rijke, M. (2006). *Why are they excited? Identifying and explaining spikes in blog mood levels*. Paper presented at the 11th meeting of the European Chapter of the Association for Computational Linguistics, Trento, Italy.

Baran, S. J. (2002). *Introduction to mass communication* (2nd ed.) New York: McGraw-Hill.

Bates, M. J., & Lu, S. (1997). An exploratory profile of personal home pages: Content, design, metaphors. *Online and CDROM Review, 21*(6), 331–340.

Bauer, M. (2000). Classical content analysis: A review. In M. W. Bauer & G. Gaskell (Eds.), *Qualitative researching with text, image, and sound: A practical handbook* (pp. 131–151). London: Sage.

Berelson, B. (1952). *Content analysis in communication research*. New York: Free Press.

Berelson, B., & Lazarsfeld, P. F. (1948). *The analysis of communication content*. Chicago/New York: University of Chicago and Columbia University.

Blood, R. (2002). Introduction. In J. Rodzvilla (Ed.), *We've got blog: How weblogs are changing our culture* (pp. ix–xiii). Cambridge, MA: Perseus.

Bush, C. R. (1951). The analysis of political campaign news. *Journalism Quarterly, 28*(2), 250–252.

Dimitrova, D. V., & Neznanski, M. (2006). Online journalism and the war in cyberspace: A comparison between U.S. and international newspapers. *Journal of Computer-Mediated Communication, 12*(1), Article 13. Retrieved from http://jcmc.indiana.edu/vol12/issue1/dimitrova.html

Efimova, L., & de Moor, A. (2005). Beyond personal web publishing: An exploratory study of conversational blogging practices. *Proceedings of the Thirty-Eighth Hawaii International Conference on System Sciences*. Los Alamitos, CA: IEEE.

Fogg, B. J., Kameda, T., Boyd, J., Marshall, J., Sethi, R., Sockol, M., et al. (2002). *Stanford-Makovsky web credibility study 2002: Investigating what makes web sites credible today*. Retrieved from http://captology.stanford.edu/pdf/Stanford-MakovskyWebCredStudy2002-prelim.pdf

Foot, K. A., Schneider, S. M., Dougherty, M., Xenos, M., & Larsen, E. (2003). Analyzing linking practices: Candidate sites in the 2002 U.S. electoral Web sphere. *Journal of Computer-Mediated Communication, 8*(4). Retrieved from http://jcmc.indiana.edu/vol8/issue4/foot.html

Gibson, G., Kleinberg, J., & Raghavan, P. (1998). Inferring web communities from link topology. *Proceedings of the 9th ACM Conference on Hypertext and Hypermedia*. Pittsburgh, PA: ACM.

Glaser, B., & Strauss, A. L. (1967). *The discovery of grounded theory: Strategies for qualitative research*. Chicago: Aldine.

Herring, S. C. (2004). Computer-mediated discourse analysis: An approach to researching online behavior. In S. A. Barab, R. Kling, & J. H. Gray (Eds.), *Designing for virtual communities in the service of learning* (pp. 338–376). New York: Cambridge University Press.

Herring, S. C., & Paolillo, J. C. (2006). Gender and genre variation in weblogs. *Journal of Sociolinguistics, 10*(4), 439–459.

Herring, S. C., Kouper, I., Paolillo, J., Scheidt, L. A., Tyworth, M., Welsch, P., et al. (2005). Conversations in the blogosphere: An analysis "from the bottom up." *Proceedings of the Thirty-Eighth Hawai'i International Conference on System Sciences.* Los Alamitos, CA: IEEE.

Herring, S. C., Scheidt, L. A., Bonus, S., & Wright, E. (2004). Bridging the gap: A genre analysis of weblogs. *Proceedings of the Thirty-Seventh Hawai'i International Conference on System Sciences.* Los Alamitos, CA: IEEE.

Herring, S. C., Scheidt, L. A., Bonus, S., & Wright, E. (2005). Weblogs as a bridging genre. *Information, Technology & People, 18*(2), 142–171.

Herring, S. C., Scheidt, L. A., Kouper, I., & Wright, E. (2006). Longitudinal content analysis of weblogs: 2003–2004. In M. Tremayne (Ed.), *Blogging, citizenship, and the future of media* (pp. 3–20). London: Routledge.

Holsti, O. R. (1969). *Content analysis for the social sciences and humanities.* Reading, MA: Addison Wesley.

Huffaker, D. A., & Calvert, S. L. (2005). Gender, identity and language use in teenage blogs. *Journal of Computer-Mediated Communication, 10*(2). Retrieved from http://jcmc.indiana.edu/vol10/issue2/huffaker.html

Jackson, M. (1997). Assessing the structure of communication on the world wide web. *Journal of Computer-Mediated Communication, 3*(1). Retrieved from http://www.ascusc.org/jcmc/vol3/issue1/jackson.html

Krippendorff, K. (1980). *Content analysis: An introduction to its methodology.* Newbury Park: Sage.

Krippendorff, K. (2008). Testing the reliability of content analysis data: What is involved and why. In K. Krippendorff & M. A. Bock (Eds.), *The content analysis reader* (pp. 350–357). Thousand Oaks, CA: Sage. Retrieved from http://www.asc.upenn.edu/usr/krippendorff/dogs.html

Kutz, D. O., & Herring, S. C. (2005). Micro-longitudinal analysis of web news updates. *Proceedings of the Thirty-Eighth Hawai'i International Conference on System Sciences.* Los Alamitos, CA: IEEE.

McMillan, S. J. (2000). The microscope and the moving target: The challenge of applying content analysis to the world wide web. *Journalism and Mass Communication Quarterly, 77*(1), 80–98.

Mishne, G., & Glance, N. (2006). *Leave a reply: An analysis of weblog comments.* Proceedings of the 3rd Annual Workshop on the Weblogging Ecosystem, 15th World Wide Web Conference, Edinburgh.

Mitra, A. (1999). Characteristics of the WWW text: Tracing discursive strategies. *Journal of Computer-Mediated Communication, 5*(1). Retrieved from http://www.ascusc.org/jcmc/vol5/issue1/mitra.html

Mitra, A., & Cohen, E. (1999). Analyzing the web: Directions and challenges. In S. Jones (Ed.), *Doing internet research: Critical issues and methods for examining the net* (pp. 179–202). Thousand Oaks, CA: Sage.

Nakajima, S., Tatemura, J., Hino, Y., Hara, Y., & Tanaka, K. (2005). *Discovering important bloggers based on analyzing blog threads.* Paper presented at WWW2005, Chiba, Japan.

Park, H. W. (2003). What is hyperlink network analysis? New method for the study of social structure on the web. *Connections, 25*(1), 49–61.

Pfeil, U., Zaphiris, P., & Ang, C. S. (2006). Cultural differences in collaborative authoring of Wikipedia. *Journal of Computer-Mediated Communication, 12*(1), Article 5. Retrieved from http://jcmc.indiana.edu/vol12/issue1/pfeil.html

Scheidt, L. A., & Wright, E. (2004). Common visual design elements of weblogs. In L. Gurak, S. Antonijevic, L. Johnson, C. Ratliff, & J. Reyman (Eds.), *Into the blogosphere: Rhetoric, community, and culture of weblogs.* Retrieved from http://blog.lib.umn.edu/blogosphere/

Schneider, S. M., & Foot, K. A. (2004). The web as an object of study. *New Media & Society, 6*(1), 114–122.

Scott, W. (1955). Reliability of content analysis: The case of nominal scale coding. *Public Opinion Quarterly, 17*, 321–325.

Singh, N., & Baack, D. W. (2004). Web site adaptation: A cross-cultural comparison of U.S. and Mexican web sites. *Journal of Computer-Mediated Communication, 9*(4). Retrieved from http://jcmc.indiana.edu/vol9/issue4/singh_baack.html

Thelwall, M. (2002). The top 100 linked pages on UK university web sites: High inlink counts are not usually directly associated with quality scholarly content. *Journal of Information Science, 28*(6), 485–493.

Trammell, K. D. (2006). Blog offensive: An exploratory analysis of attacks published on campaign blog posts from a political public relations perspective. *Public Relations Review, 32*(4), 402–406.

Trammell, K. D., Tarkowski, A., Hofmokl, J., & Sapp, A. M. (2006). Rzeczpospolita blogów [Republic of Blog]: Examining Polish bloggers through content analysis. *Journal of Computer-Mediated Communication, 11*(3), Article 2. Retrieved from http://jcmc.indiana.edu/vol11/issue3/trammell.html

Tremayne, M., Zheng, N., Lee, J. K., & Jeong, J. (2006). Issue publics on the web: Applying network theory to the war blogosphere. *Journal of Computer-Mediated Communication, 12*(1), Article 15. Retrieved from http://jcmc.indiana.edu/vol12/issue1/tremayne.html

Wakeford, N. (2000). New media, new methodologies: Studying the web. In D. Gauntlett (Ed.), *Web.studies: Rewiring media studies for the digital age* (pp. 31–42). London: Arnold.

Waseleski, C. (2006). Gender and the use of exclamation points in computer-mediated communication: An Analysis of exclamations posted to two electronic discussion lists. *Journal of Computer-Mediated Communication, 11*(4), Article 6. Retrieved http://jcmc.indiana.edu/vol11/issue4/waseleski.html

Weare, C., & Lin, W. Y. (2000). Content analysis of the world wide web – Opportunities and challenges. *Social Science Computer Review, 18*(3), 272–292.

Wikipedia. (2008). *Blog*. Retrieved on June 28, 2008, from http://en.wikipedia.org/wiki/Blog

Williams, P., Tramell, K., Postelnicu, M., Landreville, K., & Martin, J. (2005). Blogging and hyperlinking: Use of the web to enhance visibility during the 2004 U.S. campaign. *Journalism Studies, 6*(2), 177–186.

Young, J., & Foot, K. (2005). Corporate e-cruiting: The construction of work in Fortune 500 recruiting web sites. *Journal of Computer-Mediated Communication, 11*(1), Article 3. Retrieved from http://jcmc.indiana.edu/vol11/issue1/young.html

The Regulatory Framework for Privacy and Security

Janine S. Hiller

The Regulatory Framework for Privacy and Security

The intersection of privacy and the internet has a checkered past and an uncertain future in the United States. This article will begin by describing in general the ways that privacy is impacted by electronic communications and defining the terms involved – privacy, security, and confidentiality. Based on this background, the state of the law of privacy and the internet will be described. There are many statutes, and many new policies, that protect individual privacy, yet there are still areas of information collection and sharing that are not regulated in the United States. In addition, whether by statute or lack of law, individuals shoulder the burden in many cases and must take affirmative steps to protect their personal information. In fact, in some ways it is very difficult for an individual to limit the collection of personal information, as it is a condition to participating in the electronic marketplace. This article will comment briefly on the difference between the United States and the European Union views and legal protections of privacy. Lastly, while recognizing the importance of the subject of governmental access to individual information, the focus of this article is limited to the private sector's collection and use of personal information.

Background

Privacy can be defined in many ways, ranging from the ability to control decisions about one's own body or the ability of an individual to control the collection and dissemination of personally identifiable information by others (DeMarco, 2006). For purposes of the internet, and this article, the most relevant definition is the individual's ability to control the collection and use of personally identifiable information. The amount of information that is collected about individuals, fueled in large part by

J.S. Hiller (✉)
School of Business, Virginia Tech, Blacksburg, Virginia, USA
e-mail: jhiller@vt.edu

J. Hunsinger et al. (eds.), *International Handbook of Internet Research,*
DOI 10.1007/978-1-4020-9789-8_15, © Springer Science+Business Media B.V. 2010

the internet and data storage capabilities, is staggering. The collection, aggregation, and subsequent ordering of this information to create a targeted subset can be found under the term data mining. One description of the collection of information by just one of the data collection companies is as follows:

> Consider Acxiom's InfoBase profiling product. InfoBase reportedly collects data from more than 15 million data sources and provides more than 1.5 billion source records. It contains demographic information covering 95 percent of U.S. households. Clients using InfoBase can obtain a comprehensive profile of a person in "sub-second" time simply by entering the customer's name, address, and/or phone number into a computer. A brochure, now dated, for Acxiom's InfoBase profiler product lists the following types of personal information included in the database: name; address; phone number; occupation; date of birth; latitudinal/longitudinal coordinates; gender; ethnicity; age; income; net worth; polit-ical party; height and weight; education; marital status; whether subject wears corrective lenses; whether subject rents or owns dwelling; years of residence; value of home; mortgage amount and interest rate; home loan to value ratio; date home was built and date purchased; square footage of home and lot; whether home is located in a census tract where more than 50 percent of households are non-white; adult age ranges in household; number of adults in household; children's age ranges in household; number of children in household; number of generations in household; total number of occupants in household; whether there is a "work-ing woman" in household; which credit cards subject owns; range of new credit; where subject likes to shop; model and make of automobile (including a "lifestyle indicator" desig-nation based on the type of car); blue book value of vehicle; whether subject has a history of buying new cars; whether subject buys items through mail order and in what dollar amounts; whether subject owns a cat or a dog; whether subject donates to charities; whether subject owns real estate investments; whether subject has stock/bond investments; whether subject is a military veteran; whether subject likes to gamble, sew, garden, watch television, hunt, jog, sail, diet, play video games, drink wine, or read the Bible; and whether subject's over-all "lifestyle composite" classifies him/her as a "Traditionalist," "Connoisseur," "Chiphead" (like computers and science), or member of the "Intelligentsia."(McClurg, 2003, pp. 73–77)

Another program by this company groups people into 70 different categories depending on their stages in life, propensity to spend, and predicted future income, among other factors. Social Security numbers, e-mail addresses, and other informa-tion can be made available.

Privacy can be implicated when data are collected either surreptitiously or with-out permission. Examples of unique information collection by means of the internet are the use of "cookies," "web bugs," or "web beacons." Cookies are small files that are stored by a website on a user's computer so that the user is recognized upon returning to that website. Cookies can be designed so that they are only operational for one visit, can be designed so that they operate whenever the user returns to that particular website, or can be designed so that they are recognized by multiple websites. It is this last type of cookie that impacts privacy most seriously. Cookies can be useful for consumers because they allow the shopper to go back to previ-ous pages and still have his or her activities "remembered" by the site. Cookies that endure past one session allow the shopper's experience to be customized upon return. When a website greets the customer with a first name and highlights the fact that those shoes they were looking at last week are now on sale, it is because cookies let them be recognized so that the website can be personalized. This personalization can be beneficial and welcomed by the individual (DeMarco, 2006). However, when cookies are designed to be recognized across different websites, can follow the customer from one website to another, can be aggregated across websites, all without the knowledge or consent of the customer, then control by the individual becomes tenuous and privacy becomes illusive. Online advertisers can also use this information in order to post targeted ads on user's web pages as they surf through the internet. The 2008 merger of Google and Doubleclick prompted privacy complaints about the potential for increased targeted marketing (Ciocchetti, 2008) and in the same year the FTC proposed voluntary guidelines for online behavioral advertising.

Security is composed of the technical and personnel measures adopted to ensure that private information is not compromised and that unauthorized persons do not gain access. Security, then, is inextricably connected to privacy. When security fails, privacy is lost. Recent examples of security breaches range from the high tech to the no-tech, both equally damaging the entities and the effected individuals. Hackers may defeat security features in order to steal customer information, even though the business has undertaken to protect its customers. Security standards are most often incorporated into laws dealing with privacy, and so security is not discussed separately in this article but is integrated into each area. For example, security safeguards were part of the early statement of the OECD privacy guidelines issued in 1980 (see below).

Third, confidentiality is important for the protection of privacy. Confidentiality is the promise that information that has been collected in an authorized way will not be shared with others who have not been authorized. For example, the distinction between security and confidentiality can be described in this way; security is breached by unauthorized persons, and confidentiality is breached when authorized persons share the information in an unauthorized manner.

Privacy Principles

Privacy principles are not new; both domestic and global standards have been vetted and adopted over many years. Although not specifically instituted into United States law, they are instructive as a reflection of the shared values of privacy across national and international boundaries. The OECD, FTC, and EU privacy principles are described in the following sections.

OECD Privacy Principles

The OECD adopted privacy principles in 1980, long before the internet was in existence. The OECD privacy principles are

1. Collection Limitation
2. Data Quality
3. Purpose Specification

4. Use Limitation
5. Security Safeguards
6. Openness
7. Individual Participation
8. Accountability (OECD, 1980)

The basics of these international principles are that information should only be collected for a stated, limited purpose; information should only be used for that purpose and not later used for another purpose; consumers should know how the data are to be used and be able to choose, correct, and delete information; and the data collector should maintain information security and be accountable for its safety and correct usage.

In 1998 the OECD Committee for Information, Computer and Communications Policy released a study, "Implementing the OECD 'Privacy Guidelines' in the Electronic Environment: Focus on the internet." The study confirmed the usefulness of the 1980 principles, while noting that consumer confidence in electronic commerce was negatively affected by uncertain perceptions of privacy protection. Additionally, the report; identified consumer education as a necessary step to preserving privacy on the internet; exhorted businesses on the internet to adopt and post privacy policies to protect privacy; and charged governments with working together to create an international privacy framework (OECD, 1997). The principles in this report were adopted by a Ministerial Declaration on the Protection of Privacy on Global Networks in the same year (OECD, 1998).

The OECD Working Party on Information Security and Privacy continues to study and promote international cooperation for the accomplishment of these principles (OECD, 2006).

FTC Privacy Principles

While there is no official regulation specifically incorporating the Federal Trade Commission (FTC) privacy principles, they can be found in documents of the commission and are widely acknowledged. Called Fair Information Practices, they form the underlying rationale for many of the regulations that are described below, involving children's privacy and financial privacy, for example. The FTC principles are similar to the OECD principles and include

1. Notice/Awareness
2. Choice/Consent
3. Access/Participation
4. Integrity/Security
5. Enforcement/Redress (FTC, 1998)

Some of the notable differences between the OECD and the FTC privacy principles involve the extent and detail of these rights. A link to a website's privacy policy would satisfy the type of notice that is required, and the opt-out capability would satisfy the requirement of choice. The FTC principle of accountability may well be private self-regulation, although as seen later in this article the FTC has used its general powers to pursue deceptive privacy and security practices.

European Union Privacy Principles

The EU privacy principles are found in several directives and regulations, and are described in more detail below. The primary directive setting forth overarching privacy principles is the 1995 "directive on the protection of individuals with regard to the processing of personal data and on the free movement of such data," generally known as the Data Protection Directive. This directive includes the general principles of the OECD Privacy Principles, in addition to more detailed provisions, described in later sections of this article. The Data Protection Directive states as its premise the rights in the European Convention for the Protection of Human Rights and Fundamental Freedoms, Article 8, which states, "Everyone has the right to respect for his private and family life, his home and his correspondence." Therefore, the right to privacy in the EU is seen as a more comprehensive principle, one that extends both offline and online and one that is a fundamental human right.

United States Federal Privacy Laws

The US privacy laws are not comprehensive in nature, and therefore it is necessary to look at a number of laws that are applied to specific industries and types of information collection online. The discussion is not exhaustive, but includes the major federal laws regarding online privacy. The areas in which legislation exists are those most often identified as personally sensitive ones with regard to the collection of data.

Financial Privacy

Financial privacy protections are found in a section of the Financial Privacy Modernization Act, which is most commonly known as the Gramm-Leach-Bliley Act (GLBA), named for its sponsors. It regulates both online and offline privacy practices of financial institutions. Financial institutions are defined broadly and include not only banks but also any entity that collects and maintains non-public individually identifiable customer financial information. GLBA has a three-prong approach. First, financial institutions must adopt a privacy policy; second, the policy must be communicated at least annually to its customers; and third, a consumer must have the ability to opt out of information sharing with third-party unaffiliated parties. The opt-out approach means that information *may* be shared with others unless the customer affirmatively communicates his or her decision for the information *not* to be shared. Importantly, financial institutions must also adopt and implement security and confidentiality measures to protect consumer information.

The privacy policy must be clear and communicated conspicuously. This can be accomplished electronically, by means of a website, if the customer agrees. As described by the FTC in educational materials for businesses:

> For individuals who conduct transactions with you [a financial institution] electronically, you may post your privacy notice on your website and require them to acknowledge receiving the notice as a necessary part of obtaining a particular product or service. For annual notices, you may reasonably expect that your customers have received your notice if they use your website to access your financial products or services and agree to receive notices at your website, and you post your notice continuously in a clear and conspicuous manner on your website. (FTC, 2002)

The notice on a website page should be designed to call attention to the notice, both by its placement on the page and by the nature of the website design. The notice should be placed on the website that is used most often by customers or linked to from transactional pages. The design of the webpage should not detract from the prominence of the privacy notice.

The FTC has issued Security Regulations, as have the other appropriate financial regulatory agencies. The regulations require institutions to have an information security program, designated employees for security, identification and assessment of security risks, monitoring/auditing and maintenance of the security program, and implementation of any necessary updates. Portions of the regulations that particularly relate to security of customer information and the internet include

1. Use encryption when a public network is used
2. Set policies for telecommuters
3. Avoid storing sensitive information on computers connected to the internet
4. Use SSL or similar secure system for communication of information
5. Encrypt e-mails
6. If collected information online use automatic security, and "Caution customers against transmitting sensitive data, like account numbers, via e-mail or in response to an unsolicited e-mail or pop-up message."
7. Monitor amounts of data in and out so as to find unauthorized disclosure
8. Use various technical security steps related to internet connections (FTC, 2006)

Lastly, GLBA may be applied to "pretexting," an act particularly fueled by the use of e-mails or websites by persons or entities who pretend to be a financial institution, in order to fraudulently obtain individual financial information (Hardee, 2006). This information can then be used to steal from the individual's accounts or commit other acts of identity theft. Another term for this type of fraud is called "phishing." In 2004, the FTC and the Department of Justice brought a lawsuit against Zachary Hill for fraudulently obtaining consumer financial information. Hill created a fake website in the name of AOL and Paypal and then e-mailed individuals stating that their accounts would be cancelled unless they updated information on these websites. Of course, the websites were part of a scam to collect non-public financial information and to use that information to perpetrate fraud and identity theft. Hill faced criminal charges, but was also charged for obtaining the personal financial information in violation of GLBA (FTC, Pretexting).

Medical Privacy

Personal medical information is probably the most sensitive type of data that can be collected about an individual. In 1996, when the federal health billing and payment system was being switched to the electronic environment to save substantial amounts of money spent on paper processing, the Congress wisely recognized the new risks incurred to privacy when transfer of medical information is by an electronic medium. The Health Insurance Portability and Accountability Act (HIPAA) was eventually written to apply to individually identifiable health information, that is collected offline as well as online, and included standards for privacy and security and civil as well as criminal penalties. The Secretary of Health and Human Services promulgated rules for the protection of medical information privacy held by healthcare providers and their partners. Individuals must be given information about the health provider's privacy policy, the ability to access their personal information, periodic reports about its use, and the power to correct any discrepancies. Generally, health information may not be shared with outside parties without the written permission of the patient. HIPAA and the relevant rules are quite detailed and include privacy standards and security standards. Covered entities are required to undertake risk assessments and use reasonable security measures (HHS, 2003).

HIPAA is enforced by the federal government, not by private action. In 2004, a worker at a cancer treatment center was the first to be convicted of a violation of HIPAA. The worker used the information in the records of a cancer patient to open up credit card accounts and charge thousands of dollars in the patient's name. The worker received a 16 month prison term and was ordered to make restitution (Cogan, 2005).

Children's Privacy

The protection of children online has been one of the primary areas of focus for federal laws. Although content regulation has been struck down as unconstitutional, privacy regulation limiting the collection of personally identifiable information from children has not. The Children's Online Privacy Protection Act (COPPA) was passed to protect children from websites that would collect very personal information from young children. COPPA requires websites that are targeted to children, or that know that children visit their site, to post a privacy policy and refrain from collecting information from children under the age of 13 without verifiable parental consent. This is an "opt-in" framework, under which information may not be collected or used without permission, as compared with the opt-out approach that initially allows information collection yet allows an opportunity to withdraw consent. Parents also have the right to view the information collected and delete information held by the business. The FTC enforces COPPA and has adopted rules for its implementation. The FTC has certified four third-party safe harbor programs; businesses may join these self-regulatory programs to ensure that they meet the requirements of the law (Hiller, Belanger, Hsiao, & Park, 2008).

Several cases have been brought by the FTC to enforce the provisions of COPPA (Herdon, 2004). Hershey's Foods and Mrs. Field's Cookies were fined, under a consent decree, $80,000 and $100,000, respectively, for failing to either provide for parental consent or adopting inadequate procedures. The website privacy policies were also alleged to be deficient. While these fines are significant, they pale in comparison to the $1 million dollar fine imposed under a consent decree with the social networking site, Xanga, in 2006. Although the website told children under 13 that they could not join, the notice was meaningless as it did not stop children (who entered their age as under 13) from proceeding to create an account and post personal information on the website. Xanga allegedly allowed over 1.7 million children to create accounts in this manner over a 5-year period (FTC, Children).

Federal Trade Commission

As described above, the FTC has been active in enforcing privacy laws. In addition to the specific statutory authority granted to the FTC under particular privacy protecting statutes, the Commission also pursues enforcement of privacy and security promises under its general grant of authority to prevent unfair and deceptive acts in commerce. Some commentators have intimated that the FTC has become the de facto internet privacy cop, as a result. The first internet case brought by the FTC occurred in 1999, against GeoCities. GeoCities collected information from both adults and children, and the FTC alleged that it did not properly inform the consumers that the personal information would be shared with third parties, outside of the GeoCities community. Adults and children were led to believe that the information that they gave to GeoCities was necessary in order to participate in the online community and that it was only for that use. In reality, the personal data were shared with outside third parties for unrelated targeted marketing. The settlement with GeoCities required the website to post a clear privacy policy giving notice of its information collection practices, access to the information, and the ability to delete the information. The GeoCities case was followed in the same year by the Liberty Young Investors case, in which a financial firm collected quite personal financial information from children and kept it in identifiable form, under the auspices of registering for possible prizes and a newsletter. Although Liberty promised that the information provided would be anonymous, it kept the data in an identifiable form and did not even award the prizes or newsletters. Similar requirements as those in the GeoCities case were imposed in a consent decree with Liberty, and additionally, the protection of children was accomplished by requiring the website to obtain verifiable parental consent before collecting information from children aged 12 and younger.

Recent cases brought by the FTC illustrate their commitment to the protection of privacy by protecting the security of information; the FTC pursued complaints based on the deceptive practice of insecure information collection and storage. Multiple complaints from 2005 to 2008 were filed and settled because the website violated security principles and thereby compromised consumer information. DSW, a shoe discount store, failed to encrypt the credit card numbers or checking account information of its customers, along with other security lapses, leading to the theft of this information on 1.4 million consumers. DSW agreed to 20 years of monitoring, and a security audit every 2 years by an independent firm. In a high-profile case, Choicepoint, a data aggregator, gave information to individuals who claimed that they were approved entities, when in fact they were criminals who used this personal information to commit identity theft. The Choicepoint website promised that information would only be shared with properly identified, appropriate individuals and that the information was held securely and safely. This was a deceptive claim according to the FTC, and Choicepoint agreed to settle the complaint by paying $10 million in civil fines and $5 million dollars for compensation of the victims. It also agreed to a framework of security measures including bi-annual auditing by an independent firm.

Although the FTC does not have the resources to bring a large number of cases per year, the severity of the penalties indicates an intention to ensure that security practices of businesses are sufficient to protect the privacy of consumer information. Security breaches can result in identity theft, an illegal and serious consequence of a violation of privacy, and an area of consumer protection targeted by the Federal Trade Commission and increased federal penalties.

Unsolicited Bulk E-Mail: Spam

Spam is the common term for e-mail that is sent in bulk to a large number of recipients and which is unsolicited. The ability of computer programs to automatically send huge numbers of e-mails, coupled with the low cost of doing so, results in individuals receiving a large amount of spam, which invades their privacy as the e-mail is unwanted and unsolicited. The pure volume of spam that an individual can receive each day is frustrating and time consuming. AOL, a large ISP, estimated that the height of spam occurred in 2003, when on one day it blocked 2.4 billion spam messages. In 2005, it estimated that it blocked 1.5 billion spam messages to its customers per day. These statistics easily illustrate the problem (AOL, 2006).

The Computer Fraud and Abuse Act prohibits unauthorized access, or the exceeding of authorized access, to a computer that is used in interstate commerce, when the act results in damage of $5,000 or more. This act not only protects individuals from the breach of their privacy by criminal hackers but it also allows for the prosecution of cases of spam. AOL has been at the forefront of using this law to prevent the use of spam on its system. Because its Terms of Use prohibit the sending of unsolicited bulk e-mail, when spammers use the AOL network to send spam, they can violate the CFAA, as a court found early on in a 1998 case against LCGM, Inc.

The federal CAN-SPAM act also works to prohibit unsolicited e-mail from impinging on the privacy of individuals. Under this act, e-mail may not contain false header information or deceptive subject lines and must provide for a means for the recipient to opt out of future mailings. Civil fines are available for enforcement of the act, and the FTC, federal and state authorities, and ISPs may sue for violations.

Electronic Communications Privacy Act (ECPA)

Electronic communications are protected by the Electronic Communications Privacy Act. The ECPA applies to both the interception of real-time communications and the access of stored communications. As applied to the private sector, the ECPA states that no electronic communications, which would include e-mail and wireless devices, may be intentionally intercepted or monitored without the consent of the parties. The scope of the law is narrowed, however, by two exceptions: a business may access employee communications either when there is a need to protect property or if there is a valid business purpose to do so, and in any case the business may access employee e-mail when it obtains the employee's consent. Employers often obtain the consent of the employee by means of a company policy. This description of the ECPA is quite brief and there are more specific applications for service providers and more specific categorizations of the types of information that may be considered content oriented. Employee e-mail is a particularly thorny area, and courts have, sometimes reluctantly, held that they do not fall under the ECPA protections when employers view them on company-owned servers. Although general privacy protection is based on the employees this illustrates, the determination of an employee's objective reasonable expectation of privacy, which is the legally relevant inquiry, may not comport with the individual employee's subjective expectation of privacy.

Selected State Privacy Laws

States may grant greater rights than those federal rights described above. Privacy rights are granted to citizens in 10 state constitutions, for example. The common law tort of invasion of privacy is a state right and can vary from state to state. California has a unique law, the Online Privacy Protection Act of 2003, requiring commercial websites to conspicuously post a privacy policy describing their information collection practices. In order to illustrate the many kinds of different state laws that exist, two examples are described below: the first example is the substantive area of security breaches, which many states have addressed, and the second example is that of spam, unsolicited bulk e-mail.

Security Breach Laws

California was the first state to pass a Notice of Security Breach law, in 2002. The law states,

> Any person or business that conducts business in California, and that owns or licenses computerized data that includes personal information, shall disclose any breach of the security of the system following discovery or notification of the breach in the security of the data to any resident of California whose unencrypted personal information was, or is reasonably believed to have been, acquired by an unauthorized person. (CA CODE)

When Choicepoint announced that it had compromised the information of its customers, it was surmised that the announcement was forthcoming because of the California law. The California approach to privacy is more proactive than in any other state and includes an Office for Privacy and a Commissioner, who is similar to an ombudsman.

Although legislation was considered in other states subsequent to California's law, no other state passed a breach notification law until the Choicepoint release of over 100,000 consumers' personal information to unauthorized parties. In 2005, 22 states passed similar laws, and in 2006, 13 states passed such laws; by 2008 44 states had some form of a notification requirement for a security breach (NCSL, 2006). These laws differ based on the triggering event that requires notice to consumers, whether it is a risk-based or information loss-based notice and whether the notice applies to unencrypted data or any compromised personal information. The definition of personal information may also differ (UGa). Although federal legislation has been proposed, none has yet passed, and states have acted more quickly to protect the privacy of their citizens.

Spam Laws

Spam is not a legal word, but it refers to unsolicited bulk e-mail. Because spam imposes itself upon individuals without consent, clogging e-mail boxes and slowing communications, it is seen as an imposition on privacy. The federal CAN-SPAM Act of 2003 prohibits false or misleading e-mail header and subject lines, requires an opt-out mechanism, and imposes a duty to include a designation that the e-mail is an advertisement with the sender's contact information (FTC, 2004). Despite this federal law, 38 states have anti-spam laws, as of 2005 (Burgunder, 2007). Many of these statutes prohibit the use of fraudulent headers to citizens within their jurisdiction. In many cases, the laws impose criminal penalties for the use of fraudulent or misleading headers in bulk e-mail, yet if the laws are too broad they may be subject to constitutional challenge. While in 2006, the first sentence for a violation of the Virginia act brought a prison term of 7 years for the spammer under the Virginia law that categorizes false or misleading spam as a felony (Jaynes v. Commonwealth, 2006), in 2008 the law was overturned because it was constitutionally overbroad; it effectively prohibited anonymous religious and political speech by requiring all such e-mails to contain header information, thereby violating the First Amendment (Jaynes v. Commonwealth, 2008).

European Union Privacy Comparison

The distinction between the protection of online privacy in the EU and the United States begins with differing conceptions of privacy. Although many US laws and statutes have been described, there is no overarching principle of privacy, whereas in the EU, privacy is viewed as a fundamental human right. The right of privacy is recognized in the European Convention on the Protection of Human Rights and Freedoms, Article 8, which states, "Everyone has the right to respect for his private and family life, his home and his correspondence." In stark comparison, the United States primarily adopts the market approach to the protection of online privacy, assuming that if consumers desire privacy then by their actions they will apply market pressure to businesses in order to gain the required amount of privacy, an approach that could be categorized as piecemeal, characterized by weak spots (Reidenberg, 2003). Whether consumers are able to process and then implement the privacy choices that they face is the subject of some debate (Nehf, 2005). The US Department of Commerce describes the differences in this way:

> While the United States and the European Union share the goal of enhancing privacy protection for their citizens, the United States takes a different approach to privacy from that taken by the European Union. The United States uses a sectoral approach that relies on a mix of legislation, regulation, and self regulation. The European Union, however, relies on comprehensive legislation that, for example, requires creation of government data protection agencies, registration of data bases with those agencies, and in some instances prior approval before personal data processing may begin. (Dept. of Commerce)

The EU Data Protection Directive (2001) places limitations on both the type and use of information collected by businesses and implements an "opt-in" standard for the collection and sharing of that information. The opt-in regime requires that the individual give clear consent before information may be collected or shared. For the most part, the EU directive mirrors the fair information practices described earlier and requires that data collection be

- Fair and legal
- For a specific purpose
- Limited to the stated purpose
- Accurate
- Stored only for the necessary time period

The Data Protection Directive also limits the sharing of information with entities outside the EU unless that country has an "adequate level of protection" for that information. This requirement and limitation led to the negotiation and establishment of a Safe Harbor agreement with the United States and the Department of Commerce, because as discussed earlier there is no comparable overarching law in the United States. For US companies to handle personally identifiable data from the EU, a commonplace occurrence over the internet and in electronic commerce, they must meet the standards of the EU directive. The Safe Harbor provides that a US company must meet seven information practice principles of notice, choice, onward transfer, access, *security*, integrity, and enforcement. The company must also be a member of a self-regulatory organization (for example, Truste), or develop its own self-regulatory compliance program. The Department of Commerce maintains a list of companies that have self-certified that they meet the safe harbor requirements. The implementation of international and cross-border privacy principles in the online context remains a challenge involving multinational negotiation (Soma et al., 2004).

Conclusion

The internet allows the collection of personally identifiable information about individuals in ways that are new and challenging. While data collection allows businesses to personalize services to consumers in the electronic environment, it also raises issues of trust and creates the potential for abuse. The technology of security also becomes essential in order to protect personal information from being disclosed in unauthorized ways. In the United States, previously existing laws are applied to these challenges to prevent unfair and deceptive practices, led by the Federal Trade Commission. New federal laws address online children's privacy, financial privacy, and medical privacy and provide penalties for unsolicited e-mail that is misleading. States also have various new laws to address spam, security breaches, and online privacy. The US approach contrasts with that of the European Union, where privacy protection is comprehensive and data collection is regulated more systematically. US companies must meet international standards to protect privacy if they intend to do business globally.

Privacy and security regulations relating to the internet are likely to continue to be issues in the future, as federal, state, and self-regulatory systems struggle to address new technology and to respond to the demand for personal privacy.

Acknowledgment This work was supported, in part, by a National Science Foundation CyberTrust Program Grant, #CNS-0524052.

References

America Online. (2006). *Hey, 'Donald Trump Wants You!!' . . . and other lies told by Spammers in 2005*. Retrieved December 4, 2006, from http://daol.aol.com/articles/spam2005
America Online, Inc. v. LCGM, Inc., 46 F. Supp. 2d 444 (E.D.Va., 1998).
Burgunder, L. (2007). *Legal aspects of managing technology* (4th ed.). New York, NY: Thomson Higher Education.
California Database Breach Notification Security Act. (2002). *California Civil Code Sections 1798.80-1798.84*. Retrieved December 4, 2006, from http://www.leginfo.ca.gov/cgibin/waisgate?WAISdocID=24968225804+0+0+0&WAISaction=retrieve

California Online Privacy Protection Act. (2003). *California Business and Professions Code, Sections 22575-22579*. Retrieved December 3, 2006, from http://www.leginfo.ca.gov/cgibin/displaycode?section=bpc&group=22001-23000&file=22575-22579

Ciocchetti, C. (2008). Just click submit: The Collection, dissemination, and tagging of personally identifying information. *Vanderbilt Journal of Entertainment & Technology Law, 10*, 553–642.

Cogan, J. A. (2005). First ever conviction highlights differing views of HIPAA's civil and criminal penalties. *Medicine and Health Rhode Island*. Retrieved November 27, 2006, from http://www.findarticles.com/p/articles/mi_qa4100/is_200501/ai_n9520488

Controlling the Assault of Non-Solicited Pornography and Marketing Act of 2003 (CAN-SPAM Act) 15 U.S.C. Sections 7701–7713 (2003).

DeMarco, D. A. (2006). Understanding consumer information privacy in the realm of internet commerce: Personhood and pragmatism, pop-tarts and six-packs. *Texas Law Review, 84*, 1013–1065.

Department of Commerce. (n.d.). *Safe harbor overview*. Retrieved December 4, 2006, from http://www.export.gov/safeharbor/SH_Overview.asp

Directive 95/46/EC of the European Parliament and of the Council of 24 October 1995 on the protection of individuals with regard to the processing of personal data and on the free movement of such data.

European Convention for the Protection of Human Rights and Fundamental Freedoms. (1950). Article 8. Retrieved December 4, 2006, from http://ec.europa.eu/justice_home/fsj/privacy/law/treaty_en.htm

Federal Trade Commission. (n.d.). *The Children's Privacy Protection Act*. Retrieved December 3, 2006, from http://ftc.gov/privacy/privacyinitiatives/childrens_enf.html

Federal Trade Commission. (n.d.). *Pretexting: Enforcement*. Retrieved December 3, 2006, from http://www.ftc.gov/privacy/privacyinitiatives/pretexting_enf.html

Federal Trade Commission. (n.d.). *Enforcement cases: FTC privacy initiative*. Retrieved December 3, 2006, from http://ftc.gov/privacy/privacyinitiatives/promises_enf.html

Federal Trade Commission. (1998). *Privacy online: A report to congress*. Retrieved December 3, 2006, from http://www.ftc.gov/reports/privacy3/priv-23a.pdf

Federal Trade Commission. (2002). How to comply with the privacy of consumer financial information rule of the Gramm-Leach-Bliley Act. Retrieved December 1, 2006, from http://www.ftc.gov/bcp/conline/pubs/buspubs/glblong.htm

Federal Trade Commission. (2004). *The CAN-SPAM Act: Requirements for commercial emailers*. Retrieved December 3, 2006, from http://www.ftc.gov/bcp/conline/pubs/buspubs/canspam.htm

Federal Trade Commission. (2006). *Financial institutions and customer information: Complying with the safeguards rule*. Retrieved December 1, 2006, from http://www.ftc.gov/bcp/conline/pubs/buspubs/safeguards.htm

Freedom, Security and Justice, Data Protection, European Union Legislative Documents. Retrieved on December 3, 2006, from http://ec.europa.eu/justice_home/fsj/privacy/law/index_en.htm

Gramm-Leach-Bliley Act. 15 U.S.C. Sections 6801–6809 (2000).

Hardee, K. A. (2006). The Gramm-Leach-Bliley Act: Five years after implementation, does the Emperor wear clothes? *Creighton Law Review, 39*, 915–936.

Health Information Privacy and Accountability Act (HIPAA), Pub. L. No. 104-191, 110 Stat. 1936 (1996).

Herdon, J. (2004). Who's watching the kids? The use of peer-to-peer programs to cyberstalk children. *Oklahoma Journal of Law and Technology, 1*(12). Retrieved December 1, 2006, from http://www.okjolt.org/articles/2004okjoltrev12.cfm

Hiller, J., Belanger, F., Hsiao, M., & Park, J.-M. (2008). POCKET protection. *American Business Law Journal, 45*, 417–453.

Jaynes, v. Commonwealth, 276 Va. 443, 666 S.E.2d 303 (2008).

Jaynes v. Commonwealth, 48 Va.App. 673, 634 S.E.2d 357 (2006).

McClurg, A. J. (2003). A thousand words are worth a picture: A privacy tort response to consumer data profiling. *Northwestern University Law Review, 98*, 63–143.

National Conference of State Legislatures. "2006 Breach of Information Legislation." Retrieved December 1, 2006, from http://www.ncsl.org/programs/lis/cip/priv/breach06.htm

Nehf, J. P. (2005). Shopping for privacy online: Consumer decision-making strategies and the emerging market for information privacy. *University of Illinois Journal of Law, Technology and Policy, 2005*, 1–53.

Organisation for Economic Co-operation and Development. (1980). *OECD guidelines on the protection of privacy and transborder flows of personal data.* Retrieved December 4, 2006, from http://www.oecd.org/document/18/0,2340,en_2649_34255_1815186_1_1_1_1,00.html

Organisation for Economic Co-operation and Development. (1997). *Implementing the OECD "Privacy Guidelines" in the electronic environment: Focus on the internet.* Retrieved December 4, 2006, from http://www.oecd.org/dataoecd/33/43/2096272.pdf

Organisation for Economic Co-operation and Development, Working Party on Information Security and Privacy. (1998). *Ministerial declaration on the protection of privacy on global networks.* Retrieved December 4, 2006, from http://www.oecd.org/dataoecd/39/13/1840065.pdf

Organisation for Economic Co-operation and Development. (2006). *Report on the cross border enforcement of privacy laws.* Retrieved December 4, 2006, from http://www.oecd.org/dataoecd/17/43/37558845.pdf

Reidenberg, J. A. (2003). Privacy wrongs in search of remedies. *Hastings Law Journal, 54*, 877–898.

Soma, J. T., Rynerson, S. D., & Beall-Eder, B. D. (2004). An analysis of the use of bilateral agreements between transnational trading groups: The US/EU e-commerce privacy safe harbor. *Texas International Law Journal, 39*, 171–227.

United States Department of Health and Human Services. (2003). *Summary of the HIPAA privacy rule.* Retrieved December 4, 2006, from http://www.hhs.gov/ocr/privacysummary.pdf

University of Georgia Office of Information Security [INFOSEC] Enterprise Information Technology Services. *State security breach notification laws.* Retrieved December 1, 2006, from http://infosec.uga.edu/policymanagement/breachnotificationlaws.php

Toward Nomadological Cyberinfrastructures

Jeremy Hunsinger

Introduction

E-science and its seemingly required cyberinfrastructure appeared as centralizing concepts of policy discourse and eventually became part of policy goals in the late 1990s and early 2000s. These new infrastructures will be the basis for the internet for years to come. US science policy has emphasized the term "cyberinfrastructure" and recentered significant funding around it with the development of the Office of Cyberinfrastructure in the United States' National Science Foundation and the addition of cyberinfrastructure to the European Union's Seventh Framework Programme. This recentering of policy in relation to a new terminological construction created new possibilities for transforming our information infrastructure and thus our developing knowledge society. Our cyberinfrastructure is the infrastructure of our future knowledge society, as well as the infrastructure of e-science.

However, our cyberinfrastructure policies are an infrastructural blackbox, much like the telecommunications policy was in the 1990s (Mansell, 1990). A blackbox is a metaphor which means to create borders that limit the interpretation of what goes on internally. That is to say, data and information enter one side of the blackbox, and on the other side of the blackbox we receive the outputs of the internal mechanisms. Cyberinfrastructure policies "blackbox" an immense amount of intellectual territory replete with ideologies, including areas of collaboration, areas of data mining, areas of archiving, and areas of the advancement of knowledge. In keeping the operations of these areas underdefined and underdetermined, the policies keep them out of view until practices are normalized and conventionalized. Thus, these policies aid to reconfigure scientific communities that use these cyberinfrastructures to develop norms, conventions, and principles that will then reconfigure the next generation of information systems along ideologically influenced trajectories.

J. Hunsinger (✉)
Center for Digital Discourse and Culture, Virginia Tech, Blacksburg, Virginia, USA
e-mail: jhuns@vt.edu

J. Hunsinger et al. (eds.), *International Handbook of Internet Research*,
DOI 10.1007/978-1-4020-9789-8_16, © Springer Science+Business Media B.V. 2010

In this article, I want to resist the tendency found in the policy documents of cyberinfrastructure and e-science policy's discursive positionality that objectifies science and its projects as products and outcomes. This objectification transforms science, its communities, and its outcomes into something that is more efficient, more informational, more controlled, and less human. Science in the end is a community and communicational process of ordering the world that occurs through the negotiations of humans, their epistemic communities, and the techniques they develop to interrogate their worlds in order to map them. Science is not a product. Scientists are not the factory workers or data processors of the new knowledge society (Chompalov, Genuth, & Shrum, 2002). Science is a social process, much like all knowledge production. Science is not a thing or an object as is often described in popular discourse, as much as it is a multiplicity that is perpetually coming to be (Deleuze, 1995).

Science policy, of which cyberinfrastructure policy is a part, similarly is a combination of concepts and practices melded and operating as an entangled whole in popular and other policy discourse. With sufficient investigation, elements of the processes of science may be disentangled and presented in simplified relations within science policy. Yet the extraction and simplification of the elements from science discourse into science policy discourse rarely does justice to the science as practiced by the myriad of scientists.

As a multiplicity, our understanding of science parallels our understanding of the state in that it is the combination of many bodies and subjectivities coming to be over time. In that unification of bodies distributed across temporal and spatial relations, science is a communicational process of capital accumulation and thus the production of subjectivities. The multiplicities of science and the state as communicative systems are intertwined through capital, but the two have no precursors in each other (Deleuze, 1988). Science does not come from the state, nor does the state derive from science, both are human processes related to our faculties that are tied implicitly to our ecological field's permanent history (DeLanda, 2000). Science and the state never began and they will never end – their origin stories are fictive and inseparable from their rhetorics. Yet we continually rewrite their histories in relation to each other over time and space and through policy discourses. Currently, both sets of histories are inscribed through reference to other ideological multiplicities that play parts in all conceptualizations of modernity, those of informationalism and capitalism.

By mapping cyberinfrastructure and e-science policies as locations of a relational re-construction of their relations to capitalism and informationalism, we can uncover trajectories hidden within the blackbox and through uncovering them learn more about the creation of the new sets of multiplicities and subjectivities that are developing. In opening this blackbox, I hope to contribute to a new possibility for or minimally a renewed reflexivity for cyberinfrastructure policy and hopefully e-science, one that allows for the resistances and mobilities necessary for the creativity and communication central to science (Hunsinger, 2005).

Discursive Tensions and Constructions
in Cyberinfrastructure Policy

Tracing the conceptual tensions of cyberinfrastructure through a series of exemplar definitions will allow us to more fully understand its discursive relations – as discursive relations are inherently social and thus political – it is important to tease out the meanings and connections where we can, given that we are working in a discursive arena where entangled meanings are plural. The tracings of concepts keys us into their deeper implications and indications of the concept's history.

> Concepts have a history, which may include their history as components of other concepts and their relations to particular problems. Concepts are always created in relations to specific problems: "A concept lacks meaning to the extent that it is not connected to other concepts and is not linked to a problem that it resolves or helps to resolve" (Deleuze and Guattari: 79). The history of concepts therefore includes the variations they undergo in their migrations from one problem to another. (Patton, 2000, p. 13)

Conceptually, cyberinfrastructure has already begun its migrations across the fields of policy. Cyberinfrastructure, while not essentially contested, does vary conceptually (Connolly, 1993; Gallie, 1956). Cyberinfrastructure as a term, like e-science, does have a particular history and a component structure. The problem that the creation of the term is meant to solve is one of making clear the constructions of the necessities for statist policy to create a parallel meaning between physical infrastructures such as roads or sewage treatment plants and information technologies in order to legitimize the continued and extensive state investment. Cyberinfrastructure through this discursive parallel makes a claim to be something that is necessary and necessarily in that it exists less than in the form that it will become. Existence as such is more important than the structuring forms that it will take (Bourdieu, 2005).

Policy discourse is situated in national environments, and cyberinfrastructure policy is similar. It is primarily found in United States science and technology policy. This situatedness of the policy allows for somewhat invariate representations of the concepts through the primary policy documents. The majority of research on cyberinfrastructure defines it in relation to the Atkin's report, also known as "Revolutionizing Science and Engineering Through Cyberinfrastructure." The conceptualization provided on the base level is

> The newer term cyberinfrastructure refers to infrastructure based upon distributed computer, information and communication technology. If infrastructure is required for an industrial economy, then we could say that cyberinfrastructure is required for a knowledge economy. (Atkins et al., 2003, p. 84)

From this description, cyberinfrastructure is required for the knowledge economy, much as infrastructure: roads, sewers, canals, water supply are required for the industrial economy. These systems that became infrastructures developed their necessity after their existence. Cyberinfrastructure claims it will become a necessity once it exists. What kind of infrastructure is this? Dooley et al. describe it as a set of technology resources:

> The term cyberinfrastructure, coined by an "NSF Blue Ribbon Panel", refers to software and
> hardware which enable scientists to exploit cutting edge technology resources, including
> compute and data servers, visualization devices, instruments and networks, for advancing
> research in science and engineering. (Dooley, Milfeld, Guiang, Pamidighantam, & Allen,
> 2006, p. 195)

These are resources that can be used and reused, much like water lines and electrical grids, but centered on enabling scientists to do advanced research in science and engineering. To get more specific than that we can turn to Finholt, who describes parts of the actual networks and systems specific as cyberinfrastructure:

> Cyberinfrastructure can be thought of as the combined environment formed from high
> bandwidth networks (e.g., internet 2's Abilene network in the U.S.), high performance
> computing (e.g., the distributed teraflop computer project), and open-source and standards-
> based "middleware" (e.g., the computational Grid, as realized through the Globus security,
> resource discovery, and data transport toolkits – for details see www.globus.org). (Finholt,
> 2003, p. 17)

The specificity of cyberinfrastructure policy in practice becomes, as we can observe, a policy of infotechnics (the technics of informationalization) and their development. Globus makes the middleware toolkits and shares them and these toolkits when run on Abilene or other research networks become cyberinfrastructure. This does not seem to be extraordinarily innovative or conducive to science as process. Contrarily, it seems to be about developing the current informational infrastructure for science until it possesses immense capacities, such as petascale computing.

The embeddedness of cyberinfrastructure within the knowledge economy is obvious. What is not clear is what the knowledge economy actually entails about what knowledge is. One of the problems with the knowledge economy is that it assumes that knowledge becomes a product of the economy (UNESCO, 2005, p. 47). While there is a long tradition of seeing knowledge as a product, as an end, as a goal to be attained, those who actually pursue knowledge know that this product is never attained, and worse once a level of knowledge is gained, it must be actively maintained or it will quickly fade (Auge, 2004; Ricoeur, 2004). The product model of knowledge then is a fiction within the discourses of capital and more recently a fiction within the discourses of information.

The way that we imagine and portray knowledge within our discourses needs to consider the way that a human comes to be knowledgeable. The interactions amongst people and with the world that we experience and learn from is what generates knowledge. The way that we describe that knowledge is extremely important for the knowledge economy, to understand pure knowledge, that which exists in our brain, as someone else's property is to enter into a new axiomatization of the human mind, one that looks disturbingly non-human. When we frame knowledge as a product, it becomes what it principally cannot be, which is property. Knowledge, once framed as an object, can commoditized, but we cannot own it, just like we cannot own the contents of anyone else's mind. We might make claims against the other persons mind, but we cannot determine the disposition or contents of that mind.

Knowledge in the knowledge economy has to then be about the flow of knowledge, the expression of knowledge, and the commoditization of expressed knowledge.

In parallel to Dooley et al., Atkins et al. describe the technologies of cyberinfrastructure. "The base technologies underlying cyberinfrastructure are the integrated electro-optical components of computation, storage, and communication that continue to advance in raw capacity at exponential rates," (Atkins et al., 2003, p. 5). They describe these technologies as exponential accelerants of the knowledge economy. However, knowledge, unlike information, is a human capacity. Human capacities take time and communication to develop. Capacities take time to realize the reality of the beliefs at hand and their relations to the ecologies in which we exist. It takes time to understand and interpret the data that we have. Indeed, most of the data that we have from science will likely never be interpreted (Bowker, 2005). The "raw materials" of empirical evidence for knowledge creation will, as such, stay raw, much like the huge databases of consumer information, physics simulation, and other data fields stay raw for years until people actually interpret and understand the relationships in the data. Faster, in terms of knowledge, is not better or more efficient. Faster only means that there is more production information. Cyberinfrastructure policy is not producing knowledge as much as it re/produces itself and produces raw information. The overproduction of information generally slows the production of knowledge because information overload limits the human capacity for interpretation. This is starting to sound very much like the issues of infrastructural production in the early industrial age, where humans were the limiting factor in what could be produced with their manual labor, now we will limit what can be produced because of our mental labor. Labor is, in the end, what determines the output of production, though infrastructure can have effects that multiplies labor immensely.

Cyberinfrastructure proposes to build the techniques to cope with its own overproduction of information. However, information is not knowledge and making the transition from one to another is no small feat for humankind. For Atkins, cyberinfrastructure has a second purpose, it performs the boundary work between technical systems and scientific cultures. Cyberinfrastructure is the "enabling layer" between scientific techniques and scientific practice.

> Above the cyberinfrastructure layer are software programs, services, instruments, data, information, knowledge, and social practices applicable to specific projects, disciplines, and communities of practice. Between these two layers is the cyberinfrastructure layer of enabling hardware, algorithms, software, communications, institutions, and personnel. This layer should provide an effective and efficient platform for the empowerment of specific communities of researchers to innovate and eventually revolutionize what they do, how they do it, and who participates. (Atkins et al., 2003, p. 5)

Throughout the report, the values of science as process, knowledge as process are overwritten with the values of capitalism, science as production, knowledge as object. The boundary work of cyberinfrastructure is supposed to be "effective and efficient" at "empowerment of specific communities of researchers." The reality is that what the report actually suggests is that in parallel to the technics of boundaries, we need to set up a new laborer that develops the systems that perform the boundary work. These new professionals will likely not be either technicians or scientists, but a hybrid. This cross-training and para-professionalization of scientific practices is usually part of the apprenticeship to scientific careers, but as science gets inscribed with informatic and communicational practices, the pressures of expertise sharpen the divide to create the new forms of workers that are envisaged. This hybrid technician will almost certainly become part of the service economy of science, much as lab technicians in medical labs have become part of the service industry to medicine. Cyberinfrastructure, by creating a new class of worker, is creating a new form of service science to work with the new form of infrastructure.

The Atkins report indicates that there will be more participation in science through cyberinfrastructure. Cyberinfrastructure, while definably a great project for the knowledge society, tends to understand itself in relation to objects instead of in relation to society. It admits the discourses of society into its world and portrays them through capitalistic understandings of the world. There is a tension between the conception of knowledge and science as processual, constructive, creative acts of minds and bodies and science and knowledge as objectified product in the world of consumptions. This tension is fundamentally about the way capitalism constructs the relations of ontology and epistemology in the world. In particular, modern capitalism, and its derivations in postmodernity, attempt to rewrite process as object, this is one of the axioms of capitalism (Patton, 2000). Capitalism recodes all other social and human functions as capitalist functions.

Royalizing Science: Controlling Science through Cyberinfrastructure in Knowledge Society

The knowledge society as realized through informationalism and capitalism is transforming the sciences by requiring new skills, creating new classes of scientific workers, and providing new ways to monitor, control, and modulate the processes of science. Part of this transformation is the new formation of the state in the age of information, as alluded to above. The state is becoming informational and humans are moving through modulations in relation to the codes they possess (Deleuze, 1990, pp. 178–179). The transformation from a disciplinary society of confinement and encapsulation to a control of movement and constant modulation transforms with it the technics of biopolitics and policy. Cyberinfrastructure policy is part of a new control system for science. The policy, while allowing distributed interaction of scientists, data, and systems to manipulate that data, actually centralizes and brings new forms of control to scientific practices by creating new powers that can mediate their actions and interactions.

Science for Deleuze and Guattari falls into a spectrum of conceptualization from royal science to nomad science. While both nomad science and royal science exist within the state, the only science which is usually supported by the state through its institutional support such as policy and capital is the royal form. The two different forms of science differ in their fundamental approach to the world as Deleuze and Guattari note:

> What we have, rather, are two formally different conceptions of science, and, ontologically, a single field of interaction in which royal science continually appropriates the contents of vague or nomad science while nomad science continually cuts the contents of royal science loose. (Deleuze & Guattari, 1988, p. 367)

The two forms of science stand in complementary relationship, each feeding the other with new knowledges and innovations. This relationship could be thought of to be the core and periphery of sciences, where royal science is the core. That reading would be typical in the sociology of science, but it would not be the reading intended. The two systems are intertwined in a way where the core and periphery as social structure makes little sense. Instead we should think of the institutions that privilege the knowledge of each form. Royal science, objectifying and measuring, is the preferred science of the state where it is viewed as definitive, meticulous, and usually true or at least truth seeking. It is the science of knowing what is there, what exists, and knowing it completely. Nomad science though is the science of what is becoming, what will be, what is being created. Nomad science is the creative and innovative side of science, the science that moves beyond mapping, measuring, discovering, and labeling the truths of the world toward innovation of those requisite truths and developing/discovering new and alternative truths.

The construction of truths that the two sides of science deal with are fundamentally different. Nomad science constructs truth from movement, whereas royal science constructs truth from placement. For nomad science, the truth is that the subject is becoming something; for royal science, the subject is something. Cyberinfrastructure and its policy is slowly migrating from a dispersed, nomadic science to its more royal version and in that transition, as we can see with the discussion of the new class of technicians, above, certain promotions and demotions occur:

> Whenever this primacy is taken for granted, nomad science is portrayed as a prescientifc or parascientific or subscientific agency. And most important, it becomes impossible to understand the relations between science and technology, science and practices, because nomad science is not simple technology or practice, but a scientific field in which the problem of these relations is brought out and resolved in an entirely different way that from the point of view of royal science. (Deleuze & Guattari, 1988, p. 367)

The diminution of nomad science is clear when we talk about the nature of science in the field or applied science; in applying science, nomad science attempts to solve real problems in the world instead of mapping the world as it is. To do that, it must reach out of its institutions, joining the communities and their local understandings to construct and understand the problem that they need to resolve. It is not just applied science, the very way that you engage and model the world in nomad science is different when compared to royal science:

> It is instructive to contrast two models of science, after the manner of Plato in the Timmaeus. One could be called *Compars* and the other *Dispars*. The compars is the legal or legalist model employed by royal science. The search for laws consists in extracting constants, even if those constants are only relations between variables (equations). An invariable form

for variables, a variable matter of the invariant: such is the foundation of the hylomorphic schema. But for the dispars as an element of nomad science the relevant distinction is material-forces rather than matter-form. here, it is not exactly a question of extracting constants from variables but of placing themselves in a state of continuous variation. If there are still equations, they are adequations, inequations, differential equations irreducible to the algebraic form and inseparable form a sensible intution of variation. (Deleuze & Guattari, 1988, p. 369)

So for nomad science, as compared to royal science, the scientist and the institution must change, must move, and then note the approximations that this causes in the world. It is change that is noted and change that becomes something new. It is change in the end that becomes our knowledge of the world, because it arises from our manipulations. This is not to say that royal science does not manipulate the world, but in manipulating the world, royal science holds the human, social, political, epistemic, aesthetic, and ethical world as a constant and manipulates something in the world. It does not admit that the very action in the world is changing the parameters of the human world and moving in relation to that which it is studying. By holding the human world and subjectivity constant in royal science, Deleuze and Guattari claim we are attempting to reproduce the world, and in a way we are:

A distinction must be made between two types of science, or scientific procedures: one consists in "reproducing," the other in "following." The first involves reproduction, iteration and reiteration; the other, involving itineration, is the some of the itinerant, ambulant sciences. Itineration is too readily reduced to a modality of technology, or the application and verification of science. (Deleuze & Guattari, 1988, p. 372)

However, on the other side, when we follow another science, we are standing on their shoulders so that we can see farther, we do not have the same vision as they do, we do not reproduce their vision, we need to construct our own. In royal science, by removing the human subjects and transforming them into at best a series of variables, we are construing them as fixed objects in the world, unchanging in time, or if changing in time, changing at fixed and known intervals. This is contrary to the modulation and fluxing of the itinerant science, where through following, and not reproducing, we are attempting to map the changes of the world in relation to the people moving through it. This becomes important when we are talking about cyberinfrastructure because as we have described cyberinfrastructure as participating in a knowledge society, one of the tasks that cyberinfrastructure attempts to do is to capture the reproduced data without admitting the existence of the data that arises from following. Cyberinfrastructure rarely admits the human aspect as a subject in the system of science, and because of that, cyberinfrastructure tends to be oriented toward royal science. If we do not capture the subjective side of science, the side that Latour and Woolgar capture in their book *Laboratory Life* (1986), then we have not captured the process of science and have only constructed yet another objectified science. This objectified science might be the product of science, but it is not science, as it misses the human-centered processes of the scientists themselves. We will not have captured the nomadological side of science and thus, we will have missed many of the important facts that feed into the processes of successful science and innovation.

The state prefers royal science, it abhors change, innovation, and creation outside of its normal frameworks. The state prefers to encapsulate the nomadological science and only recognizes it in relation to the institutions that it creates, such as cyberinfrastructure. Cresswell argues that the innovation that the state wants, the creativity that it wants is construed as a conduit, one with clear bounds.

> The state, on the other hand, is the metaphorical enemy of the nomad, attempting to take the tactile space and enclose and bound it. It is not that the State opposes mobility but that it wishes to control flows – to make them run through conduits. It wasn't to create fixed and well-directed paths for movement to flow through. Deleuze and Guattari use the nomad as a metaphor for the undisciplined – rioting, revolution, guerrilla warfare – for all the forces that resist the fortress of State discipline. (Cresswell, 1997, p. 364)

That is the disciplinary state in action. The disciplinary state attempts to confine and direct human action. In doing that, it creates a system that forces nomadological science to become royal science and in doing that it pushes some scientists in the royal science out into new conduits seeking spaces of free action and thinking. The interaction of royal science with nomad science always liberates some royal sciences. Nomad science in its iterations is always moving and testing boundaries, and some of those boundaries become interesting to royal science, but when we participate in the becoming that is part of the untested boundary we must become mobile ourselves, we must become nomadological. If cyberinfrastructure extends and replaces the informational spheres of science, the assumptions of information and control become more limiting, and the boundary systems of the control-based knowledge society will fix in place, or worse encode the boundaries of knowledge into the infrastructure systems, thus requiring scientists to become technicians in order to rewrite the system to create new knowledge.

The interactions then of the state as disciplinary society moving into a knowledge society predicated on control needs to recognize the scientific process more completely in the systems that it supports. Just as the state has undergone a system of informationalization, science has undergone the same transformation, and the same systems, the same control-based infotechnics undergird the construction of the knowledge economy's infrastructure. When we write science policy for cyberinfrastructure then we have to be aware of the nature of the infotechnics to all kinds of science. As Stengers writes, the nomadological science will not disappear within cyberinfrastructure. Nomad science might become the hacker inside the machine, their motivations might be to free the knowledge processes from the informational system (Deleuze, 1990). We should not ignore the ambitions of the practitioners, as they could end up being the newest articulation of the processes of innovation.

> Royal Science does not make the "ambulant" or "nomad" sciences that preceded it disappear. The latter do not link science and power together, they do not destine science to an autonomous development, because they were in solidarity with the terrain of exploration, because their practices were distributed according to the problems provoked by a singularized material, without having the power to assess the difference between what, from singularities, refers to "matter itself" and what refers to the convictions and ambitions of practicioners (belonging henceforth to the second world). Royal Science "mobilizes" the ambulant process. (Stengers, 2000, pp. 155–156)

The relationship between nomad science and royal science enables and mobilizes royal science and allows it to become nomad science. Science, as a process, is ambulant. The attempts to fix it in place in the disciplinary knowledge society as a royal science will only create new forms of resistance and creation. These forms of resistance and creation will not easily be reterritorialized by royal science. They will lose their recognition and become subversion as Welchman indicates:

> It is not only the absence of formal tools that has inhibited nomad science. There is, according to Deleuze and Guattari, a political pact between the State (as rigidly stratified agent of order) and what they call Royal science (characterized by an exclusive emphasis on formalisation) which has made nomad science an eternally minor activity. Correlatively, rhyzomatics is essentially subversive, a perpetual undermind of cognitive and political authority. (Welchman, 1999, p. 626)

As I have alluded above, there is a political pact through policy, institutions, and related statist tools to privilege royal science. The state and science have a strong relationship both as multiplicities that share many overlapping concepts and assemblages, but they also have an alliance to suppress certain kinds of creativity, to limit certain kinds of innovation, and to structure the scientific process and the knowledge process as capitalist products. These processes becoming objects provide an ontological reality that maps back into the measurable, objectified world of royal science. In excluding the subjective side of science, the coming to be of the scientific fact, cyberinfrastructure policy has created two significant problems above. It has created a new control revolution in science, where informationalized science can and thus likely will be funneled through large, state funded, informational regimes. The second is that these new cyberinfrastructural regimes, while requiring a new class of scientist-technicians, have created a new class for creative resistance. Once the knowledge of how the machines are supposed to operate in the world then the knowledge of how to subvert the machines exists in the world. Following that, the knowledge processes will exist in our shared subjective experiences and our reflexive relation to the perspectival appreciations of control dramatically changes our subjectivities day to day, week to week, and year to year. By constituting a new cyberinfrastructure, we have in fact supported cybercreatives, who will likely be labeled cybersubversives by the statist regimes. This process has already occurred for the pre-internet age hacker, now re-imagined as criminal (Himanen, 2001; Jordan & Taylor, 1998).

Conclusion: Toward a Nomadological Cyberinfrastructure

In this article, I have unpacked several blackboxes and discursive territories that relate to cyberinfrastructural policy in the United States. I have shown that not all that glitters is gold and that there are significant concerns for following our current path. However, I have not argued that we should not follow this path. Contrarily, I think we should, but in following the path we need to responsibly construct systems that resist the control-oriented interests in the knowledge society, resist the negative aspects of informationalization and capitalism. We need to build a somewhat different cyberinfrastructure. This cyberinfrastructure does not need to be user centered, which would be the response of royal science. Cyberinfrastructure needs to be centered on social interaction and creativity. We need, beyond a cyberinfrastructure of royal science, a cyberinfrastructure that complements it, we need a nomadological cyberinfrastructure, much like the current version of the internet. We need a system that does not fix and encode meanings, but allows people to play with them, to observe how the processes of knowledge and creativity in our sciences occur above and beyond the factual constructions of science.

This system needs to have the qualities of being open, social, and mutable. It cannot be hidden or blackboxed like most infrastructure. Hiding the infrastructure will not protect it, it will not lessen the chance for it to be subverted, what will lessen that chance is if you remove the challenges of subversions, where each subversion becomes a legitimate project. When Virginia Tech built System X, I went to a meeting about research computing at Virginia Tech, I sat behind three older gentleman who spent the whole presentation talking back and forth about how they would manage the scheduling and cost recovery on the supercomputer, that was the royal science approach to supercomputing. The nomad approach would have been to give away the resource and develop a community that innovates and creates then eventually self-manages it for the benefit of all, building up maximum creative usage, not building walls to prevent usage. Open, social, and mutable infrastructure, customizable on the fly and hackable on the fly will enable innovation and the scientific process. Especially if, when properly built, you can monitor and engage the whole social sphere around the cyberinfrastructural resources, not merely the scientific machinations that occur through the infrastructure, but the social machinations with their multiple lines of flight and subjectivities (Masakazu, 1997).

This open and mutable infrastructure does not map onto the state or royal science. Both institutions can use this type of system for their own ends, that should not be questions, but what they cannot do is control the system, remove the meaning from the information, or create products where there may be none. Because of the lack of "productivity" of the "creative" system, I fear that we will probably not witness the birth of a cyberinfrastructure for nomads, and that the public infrastructures now in place will likely move farther into the private sphere, where they can be profit centers and premium network spaces much like highways and telecommunication systems have become (Graham & Marvin, 2001, p. 291).

References

Atkins, D. E., Droegemeier, K. K., Feldman, S. I., Garcia-Molina, H., Klein, M. L., Messerschmitt, M.L., et al. (2003). *Revolutionizing science and engineering through cyberinfrastructure: Report of the National Science Foundation blue-ribbon advisory panel on cyberinfrastructure.* Washington, DC: National Science Foundation.

Augé, M. (2004). *Oblivion*. Minneapolis, MN: University of Minnesota Press.

Bourdieu, P. (2005). *The social structures of the economy*. Cambridge: Polity Press.

Bowker, G. C. (2005). *Memory practices in the sciences*. Cambridge, MA: MIT Press.

Chompalov, I., Genuth, J., & Shrum, W. (2002). The organization of scientific collaborations. *Research Policy, 31*(5), 749–767.

Connolly, W. E. (1993). *The terms of political discourse*. Princeton, NJ: Princeton University Press.

Cresswell, T. (1997). Imagining the nomad, mobility and the postmodern primitive. In G. Benko & U. Strohmayer (Eds.), *Space and social theory: Interpreting modernity and postmodernity*. Oxford: Blackwell Publishing, Incorporated.

DeLanda, M. (2000). *A thousand years of nonlinear history* (ISBN: 0942299329 ed.). New York: Zone Books.

Deleuze, G. (1990). Control and becoming. In *Negotiations 1972–1990*. New York: Columbia University Press.

Deleuze, G. (1995). *Difference and repetition*. New York: Columbia University Press.

Deleuze, G., & Guattari, F. (1988). *A thousand plateaus: Capitalism and schizophrenia*. London: Continuum.

Dooley, R., Milfeld, K., Guiang, C., Pamidighantam, S., & Allen, G. (2006). From proposal to production: Lessons learned developing the computational chemistry grid cyberinfrastructure. *Journal of Grid Computing, 4*(2), 195–208.

Finholt, T. A. (2003). Collaboratories as a new form of scientific organization. *Economics of Innovation and New Technology, 12*(1), 5–25.

Gallie, W. B. (1956). *Essentially contested concepts*. Paper presented at the Proceedings of the Aristotelian Society.

Graham, S., & Marvin, S. (2001). *Splintering urbanism: Networked infrastructures, technological mobilities and the urban condition*. New York: Routledge.

Himanen, P. (2001). *The hacker ethic and the spirit of the information age*. New York: Random House Inc.

Hunsinger, J. (2005). Toward a internet research. *The Information Society, 21*(4), 277–279.

Hunsinger, J. (2005). Reflexivity in e-science: Virtual communities and research institutions. *ACM Siggroup, 25*(2), 38–42.

Jordan, T., & Taylor, P. (1998). A sociology of hackers. *The Sociological Review, 46*(4), 757–780.

Latour, B. & Woolgar, S. (1986). *Laboratory life*. Princeton, NJ: Princeton University Press.

Mansell, R. (1990). Rethinking the telecommunication infrastructure: The new "black box". *Research Policy, 19*, 501–515.

Masakazu, Y. (1997). "Trust" and "sociable society" – In search of social infrastructure for the twenty-first century (2). *Japan Echo, 24*, 54–60.

Patton, P. (2000). *Deleuze and the political*. New York: Routledge.

Ricoeur, P. (2004). *Memory, history, forgetting*. Chicago: University of Chicago Press.

Stengers, I. (2000). *The invention of modern science (theory out of bounds)*. Minneapolis, MN: University of Minnesota Press.

UNESCO. (2005). *Towards knowledge societies*. Imprimerie Corlet, Condé-sur-Noireau, France: Author.

Welchman, A. (1999). Into the abyss: Deleuze. In S. Glendinning (Ed.), *Encyclopedia of continental philosophy*. Edinburgh: Edinburgh University Press.

Wiener, N. (1954). *The human use of human beings: Cybernetics and society (da capo paperback)* (ISBN: 0306803208 ed.). Boston: Houghton Mifflin.

Toward a Virtual Town Square in the Era of Web 2.0

Andrea Kavanaugh, Manuel A. Perez-Quinones, John C. Tedesco, and William Sanders

Introduction

Neither time nor technology has been a friend to the old town square. In an earlier time, the town square had a special place in civic life. We could walk there and see what people were doing, and with whom they were doing it. It was where people met to discuss local issues with friends and neighbors and to find out what were the current difficult choices facing a town. We could see who went in and out of the town hall and, if curious, could probably find out why without a lot of effort. The town hall may still be home to formal civil and political activity, but with the increase in workload, the emergence of information workers, change in work hours, improvement in transportation, and sprawling urbanization, the epicenter of civil and political discussion may be changing. In the United States, electronic forms of information distribution, citizen discussion, and government-to-citizen exchange, including metatags, mashups, and social software, are changing the ways that citizens access information and participate in democratic processes. Equipped with networked phones, computers, personal digital assistants, and a plethora of online information access options, we may be creating a virtual but partial or splintered equivalent (Chadwick, 2006; Shane, 2004).

What is lost in the migration from direct democracy to digital democracy? There are perils as well as opportunities to democratic life with the advent of new forms of interaction. Some traditionally politically active participants in the United States, such as the older generation, are often uncomfortable with computers. Has their access or participation declined with the migration to electronic forms of government? On the other hand, might the younger generation (which is politically less active) become increasingly drawn into civic life through advances in information technology, such as social software that could help link them and their friends together around issues they care about? Recent developments in social software give the opportunity for the town square to be recreated in at least a virtual way. How

A. Kavanaugh (✉)
Department of Computer Science, Virginia Tech, Blacksburg, Virginia, USA
e-mail: kavan@vt.edu

J. Hunsinger et al. (eds.), *International Handbook of Internet Research*,
DOI 10.1007/978-1-4020-9789-8_17, © Springer Science+Business Media B.V. 2010

would such a town square work, what functionality should it provide, and what principles would attract and sustain participation by myriad segments of the population, so as to retain the public nature and openness of the original town square? A virtual town square is not a website per se, but the aggregation across an entire community of social and political participation blending offline and online interactions and the seamless integration of online resources.

Many other US communities have imagined these goals in the recent past (see, for example, Greensboro, North Carolina, Brattleboro, Vermont, and Palo Alto, California). What we feel has been lacking in order to make these imaginings a reality has been the systematic integration of information and communication capabilities. For example, along with a government announcement that is broadcast to citizens (by e-mail, online video, or website), much more information and communication functionality can be built-in to that message, such as links to GIS maps of the locality in question, links to a discussion forum or blog aggregator that allows citizens to discuss formally or informally online the pros and cons of a given issue with each other, and direct feedback links from citizens to government staff and officials on a given issue. There are various emerging technologies that facilitate such integration across tools and online resources.

We anticipate, based on prior research described in detail below, that through sheer convenience, social context, and relevancy, a virtual town square would have several outcomes:

1) enable citizens to become more aware of and better informed about local developments, long-term planning, and governmental processes (Bimber, 2001; Cohill & Kavanaugh, 1997; Kavanaugh, Cohill, & Patterson, 2000; Larsen & Rainie, 2002; Patterson & Kavanaugh, 1994; Shane, 2004).
2) increase public engagement in various civil processes, such as public deliberation, zoning ordinance changes, special use permit requests, and public comment (Chadwick, 2006; Kavanaugh, Reese, Carroll, & Rosson, 2003; Kavanaugh, Carroll, Rosson, Reese, & Zin, 2005; Kavanaugh, Isehour et al., 2005).
3) attract a broader and more diverse citizenship than currently participates in local civic life and thereby boost deliberative democratic processes and provide more diverse feedback to government representatives and officials (Godara, 2007; Kavanaugh, Kim, Schmitz, & Péroz-Quiñones, 2008; Kavanaugh & Schmitz, 2004; Norris, 2001).
4) boost the sense of political and community collective efficacy of diverse groups through increased political knowledge and participation, especially at the local level, but possibly also at the national level (Coleman & Gotz, 2002; Coleman, Morrison, & Svennevig, 2006; Carroll & Reese, 2003; Kavanaugh et al., 2003; Rainie & Horrigan, 2007; Tedesco, 2006).

Interdisciplinary research on the social and political use and impact of community-wide computer networking in Blacksburg is motivated by recent foundational changes in democratic society due to advances in information technology. Both the government and the citizenry act as agents of change when they use community computer networking for political and civic purposes. We have found increases in broad-based, meaningful participation in the democratic processes that are so difficult to achieve when time- and place-based participation is the only available option. Specifically, we have seen changes in civic awareness, political and collective efficacy, civic engagement and knowledge sharing among diverse community members. Moreover, our findings from the comprehensive case study of Blacksburg and environs have been shown to generalize to other college towns, networked communities, and rural areas throughout the Unites States.

Information and Communication Technology (ICT) for Political Participation at the Local Level

In order to understand the extent to which existing information technology satisfies community communication and information needs and interests, we have asked (and answered) such questions as, Who is socially and politically active? What is the nature of their community involvement? How do they use information technology and how does that use seem to affect their social and political participation? What design modifications to technology help to optimize citizen-to-citizen online deliberation? (Carroll & Rosson, 2001; Cohill & Kavanaugh, 1997; Godara, 2007; Kavanaugh, 2003; Kavanaugh et al., 2000; Kavanaugh, Rosson, Carroll, & Zin, 2006; Kavanaugh, Kim, Pùrez-Quiñones, Schmitz, & Isenhour, 2006; Kavanaugh, Kim, Pùrez-Quiñones, & Isenhour, 2007; Kavanaugh & Patterson, 2001; Kavanaugh & Schmitz, 2004; Kim, Kavanaugh, & Smith-Jackson, 2007; Patterson & Kavanaugh, 1994; Tedesco, 2006).

The diffusion of community computing in the town of Blacksburg and environs has been led by various agents of change, including local institutions, citizens, government, and information technology itself. Longitudinal data that we collected over more than a decade with support from NSF (IIS-0429274, IIS-0080864, REC-9603376) and the US Department of Commerce (PTFP 510399231, NTIA 50-SBN-TOC-1033) indicate that adoption and use of new technology for social and political purposes has been predicted by education, extroversion, age, community group membership, collective efficacy, and activism (Carroll & Reese, 2003; Carroll et al., 2006; Kavanaugh, Carroll, Rosson, Reese et al., 2005; Kavanaugh, Rosson et al., 2006). The effects of internet use for social and political purposes include increased awareness and knowledge of issues, greater sharing of information, increased volunteerism and community involvement (Carroll et al., 2006; Kavanaugh & Schmitz, 2004; Kavanaugh et al., 2003; Kavanaugh, Carroll, Rosson, Zin et al., 2005; Kavanaugh, Kim et al., 2006; Kim, Kavanaugh, & Hult, 2006).

Emerging technologies are helping to support citizen-to-citizen and citizen-to-government interaction (Kavanaugh, Carroll, Rosson, Zin, & Reese, 2005; Kavanaugh, Kim et al., 2007; Kavanaugh, Zin, Rosson, Carroll, & Schmitz, 2007; Kavanaugh et al., 2008). Increasingly, US citizens are using social software for political purposes, such as discussion and deliberation in both centralized online forums (e.g., Minnesota's e-democracy) and in dispersed formats, such as blogs (Godara, 2007; Kavanaugh, Zin et al., 2006; Kim et al., 2006, 2007). Podcasting, Real Simple Syndication or RSS, and blogs provide opportunities for citizens to obtain detailed information from each other or from government sources, to engage in online discussion, and to offer feedback to government on issues of concern. (RSS is a feature of the web that makes it easier for users to track and share information by subscribing to – or offering – syndicated content.) This kind of exchange is especially effective at the local level where online communication and information can complement face-to-face interactions among citizens and between citizens and government. Knowledge sharing through social software systems might affect the participation of young adults who are currently less politically active than older adults (Godara, 2007; Tedesco, 2007).

The town government of Blacksburg (hereafter referred to as ToB) and the Blacksburg Electronic Village (BEV) are full partners in the proposed research and both have a long history of collaboration with each other and the HCI Center of Virginia Tech. Both ToB and the BEV are renowned for their innovative electronic presence, services, and infrastructure. The BEV was one of the earliest community network initiatives (established in 1993) with close collaborations with Virginia Tech computer science department and the ToB. BEV is now a mature and stable community network with online resources and support for local residents, organizations, and groups. One of the unique opportunities we have to conduct the proposed research lies in the twin presence of a mature community network (BEV) and the innovative award-winning online presence of the ToB. The ToB has initiated a citizen-subscription e-mail announcement service (Blacksburg Alert), streaming video of public meetings, including Town Council and citizen-government committees, extensive GIS mapping online linked to overlays of the town comprehensive plan, and long-term development. The ToB is interested in extending its resources into the emerging technologies and social software known as Web 2.0.

Agents of Change: Citizens, Government, Technology

Diffusion of innovation theory argues that most social changes in human behavior follow a fairly predictable process and consistent pattern. That is, the spread of new ideas, products, or technology begin with what are called "agents of change" who are risk-takers interested in whatever lies beyond and outside their current knowledge and environment (Rogers, 1995). Agents of change are the earliest adopters of an innovation, such as new agricultural products or techniques, new health behaviors, and new information and communication technology. Other people (i.e., later adopters) often hear about new ideas and practices through mass media messages and learn informally about them through direct observation of early adopters in their social networks (Katz, 1987; Katz & Lazarsfeld, 1955). It is well established by numerous studies over the past half century that agents of change are characterized by higher education (even within lower social strata), greater empathy with others (i.e., the ability to identify with or understand the perspective of someone unlike themselves), feeling cosmopolitan (i.e., a view of the world that extends beyond their individual surroundings or perspective), and finally, exposure to and use of communication media (i.e., radio, television, print media, and most recently, the internet). Agents of change are often (but not always) opinion leaders. That is, people to whom others in their social circle turn to for advice and guidance (Keller & Berry, 2003; Rogers & Shoemaker, 1971). Opinion leaders are agents of change who are well respected and highly sociable (i.e., talkative, extroverted, and likely to be affiliated with local clubs and community groups).

Opinion Leadership

Opinion leadership, summarized by Rogers and Shoemaker (1971), is "the degree to which an individual is able to informally influence other individuals' attitudes or overt behavior in a desired way with relative frequency" (p. 35). The influence is typically informal, often by word of mouth, at the local level with ideas and information spreading throughout a leader's social circle (Keller & Berry, 2003). Further, opinion leadership is earned and maintained by the individual's competence, social accessibility, and conformity to agreed-upon norms. Opinion leadership theory argues that influentials exist at all social strata and can vary somewhat by subject area (e.g., politics, technology, consumerism) although they are generally attuned to new ideas and forward thinking across the board. Extensive longitudinal research by Roper (since the early 1970s) shows that influential Americans have consistently been politically aware and socially active citizens (Keller & Berry, 2003).

Opinion leaders make up only about 10–15% of the total US population and they are that same group that is comprised of the politically active citizens (Almond & Verba, 1963; Norris, 2001; Verba & Nie, 1972;) although not all politically active citizens are opinion leaders. Roper research shows that influentials were among the early adopters of information technology, including video recorders, home computers, and the internet (Keller & Berry, 2003). Influentials used e-mail, bulletin board systems, and web browsers from the outset to stay informed and involved in political issues that interested them and to spread ideas throughout the general population. They are among the early adopters of emerging technology and its use for political and social engagement.

Political Participation and IT Use

Who participates in political processes, how, and why has been the subject of study for a long time. Political participation theory argues – and most studies have found – that education is the main predictor of political participation (Almond & Verba, 1963; Dahl, 1991; Milbrath & Goel, 1977; Norris, 2001; Verba & Nie,

1972; Verba, Schtozman, & Brady, 1995). Studies have found that other factors that are also important predictors of participation include political efficacy, access to information, group membership, and community attachment. Kim, Wyatt, and Katz (1999) have emphasized the importance of political talk as a precursor to political participation. Although others have disputed this emphasis (see, for example, Schudson, 1997), it is clear that there is no public deliberation without political talk. Political discussion precedes almost all other political activity that is social (i.e., that goes beyond the individual awareness and political cognition). Information technology plays an important role in accommodating discussion and sometimes even in fostering and supporting it.

For at least three decades, scholars and information technology experts have envisioned computer-based communication technologies as a basis for a vibrant, engaged, and informed democracy (Arterton, 1987; Larsen & Rainie, 2001); Rogers, 1986; Schudson, 1992; Schuler, 1996). Although most of these utopian hopes have not been realized, many studies have shown that computer networking has at least fostered greater participation in democratic political life in the United States (Coleman & Gotz, 2002; Coleman et al., 2006; Dahlberg, 2001; Horrigan, Garreff, & Resnick, 2004; Kavanaugh, Carroll, Rosson, Reese et al., 2005; Kavanaugh, Kim et al., 2006, 2007; Norris, 2001; Rainie, 2005; Schmitz, Rogers, Phillips, & Paschal, 1995). Electronic mailing lists and politically oriented web-based resources grew rapidly in the late 1990s. Information technology has enhanced participation through increased knowledge sharing (such as raising awareness about issues and problems and increasing capabilities for coordination, communication, and outreach) among political actors. Recent large-scale examples include the 1999 coordination of demonstrations against the World Trade Organization meeting in Seattle that were greatly facilitated by online communication. During the 2004 US presidential campaign, political groups coordinated such activities as leafleting, neighborhood canvassing, and fundraising over the internet (Williams & Tedesco, 2006). When presidential campaign volunteers from southwest Virginia sought to help distribute surplus campaign materials in Ohio, they went online to find their counterparts, establish contact with them, and coordinate rendezvous points.

ICT has a long history of utilization in local political activities dating from early campaigns to change how a city would treat its homeless waged on Santa Monica's Public Electronic Network (Schmitz et al., 1995) or the establishment of neighborhood coalitions via the Seattle Community Network (Schuler, 1996). When a group of citizens in Blacksburg, Virginia, documented controversial procedures surrounding a proposed local sewer development, they used e-mail and listservs, along with face-to-face campaigning to help ensure a record voter turnout that elected reform-minded candidates to Town Council in a landslide victory (Kavanaugh, Isenhour et al., 2005). In short, the enhanced capabilities of ICT to reach and mobilize more people, more quickly, and to share knowledge among dispersed populations have helped political actors to educate and mobilize citizens for collective action.

Knowledge Sharing in Communities of Practice

Knowledge is distributed among different individuals, tasks, and networks in any social group. Sharing knowledge is crucial for collective problem solving. The process of knowledge sharing requires continuous interaction among participating individuals or groups, sometimes referred to as communities of practice or CoP (Lave & Wenger, 1990). CoP is a group of people who share a concern, or interest in a topic, and who deepen their understanding through ongoing interaction. Traditionally, CoP has used in-person communication as a knowledge sharing mechanism, such as a town hall meeting. The advent of ICT, however, allows knowledge sharing between (and without) in-person exchange. We will investigate online mechanisms for knowledge sharing.

As noted earlier, opinion leaders have dominated much of the ICT use for political knowledge generation and knowledge sharing with members of their social circles and wider communities. Opinion leaders exist at all social strata, including those that are traditionally underrepresented in political life, such as young adults, ethnic, and class minorities. As Bandura (2002) and others (Coleman et al., 2006) remind us, however, people will use information technology for political purposes only to the extent that they feel it is efficacious to do so. Our investigation of the effect of new media use on political efficacy is tempered by this caveat that takes into consideration contextual factors, including the perceived and actual responsiveness of government (Kavanaugh, Zin et al., 2006). A person's sense of self-efficacy (Bandura, 1997) is a belief in their ability to achieve their goals despite obstacles and setbacks. Political efficacy has both internal (or intrinsic) and external (or extrinsic) dimensions (Brady, 1999). A person's belief that s/he is capable of comprehending and participating in various aspects of political life is intrinsic political efficacy. A person's belief that government is trustworthy and competent is extrinsic political efficacy. Moreover, a person's social status or ethnicity, or extensive prior experience, can affect their political efficacy (Michaelson, 2000; Perkins, Brown, & Taylor, 1996). These concepts of efficacy have been further developed to encompass a community-wide sense of "collective efficacy" (Carroll & Reese, 2003). While we are broadly interested in political and collective efficacy of diverse citizens, we are especially interested in underrepresented groups, specifically young adults, ethnic minorities, and the socio-economically disadvantaged.

Virtual Town Square 2.0

In the town of Blacksburg, Virginia, home of the land grant university Virginia Tech and the community computer network known as the Blacksburg Electronic Village (BEV), local government, businesses, community groups, and residents make use of at least the following technologies, though not necessarily in any coordinated fashion: web pages, community calendars, a television channel, a subscription-based emergency messaging service, and third party online e-government transaction services. Town government broadcasts Town Council meetings live and replays

Jennifer is a 12-year resident of Blacksburg. She keeps up with local news and information, but is not able to attend public meetings more than once or twice a year at most. She subscribes to the town "e-mail alert" service that informs her of many developments in the local area, such as planning new uses for the old middle school and the revisions to the comprehensive town plan. When she receives an announcement about an upcoming meeting in her e-mail, she is not able to attend but is able to learn more about plans through links to all the background documentation, GIS maps and zoning regulations from the town comprehensive plan. She is able to provide feedback to the government using the "feedback" button that appears with the announcement. Since Jennifer would also like to find out what other residents think about this topic, she clicks on the link to "citizen discussion" which takes her to a blog aggregator on the BEV web site where she sees a visual display of blogs on the topic of interest; she follows this up by checking the centralized discussion forum that is hosted on the BEV. She is able to use the RSS function on the announcement to ensure that she is notified any time there is an update from government on the old middle school planning issue.

Fig. 1 Virtual town square scenario

pre-recorded meetings and events on its TV channel and streams those digitized recordings over the internet with links to each relevant topic in the online town meeting agenda. While town government and the BEV make sporadic and ad hoc use of listserv announcements to the public, website GIS maps, and online video streaming of town meetings, most of the these technologies are not linked to each other or, most importantly, to citizen discussion opportunities and feedback mechanisms.

We are exploring how a Virtual Town Square (VTS) based on social networking (Web 2.0) technologies might influence participation in local political processes from young voters and members from other underrepresented groups. The Virtual Town Square is not just a website with tagging capabilities. We consider the Virtual Town Square to be the combination of information syndication, user contributed content and ratings, community groups, and the social network that connects them all. We are developing this Virtual Town Square and will study its impact.

We are using the community of Blacksburg, the surrounding rural area, local governments, and the Blacksburg Electronic Village community computer network as a comprehensive testbed and case study that has been shown to generalize to other college towns, networked communities, and rural areas throughout the United States. While Blacksburg was ahead of other communities in the early 1990s with the diffusion of community computing, today the majority of Americans (over 70%) report using the internet (Rainie & Horrigan, 2006). Further, most cities and towns have a variety of locally oriented content online in the form of local information, resources, organizations, and individuals. A scenario that describes our vision for VTS2 is illustrated in Fig. 1.

To accomplish this vision, the Virtual Town Square will consist of content syndication and user contributed content and ratings, among other tools and plug-ins that facilitate social interaction.

Content Syndication

We will use content syndication to allow information to be reused throughout the Virtual Town Square, thus allowing a social network about Blacksburg to grow. The

ToB recently updated its web presence. The new website uses content syndication in several ways. First, news and notices are available as an RSS feed. Second, meetings and events are available as a separate RSS feed. Finally, calendar events are available to download directly to a desktop calendar program. We are encouraging the town to support tagging of content on their pages. We have suggested they add links to "Digg this page," "Add to Del.icio.us," and other similar Web 2.0 ideas.

The town currently has a sophisticated GIS system where information about all of the properties in town is available. The GIS system is even linked to the town master plan, so upcoming development is visible on the map itself. We will expand this offering to have geo-related information available as either RSS feeds or links to other mapping services (e.g., Google Maps). This would allow users to keep track of personal maps, highlighting their home, where they go shopping, where they work, etc. Such functionality would allow users to e-mailing driving instructions to their property by simply e-mailing a url.

User Contributed Content and Ratings

We plan to provide a service for users to explicitly manage their online content for organizational and social purposes (Marlow et al., 2006). The service will be available in the Blacksburg Electronic Village. It will be built using open source software and made available to other communities that might want to implement it. Most of the content will not be stored in the BEV directly, instead we will use content syndication from other sites to provide richness to VTH2. Users will be able to create a picture album by taking pictures from their account in Flickr. The idea is that BEV will provide a mashup service to town residents that allows them to combine information from many sources. For example, a user could have on her home page "Today's meetings" and show a snapshot of her calendar (possible taken from Google Calendar). She could have a list of "What I am listening" and show music from last.fm, and show all the bookmarks from del.icio.us with a particular tag (e.g., "blacksburg" tag). The page can also include the "top local stories" as determined by an aggregator of news feeds collected by the BEV from different news sources and made available to their users.

With personal accounts on BEV, we will support the creation of a social network by having people identify their "friends" online. This relationship can be used to increase the *social connectivity* in the site (Marlow, Naaman, Boyd, & Davis, 2006). We will use the social connectivity to allow events and information to be shared by others. Finally, we will use content syndication of users' personal information to be served out to other services.

Community Groups: Based on the information exchange that occurs online and the social network that evolves, we will explore the use of public displays in selected strategic locations to further disseminate information to the community. The idea is to show in public places what is happening online as a way to encourage others to join the online social network. We will explore placing a public display at the county public library, the Christiansburg recreation center, the New River

Community Action Agency, and the Virginia Tech Squires student center, as examples of locations where and how we will reach underrepresented groups with online civic resources. Furthermore, we will target a few particular groups to engage their members to use the online system as a way to participate in the political process.

Social Networks: We are exploring the creation of an online social network as part of the BEV, so that groups of interested individuals can meet online through this network. We are following design principles and guidelines about supporting the development of a social network as presented in the literature (Gingersohn & Lee, 2002; Kim, 2000; Kollock, 1998; Preece, 2000). With some design and development work on these existing technologies and strategies, we expect to integrate the town, BEV and community resources, legislative processes, and listserv announcements with local blogs, podcasting, instant messaging, discussion forums, chat rooms, bulletin boards, online surveys, public opinion services, voice over the internet, and other forms of social software.

In the next section, we describe how the implementation of these activities has taken concrete form in the community, using the examples of a ToB government–citizen task force charged with revising the Comprehensive Plan (i.e., notably a ToB Blog) and a local grassroots advocacy group, known as Citizens First.

Case Studies in Blacksburg and Environs

We investigated two cases in depth that illustrate specific ways that local government and community groups are using emerging technology, including social software, to facilitate long-term government–citizen interaction and citizen–citizen interaction. These two types of interactions are illustrated in case studies, respectively, of a Town of Blacksburg task force blog (involving citizens and government officials) and a community group known as Citizens First for Blacksburg (involving citizens). Both of these are discussed in some detail below. In a fully populated virtual town square, many town and county government entities and local community groups will be using similar technologies and practices for civic participation. We expect such usage to grow, but these are some of the earliest examples already in place.

Local Government Case: Town of Blacksburg Blog

In 2006, the ToB established a task force to revise the Comprehensive Town Plan through the year 2046. The task force consisted of nine members who were either a representative of town government or a citizen volunteer. In ongoing meetings with the Center for Human Computer Interaction at Virginia Tech, the town government became interested in the idea of using a blog to handle some of the work of the task force. Also participating in those ongoing meetings, as part of a larger study of local citizen-to-citizen deliberation funded by the National Science Foundation, was the director of the Blacksburg Electronic Village (BEV) and a co-author here, Dr.

William Sanders. He volunteered to host the ToB task force blog on a secure BEV server. Not coincidentally, Dr. Sanders was also a member of the ToB task force. The town agreed that a blog would be the easiest and simplest technology to manage and would still accommodate some kind of citizen participation (Kavanaugh, Kim, or Kavanaugh, Zin et al., 2007). BEV set up the blog in April 2006 on a secure BEV server (https://secure.bev.net/townplan).

As much as the town wanted to encourage open citizen discussion and participation on the blog, like many other government entities they were a little uncomfortable about hosting public comments directly on their blog. We emphasized that it was not necessary – and possibly not even desirable – for ToB to do this. Rather, with the agreement of the town and BEV, we contacted the local blog aggregator site manager who agreed to link the ToB blog to the aggregator site (http://www.swvanews.com), which retrieves syndicated content by a web feed, such as RSS. This linkage allowed interested citizens to view the ToB task force blog, link to it, and discuss its contents within their own blogs. In this way, citizens could initiate discussion among themselves on their own blogs about the revisions that the task force was proposing to the comprehensive plan and use traditional channels, such as e-mail, letters, and telephone, to offer feedback directly to the task force or other officials in town government (Kavanaugh, Kim et al., 2007).

Citizens First Community Organization

Citizens First for Blacksburg (http://www.citizensfirstforblacksburg.org) emerged in 2003–2004 as a grassroots community group dedicated to transparency in local government and civic engagement. In spring 2004 Citizens First (CF) raised citizen awareness, public deliberation, and voter turnout for local Town Council elections through face-to-face meetings, public petitions, and notifications sent by e-mail or listserv to interested citizens. Several major issues of concern made the elections more contentious than usual, such as the decisions surrounding a town sewer project and confusion around proposed changes to the Town Charter. In the 2004 Town Council elections, with support from CF, reform-oriented candidates won contended seats in a landslide victory with record voter turnout. CF gained trust through its track record of providing interested citizens with timely information and background.

CF became a political action committee in December 2006, with a formal charter and mission to enable Blacksburg area citizens to work together, with public officials, and with other civic groups and stakeholders to research, understand, and shape the quality of life in the community. While CF is not affiliated with any political party, among its goals are to endorse and support candidates for public office and to promote responsible growth. The foundational premise underlying the CF mission is that democratic processes work best with an active electorate that is aware of community needs, uses information, respects divergent views, seeks consensus, resolves conflicts, and supports principled public policy. Citizen information takes the form of research findings, position papers, platforms, analyses of alternatives, and viewpoints to aid public information, dialogue, and advocacy. CF facilitates citizen information and involvement through the printed word, public discussion, and electronic media.

In order to reach as broad and diverse a population as possible, the CF website links to excerpts from other relevant public records, reports, and documentation that provide a basis for discussion, both online and offline. For example, CF linked excerpts from the 35-page report (released June 4, 2007) by an independent marketing firm hired by the "Blacksburg Partnership" a formal organization representing the downtown merchants of Blacksburg with representatives from the town government (also representing the public, of course), the university (Virginia Tech), and local businesses. The Downtown Market Assessment and Marketing Plan for Blacksburg (Arnett Muldrow and Associates, 2007) provides diverse information about current trends and suggestions about best practice for revitalization attempted in other similar (university) communities.

The link to these excerpts includes many helpful recommendations from the Downtown Market study that is intended to stimulate further discussion on the CF website. Such online discussion would (hopefully) spill over into face-to-face interactions (and vice versa) among citizens and could lead to greater participation in this and other important long-term deliberations and collective decision making. Similar background documentation that is helpful in fostering debate is posted on the site regarding recent developments for a "big box" store (subsequently identified in town documentation as a Wal-Mart) with opportunities for online public discussion and comment among interested citizens. In doing this, CF is attempting to supplement face-to-face discussion with an online environment that might inform and sustain further discussion with a wider population. Since the CF website is open to the public, anyone, including government and business representatives, can see what citizens are saying and contributing to the opinion formation and consensus building processes, as well as contribute themselves to the ongoing deliberations.

The CF discussion area on their site is different from traditional centralized issue forums because it is the discussion area of one local community organization. Traditional issue forum sites, such as Minnesota e-democracy, draw participants from across the community, not through a specific community group. While CF also allows anyone in the community to participate in its web discussions, there is a face-to-face component of the organization in which meetings are held, policies are discussed, and activities are planned.

In addition to the discussion that is hosted on the CF website, it would be helpful for citizens to discover similar discussion on the same topics that are taking place on other sites. We have developed and tested a blog visualization software that can be linked to the CF website (or anyone website) that takes interested citizens to local area blogs with similar content based on a keyword search (Kavanaugh, Kim et al., 2007). The blog visualization software selects blogs with similar keywords from a local aggregator site for the southwest Virginia region (http://www.swvanews.org). By linking the blogs that discuss the same topics that the CF site lists, interested citizens can gain access to additional perspectives and ideas from a diverse population in the geographic area. Moreover, most studies show that the majority of bloggers in the United States tend to be citizens who stay informed, but are not political activists (Fox, 2006; Herring et al., 2005; Kavanaugh, Zin et al., 2006a; Nardi, 2004; Rainie, 2005). Therefore, we can expect that they would tend to bring a more mainstream point of view to the discussion of any local issue.

Summary

The work we attempted to summarize in this article is distinguished from many others regarding online political discussion (Arterton, 1987; Chadwick, 2006; Coleman & Gotz, 2002; Coleman et al., 2006; Dahlberg, 2001) by the fact that it is focused on decentralized, dispersed discussion, such as that which takes place in blogs or the discussion sites of specialized community groups (e.g., Citizens First and other community organizations). Unlike centralized websites for discussion forums, such as e-democracy.org in Minnesota (http://www.edemocracy.org), decentralized discussion in blogs or community group websites is more likely than centralized forums to engage the non-activists, which is to say, a broader more diverse population.

Decentralized online discussion is more heterogeneous due to the diversity of its participants, thereby generating and sharing greater knowledge among participants (Godara 2007). Furthermore, our approach is to support online discussion through community groups with which residents are already affiliated. This makes an online discussion from the group's website a natural extension of ongoing face-to-face political talk or civic activities in which a group is already interested or engaged. The aggregation of online discussion by multiple local groups creates a community-wide dialogue and exchange of views that forms the big picture of a virtual town square.

The two cases highlighted here illustrate some of the small ways that individual organizations and groups can take advantage of emerging technologies, especially social software, to increase interaction and discussion among members. The aggregation and inter-connection of many small contributions like these will eventually populate a virtual town square in Blacksburg, Virginia, that could be replicated in other similar towns and rural areas in the United States.

References

Almond, G., & Verba, S. (1963). *The civic culture: Political attitudes and democracy in five nations*. Princeton, NJ: Princeton University Press.

Arnett Muldrow and Associates. (2007). *Downtown market assessment and marketing plan for town of blacksburg*. Greenville, SC: Arnett Muldrow and Associates.

Arterton, F. (1987). *Teledemocracy: Can technology protect democracy?* Newbury Park, CA: Sage.

Bandura, A. (1997). *Self-efficacy: The exercise of control*. New York: Freeman.

Bandura, A. (2002). Growing primacy of human agency in adaptation and change in the electronic era. *European Psychologist, 7*(1), 2–16.

Bimber, B. (2003). *Information and American democracy: Technology in the evolution of political power*. New York: Cambridge University Press.

Brady, H. (1999). Political participation. In J. Robinson, P. Shaver, & L. Wrightsman (Eds.), *Measures of political attitudes* (pp. 737–801). San Diego, CA: Academic Press.

Carroll, H. M., & Rosson, M. B. 2001. *More home shopping or new democracy? Evaluating community network outcomes.* Proceedings of CHI '01, Seattle, WA, March 31–April 5, 2001 (pp. 372–379), New York: ACM Press.

Carroll, J. M., & Reese, D. (2003). *Community collective efficacy: Structure and consequences of perceived capacities in the Blacksburg Electronic Village.* Hawaii international conference on system sciences, HICSS-36, January 6–9, Kona.

Carroll, J. M., Rosson, M. B., Kavanaugh, A., Dunlap, D., Schafer, W., Snook, J. et al. (2006). Social and civic participation in a community network. In R. Kraut, M. Brynin, & S. Kiesler (Eds.), *Computers, phones, and the internet: Domesticating information technologies* (pp. 168–183). New York: Oxford University Press.

Chadwick, A. (2006). *Internet politics: States, citizens and new communication technologies.* New York: Oxford University Press.

Cohill, A. & Kavanaugh, A. (Eds.). (1997). *Community networks: Lessons from Blacksburg, Virginia* (1st Ed.). Norwood, MA: Artech House.

Coleman, S. & Gotz, J. (2002). Bowling together: Online public engagement in policy deliberation. Available from http://bowlingtogether.net

Coleman, S., Morrison, D., & Svennevig, M. (2006). *New media use and political efficacy.* Paper presented at the tenth anniversary international symposium on information, communication and society, September 20–22, York, England.

Dahl, R. (1991). *Democracy and its critics.* New Haven, CT: Yale University Press.

Dahlberg, L. (2001). The internet and democratic discourse: Exploring the prospects of online deliberative forums extending the public sphere. *Information, Communication & Society, 4*(4), 615–633.

Fox, S. (2006). *Bloggers: A portrait of the internet's new storytellers.* Washington, DC: Pew Internet & American Life Project. Retrieved from http://www.pewinternet.org

Girgensohn, A., & Lee, A. (2002). *Making websites be places for social interaction.* In Proceedings of CSCW'02 (pp. 136–145). New York: ACM Press.

Godara, J. (2007). *Knowledge sharing in self-organizing social systems: A comparative analysis of weblogs and centralized discussion forums.* Master's thesis. Department of Industrial Systems and Engineering, Virginia Tech.

Herring, S. C., Kouper, I., Paolillo, J. C., Scheidt, L. A., Tyworth, M., Welsch, P. et al. (2005). *Conversations in the blogosphere: An analysis 'from the bottom up'.* Proceedings of the thirty-eighth Hawaii International Conference on System Sciences (HICSS-38). Los Alamitos, CA: IEEE Press.

Horrigan, J., Garrett, K., & Resnick, P. (2004). *The internet and democratic debate.* Pew Internet & American Life Project. Retrieved from http://www.pewinternet.org

Katz, E. (1987). Communications research since Lazarsfeld. *Public Opinion Quarterly, 51*, 525–545.

Katz, E., & Lazarsfeld, P. (1955). *Personal influence: The part played by people in the flow of mass communications.* New York: The Free Press.

Kavanaugh, A. (2003). When everyone's wired: Use of the Internet for networked communities. In J. Turow & A. Kavanaugh (Eds.), *The wired homestead: An MIT Press sourcebook on the internet and the family* (pp. 423–437). Cambridge, MA: MIT Press.

Kavanaugh, A., Carroll, J. M., Rosson, M. B., Reese, D. D., & Zin, T. T. (2005). Participating in civil society: The case of networked communities. *Interacting with Computers, 17*, 9–33.

Kavanaugh, A., Carroll, J. M., Rosson, M. B., Zin, T. T., & Reese, D. D. (2005). Community networks: Where offline communities meet online. *Journal of Computer-Mediated Communication, 10*(4). Retrieved from http://jcmc.indiana.edu/vol10/issue4/kavanaugh.html

Kavanaugh, A., Cohill, A., & Patterson, S. (2000). The use and impact of the Blacksburg Electronic Village. In A. Cohill & A. Kavanaugh (Eds.), *Community networks: Lessons from Blacksburg, Virginia* (Revised Ed., pp. 77–98). Norwood, MA: Artech House.

Kavanaugh, A., Isenhour, P., Cooper, M., Carroll, J. M., Rosson, M. B., & Schmitz, J. (2005). Information technology in support of public deliberation. In P. van den Besselaar, G. de Michelis, J. Preece, & C. Simone (Eds.), *Communities and Technologies 2005* (pp. 19–40), Dordrecht: Kluwer Academic Publishers.

Kavanaugh, A., Kim, H. N., Pérez-Quiñones, M., & Isenhour, P. (2007). Models of government blogging: Design trade-offs in civic participation. In C. Steinfield, B. Pentland, M. Ackerman, & N. Contractor (Eds.), *Proceedings of the third communities and technologies conference*, East Lansing, MI, June 28–30 (pp. 419–438). Surrey: Springer.

Kavanaugh, A., Kim, B. J., Pérez-Quiñones, M., Schmitz, J., & Isenhour, P. (2006). *Net gains in political participation: Secondary effects of internet on community*. Paper presented at the tenth anniversary international symposium on information, communication and society, September 20–22, York, England.

Kavanaugh, A., Kim, B. J., Schmitz, J., & Pérez-Quiñones, M. (2008). Net gains in political participation: Secondary effects of the Internet on community. *Information, Communication and Society, 11*(7), 933–963.

Kavanaugh, A., & Patterson, S. (2001). The impact of community computer networks on social capital and community involvement. *American Behavioral Scientist, 45*(3), 496–509.

Kavanaugh, A., Reese, D. D., Carroll, J. M., & Rosson, M. B. (2003). Weak ties in networked communities. In M. Huysman, E. Wenger, & V. Wulf (Eds.) *Communities and technologies* (pp. 265–286). Dordrecht: Kluwer Academic Publishers (Reprinted in 2005 in *The Information Society, 21*(2), 119–131).

Kavanaugh, A., Rosson, M. B., Carroll, J. M., & Zin, T. T. (2006). The impact of the Internet on local and distant social ties. In P. Purcell (Ed.), *The networked neighborhood: The online community in context* (pp. 217–236). Surrey: Springer.

Kavanaugh, A., & Schmitz, J. (2004). Talking in lists: The consequences of computer mediated communication on communities. *Internet Research Annual, 1*, 250–259.

Kavanaugh, A., Zin, T. T., Carroll, J. M., Schmitz, J., Pérez-Quiñones, M., & Isenhour, P. (2006). *When opinion leaders Blog: New forms of citizen interaction*. ACM international conference proceeding series, 2006 international conference on Digital Government Research 151, San Diego, CA, May 22–24 (pp. 79–88). New York: ACM Press.

Kavanaugh, A., Zin, T. T., Rosson, M. B., Carroll, J. M., & Schmitz, J. (2007, September). Local groups online: Political learning and participation. *Journal of Computer Supported Cooperative Work, 16*, 375–395.

Keller, E., & Berry, J. (2003). *The influentials*. New York: The Free Press.

Kim, A. J. (2000). *Community building on the web*. Berkeley, CA: Peachpit Press.

Kim, B. J., Kavanaugh, A., & Hult, K. (2006). Local community groups and internet use. *Journal of Knowledge, Technology and Society*. Available from http://www.ijt.cgpublisher.com

Kim, H. N., Kavanaugh, A., & Smith-Jackson, T. (2007). *Implementation of internet technology for local government website: Design guidelines*. Proceedings of HICSS-40, Waikoloa, Hawaii, January 3–6.

Kim, J., Wyatt, R., & Katz, E. (1999). News, talk, opinion, participation: The part played by conversation in deliberative democracy. *Political Communication, 16*(4), 361–385.

Kollock, P. (1998). Design principles for online communities. *PC Update, 15*(5), 58–60. Available from http://www.sscnet.ucla.edu/soc/faculty/kollock/papers/design.htm

Larsen, E., & Rainie, L. (2002). Digital town hall. Pew Internet & American Life Project. Available from http://www.pewinternet.org

Lave, J., & Wenger, E. (1990). *Situated learning: Legitimate peripheral participation*. New York: Cambridge University Press.

Marlow, C., Naaman, M., Boyd, D., & Davis, M. (2006). HT06, tagging paper, taxonomy, flickr, academic article, to read. In *Proceedings of HT'06* (pp. 31–39). New York: ACM Press.

Michaelson, M. (2000). Political efficacy and electoral participation of Chicago Latinos. *Social Science Quarterly, 81*(1), 136–150.

Milbrath, L., & Goel, M. (1977). *Political participation: Why and how do people get involved in politics?* Lanham, MD: University Press of America.

Nardi, B. (2004). Why we blog. *Communications of the ACM, 47*(12), 41–46.

Norris, P. (2001). *Digital divide: Civic engagement, information poverty and the internet.* New York: Cambridge University Press.

Patterson, S., & Kavanaugh, A. (1994, November). Rural users' expectations of the information superhighway. *Media Information Australia, 74*, 57–61.

Perkins, D., Brown, B., & Taylor, R. (1996). The ecology of empowerment: Predicting participation in community organizations. *Journal of Social Issues, 52*(1), 85–110.

Preece, J. (2000). *Online communities: Designing usability, supporting sociability.* London: Wiley.

Rainie, L. (2005). The state of blogging. Pew Internet and American life project. Available from http://www.pewinternet.org/PPF/r/144/report_display.asp

Rainie, L., & Horrigan, J. (2007). Election 2006 Online. Pew Internet & American Life. Retrieved from http://www.pewinternet.org

Rogers, E. (1986). *Communication of innovation.* New York: The Free Press.

Rogers, E. (1995). *Diffusion of innovation* (5th Ed.). New York: Simon and Schuster.

Rogers, E., & Shoemaker, F. (1971). *Communication of innovations* (2nd Ed.). New York: The Free Press.

Schmitz, J., Rogers, E., Phillips, K., & Paschal, D. (1995). The public electronic network (PEN) and homeless in Santa Monica. *Journal of Applied Communication Research, 23*(1), 26–43.

Schudson, M. (1992, Fall). The limits of teledemocracy. *The American Prospect*, 41–45.

Schudson, M. (1997). Why conversation is not the soul of democracy. *Critical Studies in Mass Communication, 14*, 297–309.

Schuler, D. (1996). *New community networks: Wired for change.* New York: ACM Press.

Shane, P. (Ed.). 2006. *Democracy online: Prospects for political renewal through the internet.* New York: Routledge.

Tedesco, J. C. (2006). Web interactivity and young adult political efficacy. In A. P. Williams & J. C. Tedesco (Eds.), *The internet election: Perspectives of the web in campaign 2004* (pp. 187–202). Lanham, MD: Rowman & Littlefield.

Tedesco, J. C. (2007). Examining Internet interactivity effects on young adults political information efficacy. *American Behavioral Scientist, 50*(9), 1183–1194.

Verba, S., & Nie, N. (1972). Participation in America: Political democracy and social equality. New York: Harper Row.

Verba, S., Schlozman, K., & Brady, H. (1995). *Voice and equality: Civic voluntarism in American politics.* Cambridge, MA: Harvard University Press.

Williams, A. P., & Tedesco, J. C. (2006). *The internet election: Perspectives on the web in campaign 2004.* Lanham, MD: Rowman & Littlefield.

"The Legal Bit's in Russian": Making Sense of Downloaded Music

Marjorie D. Kibby

Introduction

Consumers of music from online sources have a number of options. Free tracks are legally available from musicians' websites, or as samples from music stores, or tracks can be made available illegally by users who do not hold the copyright, through file-sharing or music blogs. Music files can be purchased by subscription or per track from a range of online music stores including major retailers and independent labels. Each method of acquiring music has its relative disadvantages in terms of cost, convenience, quality or legality.

Russian sites offering very cheap music files from topline artists have been in existence for some time but have become increasingly popular as peer-to-peer file sharing has become seemingly legally risky and morally reprehensible, and legitimate purchasing has become increasingly restricted by digital rights management technologies.

Users of the Russian sites seem to negotiate a position for themselves which allows them to download with impunity, making sense of the services within the specific framework of their personal experiences and cultural environment. The positioning of the Russian download sites as both legal and moral is the result of the presentation strategies of the sites and of the sensemaking processes that users apply to a music source that lies conveniently between legal/costly and illegal/free.

The best known of the Russian music sites is *allofmp3*, a site that was second only to iTunes as the most used download site for United Kingdom digital music buyers in 2006 (Smith, 2006). Other popular Russian sites include *GoMusic* and *MP3 Sugar*. On *allofmp3* many of the tracks are stored as uncompressed files, and the site encodes each track in the format the user wants at the preferred bit rate, and charges a fee according to the resultant bandwidth requirements. The better quality the song, the more expensive it is. Individual tracks cost AU

M.D. Kibby (✉)
School of Humanities and Social Science, The University of Newcastle, Callaghan, Australia
e-mail: marj.kibby@newcastle.edu.au

\$ 0.05–0.20. *MP3 Sugar* and *GoMusic* have similar-sized music collections and a similar price at around 10 cents per track and \$1 per album. All three have extensive collections of artists whose work is not available from other pay-for-download sites.

To come to an understanding of how the users of these sites make sense of the services in terms of their understanding of copyright, international reach of national laws, user rights to music ownership, the music industry as a provider of consumer wants and moral obligations to creative artists, a qualitative study was undertaken. In the first part of the study a textual analysis revealed the information given on the sites, and the impressions given off by them. The sites were analysed to determine the major signifying elements and to make an educated guess at some of the most likely interpretations that might be made of those elements. In the second part of the study, Technorati (a blog tracking service) and del.icio.us (a social bookmarks manager) were used to locate publicly available online texts where the use of Russian download sites was discussed during 2005 and 2006. These texts included weblogs, discussion forums, and services such as Digg where readers could respond to posted articles. The texts were examined for evidence of sensemaking in relation to the download sites, and the strategies used were culled from the texts, labelled and grouped.

File Sharing

> *I download music because I'm used to it. When file-sharing programs first appeared, there weren't any major lawsuits or copyright-infringement accusations. Our generation grew up with file-sharing as a way of life; it seemed to be the only logical, sensible, and easy way to acquire music.* Posted to *The Vanderbilt Torch* by lbidikov on November 7, 2005.

File sharing was one of the original civilian applications of the internet, where through file transfer protocols users could access databases such as *Archie* to search for various different kinds of filenames. With the popularisation of compressed file formats such as MP3 in the mid-1990s, and the development of peer-to-peer software, file sharing became easily available to the average internet user.

Napster became the first major peer-to-peer file-sharing tool with an estimated 26.4 million unique users at the height of its popularity (Jupiter Media Metrix, 2001). It was a localized index of MP3 files available to the users logged into the system, with the facility for chat and instant messaging. Following highly publicised criticism and legal action by the RIAA and artists such as Metallica and Dr Dre, Napster was finally shut down as a file-sharing service. However, new services were developed using a decentralized network, and today a variety of file-sharing programs are available on several different networks, with a range of features.

In September 2003, the RIAA began filing civil lawsuits against computer users uploading copyright protected music files. The highly publicised actions seem to have led to a greater awareness of issues of anonymity and privacy in file-sharing systems and may have dissuaded potential users from less secure applications. Publicity campaigns describing illegal downloading as stealing may also have encouraged music consumers to think about copyright issues for the first time and to make moral judgements on file downloading. And while the enormous number of files available on peer-to peer networks would seem to offer an advantage, in reality "with the number of duplicates, files with names that make no sense, files that cannot be downloaded, corrupt files and files with a bitrate of less than 128, the number of successful downloads is much smaller than the number of search results" (Bakker, 2005, p. 52). The growth in the number of peer-to-peer systems was also accompanied by an increase in advertising software, such as spyware or adware, which could interfere with the operation of web browsers and cause degraded system performance. Combined with the difficulty for novice users to find the files that they wanted and the distribution of potentially offensive material including pornography and racist literature, these problems have led to a level of dissatisfaction with peer-to-peer file sharing, just at a time when legal downloads have become widely available.

There is some evidence that people are less drawn to illegal file-sharing and are instead adopting legal ways of enjoying music online. Whether it's a recognition of artist's rights, dissatisfaction with the services, the fear of getting caught breaking the law, or the realization that many applications could damage the home computer, attitudes towards peer-to-peer downloads are changing (IFPI, 2005). Peer-to-peer file sharing seems to have plateaued as other music acquisition options have grown.

Legal Downloads

Occasionally, I was beset with pangs of guilt about not financially supporting the music I enjoyed and would have to visit the Terms of Service at any digitally restricted music (backcronym for DRM) store to remind myself why I didn't buy music online. Posted to *Change is Good* by Siddiq Bello on March 21st, 2006

Legal downloads are available from a range of online sources. In Australia these include Apple iTunes, Creative Music Store, Destra Music.com, MP3.com.au and Telstra Big Pond Music. iTunes features an impressive number of tracks from both local and international artists, at AU $1.69 per song, AU $16.99 per album. Files can only be downloaded in Fairplay-protected AAC format, and while they can be transferred to an unlimited number of iPods there are restrictions on burning to compact disk. Creative Music Store has similar pricing and restrictions, encouraging the use of Creative music players. Destra Music's site, one of the first in Australia to offer paid music downloads, also powers the online music stores of several leading Australian retailers, including Leading Edge, JB Hi Fi, Sanity and more. Destra allows users to burn a song up to three times onto CD and to transfer it to three portable music players that can play licensed WMA files – for AU $1.89 per song or AU $18.95 per album. With 600,000 songs BigPond has one of the biggest song lists of the Australian online stores, it is also one of the most expensive unless users have a Big Pond internet account, and the most restrictive with the computer downloaded to being the only one that can play the track. Users can copy the song an unlimited number of times to up to two portable music players. MP3.com.au is the cheapest source with fewest restrictions but the music is primarily from unsigned, unknown artists.

The international recording industry reports that illegal file-sharing of music is being kept in check while the number of legal tracks downloaded internationally tripled to 180 million in the first half of 2005. While there has been no significant decrease in the use of peer-to-peer systems to illegally share files, there has been an increase in digital music sales, which now represent approximately 6% of overall music sales worldwide (IFPI, 2006).

Russian File Download Sites

I'm not new to mp3 download sites as at one time had several thousand house music files on my pc. I got rid of it all and have started to buy legal music. What I want to know is how legal is this site as the legality bit at the bottom is in Russian. Posted to *MP3Talks.com* by Jago on 6 April 2006

Russian websites have been selling music via the internet since 2001, but have become increasingly popular in the last 2 years as American and UK downloaders look for sources other than peer-to-peer file sharing. A representative of the best known of these sites, Allofmp3, says the site targets Russian citizens inside and outside of Russia and explains that the English language version was developed for ease of access on computers outside of Russia (Vara, 2005). However, discussion forum posts suggest that significant numbers of users are from outside Russia, and Allofmp3 is "second only to iTunes as the favoured destination of UK digital music buyers during April 2006, figures from UK-based market watcher XTN Data reveal" (Smith, 2006).

Russian copyright laws enabled agencies that were members of the Russian Authors' Society to be licensed for the "collective management" of property rights of authors, signing contracts on their behalf with businesses without the prior agreement of the copyright holder. ROMS, the Russian Multimedia and internet Society entered into agreements with Allofmp3 and other download sites on behalf of Russian and international artists, without consultation, as allowed. ROMS was obliged to collect fees from the users of copyright material, but to pay royalties to only those artists who actively pursued payment. The provisions of Russian law meant that agencies could grant the use of any copyrighted work regardless of whether the original copyright holder had given permission and need not necessarily distribute fees for the use of the music (Mertens, 2005).

Another aspect of Russian copyright law that allowed copyrighted material to be distributed on music sites without permission or royalties is the ruling that "communication of the phonogram to the public by cable" shall be allowed without the consent of the copyright holders. Uploading to the web for downloading by consumers is seen as the same as broadcasting. Without a physical product copyright does not apply (Mertens, 2005). Russian copyright law does not cover digital media as the provision of a music file on a website does not constitute the creation of a "copy" of the original work.

Russia's membership of the World Trade Organization is contingent on compliance with the WTO's Multilateral Trade Agreements including the Trade Related Aspects of Intellectual Property, and changes have been made to Russian law as a consequence. One important provision came into effect in September 2006, recognising the rights of the copyright holders to decide how a work would be communicated to the public and whether or not it would be distributed via the internet. However, changes in law are easier to bring about than changes in attitude. Russia has been on the United States Trade Representative's Priority Watch List for intellectual property violations for nine straight years without showing any significant signs of improvement (Watson, 2006). With the threshold for criminal violation leaving many infringers outside the scope of criminal prosecution, fine amounts that are too low to be a deterrent, the confiscation of copies but not equipment or profits, investigations by overworked prosecutors not police, a requirement that the copyright holder must make a formal complaint before any action can be taken, and the fact that Russia has no real history of intellectual property rights or their protection and there is a level of resentment against the west (Mertens, 2005), it is unlikely that the "loophole" that makes music downloads available without the costs and restrictions of iTunes and Big Pond Music will be closed in the near future.

Making Sense of Russian Download Sites

Russian sites are legal in Russia, doesn't mean they are legal in the UK. There's this whole, sorta meek, 'what can I get away with' vibe going on here. Legal grey areas need to be navigated by an individual's moral compass. Posted to *Alex Moskalyuk Online* blog April 23rd 2006

The discussion of the Russian music download sites on online forums suggests that users are trying to make sense of these sites in a way that allows them a morally acceptable alternative to illegal free downloads and expensive, restrictive paid downloads. Research into sense-making sees it as a behaviour with both internal (i.e. cognitive) and external (e.g. procedural) elements which allows an individual to design and construct their movements through unfamiliar time and space (Dervin, 1983, p. 3). According to Dervin, "sensemaking" is more than acquiring knowledge, it is a process of bringing to bear on a new situation a host of subjective factors including intuitions, opinions, personal experiences, evaluations and emotions. While individuals exist within systems of institutions and cultures and are informed by these systems, they are not completely constrained by them as each individual navigates their own route through social structures. Social, cultural, legal and economic formations provide a general framework within which individuals make sense of their world in terms of the personal (Dervin & Clark, 2003).

In deciding whether they can personally justify downloading music from the Russian sites, visitors seem to follow a process of extraction, or gathering information from the download sites; fusion, where this information is combined with information from other sources including personal experience and the opinions of others; and re-encoding, or transforming the information to fit new schemata.

Through this sense-making process individuals create an understanding of the websites which enable them to act in a manner that they can believe is informed and principled.

The information gathered from sites such as Allofmp3 suggests a highly professional organization. From the catalogue to the order and payment mechanism to the downloading software it is well written and competently presented. The site design is streamlined, with sparse graphics and clear navigation. Currently there is just a discreet link to a Russian version, whereas on previous iterations of the sites, visitors had to negotiate a significant amount of Russian and poor-English text. The range of popular music is vast, and the quality of the music is at least the equal of anything available online. A detailed site map, and links to help files, terms of use, privacy policy and legal information, all give the impression of a legitimate business presence. Links to collections of music associated with international awards and charts such as MTV charts and the 40th Annual Country Music Awards also contribute to the impression of legitimacy. Until recently the legal information was in Russian.

Using a translation site the legal jargon that appears in Russian translates to the following... To entire phonograms and work are in accordance with the current legislation of the Russian Federation. In particular on the basis: Law about the copyright and the adjacent rights ... Posted to *MP3Talks* on 10 April 2006.

Currently there is detailed, if not particularly readable, information on Russian copyright law, including a FAQ answering a question on the site's legality. The lengthy legalese explains that the site adheres to Russian laws, but that users should refer to "the national legislation in each user's country of residence" (Allofmp3 Legal Info). The site also states that, "All third party distributors licensed by ROMS are required to pay a portion of the revenue to the ROMS. ROMS in turn, is obligated to pay most of that money (aside from small portion it needs for operating expenses) to artists, both Russian and foreign", without mentioning that ROMS was expelled from the Russian Authors' Society in 2004 and is no longer entitled to issue licences for the use of copyright works in Russia and that no mechanism exists for the transfer of royalties to foreign copyright holders. GoMusic has a brief statement under "Copyrights" saying that "All phonograms on GoMusic.Ru are placed in accordance with Noncommercial Partnership 'Federation of Authors and Rightsholders for Collective Management of Copyright in Interactive Regime'". Both GoMusic's short statement and Allofmp3's lengthier explanation suggest that downloading is probably both legal and moral, without giving unequivocal assurances.

I started using allofmp3 last week. I signed up with paypal then used that to pay xrost. Took about 10 minutes to sign up to both and get going. Not worried about xrost if I am using paypal to pay them. Posted to *Whirlpool Forum* on 5 August 2005.

Most of the Russian music sites have an account system where the user pays upwards of $10 into an account, and then purchases items against that account. Payment methods vary, but are generally systems that online purchasers would be familiar with. Allofmp3 accepts credit cards and has an image of Mastercard and Visa. Payment options seem to change, with one card or another not being accepted at various times. In mid-October 2006 Visa and Mastercard both announced that they would no longer deal with AllofMP3, to reflect "legislation passed in Russia and with basic international copyright and intellectual property norms" (Cullen, 2006). In response, the Russian company said the blacklisting was "arbitrary, capricious and discriminatory" as Visa and Mastercard had no authority to judge the legality of AllofMP3's services, and "AllofMP3 has not been found by any court in the world to be in violation of any law..." (Cullen, 2006). Users can still fund their purchases with Mastercard and Visa credit cards by way of third-party systems. Allofmp3 did accept the prepaid Xrost iCard which can be purchased using PayPal or Chronopay. This facility was removed in February 2007, though some consumers found a workaround. GoMusic and other sites that do not operate solely on a ROMS licence can process payments directly via the Dutch Chronopay system. Paypal and Chronopay accounts can be funded through major credit cards. Allofmp3 is the only Russian download site that seems affected by the credit card blacklisting. Australian users can pay AllofMP3 using SMS credits, and although the album cost is then $5.00 most users would pay something like $30.00 for $120.00 of credits prepaid, so the actual cost is reduced. The Optus/Telstra connection also adds legitimacy to the purchase.

I click "SMS order", and a window pops up with the instructions. I have to SMS a number, and then 20 seconds later I get a code SMSed back to me. It turns out I was actually charged $5 + the cost of a regular SMS, so $5.25 in total. I don't mind too much. The actual cost for me was a quarter of this, since my prepaid credit is 4 times the real money that I pay. Posted to *Tech-babble* blog on 11 April 2006.

There is information on the download sites that may give the impression that the sites are not strictly legitimate. This information includes the price of the tracks, and the implication that users can upload files for credit. The prices are justified by an explanation that users pay for the download service, not for the tracks themselves. On Allofmp3, the music files are referred to as "data" and "information" and the fees paid are for the downloading service provided – "The users pay for Services" (Allofmp3 Help). BPI, the British record industry's trade association, believes that music fans for the most part choose to ignore why the music is on sale so cheaply at these sites (Sheppard, 2006); however, the price can be justified by the belief that it is only a service that is being paid for, not the music itself.

Read the fine print. You are only paying for the download service! Not for the music! So they don't have to pay royalties. ... Posted to MP3Talks by soulxtc on 10 April 2006.

The information that users can upload files to Allofmp3 is found under Contact Us, where there is a line: "Questions on placement of audio information on the site" and an email address. The location of this information and the way that it is expressed would mean that most site users would be unaware that files can be uploaded from their own collections, and therefore would probably not use this information in determining the legality of the site.

I just uploaded a flac album to allopmp3 so I'll be getting credit - $27.72 exchange bonus Posted to *Zeropaid News* forum by shawners on 13/06/2006
I didn't realize you could get credit if you upload to allofmp3.com Posted to *Zeropaid News* forum by Jorge on 13/06/2006

Information gathered from other sources is similarly conflicting. Young people today have grown up in a culture where the product is almost immaterial. While Walter Benjamin was concerned with the aesthetic limitations of the copy, in contemporary society it is often the copy that has cachet, and downloading files from Allofmp3 provides a level of cultural capital that purchasing from Walmart cannot. There is a "relationship between new technology and a value system that seems shaped to it" (Leland, 2003) and digital technology has led to a devaluing of music in a physical form.

BPI gained permission from the UK courts to sue Allofmp3 for copyright infringement; however, the District Court of Moscow declined to press charges. At the same time the American record industry managed to propel Allofmp3 onto the agenda of the G8 economic conference in St Petersburg in 2006, with the US delegates pressing for the shutdown Allofmp3 as a demonstration of Russian respect for worldwide intellectual property rights. However, the G8 chose not to issue a public proclamation on Russian download sites specifically, instead releasing a statement on the need to combat piracy and counterfeiting of intellectual property (G8 Russia, 2006). Both events were covered extensively in the press and while the issues of copyright holders' rights were covered, the final outcomes seemed to give the go-ahead for continued trading by the Russian download sites.

On 18 October, 2006 Allofmp3 announced the launch of its "Music for Masses" program. According to their press release Allofmp3 users who choose the "Music of Masses" program can pick all the songs they wish from the huge Allofmp3 catalogue and listen to them for free. Some restrictions apply: users can only access the music through the provided software (which translates the custom DRM these songs are bundled with) on one computer; they must be connected to the internet during playback, so that advertisements can be streamed to them; and if users want to transfer these songs to an MP3 player or burn to CD, they have to pay a fee for standard DRM-free versions. However, this modification failed to placate the RIAA, and in December 2006, the RIAA, on behalf of the major labels, filed a US $1.65 trillion lawsuit against AllofMP3 (*USA Today*, 2006). Allofmp3's response to the lawsuit was, "AllofMP3 understands that several U.S. record label companies filed a lawsuit against Media Services in New York. This suit is unjustified as AllofMP3 does not operate in New York. Certainly the labels are free to file any suit they wish, despite knowing full well that AllofMP3 operates legally in Russia. In the mean time, AllofMP3 plans to continue to operate legally and comply with all Russian laws"(Mennecke, 2006).

The Russian legal system continued to support the music sites' operations. A Moscow court ruled in July 2007 that Visa's decision to cut off payments to allTunes was unlawful, and Denis Kvasov, head of the company which owned AllofMP3.com, was acquitted of all charges stemming from a copyright infringement prosecution brought by Russian Prosecutors in what was seen as a test case. AllofMP3, however, became a music news site in mid-2007 and the operators established MP3Sparkes.com, transferring consumer's usernames and account balances to the new site. A number of other sites also opened offering "alternatives to AllofMP3".

News coverage of the Russian download sites generally seems to provide ambivalent or ambiguous information on their legal status. An article in the Sydney Morning Herald, after discussing how the prices imply digital burglary, said that "We can't see any legal or moral objection to using the site" (Wright, 2004), while a New York Times article discussed the Russian legal loophole that facilitates a service that would otherwise be illegal (Crampton, 2006).

Most of the information available on the legality or otherwise of Russian music download sites comes from other users on blogs and discussion forums. Sensemaking is a social process (Resnick, Levine, & Teasly, 1991), which unfolds as a conversational exchange of information and opinion while a sense of order is gradually constructed around changing circumstances through the social process of interpretation and adaptation. This process is evident in the online discussions, where users attempt to make sense of systems of copyright and royalty payments and to uncover who benefited from the payment of the fee on the download sites.

> *I don't want to give my money to some Russian guys that abuse the law. I'd rather download it off some p2p-network instead. The only reason I buy songs is that the artists get money, which isn't the case for allofmp3.* Posted to digg – Russian MP3 sales site AllofMP3.com second only to iTunes by noof on 12 May 2006.

> *Allofmp3 pays everything they are legally required to pay to ROMS (the Russian equivalent to the RIAA).* Posted to *digg – Russian MP3 sales site AllofMP3.com second only to iTunes* by Inxaddct on 12 May 2006.

> *Now don't feed me any of that ROMS crap, since my artist friends haven't seen a single check from ROMS.* Posted to *digg – Russian MP3 sales site AllofMP3.com second only to iTunes* by redcard on 12 May 2006.

> *It's my understanding that allofmp3 does pay royalties based on Russian law. They consider the playing of the song over the Internet a "performance" and they pay the songwriters some set fee.* Posted to *digg – Russian MP3 sales site AllofMP3.com second only to iTunes* by dognose on 12 May 2006.

The ideas expressed in these forums are a fusion of experiences, assumptions, intuitions and value judgements. Digital technologies and networked communications are transforming the experience of music in ways that have the potential to reconfigure the relations between music producers, distributors and consumers. By making it possible to record, store, copy, edit and transmit sound files of good to high quality via the internet – in ways that are relatively easy and affordable – these new technologies should allow creators and consumers alike to share in a frictionless "arena of exchange in which everyone wins" (McCourt & Burkart, 2003, p. 334). In fact, however, restrictive policies have developed rapidly in response to initiatives by music industry representatives, creating legal regimes and marketplace economics that limit access by consumers and enhance profits for music distributors (McCourt & Burkart, 2003).

Music consumers have witnessed changes in the music industry that support a belief that recordings and the right to profit from recordings are owned by the companies that finance and market them, not the artists that produced them. There has also been a significant increase in the apparent aggressive protection of profits by the record companies and a highly litigious approach to the safeguard of distribution rights. And, while music production and distribution costs have decreased, the cost to the consumer has grown as record companies increased their profit margins to accommodate declining sales (McCourt & Burkart, 2003, p. 340). Digital music is widely available on a pay-per-download basis, but in many cases it is more expensive than the physical product. The music consumer might well feel that they are paying more and getting less.

Digital rights management technologies (DRM) control the way in which digital music can be accessed and used. Encryption, watermarking, metadata and other technologies place limits on how users can listen to the music files they have purchased and on how they can copy, distribute or modify them. DRM technologies are "being implemented and enforced in a way that overrides the legal rules set by copyright law" (Noguchi, 2006 p. 9) denying users' rights to fair-dealing and other non-infringing uses of copyrighted material. DRM has disturbed what was a "reasonably legitimate politico-legal settlement over 'fair-use', challenging the existing balance between the rights of 'creators' and the interests of users" (May, 2003, p. 1). The types of music use that was once covered by "fair-use" have continued; music consumers still time-shift, format-shift, and copy as back-up and not-for-profit distribution, "but it is now seen as a political blow against a set of private interests that are not regarded as legitimate" (May, 2003, p. 19).

Contemporary music consumers live in culture that values cutting, pasting, cloning, sampling, quoting, airbrushing, customizing, recycling and re-circulating. Djs, bloggers, the cloners of designer labels, political report writers and student plagiarists alike follow Nike's example to acquire product as cheaply as possible and add their own signature (Leland, 2003). Within a copy/paste society the internet reinforces the "deep cultural belief that information is, legitimately, copyable and redistributable. Copying is . . . a defining, multifaceted feature of Internet behaviour and culture" (Allen, 2003 p. 26). As a consequence, music file downloaders do not think of their actions as stealing music, they look at it as creating a personalized music product, something that cannot be purchased.

Digitized music has also led to "a desire for a sort of musical 'affluence' where the size and currency of the collection is valued, rather than the constituent components of the collection" (Kibby, 2003 p.1). Collections of 1000–2000 music files are common, taking up 5–10 GB of storage space (*BBC News*, 2004). There is cultural capital to be gained in having not only an extensive collection of music files but also an up-to-date collection with new tunes added on (or before) the track's official release date.

The combination of the factors, a free exchange mindset; a culture of copying; an increase in cost and decrease in functionality of paid-for music files; increasing litigation against illegal file-sharing and increasing disadvantages associated with shared files; and a desire for large, current music collections, leave users looking for cheap, reliable, legal alternatives, predisposed to make sense of the Russian music download sites in these terms. In order to re-encode what they know about these sites, the users seem to employ both values about right and wrong and expectations of consequences.

Legal and/or Ethical

The use of deontological norms and teleological principles is the basis of ethical decision making, and consumer research shows that consumers rely on both ethical norms (deontology) and perceived consequences of behaviours (teleology) in forming their moral judgements and in determining their behaviour in situations involving ethical issues (Vitell, Singhapakdi, & Thomas, 2001). Where the consumer actively seeks an advantage, where the activity could be perceived as illegal, and where some direct harm could result then there is a difficulty in rationalizing the behaviour as ethical (Muncy & Vitell, 1992). Cohn and Vacarro explain that in these situations "it was expected that consumers would employ neutralization techniques to assuage the guilt in the unethical acquisition" (2006, p. 71).

As the music consumer is actively seeking out Russian downloads where the price per track implies that the service cannot be totally legal, and the disclaimers on the sites leave the impression that non-Russian copyright holders will receive little or nothing in the way of royalties, it would be difficult to come to the conclusion that downloading from the sites is ethical, without an elaborate sense-making process that re-encodes these factors.

One of the most apparent neutralization techniques in postings on Russian downloads is that of "condemn the condemners" (Cohn & Vaccaro, 2006, p. 72) where downloaders shift blame for their activity to those most critical of their actions, the record companies.

> *The amount of money artists make per CD is usually less than $.05 per CD, with the RIAA/Label taking a cut of 80%.* Posted to *digg – Russian MP3 sales site AllofMP3.com second only to iTunes* by themack on 15 July 2006.

> *The pigopolist record companies don't like it because it cuts them out of the loop.* Posted to *Alex Moskalyuk Online* blog by Alice 28 March 2006

> *I am quite sure that Allofmp3 doesn't pay much, if anything, in royalties, and this is what gives me a twinge of guilt when I download an album from them that I have not previously purchased, but I know times have changed and the music business has to change with the times and technology. The current arrangement is just not working.* Posted to *White Man Stew* blog by Patrick Crossley 27 May 2006

> *The "music industry" doesn't need to make more money.* Posted to *MP3Talks* forum by Lyph4 on 13 April 2006.

Another neutralization technique that appears frequently is that of "denial of responsibility" (Cohn & Vaccaro, 2006, p. 72) where downloaders rationalize their use of the Russian music sites by believing that they are doing no more than they are entitled to do.

> *I was looking for an album "the hunting of the snark' by Mike Batt. I own it on vinyl, but don't have a record player, hence wanted an MP3 – which I reckon I have a right to.* Posted to *Whirlpool* discussion forum by DisasterArea on 7 August 2006.

> *I use this service because I am willing to buy music at a reasonable price. What I am not willing to do is pay $15+ for a CD.* Posted to *Zeropaid* forums by status quo on 11 April 2006.

Filtering Information

Downloaders' rationalization of their use of the Russian sites is facilitated by a subconscious filtering system. Sensemaking is an ongoing process; as the situation unfolds the individual will continue to abstract cues to assist in making sense of the situation. However, in most situations individuals are faced with too many cues to pick up on them all; they will select a few cues as important, filtering out the others (Weick, 1995, p. 62). The perceptual filters identify the salient information on the basis of immediate context and personal dispositions so that the individual will recognize as cues only those bits of information that mesh with her or his current attitudes and predisposed behaviour patterns. In addition, sensemaking is driven by plausibility rather than accuracy. When people have found a credible answer, they generally stop looking for additional information and no longer consider alternative explanations.

It seems that, for those downloading music from the Russian sites, the primary filter used is an emotional response to recording industry practices. A review of responses to article postings on Slashdot and Plastic, of contributions to forums on technology or music, and of the postings to music blogs reveals that many consumers now view the record industry as the equivalent of the evil empire.

> *The enemy is the music industry, the bloated parasitic slug that owns copyright and controls distribution.* Posted to Plastic DRM + DMCA = FU by Ben on 5 September 2006.

> *DRM provides a moral get-out clause for illegal downloading.* Posted to DRM + DMCA = FU on *Plastic* by cutta on 5 September 2006.

Among the lists of complaints against the industry are restricting releases by arbitrary dates and geographical borders, so that CDs must be bought at import rates of AU $30.00; promoting only a small section of their stable of artists so that less mainstream bands go unknown; selling tracks on the basis of a 30-second sample, which in some genres is still the instrumental introduction; adhering to a 12–15 track, one artist, CD format when consumers want, and technology allows, an editable 2 hour stream of music on a theme; a pricing system that forces consumers to pay repeatedly for the same music in different formats, from live performance to compact disk to music file; and imposing restrictions on how consumers may use the music they have purchased, which often prevents them from using it at all.

As Glen McDonald's open letter to the music industry says,

> *If you try to rely on deliberate obscurity, you will lose. If you bank on valueless repackaging, we will show you another sense of "valueless". If you copy-protect CDs knowing full well that law-abiding listeners want to play them on laptops and iPods and Linux boxes, you precipitate morally correct resentment and defiance. If, with the resources of an entire industry of full-time workers and decades of catalogs and data and precedent, you serve music listeners less well than listeners and their hacked-together tech kludges serve each other, then you are defeated by your own market forces, and by your own market.* Posted to *The War Against Silence* blog by Glen McDonald on 2nd June 2006.

Given that the websites of MP3Sparks GoMusic and MP3Sugar look and feel like legal pay-per-download sites; that they overtly say that they are completely legal inside Russia, and imply that they are legal outside Russia; given that media coverage of the sites uses terms such as "loophole in the law" to explain away the too-good-to-be-true fees for downloading, and publicizes their legality in countries with user-centred copyright laws; given that music consumers believe they are justified in ignoring or rejecting information provided by the recording industry; and given that on the whole the music industry has failed to provide the product that many consumers wish to buy, it is not surprising that consumers downloading from the Russian sites make sense of their actions as both legal and moral.

Personally I use allofmp3 which has an interesting system unlike iTunes, Napster, et al. The songs are DRM-free, you can choose the encoding of the file (ogg, flac, mp3, etc.) and they charge by the megabyte ($.02). Best of all they are legal due to a loophole in Russian copyright law. Posted to DRM + DMCA = FU on *Plastic* by gr3g on 5 September 2006.

References

Allen, M. (2003). Dematerialised data and human desire: The internet and copy culture, Second international conference on cyberworlds (CW'03). Accessed October 18, 2006, from http://doi.ieeecomputersociety.org/10.1109/CYBER.2003.1253431

Bakker, P. (2005). File-sharing – Fight, ignore or compete: Paid download services vs. P2Pnetworks. *Telematics and Informatics, 22,* 41–55.

BBC News. (2004). *Britons growing "digitally obese".* Thursday, December 9. Accessed October 10, 2006, from http://news.bbc.co.uk/2/hi/technology/4079417.stm

Cohn, D. Y., & Valerie, L. V. (2006). A study of neutralisation theory's application to global consumer ethics: P2P file-trading of musical intellectual property on the internet. *International Journal of Internet Marketing and Advertising, 3*(1), 68–88.

Crampton, T. (2006). On a Russian site, cheap songs with a backbeat of illegality. *New York Times.* June 5, Monday, Section C, Page 4, Column 4.

Cullen, D. (2006). Blacklisted AllofMP3 slams 'capricious' Visa and Mastercard. *The Register.* Thursday October 19. Accessed October 20, 2006, from http://www.theregister.co.uk/2006/10/19/allofmp3_attacks_visa_and_mastercard/

Dervin, B. (1983). *An overview of sensemaking research: Concepts, methods, and results to date.* international communication association conference, Dallas, TX. Retrieved from http://communication.sbs.ohio-state.edu/sense-making/art/artabsdervin83smoverview.html

Dervin, B., & Clark, K. (2003). Communication and democracy: A mandate for procedural invention. In B. Dervin, L. Forman-Werdnet, & E. Lauterbach (Eds.), *Sense-making methodology reader* (pp. 165–193). Cresskill, NJ: Hampton.

G8 Russia (2006). *Combating IPR piracy and counterfeiting.* Official Website of the G8 Presidency of the Russian Federation in 2006. St. Petersburg, July 16. Accessed October 10, 2006, from http://en.g8russia.ru/docs/15.html

IFPI (International Federation of Phonographic Industries). (2005). *Fact sheet: The legitimate download market.* July 21. Accessed October 5, 2006, from, http://www.ifpi.org/sitecontent/press/20050721.html

IFPI (International Federation of Phonographic Industries). (2006). *The Digital Music Report 2006 – Facts and Figures.* January 19. Accessed October 5, 2006, from http://www.ifpi.org/sitecontent/press/20050721.html

Jupiter Media Metrix. (2001). *Global napster usage plummets, but new file-sharing alternatives gaining ground.* Press Release. July 20. Accessed October 5, 2006, from http://www.comscore.com/press/release.asp?id=249

Kibby, M. (2003, April 23). Shared files. *M/C: A Journal of Media and Culture, 6.* Accessed October 5, 2006, from http://www.mediaculture.org.au/0304/05-sharedfiles.php

Leland, J. (2003, September 14). Beyond file-sharing: A nation of copiers. *New York Times.* Accessed October 5, 2006, from http://www.nytimes.com/2003/09/14/fashion/14COPY.html

May, C. (2003, November). Digital rights management and the breakdown of social norms. *First Monday, 8*(11). Accessed October 7, 2006, from http://firstmonday.org/issues/issue8_11/may/index.html

McCourt, T., & Burkart, P. (2003). When creators, corporations and consumers collide: Napster and the development of on-line music distribution. *Media, Culture & Society, 25,* 333–350.

Mennecke, T. (2006, December 27). AllofMP3.com responds to the $1.64 trillion lawsuit. *Slyck.com.* Accessed January 11, 2007, from http://www.slyck.com/story1368.html

Mertens, M. F. (2005). Thieves in cyberspace: Examining music piracy and copyright law deficiencies in Russia as it enters the digital age. *ExpressO Preprint Series Paper 663,* The Berkeley Electronic Press. Accessed October 6, 2006, from http://law.bepress.com/expresso/eps/663

Muncy, J., Scott, A., & Vitell, J. (1992). Consumer ethics: An investigation of the ethical beliefs of the final consumer. *Journal of Business Research, 24*(4), 297–311.

Noguchi, Y. (2006). The problem of freedom override by digital rights management technologies: The market mechanisms and possible legal options. *ExpressO Preprint Series Paper 1355,* The Berkeley Electronic Press. Accessed October 17, 2006, from http://law.bepress.com/expresso/eps/1355

Resnick, L. B., Levine, J. M., & Teasly, S. D. (Eds.). (1991). *Perspectives on socially shared cognition.* American Psychological Association, Washington, DC.

Sheppard, F. (2006, July 4). BPI wins first round in battle to beat cheap music sales on Russian site. *The Scotsman.* Tuesday. Accessed October 5, 2006, from http://news.scotsman.com/uk.cfm?id=973422006

Smith, T. (2006, May 12). Russian MP3 sales site "more popular in UK than Napster". *The Register,* Friday. Accessed October 20, 2006, from http://www.theregister.co.uk/2006/05/12/alllofmp3_uk_download_demand/

USA Today. (2006, December 20). *Record labels sue operator of Russian music Web site AllofMP3.com.* Accessed January 11, 2007, from http://www.usatoday.com/tech/news/2006-12-20-allofmp3-suit_x.htm

Vara, V. (2005, January 26). Russian web sites offer cheap songs, but piracy is issue. *Wall Street Journal.* D10.

Vitell, S. J., Anusorn, S., & James, T. (2001). Consumer ethics: An application and empirical testing of the Hunt-Vitell theory of ethics. *Journal of Consumer Marketing, 18*(2), 153–178.

Watson, D. E. (2006). *Russian intellectual property violations must be addressed at G-8 Summit.* Press Release. Accessed October 8, 2006, from http://www.house.gov/apps/list/press/ca33_watson/060714.html

Weick, K. E. (1995). *Sensemaking in organizations.* Thousand Oaks, CA: Sage.

Wright, C. (2004, April 27) Russian site is music to the ears. *The Sydney Morning Herald.* Accessed October 16, 2006, from http://www.smh.com.au/articles/2004/04/26/1082831475556.html

Understanding Online (Game)worlds

Lisbeth Klastrup

Online worlds have engaged millions of internet users, both as a new genre of entertainment and play, as well as sites for intense social interaction, since the mainstream breakthrough of graphical online worlds in the very late 1990s and early 2000s.[1] Despite their popularity, also within certain academic field of studies, we still need a coherent framework of analysis with which to approach them as a particular form of engaging online experience. This article presents one such framework, taking its point of departure in a discussion of what online worlds are, which forms of online worlds exist and how using them can be understood as a new form of engaging experience similar to the type of experience we have when we are captivated by the fictional universes of novels, films and tabletop roleplaying games. They are, in other words, a new form of *cultural entertainment systems*. To describe how these systems work, the proposed framework is grounded in an aesthetic, communicative and social approach to digital phenomena, with the primary objective of describing how online gameworlds function as systems that create meaning through the production of a specific form of "worldness", a concept which will be introduced and explained further below.

Defining Online Worlds

Any analysis of an online "media product" must start with a consideration of what defines the object of study at hand in comparison with other similar products, and whether they can be categorised into one or more (sub)genres. Though the research community will likely never agree completely on a definition, at this point in time general consensus seem to exist that as phenomena online worlds are characterised by the fact, that they are shared, persistent, large and explorable 3D-environments,

L. Klastrup (✉)
Innovative Communication Research Group, IT University of Copenhagen,
Copenhagen S, Denmark
e-mail: klastrup@itu.dk

[1] See also Bartle's article elsewhere in this volume.

J. Hunsinger et al. (eds.), *International Handbook of Internet Research*,
DOI 10.1007/978-1-4020-9789-8_19, © Springer Science+Business Media B.V. 2010

in which multiple users are represented by an in-world entity, typically a virtual body, in the form of a so-called "avatar" or character. Characteristic of an online world is also the fact that spatially it seems world-like in geographical size, which means that players cannot explore all of it in one visit. Technically, player data (logs of and information about the player's characters) usually are kept on the central servers between use sessions, which make it possible for that player to have many characters in one world which continuously develop over time, independent of the players' computer. Overall, these characteristics make online worlds different from chat rooms, which might be persistent, but are not spatially extended and where you are often represented just as a "handle" (nickname) or icon but not as body; and from multiplayer games such as *Counter-Strike* and *Battlefield 1942*, which have some spatial extension, but can only hold a limited number of players, and of which it is an essential trait that characters do not change between sessions but always "respawn" exactly the same (they are functions rather than people).

Regarding the question of genre, historically it seems that online worlds can be divided into two main genres: gameworlds and social worlds. Gameworlds, or MMORPGs (Massively Multiplayer Online Roleplaying Game) as they are commonly referred to, are essentially based on the early tabletop Dungeon & Dragon game system. They are characterised by the fact that like in other game genres, the world or "game" presents the users with clear and obtainable goals, mainly to level their character to the highest level possible by fulfilling a number of missions ("quests"), which earns them some form of "experience points" and by improving the skill of their characters. In the currently most popular subgenres, skill improvement typically involves combat and killing of computer-controlled characters, monsters and other player characters, as well as more general testing of the general game mechanics in order to "play the world" as optimally as possible. To control the gaming experience and make sure that some players do not get unfair advantages, it is normally not possible for gameworld players to add significantly to the design of a gameworld by expanding it or programming in-world objects. Though the game mechanics of gameworlds encourage and enforce social interaction, and indeed much activity in gameworlds are highly social, players who prefer to play the world on their own, especially in the lower levels, usually can do it a significant part of their in-world time. In fact, a quantitative research project carried out by Duchenaut et al. in 2006 showed that players of the very popular gameworld *World of Warcraft* preferred the more soloable classes and up until the end-level of the game spent at least 60% of their time outside groups. The study also showed that while 66% of the players were members of a guild, only a fraction (10%) of guild members engaged in joint activities. Overall, their observations lead these researchers to conclude that the social presence of others which can serve as audience and spectators to one's activities might be more important to players than actual social gaming with others (Duchenaut, Yee, Moore, & Nickell, 2006).

In comparison, social worlds normally do not usually have an explicitly levelling system and players do not collect experience points, though some form of status system might exist. Players can normally add content to social worlds in terms of for instance new buildings or areas of the world, and they are allowed to modify and program objects in the world. Since social worlds appear to exist mainly to provide a space for socialising and self-presentation, they might in comparison with gameworlds therefore not be very interesting to use regularly, if as a player, you are more interested in exploring and using a world on your own. Additionally, it should be noted that the individual endeavour of earning money, for some players, might have become a more recent reason for using some social worlds such as *Second Life*. Finally, one should also be aware that some social worlds also include educational sections, in which case players' main motives for world use typically are a given learning objective such as learning programming (by building objects) or collaboration skills. A well-known example of this subgenre of social worlds is the *Eduverse* sub-universe, part of the more than 10-year-old *Activeworlds* enterprise.

However, the distinction between gameworlds and social worlds can be difficult to maintain. On one hand, we may find "gaming" worlds which downplay or exclude the element of combat and killing, such as the world of *A Tale in the Desert*, which is generally categorised as a "MMORPG", but focuses on the development of society and economy; or social and educational worlds which also have elements of competition and quests embedded in their design or added by users (such as Treasure Hunt quests in *Second Life*). This article primarily focuses on gameworlds, but since one of the main points of the article is that we always need to look beyond the pure gaming elements of a world in order to understand what makes us experience it as *a world*, the analytical framework presented in the article should also in many ways be applicable to social worlds as well.

Online (Game)worlds as Worlds

Much research has in fact already been done on online worlds, particularly by researchers with a background in social sciences and social psychology (see, for instance, Taylor, 2006; Williams, Consalvo, Caplan, & Yee, 2009; Yee, 2006) and Human–Computer Interaction and CSCW studies (Duchenaut, Moore, & Nickell, 2007, Nardi & Harris 2006) who are also interested in game studies. Gameworlds have also caught the attention of economists (Castranova, 2005, 2008), and politics and law researchers (see, for instance, Lastowka & Hunter, 2003), and obviously it has been the object of study of the emergent field of dedicated game research (Aarseth, 2008; Juul, 2005). In many of these studies, the worlds are approached primarily as social phenomena rather than worlds as such. Hence, even if much of the research takes its point of departure in a particular world, researchers rarely engage in a discussion of what makes this particular world special, whether it be its game design or its social architecture. There is no doubt about the importance of sociality when it comes to describing the attraction of online worlds, but if the approach to online gameworlds is mostly focused on the social- and community-oriented aspects, we might not be able to explain why, as discussed above, some players enjoy playing and engaging with a gameworld mostly as a solitary endeavour. Furthermore, even though some researchers with a background in film, media and

L. Klastrup

cultural studies have also engaged in gameworld studies (see f.i., Corneliussen & Walker, 2008; Krzywinska, 2008; Mortensen, 2002, 2006), discussing aspects such as the importance of micronarrative structures (Walker, 2008) and mythology in these worlds (Krzywinska, 2006, 2008), very little research has to this day been done on online worlds *as worlds* and *cultural entertainment systems* created with the purpose of engaging us in an universe that we know is not real. Following, given the problems of singular perspectives in research on gameworlds, I apply a hybrid methodology which combines a traditional literary aesthetic perspective and "reading" of the world, with cultural ethnography and game studies in order to describe what I have previously defined as the player's experience of *worldness* (Klastrup, 2003, 2006, 2007). The experience of worldness emerges from the interplay between world design choices, world aesthetics, a specific gameworld culture and the player's world experience. This perspective therefore also addresses the process of the elements which help a player make meaning of an online world.

This inquiry into the aspects which helps define the experience of the worldness on online worlds is inspired by similar efforts by a number of literary theorists in the early 20th century who sought to define those specific aspects of works of literature, which defined the "literariness" of literature. Following Tzvetan Todorov's definition of literary poetics as an academic endeavour that focuses on the general and unique properties of this discursive genre, its literariness (Todorov, 1977), the study of "worldness" is therefore the "systematic study of virtual worlds as virtual worlds" (Klastrup, 2003, p. 262), which includes the process of examining and generalising some of the properties that defines online worlds as a particular new *genre of fictional universes*. In this context, it should be emphasised that the concept of worldness is applicable on two levels which continuously inform each other: we can speak of worldness on a very abstract level as a number of essential aspects applicable to all worlds and on a specific level as the defining characteristics of an individual world, reflected in the way the general properties are set into motion and transformed by the world in question, and as they are perceived by the players.

Online World as Fictional Universes

Turning now to the question of the general traits that defines the experience of the "worldness" of online worlds, we might begin by asking what is prominently different and new about gameworlds as a form of cultural entertainment systems? First and foremost, online worlds are characterised by the fact *that they are realised, alterable and permanent fictional universes which real people can explore from within and with each other.* It is thus a representation of a world in the form of a simulation. As an effect of this, the nature of the *reality of the gameworld* is essentially different from previous forms of fictions and as sociologist T.L. Taylor and economist Edward Castranova have pointed out, the border between the fictional or virtual ("non-real") realm and the "real world" is hard to define and is continuously transgressed. Indeed, as Castranova in his analysis of the relation between "real world" economy and online world economies puts it: "Synthetic worlds are becoming important because events inside them can have effects outside them" (Castranova, 2005, p. 7). One reason for this transgression of borders is that the characters we meet and interact with in the world are controlled by real people, and our communication with them takes place in "real time". As our knowledge of them increases, our social world in the gameworld becomes closely interwoven with our social offline world, as T.L Taylor has aptly pointed out in *Play between Worlds* (Taylor, 2006). Another area in which the online world blends with the offline world is that of economy. As we have seen in the case of *World of Warcraft* and *Second Life* the virtual economies of the online worlds are fused with real-world economies in a variety of ways. For instance, the so-called Chinese goldfarmers employed to level gameworld characters and amass in-world currency are in fact, when they are playing, earning real money. Finally, as indicated, an online world is a permanent, alterable and realised universe, based on software, and in that sense both much more concrete and much more changeable than non-digital fictional universes. Unlike for instance the novel, it is not just a purely imaginary universe, but has an actual existence. For instance, the online gameworld version of *Lord of the Rings* (*LOTRO*, Turbine, 2007) is part representation, part simulation of a Tolkien-inspired universe. The user can enter it, and *live* and *perform* the life of a Tolkien-inspired character class, in keeping with the codex of conduct and morality known from the other instances of the Tolkien universe (for a further discussion of transmedial worlds including Tolkien's, see Klastrup & Tosca, 2005). The world is a mental projection, but also a responsive piece of software than allows us to step inside it and live the ethos and mythos of the world. Perhaps this fundamental characteristic is also part of the reason why, as I have observed in my own studies of the worlds of *EverQuest* and *World of Warcraft*, players themselves seem to have no problem stepping in and out of the fictional frame of the (game)world. While players do, as will be shortly discussed, engage in a very basic game of make-believe when they enter a gameworld, they do also, particularly through their social interaction both inside and outside the world, demonstrate a very conscious and instrumental approach to the world, occasionally treating it and talking about it as any other kind of software. For instance, one moment players might be performing as mages in the world, the next moment they may rationally be discussing the technicalities of a new cool feature of the spell system. This oscillation between pretending to be *in* the world and then the next moment stepping outside the world to discuss it as a system indicates that constant immersion in the fiction does not play as important a role in producing *engagement* in a (game)world as it does in non-digital fictions, for which the experience of immersion has traditionally been the main objective. This phenomena might not only be applicable to gameworlds alone, because as Mackey points out in her study of the way young people engage with fictions, this "play on the border of the diegetic" seems to become more and more widespread. In her article (Mackey, 2003), she identifies a number of contemporary text forms and genres which opens themselves to exactly this kind of borderplay (including video games).

Having listed some important differences between previous forms of fictional universes, let us now look at some of the noteworthy similarities between non-digital fictional universes and gameworlds. The most important similarity is what we in a Scandinavian tradition refer to as the act of willingly accepting the "fictional contract" set up between user and world-producer. When we enter an online world, through the explicit act of logging on and logging in to it, we engage in a game of make-believe which disregards the obvious fact that we all know and share: that the world we move in is not real – this is what is known (but rarely quoted correctly) as the *"willing* suspension of disbelief" with reference to a statement by the English poet Samuel Coleridge.[2] Even if we know that monsters do not exist in reality, we *pretend* that we are elves or trolls, magicians or warriors living in a world where orcs, wandering skeletons and dragons are as real as we are, and we consciously and continuously perform a series of *feigned acts*: we are well aware that when we deal a death blow to another player's character and thereby kill him, it does not mean that the other player behind the screen somewhere else in the offline world drops dead. The act only has meaning within the framework of the world, and only affects our virtual bodies, but nevertheless, we might still exclaim "I killed you!". Part of the cultural conventions of acting in an online world is that we deal with it, as if it were, to a certain degree real, with the shared knowledge that what happens is, on a certain level, not real at all. We are, in other words, co-creators of the world as a form of fictional discourse:

> What distinguishes fiction from lies is the existence of a separate set of conventions which enables the author to go through the motions of making statements which he knows to be not true even though he has no intention to deceive (Searle, 1975, p. 326)

One could following argue that our understanding of the *ontology* of the world is that we know it is a fiction, but we are at the same time well aware that what goes on inside it is indeed a *social and materially coded reality*.

Furthermore, what online worlds share with other fictional universes is the fact that they function as symbolic frames for a special form of experience which we associate with the promise of emotional engagement or flow we have come to expect from the engagement with novels, films and adventure games. One of the reasons why we might easily engage in these fictions is the fact that in these worlds all that is irrelevant to the immediate story or all elements too mundane to bother with have been filtered out of the representation. Like the worlds of novels or films, the online world is never a complete simulation of the real world (the map which covers the entire territory of the world it represents), rather it is a condensed presentation of what a world can be like; and part of the experience of being in this world is

---

[2]The quote is taken from Chapter XIV of the English poet Samuel Coleridge's manifestlike autobiography, *Biographia Literaria* from 1817 and in context reads: "In this idea originated the plan of the "Lyrical Ballads"; in which it was agreed, that my endeavours should be directed to persons and characters supernatural, or at least romantic; yet so as to transfer from our inward nature a human interest and a semblance of truth sufficient to procure for these shadows of imagination that *willing suspension of disbelief* for the moment, which constitutes poetic faith." (my italics)

also accepting and perhaps reflecting on the choices that have been made regarding which aspects of life to include and which to exclude, which events to speed up and which to keep in real time, etc. For instance, just like in films or novels, *ellipsis* (in literary theory defined as non-narrated passages of time or "leaps forward" in time)[3] is applied as a configurative strategy in the way the online world as a the simulation is configured: travelling vast distances can be done in a much shorter time than in the physical world, gameworld characters never go to the bathroom, brush their teeth or take off their pyjamas (unless it is an explicit part of the game mechanics as in *The Sims* franchise), and likewise similar kinds of actions which are normally excluded from most fictional universes, because they are tedious both to perform and watch, are also weeded out. Though gaming in a gameworld do contain a lot of trivial work because you have to do the same thing over and over again (often referred to as "grinding"), gameworld designers have made sure that all the not so interesting aspects of our everyday offline lives do not stand in the way of "fun" experiences in the worlds they make (at least you get to "kill" a lion 100 times instead of having to make dinner 100 times). The attraction of online worlds is, I would argue, similar to that of other forms of fiction, that they are *not* like our offline world, because they present a compact and intensified version of the real world.

Finally, we can learn much about the way online worlds function by looking at how it as a genre of representation, just like in literature, movies and games, help frame our experiences and expectations. Genre is here understood in the sense that Carolyn Miller has defined it, as

> a rhetorical means for mediating private intentions and social exigence; it motivates by connecting the private with the public, the singular with the recurrent. (Miller, 1984, p. 163)

That is, as a social discourse that informs the actions and understandings of the individual. Curiously, genre studies are generally missing in online gameworld research, and since I have not yet conducted empirical studies in this area, statements about the importance of genre can therefore only be speculative. Nevertheless I suggest that engagement in an online world is also related to our knowledge and expectations of the genre of fictional universes the world taps into. This includes the conventions of representation and type of content that is attached to this genre, for instance the so-called backstories of the worlds (that serve to frame the in-world story arc and conflicts) will be quite different, depending on whether you are entering a science fiction or a fantasy world. In other words, our awareness of genre conventions will also serve as an "interpretative framework" against which we can test the consistency, embedded values and symbolic foci of a world. If a gameworld belongs to the fantasy world genre, we will expect that the representation-simulation of the world is consistently "fantasylike", and it would be considered out-of-place if spaceships or futuristic social housing suddenly appear in, for instance, *World of Warcraft*. Instead the players entering a world like *World of Warcraft* will expect

---

[3] I here refer to the concept of ellipsis as defined by Gerald Genette (p. 43 and following) in his book *Narrative Discourse – An Essay in Method*.

a medieval aesthetics: dragons, orcs and magic will be perceived as "natural" elements in this world, as cars and antibiotics are in our world; and it would go against conventions if a character could buy modern guns to slay the dragons or Formula-1 cars to chase the orcs. These expectations do not only inform what we expect to find but also what we expect to be able to do, and what we expect will happen as the overall story of the world unfolds. Accordingly, events in the online worlds will, in keeping with the genre of the world universe, be interpreted according to what we as players conceive of as the inner logic of this world, both in relation to the tradition of fictional representation it draws on and the type (genre) of game mechanics it applies. In a previous study of the implementation of "death" in gameworlds, one of my findings was that fantasy worlds studied in general implemented a game mechanics where players have to resurrect their dead character's body by running back to and identifying it on the battlefield (or let it be resurrected by another character with magical abilities), whereas in the science-fiction worlds, characters were normally resurrected through the use of smart machines or city-based resurrection facilities (Klastrup, 2007). In both cases, the game mechanics tie in well with the role technologies plays (or does not play) in fantasy and science-fiction genres in general.

"Measuring" Experience

While a knowledge of the genre types and genre conventions of fictional universes should be the point of departure of any in-depth study of a given world, we need to study "experience" also on a more local and personal level, if we want to reach an deep understanding of the worldness experience of the individual player. Before I present the concrete framework of analysis with which I propose that we study (game) world experience, it is necessary to make clear exactly how "experience" in this context is understood.

Writers seem to agree that within the digital realm experience grows out of the interplay between the qualities and characteristics of the digital artefact (in our case "the world") at hand, previous similar experiences (this includes genre expectations) and the social and cultural setting within which the individual user moves. It is therefore not enough to just look at the interaction between the player and the digital artefact. We need to examine the complex interplay between people's personal repertoire of experiences, the context of experience (physical and social) in combination with the actual design of, for instance, a gameworld if we want to understand in-depth the nature of one individual player's experience of the world. It is only by exploring the relation between all these aspects of experience that we can begin to understand what makes digital experiences in their many forms truly unique and engaging. However, we face a challenge: if we as a starting point assume that all experience is subjective, it follows that world designers cannot design a specific experience that everybody using their world will have. Nor can we as researchers generalise the nature of an experience, even if we through interviews, cultural probes and similar methods might get a good understanding of the nature of some particular player's experiences. Designers can however provide a structure for experience *types*, intended to provide a certain set of experiences (a game designed to be "fun" will hopefully not be experienced as "sad" by many players). To return to the example of the design of death, gameworld designers cannot stage death in a way that is bound to guarantee a very specific experience of dying. But through their design, understood as both game mechanics and aesthetics, they are able to *affect* people's experience of gameplay and death. Likewise, as researchers we can study the effect of the framework, rather than individual experiences as such. For instance, my studies have shown that designers assume that death and its penalty will be considered as an unpleasant aspect of playing by the players, yet nevertheless they consider it an indispensable part of the design of the gaming experience in game genres in which players have a high degree of attachment to their characters.[4] Richard Bartle puts it bluntly in his book on gameworld design: "some of the more primitive and tedious aspects of the real world that players don't want to experience act, unfortunately, to set up some of the more advanced and enjoyable aspects that they do want to experience." (Bartle, 2003, p. 386). My study of gameworld death however showed that the stories players tell about their characters' death experiences reveal that "death" is in reality not always considered an unpleasant experience, but might just be considered trivial, or in some cases even heroic and exiting.

In sum, as online (game) world researchers, even if we cannot generalise experience, also that of a world's "worldness", we can try to understand how it is shaped, and how it is likely to fall in either the category of being pleasant or unpleasant, fun or boring and so forth. When it comes to the question of how we "measure" experience, it is important to point out the difference between behaviour and experience. Experience is an active and reflective engagement with something that has happened; behaviour is what you do in a concrete situation, and as such something that the design of a game encourages. The anthropologist Edward Bruner phrases it succinctly: "An experience is more personal, as it refers to an active self, to a human being who not only engages in but shapes an action . . . It is not customary to say, 'Let me tell you about my behaviour'; rather, we tell about experiences, which include not only actions and feelings but also reflections about those actions and feelings" (Bruner, 1986, p. 5). Experience is what we tell stories about, and therefore, by looking at the interplay between game mechanics (as that which shapes behaviour, which results in experiences) and the stories players tell about their gameworld experienc*es* (as manifest reflections on experience), we should be able to identify at least some typical experience characteristic of the world or world genres

---

[4]It should be noted that the care for one's character is much more developed in game genres that focus on continuous character advancement, such as role-playing games (where information about character level and character stats are saved in between gaming sessions). "Character" does, for instance, not really matter in games of the first-person shooter genre, where characters are largely iconic and have no personal characteristics.

that are our object of study. The study of player stories short or long, not as distinct narratives per se, but as mediated reflections of experience, therefore becomes a very important part of the study of worldness.

Identifying and Analysing an Online World

Having outlined a more general framework of understanding of what kind of cultural and fictional "text" (in a broad sense) an online gameworld is, and how we should work with the concept of experience, I will in the last part of this article present a more concrete analytical guideline for the analysis of what shapes the experience of a (game)world's worldness. This is thus a type of analysis, which approaches a world as an "experience producing system". It can be carried out in several ways, depending on whether the goal is to identify more general aspects of "worldness" or to identify defining aspects of the worldness of *one* gameworld. Thus, one could examine the experience design and reception of one experience element in one world such as death (see Klastrup, 2008) or fashion (see Tosca & Klastrup, 2009; one element in many worlds such as the similarities and likeness in the staging of death (see Klastrup, 2006, 2007), or recurring experience frameworks in many worlds – a hypothetical example could here be a study of the social and aesthetic design of, and forms of interaction taking place in inns, bars and "canteens" across worlds.

Before embarking on an analysis, however, it is important to pause and consider exactly what the extent of the world in question is. In *Play between Worlds*, T.L. Taylor points out that

> it is not just the first-hand, real-time interpersonal relationships and groups that constitute the social world of the game, but also the collection of message boards, databases, comics, fan arts and stories, and even game modifications that contribute to players feeling a bond and connection to the EQworld [EverQuest] and their fellow gamers. (Taylor, 2006, p. 57)

The "world" and the associated worldness experience of an online gameworld is not only the world that characters can move in but also the world that players talk about and imaginarily expand outside the realised "gameable" world. Deciding which corpus of cultural artefacts and texts surrounding a gameworld to include in an analysis can be a tricky question, since the most popular worlds have millions of satellite texts in their orbit.[5] It must therefore be a question of case-to-case evaluation to decide which artefacts might form a representative sample. Official developer-supported forums and popular user-generated portals that list and discuss areas or objects in world are often good places to start harvesting.

---

[5]Mackey refers to satellite texts as all forms of "texts" that support the "same fictional domain" (Mackey, 2003, p. 9, webprint).

Elements of Analysis

Once the gameworld(s) to be analysed have been identified and delimitated, a worldness analysis should consider the following elements:

The World as Instrument

This part of the analysis concerns the material aspects of the world and the ways players relate to this. Does the world software come on CD-ROMs, combined with online patches, and run in its own separate window, or is based on an online download and played from within a browser? Which modifications of the world exist, both as official expansions of the world, or perhaps as more or less legal player "add-ons"? What does the interface to the world look like and how may interface elements affect experience? For instance, in *EverQuest* the player is not informed how many experience points are needed before the next character level is reached. In *World of Warcraft*, the experience point progress bar lists exactly how many experience points are needed. Do these different ways of communicating progress make a difference in player engagement and style of play?

This aspect of analysis is also concerned with the oscillation between "pretend play" (pretending to be in-character and in-world) and "reality talk". How do players speak of the world as a game? One way to study this could be by asking: is the world well known for particular types of bugs and how do players in writing and social interaction refer to and discuss these bugs? Is it an integral part of the social interaction in the world, a guild or a group that one pauses to discuss game mechanics?

The Aesthetics of Genre and World

This part of the analysis relates to the importance of genre as discussed above and the importance of aesthetics and style in framing the players' expectations and interactions with each other and the world. What is the representational aesthetics of the world and how is it framed as a fiction – this includes looking at how the world is represented in trailers and backstories. How do you enter the world for the first time, and what are the rituals of entry and exit provided in general – that is, how is the fictional contract realised? To which degree does the world draw on representational conventions of the genre to which it claims to belong? For instance, if it is a world based on the fantasy genre, how are the fantastical elements rendered? As an example one could, by asking players of both worlds, examine whether there is a perceivable experiential difference in the experience of the soft, almost cartoonish aesthetics of the *World of Warcraft*-universe and the slightly more photo-realistic and hard-edged aesthetics of the *Lord of the Rings Online* universe? If the world draws on aesthetic genre conventions not hitherto applied in an online world, how do they play with and transform this aesthetics? As an example one could examine in which ways a world like *City of Heroes* relate to the superhero comics genre and aesthetics and which other representational paradigms the designers of this world have drawn on.

The Performative Range of the Character

This aspect of analysis relates to the study of experience as concrete action and performance primarily in relation to other players. How can players express themselves in the world, how can they interact with other players and how can they influence other players' experience of his character(s)? This could include looking at possibilities of character selection and customisation and the production and availability of clothing, fashion-trends and dress conventions in the world. Furthermore, one should identify which communication channels are available to players (which chat channels are for instance available and what are they in practice used for?); can players use "emotes" (pretend-play actions typed in by the player); which preset character animations are available and do the range of animations tell us anything about which forms of socially acceptable (inter)actions are enforced by the designers? Are other means of self-expression available this could include looking at the conventions for naming characters (for an example of one such study, see Hagström, 2008)? Is role-play enforced and on which level do this enforcement take place? For instance, role-play can be enforced on server-level ("this is a role-playing server"), as well as in-game: in guilds, particular areas of the world, or through general conventions for which chat channels to use for respectively in-character and out-of-character talk.

Interaction Forms and Scope

This aspect of analysis relates to the study of experience as it unfolds in the relation between player and the world, both as a realised concrete space (universe) and as a (game) system. What can players do to the world? Is it in any way possible to make a lasting mark on the world, through for instance the addition of buildings or objects? How is the game mechanics implemented and how is it communicated to the player? In many worlds, for instance, the effect of the players' game behaviour is communicated to the players as on on-screen "voice", which informs the player that he or she "dies", "cannot do that", "is running out of food", etc. How does this voice influence the play experience? And how do players express their experiences with the game system? Do they talk about it as rigid and unfair? Or exploitable and soft? In which ways do the game architecture encourage, or perhaps even make (instrumental) social interaction between players necessary?

The Social Culture of the World

Evidently an analysis of this type can only touch on certain aspects of the social culture of the world, since an in-depth cultural study of an online world in itself requires an extensive analysis. However, in a worldness experience-oriented analysis of culture, the focus should be on the stories and myths about the world players themselves tell and share. For instance, which stories about player-behaviour are circulated on guild websites, forums and player-story portals and what do these stories tell us about which experiences are the most popular or remarkable in the world? Do they help enforce certain social behaviors? Which guilds are the most revered and spoken on the server and for which social or cultural reasons?

The Experience of Lived Life

Finally, an important part of any analysis of an online world is the experience of the world "through time". That the researcher him- or herself, as part of the analysis, spends substantial time in the world is pivotal. Most gameworlds have a steep learning curve, both when it comes to learning how to "game" it instrumentally and when it comes to learning how to perform socially inside it. Essentially, the experience of worldness emerges from long-time exposure to the world, during which all the previously mentioned aspects of analysis comes into play, and not the least through the process of getting a sense of the typical phases a player in the world goes through, by levelling one, but more typically, several characters. Typical phases, following the levelling process seems to be the following: being a newbie not familiar with the world, its game-mechanics and customs, then a low-level player with some knowledge of these, a mid-level player and finally (for some) an end-game high level player (which might also start to go through the entire levelling process again with a new character, but typically at a somewhat quicker pace). Not alone should you as an analyst try to go through all these phases yourself and ask yourself which stories *you* want to tell about them, but you should also ask: how do other players of the world deal with these phases, for instance how do they in their stories describe the "rites of passage" from one phase to the other?

Understanding Worlds, Understanding Worldness

Above, I have presented six aspects of the design and experience of an online world that I believe should be addressed as part of any general analysis of an online world – and hopefully it will help point to certain aspects of one particular world which one should address in more detail, depending on the genre, aesthetics and social architecture of that world. Much work still needs to be done when it comes to understanding the interplay between fictionality, world genre, world design, interaction and performance within the world, and the culture. How do all these elements shape the world experience of the individual user? What we need at this point in time are many more dedicated case studies which can broaden our understanding of the interplay between these aspects and encourage further studies of how from this constant interplay emerges the unique characteristics of a world, its "worldness", that which makes it different from all worlds of the same genre, whether we consider it a game, a culture or a social place; that which makes us want to spend so many hours inhabiting and sharing them with others.

References

Aarseth, E. (2008). A hollow world: World of warcraft as spatial practice. In H. Corneliussen & J. Walker (Eds.), *Digital culture, play and identity – A world of warcraft reader* (pp. 111–122). Cambridge, MA: MIT Press.

Bartle, R. (2003). *Designing virtual worlds*. Indianapolis, IN: New Riders.

Bruner, E. M. (1986). Experience and its expressions. In. V. W. Turner & E. M. Bruner (Eds.), *The anthropology of experience* (pp. 3–32). Urbana, IL: University of Illinois Press.

Castranova, E. (2005). *Synthetic worlds – The business and culture of online games*. Chicago: University of Chicago Press.

Castranova, E. (2008). *Exodus to the virtual world: How online fun is changing reality*. New York: Palgrave Macmillan.

Duchenaut, N., Moore, R. J., & Nickell, E. (2007). Virtual 'third places': A case study of sociability in massively multiplayer games. *Computer Supported Cooperative Work, 16*(1–2), 129–166.

Duchenaut, N., Yee, N., Moore, R. J., & Nickell, E. (2006). *Alone Together?: Exploring the social dynamics of massively multiplayer online games*. Proceedings of ACM CHI 2006 conference in human factors in computing systems 2006 (pp. 407–416).

Hagström, C. (2008). Playing with names. Gaming and naming in world of warcraft. In H. Corneliussen & J. Walker, (Eds.), *Digital culture, play and identity – A world of warcraft reader*. Cambridge, MA: MIT Press.

Juul, J. (2005). *Half real: Video games between real rules and fictional worlds*. Cambridge, MA: MIT Press.

Klastrup, L. (2003). *Towards a poetics of virtual worlds – Multi-user textuality and the emergence of story*. Copenhagen: IT University of Copenhagen.

Klastrup, L. (2006). *Death matters: Understanding gameworld experiences*. Proceedings from the advances in computing entertainment conference (ACE) 2006. ACM digital library: http://portal.acm.org/citation.cfm?id=1178859&coll=ACM&dl=ACM&CFID=12434038& CFTOKEN=73705961

Klastrup, L. (2007). Why death matters: Understanding gameworld experience. *Journal of Virtual Reality & Broadcasting, 4*(3).

Klastrup, L. (2008). What makes world of warcraft a world? A note on death and dying. In H. Corneliussen & J. Walker (Eds.), *Digital culture, play and identity – A world of warcraft reader*. Cambridge, MA: MIT Press.

Klastrup, L., & Tosca, S. (2005). Transmedial worlds – Rethinking cyberworld design. In Klastrup, L. and Tosca, S. (Eds.), *Proceedings International Conference on Cyberworlds 2004*. IEEEE Computer Society, Los Alamitos, CA, 2005.

Krzywinska, T. (2006). Blood scythes, festivals, quests and backstories: World creation and rhetorics of myth in world of warcraft. *Games and Culture, 1*, 383–396.

Krzywinska, T. (2008). World creation and lore: World of warcraft as rich text. In H. Corneliussen, & J. Walker (Eds.), *Digital culture, play and identity – A world of warcraft reader*. Cambridge, MA: MIT Press.

Lastowka, F. G., & Hunter, D. (2003). The laws of virtual worlds. Research Paper No 03-10, Institute for Law and Economics. Available at the Social Science Research Network Electronic Paper Collection.

Mackey, M. (2003). At play on the borders of the diegetic: Story boundaries and narrative interpretation. *Journal of Literacy Research, 35*(1), 591–632.

Miller, C. (1984). Genre as social action. *Quarterly Journal of Speech, 70*, 151–167.

Mortensen, T. (2002). Playing with players: Potential methodologies for MUDs. In E. Aarseth (Ed.), *Game Studies* (issue 2), at http://gamestudies.org

Mortensen, T. (2006, October). WoW is the new MUD, social gaming from text to video. In D. Thomas (Ed.), *Games and Culture, A Journal of Interactive Media*, 1(4), Sage Publications.

Nardi, B., & Harris, J. (2006). *Strangers and friends: Collaborative play in world of warcraft.* Paper presented at CSCW'06, November 2006, Banff, AB, Canada.

Searle, J. R. (1975). The logical status of fictional discourse. In *Expression and meaning: Studies in the theory of speech acts.* Cambridge: Cambridge University Press.

Taylor, T. L. (2006). *Play between worlds: Exploring online game culture.* Cambridge, MA: MIT Press.

Todorov, T. (1977). *The poetics of prose* (R. Howard, Trans.). Oxford: Blackwell.

Tosca, S., & Klastrup, L. (2009, February). 'Because it just looks cool!' – Fashion as character performance: the case of WoW. *Journal of Virtual Worlds, 1*(3).

Walker, J. (2008). Quests in world of warcraft: Deferral and repetition. In H. Corneliussen & J. Walker (Eds.), *Digital culture, play and identity – A world of warcraft reader* (pp. 167–184). Cambridge, MA: MIT Press.

Williams, D., Consalvo, M., Caplan, S., & Yee, N. (2009). Looking for gender (LFG): Gender roles and behaviours among online gamers. Accepted for publication in *Journal of Communication*, 2009. Available at http://dmitriwilliams.com/GenderDifferencesTN.doc

Yee, N. (2006). The demographics, motivations and derived experiences of users of massively multi-user online graphical environments. *Presence: Teleoperators and Virtual Environments, 15*, 309–329.

Strategy and Structure for Online News Production – Case Studies of CNN and NRK

Arne H. Krumsvik

Introduction

The initial interest of the topic originated from the observed practice of online journalism in large traditional media firms, which was, in contrast to the revolution in journalism assumed by many new media researchers after the introduction of hypertext, interactivity and multimedia (Deuze, 2001; Engebretsen, 2001; Harper, 1998; Pavlik, 1999). Technological assets of new media were for the broader part ignored in online journalism (Domingo, 2004; Matheson, 2004; Schroeder, 2004) or at least implemented at a much slower rate then earlier suggested (Boczkowski, 2004; Steensen, 2005). The interrelationship between the strategy of the firm and the development of online journalism was de facto ignored by most media researchers.

The purpose of this project is to contribute to the understanding of the implications of corporate strategy and organizational structure on the journalism production process within the context of digitalization and convergence by conducting a cross-national comparative case study of online news production and to analyze the strategies and structures of Cable News Network (CNN) and the Norwegian Broadcasting Corporation (NRK).

News production and distribution has been the core activity of journalism and often the most cost-intensive part of the in-house production in traditional television corporations. Due to the level of investment and prestige of this content, strategies for news distribution and development are central to these corporations' overall strategies (Krumsvik 2006; 2008).

Internet is quite different from broadcasting, but for TV and radio channels it has been a matter of course to establish online activities (Rasmussen, 2002). Because of their traditional content these players have been the frontrunners in developing multimedia services in the same framework as online newspapers. And because of their ability to use more of the possibilities of new media with less need to invest heavily on new equipment and skills, broadcasters are interesting objects of study in the current phase.

A.H. Krumsvik (✉)
Department of Media and Communication, University of Oslo, Oslo, Norway
e-mail: a.h.krumsvik@media.uio.no

J. Hunsinger et al. (eds.), *International Handbook of Internet Research*,
DOI 10.1007/978-1-4020-9789-8_20, © Springer Science+Business Media B.V. 2010

Theoretical Framework

The organization, more specifically corporate strategy, represents the independent variable of this study. The focal point is how strategy at the corporate level influences the role of the journalist.

The dependent variable of this study is the production *process* of online news, more specifically the role of the producers (journalists) on the basic level of job content and the use of technology. The aim is to better understand how changes in corporate strategy and organizational structures affect cultural production.

Companies' adjustments to altered external conditions are complex and dynamical processes. By studying different industries, Miles and Snow (2003) identify four archetypes. Each of these has its own strategy in responding to changes in the surroundings, as well as its typical configuration for technology, structure, and process consistent with its strategy. Three stable situations are named *"Defender,"* *"Analyzer,"* and *"Prospector,"* where the company is competitive over time if organized according to its strategic type. The last category called *"Reactor"* represents an unstable situation (Miles & Snow 2003, p. 29).

> *Defenders* are organizations which have narrow product-margin domains. Top managers in this type of organizations are highly experts in their organization's limited area of operations but do not tend to search outside their domain for new opportunities. As a result of this narrow focus, these organizations seldom make major adjustments to their technology, structure, or methods of operations. Instead, they devote primary attention to improving the efficiency of their existing operations.
>
> *Prospectors* are organizations which almost continually search for market opportunities, and they regularly experiment with potential responses to emerging environmental trends. Thus, these organizations often are the creators of change and uncertainty to which their competitors must respond. However, because of their strong concern for product and market innovation, these organizations are not completely efficient.
>
> *Analyzers* are organizations which operate in two types of product-market domains, one relatively stable, the other changing. In their stable areas, these organizations operate routinely and efficiently through use of formalized structures and processes. In their more turbulent areas, top managers watch their competitors closely for new ideas, and then they rapidly adapt those which appear to be most promising.
>
> *Reactors* are organizations in which top managers frequently perceive change and uncertainty occurring in their organizational environments but are not able to respond effectively. Because this type of organization lacks a consistent strategy–structure relationship, it seldom makes adjustments of any sort until forced to do so by environmental pressures.

Miles and Snow's model was an important contribution to the development of strategic management as a field of study, founded, inter alia, on the works of Alfred

Chandler (1962). Chandler's analysis of large American enterprises documented how changes of strategy are followed by changes of structure. Miles and Snow's contribution has been vital in the formation/development of what is known as "the configurational view of strategy," which explains that there is not an infinite number of alternative routes toward the goal, but rather a handful of fundamental alternatives to choose between in order to achieve what one wants. Porter (1980) is among those who, following the typologies developed by Miles and Snow, has presented his set of generic strategies (*cost leadership, differentiation,* and *focus*) (Hambrick, 2003).

The core activity of a broadcasting corporation seems basically to fit in with the *defender* category. The focus is on publishing television and radio, and the executives are usually experts on precisely that, besides having worked a long time in the business. The executives do not actively seek opportunities outside of their domain or line of business, and their main focus remains on improving management of the core activity. The large investments that have been made to digitalize the production process seem mostly to be about producing the same thing in a more efficient way.

However, the digitalization of production, storage, and distribution of media content paves the way for a new understanding of the line of business within which one operates and the competition one partakes in. In this situation, the broadcasters have an advantage because of their rich content and well-established channels for marketing new products and services.

The establishment of online news services can be seen as a shift from *defender* toward the category *analyzer*, with operations in one relatively stable part of the market and one rather unstable. In the traditional line of operations focus is on routine and efficiency, whereas one in the new line of business seeks to adapt good and promising ideas. Based on the historical development and the typology designed by Miles and Snow, a hypothesis of *analyzer* as the main strategy chosen will be the most reasonable. The structure and processes of the organization are differentiated to be able to account for both stable and dynamic spheres of activity.

Research suggests that technological assets of new media for the broader part are ignored in online journalism (Domingo, 2004; Matheson, 2004; Schroeder, 2004) or at least implemented at a much slower rate then earlier suggested (Boczkowski, 2004).

Bolter and Grusin explain the development of new media through the process of *remediation*. New media remediate old media, and old media is remediated by new media, driven forward by the strive for transparent immediacy (Bolter & Grusin 1999). Social theory, addressing the human factor and the view of news production as acts of social construction, might be used to understand the relative delay in the process of remediation.

To study actions preformed by the journalist in reliance to the duties and rights established by the profession, the sociological dichotomy of structure and agency is included in the theoretical approach. Giddens defines structure as "rules and resources, recursively, implicated in the reproduction of social systems" (Giddens, 1984). The structure provides both opportunities and limitations for actions – this duality is what Giddens labels social practice.

In a modern industrialized society and democracy media development will be a compromise between the market, political decision processes (e.g., ownership limitations), local newsroom culture and social institutions, including unions (Ottosen, 2004).

Nygren (2008) presents a model for analysis of the role of journalists on four levels:

1. Journalist's role in the news production, what they do in their daily work, and their relations to other groups in the media organization.
2. The norms and routines developing in the daily work, both conscious norms built in to the work flow and unconscious norms in the silent knowledge of the profession.
3. Conscious ideals and values of the journalist, giving meaning to the work and direction for decisions taken in the work process.
4. The role of the journalist in society outside the daily operations in the news room. Journalism has created a role in society both as actor and an arena in the democratic processes, and as narrator of contemporary history. Each journalist is a carrier of this role, and it is an important part of the values influencing professional decisions.

The technological framework for the development of journalism and the role of journalists represents one of several lines of conflict in relation to the commercialization of media (Ottosen, 2004). McManus argues there are four interested parties in the production of news: news sources, advertisers, consumers, and corporate investors. Market-driven theory of news production implies fundamentally different goals than the traditional journalism theory of news production. The market-driven theory is economically centered around pleasing advertisers and attracting the largest possible audiences while minimizing newsroom labor and production costs, McManus (1994) asserts.

My objective is to develop this further by introducing the role of corporate strategy in the equation. In order to understand how new media development in a traditional media organization is affecting the journalism production process, it is necessary to understand the strategic role of new platforms, and the commercial rationale for multi-platform product portfolio development.[1]

Research Questions

Starting out with the production *process* of online news as the dependent variable, the interest of this study is the interplay between strategy and process – in the context

---

[1]Picard (2005) identifies five rationales for the development of media product portfolios: Risk Reduction, Managing Product Life Cycles, Market Exploration and Company Growth, Breath of Market Service, and Efficiency.

of external factors changing technology, regulation, and values in society (Roos & van Krogh 1996).

Q1) How does the strategic role of new media development in a traditional media organization affect the journalism production process?

Q2) What kind of journalists and journalism are shaped under changing individual, institutional, and technological frameworks?

Methodology

A multi-disciplinary approach in developing new concepts, within the traditions of empirical sciences such as communication studies, sociology, and economics, places this project, in terms of Mjøset's six notions of theory (2006), in a *pragmatist tradition of social science,* with an explanation-based notion of theory.

This cross-national comparative case study of online news production analyzes the strategies and structures of Cable News Network (CNN) and the Norwegian Broadcasting Corporation (NRK), based on 35 in-depth interviews in 2005–2007 with current and former producers and news executives of CNN and NRK, academics, and industry specialists.

The main reason for choosing these traditional television organizations as objects of study is their positions as leading news gathering organizations. NRK controls Norway's largest news organization, while CNN operates the world's largest news gathering network. This represents a "most different cases" approach (Andersen 1997). The focus of the study will be on specific scope conditions, while the contiguous variables are very different: public service[2] vs. commercial, Scandinavian vs. American, national vs. global, traditional terrestrial vs. cable and satellite, online pioneer vs. late starter, etc. The aim is then to discover decontextualized stabile patterns, indicating general coherence.

The Two Cases

CNN.com, launched in 1995, is among the world's leaders in online news and information delivery,[3] relying heavily on CNN's global team of almost 4,000 news professionals. The site is updated continuously through a "follow the sun" model by the production facilities in Atlanta, London, Hong Kong, and Sydney, financed by advertising.

The NRK (the Norwegian Broadcasting Corporation) is Norway's major broadcasting institution with nine radio channels and three TV channels. There are NRK

---

[2] While NRK traditionally is a public service broadcaster of radio and television, the online activity is defined as a commercial activity since 2000.

[3] In 1980, Ted Turner launched CNN, the world's first live, 24-hour global news network.

offices in 50 different places in Norway in addition to 10 correspondents abroad.[4] The NRK began experimenting with the world wide web in 1995, starting with offering a selection of program-related material. Due to advice from the European Broadcasting Union (EBU) not to invest too much on internet activities, they started rather low scale. This was later used as an explanation of why NRK is not in a leading national position, as is the case in every other market they operate. The online service was initially 100% financed by the public broadcasters' license fees.

The First Phase (1993–1999)

CNN's online activities started on the proprietary online service CompuServe in 1993 with an online forum set up around the live Talk Back program. In 1994 CNN started to deliver news headlines to CompuServe, and this activity initiated a process of setting up a business plan for the online activities of the CNN. At the time, projecting forward was based on production for either CD-ROM or proprietary online services. It was not until March 1995 CNN discovered the world wide web as an opportunity to reach the whole world, which was important for CNN, and something they could not achieve in an offering to the contained audience of CompuServe. The DC-ROM production cycle was also less compelling to the style of CNN reporting.

The web answered the concerns of production cycle and market reach, and in August 2005 they launched CNN.com. The CNN Interactive staff had grown from 5 people in March to about 60 at the time of the launch.

Due to the lack of a content management system for online publishing, the number of staff continued to grow. Every web page was made and updated manually by webmasters. At the most, CNN.com employed 45 technical staff members in Atlanta.

CNN.com expanded internationally with special editions for Europe, Asia, Middle East, and in association with partners, local language editions was launched in Arabic, Danish, Italian, Norwegian, Spanish, Swedish, and Turkish.

NRK's first online organization had three employees. They got resources to finance their own salaries, and a "license to beg" for production funding from the other departments at NRK. This led to an online offering dependent on the willingness to pay in various parts of the organization. The most prestigious part of the programming felt no need to invest in new media development, hence there was no online news offering for the first 5 years (1995–2000). For a license fee financed broadcaster, the income was fixed, and new ventures had to compete alongside existing activities for resources.

---

[4] NRK's program activities are organized according to a so-called broadcaster model. One section of the organization, Broadcasting, plans programs and the contents of the program schedules. This part of the organization sends requests and is responsible at all times for what is actually transmitted via television and radio and for what is published on the internet. Another section of the organization, the Program Division, develops and produces programs and contents according to the requests from the Broadcasting section.

The Second Phase (1999–2004)

After the Time Warner/America Online merger[5] and the dot com downfall in 2001, a major downsizing of the CNN Interactive organization took place, and the activities of CNN.com were refocused.

In 2005 the technical staffs were reduced by more than 70%, to 12 of the 60 people then employed in Atlanta and the international desks in London, Hong Kong, and Sydney in total had an editorial staff of 8 senior news editors. In addition to the domestic CNN.com, CNN's international editions are comprised in one international website. All local language initiatives were closed down after the internet crisis in 2001, but an edition translated into Arabic was launched after 9/11.

> I always viewed it as another channel, just like you [...] might use CNN headline news to get a quick take on the news versus watching CNN were you might spend more time. I thought of CNN.com as a place you can go when you are online or you want to search for something, interact with the news. I think when I left it certainly shifted more to being a support mechanism for the television channels, which I think is the wrong direction to go, because [...] it should not be the primary purpose, it really needs to stand alone. And I think the successful sites out there, BBC News is the one I would point to the most, does not have a channel identity at all, it really does stand alone. (Scott Woelfel, founding Executive Producer of CNN.com, interviewed in Atlanta, 2005)

Some of the online staff laid off in Atlanta had news wire[6] background and were recruited to the internal CNN Wire service, then growing to become a 24/7 operation servicing all CNN channels and shows. This service has become an important part of the centralized news production at the CNN.

The general online optimism leading up to the millennium, and advertising financing of parts of selected BBC products online, BBC being the role model of all public service organizations, led to a new strategy at the NRK. There was a need to allocate more resources to the online service, and advertising was identified as the solution. In order to open for such revenue, the online offering had to be defined outside the public service mission of NRK. A new division named NRK Futurum was established with a mission of creating new streams of revenue for the public broadcaster, and an ambitious goal of taking a dominant place in the online space was proclaimed in 2000. News then became a part of the online offering.

The dot com implosion of 2001 limited the potential of online revenue, and the online organization was reorganized. Online production became an integrated part of the various production departments. The videotext organization was expanded

---

[5] AOL purchased Time Warner for US $164 bn in 2000. Each original company merged into a newly created entity, where the shareholders of AOL owned 55% and Time Warner shareholders 45%. After the merger, the profitability of the former America Online decreased, and the market valuation of similar independent internet companies fell. This forced a goodwill write-off, causing AOL Time Warner to report a loss of $99 billion in 2002 – at the time, the largest loss ever reported by a company.

[6] Wire services supply news reports to newspapers, magazines, and radio and television broadcasters. These news agencies can be corporations (Reuters and AFP) or cooperative organizations (AP, UPI).

with some temporary employment to serve the new online channel and became a part of the radio division. A niche channel for news was also launched for terrestrial radio based on repurposing of material from the traditional radio operation, and these activities were located on the same floor. Original news reporting for NRK.no was prohibited due to the fear of exhausting sources needed for radio and television.

Site management and editing of the home page of NRK.no became the responsibilities of the Online Broadcaster. In principle the Broadcaster defines the offering and contracts content from the production departments, but in practice a conflict of front page space raised as the richness in content grew. Partly as a compromise the home page was divided in three sections: (1) program information and promotion, (2) online news, and (3) live and on-demand distribution of radio and television.

In 2004 the decision was made to make all regional transmissions, both radio and television, available on the internet across all national borders. In the case of major news events, the NRK website transmits live from the sites where events are taking place.

The same year NRK became one of the most visited websites in the country, but still not on the top 10 list. The Online Broadcaster had high hopes for better market positions as video consumption was expected to grow substantially due to increased online penetration.

The Third Phase (2005–2007) of CNN

In 2005 no CNN channels, including CNN.com, any longer had their own reporters and correspondents. All news packages were delivered to the main news room in Atlanta, and approved, before being available to all CNN channels simultaneously.

This can be seen as consistent with the traditional CNN approach to efficient news productions, which has made it possible for the CNN organization to deliver several 24 hour television channels for a far lower total cost than the resources available for news departments at the traditional US television networks with only a few hours air time (Küng-Shankleman, 2000).

All original reporting for CNN.com follow the same approval process via the senior editors at "The Row" in Atlanta.

> A broadcast network is very much about polished news, and that's what we have to rely on, [. . .] what's legally been approved [. . .] We still have to meet that standard, because it is a brand promise. (CNN interviewee, Atlanta, 2005)

It is an important part for CNN's strategy to be available for the consumer at any given time:

> CNN is about communicating news and information to as many people as possible and in as many ways as possible. And what CNN stands for is giving people accurate, reliable, timely, comprehensive news and information, and that there are multiple ways to do that. CNN does that over the cell phone, we do it over the computer, we do it over televisions, we do it over radio, [and] we do it in pre-programmed features that run in doctors' offices. CNN is about communicating news and information regardless of the vehicle through which it is communicated. (Mitch Gelman, Executive Producer, CNN.com, interviewed in Atlanta, 2005)

Even though the core reporting is standardized, the packaging is individual for each channel, based on the target group and the consumer's needs in the various situation of consumption. Broadcasting on the CNN Airport Network is delayed in order to avoid reports of aviation disasters, and on CNN.com you do not find talk shows.

In New York a new edition of the CNN Money section was relaunched in February 2006 as an online joint venture with Fortune, Money, Business 2.0, and Fortune Small Business. All Time Warner properties joined forces to increase the market share in the lucrative niche market for business news and information, and CNN.com is used to generate traffic to the new site, that is both a section of the domestic CNN.com and at the same time marketed as CNNMoney.com.

Online video had its breakthrough in 2005 when CNN left the online video subscription model and introduced free video, financed by advertising, on CNN.com. This was possible to do in a very efficient manner due to the centralized news production. But adding to the portfolio of channels has some consequences for traditional television.

> [Internet] has changed forever the dynamic of television journalism, because no longer do most people get their news when they get home in the evening or on the radio in the car on the way home. They are peeking at it at work during the day. They know what the news is when they get to the house. So, if you are going to deliver something in primetime, you have to deliver something that takes the viewer beyond basic news, the commodity news of the day. (Richard T. Griffiths, Editorial Director CNN, Atlanta, November 2005).

Prime time shows are now demanding stories going behind the news in contrast to what Griffiths define as "here-they-come-here-they-go journalism."

> ...in prime time, they do not really seem to care about speed. They care about quality of the storytelling, is it a compelling story, is it an interesting story, is it well told, is it pulled together well? [...] What is the choice of the story? Is it going to draw an audience, is it going to draw the prime time audience? And some of that is in play, whereas the website, and daytime programming and headline news are all about speed, and getting the information on very, very quickly. So, we have two different customer styles happening within the company right now. (Richard T. Griffiths, Editorial Director CNN, Atlanta, November 2005)

This leads to a situation where the American prime time shows aired from Time Warner's New York Headquarter are asking for more exclusive use of the correspondents controlled by the centralized news operation in Atlanta.

The Third Phase (2005–2007) of NRK

The year 2005 became the breakthrough for online video. But NRK did not manage to realize the potential. Mandatory registration of video users[7] was removed to

---

[7] NRK and CNN did both require registration of video users; however, only CNN charged for videos initially.

enhance usability, but the automated production was detached from the online news staff, and the integration of video in online news developed slowly.

The Norwegian online market is unique in the sense that online newspapers have a strong national position. Three of the top 10 sites are national print newspapers with a wide range of service. All started web-tv offerings in 2006, and the largest newspaper, national tabloid VG, also became the leading online broadcaster, to the frustration of the nation's dominating broadcaster, NRK.

The leading commercial broadcaster, TV 2, had become a major player in online news through the purchase of the online-only Nettavisen (Online Newspaper) in 2002, but this was a first-generation online news service with limited multimedia content. TV 2's strategy was to offer online video as premium service requiring a paid subscription. As the dominant player in this niche, this became a profitable venture based on on-demand news and entertainment previously aired on television. Hence the major print newspapers took the lead in development of original multimedia news content for the web.

NRK had the richest video content offering, but presented it mainly in an archive format. The online news department was moved from the radio division to television in an attempt to facilitate breaking news video production for NRK.no. The access to moving images has become better, but all interviewees agree that this has not reached its potential.

As digital terrestrial television (DTT) was about to be introduced in 2008 and analogue shut off was decided, a new situation emerged for the traditional television channels. NRK and TV 2 would not be the only channels with full national distribution. In preparing for increased competition the traditional market leaders introduced niche channels. TV 2 went from being a family channel to offering a family of channels, with sports, news, and movies as part of its new portfolio.

NRK decided to re-launch NRK2 as a news channel in competition with TV 2 and to establish a children's channel in addition. As TV 2 launched the news channel in February 2007, NRK did a soft launch of their news channel online and reorganized the news department in order to realize the new strategy on continually publication of online news in all three channels.

Internal conflicts led to a compromise of two news organizations, one responsible for all traditional prime time news shows on radio and television, the other for the continuously updated news offerings in all channels. The latter was supposed to control the news gathering resources, but the traditional shows were struggling for control over dedicated reporters.

One of the objectives of reorganizing was to produce more without increasing the total costs. As more people are dedicated to specific program offerings, fewer resources are available for a centralized multi-channel production. At the same time the union at the prime time "Dagsrevyen" is struggling to stop proposed strategic alliances with a major business print daily in the business coverage in new channels. Strong unions demand more resources for the new news operation. But for a public broadcaster the revenue stream is still fixed. The definition of online to be outside the public service domain in order to sell advertising has not resulted in a revenue stream substantially to finance new ventures.

The Online Broadcaster and the online news department are integrated in the public service organization, and the commercial NRK Aktivum is selling advertising on the offerings made available. There is no tradition for developing business plans before launching news concepts online.

Strategies of Change

Economies of scale and scope provide a compelling case in favor of providing media content online (Doyle, 2002). By utilizing a system of centralized news gathering to serve a growing number of channels, CNN is able to hold the marginal cost of each new channel in check.

Historically CNN comes out of a tradition of business development that might be characterized as a *prospector* strategy. Ted Turner inherited his father's business of advertising boards in the southeastern USA and built a media empire by responding to emerging trends. He is still an entrepreneur continually in search for market opportunities.[8]

In 1995 CNN was the world's news leader, and ran a global news operation with several output channels very efficiently. Even with an innovating approach to news gathering (one-man teams with satellite phones in war zones, etc.), it might be argued that the main focus was on improving the efficiency of their existing operations, and therefore should be analyzed as a *defender*. However, the innovative approach also in the development of new output channels suggests an *analyzer* strategy.

The *analyzers* would operate routinely and efficiently in their stabile area through use of formalized structures and processes, and in their more turbulent areas watch their competitors closely for new ideas, rapidly adapt those that appear to be most promising (Miles and Snow).

The problem with such an analysis is the period when CNN.com was launched. In 1995 there was no proven business model for online activities. CNN was not the only large media organization to launch major online operations at this time, but the first major television operation to invest heavily in this new field. Rather than watching out for success-stories to copy, CNN was a creator of change in the whole industry – playing part of the same role as it did in the traditional television market, especially with the emphasis on breaking news.

In relation to the continuously experimentation with new output channels, it might be argued that CNN to a certain degree remained a *prospector*.

The merger AOL/Time Warner might represent a moment of significant change. Ted Turner did not any longer play a part in the development of CNN, and a major downsizing led to streamlining of the total news operation. Promotion of CNN television and other Time Warner products became an increasingly important part of the

---

[8] A restaurant chain serving fresh bison meat is one of Ted Turner's last ventures.

CNN.com product. And new revenue was created by introducing sponsored special reports.

CNN is maintaining the brand promise of delivering polished content in every available channel. And television content is an increasingly important part of the product offering online.

They do have plans to continue development of new market opportunities in digital television, but the need to operate within the limits of a brand promise does prohibit a typical *prospector* strategy.

Using new technology primary as a tool for distribution, with very little emphasis on the development of original online journalism, CNN strategy today will be classified as a *defender*.

In comparison, NRK entered the online market with a *defender* strategy. The focus was on publishing television and radio, and based on advice from the European Broadcasting Union, the online activities were limited and the funding led to a not-so-coordinated portfolio of promotional activities.

The second phase represented a rhetorical shift toward an *analyzer* strategy. A new market had emerged and NRK had the content and competence needed. Online was defined outside the area of public service, and a new commercial division had high ambitions of creating new revenue from a rapidly growing online market.

However, the structure of production and publishing remained integrated in the traditional organization with dedicated resources for every platform and online on a third place in prioritization behind television and radio. Journalists were internally recruited. New talent started in radio and aspired to television. There is a strong consensus in the editorial staff of public service as the brand promise in all platforms; hence the commercial online zone consisted of public service content with advertising.

The commercial division is limited to advertising sales in a strong church and state separation from concept development and production. The strategy might be formulated as an *analyzer*, but the structure remains that of a *defender*. Their lack of success in the Norwegian online market led to a conflict where the news department, the online broadcaster, and the commercial division played a typically blame game rather than cooperating to gain the expected market share.

This may suggest that the formula is yet to be found and that the balance between traditional and new activities in an *analyzer* model has not been established in a satisfactory way. Hence it is possible to discuss whether NRK is a *defender* with some symptoms of a *reactor*.

Miles and Snow (2003, p. 93) identify three main reasons why an organization acts as *reactor*:

1. Top management may not have clearly articulated the organization's strategy.
2. Management does not fully shape the organization's structure and processes to fit a chosen strategy.
3. There is a tendency for management to maintain the organization's strategy–structure relationship despite overwhelming changes in environmental conditions.

Rapid reorganization processes indicate the willingness to shape the organization's structure and processes, but the strategic choice to define online as a commercial field outside the public service domain has not led to major changes to the overall strategy–structure relationship. "An organization is seldom able to veer substantially from its current course without major structure-process alternations" (Miles & Snow 2003, p. 8).

A major downsizing in 2001 led to changes in the CNN production structure toward a centralized news production, efficiently serving a growing number of platforms. CNN has developed from a *prospector* tradition experimenting with new technology of production, distribution, and content formats to a *defender,* using new media channels primarily for distribution of centralized produced content. NRK came to the game as a *defender* and is struggling to find organizational structures to balance traditional and new platforms in a news productions moving toward a centralized model.

Despite all differences between CNN and NRK, both have developed *defender* strategies. The operationalization of this strategy is to develop an organizational structure to realize the efficiency of centralized news production, enabling an increased *breath of market service* and to hold the marginal cost of each new channel in check.

Multi-platform Defender Strategies

The *multi-platform* production leads to standardized content being adjusted for different output channels in the newsroom. If unique content is produced, the most prestigious channel will have priority. This leads to a situation where *cross-media* concepts with interplay between media types are less likely to be developed in news operations, and interactive *multimedia* content utilizing the full online toolbox rarely will be present. In the *defender* cases of CNN and NRK, the rationale for a product portfolio strategy (Picard, 2005) is *breath of market service*, and *efficiency,* irrespective of all the differences between CNN and NRK.

Cross-media concepts might be tools to move the user between platforms and maximize the total time spent on the brand portfolio – by creating a total experience cross-media that each channel will not be able to offer by itself. The operationalization will however demand major organizational change in the news production. A defender strategy with a structure of integrated production will probably be preferred. But as we have seen, traditional news organizations adapting such strategies and structures are likely to be perusing the efficiency of *multi-platform* production rather than matrix structures for *cross-media* concepts. Hence the future for this approach to online journalism is not very bright.

The *defender* strategies of CNN and NRK do have implications for the professional role of the journalists. On the basic level the centralized and efficient approach to news production leads to the development of standard formats fitting a growing number or output channels. Rather than utilizing the comparative storytelling advantage of each channel or platform, there will be a higher focus on the lowest common denominator. The identity of the journalist working in a centralized news gathering organization will be strongest linked to the most prestigious output context (i.e., channel or platform) for the content produced. In broadcasting this tends to be the main television channel, while in newspapers the morning edition on paper.

Hence the professional role of the journalist on the higher levels (Nygren, 2008), defined by the norms, ideas, and values related to the main output channel, becomes part of the structure for the professional role in new and developing platforms for news mediation.

Conclusion

This cross-national comparative case study of online news production has demonstrated the importance of the strategy–structure relationship in developing new platforms within a traditional media organization.

Decontextualized stabile patterns identified in the two most different cases of CNN and NRK might indicate general coherence in the strategy, structure, and rationale for the development of media product portfolios in large incumbent news organizations.[9] *Defenders* tend to choose a structure of centralized and integrated news gathering, aiming to increase the *breath of market service* and to hold the marginal cost of each new channel in check. On a basic level of job content and use of technology, the implications of the role of the journalist is industrialized production of standardized content elements applying the lowest common denominator rather than the unique storytelling tools of each output channel – with the most prestigious output channel playing a defining role.

However, this Tayloristic image of the situation after the first 10 years of online news production does not represent a static situation. Social structures are changing over time, and the CNN case illustrates how the new environment of multi-platform portfolios leads to the need for product development in traditional prime time television.

Changes toward analyzer strategies and utilizing the unique storytelling features of each channel might be a scenario if a higher degree of product differentiation is needed to meet competition and increase the total viewer time on own brand. But the conflict of the need for differentiation and limited resources to develop these attributes is typical for the situation of mainstream online media in a time where

---

[9] The competitive case of Norwegian national newspapers represents a deviant case in the same time period, with several players developing analyzer strategies resulting in different structures and processes (Krumsvik, 2008). In 2008 also the majority of these players are integrating news gathering to gain higher efficiency.

digitalization has dramatically lowered the barriers of entry, and the fragmentation of the media market is increasing.[10]

The growing importance of online channels in attention and economic value does also have implication for the social structure of the development of online journalism. This might be the most likely scenario for a larger degree of utilizing the online toolbox. For new platforms to come, history might repeat: The journalists' own understanding of their professional role will probably continue to be a conservative force.

References

Andersen, S. S. (1997). *Case-studier og generalisering*. Bergen: Fagbokforlaget.

Baker, C. E. (1994). *Advertising and a democratic press*. Princeton, NJ: Princeton University Press.

Boczkowski, P. J. (2004). *Digitizing the news: Innovation in online newspapers*. Cambridge, MA: The MIT Press.

Bolter, J. D., & Richard, G. (1999). *Remediation understanding new media*. Cambridge, MA: The MIT Press.

Chamberlin, E. H. (1933). *Theory of monopolistic competition*. Cambridge, MA. Harvard University Press.

Chandler, A. D. Jr. (1962). *Strategy and structure: Chapters in the history of the American industrial enterprise*. Cambridge: The MIT Press.

Deuze, M. (2001). Understanding the impact of the internet: On new media profesionalism, mindsets and buzzwords. *Ejournalist* 1(1), http://www.ejournalism.au.com/ejournalist/deuze.pdf

Domingo, D. (2004). *Comparing professional routines and values in online newsrooms: A reflection from a case study*. Paper for the Media Production Analysis Working Group, IAMCR Conference, Porto Alegre.

Doyle, G. (2002). *Understanding media economics*. London, Thousand Oaks, CA, New Delhi: Sage.

Engebretsen, M. (2001). *Nyheten som hypertekst: Tekstuelle aspekter ved møtet mellom en gammel sjanger og ny teknologi*. Kristiansand: IJ-forlaget.

Giddens, A. (1984). *The constitution of society: Outline of the theory of structuration*. Berkeley, CA: University of California Press.

Hambrick, D. (2003). Foreword to the classic edition. In R. Miles & C. Snow (Eds.), *Organizational strategy, structure, and process. Stanford business classics*. Stanford, CA: Stanford University Press.

Harper, C. (1998). *And that's the way it will be: News and information in a digital world*. New York: New York University Press.

Krumsvik, A. H. (2006). The strategic role of online newspapers. *Nordicom Review, 27*(2), 283–295.

Krumsvik, A. H. (2008). Forholdet mellom kanalstrategi og journalistrollen i NRK og CNN. In R. Ottosen & A. H. Krumsvik (red), *Journalistikk i en digital hverdag. Høyskoleforlaget/IJ-forlaget*. Kristiansand: Norwegian Academic Press.

---

[10]Chamberlin (1933) introduced the term Monopolistic Competition to explain a situation between the polar cases of perfect competition and monopoly. In this market structure there are many firms selling a differentiated product, and there are low barriers to entry and exit in the industry. It is similar to monopoly in the sense that the firm has some control over the price it charges, since products are differentiated. But because there are many sellers, it is similar with perfect competition in that the free entry and exit of other firms in the industry pushes each firm's net profit toward zero.

Küng-Shankleman, L. (2000). *Inside the BBC and CNN – Managing media organisations*. London, New York: Routledge.

Matheson, D. (2004). Weblogs and the epistemology of the news: Some trends in online journalism. *New Media & Society, 6*(4), 443–468.

McManus, J. H. (1994). *Market-driven journalism: Let the citizen beware?* Thousand Oaks, CA: Sage Publications.

Miles, R., & Snow, C. (2003). Organizational strategy, structure, and process. Stanford business classics. Stanford, CA: Stanford University Press [Originally Published in 1978. New York: McGraw-Hill].

Mjøset, L. (2006). Can grounded theory solve the problems of its critics. *Sosiologisk tidsskrift, 4*(13), 379–408.

Nygren, G. (2008). *Nyhetsfabriken. Journalistiska yrkesroller i en förändrad medievärld*. Lund: Studentlitteratur.

Ottosen, R. (2004). *I journalistikkens grenseland – Journalistrollen mellom marked og idealer*. Kristiansand: IJ-forlaget.

Pavlik, J. (1999). *Journalism and new media*. New York: Colombia University Press.

Picard, R. G. (red). (2005). *Media product portfolios: Issues in management of multiple products and services*. Mahwah, NJ: LEA.

Porter, M. (1980). *Competitive strategy: Techniques for analyzing industries and competitors*. New York: The Free Press.

Rasmussen, T. (2002). Nettmedier. Journalistikk og medier på Internett. Bergen: Fagbokforlaget.

Roos, J., & von Krogh, G. (1996). *Managing strategy processes in emergent industries: The case of media firms*. London: MacMillan Business.

Schroeder, R. (2004). Online review. *Journalism Studies, 5*(4), 563–570.

Steensen, S. (2005). *All about text – Why online journalists seem reluctant to implement newmedia technology*. Paper presented at the First European Communication Conference in Amsterdam, 24–26 November 2005.

Political Economy, the Internet and FL/OSS Development

Robin Mansell and Evangelia Berdou

Introduction

There is a growing amount of research on Free Libre/Open Source Software (FL/OSS) development. Despite this, we still have a rather fragmented view of how structural factors associated with institutions influence the patterns of software developer activity in this area. What are some of the institutional dynamics of the development of this particular type of software? Are these dynamics mainly associated with features of the 'gift economy' such as a strong voluntary ethos and a deeply rooted cooperative spirit, as is frequently suggested in the literature? Should we conclude that features of the 'exchange economy' such as the hierarchical structuring of economic power are evaded by most of the participants in FL/OSS developer communities?

In this article we present an examination of patterns of contribution and 'maintainership' in a large FL/OSS project. The results provide a basis for considering the extent to which structural factors such as institutional support can be taken as an indication of economic power and as important features of the emerging dynamic of FL/OSS development. We suggest that a careful assessment of the dynamic of FL/OSS requires a detailed empirical analysis of the different patterns of software contributors, depending upon whether their contributions are voluntary or paid. We reflect upon the distinctiveness of the patterns of contribution and on some of their implications.

A political economy perspective is sometimes regarded as being antithetical to theoretical traditions that focus on the highly situated nature of the activities of individuals and their communities of practice in the FL/OSS area. However, as the analysis in this article suggests, there can be a productive interplay between these traditions (see Mansell, 2004). We link these two traditions in the investigation of the case study which we present in the section 'The Case of GNOME' in order to reveal aspects of developments in the FL/OSS arena that might otherwise remain

R. Mansell (✉)
Department of Media and Communications, London School of Economics and Political Science, Houghton Street, London, UK
e-mail: r.e.mansell@lse.ac.uk

J. Hunsinger et al. (eds.), *International Handbook of Internet Research*,
DOI 10.1007/978-1-4020-9789-8_21, © Springer Science+Business Media B.V. 2010

hidden from view. In the following section we highlight some of the theoretical insights that a political economy perspective brings to the analysis of FL/OSS.

Determinations in FL/OSS Development

In the political economy tradition of research we are led, following Golding and Murdock (1978), to approach questions relating to the dynamics of FL/OSS development from a position that investigates whether there is the potential for inequality to emerge in relationships between those contributing to this growing arena of software development. If we acknowledge that social and economic relations are not egalitarian within society as a whole, would we not expect such relations to be present within the FL/OSS developer communities? From a political economy perspective, we might expect new articulations of power relations to emerge and shape the activities of many of those who, nevertheless, remain deeply committed to reciprocity and the sharing of knowledge through cooperation that characterises the 'gift economy' relationships that have been documented in the literature (Kollock, 1999; Lampel & Bhalla 2007; Weber, 2004).

Studies of FL/OSS development often emphasise the abundance and variety of the contributions of developers but pay little heed to the structures and processes of power that may be associated with the organisation of institutions with which these individuals are involved. There are interesting features of the development of FL/OSS that do not appear to be mediated by the values of market exchange. But there may also be mediation by at least some of the features of exchange models of the economy. These features may be visible if we orient our investigation to areas in which there may be conditions of scarcity – whether of money, skills, or time – in relation to FL/OSS development (Mansell, 1999). Conditions of scarcity might be expected to give rise to articulations of power that create tensions within the communities of software developers.

At its core, a political economy perspective on FL/OSS should be particularly concerned with the specific institutional circumstances under which the software is being developed (Mansell, 2004). Research highlighting the voluntary aspects of FL/OSS communities has its parallel in research on the internet which assumes that the present-day generation of the internet 'automatically' empowers people to engage in new social and economic relationships. While the internet may be characterised as a postmodern medium (Murphy, 2002; Poster, 2001), as being technologically progressive (Patelis, 2000), or as a new public space for communities (Wellman & Haythornthwaite, 2002), these are not the only perspectives on its development. Others have emphasised the commercialisation of the internet and its characteristics as a commercial space for advertisers and new media businesses (Ettema & Whitney, 1994; Roscoe, 1999; Webster & Phalen, 1997). Like other forms of mediation, the internet is being socially constructed (Lievrouw & Livingstone, 2006; Livingstone, 2002; Miller & Slater, 2000). This construction is likely to favour certain social and economic values over others (Castells, 2001). David's (2001) review of the origins of the internet demonstrates the extent to which policy intervention by the US government played a major role in encouraging the flat configuration of the internet protocol, but this does not mean that this configuration will always remain in place (David, 2007). Choices about the values, such as the flat, non-discriminatory design of the internet protocol associated with the absence of hierarchy and with collaboration and sharing, are being contested by those favouring discriminatory treatment of internet traffic, for example, in the interests of efficiency and quality of service.

Similarly, in the case of FL/OSS, power is embedded in the institutions associated with its development and this software is also being socially constructed by a wide range of participants with different values, skill levels, employment arrangements, etc. Dalle, David, Ghosh, and Steinmueller (2005) provide survey-based evidence suggesting that there are many potential variations and patterns in the roles and activities of these participants. von Hippel and Lakhani (2000) also found substantial variations in the levels of contributions to software projects by software developers. These studies suggest that there is something considerably more complicated about the structuring of FL/OSS communities than a gift exchange explanation can provide. Like other new media, FL/OSS is developing within capitalism and it is likely that there will be a blending of features of the older and newer modes of software development, especially when software is being developed and used in relatively large-scale and widely dispersed contexts.

Contributors to the analysis of the political economy of the media and communication industries from Smythe (1960) to Garnham (1986) have paid close attention to emerging structures and hierarchies of power. If resources of various kinds are scarce and insofar as power is unequally distributed in society, then the key issues are how those scarce resources are controlled and with what consequences. Although, FL/OSS is being developed within the broader context of capitalism and of the exchange economy, we follow Garnham in insisting that this context should not be regarded as an overwhelming determination. As Garnham put, it "there is then, and this cannot be sufficiently stressed, *no necessary coincidence between the effects of the capitalist process proper and the ideological needs of the dominant class*" (emphasis added) (Garnham, 1986, p. 23). The values and needs for institutional support, for example, of the most active FL/OSS developers may differ from those with more peripheral involvement and their need for institutional support may also differ as a result. There may be many other variations as well. Therefore, empirical research is needed to suggest how power is structured and differentiated within the communities of developers who participate in FL/OSS (Garnham, 2000; Melody, 1994).

To understand these specific circumstances in the case of FL/OSS we need an analysis of how values and control processes are becoming embedded in the institutions and procedures adopted by participants in FL/OSS communities. The need to seek ways of differentiating between participants is emphasised in approaches to innovation associated more generally with new information and communication technologies (ICTs). Freeman (1992) and Freeman and Louçã (2001), for example, argued that when new technologies emerge, their widespread appropriation begins to challenge the hegemony of earlier modes of social and economic organisation.

In the case of FL/OSS they might not be surprised by the emergence of the values associated with the gift economy. Freeman argued that an emergent technological paradigm, such as that associated with new ICTs (and therefore with FL/OSS) may involve a new set of principles or values or common sense practices, but that this would not necessarily mean that new values and practices become the dominant ones. Instead, both the new and the old may mutate, recede, or become dominant. At any given time the new combinations of values and practices need to be investigated through empirical studies to provide insight into the process of change. Thus, we need empirical studies of the many contexts in which FL/OSS is being developed (David & Shapiro, 2008). We suggest that research needs to give greater attention not only to micro-processes involved but also to the links between these and the development of institutions and their associated power relations.

As is the case in the 'administrative' tradition of research on older media and communication industries (Melody & Mansell, 1983), the predominant focus in the study of the internet and FL/OSS development has been to develop a rather unproblematised account of the internet's growth and of the new institutions of governance that are emerging. We know from research in the media and communication field that new ICTs are implicated in many contradictory ways in enabling or disabling various forms of sociability (Lievrouw & Livingstone, 2006; Silverstone, 1999; Silverstone & Hirsch, 1992). There seems to be no reason to assume that software should be different. We also know from research in the information systems field that power and negotiation are important aspects of the development of new kinds of network relationships, including those associated with FL/OSS (Koch & Schneider, 2002). Yet in studies of communities of practice, and especially those focusing on software development processes, issues of power are being addressed only indirectly and partially (Berdou, 2003). Two of the major contributors to this literature, Lave and Wenger (1991, p. 42), have acknowledged that "unequal relations of power must be included more systematically..." in the analysis of these communities. Until recently this neglect of power was still a feature of this tradition of research (Wenger, 1999; Fox, 2000).

The study of communities or networks of practice is helping to identify how knowledge accumulates and is shared in FL/OSS contexts (see, for example, Samer & Wasko 2002), but again with little attention to power relationships. Bergquist and Ljungberg (2001) have addressed issues of unequal participation and power in FL/OSS communities, but much of the literature assumes the spread of an all-pervasive gift-giving, non-hierarchical culture (Kollock, 1999; Raymond, 2001a). Bergquist and Ljungberg (2001, p. 315) argue, in contrast, that "some of the user/developers experience power relationships that are expressed as an elitism of the inner circle and exercised as the right to hinder a person in contributing to the common good".

In summary, the FL/OSS development model is regarded by some analysts as a counterpoint to the hegemony of the power of traditional proprietary software producers (Bezroukov, 1999; Feller & Fitzgerald, 2002; Raymond, 2001b). It may indeed be a new platform for user-driven innovation (von Hippel, 2002) and it may provide a platform for a wide range of new business models (Mansell &

Steinmueller, 2000; Feller & Fitzgerald, 2002) as well as offering a new mode of online collaborative and distributed working (Bezroukov, 1999; Feller & Fitzgerald, 2002; Gallivan, 2001; Ljundgberg, 2000; Moon & Sproull, 2002). However, if we are to understand the dynamics that are at work in FL/OSS communities, we need to deepen and extend the work of those who have begun their investigations from a political economy perspective (see, for example, Weber, 2004; Healy & Schussman 2003; Lancashire, 2001).

In the next section, we take the example of the FL/OSS GNOME project as a case study through which to begin the task of exploring the distinctiveness of software developer contributions and the way differences may be associated with scarce resources such as skill and with institutional affiliation. The latter is examined by focusing on the governance institution created for GNOME and the former by analysing the contributions of those who develop and maintain various modules of the GNOME project's software.

The Case of GNOME

The results of an examination of patterns of contribution and maintainership in a FL/OSS project are presented in this section. Contributors to the GNOME project[1] aim to create a complete desktop environment and a development platform for the Unix operating system.[2] A study was undertaken by Berdou (2007) to investigate the patterns of contribution between affiliated and non-affiliated contributors to GNOME, focussing specifically on the GNOME Foundation members and on those involved in the project's maintainer network. The study gave particular attention to those who not only contribute software code to the project but also are involved in more peripheral roles such as translation, documentation, or conference organization. In this section, we highlight the central roles of paid software developers in the GNOME project and the characteristics of members of the volunteer and peripheral communities participating in the project. We also draw attention to interesting differences between paid contributors who are employed to work on GNOME and those who are employed to contribute to other FL/OSS projects.

Background to the Empirical Study

The GNOME Foundation was established in 2000.[3] It is comprised of a Board of Directors, an Executive Director, an Advisory Board, and the GNOME Membership Committee. The Foundation coordinates GNOME releases, specifies which projects

---

[1] See http://www.gnome.org.

[2] See research on the dynamics of commercialization and peripheral participation in mature, community-led free/open source software projects, Berdou (2007).

[3] See http://foundation.gnome.org/

belong in GNOME, and acts as the official voice of the project community. At the time the investigation of GNOME was conducted (June 2005), the Foundation had 335 members. Membership, which is renewed every two years, is available to individuals who have contributed a 'non-trivial' improvement to the project.

The extent of an applicant's contribution is confirmed by a long-term GNOME contributor and status as a member is decided by the membership committee. A Foundation member can stand for election to the Board of Directors, vote in elections, and issue or approve referenda. In examining GNOME at the level of the Foundation, we are therefore considering the characteristics of experienced contributors whose work has been recognized by others and who are interested in participating in the institutional and administrative aspects of the GNOME project.

The empirical results set out in the following discussion are based on data collected using a questionnaire which was distributed at the GNOME Foundation meeting in GUADEC 2006 (GNOME Users and Developers Conference) in Stuttgart, Germany, and by email.[4] The survey resulted in 199 responses (152 via email and 47 at the conference) from the 335 members of the Foundation, yielding a 59.4% response rate.

As indicated above, this research also examined participants in the maintainer network. Maintainers in FL/OSS projects assume a variety of duties and responsibilities. A maintainer is responsible for answering queries and responding to problem reports and is usually the point person for coordinating with the individual(s) in charge of software releases. Maintainers are highly skilled and are recognized authorities in their area of expertise. As such, they influence the technical direction of their project, providing the vision behind its development. Maintainers have the right to peer-review, approve, and incorporate patches into the code base. In some instances an individual may have the right to commit changes to the code base, but it is generally considered 'bad form' to forgo a maintainer's approval. Given the importance of the role of the maintainer, instead of using the term 'maintenance' which may suggest that the maintenance of code is a passive activity, we use the term 'maintainership' in this article.

In order to examine the patterns of maintainership activity, the research focused on the 2.10.0 release of GNOME and, specifically, on the Platform and Desktop Sources. In GNOME, the names of the maintainers are usually included in a text file called 'MAINTAINER(S)' which can be found in the release tar archives.[5] The data compiled as the basis for the analysis in this article included 110 modules maintained by 92 individuals.[6] As in the case of the GNOME Foundation members, the analysis of GNOME maintainers focuses on experienced and committed

---

[4] See Berdou (2007) for details of the methodology. Questions were asked about members' overall and principal areas/modules of contribution, affiliation, GUADEC attendance, city of residence.

[5] A tar archive, or tarball in jargon terms, is a group of files compressed together as one, which is used to package source code distributions.

[6] The data were validated by two long-term GNOME contributors. See Berdou (2007) for details of the methodology. This data coding scheme was also validated by two long-term contributors.

contributors. Unlike the case of the Foundation members where non-coders can participate, the maintainer network consists only of programmers and is therefore more technical in character.

The survey respondents were invited to report modules/projects to which they had made a contribution. For analytical purposes, the modules were grouped into five hierarchical areas of development. The same scheme was applied for the classification of maintained modules.

Core/Platform modules. These comprise the main development libraries of the GNOME platform. These include the graphical libraries, the component model, the accessibility libraries, Configuration and Lockdown, printing, and the main gnome desktop library, libgnomeui.

Main Desktop modules. These include the main components of the GNOME desktop environment, such as the file manager, panel, and window manager as well as Evolution, GNOME's primary groupware and personal information manager, and the multimedia framework (Gstreamer).

Secondary desktop modules. These include secondary libraries and secondary elements of the GNOME desktop as well as the end-user productivity applications included in the GNOME release.

Development tools and processes. This comprises tools for development as well as tasks related to releases, issues of quality control, and unspecified bug fixes.

Peripheral activities. This comprises the non-coding aspects of contribution, such as documentation, translation, and artwork.

Patterns of Contribution and Participation of GNOME Foundation Members

The analysis of the GNOME data indicates a clear split in the distribution of volunteers and paid contributors. The respondents in the sample reported that 98 were volunteers and 101 were affiliated individuals.[7] Furthermore, as shown in Fig. 1, the data allow for a more detailed categorization of paid developers based on whether they have been employed to contribute exclusively to GNOME, other FL/OSS projects, or both to GNOME and other FL/OSS projects.

The data indicate that GNOME has a rich ecology of contributing organizations. The paid developers in the sample were employed by 41 institutions, including small- and medium-sized enterprises, large companies, and research institutions. The three most important employers were Novell Inc. and Red Hat Inc. with 16 developers each, and Sun Microsystems Inc. with 12 developers working on GNOME and on FL/OSS development. The two biggest companies represented in

---

[7] 'Affiliated' or 'paid' refers in this context to a developer employed by an organization actively involved in FL/OSS development. A volunteer is a contributor who is not employed by such an organization. This therefore does not mean that all volunteers are unemployed, but simply that they are not remunerated to participate in FL/OSS development.

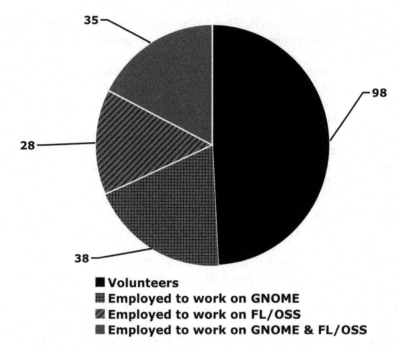

Fig. 1 Number of GNOME Foundation respondents according to their employment status
Source: GNOME Foundation survey, N=199.

the sample, IBM and Nokia, were participating only marginally in the project, at
least at the level of the Foundation, with one contributor each. The sample also features a considerable number of developers, eight in total, who were self-employed
and were undertaking subcontracting jobs.

Figure 2 shows a breakdown of the involvement of the respondents according to
their main area of contribution, i.e. the module/activity they reported to have been
most active in during the six months leading up to the survey. What stands out in
Fig. 2 is the overwhelming presence of paid developers in *Core/Platform modules*
and the very strong presence of volunteers in *Secondary Desktop* and *Peripheral
Activities*. Specifically, 85.7% (53.6 + 32.1%) of all the contributors involved in
Core/Platform Modules are developers employed to work on GNOME and more
than 60% of the contributors who were primarily active in *Peripheral Activities* are
volunteers. In *Secondary Desktop*, 64.1% of the respondents are volunteers and in
Main Desktop, more than 70% of developers are employed.

Figure 3 presents the distribution of the respondents' effort in the five main areas
of contribution. Volunteers and contributors paid to work on FL/OSS but not on
GNOME have very similar patterns of participation: they contribute equally intensively to *Secondary Desktop* (42%) and *Peripheral Activities* (35.7%). Similarly,
dedicated GNOME contributors (Paid to work on GNOME and Paid to work on
GNOME and on FL/OSS) appear to have nearly identical patterns of involvement

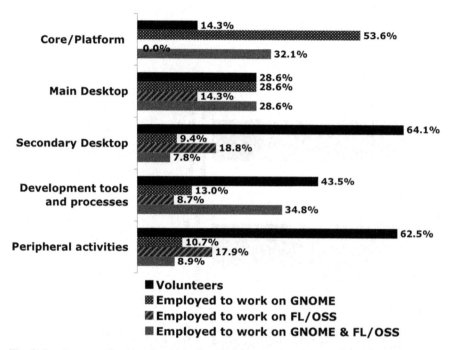

Core/Platform — 14.3%, 53.6%, 0.0%, 32.1%

Main Desktop — 28.6%, 28.6%, 14.3%, 28.6%

Secondary Desktop — 9.4%, 18.8%, 7.8%, 64.1%

Development tools and processes — 13.0%, 8.7%, 34.8%, 43.5%

Peripheral activities — 10.7%, 17.9%, 8.9%, 62.5%

■ Volunteers
▨ Employed to work on GNOME
▨ Employed to work on FL/OSS
■ Employed to work on GNOME & FL/OSS

Fig. 2 Involvement of paid and volunteer contributors according to main area of contribution
Source: GNOME Foundation survey, N=199.

in four out of five areas of development (*Core/Platform, Main Desktop, Secondary Desktop, and Peripheral Activities*).

In the following, we examine whether these differences are statistically significant. Table 1 reports the results of a cross-tabulation of the results for volunteers and affiliated contributors by main area of contribution. The cross-tabulation has a χ^2 value (df=8 and N=199) of 53.372, p<0.0001, indicating a significant association between the selected groups and the specified areas of development. The adjusted residuals inform us that the most significant patterns of association are to be found between volunteers and *Core/Platform* modules (-4), volunteers and *Main Desktop* modules (-2.4), volunteers and *Secondary Desktop* modules (2.9), volunteers and *Peripheral Activities* (2.3) employed to work on GNOME and on GNOME and FL/OSS and *Core/Platform* modules (5.8) employed to work on GNOME and on GNOME and FL/OSS and *Secondary Desktop* (-3.9) as well as *Peripheral Activities* (-3.1). There is a larger proportion of paid developers who contribute to *Core/Platform* and *Main Desktop* modules than would be expected if the variables were independent. By contrast, volunteers clearly contribute more to *Peripheral Activities* and to the *Secondary Desktop*. The only area of development that is significant for developers paid to work on FL/OSS is *Core/Platform* (-2.3).

We next consider how these results relate to GNOME event attendance. Figure 4 indicates how frequently volunteers and paid developers participate in

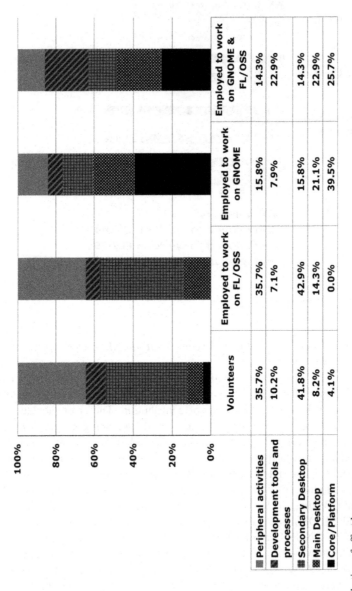

Fig. 3 Distribution of effort by group
Source: GNOME Foundation survey, N=199.

Table 1 Main area of contribution, affiliated and volunteers

		Main area of contribution					
		Core/ platform	Main desktop	Secondary desktop	Development tools and processes	Peripheral activities	Total
Volunteers	Count	4	8	41	10	35	98
	Percentage within the Group	4.1	8.2	41.8	10.2	35.7	100.0
	Percentage within the Area	14.3	28.6	64.1	43.5	62.5	49.2
	Adjusted Residual	−4	−2.4	2.9	−0.6	2.3	
Paid to work on GNOME and GNOME and FL/OSS	Count	24	16	11	11	11	73
	Percentage within the Group	32.9	21.9	15.1	15.1	15.1	100.0
	Percentage within the Area	85.7	57.1	17.2	47.8	19.6	36.7
	Adjusted Residual	5.8	2.4	−3.9	1.2	−3.1	
Paid to work on FL/OSS	Count	0	4	12	2	10	28
	Percentage within the Group	0.0	14.3	42.9	7.1	35.7	100.0
	Percentage within the Area	0.0	14.3	18.8	8.7	17.9	14.1
	Adjusted Residual	−2.3	0	1.3	−0.8	1	

Source: GNOME Foundation survey, N=199.

GUADEC, the GNOME Users and Developers' Conference, the leading event for the developer community. Figure 4 shows that 64.5% (38.2+26.3%) of those who are paid to work on GNOME have participated in all three GUADEC conferences between 2003 and 2005, whereas 66% of volunteers and 57% of those contributors hired to develop FL/OSS but not to work on GNOME have not participated in any event. The Chi-Square statistic has a value of χ^2 (df=6 and N=199) 51.425, p<0.0001, indicating that the relationship between affiliation and conference attendance is indeed significant.

The adjusted residuals in Table 2, which include the results of the events affiliation cross-tabulation, allow us to identify the most significant patterns of attendance. There is a considerable proportion of volunteers who have not attended any event between 2003 and 2005 (5.5) and a very small proportion of volunteers who have

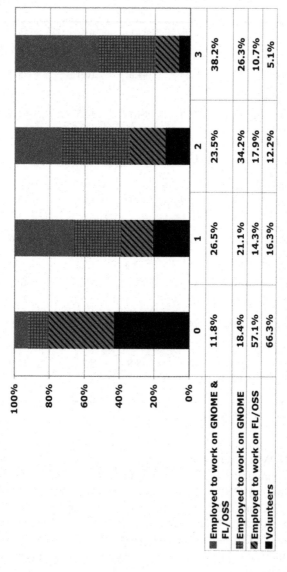

Fig. 4 Participation in GUADECs taking place between 2003–2005 for volunteers and affiliated
Source: GNOME Foundation survey, N=199.

Table 2 Number of GUADECs attended by affiliated and volunteers

		Number of attended GUADECs (2003-2005)			
		0	1	2	3
Volunteers	Count	65	16	12	5
	Percentage within the Group	66.3	16.3	12.2	5.1
	Percentage within the Event	69.9	43.2	31.6	16.1
	Adjusted Residual	5.5	−0.8	−2.4	−4
Paid to work on GNOME and GNOME and FL/OSS	Count	12	17	21	23
	Percentage within the Group	16.4	23.3	28.8	31.5
	Percentage within the Event	12.9	45.9	55.3	74.2
	Adjusted Residual	−6.5	1.3	2.6	4.7
Paid to work on FL/OSS	Count	16	4	5	3
	Percentage within the Group	57.1	14.3	17.9	10.7
	Percentage within the no. of Events	17.2	10.8	13.2	9.7
	Adjusted Residual	1.2	−0.6	−0.2	−0.8

Source: GNOME Foundation survey, N=199.

attended all three events (−4). By contrast, the adjusted residuals for paid developers suggest that the majority of the members of this group rarely miss a major community event (4.7 for 3 attended GUADECs and −6.5 for non-attendance).

Table 3 indicates the significance level for event attendance by combinations of groups. One interesting pattern is that between volunteers and those employed to work on FL/OSS but not on GNOME. The analysis shows the differences between

Table 3 Patterns of GUADEC conference attendance by volunteers and affiliated for different group combinations

	Paid to work on FL/OSS	Paid to work only on GNOME	Paid to work on GNOME and FL/OSS	Paid to work on GNOME and GNOME and FL/OSS	All paid
Volunteers	Not significant	***	***	***	***
Paid to work on FL/OSS		***	Not significant	***	
Paid to work only on GNOME			Not significant		

Source: GNOME Foundation survey, N=199.
***, significant at p<0.001; **, significant at p<0.01; *, significant at p<0.05.

the two groups to be insignificant. But it confirms that the most important differences are between volunteers and those employed to work on GNOME, and those employed to work on FL/OSS and those employed to work on GNOME and on GNOME and FL/OSS.

We look next at the way these results compare with the analysis of maintainership patterns.

Patterns of Maintainership

As in the case of the GNOME Foundation members, the GNOME maintainer network is characterized by an almost even split between affiliated and non-affiliated[8] developers.[9] Specifically, the 2.10.0 release was done by 42 non-affiliated and 50 affiliated maintainers. Figure 5 presents the distribution of maintainership activity between affiliated and non-affiliated developers. The figure shows that 61% of the modules were exclusively maintained by affiliated developers, 33% of the modules were maintained solely by non-affiliated developers, and only 6% of the modules were cooperatively maintained by affiliated and non-affiliated programmers.

As Fig. 6 indicates most of the *Core/Platform* and *Main Desktop* modules are maintained exclusively by affiliated developers. This is consistent with the analysis of the data for the GNOME Foundation members' network. In contrast to the results for the Foundation members where *Secondary Desktop* (which included Applications) was mostly developed by volunteers, however, maintainership in this area is divided evenly between non-affiliated and affiliated contributors. At the same

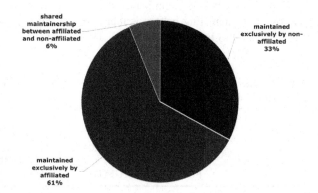

Fig. 5 Modules maintained by affiliated and non-affiliated developers Source: Online search, N=110 (modules).

shared maintainership between affiliated and non-affiliated 6%

maintained exclusively by non-affiliated 33%

maintained exclusively by affiliated 61%

---

[8] As in the case of the GNOME Foundation members 'affiliated' or 'paid' refers in this context to a developer employed by an organization involved in FL/OSS development.

[9] In terms of the overlap between the two networks there were 27 maintainers who were not members of the GNOME Foundation and 42 maintainers who were not among the Foundation respondents.

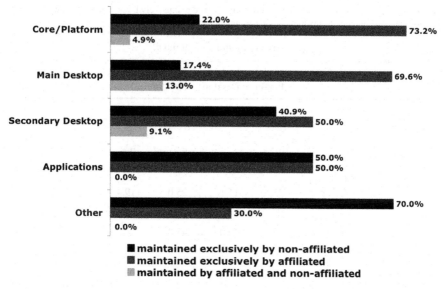

Fig. 6 Modules maintained by affiliated and non-affiliated contributors in principal areas of development
Source: Online search, N=110 (modules).

time, non-affiliated developers appear to maintain more *Peripheral* modules, such as the ones related to developer tools and documentation (grouped under 'Other').

The analysis of the significance of the relation between maintainership and affiliation concentrates on cases of exclusive maintainership.[10] The Chi-Square test for the cross-tabulation (see Table 4) of cases of exclusive maintainership with the main areas of the code base has a value χ^2 (df=4 and N=103) 12.071, p<0.05. There is a connection between this type of maintainership and affiliation. A closer look at each area of the code base reveals, however, that the relationships that are statistically significant are only those for *Core/Platform* (adjusted residuals=−2,2) and *Other (Peripheral) Modules* (adjusted residuals=−2.4,2.4). This indicates that there is a significant association, one that could have not been observed by chance, between exclusive maintainership and affiliation only in the cases of *Core/Platform* and *Other (Peripheral) Modules*.

Another interesting relationship is that between affiliated and non-affiliated developers and the number of modules maintained. To discover whether this relation is statistically significant, maintainers were divided into two groups: those who maintained up to two modules and those maintaining more than two. The association is significant at the p<0.05 level (Chi-Square (df=1, N=92) = 5.650), which

---

[10]This is necessary since taking into account all three categories of maintainership results in too high a percent of expected frequencies under 5, resulting in a loss of statistical power (for an explanation, see Field (2005)).

Table 4 Exclusive maintainership (modules maintained exclusively by non-affiliated and modules maintained exclusively by affiliated) with areas the modules belong in

		Area of module maintained					
		Core/ Platform	Main Desktop	Secondary Desktop	Applications	Other	Total
Maintained exclusively by non-affiliated	Count	9	4	9	7	7	36
	Percentage within the Group	25.0	11.1	25.0	19.4	19.4	100.0
	Percentage within the Area	23.1	20.0	45.0	50.0	70.0	35.0
	Adjusted Residual	−2	−1.6	1	1.3	2.4	
Maintained exclusively by affiliated	Count	30	16	11	7	3	67
	Percentage within the Group	44.8	23.9	16.4	10.4	4.5	100.0
	Percentage within the Area	76.9	80.0	55.0	50.0	30.0	65.0
	Adjusted Residual	2	1.6	−1	−1.3	−2.4	

Source: Online search, N=103 (modules).

indicates that the two variables are dependent. The odds ratios[11] calculated on the basis of counts indicated in Table 5 indicate that an affiliated developer is 4.5 times more likely to maintain more than two modules than a non-affiliated developer.

Distinctiveness of GNOME Contributor Patterns

The analysis of the GNOME Foundation member survey data suggests that despite the even split between paid developers and volunteers among its members, paid developers who are employed to work on GNOME and on GNOME and on other FL/OSS projects are more involved in the infrastructure aspects of the platform

---

[11] The calculation of the odds ratio allows us to gauge the effect size, how strong a relation is, for categorical data. See Field (2005, p. 693).

Table 5 Affiliation by number of modules maintained

		Maintaining up to two modules	Maintaining more than two modules	Total
Non-affiliated	Count	39	3	42
	Expected Count	34.7	7.3	42
	Percentage within each Group	92.9	7.1	100.0
	Percentage within each Group category	51.3	18.8	45.7
	Adjusted Residual	2.4	−2.4	
Affiliated	Count	37	13	50
	Expected Count	41.3	8.7	50
	Percentage within Volunteer vs. affiliated	74.0	26.0	100.0
	Percentage within each Group Category	48.7	81.3	54.3
	Adjusted Residual	-2.4	2.4	

Source: Online search, N=92 (maintainers).

(Core/Platform Modules) and of the desktop *(Main Desktop Modules)* than volunteers. Volunteers, on the other hand, are concentrated in secondary areas of development, such as in *Secondary Desktop Modules* that include many user-oriented applications, and in *Peripheral Activities* that include non-coding activities. The volunteer patterns of contribution and conference attendance are not dissimilar from those of developers who are employed to work on FL/OSS projects other than GNOME. This suggests that the most important differentiating factor between the four groups (Volunteers, Paid to work on GNOME, Paid to work on GNOME and FL/OSS, and paid to work on FL/OSS) is being employed to work on GNOME.

The patterns of maintainership between affiliated and non-affiliated developers are consistent with the patterns of contribution for the GNOME Foundation network. Developers affiliated with an organization involved in FL/OSS development maintain predominantly *Core/Platform* modules. Non-affiliated developers, on the other hand, maintain mostly *Peripheral* Modules, that is, parts of the code base that are associated with *Development Tools*. Paid developers also maintain more modules than non-affiliated contributors. In addition, the absence of cooperatively maintained modules between affiliated and non-affiliated developers supports the argument that the two groups are quite distinct.

The analysis of the GNOME data indicates that the volunteer and affiliated communities are distinctive and that institutional support is an important factor in the continuous involvement of developers at the highest technical level and with respect to their participation in the life of the GNOME community. Two important factors need to be taken into account in drawing conclusions about the implications of these results. First, paid developers often maintain code modules that they are not directly paid to contribute to. This is especially the case for maintainers with strong community ties. Second, there are other layers of institutional support that need to be further investigated before we can fully understand the relationships between affiliation, contribution, and maintenance. For instance, the process of identifying maintainers and their affiliation indicated that many of them are associated with higher level education and research institutions, either as students (many of whom were studying at the postgraduate level) or employees, but the analysis in this article did not take these types of affiliation into account.

Conclusion

The picture that emerges from the GNOME case study raises interesting issues with respect to the relationship between gift and exchange economies. What this case study suggests is that the ways in which the values and practices of both economies are becoming intertwined with each other are suggestive of new power relationships, some of which may be more consistent with those of the exchange economy. There are differences in the extent and types of contributions to FL/OSS in the case of GNOME that appear to be influenced to some extent by types of institutional affiliation, employment status, and skill levels. These differences may be explained by emergent power relationships which operate at both the level of the micro-practices of individual contributors within their communities of practice and at the level of governance institutions, such as those emerging within the GNOME Foundation. There are also signs of hierarchy in the GNOME maintainers' network where tacit acknowledgement is given to the need to seek permission of maintainers when they contribute code even when a developer has acquired the substantial level of expertise needed to commit changes to the code base.

This article emphasises the need for further investigation of FL/OSS in terms of the specific circumstances of its development. We have argued that power relationships need to be examined explicitly in the light of their articulation through the features of the economy more generally. By examining the case of the GNOME project, we gain a deeper understanding of some of the pressures favouring values and practices associated with the exchange economy but we also see evidence of features of the gift economy. Further research is needed to explore how companies operating within this increasingly mixed economy will fare as they seek to further develop FL/OSS (see also Sharma, Suguraman, & Rajagopalani, 2002). As its development scales up, the resources of skill, money, and time are likely to experience various degrees of scarcity. The way this is addressed by those involved with FL/OSS seems very likely to lead to the continuing emergence of some of the attributes of the exchange economy within the communities of practice that constitute the FL/OSS developer communities.

As Lindblom has argued, "there remain, however, fundamental aspects of social problem solving that not even a revolution in the technology of computation and information processing can turn into scientific problems lying within the competence of persons of sufficient expertise" (Lindblom 1990, p. 9). If we regard FL/OSS communities as a relatively new arena for social problem solving with respect to the rights, obligations, and responsibilities of those who develop or use

FL/OSS platforms and applications, then we should not consider the question of power relationships among the participants and institutions involved simply to be one concerning those who have acquired FL/OSS experience through their various contributions as coders, translators, or conference organizers.

FL/OSS is becoming ever more central to the infrastructure and operations of a huge array of social and economic processes. A failure to interrogate its structural dynamics from a political economy perspective would leave the extent and potential for changes in power relationships unexplored. Given the centrality of this model of software development in the first decade of the twenty-first century, the internet Research community would be well advised to encourage research in this tradition alongside the rich insights emerging from studies of the micro-practices of those involved in the FL/OSS developer communities. It is essential to approach claims embodied in utopian discourses that promise a better world due to technology, in this case FL/OSS and its gift economy values, from a critical perspective that acknowledges the reality of struggles for control of the technologies that mediate our lives and in which the values of the exchange economy are embedded. As Mattelart (1996/2000, p. 107) puts it, "the emphasis placed on mediations and interactions must not cause us to forget that contemporary universalisation of a productive and technoscientific system remains, more than ever, marked by the inequality of exchanges".

Even though FL/OSS benefits from many voluntary contributions associated with the gift economy, like software developed within the traditions of the proprietary software model which is aligned with the values of market exchange, the FL/OSS also has a high fixed cost, especially in relation to the more technically demanding aspects of development. To produce the first copy of a major release still requires substantial resources, a considerable component of which is contributed by the employees of companies as our case study has shown. The case study reported in this article raises many questions about how voluntary effort can be mobilised when the scale of developer activity increases and about how effectively this emerging mixed economy will operate. Future research is needed to discern the dominant values and power relations and what their consequences will be.

References

Berdou, E. (2003). *Open source: Community, creativity, participation and evolving patterns of work and power at the intersection of online and offline worlds.* Paper prepared for research seminar for media communication and culture, London School of Economics and Political Science, 25 April.

Berdou, E. (2007). Managing the bazaar: Commercialization and peripheral participation in mature, community-led Free/Open Source Projects. Unpublished PhD Thesis, Department of Media and Communications, London School of Economics and Political Science, June.

Bergquist, M., & Ljungberg, J. (2001). The power of gifts: Organizing social relationships in open source communities. *Information Systems Journal, 11*(4), 305–320.

Bezroukov, N. (1999). Open source software as a special type of academic research (critique of vulgar raymondism). *First Monday, 14*(10). Accessed September 27, 2008, from http://firstmonday.org/issues/issue4_10/bezroukov/index.html

Castells, M. (2001). *The internet galaxy: Reflections on the internet, business, and society*. Oxford: Oxford University Press.

Dalle, J.-M., David, P. A., Ghosh, R. A., & Steinmueller, W. E. (2005). Advancing economic research on the free and open source software mode of production. In M. Wynants & J. Cornelis (Eds.), *How open is the future? Economic, social & cultural scenarios inspired by free & open-source software* (pp. 395–426). Brussels: Vrjie Universiteit Brussels (VUB) Press.

David, P. A. (2001). The evolving accidental information super-highway. *Oxford Review of Economic Policy, 17*(2), 159–187.

David, P. A. (2007). Economic policy analysis and the internet: Coming to terms with a telecommunications anomaly. In R. Mansell, C. Chrisanthi, D. Quah, & R. Silverstone (Eds.), *Oxford handbook of information and communication technologies* (pp. 148–167). Oxford: Oxford University Press.

David, P. A., & Shapiro, J. S. (2008). Community based production: What do we know about the developers who participate? *Information Economics and Policy, Special Issue, 20*(4), 364–398.

Ettema, J. S., & Whitney, D. C. (1994). The money arrow: An introduction to audiencemaking. In J. S. Ettema & D. C. Whitney (Eds.), *Audiencemaking: How the media create the audience* (pp. 1–18). Thousand Oaks CA: Sage.

Feller, J., & Fitzgerald, B. (2002). *Understanding open source software development*. New York: Addison Wesley.

Field, A. (2005). *Discovering statistics using SPSS*. London: Sage.

Fox, S. (2000). Communities of practice, Foucault and actor network theory. *Journal of Management Studies, 37*(6), 853–867.

Freeman, C. (1992). Technology, progress and the quality of life. In C. Freeman (Ed.), *The economics of hope: Essays on technical change, economic growth and the environment* (pp. 212–230), London: Pinter Publishers.

Freeman, C., & Louça, F. (2001). *As Time goes by: From the industrial revolutions to the information revolution*. Oxford: Oxford University Press.

Gallivan, M. J. (2001). Striking balance between trust and control in a virtual organization: A content analysis of open source software studies. *Information Systems Journal, 11*(4), 277–304.

Garnham, N. (1986). Contribution to a political economy of mass-communication. In R. Collins, et al. (Eds.), *Media, culture and society: A critical reader* (pp. 9–32). London: Sage.

Garnham, N. (2000). *Emancipation, the media and modernity: Arguments about the media and social theory*. Oxford: Oxford University Press.

Golding, P., & Murdock, G. (1978). Theories of communication and theories of society. *Communication Research, 5*(3), 339–356.

Healy, K., & Schussman, A. (2003). *The ecology of open source software development (draft)*. Department of Sociology, University of Arizona, Unpublished Working Paper. Accessed September 27, 2008, http://opensource.mit.edu/papers/

von Hippel, E. (2002). *Horizontal innovation networks-by and for users*. Cambridge, MA, MIT Sloan, Working Paper No. 4366-02.

von Hippel, E. A., & Lakhani, K. (2000). *How open source software works: 'Free' user-to-user assistance?* May, MIT Sloan Working Paper No. 4117-00. Accessed September 27, 2008, from SSRN: http://ssrn.com/abstract=290305

Koch, S., & Schneider, G. (2002). Effort, co-ordination and co-operation in an open source software project: GNOME. *Information Systems Journal, 12*, 27–42.

Kollock, P. (1999). The economies of online cooperation: Gifts and publics goods in cyberspace. In M. Smith & P. Kollock (Eds.), *Communities in cyberspace* (pp. 220–242). London: Routledge.

Lampel, J., & Bhalla, A. (2007). The role of status seeking in online communities: Giving the gift of experience. *Journal of Computer Mediated Communication, 12*, 434–455.

Lancashire, D. (2001). Code, culture and cash: The fading altruism of open source development. *First Monday, 6*(12). Accessed September 27, 2008, from http://firstmonday.org/issues/issue6_12/lancashire/index.html

Lave, J., & Wenger, E. (1991). *Situated learning: Legitimate peripheral participation*. Cambridge: Cambridge University Press.

Lievrouw, A., & Livingstone, S. (Eds.). (2006). *The handbook of new media* (Updated Student Edition). London: Sage.

Lindblom, C. E. (1990). *Inquiry and change: The troubled attempt to understand & shape society.* New Haven, CT: Yale University Press.

Livingstone, S. M. (2002). *Young people and new media: Childhood and the changing media environment.* London: Sage.

Ljundgberg, J. (2000). Open source movements as a model of organizing. *European Journal of Information Systems, 9*(4), 208–216.

Mansell, R. (1999). New media competition and access: The scarcity-abundance dialectic. *New Media & Society, 1*(2), 155–182.

Mansell, R. (2004). Political economy, power and new media. *New Media & Society, 6*(1), 74–83.

Mansell, R., & Steinmueller, W. E. (2000). *Mobilizing the information society: Strategies for growth and opportunity.* Oxford: Oxford University Press.

Mattelart, A. (1996/2000). *Networking the world: 1794–2000* (J A Cohen, Trans.). Minneapolis, MN: University of Minnesota Press.

Melody, W. H. (1994). The information society: Implications for economic institutions and market theory. In E. Comor (Ed.), *The global political economy of communication* (pp. 21–36). London: St. Martin's Press.

Melody, W. H., & Mansell, R. (1983). The debate over critical versus administrative research: Circularity or challenge? *Journal of Communication, 33*(3), 103–117.

Miller, D., & Slater, D. (2000). *The internet: An ethnographic approach.* Oxford: Berg.

Moon, Y.-J., & Sproull, L. (2002). Essence of distributed work: The case of the linux kernel. In P. Hinds & S. Kiesler (Eds.), *Distributed work* (pp. 381–404). Cambridge MA: MIT Press.

Murphy, B. (2002). A critical history of the internet. In G. Elmer (Ed.), *Critical perspectives on the internet* (pp. 27–48). Lanham, MD: Rowman & Littlefield.

Patelis, K. (2000). The political economy of the internet. In J. Curran (Ed.), *Media organisations in society* (pp. 84–106). London: Arnold.

Poster, M. (2001). *What's the matter with the internet?* Minneapolis, MN: University of Minnesota Press.

Raymond, E. S. (2001a). The magic cauldron. In *The cathedral and the bazaar: Musings on Linux and open source by an accidental revolutionary* (pp. 113–166). Sebastopol, CA: O'Reilly.

Raymond, E. S. (2001b). The cathedral and the bazaar. In *The cathedral and the Bazaar: Musings on Linux and open source by an accidental revolutionary* (pp. 19–64). Sebastopol, CA: O'Reilly.

Roscoe, T. (1999). The construction of the world wide web audience. *Media, Culture & Society, 21*(5), 673–684.

Samer, F., & Wasko, M. M. (2002). The web of knowledge: An investigation of knowledge exchange in networks of practice. Accessed September 27, 2008, from http://opensource.mit.edu/papers/Farajwasko.pdf

Sharma, S., Suguraman, V., & Rajagopalani, B. (2002). A framework for creating hybrid open source communities. *Information Systems Journal, 12*(1), 7–25.

Silverstone, R. (1999). *Why study the media?* London: Sage.

Silverstone, R., & Hirsch, E. (Eds.). (1992). *Consuming technologies: Media and information in domestic spaces.* London: Routledge.

Smythe, D. W. (1960). On the political economy of communications. *Journalism Quarterly, 37*(4), 461–475.

Weber, S. (2004). *The success of open source.* Cambridge, MA: Harvard University Press.

Webster, J. G., & Phalen, P. F. (1997). *The mass audience: Rediscovering the dominant model.* Mahwah, NJ: Lawrence Erlbaum Associates.

Wellman, B., & Haythornthwaite, C. (2002). The internet in everyday life: An introduction. In B. Wellman & C. Haythornthwaite (Eds.), *The internet in everyday life* (pp. 3–41), Oxford: Blackwell.

Wenger, W. (1999). *Communities of practice: Learning, meaning, and identity.* Cambridge: Cambridge University Press.

Intercreativity: Mapping Online Activism

Graham Meikle

Introduction

How do activists use the internet? Versions of this question have attracted substantial attention (e.g. Atton, 2004; Bruns, 2005; De Jong, Shaw, & Stammers, 2005; Jordan & Taylor, 2004; McCaughey & Ayers, 2003; Meikle, 2002; Shirky, 2008; Van de Donk, Loader, Nixon, & Rucht 2004). An analysis of activists' uses of the net offers an important opportunity to test and refine some of the most pervasive claims made for the democratic potential of new media. It also offers a valuable index of wider shifts in the media environment: what Jenkins (2002, 2003) has termed 'participatory culture', and what Lessig (2004) has argued marks a shift from 'read-only' to 'read-and-write' media.

The literature on internet activism draws together a range of disciplinary and methodological approaches. Much of this work engages with questions of *who, what, where, when* and *why*, generating a substantial range of emphases: there are, for example, studies of environmental activism (Pickerill, 2003), disability social movements (Cheta, 2004), the Far Right (Atton, 2004) and transsexual representation online (O'Riordan, 2005). This article emphasises the question of *how*. It synthesises the literature on the question of how activists use the net, focusing on representative tactics and strategies and maps a wide range of activist practice and research. As a lens through which to focus this diverse literature and practice, the article applies and develops Tim Berners-Lee's concept of 'intercreativity':

> We ought to be able not only to find any kind of document on the Web, but also to create any kind of document, easily. We should be able not only to follow links, but to create them between all sorts of media. We should be able not only to interact with other people, but to create with other people. *Intercreativity* is the process of making things or solving problems together. If *interactivity* is not just sitting there passively in front of a display screen, then *intercreativity* is not just sitting there in front of something 'interactive'. (Berners-Lee, 1999, pp. 182–183, emphasis in original)

G. Meikle (✉)
Department of Film, Media & Journalism, University of Stirling, Stirling, FK9 4LA, Scotland
e-mail: graham.meikle@stir.ac.uk

J. Hunsinger et al. (eds.), *International Handbook of Internet Research*,
DOI 10.1007/978-1-4020-9789-8_22, © Springer Science+Business Media B.V. 2010

This idea of intercreativity is key in analysing net activist campaigns: the projects discussed in this article are all, on one level, about activists not only interacting but creating together. This article identifies four dimensions of net activism: intercreative texts, tactics, strategies and networks.

- intercreative texts: forms of activism which re-work and re-imagine existing media texts and images, creating new texts — or rather, hybrid subversions of existing texts;
- intercreative tactics: approaches which develop new variations on established tactics and protest gestures and perhaps, ultimately, new tactics; in this case, the discourses and practices of electronic civil disobedience;
- intercreative strategies: activism which draws upon the traditions of alternative media, creating a strategic alternative to the established media — an alternative that is an open, participant-centred media space;
- intercreative networks: forums and practices which link open source software to experimental online publishing models in activist campaigns, creating a new media network model.

This article will develop these four aspects of net activism through examples of their manifestations around one cluster of issues: support campaigns for refugees and asylum seekers.

Intercreative Texts

This section focuses on intercreative texts — the collaborative, creative re-working and re-imagining of existing media texts and images as part of attempts to effect social or cultural change. As Manovich (2006) argues, the remix aesthetic has become the fundamental logic of all cultural production, and much internet activism applies this remix aesthetic in the collaborative creation of new hybrid media texts and media images and in the subversion of texts and images already in circulation. Such practices are often labelled as 'culture jamming' (Meikle, 2007). This can be understood as being what happens 'when a population bombarded with electronic media meets the hardware that encourages them to capture it' (Negativland, 1995, p. 251). Culture jammers rework existing media images and media forms to make a cultural or political statement. Most often, jamming is self-reflexive media activism, in that it uses the media to address questions of media representation (Klein, 2000; Lasn, 1999). Moreover, it is often intended to draw media attention to media-related issues. Culture jamming, in short, is the practice of taking familiar signs and reshaping these into question marks.

Credit for the term 'culture jamming' is claimed by the experimental rock group Negativland (Joyce, 2005). An early influential discussion of jamming was a 1993 pamphlet by cultural critic Mark Dery, who described jamming as 'guerrilla semiotics' (1993, p. 11), and the shape of 'an engaged politics [...] in an empire of signs' (1993, p. 6). The concept of jamming here can connote obstruction, blockage, interference, but it can also connote the musical sense of jamming, of playful collaboration around a pre-existing theme: DJ Spooky (aka Miller, 2004) captures this latter sense in his description of creativity as a matter of remixing, reworking, restating, recombining — 'play and irreverence toward the found objects that we use as consumers and a sense that something new was right in front of our oh-so-jaded eyes' (Miller, 2004), p. 45).

A key antecedent to the culture jammers' approach of applying media techniques to media images is the work of the Situationist International (Debord, 1987; Debord & Wolman, 1981; Knabb, 1981; McDonough, 2002; Marcus, 1989; Plant, 1992; Sussman, 1989; Wark, 2008). One Situationist response to the commercial space that they labelled the *spectacle* was the practice of detournement: this can be understood as the sampling of texts or images from one context and their embedding in a new one. Detournement creates a synthesis that calls attention to both the original context and the new result. It takes familiar signs and reshapes these as question marks (autonome a.f.r.i.k.a. gruppe, 2002; Critical Art Ensemble, 1994; Meikle 2007, 2008b).

At one level, activist detournement can be seen in individual texts and images circulated online (Meikle, 2008b). Some important examples of this can be seen in Australian activists' responses to government policy on asylum seekers under Prime Minister John Howard (who headed the government from 1996 to 2007). In particular, the 2001 Australian Federal Election was fought almost entirely around the theme of 'border protection', triggered when the Howard government attempted to deny entry to a Norwegian freighter, the *Tampa*, which was carrying 433 asylum seekers it had rescued after their ferry had sunk en route to Australia. The *Tampa* proved to be only the first of a series of such controversies, with the subsequent introduction of the so-called Pacific Solution (the exporting of asylum seekers to small island states such as Nauru for processing); the drowning off Indonesia of more than 350 other asylum seekers bound for Australia on 19 October 2001; and the 'children overboard' affair, in which government ministers falsely claimed that asylum seekers at sea had flung their own children into the ocean in order to force Australian officials to rescue them. In response to this climate of politicised exclusion, one group of Australian activists projected a 15-m high image of an eighteenth century First Fleet settlers' ship above the words 'boat people' onto the Sydney Opera House, drawing Paraels between 'legitimate' and 'illegitimate' migration, and making this image the central hook of a website which was built around providing information on the issues (Meikle, 2003). Other activists made available for download a stencil kit which could be used to detourn pedestrian traffic safety road signs: ordinarily, these signs are yellow diamonds with the words 'Refuge Island' above an image of an adult human figure shepherding a child across the road; using these downloaded stencils to add a letter 'E', a gun, and a map of Australia, road crossings could be altered to read 'Refugee Island', their figures of pedestrians reworked as armed detainer and detainee. Images of both examples from this paragraph can be viewed at < http://www.boat-people.org.>

One particularly sophisticated activist detournement is the *Escape From Woomera* videogame. This is a first-person 3D adventure, in which the player controls the character of an asylum seeker in a remote immigration detention centre. To progress through the game, the player has to take part in conversations with various non-player characters, gathering clues while fully exploring the Woomera complex. Items and scraps of information, which draw upon interviews and media archives to recreate the camp and incorporate real-life events and anecdotes, are fed steadily to the player, who must work out how to fit these together: indeed, the game play is structured to make it necessary for the player to pay attention to these anecdotes in order to progress, thus incorporating an educational function into the actual gameplay.

The *Escape From Woomera* game makes use of principles of detournement in two especially important senses: first, it invites its players to re-think the detention centre which gives the game its title. Such centres are closed, remote, secretive, carceral environments; their nature, structure and location combine to forbid access, and hence to deny inspection, scrutiny or knowledge. *Escape From Woomera* proposes this space instead as one for exploration, mapping and awareness. Second, *Escape From Woomera* takes the familiar sign of the videogame and proposes it not as a diversion, but rather as a space of political engagement, contestation and debate.

At another level, activist detournement can be seen in the creation of spoof websites. 'Image has become capital,' as one group of activist theorists argue, 'and on the terrain of image, communication guerrillas can easily subvert the messages of power' (autonome a.f.r.i.k.a. gruppe, 2002, p. 169). A major example here is the Deportation Class website <http://www.deportation-class.com>, which critiques the involvement of major European airlines in the forced deportation of asylum seekers whose claims to refugee status have been denied by national governments: 'See the world through different eyes! Travel in exotic style with Lufthansa's Deportation Class service.' The site replicates the typical imagery and mode of address of a passenger airline, complete with an activist frequent flyer program, and combines the standard visual imagery of attractive destinations, special offer prices and exhortations to 'book now' with texts which highlight the horrors of the physical restraints often used on forced deportees: 'adjust to the delights of your travel destination in an atmosphere relaxed by obligatory sedative usage.'

Intercreative Tactics

On 20 June 2001, activists targeted Lufthansa's Annual General Meeting, to protest about the airline's involvement in the forcible deportation of asylum seekers. As well as physical protests at the meeting itself, an online demonstration was organised — a 'virtual sit-in' of the Lufthansa website <http://go.to/online-demo>. While demonstrators in Cologne crowded the meeting venue, others around the world crowded the company's website in a distributed denial-of-service action: 'a hybrid of immaterial sabotage and digital demonstration' (Schneider, 2002, p. 178). Such actions can be seen as vehicles for capturing the attention of the established news media, in order to force a cause onto the news agenda: activists can exploit the appetite for sensationalism (Vegh, 2003, p. 92). However, there is a dilemma here for activists, in that while the news media are drawn to novelty and disruption, their coverage is also more likely to focus on that very novelty and disruption than on the underlying issues or causes involved, which may in fact work against the activist cause (Scalmer, 2002, p. 41). This dilemma is especially pertinent in relation to the example of the virtual sit-in and its discourse of electronic civil disobedience: this is often referred to as hacktivism, and on some occasions this has enabled an unfortunate linkage between its practices and terrorism (e.g. Denning, 1999, 2001; Meikle, 2008a).

The central discourse here is that of tactical media (Boler, 2008; CAE, 2001; Garcia & Lovink, 1997, 1999; Lovink, 2002). Tactical media combine creative sub-version with subversive creativity. The discourse of tactical media emphasises the technological, the transitory and the collaborative. A particular emphasis in this discourse is on media projects that are characterised by mobility and flexibility, by novelty and reinvention, and by a certain transient and temporary dimension — 'hit and run, draw and withdraw, code and delete', as Lovink and Schneider put it (2001). The most important example of both the strengths and limitations of tactical media remains the use of the internet by Belgrade independent radio station B92 to circumvent censorship by the Milosevic regime (Lovink, 2003).

Electronic civil disobedience was first proposed in 1994 by Critical Art Ensemble (CAE) a small group of digital theorists and artists (CAE, 1994, 1995). In their definition, electronic civil disobedience is 'hacking that is done primar-ily as a form of political resistance rather than as an idiosyncratic activity or as a profit- or prestige-generating process' (CAE interviewed in Little, 1999, p. 194). The group's involvement with the AIDS activism of ACT UP in the 1980s had suggested to them that the established repertoire of protest gestures had lost their efficacy. Their response was to call for new alliances between hackers and activists and for hacker actions against the cyberspace presence of institutions.

In naming this proposed practice, CAE aligned the concept of electronic civil dis-obedience with the widely understood principles of traditional civil disobedience, in a conscious attempt to draw legitimacy from the legacy of such figures as Thoreau, Gandhi and Martin Luther King. There were certain continuities with the established traditions of civil disobedience, such as the use of trespass and blockades as central tactics. However, there were also certain discontinuities, such as the de-emphasising of mass participation in favour of decentralised, cell-based organisation, using small groups of from four to ten activists, and in particular the argument that electronic civil disobedience should be surreptitious, in the hacker tradition. Where practition-ers of civil disobedience have been transparent about their opposition to the laws they break (Gandhi, 2000, p. 410), CAE argued for a clandestine approach, propos-ing electronic civil disobedience as 'an underground activity that should be kept out

of the public/popular sphere (as in the hacker tradition) and the eye of the media'
(2001, p. 14).

The concept of electronic civil disobedience was developed further by
the Electronic Disturbance Theater (EDT) <http://www.thing.net/~rdom/ecd/ecd.
html>, a four-person group founded by one-time CAE member Ricardo Dominguez.
The EDT moved away from CAE's emphasis on the clandestine exercise of elite
hacker skills towards a more transparent public spectacle which aimed to draw
as many participants together as possible (Wray, 1998). They developed a piece
of software called FloodNet, which both simplifies and automates distributed
denial-of-service attacks or, as the EDT labelled them, virtual sit-ins. Where CAE
envisaged a small number of hackers with significant expertise, the EDT created a
situation in which the more participants the better, and in which being able to click
on a hyperlink was sufficient technical ability. These actions, as Dominguez puts it,
are about 'creating the unbearable weight of human beings in a digital way' (quoted
in Meikle, 2002, p. 142).

The EDT initially formed to support the Mexican Zapatistas, although FloodNet
has been used in actions for a large number of causes, including for anti-deportation
campaigns such as that against Lufthansa. Other uses of the virtual sit-in tactic have targeted the US Republican National Committee, Dow Chemical, the
Michigan State Legislature, and the infamous website of the Westboro Baptist
Church of Topeka, Kansas, at <http://www.godhatesfags.com>. In May 2005, a
claimed 78,500 people joined a virtual sit-in against the website of the Minutemen
Project, a vigilante organization which opposes immigration to the US, particularly from Mexico and Latin America (Dominguez, 2005; Kartenberg, 2005; Jordan,
2007). The EDT were also key participants in the 1999 Toywar, in which an online
toy retailer with the domain name <etoys.com> disputed the right of the pre-existing
European art group etoy to use their own domain name <etoy.com>. Legal action by
the retailer was met with a sophisticated suite of tactical media responses, including
a virtual sit-in of the toy store's website. The retailer capitulated in January 2000,
shortly before filing for bankruptcy (agent.NASDAQ, 2001; Jordan & Taylor, 2004;
Meikle, 2002; Wark, 2003; Wishart & Bochsler, 2002).

While the virtual sit-in and the wider discourse of tactical media both emphasise
novelty and re-invention, it is important to note that there are continuities here as
well as transformations. On the one hand, the sit-in is a tactic with a long history.
Sharp traces its uses as far back as 1838 and emphasises its association with the US
Civil Rights movement and, before that, with Abolitionist campaigns (Sharp, 1973,
pp. 371–374); Ackerman and Du Vall document a successful use of the tactic against
the Nazis in 1943 (2000, p. 237). Such history can offer pedagogical possibilities
for internet activists introducing virtual versions of familiar tactics. Yet at the same
time, the virtual sit-in is significant in that it takes cyberspace as the actual site of
action: 'Hacktivists are the first social movement of virtuality', suggest Jordan and
Taylor (2004, p. 172). In this sense, the virtual sit-in also represents a move towards
using the technical properties of new media to formulate new tactics for effecting
social change.

Intercreative Strategies

internet activism commonly involves the creation of alternative media spaces: strategic alternatives to the established news media; open, participant-centred media forums and projects. One example is Make Borders History <http://makebordershistory.org>. Created in 2005 as part of the protests against the G8 meeting in Scotland, this site presents itself as

> a tool/interactive platform for grassroots activists and groups who work on immigration- and asylum-related issues and struggle for the freedom of movement for all people, against repression and the many controls that multiply the borders everywhere in all countries. <http://makebordershistory.org/workspace/MissionStatement>

It is a moderated site using the same Mediawiki software as Wikipedia, which allows anyone to create an account and log in to contribute or edit information on the goals of the project. There are announcements, alerts and updates on direct actions, as well as news reports and features contributed by users and moderators. The site also offers background information on asylum and immigration laws (with a UK emphasis) and on private companies involved in detention programs.

The burgeoning literature on alternative media becomes central to an analysis of such projects (Atton, 2002; Couldry & Curran, 2003; Coyer, Dowmunt, & Fountain, 2007; Downing, 2001). The concept of 'alternative' media demands care, as it needs to be defined and used more strictly than simply in opposition to 'mainstream'. Atton refers to 'a range of media projects, interventions and networks that work against, or seek to develop different forms of, the dominant, expected (and broadly accepted) ways of "doing" media' (Atton, 2004, p. ix). While this opens up a large range of issues, this section will confine itself to four points which are salient in the analysis of internet activists and their intercreative strategies.

First, there is the acknowledgment of history — the precursors, traditions and models upon which contemporary alternative media build (Atton, 2002; Curran & Seaton, 2003; Downing, 2001; Drew, 2005). Much internet commentary focuses on transformation, on the shock of the new and on the possibilities for developing new modes of media production, distribution, reception — and analysis. However, the continuities are at least as important as the transformations. This is particularly true in the case of networked social movements and those who study them, with much to be learned from comparison with the past and from situating internet activism in longer-term historical contexts than simply that of the internet era (Jordan & Taylor, 2004). It is also important to maintain consideration of some of the earliest examples of activist computer use and of their study by researchers, in particular those that pre-date the web (Cordero, 1991; Docter & Dutton, 1998; Downing, 1989; Frederick, 1993; Gurak & Logie, 2003; Mele, 1999; Rheingold, 1993; Salter, 2003).

Second, there is the emphasis within the alternative media literature on modes of organisation, in particular upon independence and self-management or self-organisation (Downing, 1995; Fuchs, 2006). The question of alternative media has often been addressed in terms of control and ownership, of political economy, and such issues have their own specificity in relation to the internet. It is of course true that the internet remains far from universally available: Sparks points out that even electricity is beyond the reach of vast sections of the global population (2005). Nevertheless, for those who do have ready access to the net, the obstacles to establishing an online presence are significantly different from those involved in creating a broadcast network.

Third, such projects can be approached in terms of their content: textual forms, narrative strategies, modes of address, visuality, and/or ideological orientation. Of particular significance are the ways in which internet activists construct forums for viewpoints which are not usually expressed within the established media consensus about what counts as news and who counts as an authoritative source. A site such as Make Borders History illustrates Atton's analysis of the style of activist journalism that is emerging online: 'Its practices emphasise first-person, eyewitness accounts by participants; a reworking of the populist approaches of tabloid newspapers to recover a "radical popular" style of reporting' (Atton, 2004, p. 26).

A fourth important dimension of online alternative media strategies is the extent to which these emphasise and foster horizontal connections and open participation, in contrast to the vertical flows of the established news media — a common emphasis is on the potential of communication between participants, rather than to audiences (Downing, 1995, 2001, 2003a). As Atton and Couldry note (2003), those who create alternative media are those who are dissatisfied with the established relations of symbolic power. The open access provisions of projects such as Make Borders History, and their collaborative, intercreative ethos, enact particular visions of journalistic potential: '... collective and anti-hierarchical forms of organisation which eschew demarcation and specialisation — and which importantly suggest an inclusive, radical form of civic journalism' (Atton, 2004, p. 26).

Of particular use here is Rodriguez's concept of 'citizens' media' (2001, 2002). Rodriguez argues for a participation-centred approach to alternative media, proposing that such projects must be analysed 'in terms of the transformative processes they bring about within participants and their communities' (2002, p. 79). Rodriguez's concept has three central tenets:

> ... 'citizens' media' implies first that a collectivity is *enacting* its citizenship by actively intervening and transforming the established mediascape; second, that these media are contesting social codes, legitimized identities, and institutionalized social relations; and third, that these communication practices are empowering the community involved, to the point where these transformations and changes are possible (Rodriguez, 2001, p. 20, emphasis in original).

From this perspective, the significance of online activist spaces such as the Make Borders History website may lie in the resources that they offer to users to create their own media, to participate in debates, and to act as citizens as well as audiences — with citizenship thought of here as a concept defined 'on account of one's ability to gather forces that shape one's symbolic and material world' (Rodriguez, 2002), p. 79).

Intercreative Networks

A previous section discussed the virtual sit-in action against Lufthansa. This was organised by, among others, the German-based activist group 'Kein mensch ist illegal' <http://www.contrast.org/borders/kein> or, in English, 'No one is illegal'. This phrase has been used as a rallying cry, a slogan, and as the name for organisations of varying degrees of longevity. It has been taken up by activists in Canada, Australia, the UK, and used in coordinating actions and camps on the German-Polish border, the US-Mexican border, and at Australian detention centres. Its multiple appearances and reappearances in different contexts illustrate the intercreative network logic — flexible, autonomous, decentralised and yet connected.

The image of the network is now central to much writing on new media, in large part due to the work of Manuel Castells. Castells identifies the network paradigm as a new form of social organisation, one characterised by strategic capitalist expansion on a global level, by post-fordist production and labour management and by shifts in the experience of both space and time (2000). This new paradigm, incorporating the economic, the social and the cultural, is spreading across the globe, but is meeting with significant resistance: 'the widespread surge of powerful expressions of collective identity that challenge globalization and cosmopolitanism on behalf of cultural singularity and people's control over their lives and environment' (Castells, 1997, p. 2). Such 'expressions of collective identity' characterise much networked activism. Indeed, Castells contends that contemporary social movements increasingly operate in a manner which inverts the once-popular environmentalist slogan 'think global, act local'. Now, writes Castells, 'social movements must think local (relating to their own concerns and identity) and act global — at the level where it really matters today' (2001, p. 143).

The intercreative network that has attracted the most attention is the Indymedia movement (inter alia Atton, 2004; Castells, 2007; Coyer, 2005; Downing, 2002, 2003a, 2003b; Garcelon, 2006; Lovink, 2003). Indymedia is a global network of independent news websites, each using a local version of the common domain name <indymedia.org>, as in, for example, <ecuador.indymedia.org> or <japan.indymedia.org>. Each site publishes news stories and other items submitted by anyone who wishes to contribute; while this policy is evolving and subject to local variation, the defining principle of Indymedia is this ethos of 'open publishing' (Arnison, 2001; Bruns, 2005; Meikle, 2002). Open publishing can be thought of as an ethos of transparency as well as one of access and has conceptual roots in the open source software movement. Downing (2002) has argued that its news service is only part of Indymedia's significance, suggesting that its activist focus and direct involvement with campaigning 'represent an interventionist strategy well beyond the purely service offerings of a progressive news service' (p. 227).

The first Indymedia website <http://www.indymedia.org> was established as an online focal point for the demonstrations against the World Trade Organisation meeting in Seattle in November 1999 (Kahn & Kellner, 2004; Kidd, 2003; Meikle, 2002; Platon & Deuze, 2003). In the following months, the site was refocused around several subsequent protests, before local collectives began to appear and form their own Indymedia centres (IMCs). Within a year of the first IMC, a network of more than 30 had been established. By March 2002 there were more than 70 nodes in the network, with IMCs established in Africa and India, as well as many European countries. By January 2004 there were more than 120 IMCS in locations as diverse as Argentina, Indonesia, Poland, South Africa and Japan (Meikle, 2004), although Indymedia China has yet to appear. By September 2006 there were 136 active Indymedia centres, while a further 22 sites were no longer operating (Coopman, 2006). One thing that is particularly striking about the speed and scope of this development is that the Indymedia network has been established largely by volunteers and donations (Halleck, 2003; Pickard, 2006).

Indymedia has not always maintained the standards set in its first few years. Bruns suggests that, by 2008, the main Indymedia newswire had been reduced to 'a mere clearing-house for activist press releases' (2008, p. 250). Nevertheless, the network still demands serious attention — as one of the longest established participatory online projects, it offers great scope for analysis and for gaining perspective on newer developments that follow in its wake.

As with all other examples of net activism in this article, there are important precursors and antecedents here. For example, Jesse Drew offers an account of alternative TV and video networks, tracing connections from Paper Tiger TV and the Deep Dish network to the Indymedia network. Drew stresses the importance of recognising the social and cultural dimensions to the success of these earlier networks. On the one hand, Deep Dish depended on the proliferation of camcorders to enable community groups to contribute reports on ongoing projects or campaigns or issues. In this, there is a technological analogue to the role of the net in making Indymedia possible. On the other hand, Drew emphasises the need to interrogate structures and organisations in networks, to go beyond the usual easy assumption that networks are necessarily positive. 'Networks', writes Drew, 'must be scrutinized for their social impact, and not just their technical achievement' (2005, p. 222).

An important analysis here is the concept of 'social netwar', developed by Arquilla and Ronfeldt (1997, 2000a, 2001b, 2001c; De Armond 2001). This describes what its authors view as an emerging form of informational conflict, involving networked non-state actors: 'The information revolution is leading to the rise of network forms of organization, whereby small, previously isolated groups can communicate, link up, and conduct coordinated joint actions as never before' (Arquilla, Ronfeldt, Fuller, & Fuller, 1998, p. xi). The discourse of netwar is a problematic discourse for some activists, who may be unwilling to view themselves as 'combatants'. However, it is significant in its sustained analysis of network models of organisation and communication and in its comparison between hierarchical, institutional forces and flexible, decentralised ones: 'Institutions can be defeated by networks. It may take networks to counter networks. The future may belong to whoever masters the network form' (Arquilla & Ronfeldt, 1997, p. 40).

Conclusion

Here, then, are four central dimensions of online activism: the collaborative re-working of existing media texts and images, which this article has discussed as intercreative texts; the collaborative development of tactical uses of the net, such as the virtual sit-in, which this article has discussed as intercreative tactics; the collaborative development of ongoing online media spaces for the expression of dissonant perspectives, sites of strategic alternative media, which this article has discussed as intercreative strategies; and the collaborative development of networks of influence, exemplified in this article's discussion of the Indymedia movement as intercreative network.

There remains, of course, a great deal of scope for further research in all of the areas outlined above. To illustrate this, one might invoke Resnick's useful distinction between three forms of internet politics: 'politics within the Net, politics which impacts the Net, and political uses of the Net' (1998, p. 55). This article has concentrated on the third of these, but there remains scope for further research which draws upon the first and second categories also, and above all for research which examines the inter-relationships between these three forms of politics online. For example, there is an ongoing need for work which explores the relationships between the politics which 'impacts' upon the net and the emerging repertoire of cybercultural activist tactics and strategies, as cyberspace(s) are drawn more precisely within legal and regulatory frameworks; this is especially pressing in the context of an internet environment which is, as Goldsmith and Wu argue (2006), increasingly shaped and re-shaped by national governments.

References

Ackerman, P., & Du Vall, J. (2000). *A force more powerful: A century of nonviolent conflict.* Basingstoke: Palgrave.

agent.NASDAQ (aka Reinhold Grether). (2001). How the etoy campaign was won: An agent's report. In P. Weibel & T. Druckrey (Eds.), *net_condition: Art and global media* (pp. 280–5). Cambridge, MA: MIT Press.

Arnison, M. (2001). Open publishing is the same as free software. Accessed February 23, 2004, from http://www.cat.org.au/maffew/cat/openpub.html

Arquilla, J., & Ronfeldt, D. (1997) [1993]. Cyberwar is coming! In J. Arquilla & D. Ronfeldt (Eds.), *In Athena's camp: Preparing for conflict in the information age* (pp. 23–60). Santa Monica, CA: RAND Corporation. Accessed February 23, 2004, from, http://www.rand.org/publications/MR/MR880

Arquilla, J. & Ronfeldt, D. (2001a). Fighting the network war. *Wired* 9.12, December. Accessed January 10, 2008, from, http://www.wired.com/wired/archive/9.12/netwar.html

Arquilla, J., & Ronfeldt, D. (Eds.). (2001b). The advent of netwar (revisited). In *Networks and netwars: The future of terror, crime, and militancy* (pp. 1–25). Santa Monica, CA: RAND Corporation. Accessed January 10, 2008, from http://www.rand.org/pubs/monograph_reports/MR1382

Arquilla, J., & Ronfeldt, D. (Eds.) (2001c). *Networks and netwars: The future of terror, crime, and militancy.* Santa Monica, CA: RAND Corporation. Accessed January 10, 2008, from, http://www.rand.org/pubs/monograph_reports/MR1382

Arquilla, J., Ronfeldt, D. F., Fuller, G. F., & Fuller, M. (1998). *The Zapatista 'social net-war' in Mexico*. Santa Monica, CA: RAND Corporation. Accessed February 23, 2004, from, http://www.rand.org/publications/MR/MR994

Atton, C. (2002). *Alternative media*. London: Sage.

Atton, C. (2004). *An alternative internet*. Edinburgh: Edinburgh University Press.

Atton, C., & Couldry, N. (2003). Introduction to special issue of media, culture & society on alternative media. *Media, Culture & Society, 25*(5), 579–86.

autonome a.f.r.i.k.a. gruppe. (2002). Communication guerrillas: Using the language of power. In E. Lubbers (Ed.), *Battling big business: Countering greenwash, infiltration and other forms of corporate bullying* (pp. 166–76). Melbourne: Scribe Publications.

Berners-Lee, T. (1999). *Weaving the web*. London: Orion Business Books.

Boler, M. (Ed.). (2008). *Digital media and democracy: Tactics in hard times*. Cambridge, MA: MIT Press.

Bruns, A. (2005). *Gatewatching: Collaborative online news production*. New York: Peter Lang.

Bruns, A. (2008). *Blogs, Wikipedia, second life and beyond*. New York: Peter Lang.

Castells, M. (1997). *The power of identity*. Oxford: Blackwell.

Castells, M. (2000). *The rise of the network society* (2nd ed.). Oxford: Blackwell.

Castells, M. (2001). *The internet galaxy: Reflections on the internet, business and society*. Oxford: Oxford University Press.

Castells, M. (2007). Communication, power and counter-power in the network society. *International Journal of Communication, 1*(1), 238–66.

Cheta, R. (2004). Dis@bled people, ICTs and a new age of activism. In W. Van De Donk, B. D. Loader, P. G. Nixon, & D. Rucht (Eds.), *Cyberprotest: New media, citizens and social movements* (pp. 207–32). London: Routledge.

Coopman, T. (2006). Indymedia as a global free media infrastructure. Paper presented to the Association of Internet Researchers conference in Brisbane, September 29.

Cordero, A. (1991). Computers and community organizing: Issues and examples from New York City. In J. Downing, R. Fasano, P. A. Friedland, M. F. McCullough, T. Mizrahi, & J. J. Shapiro (Eds.), *Computers for social change and community organizing* (pp. 89–103). New York: Haworth Press.

Cordero, A., & Curran, J. (Eds.). (2003). *Contesting media power: Alternative media in a networked world*. Lanham, MD: Rowman & Littlefield.

Couldry, N., & Curran, J. (Eds.). (2003). *Contesting media power: Alternative media in a networked world*. Lanham, MD: Rowman & Littlefield.

Coyer, K. (2005). If it leads it bleeds: The participatory newsmaking of the independent media centre. In W. de Jong, M. Shaw, & N. Stammers (Eds.), *Global Activism, Global Media*, (pp. 165–178). London: Pluto.

Coyer, K., Dowmunt, T., & Fountain, A. (Eds.). (2007). *The alternative media handbook*. London: Routledge.

Critical Art Ensemble. (1994). *The electronic disturbance*. New York: Autonomedia.

Critical Art Ensemble (1995). *Electronic civil disobedience and other unpopular ideas*. New York: Autonomedia.

Critical Art Ensemble (2001). *Digital resistance: Explorations in tactical media*. New York: Autonomedia.

Curran, J., & Seaton, J. (2003). *Power without responsibility: The press, broadcasting, and new media in Britain* (6th Ed.). London: Routledge.

De Armond, P. (2001). Netwar in the emerald city: WTO protest strategy and tactics. In J. Arquilla & D. Ronfeldt (Eds.), *Networks and netwars: The future of terror, crime, and militancy* (pp. 201–35). Santa Monica, CA: RAND Corporation. Accessed January 10, 2008, from http://www.rand.org/pubs/monograph_reports/MR1382

Debord, G. (1987) [1967]. *The society of the spectacle*. Exeter: Rebel Press.

Debord, G., & Wolman, G. (1981) [1956]. Methods of detournement. In K. Knabb (Ed.), *Situationist international anthology* (pp. 8–14). Berkeley, CA: Bureau of Public Secrets.

De Jong, W., Shaw, M., & Stammers, N. (Eds.). (2005). *Global activism, global media*. London: Pluto.

Denning, D. (1999). Activism, hacktivism and cyberterrorism: The internet as a tool for influencing foreign policy. Accessed February 23, 2004, from http://www.nautilus.org/info-policy/workshop/papers/denning.html

Denning, D. (2001). Cyberwarriors: Activists and terrorists turn to cyberspace. *Harvard International Review, 23*(2), 70–75.

Dery, M. (1993). *Culture jamming: Hacking, slashing and sniping in the empire of signs*. Westfield, NJ: Open Magazine Pamphlet Series no. 25.

Docter, S., & Dutton, W. H. (1998). The first amendment online: Santa Monica's Public Electronic Network. In R. Tsagarousianou, D. Tambini, & C. Bryan (Eds.), *Cyberdemocracy: Technology, cities and civic networks* (pp. 125–51). London: Routledge.

Dominguez, R. (2005). SWARM the minutemen – Post action update May 30, 2005, posted to the Nettime list, May 31. Accessed January 10, 2008, from http://www.nettime.org/Lists-Archives/nettimel-0505/msg00071.html

Downing, J. D. H. (1989). Computers for political change: Peacenet and public data access. *Journal of Communication, 39*(3), 154–62.

Downing, J. D. H. (1995). Alternative media and the Boston tea party. In J. Downing, A. Mohammadi, & A. Sreberny-Mohammadi (Eds.), *Questioning the media* (2nd ed., pp. 238–52). Thousand Oaks, CA: Sage.

Downing, J. D. H. (2002). Independent media centres: A multi-local, multi-media challenge to global neo-liberalism. In M. Raboy (Ed.), *Global media policy in the new millennium* (pp. 215–32). Luton: University of Luton Press.

Downing, J. D. H. (2003a). Audiences and readers of alternative media: The absent lure of the virtually unknown. *Media, Culture & Society, 25*(5), 625–45.

Downing, J. D. H. (2003b). The independent media center movement and the anarchist socialist tradition. In N. Couldry & J. Curran (Eds.), *Contesting Media Power: Alternative Media in a Networked World* (pp. 243–57). Lanham, MD: Rowman & Littlefield.

Downing, J. D. H., Ford, T. V., Gil, G., & Stein, L. (2001). *Radical media: Rebellious communication and social movements*. Thousand Oaks, CA: Sage.

Drew, J. (2005). From the Gulf war to the battle of Seattle: Building an international alternative media network. In A. Chandler & N. Neumark (Eds.), *At a distance: Precursors to art and activism on the internet* (pp. 210–24). Cambridge, MA: MIT Press.

Frederick, H. (1993). Computer networks and the emergence of global civil society. In Harasim, L. M. (Ed.), *Global networks: Computers and international communication* (pp. 283–295). Cambridge, MA: MIT Press.

Fuchs, C. (2006). The self-organization of cyberprotest. In K. Morgan, C. A. Brebbia, & J. M. Spector (Eds.), *The internet society II: Advances in education, commerce & governance* (pp. 275–295). Southampton: WIT.

Gandhi, M. K. (2000) [1920]. A selection from his writings. In P. Lauter (Ed.), *Walden and Civil Disobedience* (pp. 407–22). Boston: Houghton Mifflin.

Garcelon, M. (2006). The "Indymedia" Experiment. *Convergence, 12*(1), 55–82.

Garcia, D., & Lovink, G. (1997). The ABC of tactical media. Posted to the <nettime> list on 16 May 1997. Accessed December 21, 2006, from http://www.nettime.org/Lists-Archives/nettime-l-9705/msg00096.html

Garcia, D., & Lovink, G. (1999). The DEF of tactical media. Posted to the <nettime> list on 22 February 1999. Accessed December 21, 2006, from http://www.nettime.org/Lists-Archives/nettime-l-9902/msg00104.html

Goldsmith, J., & Wu, T. (2006). *Who controls the internet? Illusions of a borderless world*. New York: Oxford University Press.

Gurak, L. J., & Logie, J. (2003). Internet protests, from text to web. In M. McCaughey & M. D. Ayers (Eds.), *Cyberactivism: Online activism in theory and practice* (pp. 25–46). New York: Routledge.

Halleck, D. (2003). Indymedia: Building an international activist internet network. *Media Development, 50*(4), 11–15.

Jenkins, H. (2002). Interactive audiences? In D. Harries (Ed.), *The New Media Book* (pp. 157–70). London: British Film Institute.

Jenkins, H. (2003). Quentin Tarantino's star wars? Digital cinema, media convergence, and participatory culture. In D. Thorburn & H. Jenkins (Eds.), *Rethinking media change* (pp. 281–312). Cambridge, MA: MIT Press.

Jordan, T. (2002).*Activism! Direct action, hacktivism and the future of society*. London: Reaktion Books.

Jordan, T. (2007). Online direct action: Hacktivism and radical democracy. In L. Dahlberg & E. Siapera (Eds.), *Radical democracy and the internet* (pp. 73–88). Basingstoke: Palgrave Macmillan.

Jordan, T., & Taylor, P. (2004). *Hacktivism and cyberwars: Rebels with a cause*. London: Routledge.

Joyce, D. (2005). An unsuspected future in broadcasting: Negativland. In A. Chandler & N. Neumark (Eds.), *At a distance: Precursors to art and activism on the internet* (pp. 176–89). Cambridge, MA: MIT Press.

Kahn, R., & Kellner, D. (2004). New media and internet activism: From the "battle of Seattle" to blogging. *New Media & Society, 6*(1), 87–95.

Kartenberg, H. P. (2005). *A transparent and civil act of disobedience*. Accessed January 10, 2008, from http://post.thing.net/node/304

Kidd, D. (2003). Indymedia.org: A new communications commons. In M. McCaughey & M. D. Ayers (Eds.), *Cyberactivism: Online activism in theory and practice* (pp. 47–69). New York: Routledge.

Klein, N. (2000). *No logo*. London: Flamingo.

Knabb, K. (Ed.). (1981). *Situationist international anthology*. Berkeley, CA: Bureau of Public Secrets.

Lasn, K. (1999). *Culture jam: The uncooling of America^{TM}*. New York: Eagle Brook.

Lessig, L. (2004). *Free culture*. New York: Penguin.

Little, M. (1999). Practical anarchy: An interview with critical art ensemble. *Angelaki, 4*(2), 192–201.

Lovink, G. (2002). *Dark fiber: Tracking critical internet culture*. Cambridge, MA: MIT Press.

Lovink, G. (2003). *My first recession: Critical internet culture in transition*. Rotterdam: V2_Publishing/Nai Publishers.

Lovink, G., & Schneider, F. (2001). New rules of the new actonomy. Posted to the Nettime list, 25 June. Accessed February 23, 2004, from http://amsterdam.nettime.org/Lists-Archives/nettime-l-0106/msg00114.html

Manovich, L. (2006). Generation flash. In W. H. K. Chun & T. Keenan (Eds.), *New media old media: A history and theory reader* (pp. 209–218). New York: Routledge.

Marcus, G. (1989). *Lipstick traces: A secret history of the twentieth century*. London: Picador.

McCaughey, M., & Ayers, M. (Eds.). (2003). *Cyberactivism: Online activism in theory and practice*. New York: Routledge.

McDonough, T. (Ed.). (2002). *Guy debord and the situationist international: Texts and documents*. Cambridge, MA: MIT Press.

Meikle, G. (2002). *Future active: Media activism and the internet*. New York: Routledge.

Meikle, G. (2003, May). We are all boat people: A case study in internet activism. *Media International Australia, 107*, 9–18.

Meikle, G. (2004). Networks of influence: Internet activism in Australia and beyond. In G. Goggin (Ed.), *Virtual nation: The internet in Australia* (pp. 73–87). Sydney: University of New South Wales Press.

Meikle, G. (2007). Stop signs: An introduction to culture jamming. In K. Coyer, T. Dowmunt, & A. Fountain (Eds), *The alternative media handbook* (pp. 166–79). London: Routledge.

Meikle, G. (2008a). Electronic civil disobedience and symbolic power. In A. Karatzogianni (Ed.), *Cyber-conflict and global politics* (pp. 177–87). London: Routledge.

Meikle, G. (2008b). Whacking bush: Tactical media as play. In M. Boler (Ed.), *Digital media and democracy: Tactics in hard times* (pp. 367–82). Cambridge, MA: MIT Press.

Mele, C. (1999). Cyberspace and disadvantaged communities: The internet as a tool for collective action. In M. A. Smith & P. Kollock (Eds.), *Communities in cyberspace* (pp. 290–310). New York: Routledge.

Miller, P. D. aka DJ Spooky That Subliminal Kid. (2004). *Rhythm science.* Cambridge, MA: MIT Press.

Negativland. (1995). *Fair use: The story of the letter u and the numeral 2.* Concord, CA: Seeland.

O'Riordan, K. (2005). Transgender activism and the net: Global activism or casualty of globalisation. In W. de Jong, M. Shaw, & N. Stammers (Eds.), *Global activism, global media* (pp. 179–93). London: Pluto.

Pickard, V. W. (2006). United yet autonomous: Indymedia and the struggle to sustain a radical democratic network. *Media, Culture & Society, 28*(3), 315–36.

Pickerill, J. (2003). *Cyberprotest: Environmental activism online.* Manchester: Manchester University Press.

Plant, S. (1992). *The most radical gesture: The situationist international in a postmodern age.* London: Routledge.

Platon, S., & Deuze, M. (2003). Indymedia journalism: A radical way of making, selecting and sharing news? *Journalism: Theory, Practice and Criticism, 4*(3), 336–55.

Resnick, D. (1998). Politics on the internet: The normalization of cyberspace. In C. Toulouse & T. W. Luke (Eds.), *The politics of cyberspace: A new political science reader* (pp. 48–68). New York: Routledge.

Rheingold, H. (1993). *The virtual community: Homesteading on the electronic frontier.* Reading, MA: Addison-Wesley.

Rodriguez, C. (2001). *Fissures in the mediascape: An international study of citizens' media.* Cresskill, NJ: Hampton Press.

Rodriguez, C. (2002, May). Citizens' media and the voice of the angel/poet. *Media International Australia incorporating Culture and Policy*, 103, 78–87.

Salter, L. (2003). Democracy, new social movements, and the internet: A habermasian analysis. In M. McCaughey & M. D. Ayers (Eds.), *Cyberactivism: Online activism in theory and practice* (pp. 117–44). New York: Routledge.

Scalmer, S. (2002). *Dissent events: Protest, the media and the political gimmick in Australia.* Sydney: UNSW Press.

Schneider, F. (2002). Virtual sabotage. In E. Lubbers (Ed.), *Battling big business: Countering greenwash, infiltration and other forms of corporate bullying* (pp. 177–180). Melbourne: Scribe Publications.

Sharp, G. (1973). *The politics of nonviolent action* (in 3 Vols.). Boston: Porter Sargent.

Shirky, C. (2008). *Here comes everybody.* London: Allen Lane.

Sparks, C. (2005). Media and the global public sphere: An evaluative approach. In W. de Jong, M. Shaw, & N. Stammers (Eds.), *Global activism, global media* (pp. 34–49). London: Pluto.

Sussman, E. (Ed.). (1989). *On the passage of a few people through a rather brief moment in time: The situationist international, 1957–1972.* Cambridge, MA: MIT Press.

Van de Donk, W., Loader, B. D., Nixon, P. G., & Rucht, D. (Eds.). (2004). *Cyberprotest: New media, citizens and social movements.* London: Routledge.

Vegh, S. (2003). Classifying forms of online activism: The case of cyberprotests against the World Bank. In M. McCaughey & M. D. Ayers (Eds.), *Cyberactivism: Online activism in theory and practice* (pp. 71–95). New York: Routledge.

Wark, M. (2003). Toywars: Conceptual art meets conceptual business. *M/C Journal, 6*(3). Accessed January 24, 2007, from http://journal.media-culture.org.au/0306/02-toywars.php

Wark, M. (2008). *Fifty years of recuperation of the situationist international.* New York: Princeton Architectural Press.

Wishart, A., & Bochsler, R. (2002). *Leaving reality behind.* London: Fourth Estate.

Wray, S. (1998). *On electronic civil disobedience.* Accessed January 24, 2007, from http://www.thing.net/~rdom/ecd/oecd.html

Internet Reagency: The Implications of a Global Science for Collaboration, Productivity, and Gender Inequity in Less Developed Areas

B. Paige Miller, Ricardo Duque, Meredith Anderson, Marcus Antonius Ynalvez, Antony Palackal, Dan-Bright S. Dzorgbo, Paul N. Mbatia, and Wesley Shrum

Introduction

Both deplored and celebrated, globalization is altering social experiences and realities in developed and less developed countries. Although typically discussed in terms of economics, the process of globalization also holds significant implications for the structure of domestic *social* arrangements (Scholte, 2005, p. 8). With the widespread diffusion of information and communication technologies (ICTs)—a key dynamic of globalization—the structure of knowledge production in universities and research institutions may be altered. The internet, in particular, possesses the greatest potential for producing change within the scientific community. With its capacity to support synchronous and asynchronous communication, the internet is distinguished from traditional development projects as one centered on data sharing, collaboration, and networking. By eliminating the criterion of co-presence for interaction, use of the internet may ease the constraints of time and place that affect the ability of researchers to engage in more intense formal and informal interactions.

The potential change wrought by the internet on the structure of science and less developed areas more generally is not an uncontested issue. A debate exists between those who see the internet as an unproblematic good—the elixir argument—and those that see the internet as producing a new divide between rich and poor—the affliction argument (Davidson, Sooryamoorthy, & Shrum, 2002; Schech, 2002; Uimonen, 2001). The internet as Elixir argument suggests that by providing less developed areas with the technology and infrastructure they will be able to "reap the fruits" of the information society and leapfrog the development process, skipping intermediate "stages" of economic growth (De Roy, 1997; Uimonen, 2001, p. 92). Proponents of the internet as Affliction argument argue that social inequality both between and within countries will be exacerbated by the introduction of a new resource required for success in the information age. Applied to the institution

B.P. Miller (✉)
University of Wisconsin, River Falls, Wisconsin, USA
e-mail: paige.miller@uwrf.edu

J. Hunsinger et al. (eds.), *International Handbook of Internet Research*,
DOI 10.1007/978-1-4020-9789-8_23, © Springer Science+Business Media B.V. 2010

of science, this perspective predicts that the internet will have trivial or negative impacts on the research careers of scientists in less developed areas.

This article addresses the question of internet effects on science in developing areas, reviewing findings from an international research project first implemented in the "pre-internet" era. In examining this relationship, we maintain that the elixir and affliction arguments do not adequately capture the contemporary advances in information technologies insofar as they are grounded in traditional development discourses of modernization and dependency (Schech, 2002). Because these discourses predate the widespread advancements in and diffusion of the internet, they are not adequately equipped to account for the nature of contemporary social changes (DiMaggio, Hargittai, Neuman, & Robinson, 2001; Uimonen, 2001).

The perspective taken here is not of the internet as affliction or elixir but of the internet as reagentive. Due to the collaborative nature of the internet, we argue that it has the potential to reagentize science in a fundamentally new way than previous development projects. While the internet presents the possibility for collaboration, reagency emphasizes the unpredictable reactions brought about by the variable nature of time, place, and identity in the information age (Emirbayer & Misch, 1998; Shrum, 2005).[1] Use of the internet may make it easier for researchers to establish contacts with one another, but this effect is contingent on both the context in which it is used and the identities of its users.

We begin this discussion by exploring the dominant perspectives within the development literature, including dependency and world system, modernization, and neo-institutionalism. We critique these approaches for their assumptions that development, dependency, or both are the consequences of either place-bound identities and norms or the unidirectional flow of influence from core to peripheral countries. Next, we examine the concept of globalization in order to discuss the impact of the internet on the formation of global scientific relations. We suggest that globalization should be understood as a process that is shaped locally in unique ways, creating change within continuity or hybrid cultural forms (Nederveen Pieterse, 2004; Scholte, 2000) and introduce the concept of reagency to "re-place" development. Finally, we discuss the potential change in the structure of science as a result of the diffusion of the internet. By connecting researchers in developed and less developed institutions, the internet may create a truly global science.

In the second part we review the empirical findings of the project along six dimensions. The first two dimensions address the disparities between researchers working in different national contexts in terms of personal computer and internet use, access, practice, and experience. Moving beyond the simple access/no access dichotomy, as many internet researchers are now doing, provides a very different picture of the digital divide. The third dimension focuses on the outcomes of scientific research by elaborating on the relationship between internet use and publication output in scholarly journals. Connected to this is the issue of collaboration

---

[1] The concept of reagency has been used on this project beginning in 2000 to describe the dual nature of connectivity, not only as a conventional development project (generating activities through innovations and funding from distant lands) but also as an interactive technology that changes the conditions for establishment and maintenance of social relations.

and productivity. While studies have found a relationship between collaboration and productivity in developed scientific communities, our study indicates that for researchers in less developed areas this association may not be so straightforward. Next, we examine the degree of which use of e-mail and collaboration are associated with research problems. Finally, we look closer at disparities between men and women in terms of internet access, publication, and professional contacts.

Development

The role of science and technology in less developed areas is usually discussed in the context of the development project. Development as a project is comprised of institutions and national policies designed to create sustained economic and social growth. It is also associated with a discursive framework for talking and thinking about African, Asian, and Latin American countries (Escobar, 1995; McMichael, 2000; Meyer, Boli, Thomas, & Ramirez, 1997). From its inception the expansion of science and technology was an integral component of the development project (Escobar, 1995; Meyer et al., 1997; Shahidullah, 1991; Shrum & Shenhav, 1995; Uimonen, 2001; Yearley, 1988). For adherents to the modernization perspective, in particular, the ability to produce and use scientific knowledge and Western technology mark a country as modern.

Over time, however, skepticism grew over the suitability of these largely Western artifacts for the creation of sustained economic growth or social progress. In part a reaction to this, dependency and world system perspectives argue that development and underdevelopment are part of the same system: the world capitalist system (Chirot & Hall, 1982; Wallerstein, 1974). Adherents to this perspective argue that underdevelopment has been created and maintained through foreign investment and aid and international trade. Science and technology, as a form of foreign aid, are simply part of the world capitalist system that created dependence on the West.

Regardless of whether or not development is inevitable or whether science and technology are necessary tools for such development, most countries are committed to both (Shrum & Shenhav, 1995; Drori, Meyer, Ramirez, & Schofer, 2003; Schofer, 2004). According to neo-institutionalism, in order to be recognized as rational actors on the world stage in the post-war period, newly formed nation states and the organizations and associations that comprise them adopted identities centered on certain goals. Scientific knowledge and technological progress are part of the wider global cultural framework adopted by less developed areas (Drori et al., 2003: 3; Meyer et al., 1997).

With the advent and widespread diffusion of ICTs, advancements largely postdating traditional development perspectives, the focus of developmental discourse has shifted from one centered on technology transfer to one centered on collaboration and mediated relationships across national boundaries. In addition, culture, from these perspectives, is of secondary importance (Harrison, 1988, p. 145). The people inhabiting core and peripheral countries are generally treated as "agency-less." New treatments of globalization reveal the weaknesses of traditional concepts and the need to understand development processes as "reagentive."

Globalization and Reagency

The shift from the development project to the globalization project in the late 1970s marked a move from nationally managed social and economic growth to the positioning of countries in the *global* economy (McMichael, 2000). While economic dynamics are given the most attention as the primary force behind globalization, it is also technologically driven in the sense that changes in communication infrastructure aid the creation of the network society (McMichael, 1996; Uimonen, 2001; Wellman, 2001). But globalization operates at a local level as well, shaping and shaped by organizational environments and the identities of individual actors resulting in mixed cultures (Held, McGrew, Goldblatt, & Perraton, 1999; Nederveen Pieterse, 2004; Roberston, 2000; Schott, 1993; Uimonen, 2001).

How does this idea of hybrid cultural forms and mixed identities apply to the introduction of the internet into less developed areas? With some areas of the developing world exhibiting little economic growth in the last 50 years, it is peculiar to use the concept of "development" in a descriptive sense. This fact, in conjunction with rapid advancements in internet technology, poses a challenge to the way development is conceived. For these reasons, we argue that the concept of development needs to be replaced with "reagency."

Reagency refers to processes set in motion when projects originating in areas with high levels of resources are disseminated into areas with fewer resources. It seeks to describe what is occurring not as a simple matter of diffusion, domination, or imitation but as situated action within a dynamic interplay of development initiatives. Our understanding of reagency builds on Emirbayer and Misch's (1998) definition of agency as structurally embedded social engagement unfolding within the flow of time, with any given action exhibiting orientation to its past, future, and present components. Emirbayer and Misch's understanding of agency, however, is both un-placed and un-identified because it fails to identify the relational aspect of agency. The individuals, groups, and organizations occupying a given place do not passively accept development projects. They redirect the action using resources stemming from development agencies. In this way, development initiatives of all kinds create a reaction on the part of the actors involved and are thus reagentive.

Yet the internet is different from most other initiatives due to the potential change in the interaction patterns of donors, aid agencies, NGOs, and those people at whom these projects are aimed. Most development programs are quickly absorbed by target communities once resources are gone and external identities have vanished. But if action is understood as unfolding within the temporal orientations of actors in distinct structural contexts, the internet, by eliminating the criterion of co-presence for interaction, alters the nature of space and time. In this way, it allows for continued actions and reactions beyond the initial contact.

Programs designed to elicit "progress" or growth are carried by organizational representatives who enter a context with pre-existing identities that may have an interest in aid programs only as a means of acquiring resources or as allies in local struggles. While globalization has entailed a greater degree of interconnectedness, identities are still formed in places and relations with outsiders are structured via local interdependencies, but now they are embedded in an increasingly inter-connected world (Escobar, 2001; Gieryn, 2000; Henke, 2000; Scholte, 2000). The concept of reagency provides a way of seeing globalization that leaves room for variability and individual actors. More importantly, reagency provides a framework for understanding the implications of the internet for global science.

The Social Network Approach to Knowledge Production and Globalization

We approach the study of science and the internet in less developed areas through a network perspective, which views human behavior as constrained or enabled by social ties (Marsden, 1990; Scott, 1991). Adopting a network approach to the study of science allows one to go beyond development discourses centered on bounded identities and places to examine boundary crossings and the intersection of internal and external relationships.

The features of the internet mentioned throughout this article—the mediation of formal and informal communication and access to information—make it uniquely capable of attenuating the constraints on establishing and maintaining global col-laborations. Computer use, particularly the use of e-mail, instant messaging, and message boards, connects people who turn to online relationships seeking support, information, and commonality from others (Wellman, 2001; Wellman, Garton, & Haythornwaite, 1997). Collaboration between researchers is also thought to increase the visibility of scientists through increased publication (Lee & Bozeman, 2005; Luukkonen, Tijssen, Persson, & Sivertsen, 1993; Schott, 1993; Shrum, Genuth, & Chompalov, 2007). The argument for collaboration is most compelling for those in places with low levels of resources, providing a means for researchers to con-nect without the expense associated with co-presence. These are precisely the areas where developmental or reagentive processes occur.

For us, then, the most interesting question is what effects the internet will have on the way knowledge is produced, when rapid and reliable connections are avail-able between people working in different regions, fostering communication and collaborations not bound by time and space? Our study was designed to address, through a longitudinal and comparative design, whether the internet is changing the communication and productivity patterns of researchers in developed areas.

Context and Method

In the early 1990s, three locations in Africa and Asia were selected to represent vary-ing degrees of social and economic progress: Kerala, India (high), Kenya (medium), and Ghana (low).[2] In 2005, the per capita gross national income for India, Kenya,

---

[2]These locations were selected by the Dutch organization that initially funded the project in 1993, the Advisory Council for Scientific Research in Development Problems.

and Ghana was $720, $530, and $450, respectively. In 2004, India reported a 61.0% literacy rate for those over the age of 15, compared to the high in Kenya of 73.6% and the low in Ghana of 57.9%. For the same year, the number of fixed line and mobile phone subscribers and internet users in India was 84.5 and 32.4 per 1,000 people. The corresponding figures for Kenya were 85.0 fixed line and mobile phone subscribers and 44.8 internet users per 1,000 people. Ghana, while reporting the fewest number of internet users (17.0), also reported the highest number of fixed line and mobile phone subscribers (92.7) (The World Bank Group, 2006).

Within India, we focus on the southwestern state of Kerala. Often referred to as a model of development, Kerala presents a paradox. On the one hand, the country ranks relatively high on indices of social growth in terms of both demographic and educational characteristics. In terms of fertility, infant mortality, and life expectancy rates, Kerala mirrors that of many Western European and North American countries. Further, the status of women in the state is considered by many to be relatively high in terms of their high rates of educational attainment and literacy rates (Jeffrey, 1992). On the other hand, Kerala also ranks low on measures of economic progress leading some to argue that the Kerala model of development may not be sustainable. As proof, they note the high level of unemployment, even among the highly educated, and the low level of external economic investment (Iyer and MacPherson, 2000).

Kenya, selected to represent a medium level of economic and social development, has been plagued with corruption and anti-democratic politics since gaining independence in the 1960s. These problems have at various points caused international donors and aid groups to withhold funds from the country, in turn causing the Kenyan currency to drop in value (Barkan & Ng'ethe, 1998). At the same time, and more importantly for the purposes of this article, the country also possesses one of the largest research systems in Africa and is also one of only seven countries on the continent to possess more than 10 internet Service Providers (Duque et al., 2005).

Finally, Ghana, selected to represent a low level of economic and social development, ranks lower than Kenya on most development indicators. In spite of this, the country has consistently set itself apart as one of the leading economies in the region, in part due to the restructuring loans it has received from outside agencies. While its academic and research systems are relatively old, a carryover from the colonial period, corruption and economic downturns have slowed the level of growth in research output. The country has also invested heavily in developing its IT sector and as a consequence has internet connectivity at a rate consistent with Kenya.

The data for this project were collected in several waves: the first in 1994 and the second over a 3-year period extending from 2000 to 2002.[3] In the first wave of the study, respondents working in national and international research institutions,

---

[3]In 2005, we conducted another wave of the survey in Ghana, India, and Kenya, attempting to reach each member of the earlier survey for a true panel design. In addition, we conducted the study for the first time in South Africa, Chile, and the Philippines. However, these new locations have only been analyzed in a preliminary way.

non-governmental organizations (NGOs), and universities were asked a variety of questions related to their educational, occupational, and demographic backgrounds. They represented researchers employed in a number of fields including agriculture, bioscience, information technology, engineering, math, chemistry, physics, geology, and social science.

The second wave of the study was conducted on a subset of the original institutions—NGOs were excluded to ensure more intensive coverage of a smaller number of institutions. Respondents employed in national research institutions and universities were interviewed in 2000 (Kerala, n=303), 2001 (Kenya, n=315), and 2002 (Ghana, n=300) for a total of 918 respondents. Because the first wave of the study was "pre-internet," the second wave included a number of additional questions regarding access to and use of ICTs. The summary below focuses primarily on the results from the 2000–2002 data. To examine gender differences in the three original countries we have conducted a longitudinal analysis of changes in women's research careers relative to men's across the two waves of the survey (1994 and 2000–2002). We also examined 90 qualitative interviews with researchers in Kerala conducted between 2003 and 2004.

Results

In a series of papers and unpublished findings, we have examined a number of issues related to the diffusion of the internet and its impact on the research careers of scientists in less developed areas. First, because the advent and diffusion of the internet is a relatively recent phenomenon, we have evaluated the degree to which researchers report adopting both the physical hardware required for internet access, i.e., personal computers as well as the internet itself. By "the internet" we mean a combination of information retrieval (web browsing) and information sharing and communication (e-mail). While a region may have the capacity for connectivity, without the physical hardware this means very little.

In this context, we have examined patterns of internet access and use in terms of being a self-defined current user, possessing ready access to e-mail, internet practice—a measure of e-mail and web use diversity, and internet experience—a measure of the length of time respondents have been using the web and e-mail. Consistent with the reagency argument, our second focus has been on the disparities in access and use between the three countries as well as within them. As such, we have examined differences on those four dimensions of internet adoption just mentioned according to the ascribed and achieved identities of the researchers in our three locations.

The third topic we have addressed is the extent to which internet use is associated with research output in domestic and foreign journals. Related to this, the fourth and fifth issues we have focused on examine the association between collaboration and productivity and the extent to which the internet was used by researchers to alleviate the problems associated with collaboration. Finally, the sixth topic we have attended to takes a specific focus on the implications of the internet for gender inequities in science. Culturally and socially informed gender identities as well as social norms, we argue, have an important impact on the way individuals interact with new technologies.

Adoption of Personal Computers and the Internet

The approach outlined above insists that in order to understand the potential impact of internet diffusion on the research practices in less developed areas one must be sensitive to variations in context, organizational background, and differences in individual identities. When examining the extent to which ICTs have been adopted we considered the organizational context (national research institute or university), the level of socio-economic development (regional location), and status characteristics of the scientists. As expected, there were a number of variations within each country and between research environments in terms of access to personal computers. For instance, while the majority of our sample had access to a personal computer at work, Malayalis were most likely to report such access and Ghanaians least likely. By sector of employment, scientists in research institutions tended to have greater access to computers in work settings than academics.

A qualification should be added to this general picture of work access to computers. While respondents from Ghana were least likely and respondents from Kerala most likely to possess access to a computer at work, Malayalis were also least likely to report having access in their office and vice versa for Ghanaians. The number of researchers reporting *private* access to a computer, access within their personal office, was quite small. This finding is telling as it indicates that even with access to personal computers within an organization, researchers working in less developed areas, regardless of organizational context, tend to share hardware. Consequently, at the time that we gathered the data for this study, they were limited in internet access, regardless of connectivity.

Support for this was seen in the disparity between the researchers' view of themselves as current e-mail users and the extent to which they actually had access to the technology. In other words, the majority of the respondents, regardless of socio-economic differences and sectoral context, viewed themselves as current e-mail users. However, far fewer had ready access to the technology (a consequence of sharing the computer hardware) and most reported difficulty using e-mail due to technical problems.

Disparities in ICT Access and Use

Our second focus has been the degree to which disparities exist within countries between researchers based on their educational, professional, and demographic backgrounds. Most respondents viewed themselves as users of the internet. But generally speaking, regardless of personal characteristics, they reported limited experience and low diversity in their use of the internet. When we examined more descriptive aspects of their ICT use along the lines of ready access, experience, and practice, a different image of the digital divide began to emerge. We found differences among locations, but few differences between institutional contexts.

In terms of the individual characteristics, differences existed on most dimensions of internet practice and experience based on age and marital status, as well as gender and educational attainment, in terms of both the degree held and the location where they received their degree. Men, those possessing a doctorate, and those educated in developed countries reported more diverse e-mail and web use as well as internet experience. Indians reported greater diversity of practice and experience than Africans. Our qualitative interviews strongly suggest this was due to their greater ability to access the internet in the domestic setting. To summarize our experience in the past several years of observation and analysis, "mere" access or "connectivity" is not generally the most important issue. The digital divide is better viewed in terms of the conditions of access, as well as by issues of experience and practice.

ICT Use and Productivity

We documented disparities in internet adoption, practice, and experience based on the place, context, and identities of internet users. What are the consequences of adoption, practice, and experience for the career outcomes of scientists in Africa and Asia? The general assumption in the literature on internet diffusion is that use of ICTs will provide individuals and organizations improved efficiency and effectiveness. In the research sector this translates to visibility in the scientific community through increased publication productivity. Does this assumption hold true in Kerala, Kenya, and Ghana?

We examined productivity along two dimensions, domestic productivity (publications in local journals) and foreign productivity (publication in international journals). The aggregated results by location suggest that Malayalis were the most productive researchers in our sample, followed by Ghanaians, and finally Kenyans. The association between ICT use and productivity at the local level showed no clear pattern of association between internet adoption and research output. Instead what we found were variations according to the level of socio-economic development, the specific aspect of internet adoption, and the social and demographic background characteristics of the respondents. For instance, there was no apparent benefit for local productivity or foreign productivity based on ICT adoption for Ghanaian researchers. Kerala and Kenya both exhibited some benefits for local productivity but only on the current use and experience dimensions (Kerala) and e-mail diversity (Kenya). The association between foreign productivity and ICT adoption for Kerala and Kenya was significant, but only for e-mail diversity (both Kenya and Kerala) and e-mail experience (Kerala only). Our results do not support any generalized association between internet adoption and research output.

Productivity and Collaboration

Two kinds of relationships support knowledge production, reflecting two important sources of assistance and information that are used in the course of answering research questions. Hence, the conceptualization of collaborative ties from the standpoint of an individual scientist must include both organizational colleagues and those outside of the immediate work context—inter-organizational ties. Our findings have not been consistent with expectations based on the level of social and economic development or with the hypothesized relationship between productivity and collaboration. While the Indians in our study have generally been the most productive they were also least likely to collaborate, both within and outside of their immediate work environment. Kenyan scientists, as a group, reported the most external collaboration owing to the large number of international organizations located in the country and the amount of external aid—but were least productive on standard output measures.

When we examined the output by research sector, we found that collaboration was positively related to publication output only in academic institutions: in government research institutes there were actually negative correlations between collaboration and productivity. Combining collaboration and the respondent's ascribed and achieved statuses gave an even clearer picture of the association between collaboration and productivity. When we controlled for research sector, marital status, level of education, and professional status, the only positive association between collaboration and research output was for Kenyan academics. Most scientists did not appear to benefit from collaboration, at least in terms of higher publication productivity. This finding is not consistent with the traditional approach, which views collaborative activities as well as relationships with international colleagues and funding agents as enhancing scientific effectiveness. However, it is consistent with a reagency perspective that views collaboration as the acquisition of resources as an end in itself, without output objectives. In less developed areas such as Kenya and Ghana, collaborations are valued for their resource potential. The traditional publication productivity of scientists is de-emphasized in favor of generating new projects and sources of income. When collaborations become costly in terms of time and energy and do not offer significant resource benefits, they are viewed as unwarranted.

Does the Internet Facilitate Collaboration?

These results raised two questions. First, is collaboration in less developed areas actually associated with research difficulties, as the findings reported above seem to suggest? And second, does use of the internet actually reduce the difficulties establishing and maintaining contacts with other researchers? Significant differences emerged in four problem areas: contacting people when needed, transmitting information, keeping others informed, and security of information. Initial results appeared to support the idea that developmental context made a difference. Kenyans, who collaborated a lot, reported the greatest difficulties. Indians, who had greater access to e-mail, reported the fewest research difficulties. As indicated above, however, Indians have not been as active in forming and maintaining collaborative relationships. When we took into account both the social and organizational context, the association between collaboration and research problems disappeared, suggesting that research difficulties and collaboration were not as intimately related as the place in which research is practiced. However, we did find a consistent relationship between greater e-mail use and fewer research problems across all three locations and controlling for organizational context.

ICT Use and Gender Inequality

It seems clear that the ability to collaborate, productivity levels of individuals and groups, and access to resources and information, vary intra-culturally as well. Women in particular may benefit from certain features of the internet in terms of their informal communication patterns, access to information resources, and productivity levels. Much of the work on women and science has focused on women employed in highly functioning research systems, although the research that is available suggests that the experiences of women in less developed areas may be similar if not exacerbated (Fox, 1999; Long, 1992; Xie & Shaumann, 2003).

Gupta and Sharma (2002) argue that women in India, even if they remain in the scientific pipeline, experience a number of difficulties establishing and maintaining contacts with fellow researchers due to the patrifocal nature of Indian society, which restricts the interactions of women with males outside the kinship context. Our interest in this subject has been guided by the idea that ICTs may provide an environment for women to establish contacts with other researchers by circumventing the constraints on their interaction patterns, thus providing an alternate means to develop and maintain social capital.

We employed both qualitative and quantitative methodologies for examining gender differences in less developed areas. Our initial studies, focusing specifically on gender differences, corroborated the above finding of increased access to the internet and e-mail, with no significant differences emerging along gender lines. In less than a decade, there was also increased access to human capital (as measured by possession of the Ph.D.). The gender gap in educational attainment closed, with women scientists equally likely to have reported possession of the Ph.D. Indeed, results from both the full sample and the qualitative interviews among Kerala women provided initial support for the hypothesis that increased access to ICTs may be a means for women to circumvent constraints placed on their physical mobility. Malayali women, while they displayed virtually no change in their educational localism, did discuss a number of short trips abroad.[4] What emerged as problematic was that the

---

[4]We measure orientation to career by asking respondents to report the number of years spent in developed areas for education or in general and the number of days spent away from their parent organization or the organization in which they are employed.

full sample actually displayed increased localism over time. Initially, we thought it could be that ready internet access reduced the need to travel, but at the time of our second wave, internet connectivity was significantly below Western levels. Even if the internet served to replace face-to-face interaction in some contexts—which is anything but certain—it was difficult to argue that the internet had reduced the need to travel.

Most interesting for future work was a seeming contradiction that emerged between the qualitative and quantitative analyses regarding the degree to which increased access to e-mail might actually enable women, in particular Indian women, to circumvent constraints on physical mobility and create professional contacts. Increased access to e-mail reported by female researchers between 1994 and 2000–2002 was not associated with increased international contacts but actually a decrease. Qualitative interviews with Malayali researchers, on the other hand, created a very different picture. Although we did not directly measure the number of professional contacts, in interviews women researchers placed more emphasis on their foreign contacts than men and viewed the internet as a valuable source for gathering information on international opportunities, including travel abroad. Our most recent survey may allow us to assess whether this is the result of an actual shift that has been slow in coming or, alternatively, whether the emphasis on foreign contacts is perceptual in nature, perhaps due to the enhanced salience of contacts where they are limited in nature.

Internet and Science in the Philippines, Chile, and South Africa

In 2005 we expanded the project to Chile, South Africa, and the Philippines—three new areas that will allow comparisons across contexts. Preliminary findings also show differences in internet use, collaboration, and productivity, but in 2005 the overall level of connectivity had increased substantially. For scientists in the Philippines, Chile, and South Africa, internet access is almost a given, as it is in the United States and Europe. The primary source of variability now lies in advanced internet use and habits or practices.

The Philippine case offers a contrast to India as an Asian country with a research system more dependent on development aid. Scientists in the Philippines engage predominantly in domestic collaboration, but when they do engage in foreign collaboration, there is no effect on productivity. What matters are advanced computer–user interaction skills, larger networks, and contacts in developed areas (Australia, Japan, the United States). Unlike the Indian scientists we had long studied, researchers in the Philippines were quite likely to go abroad for advanced training and that experience matters for the development and maintenance of informal networks. In particular, doctoral training in Japan is associated with close ties to mentors and the maintenance of those linkages after graduation, a routine and explicit element of Japanese cultural practice.

Our interest in South Africa was generated by the fact that it is the most highly developed research system in sub-Saharan Africa and offered a regional counter-point to Ghana and Kenya. Here, internet use, as measured by time spent on e-mail, is positively associated with collaboration, but collaboration is *not* generally related to publication productivity, and there is little evidence that academics benefit from international collaboration. While scientists who use e-mail intensively are slightly more productive, this is not the case for foreign productivity in the case of academic scientists.

Chile has one of the strongest economies and one of the most advanced research systems in Latin America. Nearly one-third of collaborations reported by scientists included foreign partners, but in contrast to other regions of the study, higher levels of collaboration are reliably associated with productivity, an effect most pronounced among academics. Moreover, collaboration with foreign partners is associated with higher international productivity, the kind most valued by research administrators. In terms of training, about half of Chilean scientists received their doctorate in a developed country, but this is associated with fewer foreign publications. Domestic training would seem to limit, at least initially, the number of international con-tacts, but this does not translate into a long-term disadvantage. We are investigating the extent to which internet practice may explain this: those who do not have the opportunity to establish foreign ties early in their careers may be more active in initiating collaborations that increase productivity.

Conclusion

From its inception the internet has been viewed as a means to link researchers around the world and provide new avenues for the acquisition of information and resources (Davidson et al., 2002; Uimonen, 2001). By removing the need for geo-graphic proximity to colleagues and facilities, it has been hypothesized that the internet will transform the way researchers work, gather information, and interact with one another (DiMaggio et al., 2001; Uimonen, 2001). Because the internet combines a multiplicity of features that include interactional components as well as different content formats, its impact on social change is distinct from other techno-logical innovations such as the television and the telephone (DiMaggio et al., 2001). The nature and speed of these effects are far from certain, particularly with respect to less developed areas of the world. internet research must focus significant attention on the broad questions of (1) whether the overall impact of the internet is to increase or decrease inequality and, equally important, (2) how it impacts the lives of those in the developing world. These questions cannot be accomplished by "usage" studies that simply ask how the internet is used by those who use it.

Will the internet lead to social isolation, a world dense with transnational inter-connections, or something else? In what way will the internet impact women as compared to men? Will rural areas, less developed countries, and the marginalized be left out of this technological revolution? What will the internet mean for the production of knowledge in areas of the world that have been remote from the centers of scientific and technological advance? These questions are particularly vital for an information age discourse that views knowledge as the new form of capital. Individuals and countries with access to information technologies—the information rich—are in a better position to develop knowledge-based institutions and the information economy as well. Knowledge and power, it is argued, are linked in contemporary societies.[5]

Elixir, utopian, and modernization views of the impact of the internet are incomplete because they focus on the extent to which connectivity and ICTs have diffused to developing areas. There is little discussion of costs and trade-offs. When benefits are assumed, the primary empirical issues simply focus on whether and to what extent the connectivity project has been extended to, for example, research institutes and universities in the less developed world. But connectivity itself is one in a long line of initiatives that have been implemented by multilateral agencies and NGOs that promote dependency and maintenance of a set of developmental institutions. Focus on connectivity and access presumes that interactive and information technologies themselves are the means to productivity and betterment—notwithstanding the set of identities that implement and maintain these technologies. The reagency perspective is a micro-sociological view that highlights the development organizations themselves, as they interact with local identities with non-local resources.

Earlier views do not examine the negative consequences that can occur with the diffusion of technology to less developed areas, while affliction, dystopian, and dependency theories fail to examine the different kinds of agency involved in multilateral and international initiatives and programs. We must look more to local as opposed to global theories to explain the consequences of internet diffusion (Agnew, 1982). The internet should be viewed as a cultural construct both endowed with the characteristics of the environment in which it was created and embedded in different cultural spaces (Uimonen, 2001). This is consistent with the idea that place, identity, and time are critical factors in the social realities of persons, notwithstanding accelerated globalization processes. Individuals do not cease to exist in the spatio-temporal world when they enter "cyberspace." The internet does facilitate communication across great distances, creating the potential for collaboratories that provide geographically distributed "access to equipment, colleagues, and databases" (Walsh et al., 2000). Access to ICTs may provide disadvantaged actors with the tools for advancement, but at its core, our argument is that the benefits of such technologies

---

[5]Parayil (2005), for instance, demonstrates the way in which the information age has been marked by an increase rather than a decrease in inequality measured in terms of the income levels both within and between countries. Those countries and people able to produce and use knowledge, primarily scientific and technical knowledge, are in a dominant position compared to those unable to. He argues that this results from most people being left out of the information revolution, but concludes that this is caused by the political and economic context in which the internet is used not due to something inherent within the technology itself.

must be viewed with a critical eye. Empirical studies are required to monitor the microsocial processes that address these issues.

Acknowledgments This article presents results from a series of studies conducted between 1994 and 2002 in Kerala, Kenya, and Ghana funded by the Netherlands Development Assistance Research Council and the US National Science Foundation under Grant No. 0113545 (International Program; STS Program; Program on Information Technology Research).

References

Agnew, J. A. (1982). Technology transfer and theories of development. *Journal of Asian and African Studies, 17*(1–2), 16–31.

Barkan, J. D., & Ng'ethe, N. (1998). Kenya tries again. *Journal of Democracy, 9*(2), 32–48.

Chirot, D., & Hall, T. (1982). World-system theory. *Annual Review of Sociology, 8*, 81–106.

Davidson, T., Sooryamoorthy, R., & Shrum, W. (2002). Kerala connections: Will the internet affect science in developing areas? In B. Wellman & C. Haythornthwaite (Eds.), *The internet in everyday life* (pp. 496–519). Malden, MA: Blackwell.

De Roy, O. (1997). The African challenge: Internet, networking and connectivity activities in a developing environment. *Third World Quarterly, 18*(5), 883–899.

DiMaggio, P., Hargittai, E., Neuman, W., & Robinson, J. (2001). Social implications of the internet. *Annual Review of Sociology, 27*, 307–336.

Drori, G., Meyer, J., Ramirez, F., & Schofer, E. (2003). *Science in the modern world polity: Institutionalization and globalization.* Stanford, CA: Stanford University Press.

Duque, R. B., Ynalvez, M. A., Soorymoorthy, R., Mbatia, P., Dzrogbo, D. B., & Shrum, W. (2005). Collaboration paradox: Scientific productivity, the internet, and problems of research in developing areas. *Social Studies of Science, 35*(5), 755–785.

Emirbayer, M., & Mische, A. (1998). What is agency? *American Journal of Sociology, 103*(4), 962–1023.

Escobar, A. (1995). *Encountering development: The making and unmaking of the third world.* Princeton, NJ: Princeton University Press.

Escobar, A. (2001). Culture sits in places: Reflections on globalism and subaltern strategies of localization. *Political Geography, 20*(2), 139–174.

Fox, M. F. (1999). Gender, hierarchy, and science. In J. S. Chafetz (Ed.), *Handbook of the sociology of gender* (pp. 441–458). New York.

Gieryn, T. F. (2000). A space for place in sociology. *Annual Review of Sociology, 26*, 463–496.

Gupta, N., & Sharma, A. K. (2002). Women academic scientists in India. *Social studies of science, 32*(5–6), 901–915.

Harrison, D. (1988). *The sociology of modernization and development.* London: Unwin Hyman.

Held, D., McGrew, A. G., Goldblatt, D., & Perraton, J. (1999). *Global transformations: Politics, economics, and culture.* Stanford, CA: Stanford University Press.

Henke, C. R. (2000). Making a place for science: The field trial. *Social Studies of Science, 30*(44), 483–511.

Iyer, S. R., & MacPherson, S. (2000). *Social development in Kerala: Illusion or reality?* Aldershot: Ashgate.

Jeffrey, R. (1992). *Politics, women, and well-being: How Kerala became a model.* London: Macmillan.

Lee, S., & Bozeman, B. (2005). The impact of research collaboration on scientific productivity. *Social Studies of Science, 35*(5), 703–723.

Long, J. (1992). Measures of sex differences in scientific productivity. *Social Forces, 71*(1), 159–178.

Luukkonen, T., Tijssen, R., Persson, O., & Sivertsen, G. (1993). The measurement of international scientific collaboration, *Scientometrics, 28*(1), 15–36.

Marsden, P. (1990). Network data and measurement. *Annual Review of Sociology, 16*, 435–463.

McMichael, P. (1996). Globalization: Myths and realities. *Rural Sociology, 61*(1), 25–55.

McMichael, P. (2000). *Development and social change: A global perspective* (2nd ed.). Thousand Oaks, CA: Pine Forge Press.

Meyer, J. W., Boli, J., Thomas, G. M., & Ramirez, F. (1997). World society and the nation state. *The American Journal of Sociology, 103*(1), 144–181.

Nederveen Pieterse, J. (2004). *Globalization and culture: Global mélange.* Lanham, MD: Rowman and Littlefield Publishers.

Parayil, G. (2005). Digital divide and increasing returns: Contradictions of informational capitalism. *The Information Society, 21*(1), 41–51.

Robertson, R. (2000). Globalization theory 2000+: Major problematics. In G. Ritzer & B. Smart (Eds.), *Handbook of social theory* (pp. 458–471). Thousand Oaks, CA: Sage Publications.

Schech, S. (2002). Wired for change: The links between ICTs and development discourses. *Journal of International Development, 14*(1), 13–23.

Schofer, E. (2004). Cross-national differences in the expansion of science, 1970–1990. *Social Forces, 83* (1), 215–248.

Scholte, J. A. (2005). *Globalization: A critical introduction* (2nd ed.). London: Macmillan.

Schott, T. (1993). World science: Globalization of institutions and participation. *Science, Technology and Human Values, 18*(2), 196–208.

Scott, J. (1991). *Social network analysis.* London: Sage Publications.

Shahidullah, S. M. (1991). *Capacity-building in science and technology in the third world: Problems, issues, and strategies.* San Francisco: Westview Press.

Shrum, W. (2005). Reagency of the internet, or, how I became a guest for science. *Social Studies of Science, 35*(5), 723–754.

Shrum, W., & Shenhav, Y. (1995). Science and technology in less developed countries. In S. Jasanoff, G. E. Markle, J. C. Petersen, & T. Pinch (Eds.), *Handbook of science and technology studies* (pp. 229–256). Thousand Oaks, CA: Sage Publications.

Shrum, W., Genuth, J., & Chompalov, I. (2007). *Structures of scientific collaboration.* Cambridge, MA: MIT Press.

Uimonen, P. (2001). *Transnational dynamics@development.net: Internet, modernization and globalization.* Stockholm: Department of Social Anthropology, Stockholm University.

Wallerstein, I. (1974). *The modern world system.* New York: Academic Press.

Walsh, J. P., Kucker, S., Maloney, N. G., & Gabbay, S. (2000). Connecting minds: Computer-mediated communication and scientific work. *Journal of the American Society for Information Science, 51*(14), 1295–1305.

Wellman, B. (2001). Computer networks as social networks. *Science, 293*(5537), 2031–2034.

Wellman, B., Garton, L., & Haythornwaite, C. (1997). Studying online social networks. *Journal of Computer Mediated Communication, 3*(1). Retrieved from http://jcmc.indiana.edu/vol3/issue1/garton.html

The World Bank Group (2006). *Key development data and statistics.* Retrieved October, 2006, from http://www.worldbank.org/

Xie, Y., & Shaumann, K. A. (2003). *Women in science: Career processes and outcomes.* Cambridge, MA: Harvard University Press.

Yearley, S. (1988). *Science, technology and social change.* London: Unwin Hyman.

Strangers and Friends: Collaborative Play in World of Warcraft

Bonnie Nardi and Justin Harris

Introduction

Understanding changing social relations as they are developing within the context of the internet is an important task for CSCW research (Brown & Bell, 2004). A new and rapidly growing site of online collaboration is massively multiplayer online games (MMOGs). MMOGs are part of a larger group of video games that have surpassed films in box office revenue, with MMOGs accounting for about half of the total game revenue (Kushner, 2005). MMOGs connect hundreds or thousands of players through the internet in persistent game worlds. In this article we describe diverse types of collaborative play in *World of Warcraft*, ranging from lightweight encounters with strangers to highly organized groupings with well-known friends. We argue that together these collaborations constitute a distinctive space of play made possible by the capabilities of the internet, the design of *World of Warcraft*, and the culture created by players. Many collaborations spontaneously take place with strangers – a striking phenomenon that seems unusually prevalent in multiplayer games and suggests the emergence of new kinds of social relations developing within contexts provided by the internet (Brown & Bell, 2004). At the same time, many play *WoW* (as it is known) with offline friends and family, so the game also appears to reinforce existing social ties for these players.

Now that games are an important part of internet use, we have an opportunity to recognize the collaborative aspects of online fun, to expand "CSCW" to include activities that provide entertainment (Brown & Bell 2004; Bainbridge, 2007; Ducheneaut & Moore 2004; Ducheneaut, Yee, Nickell, & Moore, 2006; Steinkuehler & Williams 2006; Twidale, Wang, & Hinn, 2005). Though the outcome of such activities is amusement and not a work product, there is a collective object-oriented activity (Leontiev, 1974), i.e., having fun. Even when players are competing, the object of having fun by playing the game is a form of collaboration;

B. Nardi (✉)
Department of Informatics, University of California, Irvine, UK
e-mail: nardi@ics.uci.edu

J. Hunsinger et al. (eds.), *International Handbook of Internet Research*,
DOI 10.1007/978-1-4020-9789-8_24, © Springer Science+Business Media B.V. 2010

players could not compete if there were no one to play with. As in any game or sport, the larger field of collaboration is constituted by engaging in the game.

World of Warcraft

Based on a Tolkienesque high-fantasy motif, *World of Warcraft* is a MMOG in which players create characters with distinctive looks and qualities such as intellect, strength, stamina, and agility. Characters advance through 80 levels of play. They acquire equipment such as swords, armor, and jewelry; develop skills such as attacking and healing; and slay an array of imaginative monsters dwelling in caves, dungeons, and encampments in varied landscapes in the land of Azeroth. The game can be likened to an animated cartoon in which the player controls the character with mouse and keyboard. Characters travel on foot, by boat, or air through fields, farms, deserts, mountains, seas, and other distinctive scenery for which *WoW* is known. Lyrical or haunting music often plays as the character adventures.

Players are divided into "realms" which are servers of about 20,000 players (warcraftrealms.com). The first key decision a player makes is which race and class to play. The "races" in *WoW* are Night Elf, Dwarf, Gnome, Human, Dranei, Troll, Orc, Tauren, Undead, and Blood Elf. Classes are druid, priest, warrior, rogue, mage, hunter, paladin, shaman, warlock, and death knight. Each class entails a different style of play – for example, the priest is physically weak but able to cast deadly spells or heal fellow players while the warrior can take a beating from powerful monsters, keeping them at bay as other players struggle to defeat them. The classes' asymmetrical strengths and weaknesses encourage collaboration during battle as well as in brief encounters, such as asking a rogue to use his lock-picking ability to open a chest buried at sea or requesting conjured water from a mage.

World of Warcraft entails killing monsters, exploration, quests, and playing in battlegrounds as well as more restful pursuits such as crafting, chatting with friends, and spending time in cities for banking, training, and trading. In a quest, the key form of play, a computer character gives the player a goal, for example, slaying the traitorous Edwin VanCleef. The player must travel to a certain area, kill a series of monsters, and finally battle VanCleef. Once the quest is completed, the player receives "experience points" which count toward reaching the next level of play, and possibly a reward such as equipment, in-game money, or fanciful items like a bouquet of flowers or a flagon of beer.

Game activities include practicing professions such as herbalism or blacksmithing, buying and selling items at the Auction House or through a trade chat channel, and socializing in many venues. Players establish guilds which are named groups that socialize and play together. Guilds can be designed to create somewhat customized play experiences. For example, an LDS (Church of the Latter Day Saints) guild stated on an online guild recruitment forum, "We welcome all players as long as they can respect our standards (i.e., no dirty language/swearing). If you wish to have fun in a clean gaming environment, contact us." The second author's guild was "The Grand Threat" (a pseudonym), discovered in an online guild recruitment forum, and chosen for its gay-friendly status because of the author's interest in the GLBT (gay–lesbian–bisexual transgender) community online. The other author was recruited in-game to "The Legion of Darkness."

Methodology

We studied *World of Warcraft* through immersive ethnographic fieldwork including participant observation; semi-structured in-depth interviews offline and online (through an in-game chat channel or e-mail); the collection of chat logs (using a function supplied in the game); and reading documents such as *WoW*-related forums and websites. Late in 2005, we each created a character and logged on several times a week, playing intensively through the Christmas break, with ongoing play and observation continuing. One of us chose a druid and the other a priest for our characters. To gain as much knowledge of the game as possible, one of us joined a "player vs player" (PvP) server and the other a "player vs environment" (PvE) server. On player vs player servers, players can attack and kill other players of the opposing "faction," Alliance or Horde. On PvE servers, players must intentionally flag themselves for PvP combat. PvP and PvE play are about evenly divided in number of characters (warcraftrealms.com). Each of us experimented with alternative characters, or "alts," to gain further understanding of the classes and explore parts of the world inhabited by the two factions. We conducted 26 in-depth, semi-structured interviews, 12 with our guild members, 8 with players we met and interviewed offline, and 6 with players we met online who were not in our guilds. Nineteen players were male and seven female. We asked people when and why they started to play *WoW*, how they learned the game, what they liked and disliked about it, how many characters they had, details regarding the characters, and whether they played offline with friends and family. All guild and player names used are pseudonyms. Orthography in quotations from chat logs is unaltered.

Types of Collaboration in World of Warcraft

In this section we describe types of collaborative play in *WoW* ranging from fleeting lightweight encounters to highly structured collaborations in guilds. In the section "Strangers in the Fight" we point out collaborations that take place with strangers to support Brown and Bell's argument regarding the ease of collaborating with strangers in at least some MMOGs. In the section "Structured Collaborations with Friends and Strangers" we discuss the formal structures for collaborative support provided by game mechanics. In "Random Acts of Fun" we describe playful non-structured collaborations. In both, friends and strangers may collaborate.

Strangers in the Fight

A new player is suddenly surprised by a soft whooshing noise. A colorful icon appears near the top of her screen, and she experiences a moment of alarm. Was that a game-generated attack? No – the player has been "buffed," that is, she is the recipient of a beneficial spell cast by a nearby player. A buff increases an ability for a short period of time so that while in combat the player has a small advantage. Buffs are the simplest form of engagement between players we observed in *World of Warcraft*. While they are frequently used in formal groups, buffs are also a gesture of goodwill cast in passing on players with whom the caster has no relationship. Buffs are part of the culture of the game in which players commit small acts of kindness to maintain a mutually beneficial atmosphere even though no immediate reciprocity is in the offing and no rewards such as experience points are gained.

A "kill assist" is another common favor. While traveling, a player notices someone about to expire while battling a monster. Instead of continuing on, he stops to help make the kill, leaving a grateful player who avoids a dreary run back from the graveyard (the penalty for "death" in *WoW*). Or, a player has died before help could arrive. A nearby player who can return others to life resurrects the player.

Players offer assistance in other ways. A player finds himself in hostile territory with monsters too high-level for him to fight. He asks the help of a more advanced player and is escorted to safety – which can take several minutes and is a generous gesture. A frequent favor is to answer questions players ask in a chat channel. Players are constantly in need of information on how to play. For example, a player sends a message for the location of a particular computer-controlled character, receiving a reply giving directions.

It is likely that players in these encounters do not know one another. Players routinely offer unsolicited help to strangers as well as responding when asked. Because characters are labeled with their name and guild, and mousing over the character reveals class and level, players have enough information to make appropriate requests. A collaborative atmosphere of "respect" for all players is a desired aim articulated by many guilds and reinforced as players help others, mindful of help they have received.

Not all interactions with strangers are beneficial. A level 20 character runs through a contested area on a PvP server and suddenly a mounted character appears on the road before him. The level 20 clicks on the character only to see a skull icon next to her name – *WoW*'s way of saying that a fight with this person will surely bring death. As the first hit from the opponent drains half the character's life, he runs but is quickly defeated.

The level 20, now recovered, is in a close fight with a monster. As the moment of victory is reached he breathes a sigh of relief, only to be attacked from another quarter. A level 20 from the opposing faction has decided to take advantage of his weakened state for an easy kill. These activities are called "ganking." Not only are they allowed by game mechanics, they are considered fair play, as explained on the Blizzard website. Unlike offline strangers, in the *World of Warcraft* unknown others are more than just part of the landscape. Players actively pursue engagements with them, both beneficial and combative. These informal, unplanned collaborations with other players bring added depth to the game as players fight their way through the computer-generated world.

Structured Collaborations with Friends and Strangers

World of Warcraft provides several means of structured collaboration where much play takes place. Players may play with players they do not know, with friends and family from offline life, or with in-game friends.

Parties, Raids, and the Friends List

Parties and raids are temporary groups formed to accomplish a short-term goal such as a quest or defending against the opposite faction in PvP. They have a leader who invites players and can remove them. When conducting quests there are specific means by which experience points and treasure, or "loot," are shared so members know in advance what to expect. A party, composed of two to five players, has its own chat channel. Party members may or may not know one another. For example, a party may set out at half-strength with players who know each other. They begin a quest and then add new members as needed as they meet other players doing the same quest. If party members enjoy playing together they may share their other quests. Quests are normally obtained from a computer-character but quest-sharing allows players to continue to play together after the initial quest that brought them together is complete. If they like one another, players add each other to their friends list for future play.

The friends list is maintained individually by each player and contains a collection of people who usually do not know one another; they are known individually to the maker of the list. The friends list is one-way; adding a friend does not reciprocally add the player to the other's list. The friends list alerts the player when a friend logs in or out and provides information on their current level and location. Friends often "whisper" to one another, that is, communicate in a private chat channel. Friends are not weak ties as posited by Granovetter (1973) because they typically do not link to other parts of a network as weak ties do, but remain one-to-one relations.

For bigger challenges than can be handled by parties, raids are formed. A raid is a group of up to eight parties. Each party within the raid has its own chat channel and a raid channel connects the members of the entire raid. Usually at least some raid members know one another. New members may also be added. *WoW* facilitates finding other players to party or raid with through a chat channel where people advertise the quests they wish to do. As with "pick-up groups" where parties are formed in the field, the chat channel can bring together players who do not know one another.

Guilds

Guilds are long-term groups which range in size from a small handful to a couple of hundred players (Ducheneaut et al., 2006). Players can belong to only one guild. There may be no specific goal for a guild other than for players to have a group to identify with, or guilds may be highly organized and goal-driven (especially at higher levels). There is a guild chat channel and hierarchical ranks within the guild.

Middle-level ranks can invite new members. This is a trusted responsibility because allowing the wrong people into a guild can ruin its social dynamics. The highest ranks can remove members, post messages that guild members see when they log in, and promote members to higher ranks.

Guilds often organize guild-only raids and guildmates often group together. Much of the sociable non-game-related chat takes place in the guild channel. Most is informal, humorous, or downright silly although in one of the author's guilds, chat occasionally turned to more serious topics such as news reports of a player in China who had died because he did not get up from his keyboard. ("If we see anyone online that much, we'll stage an intervention," said the social worker in the guild.) Often players would report on their local weather, remark that they had a test to study for, or give other small details that revealed something of their lives. Over time, personal details about family, significant others, and so on entered the conversation. Though such messages were brief, they provided enough information so that guildmates had a sense of each others' lives. Friends engaged in similar chat. Many guilds have websites with player profiles, sometimes with photos, so guildmates have another source of information about one another.

Battlegrounds

Battlegrounds host structured PvP campaigns. Players enter a queue and then join a team to play a game such as capture the flag. PvE players can also enter battlegrounds where they will be flagged PvP for the duration of the battle. While the goal of the game is to capture the flag (or similar goals), players can kill each other during play.

Duels and Trades

Duels and trades involve one-to-one engagements. Players in the same faction challenge each other to fight but not to the death. Duels are common even on PvE servers. Duels may take place between strangers or friends.

Players trade raw materials that have been collected with the gathering professions, as well as crafted items, enchantments, and loot they may not want. Trades can be accomplished through the trade chat channel or the Auction House where players put items up for bid. Players can also trade directly with one another through a trade window. Usually trading partners do not know one another and are brought together through the trade channel or Auction House.

Random Acts of Fun

We return in this section to impromptu, less structured collaborations in *World of Warcraft* because they are interleaved with more structured collaborations, giving the game its sense of delight and unpredictability. When not engaged in battle, players come together to flirt, dance, drink, hug, joke, smile, laugh, and cheer. These actions, and many others, are supported by several dozen typed emote commands. For example, a player with a character named Annina types "/dance." The prompt says "Annina bursts into dance" and Annina begins a gender- and race-specific dance. Each race has a distinctive dance – slinky, earthy, humorous, ghoulish. Chances are Annina has joined a group of dancers carousing outside an inn or on the village green. Someone may have whispered, "Come dance with us." A group of players of different races and levels dancing together provides a welcome bit of levity after a difficult quest or narrow escape.

Players have fun in creative ways probably not envisioned by Blizzard designers. For example, we observed someone "teasing" a large dragon from the countryside into Stormwind, one of the major cities, and from there into the Auction House. Players sometimes mount up in capital cities, inciting others to join them in riding in circles, their enchanted weapons glowing and throwing off colorful sparkles. Guilds may host activities such as treasure hunts and parties. One of our guilds held a slumber party in which characters formed what they called a "conga line" using the /follow command.

These entertainments are intensified by the freer atmosphere common in online interactions (Reid, 1991) where the strictures of daily life are loosened. For example, one evening in Northshire Abbey we observed a group of characters who had discarded their clothing and were dancing in their undergarments in a fountain outside the Abbey. Such occurrences are rare offline but not in the fantasy play of *WoW*. Players may flirt or dance with same-sex players (regardless of the gender of the character). Both of us have observed such interactions in guild settings where we know the actual gender and sexual orientation of the player and we know they are known to the respective players because they have been revealed in guild chat or the players are offline friends. In such encounters gender does not matter the same way it does offline, and a less inhibited ambience prevails.

Misbehaving in WoW

Because our analysis focuses on collaboration, it may misleadingly suggest a constant friendliness. *WoW* generally maintains a congenial atmosphere, but there are a number of player actions that upset other players and are the source of player complaints. We have discussed ganking. While it is fair play according to Blizzard, ganking is annoying to players, as is "corpse camping." In PvP, a player may kill another player and "camp" the corpse, remaining by the corpse and killing the player after he resurrects and is in a weakened condition, sometimes repeating the action to the intense frustration of the defeated player. One player we talked to was paid to avenge a lower level player whose corpse had been camped by repeatedly killing and camping the corpse of the first attacker. Other causes for complaint are spamming chat channels with trade items or the use of mocking language in a general chat channel.

Offline Social Connection Through World of Warcraft

While arguments about social life on the internet suggest that it may lead to social isolation (Kraut et al., 1998; Nie & Erbring, 2002; Putnam, 2000) or, at best, weak social ties (Driskell & Lyon, 2002), it is common for *WoW* players to play with offline friends and family. Of the 26 people we interviewed, 20 currently played with offline friends and/or family and 2 others had in the past. Observations in both guilds showed this to be common among those not interviewed. Our interview sample may report a higher percentage of play with family and friends than actually exists because two informants were married to each other and two others played together in a guild.

WoW promotes offline social connection by providing a shared activity. College roommates and friends often play. Friends who live in different cities may keep their friendships going in part by playing together. One player we interviewed had a set of eight friends in different parts of the Western United States with whom he played. Another played with a friend in Germany, despite time zone differences. Nightflower, one of our guildmates who is a 53-year-old mother of seven, said in an online interview, "My oldest son just started playing last week and i am thrilled! he lives in NC and we haven't been close for a while...but now we talk a lot more ig and irl [ingame and in real life]." One player, who had two siblings and a nephew in the guild, said that they often used a voice chat program to talk while they played. It was, "like all being in the same room playing for a few hours a day." She also reported that she had a brother who played with his wife and their 9- and 14-year-old daughters on a role-playing server, recreating the family through the characters. In the other guild, a mother of two who home schooled her children used *WoW* as part of the curriculum to study typing and math. The married couple we interviewed played together and had chosen character names, "Toast" and "Jam," to identify themselves as linked. We observed this playful naming convention in other family groups as well.

Another avenue of increased social connection is that *WoW* can be a topic of offline conversation for people who play together, and even for those who play, but not together. One level 60, an officer of The Grand Threat, related that he had gotten his brother to start playing, "and as a result we have new things to talk about, like in-game stuff." Another player, introduced to the game by his brother who was several years older, said, "Now we finally have something to talk about."

This is not to say that *WoW* necessarily always provides increasing offline social connection. Players sometimes value the ability to get away from offline relationships through the game. Halbarde said, "i think [playing *WoW*] has made me less social in real life. i will quite often pass on doing things to stay home and play. however, that isn't a bad thing, as before, I was quite the opposite and was having to learn to be by myself and enjoy my own company." Nightflower saw play as a way to reconnect with her children, but she also sometimes used the game to get a break. She said that offline she only had friends that she was very close to. Her in-game friends were refreshingly casual. Even then she said, "and to be honest sometimes i don't even want to do that [be tied to people in game] so i have a couple of horde char on another server that are not guilded that i play all alone."

Social Organization in World of Warcraft

We have described the many kinds of collaboration in *World of Warcraft*, grounding the discussion in the particularities of the game. We can analyze the collaborations in three categories: (1) communities, (2) "knots," and (3) pairwise collaborations with friends. We will argue that two key game activities – having fun and learning the game – are enhanced by actions carried out in these arenas of collaboration, each with its own advantages. Having multiple arenas of collaboration, rather than just one, such as a community, provides a versatile, robust environment for play and learning.

Communities

We consider guilds to be communities. While the term "community" has been used in myriad ways (Hillery, 1955), we adopt Driskell & Lyon's formulation that a community involves "common ties" and "social interactions" (Driskell & Lyon, 2002). Common ties include a shared interest, bonds, commitment, a set of shared values, a culture, history, and shared identity.

Knots

Engeström, Engeström, & Vähäaho, (1999) defined "knots" as unique groups that form to complete a task of relatively short duration. Examples of knots are an airline crew or personnel in a courtroom. Knots may also bring together strangers who spontaneously voluntarily agree to collaborate. In knots strangers "tie a knot" to accomplish something together, as opposed to teams where members know one another and have persistent relationships. Parties in *WoW* are often knots (of the voluntary sort). So are battleground teams, trading partners, duelists, those who ask and answer questions in chat channels, and players who spontaneously cavort together.

The following chatlog shows portions of an hour's play between a priest and a hunter, both level 29, who do not know one another, but form a party. They approach a dungeon at the same time, each alone. They have a quest that requires slaying Taneel Darkwood, Uthil Mooncall, and Mavoris Cloudsbreak. (The players switch from a local area chat to party chat at about 21:38.)

> 1/8 20:59:41.690 To Delbarth: are you doing insane druids [a quest]?
> 1/8 21:02:13.481 Delbarth says: do you want to party up?
> 1/8 21:02:20.599 Delbarth has invited you to join a group.

1/8 21:02:50.556 Delbarth says: what point in the quest are you at?

1/8 21:03:02.604 Annina says: starting

1/8 21:03:12.441 Annina says: how about you?

1/8 21:03:24.256 Delbarth says: I have killed two of them—need taneel still

1/8 21:03:30.935 Annina says: ok

1/8 21:03:32.444 Delbarth says: lets give it a go :)

1/8 21:03:35.112 Annina says: k

[many monsters are slain including finally taneel]

1/8 21:38:11.186 [Party] Annina: ok got taneel!

1/8 21:38:11.809 [Party] Delbarth: oh yeah!

1/8 21:38:37.388 [Party] Delbarth: I am done with the quest, but you want to keep going?

1/8 21:38:44.612 [Party] Annina: yes!

[several monsters later]

1/8 21:41:41.345 [Party] Delbarth: you ok with mana?

1/8 21:41:46.243 [Party] Annina: yes

1/8 21:43:53.959 [Party] Delbarth: DING

1/8 21:44:00.636 [Party] Delbarth: 30th—wooh!

1/8 21:44:05.665 [Party] Annina: hurray!

[yet more monsters]

1/8 21:54:00.856 [Party] Delbarth: shall we keep going?

1/8 21:54:06.858 [Party] Annina: yes

[Annina gets one more of the monsters she needs]

1/8 21:55:32.578 [Party] Delbarth: thanks for the healing :)

1/8 21:56:46.311 [Party] Delbarth: I need to stop for the night—my wife is getting ancy :)

1/8 21:57:03.302 [Party] Annina: ok. thanks a lot for helping. and congrats on 30

1/8 21:57:20.881 [Party] Delbarth: thanks for the help, as well—can't do that dungeon solo, for sure!

By forming a knot, they collaborated to accomplish their goals and enjoyed a typical *WoW* experience. *WoW* makes such collaborations easy and the spirit of adventure and mutual aid created by players makes them fun.

Pairwise Collaborations with Friends

The friends list enables players to keep in touch with friends by being notified when they come online and go offline. Players chat with friends, they seek and give advice, and may group with them. Friends occasionally arrange a meeting if they have not seen each other's characters for awhile to check out new gear or to give each other gifts using the trade window. Gifts may also be sent through the mailbox system which only allows one-to-one mailings.

Discussion

A Multiplicity of Interleaved Collaborations

Participation in a guild, collaboration in knots, and pairwise collaborations with friends lend the game variety, novelty, and surprise. These interleaved collaborations create a richly textured space in which play flows between community-based and lighter weight collaborations. One player with several characters said, "I like that you kind of feel a part of this bigger world. You have to go and explore and find out things and meet people." Another player said, "I have a lot of favorite things, especially selling enchantments. I like negotiating with other people and trying to make the most profit."

Community-based relations in guilds are desirable and sought in the game. But the closer relationships can lead to what is often referred to as "drama." For example, a player may get upset if one of his friends is not invited into his guild, even though the guild cannot accommodate a player of his class. Or a player may be disruptive, running at a monster in what should be a carefully orchestrated attack, ruining play for everyone else.[1] The Legion of Darkness experienced a wrenching change of leadership as the founding leader left to start a new guild, taking several good players with him. One day he simply disappeared, upsetting remaining players.

Such dislocations are part of guild life as we discovered in our own guilds and heard from informants in interviews. Driskell and Lyon (2002) observed that it seems we never cease to pine for the tightknit communities putatively found in the small villages of Europe in the nineteenth century. Such villages were the inspiration for Tönnies's concept of *Gemeinschaft* – the intimate, close relations of a group of people who know one another well and share history and tradition (Tönnies, 1957). But MMOGs provide an occasion to reflect on whether such communities should be the gold standard (Driskell & Lyon, 2002). While *Gemeinschaft*-style social groups provide deep bonds, such bonds can be constraining as well as fulfilling. People may feel constrained to certain relationships and specific roles that may not actually suit them (Bargh, McKenna, & Fitzsimons, 2002). In *WoW*, the guild community is important for many, but not the only choice for collaboration. Many players value their friends list which represents an ego-centered personal social network in which a player's friends may know one another but usually do not. One player who was not in a guild said, "[I like] meeting good people online and being able to put them on my friends list." None of the players on his list knew one another. A player active in her guild said she still made other friends: "I have around fifteen on the list, three of whom are very good friends by now who I regularly talk to in-game."

As suggested by the Legion of Darkness's troubles, guild communities are often fragile. Driskell and Lyon noted that online communities are less robust than offline communities. Many in our study reported that they had been in several guilds,

---

[1]This particular disruption was made famous in *WoW* lore in a humorous video called Leeroy Jenkins, available online at www.leeroyjenkins.net.

which, for one reason or another, did not work out. The normalcy of collaborating with strangers means that finding others to collaborate with is not as difficult as it may be in more *Gemeinschaft*-like environments.

WoW's interleaved collaborations advance the object of playing a game to have fun. That *WoW* is fun is expressed in players' wry use of the word "addicting" to describe the game, a word we heard repeatedly in interviews and one used so often on game forums that it is a cliché. As one of our guildmates said, "If only real life was this addicting."

While players like many things about *WoW* such as leveling, virtually all of our informants mentioned the social aspects of *WoW* as crucial to their enjoyment. One player said, "[*WoW*] is fun on many levels, and it's like a real world because you know you are playing with other real human beings rather than AI. . ... It's addicting." Another said, "I like the social aspects of *WoW* and playing with other people gives it an added unpredictability." In the following interview segment, Dreadlock, a young male player, connected the fun of *WoW* to opportunities for meeting people. (The :D icon means "grin." Instances are quests in "private" dungeons where only the party or raid members are present.)

> To Dreadlock: what do you like about the game?
> Dreadlock whispers: its fun :D
> To Dreadlock: right! but why?
> Dreadlock whispers: cant feal lonly while playing it!
> Dreadlock whispers: to meet people, etcw
> Dreadlock whispers: i love instances
> To Dreadlock: why do you love them?
> Dreadlock whispers: because they make it so you MUST group
> Dreadlock whispers: its not an option
> To Dreadlock: how do you find people to group with?
> Dreadlock whispers: advertising in the chat channels, guild and asking my friends
> Dreadlock whispers: also instances are an oppertuniy to meet people

Ducheneaut et al. (2006) described *World of Warcraft* as a game in which people spend significant amounts of time alone, in the presence of others, but not interacting with them. Using logging software, they measured sociability as time spent grouping in parties, raids, and battlegrounds. Because these are only a portion of many social activities in *WoW*, it appeared that players were "alone" much of the time since grouping accounted for 30–40% of play.

However, the totality of collaborative play should be analyzed. Our analysis enumerated the many different kinds of collaborative play in *WoW* including parties, raids, friends, guilds, duels, battlegrounds, trades, as well as informal collaborations such as kill assists, answering questions, impromptu dancing and flirting, chatting, and PvP play. Taken together, these activities comprise a sociable experience, as our informants reported and we observed in-game. Raw time is a problematic metric for capturing sociability. Duels, for example, take only a short time but offer an enjoyable challenge and one that provides the stuff of stories players tell each other. Players may spend only a few minutes dancing on the village green, but those few vivid minutes are the difference between a single-player game and a multiplayer game such as *World of Warcraft*.

Perhaps most important, chatting is a key aspect of socializing in *WoW* that is not captured in the metrics that measure time in formal groups. Chatting takes place when grouping, but also while people are soloing, crafting, spending time in cities, or traveling. For example, traveling is time consuming, but many put their character on "auto-run" and chat while moving on foot around Azeroth, or while traveling on the slow transportation network. In fact, much sociable chat takes place during exactly such times when people are not in battle. Ducheneaut et al. argued that grouping was an obvious metric for sociability in *World of Warcraft*, but chatting and the multiplicity of collaborations we reported are central to game experience. Such metrics cannot capture the sociability of play between family members and offline friends. The authors suggested that offline friends who play together may get "separated" as they level at different rates, but it is common to have alts which the logging cannot account for. Because of alts, offline friends may still play together, providing a highly social experience. We had several such cases among our informants. If offline friends and family spend 30–40% of game time grouping together, we might interpret this metric to suggest that such time together is considerable, intensifying already close social relationships.

We emphasize that much socializing in *WoW* is brief, lightweight, informal fun. At the same time, as play progresses, many players spend more and more time in dungeons which require groups. Our informants mentioned the satisfaction of "teamwork" in these groups. Ducheneaut et al. found that grouping increased as players progressed through the levels. Players who do not enjoy socializing have many other games from which to choose.

Learning

We have discussed the many ways *WoW* players collaborate to have fun. The interleaved collaborations also have important implications for learning. As with most MMOGs, there is a lot to learn. For example, players must understand different spells and when to use them; have some comprehension of the different classes so that when playing with others the character is positioned correctly and acts in a way that complements others' abilities; be able to predict how monsters will react; and know which equipment is best for the specific way the character has been created and for different contexts of battle (to mention only a few aspects of the game).

Guildmates are an important resource for learning. But many players also ask strangers for help in chat channels or if a player is standing nearby. They may ask players on the friends' list, using their personal social networks. One player said, "I was trying to find my way into the Badlands and couldn't so I asked one of my friends and she explained how to. I don't know how long it would have taken me to find it on my own."

Gamers' use of learning resources such as websites and forums has been well documented (Gee, 2003; Steinkuehler, 2005). The players in our study consulted sites such as Thottbot, Allakhazam, the Blizzard website and forums, online guides to playing a particular class, and various FAQs. A player can find finely detailed descriptions of game minutiae such as how to use a fishing pole or the way lower level players can make their way to the large cities when traveling through dangerous territory. Several sites provide useful user interface modifications or "mods" (e.g., CTMod) that many in our study took advantage of. Based on their own experiences, players write guides, FAQs, and mods well-matched to players' needs.

In *WoW*, the individual learner coordinates the diverse resources in the collaboration space. The learner has agency in choosing and deploying learning resources—learning is not controlled by an organization, peer, teacher, curriculum, or community. Learning occurs when the learner needs and wants it, in the context of solving a problem the learner genuinely wishes to solve (see Dewey, 1938). A multiplicity of collaboration types offers redundant sites of learning. The opportunity to receive an answer to a question or obtain advice quickly and in context does not depend on the requirement that a player draw on *Gemeinschaft* relations as in, for example, apprenticeship learning (see Lave & Wenger, 1991). Resources are distributed and easily accessed by the learner who can seek advice and information from in-game friends and strangers, online sources, guildmates, and often offline friends and family. The atmosphere of mutual benefit that begins with the player's first buff provides an environment in which players have established an ethos of helping and asking for help. Players who write guides and contribute to forums found on the internet extend this ethos outside the game, to online venues that are valued by players.

Vygotsky spoke of the "zone of proximal development" in which a learner advances by being offered a challenge and the appropriate resources to meet the challenge. The resources are supplied by a teacher or more experienced peers (Vygotsky, 1938). The zone is the difference between what the learner can do with and without the aid of the teacher or more experienced peers. In *WoW*, the zone of proximal development is unusually flexible because aid from more experienced peers is available from so many sources. While it is not possible here to undertake a detailed comparison to other learning environments such as traditional classrooms, apprenticeships, or online tutorials, we cannot think of another context of learning with the access and flexibility we observed within *World of Warcraft* and its associated online resources.

Conclusion

Social activity in *World of Warcraft* challenges discourse that asserts that the internet leads to isolation or is simply community moved online (see Nardi, 2010). A space of mixed collaborations provides variety in play experience and flexibility in learning. Our findings suggest that lightweight collaborations can be enjoyable and enlightening and need not be negatively valued. The design of *World of Warcraft* and the player culture that have developed within the game provide an innovative space in which strangers collaborate and can become friends. At the same time, *WoW* joins a long tradition of card and board games in which family and friends of different ages and genders may play together.

References

Bainbridge, W. (2007). The scientific research potential of virtual worlds. *Science, 317*, 472–476.

Bargh, J., McKenna, K., & Fitzsimons, G. (2002). Can you see the real me? Activation and expression of the "true self" on the internet. *Journal of Social Issues, 58*, 33–48.

Brown, B., & Bell, M. (2004). CSCW at play: 'there' as a collaborative virtual environment. *Proceedings CSCW 2004* (pp. 350–359). New York: ACM Press.

Dewey, J. (1938). *Experience and education.* New York: Macmillan.

Driskell, R., & Lyon, L. (2002). Are virtual communities true communities? Examining the environments and elements of community. *City and Community, 1*, 373–390.

Ducheneaut, N., & Moore, R. (2004). The social side of gaming: A study of interaction patterns in a massively multiplayer online game. *Proceedings CSCW 2004* (pp. 360–369). New York: ACM Press.

Ducheneaut, N., Yee, N., Nickell, E., & Moore, R. (2006). "Alone together?" Exploring the social dynamics of massively multiplayer online games. *Proceedings CHI06* (pp. 407–416). New York: ACM Press.

Engeström, Y., Engeström, R., & Vähäaho, T. (1999). When the center doesn't hold: The importance of knotworking. In S. Chaiklin, M. Hedegaard, & U. Jensen (Eds.), *Activity theory and social practice.* Aarhus: Aarhus Press.

Gee, J. (2003). *What video games have to teach us about learning and literacy.* New York: Palgrave Macmillan.

Granovetter, M. (1973). The strength of weak ties. *American Journal of Sociology, 78*, 1360–1380.

Hillery, G. (1955). Definitions of community. *Rural Sociology, 20*, 779–791.

Kraut, R., Patterson, M., Lundmark, V., Kiesler, S., Mukhopadhyay, T., & Scherlis, W. (1998). Internet paradox: A social technology that reduces social involvement and psychological wellbeing? *American Psychologist, 53*, 1001–1031.

Kushner, D. (2005). Engineering everquest. *IEEE Spectrum Online.* Retrieved July, 2005, from http://www.spectrum.ieee.org/jul05/1561

Lave, J., & Wenger, E. (1991). Situated learning: Legitimate peripheral participation. Cambridge: Cambridge University Press.

Leontiev, A. (1974). The problem of activity in psychology. *Soviet Psychology, 13*, 4–33.

Nardi, B. (2010). My life as a night elf priest: An anthropological account of world of warcraft. Ann Arbor, MI: University of Michigan Press.

Nie, N. H., & Erbring, L. (2002). Internet and society: A preliminary report. *IT & Society, 1*, 275–283.

Prince, M., Harwood, R., Blizard, R., Thomas, A., & Mann, A. (1997). Social support deficits, loneliness and life events as risk factors for depression in old age. *Psychological Medicine, 27*, 323–332.

Putnam, R. (2000). Bowling alone: The collapse and revival of American Community. New York: Simon and Schuster.

Reid, E. (1991). *Electropolis: Communication and community on internet relay chat.* Honours Dissertation, University of Melbourne.

Squire, K. (2005, August/September). Changing the game: What happens when video games enter the classroom? *Innovate: Journal of Online Education, 1*(6).

Steinkuehler, C. (2005). *Cognition and learning in massively multiplayer online games: A critical approach.* Ph.D. Thesis, University of Wisconsin, Madison.

Steinkuehler, C., & Williams, D. (2006). Where everybody knows your (screen) name: Online games as "third places." *Journal of Computer-Mediated Communication, 11*(4), 885–909.

Tönnies, F. (1957). Community and society: Gemeinschaft and Gesellschaft. East Lansing, MI: Michigan State University Press, 1887/1957.

Twidale, M., Wang, X., & Hinn, D. (2005). CSC: Computer supported collaborative work, learning, and play. In T. Koschmann, D. Suthers, & T. Chan (Eds.), *Proceedings, computer supported collaborative learning 2005*. Hillsdale, NJ: Lawrence Erlbaum.

Vygotsky, L. (1978). Mind and society: The development of higher mental processes. Harvard University Press, Harvard.

Vygotsky, L. (1986). Thought and language. Cambridge: MIT Press. Retrieved from http://www.warcraftrealms.com/census.php

Trouble with the Commercial: Internets Theorized and Used

Susanna Paasonen

The introduction of the graphic web browser Mosaic in 1993 brought forth drastic transformations in media economy, forms of possible and available content, user demographics, as well as the general visibility and the cultural role of the internet as a medium with a global reach. Nevertheless, the web remained under-represented in scholarly investigations throughout the 1990s: scholars simply found the web less interesting than Usenet or e-mail (Jones, 2000, p. 171). While this situation has changed with the more recent scholarly attention toward online fandom, blogging, and other forms of social media discussed under the umbrella term Web 2.0, a certain disequilibrium is still present in the existing body of internet research – especially in terms of those practices and phenomena that have been relabeled as "Web 1.0."

Browsing through readers, anthologies, and textbooks on internet research published in the 1990s makes evident the endurance of intellectual engagements with practices of community building and reworking of identity in online spaces (e.g., Bell, 2001; Jones, 1994, 1998; Smith, 1999). Given the variety of available applications, practices of production and usage involved with the internet, it is fair to state that MUDs and MOOs, for example, remain somewhat over-represented in research literature in respect to the volume of their active usage. If a future archeologist were to reconstruct internet cultures of the 1990s on the basis of available research literature written during the decade in question, what shape would the resulting "internet" take? How would it correspond to the widely used internet applications, popular discourses, or everyday experiences of usage? Taking these hypothetical questions as starting point, this article investigates Internets presumed and produced in scholarly investigations and their relationship to the ever-transforming research object of the internet. I argue that more or less pronounced premises concerning the internet as a communication medium and publishing forum can be deciphered from existing research literature and that these premises bring rise to ideals and norms that have a continuing legacy for internet research. More specifically, my interests lie in how the

S. Paasonen (✉)
Helsinki Collegium for Advances Studies, University of Helsinki, Helsinki, Finland
e-mail: susanna.paasonen@helsinki.fi

J. Hunsinger et al. (eds.), *International Handbook of Internet Research*,
DOI 10.1007/978-1-4020-9789-8_25, © Springer Science+Business Media B.V. 2010

internet became conceptualized as a medium in the 1990s and the kind of influence that these conceptualizations have in the present.

A Tale of Two Paradigms

At the general discussion following a keynote presentation at the second annual Association of internet Researchers conference in Minneapolis in 2001, a dividing line was drawn between the "first" and "second" generation of internet researchers. The introduction of the web was posed as the borderline marking the two generations – or paradigms – apart. The debate identified the first generation active since the 1980s as engaged with text-based networked communications, community formation, and exchange of information. These studies focused on the novel communication forms brought forth by information networks, their differences to more traditional media, as well as their possibilities in creating alternative information economies. Newsgroups and bulletin board systems, characterized by the open free exchange and accessibility of information in networks void of centers or hierarchies of the kind that structure print media or broadcasting, came to stand for a potential counter-medium. These text-based solutions then came to stand for a kind of original or true form of the internet in respect to which the web symbolized an ultimate watering-down of the ideal open and democratic network operating outside the media industry. Due to this, studies of the web (representative of the second paradigm), decidedly more multi-medial in nature and involving analyses of graphic interfaces, intermedial connections, commercial service providers, advertisers, and media corporations, were categorized as ones of secondary importance to the degree of being frivolous. What I found disturbing in this model of two generations was not so much the strictness of the divide as the ideological underpinnings implied in it.[1]

The discussion sensitized me to the ways in which understandings of the internet as a medium, as articulated by researchers, involve more or less pronounced ideals that effect ways of conceptualizing the medium studied: through them, the internet is performed into being as certain kind and studied in certain ways. Taking one historical moment in the development of the internet as an ideal against which later developments can be measured is not merely a means of making visible

---

[1] David Silver's (2000) well-known model of three internet research generations operates with a different understanding of the field. Silver's three generations – ranging from journalistic enthusiasm of the early 1990s to studies of virtual communities in the mid-1990s and "critical cyberculture studies" of the new millennium encompassing more multimedial and interdisciplinary investigations – all fit in a decade and describe a field evolving toward increased complexity. Research generations were also the theme of the annual Association of internet Researchers conference in 2005. As I have argued elsewhere (Paasonen, 2005b, 2007), the widely used and pedagogically appealing model of research generations is both specific to developments in the Anglophone academia and not the best of models for describing continuities within the field. It also risks locking individual scholars into figures of a certain historical moment or generation, independent of their later intellectual trajectories.

alternative possibilities and promises that may have been overshadowed by more recent developments but also a means of dismissing studies of these developments, and hence the contemporary medium, as ones of less weight or significance. The question of commercialization, along with the web, then becomes associated with homogenization and predictability in ways that do not aim to capture the complexity of the medium or the diversity of its user cultures.

A certain paradox seems to lie at the heart of the tale of two paradigms. Since the 1980s, hacker cultures have emphasized the accessibility of information, the general right of accessing it, and the importance of making the medium accessible to "the people" (meaning the general population). Questions concerning access to information and possibilities of freely distributing it were central in early studies of online communications and in articulations of the internet as a new medium. Such democratic possibilities, as well as novel forms of communication and community building, were primarily associated with text-based interfaces since the early studies of bulletin boards and electronic conferencing systems (cf. Rheingold, 1991/1995). In the 1980s, mainly people working in research institutions – scientists, scholars, programmers, and other experts residing in the United States – were using information networks. International connections were drawn to universities within the NATO countries, which made the demographics of internet users highly selective (or structurally biased in terms of the general international population). The deregulation of the internet in the early 1990s coincided with the introduction of the Web and together these developments meant the creation of a more visual and decidedly more commercial medium with a manifested presence of not just public institutions but also telecoms, advertisers, and media conglomerates. The web became the interface – a kind of colorful shop window – through which new users were introduced to the internet. However, as "the people" started increasingly using the internet, their preferred uses were not exactly identical to those envisioned in discourses of e-democracy or alternative information spheres.

Pornography has been identified as the first commercially profitable area of online content production. Other forms of online business began to establish a customer base while users started tinkering with personal home pages, online diaries, and fan pages. In other words, "the people" were interested in different kinds of content than assumed by or at least presented in hacker discourses or cyberspace formulations. Popular culture, commerce, casual and leisurely uses proved far more appealing to most than political organization or countermedia activism (which, of course, is not to say that these practices would not have taken fire as such). Hypertext fictions rendering readers into active coauthors or various online role-playing communities enabling experimentations with different characters and interaction styles were popular topics of research through the 1990s, even if their uses remained somewhat marginal in terms of networked communications in general. This makes evident a paradoxical gap between Internets *theorized* and Internets *used*: it appears that studies of the internet have been influenced by certain ideal figures of the medium and that have not been easy to balance with the ways in which the medium has been developed and used. Some uses (like MUDs) have been studied in great detail whereas others (like commercial online pornography) have been left with considerably little attention. Furthermore, online phenomena have been largely studied from the perspective of sociology and psychology whereas other disciplinary traditions have had less of a footing in defining the field, its methodology or ethics (Sterne, 2005; White, 2002). In some parts of the world, like the Nordic countries, the discourse of the information society and the public sphere has, in a different yet parallel way, worked to efface leisurely, "useless" uses from view while emphasizing assumedly more rationally motivated online practices, such as civic participation.

The situation is familiar from histories of other media technologies. According to media archeologist Erkki Huhtamo (1995, p. 68), critics of commercial media technology have framed media users as puppets controlled by corporate interests without any possibility to influence the operating principles of the technologies they are using. This history of juxtaposing media production and consumption makes it perhaps easier to understand the skepticism that accompanied web-based solutions and services in comparison to the more DIY-style networks of the 1980s. Programming and coding have become increasingly complex and they are no longer part and parcel of regular computer hobbyism. In comparison to mid- or even late 1990s, web design has developed into a field of specialized skills that is accessible to the majority of users through ready-made, albeit customizable templates. Information and communication technologies have grown increasingly "user friendly," and various platforms and applications for user-generated content are mushrooming with Web 2.0. However, at the same moment when the threshold of online publishing, participation, and customization is lower than perhaps ever before, users have less access to the technical basis of the medium.

Like video, an earlier media technology with military origins that became appropriated as a tool for social activism and the construction of alternative media culture, the internet has become a globally used mass medium through a process of privatization, commercialization, and popularization. This development has relied on the dismantling of US government control and the rise of commercial service providers, as well as the increasing accessibility of media technology. Both affordable personal computers and internet connections outside of public institutions enabled the de-centralized use and content production of "new media." To make a historical parallel, the launch of Sony's open-reel video camera Portapak in 1967–1968 made video technology relatively affordable for groups and individuals and spurred media activism aiming at the creation of an alternative information sphere that would challenge the hegemony of network television in the United States (Boyle, 1997, p. 4; Hill, 1996, p. 5). In spite of the strong anti-commercial tone of the video movement, its working practices owed much to the commercialization of media as affordable and relatively easy to use. The situation is similar with internet technology, user friendly applications, interfaces, and affordable prices. Media access means participation in media economy. There are no easy outsides or unambiguously non-commercial positions available: as internet users, we are all implicated in the hardware manufacture, software development, and network structure. As Brian Winston, addressing the military connections and corporate underpinnings of the internet hype of the early 1990s, dryly notes, "[t]hose who seriously believed they were in a brave new world of free and democratic communications were simply ignoring the reality of their situation" (Winston, 1998, p. 333).

Online vs. Offline

Studies of the internet were, through the 1990s, more focused on mapping the novelty of the internet than considering its ties to other fields of media culture. The internet was broadly theorized as a cyberspace of alternative fluid identities and novel interaction forms (Benedikt, 1991). The independence of the internet from physical locations, embodiments, or acts of regulation, as suggested by internet enthusiast and free speech lobbyist John Perry Barlow, has both helped to mark the internet apart from other media and to separate the online from the offline: "We are creating a world that all may enter without privilege or prejudice accorded by race, economic power, military force, or station of birth. We are creating a world where anyone, anywhere may express his or her beliefs, no matter how singular, without fear of being coerced into silence or conformity" (Barlow, 1996). This formulation envisions the internet as more than a medium – an alternative world titled cyberspace. The term is famously derived from William Gibson's cyberpunk fictions (particularly the 1982 short story "Burning Chrome" and the 1984 novel *Neuromancer*), where cyberspace describes the computer user's hallucinatory immersion in graphic 3D environments. Barlow claims having been the first one to apply it to the internet (Paasonen, 2005a, p. 2). Dreams of entering "the realm of pure intellect in cyberspace" (Adam, 1998, p. 169) and abandoning the sphere known as physical reality have been widely reiterated as descriptions of internet usage, rooting a mind–body split into studies of the medium. The term cyberspace was coined before the invention of hypertext, the WWW, or the popularization of the internet. In this sense, Gibson's fictions did not so much depict an existing medium as produce a framework through which the internet and its possible future forms have since been conceptualized.[2] Rob Shields (2000, p. 67), for example, describes cyberspace as a "self-fulfilling prophesy, slowly coming into existence as more and more computers are 'wired' to the Internet." Research, development, and theorization of the internet have drawn from fictitious and speculative descriptions of information networks as new disembodied spatial and mental dimensions. Gibson's fictions of the 1980s have been given the power to foretell future developments, which are then posed as unavoidable.

At the core of the articulations of internet as cyberspace lies the notion of freedom – freedom from the everyday, embodiment and identity alike. Online, people are said to "express multiple and often unexplored aspects of the self," to "play with their identity and try out new ones" (Turkle, 1995/1997, p. 12). Freedom

---

[2]It should be noted that cyberspace discourse has not had universal appeal but remains largely specific to the Anglophone academe (discussed in Paasonen, 2009).

and play, which have "preoccupied the more high-profile literature, as well as much public discussion and common sense about the net" (Miller & Slater, 2000, p. 4), have been influential in articulations of the assumedly revolutionary potential and attraction of the internet (discussed as cyberspace). Figuring the internet as an alternative spatiality unlimited by geography has facilitated an analytical division of online phenomena from offline ones. Consequently, internet users are considered to be "either online or offline, but rarely both" (McGerty, 2000, pp. 896–897). This notably artificial division has diverted attention from the physical contexts and locations of internet use—from the ways in which access, usage, and content production are conditioned by the kind of access that one has and the kinds of spaces in which these uses are situated. Furthermore, the discourse of cyberspace has worked to efface the role and meaning of physical bodies. Although bodies cannot be seen in many forms of online communication, this does not mean that bodies would have somehow disappeared. The legacy of the rhetoric of cyberspace disembodiment is evident in the long-standing discussions of whether identity categories such as gender, "race," or class matter online. The answer to such a categorical question may seem obviously affirmative. However, the 1990s research on identity play suggesting that identity categories have become radically redefined online, and that users are freed from their bodies and able to take up any persona they desire, continues to have a considerable legacy.

Studies in the 1990s on gender bending and identity play in online communities formed an intellectual center for theorizations of the medium (Kolko, Nakamura, & Rodman, 2000, p. 5). The figure of an internet user crafting various "virtual selves" and blurring the categories of identity, as introduced in the studies of Sherry Turkle or Allucquére Rosanne Stone, have been central starting points for studying identity and social relations on the internet (cf. Bolter, 2000, pp. 24–25; Danet, 1998; Dietrich, 2000; Hayles, 1999, pp. 27–28). The specificity of the case studies and research material on which these theorizations were based is perhaps less often remembered. Sherry Turkle's research, for example, drew heavily from conversations with MUDders. Although she also investigated IRC, newsgroups, bulletin boards, and online services (Turkle, 1997, p. 323), her focus was on the heavy MUD users in the Boston area in the early 1990s. During this pre-web period, around 10% of Americans used the internet whereas the people Turkle interviewed spent considerable amounts of time online on a daily basis. This highly specific demographic can hardly be considered representative of internet use experiences at the time. The study has since been established as classic and a central point of reference for studies of identity online – or even emblematic of the experiences and implications of internet use in general – without necessarily dwelling on its partiality.

The widely read and referenced studies of virtual communities involve a somewhat limited selection of online interaction and self-performance that have nevertheless been taken as descriptive of internet usage as a whole. Eleanor Wynn and James E. Katz (1997, p. 300) have pointed to this, arguing that the data used in Turkle or Stone's work, "come[s] from within the target community of computer users that most exemplify the extremes of behavior upheld as social trends. Without social theory and more grounded methods, the internet is plausibly portrayed as fantastic and unreal rather than practical." Some issues also lie in the uses of interview material, personal experiences, and individual examples as a basis for generalization and theoretical speculation concerning identity and the internet. Authors like Turkle, Stone, or Howard Rheingold drew extensively from their own experiences and the kinds of online practices they were interested in. As Daniel Miller and Don Slater have pointed out, in this paradigm the internet becomes articulated as "a kind of social laboratory in which the performative character of all social realities and identities can be brought to light, deconstructed and transcended." Such theorizations may have more to do with the needs of intellectual projects in question than they do with the medium studied, its forms, or uses (Miller & Slater, 2000, p. 5).

From Media Specificity to Intermedia

Discussing internet use, or experiences thereof, on a general level is destined to fail. The diversity of user practices guarantees that ways of understanding the medium, its forms and possibilities, and meanings are equally contingent. To a degree, researchers necessarily operate on the basis of their own experience and understanding of the medium, its meanings, and significance. Consequently, the situational and situated nature of internet usage has important implications for scholarly practice. Scholars understand and conceptualize the internet through different disciplinary, personal, ideological, and geographical frameworks. Doing this, they encourage some histories of the internet – and internet research – while possibly preventing others (White, 2002, p. 250). Jonathan Sterne (1999, p. 278) even argues that "internet scholars have a tendency to universalize their own subjective impressions and dispositions, thereby grossly overestimating the impact, magnitude, accessibility, and universality of their object of study." It certainly seems that researchers have downplayed online phenomena that they have not considered interesting or progressive, as is evident in the shortage of studies of mainstream web interfaces or popular practices throughout the 1990s.

Online pornography is perhaps the most striking singular example of such scholarly aversion. It is widely acknowledged that pornography was the first, and for some years even the only economically profitable, form of online content production. While pornography (both amateur and commercial) was abundantly available already in Usenet, the web enabled the distribution of images, texts, and videos to a far wider audience. The needs of the porn industry have shaped the technical development of the WWW and the range of currently available solutions and business practices from web hosting services to credit card processing, banner advertisement, web promotion, and streaming video technology (Bennett, 2001, p. 381; Filippo, 2000, p. 125; O'Toole,1998, p. 285; Perdue, 2002). Although the relative proportion of porn sites has decreased during the past decade due to the drastic increase of new domains, porn remains perpetually popular while the range of available niches seems to be forever expanding. This popularity is rendered invisible in the published listings of top search terms and sites that systematically efface porn. Pornography is seldom mentioned in studies of e-commerce, information society, online communications, or internet history as other than anomaly or a social problem of some sort. This silence supports the general status of pornography as a kind of public secret that is addressed mainly from the perspectives of child protection and the necessity of controlling access to so-called adult content.

The aversion toward pornography also involves a more general emphasis on rational uses (and assumedly rational users) in public discussions concerning the internet. As Blaise Cronin and Elisabeth Davenport (2001, p. 34) argue, "entertainment, sport, games and play (specifically play that involves the body) have been expunged from 'official' narratives of the information society." While this goes for information society discourses, the exclusion of play or embodiment has not really been the case in internet research – for, as suggested above, these have been central concerns since the early 1990s. The relative invisibility of commercial pornography in the field has more to do with cultural hierarchies and questions of taste: as a popular genre, pornography has considerably low cultural status as that which, according to various US court decisions, lacks in social, cultural, or artistic value. Furthermore, the relatively sparse attention to porn is telling of an attachment to representations and exchanges considered novel over more familiar and predictable ones, and independent over commercial ones, in studies of new media more generally. Hence various forms of cybersex, cyborgasms, and e-rotics have been objects of study, and porn less so. In addition to child protection, freedom of speech, and search practices (Jansen & Spink, 2006, pp. 258–259; Spink, Partridge, & Jansen, 2006), internet porn has been addressed in the perspective of business and technology development (Lane, 2001; Perdue, 2002), the redefinition of the gendered codes of erotica and porn (Kibby, 2001; Kibby & Costello, 2001; Villarejo, 2004; Patterson, 2004), and the meanings of alternative pornographies (Attwood, 2007; Jacobs, Janssen, & Pasquinelli, 2007; Magnet, 2007; Waskul, 2004). Analysis of commercial porn has been a less popular preoccupation. This may also have to do with the highly polarized and politicized nature of porn debates in the United States, which have divided lines of debate as either for or against, for freedom of speech or censorship. The recent US "war on porn" has added yet another twist to these battle lines while making the need for analytical investigations on an international scale ever more pertinent.

Alternative, artistic, amateur, and independent pornographies are perhaps obviously more attractive case studies than mainstream commercial porn in terms of their aesthetics, economies, and departures from the established conventions and norms of the genre. Nevertheless, the tendency to overlook commercial porn and its role in the development of the internet risks leading to voluntary blindness toward online economies and popular uses alike. Pornographic representation online tends to follow generic models developed in other media, and business ventures remain highly irreverent to media specificity. Print magazine brands such as Playboy and Hustler have made their presence known in a range of media, the internet included, whereas online ventures have launched DVD production and their contents have been published in print. Taking such intermedial connections seriously, analyses of online pornography make evident the analytical shortcomings of binary divisions (old and new, analogue and digital, offline and online) prevalent in studies of so-called new media. In other words, investigations of commercial porn and its ties to the porn industry and other distribution formats necessitate breaking away from the divisions of "online" and "offline" or "new" and "old" media as analytical frameworks.

Open Windows

All this is not to say that popular uses or contents need automatically become objects of study. After all, it can hardly be argued that television studies need to simply mirror the top ratings within current broadcasting. But neither can research simply turn a blind eye toward contents and practices of central cultural, social, economic, and political influence is it to have either explanatory power concerning the medium discussed, or broader cultural significance (Nakamura, 2006, p. 33). Public discussions concerning the internet tend to be polarized (beyond the discussion on pornography) and it is repeatedly depicted as a two-faced beast or a Janus-faced entity that is either "good" or "bad" (Paasonen, 2005a, pp. 259–260). The internet has been hyped up as the agent of societal revolution but equally labeled as a realm of addiction, pedophilia, and anti-social networks. In my view, internet researchers studying the medium can and should add complexity to the simplified debate, rather than replicate its dynamics. Such public intellectualism necessitates analysis of commercial, mainstream, and in some ways predictable forms of content, services, and uses without being reductive in interpretations concerning their social or cultural meaning.

The current interest toward the virtual world *Second Life* among internet researchers marks a continuing interest in role-playing communities and the crafting of alternative personalities in virtual spaces. *Second Life* may not be the most popular or densely populated of social networked spaces, yet it is one that seems to speak to particular intellectual concerns. Scholarly gravitation toward *Second Life* is telling of a continuum from studies of MUDs and MOOs to those of exchanges taking place in increasingly graphic environments, even if these continuities are not necessarily always made explicit. Possibilities of role and identity play, character construction, and the crafting of alternative virtual worlds remain topics of notable interest among internet researchers. Blogs, a research topic of equal appeal, can be connected to the tradition of online diaries and journals, handcrafted with HTML, and later developed with the aid of templates. Their appeal may also have to do with the possibilities of open exchange of information outside the nodes of mainstream media, as expressed in the context of Usenet in the 1980s (seen by some as characteristic of the "first generation" of internet research). Considered more broadly, however, the recent scholarly embrace of Web 2.0 also points to a possible reconfiguration of intellectual agendas. As an industry-generated term, Web 2.0 describes the role of user-generated content in and for online business. The discourse of Web 2.0 postulates a rather unhistorical separation from "Web 1.0," expressed through the logic of upgrades. This unfortunate terminology aside, considerations of social media open up a different space from which to study the development of the medium – one that acknowledges users as engaged participants and producers (rather than puppets manipulated by the industry) since the launch of the WWW (as well as before). Extending this logic to "Web 1.0," its personal home pages, online journals, gaming, and fan communities help in mapping out continuities and transformations in acts and social environments of self-representation, interaction, and play, as they have occurred since the early 1990s till today. Such a revisionary move brings forth more complex interrelations between users and producers, technology and economy, user experience and content production that make the binary division of the commercial and non-commercial untenable. Media economy, commercial content production, internet service provision, or the business of hardware and software are not external to internet cultures but frame, condition, facilitate, and enable them in certain ways, while being inevitably influenced and shaped by these cultures in return.

To conclude, researchers take active part in giving shape to the internet as a medium, outlining its current trends and possible futures on the basis of their own understanding of how the internet will evolve. Doing this, scholars are shaping popular opinion as well as participating in the writing of internet history (Costighan, 1999, p. xx). Doing internet research means participation in historiography as well as the definition and negotiation of the meanings of the medium studied. All this makes accountability for the kind of research one produces a crucial issue. What we, as internet researchers, remember and what we forget of the internet, its histories, uses, and conceptual frameworks influence the shape we give to the medium, as well as the kinds of histories and futures we render visible. The practice of *critical revisiting*, analyzing the premises of earlier research, and considering its productivity in terms of contemporary questions is crucial for understanding the field of research that one is situated in. Such critical dialogue concerns self-reflexivity in both an individual and disciplinary level. It is a means of situating oneself in disciplinary histories and figuring out the historical construction – and hence the contingency – of research terminology and premises. Contemporary studies require analysis of the legacy of the existing body of internet research, its focus, research material and methodology, as well as the kinds of understandings concerning the medium it has subscribed or given rise to.

My second, and final, concluding remark concerns intermedia and the problems inherent in analyzing the internet in isolation from media history or media industry. Terms such as internet research or internet studies evoke understandings of a discipline defined in technical terms and even risk to frame out such intermedial phenomena as gaming or mobile communications. Perhaps it is a general desire to identify practices as specific to the internet that has oriented research toward speculations of cyberspace. This risks not only foregrounding some uses over others but also disabling understandings of the intermedial nature of media culture (be this past or present) and the position of online practices within it. internet research needs studies of all kinds of applications, user cultures, production practices, discourses, and policies in mapping the range and implications of networked communications. The important thing is not to put these in a hierarchical order in which some questions or forums are considered more interesting, important, or general than others.

References

Adam, A. (1998). *Artificial knowing: Gender and the thinking machine*. London: Routledge.

Attwood, F. (2007). No money shot? Commerce, pornography and new sex taste cultures. *Sexualities, 10*(4), 441–456.

Barlow, J. P. (1996). *A declaration of the independence of cyberspace*. Retrieved November 24, 2006, from http://www.eff.org/~barlow/Declaration-Final.htm

Bell, D. (2001). *An introduction to cybercultures*. London: Routledge.

Benedikt, M. (Ed.). (1991). *Cyberspace: The first steps*. Cambridge: MIT Press.

Bennett, D. (2001). Pornography-dot-com: Eroticising privacy on the internet. *The Review of Education/Pedagogy/Cultural Studies, 23*(4), 381–391.

Bolter, D. J. (2000). Identity. In T. Swiss (Ed.), *Unspun: Key concepts for understanding the world wide web* (pp. 17–29). New York: New York University Press.

Boyle, D. (1997). *Subject to change: Guerrilla television revisited*. New York: Oxford University Press.

Costighan, J. T. (1999). Introduction: Forests, trees, and internet research. In S. Jones (Ed.), *Doing internet research: Critical issues and methods for examining the net* (pp. xvii–xxiv). London: Sage.

Cronin, B., & Davenport, E. (2001). E-rogenous zones: Positioning pornography in the digital economy. *The Information Society, 17*(1), 33–48.

Danet, B. (1998). Text as mask: Gender, play, and performance on the internet. In S. Jones (Ed.), *Cybersociety 2.0: Revisiting computer-mediated communication and community* (pp. 129–158). London: Sage.

Dietrich, D. (2000). Performance. In T. Swiss (Ed.), *Unspun: Key concepts for understanding the world wide web* (pp. 100–119). New York: New York University Press.

Filippo, J. (2000). Pornography on the Web. In D. Gauntlett (Ed.), *Web.studies: Rewiring media studies for the digital age* (pp. 122–129). London: Arnold.

Hayles, N. K. (1999). *How we became posthuman: Virtual bodies in cybernetics, literature, and informatics*. Chicago: University of Chicago Press.

Hill, C. (1996). "Attention! Production! Audience!" Performing video in its first decade. In C. Hill, K. Horshfield, M. Troy, & D. Boyle (Eds.), *Rewind: Video art and alternative media in the United States 1968–1980* (pp. 5–36). Unpublished book manuscript by the School of the Art Institute of Chicago Video Data Bank.

Huhtamo, E. (1995). *Taidetta koneesta: Media, taide, teknologia (Ars ex machina: Media, Art, Technology)*. Turku: University of Turku.

Jacobs, K., Janssen, M., & Pasquinelli, M. (Eds.). (2007). *C'Lick me: A netporn studies reader*. Amsterdam: Institute of Network Cultures.

Jansen, B. J., & Spink, A. (2006). How are we searching the world wide web? A comparison of nine search engine transaction logs. *Information Processing and Management, 42*(1), 248–263.

Jones, S. (Ed.). (1994). *CyberSociety: Computer-mediated communication and community*. London: Sage.

Jones, S. (Ed.). (1998). *CyberSociety 2.0: Revisiting computer-mediated community and technology*. London: Sage.

Jones, S. (2000). The bias of the web. In A. Herman & T. Swiss (Eds.), *The world wide web and contemporary cultural theory* (pp. 171–182). New York: Routledge.

Kibby, M. (2001). Women and sex entertainment on the internet: Discourses of gender and power. *Mots Pluriels, 19*. Retrieved November 24, 2006, from http://www.arts.uwa.edu.au/MotsPluriels/MP1901mk.html

Kibby, M., & Costello, B. (2001). Between the image and the act: Interactive sex entertainment on the internet. *Sexualities: Studies in Culture and Society, 4*(3), 353–369.

Kolko, B. E., Nakamura, L., & Rodman, G. B. (Eds.) (2000). Race in cyberspace: An introduction. *Race in Cyberspace* (pp. 1–14). New York: Routledge.

Lane, F. S. III. (2001). *Obscene profits: The entrepreneurs of pornography in the cyber age.* New York: Routledge.

Magnet, S. (2007). Feminist sexualities, race and the internet: An investigation of suicidegirls.com. *New Media & Society, 9*(4), 577–602.

McGerty, L.-J. (2000). "Nobody lives only in cyberspace": Gendered subjectivities and domestic uses of the internet. *CyberPsychology & Behavior, 3*(5), 895–899.

Miller, D., & Slater, D. (2000). *Internet: An ethnographical approach.* Oxford: Berg.

Nakamura, L. (2006). Cultural difference, theory, and cyberculture studies: A case of mutual repulsion. In D. Silver & A. Massanari (Eds.), *Critical cyberculture studies* (pp. 29–36). New York: New York University Press.

O'Toole, L. (1998). *Pornocopia: Porn, sex, technology and desire.* London: Serpent's Tail.

Paasonen, S. (2005a). *Figures of fantasy: Women, internet, and cyberdiscourse.* New York: Peter Lang.

Paasonen, S. (2005b). Net years, pioneers and flat perspectives: Temporality and internet research. In M. Allen & M. Consalvo (Eds.), *Internet research annual* (Vol. 2, pp. 3–14). New York: Peter Lang.

Paasonen, S. (2007). Family romance: Generation, kinship, and internet research. In M. Consalvo & C. Haythorntwhite (Eds.), *Internet research annual* (Vol. 4, pp. 9–13). New York: Peter Lang.

Paasonen, S. (2009). What cyberspace? Traveling concepts in internet research. In G. Goggin & M. McLelland (Eds.), *Internationalizing internet studies: Beyond Anglophone paradigms* (pp. 18–31). New York: Routledge.

Patterson, Z. (2004). Going on-line: Consuming pornography in the digital era. In L. Williams (Ed.), *Porn studies* (pp. 104–123). Durham: Duke University Press.

Perdue, L. (2002). *EroticaBiz: How sex shaped the internet.* New York: Writers Club Press.

Rheingold, H. (1994/1995). *The virtual community: Finding connection in a computerized world.* London: Minerva.

Shields, R. (2000). Cyberspace. In T. Swiss (Ed.), *Unspun: Key concepts for understanding the world wide web* (pp. 66–72). New York: New York University Press.

Silver, D. (2000). Looking backwards, looking forwards: Cyberculture studies 1990–2000. In D. Gauntlett (Ed.), *Web.studies: Rewiring media studies for the digital age* (pp. 19–30). London: Arnold.

Smith, M.A. (1999). *Communities in cyberspace.* New York: Routledge.

Spink, A., Partridge, H., & Jansen, B. J. (2006). Sexual and pornographic web searching: Trend analysis. *First Monday, 11*(9). Retrieved November 24, 2006, from http://www.firstmonday.org/issues/issue11_9/spink/

Sterne, J. (1999). Thinking the internet: Cultural studies versus the millennium. In S. Jones (Ed.), *Doing internet research: Critical issues and methods for examining the net* (pp. 257–288). London: Sage.

Sterne, J. (2005). Digital media and disciplinarity. *The information society, 21*, 249–256.

Stone, A. R. (1995). *The war of desire and technology at the close of the mechanical age.* Cambridge: MIT Press.

Turkle, S. (1995/1997). *Life on the screen: Identity in the age of the internet.* New York: Simon and Schuster.

Villarejo, A. (2004). Defycategory.com, or the place of categories in intermedia. In P. Church Gibson (Ed.), *More dirty looks: Gender, pornography and power* (2nd ed., pp. 85–91). London: BFI.

Waskul, D. D. (Ed.). (2004). *Net.seXXX: Readings on sex, pornography, and the internet.* New York: Peter Lang.

White, M. (2002). Representations or people? *Ethics and Information Technology, 4*(3), 249–266.

Winston, B. (1998). *Media technology and society. A history: From the telegraph to the internet.* London: Routledge.

Wynn, E., & Katz, J. E. (1997). Hyperbole over cyberspace: Self-presentation & social boundaries in internet home pages and discourse. *The Information Society, 13*(4), 297–328.

(Dis)Connected: Deleuze's Superject and the Internet

David Savat

Unlike Lyotard, Baudrillard, Virilio, and to a lesser extent Guattari, Deleuze never really theorised so-called digital or new media, certainly not that collection of machines and ideas that we refer to as the internet. Yet, many have used aspects of Deleuze's work to do just that. Most notably it is Deleuze and Guattari's use of the concept of the 'rhizome' that has been most made use of in attempts to describe and conceptualise the internet and the use thereof (Buchanan, 2009), though not always in the sense that Deleuze and Guattari employed it. In this article I want to explore a different way in which one can make use of aspects of Deleuze's work when it comes to thinking about, or even theorising, the internet or aspects thereof.

My initial focus here is on Deleuze's use of the concept of the assemblage and his understanding of machines and technology that is tied in with this. Notably, as I will elaborate further on, for Deleuze, any question concerning machines is also immediately a question about human existence. To perhaps state it somewhat more accurately, for Deleuze any question about human being or human existence is immediately a question about machines and the assemblages that constitute them. It is in this context that in this article I want to consider more closely that techno-logical assemblage referred to as the internet, especially in terms of considering the human component within that assemblage. It is in that context that I want to offer some suggestions as to how it constitutes itself by way of and within that specific assemblage.

The Assemblage

In a much quoted short essay entitled 'Postscript on the Societies of Control', Deleuze states that

> It is easy to set up a correspondence between any society and some kind of machine, which isn't to say that their machines determine different kinds of society but that they express the social forms capable of producing them and making use of them.(Deleuze, 1995, p. 180)

D. Savat (✉)
Humanities and Social Sciences, The University of Western Australia, Perth, Australia
e-mail: Savat@cyllene.uwa.edu.au

J. Hunsinger et al. (eds.), *International Handbook of Internet Research*,
DOI 10.1007/978-1-4020-9789-8_26, © Springer Science+Business Media B.V. 2010

From such a perspective any technological object or practice, including the internet, exists as part of a given social context, and one cannot expect to be able to remove it from this social context and still be capable of understanding it or using it in the manner one did previously. The discipline of archaeology, for example, especially experimental archaeology, provides countless examples of this, whether one considers the pyramids in Egypt, Roman bridge building, or Archimedes' 'shipshaker'. Even using the engineering techniques and practices people have at hand today we struggle in our attempts to reproduce many ancient objects and techniques. This suggests that a different and specific knowledge functions within different and specific technological and societal contexts.

However, instead of referring to it as 'contexts', or 'cultures', it is perhaps more productive and more precise to consider them as assemblages:

> We will call an assemblage every constellation of singularities and traits deduced from the flow [of matter and energy] – selected, organised, stratified – in such a way as to converge...artificially or naturally...Assemblages may group themselves into extremely vast constellations constituting 'cultures', or even ages...We may distinguish in every case a number of different lines. Some of them, phylogenetic lines, travel long distances between assemblages of various ages and cultures (from the blowgun to the cannon? From the prayer wheel to the propellor? From the pot to the motor?); others, ontogenetic lines, are internal to one assemblage and link up its various elements, or else cause something to pass...into another assemblage of a different nature but of the same culture or age (for example the horseshoe which spread through agricultural assemblages). (Deleuze in De Landa, 1991, p. 140)

To take a technology outside of the assemblage of which it is a part is for its existence, as that technology, as that specific practice, to cease to exist. The reason for that is because any machine is 'the ensemble of the interrelations of its components, independent of the components themselves' (Valera in Guattari, 1993, p. 16). In short, one cannot take a laptop, nor the internet for that matter, outside of its larger societal ensemble, put it into another and then still expect it to continue to be a 'laptop'. Doing so would mean that it simply ceases to exist as that technology, as that machine or set of practices. In short, as both Deleuze and Guattari maintain, the manner in which a machine is organised and its actual materiality do not have much to do with one another. Technology, as Marx, Mumford, Heidegger, and Guattari pointed out in their different ways (Guattari, 1995; Heidegger, 1993; Marx, 1973, Mumford, 1995), is not only the actual material component but, importantly, also a set of social practices, including, importantly, the various machinic needs and social needs and interests that a particular component within an assemblage serves, which applies to the internet as much as it applies to any other technology or set thereof.

Of course, the distinction between various societal assemblages, or what Marx called 'epochs of production' and Mumford called 'megamachines' (Marx, 1973, p. 85; Mumford, 1995, p. 324) is not clear cut. As Deleuze indicates in the above-quoted passage, different assemblages of different forms and scales can exist over time and, indeed, can form part of other assemblages. Mumford (1995) too, for example, was very much aware of how the civilisation he was part of contained habits, ideas, and ways of doing things that formed part of other civilisations. This is not to say that one cannot discern a specific unity to larger societal assemblages, and of course the criteria one uses is critical in such an exercise, but, even focusing on the types of machines, as Deleuze recognised, does not actually explain anything about a given society and how people exist within it. As Deleuze strongly emphasised 'the machines don't explain anything, you have to analyse the collective arrangements of which the machines are just one component' (Deleuze, 1995, p. 175). The components that these collective arrangements consist of can vary, ranging from

> Material and energy components; semiotic, diagrammatic and algorithmic components (plans, formulae, equations and calculations which lead to the fabrication of the machine); components of organs, influx and humours of the human body; individual and collective mental representations and information; investments of desiring machines producing a subjectivity adjacent to these components; abstract machines installing themselves transversally to the machinic levels previously considered (material, cognitive, affective and social. (Guattari, 1995, pp. 35–36)

The Assemblage of Subjectivity

One of the components in these collective arrangements is 'subjectivity'. Deleuze and Guattari, however, view what is called subjectivity not only as a component within a larger assemblage or set of assemblages but also as an assemblage itself. Their view is that there is a 'diversity of components of subjectivation' (Guattari, 1995, p. 16) that passes through any one person or rather of which any one person consists. For example, there may be components of subjectivation that originate with the disciplinary mode of power, which Foucault (1979), following Deleuze and Guattari (1977), saw as a machine for producing that form of subjectivity we call individuality. At the very same time, there may also be components of subjectivation that originate with what Deleuze termed a modulatory mode of power (Savat, 2009). Alongside this, and as part of this, we should not forget other components, including the various machines we connect to, including the internet. For Guattari, as well as for Deleuze, what we refer to as 'subjectivity', then, is an ongoing production and maintenance of a relative sense of unicity. As Deleuze explains it, subjectivity is a question of how a person maintains a specific form of existence in a given assemblage or ensemble (Deleuze, 1995), thereby making the question of subjectivity immediately a political and ethical question.

Taking such a view of subjectivity, and keeping in mind that technology is an expression of human being as human doing, it then makes sense that subjectivity, that is, the form or manner of existence one maintains in a given context or ensemble, is in great part a function of the different components of subjectivation that exist at any point in time. Subjectivity, in other words, changes depending on the numerous and varying forces and pressures that produce it, as well as those by which, importantly, it produces itself. As pointed out above, one of these components is the actual machine component or technology. It is a significant component that, as an expression of a given form of subjectivity, enables, and in a sense requires, one to act in the world in some ways while not in others. Different technologies, in short, whether they be a knife, a printing press, a car, or the internet,[1] can alter one's sense of being an actor in the world because of the manner in which they enable a different doing, and in the process can come to constitute and reflect, as well as require, a different sense of self. As Schivelbusch pointed out in his study of the railway, 'If an essential element of a given socio-cultural space-time continuum undergoes change, this will affect the entire structure; our perception of space-time will also lose its accustomed orientation' (Schivelbusch, 1986, p. 36).

Technological shifts, in other words, that on the one hand often constitute a quantitative change, can, on the other hand, result in qualitative shifts in how people perceive and experience the world. For example, a shift to the use of a new form or type of technology, such as the shift from the carriage to the railway, and, more broadly, to the steam engine, can come to constitute what Kirby refers to as a shift in the accepted space–time continuum:

> Any artificial means of motion – horseback riding, for example, or travel by horsedrawn carriages – would dictate new strategies of perception, but the phenomenological adjustment required by railway movement proved to be far more extreme. In walking, running, and riding, the perception of the landscape has a physical correlate in human muscular activity. To a lesser extent, the same is true of animal propulsion...there is a sense of bodily displacement that matches one's actual spatial displacement. Older transport technology preserved the traditional space-time continuum. (Kirby, 1996, p. 74)

In other words, in shifting from muscle, water and wind power to the steam engine, which essentially is a shift in the generation and distribution of energy (Castells, 1996, p. 38), people gained an autonomy and degree of independence, which some perceived as a 'disconnection' from the world (Carlyle, 1984) that was previously not possible. The introduction of the steam engine, or rather, of motorisation if we follow Virilio's thinking, constituted a major form of what in more Deleuzian terms might be called a 'deterritorialisation'. For example, Marx argued that

> Not till the invention of Watt's second and so-called double-acting steam-engine was a prime mover found which drew its own motive power from the consumption of coal and water, was entirely under man's [sic] control, was mobile and a means of locomotion, was urban and not – like the water-wheel – rural, permitted production to be concentrated in towns instead of – like water wheels – being scattered over the countryside and, finally, was of universal technical application, and little affected in its choice of residence by local circumstances. (Marx, 1990, p. 499)[2]

---

[1] It should be clear by now that any machine is multiple; for example, the train is itself an assemblage of other machines and practices, including control technologies, but all of this is encapsulated in the assemblage that people refer to as the train. The same goes for the internet. Here it is often talked about as if it is a unitary or singular machine, but it is important to recognise that it is a collection of machines and practices, which is not to say that it does not have a unity to it.

[2] Of course, a similar deterritorialisation was experienced with the use of the windmill and the water wheel at its time. Notably, this deterritorialisation resulted in a reterritorialisation of another kind, and took some of the worst forms in terms of how people's capacity for action became, while more autonomous from the so-called natural world, quite limited in being connected to the machines of the factory.

Where sail ships, and therefore trade, had previously been dependent on the weather, steam ships were more or less independent of the wind and currents. Likewise, production could be concentrated much more easily, and therefore concentrated living in the form of the city as well, with goods and people transported much more easily by way of rail. With the use of the steam engine came an entirely new production of space and time, keeping in mind that 'space is a material product...a concrete expression of each historical ensemble in which a society is specified' (Castells in Soja, 1989, p. 830). In short, different technologies can alter our sense of being able to act in the world in very significant ways, whether we consider a simple difference in speed of movement (Virilio, 1986, 1991), like comparing walking to riding a bicycle, or a difference in vision, such as the invention of linear perspective vision (Romanyshyn, 1989). In other words, both different machines and technologies are an expression of specific forms or aspects of subjectivity, and they are what enable certain forms and aspects of subjectivity to be produced (Guattari, 1992, 1993).

Notably, the different components of subjectivation have to be arranged in such a manner that one can come to act in a specific technological ensemble. Stated differently, in order to be capable of effective action in the context of any larger technological assemblage one has to constitute a specific form of unicity, that is, subjectivity or, less broadly, sense of self. It is at this point that we need to consider the formation of what I will here term a digital ensemble, central to which is the internet, and how it affects and effects the different components of subjectivity, as well as the form of unicity that is characteristic of it.

The Digital Ensemble and the Internet

A number of people have made the claim that the use of digital technologies, and especially the advent of the internet, constitutes a social transformation of the same order as the steam engine initiated. Indeed, Deleuze (1992) too saw the emergence of a new type of machine or technology that operated by way of a digital language as very significant. It is partly because of the use of these machines in different aspects of people's life, including the use of the internet, that something has changed in the way people function in the world and in the ways they relate to one another. Indeed, many people describe the general process that goes on as an annihilation of space. Of course, as it was with similar claims that accompanied the introduction of the railway, this is not quite correct. What is occurring is that one specific understanding or perception of space, and thereby time, is being replaced by another understanding or perception. This is an understanding of space and time which to many may be experienced as quite natural but, that, in the context of digital technologies, especially when these form part of a network, ceases to have much meaningful sense or, rather, comes to have a very different sense. At the same time, however, we do not necessarily have the conceptual tools to be able to adequately come to terms with this different construction of space and time.

In the first instance, what we are dealing with when we are dealing with digital technologies, of which that collection of technologies that is the internet is most exemplary, is a whole new range of practices or new ways of doing. Certainly when compared to the machines and practices that exemplify what might best be termed the industrialised or motorised mechanical ensemble, in the digital ensemble we deal with machines and practices that are qualitatively different. This is not to suggest that the digital ensemble is necessarily replacing the industrialised ensemble. Nor to suggest that it did not emerge out of the machines and practices of the industrialised mechanical ensemble. Indeed, both ensembles operate concurrently and, significantly, cannot operate without each other.[3] However, this is not to deny that the machines and practices that digital technologies constitute are significantly different ones from those of other technological ensembles. As a range of authors have pointed out, there is a shift occurring. Irrespective of whether one subscribes to more negative views on the consequences of that shift, or more positive views, Virilio's point is that it constitutes a 'disturbance in the perception of what reality is' (Virilio, 2001, p. 24).

While there is no space here to fully explore some of the key features of the digital ensemble, I here want to point to some of those that may be especially significant. I specifically want to emphasise those features that are relevant in considering how they express, or are an expression of, any newly emerging production of a sense of unicity as it is experienced by way of the assemblage referred to as the internet.

One notable characteristic of digital machines, one also identified by Deleuze, is that even while they might be said to operate at the speed of light (Haraway, 1991; Virilio, 2001, p. 23), they do not actually move. Unlike the machines of the industrialised or motorised ensemble they have no mobility or motion. What this is more widely reflective of is that the digital ensemble makes use of energy in a very different way than the industrialised or motorised ensemble. Instead of engaging in the production and/or distribution of energy, instead of dealing with kinetic energy, the machines of the digital ensemble reproduce energy and are, as Castells (1996) points out, engaged in 'the action of knowledge upon knowledge itself as the main source of productivity'. This different use of energy is clearly reflected, for example, in how the machines of the digital ensemble possess a very different capacity for representation. As Jameson pointed out so well,

> It is immediately obvious that the technology of our own moment no longer possesses this same capacity for representation: not the turbine, nor even Sheeler's grain elevators or smokestacks, not the baroque elaboration of pipes and conveyor belts, nor even the streamlined profile of the railroad train - all vehicles of speed still concentrated at rest - but rather the computer, whose outer shell has no emblematic or visual power, or even

---

[3]For example, processes of industrial production, and very importantly, processes of distribution and consumption, have been transformed through the use of digital technologies, including the internet. At the same time, our digital machines run on oil and are produced by the factory form of organisation that is so central to the industrial ensemble. This is partly what Deleuze and Guattari refer to in their earlier quoted text in this piece defining the assemblage. Lines can cross or traverse various assemblages, and an assemblage never stands alone.

the casings of the various media themselves, as with that home appliance called television which articulates nothing but rather implodes, carrying its flattened image surface within itself. (Jameson, 1991, pp. 36–37)

Many refer to this process of, on the one hand, having reached the speed of light (Haraway, 1991; Virilio, 2001), that is, electricity, while no longer being engaged in physical motion as an annihilation of space and time. With such a claim they simply echo similar claims that were made with the advent of motorisation by way of the steam engine. In many respects, then, one could well argue, following Marx (1973, pp. 533–534), that such a shortening of the temporal and spatial moment is simply a product of the development of productive forces, that is, capitalism.[4] Here, however, it would be more precise to state that a new 'spatiality' and 'temporality' are being constructed, for which we simply have not developed as yet the 'perceptual equipment' to recognise it (Jameson, 1991, pp. 38–39).[5]

Invariably, people refer to this newly emerging 'spatiality' or temporality as virtual reality, hyperspace, and cyberspace. What seems to be crucial, however, is that with the machines of the digital ensemble our current understandings of space and time are collapsed. As a number of authors have pointed out in different ways, in this assemblage space *is* time (Chesher, 1997; Mihalache, 2002; Virilio, 1991, 2001). To explain this somewhat differently, there is no depth. Nor does one inhabit it, or move from location to location. Instead, it inhabits us. In short, it is in our heads, it is a construct, it is information. Information has no perspective and, as Nunes (1997) has pointed out, it is not a place we can visit.

Taking such a view, then, when functioning purely as part of the digital ensemble, distinctions of 'near', 'far', 'here', and 'there' cease to make much sense or, rather, are placed in doubt, which is precisely, as Baudrillard (1994, p. 3) pointed out, the effect of any simulation. Indeed, one can be both 'here' and 'there' in the same moment, which is why the internet, and especially the World Wide Web (WWW), can be seen as a key expression of the development of capitalism, in that the site of production and the site of circulation effectively become one and the same (Hardt & Negri, 2001, p. 298). In that respect, one should not focus so much on the so-called spatial moment of circulation but, rather, place emphasis on the temporal moment. Stated differently, virtuality and action within that context are better understood and discussed by way of a focus on temporality rather than spatiality, which is what so far has been the case.[6]

---

[4]See Schivelbusch (1986) on this in relation to the emergence of railroad space and railroad time. Virilio (1986) has argued that this 'annihilation' of space was foreshadowed by ballistics technology, to which the development of computing is not simply incidental.

[5]At this point I really want to highlight that for the time being the use of the word 'space', or any spatial metaphors for that matter, to describe action in the context of the digital ensemble is increasingly problematic, though, as Kirby (1996) has argued so effectively, a language without spatial overtones may well not be a possibility for human beings.

[6]Deleuze's work, of course, is worth exploring in terms of building a more critical understanding of the virtual, as Deleuze does not draw a distinction between the virtual and the real, but rather, between the virtual and the actual. On this see Levy (1998) and Bogard (1996, pp. 14–15).

Indeed, not only distinctions of 'near' and 'far', and 'here' and 'there' are put into doubt but a whole range of other distinctions so familiar to us are according to many put into doubt as well. These include distinctions such as present/future, author/text, actor/action, presence/absence, real/unreal, original/copy, medium/message, form/ expression, style/content and subject/object (Baudrillard, 1994; Der Derian, 2001; Giese, 1998; Haraway, 1995; Mihalache, 2002; Poster, 1995; Stone, 2001). Indeed, the very status of knowledge some argue shifts (Lyotard 1984). The principal reason being that analogue representations can always in some form be traced back to what they represent, while with digital encoding this is not possible. Everything is effectively reduced to the binary bit, thereby making everything within the digital ensemble potentially interchangeable (Chesher, 1997, p. 87). As Smith (1986, p. 161) has argued, because the basic unit of knowledge is the bit there is 'no longer a line of validation back to a pure text'. At least when operating within the context of the digital ensemble, to the extent that there are distinctions of near/far, subject/object and actor/action, these are simulations or virtuality. In many respects the one distinction or difference that does matter is whether the switch is either on or off.

One thing that can be observed, then, is that there appears to be a general smoothing over of difference by and within the digital ensemble. This can be observed in a number of different ways. For example, production in the context of the industrialised or motorised ensemble is characterised by a very high degree of functional differentiation and spatial fragmentation, where every machine has its function, or rather, every function has its specific machine, with each function being spatially organised. This is what Adam Smith's 'division of labour', so central to the factory form of organisation, is all about, which Marx in turn saw as destructive of human existence. The machines of the digital ensemble, however, more often than not contain a variety of functions and, provided one has access to 'the network' one's location is to a large extent irrelevant. As Hardt and Negri point out, the digital computer is now 'the universal tool, through which all activities must pass' (2001, p. 292). It is on this point that Poster's comparison between the typewriter and the word processor is particularly useful as it is not simply that one can perform very different actions with the latter but, more significantly, this very difference in action is a very different form of doing. This suggests that

[t]he shift from the typewriter keyboard to the computer keyboard is ontological: the former instantiates and reinforces a subject-object. The paper page receives the mechanical blows of the keys as the writer presses on the machine to produce the inked page. The typewriter merely improves the legibility of the page over the hand-manipulated quill, ink pen, or pencil, where one scratches inscriptions into the paper. The computer keyboard, by contrast, sends digital signals to the central processing chip through the word processing program, producing letters on the screen that lack the material properties of the typed paper page. The letters on the screen are fluid, easily changeable and moveable. (Poster 2002, pp. 754–755)

The machines of the digital ensemble, then, enable a very different form of 'doing' than the machines of the industrialised ensemble. For one thing, they construct or enable a spatial and temporal experience that is entirely different from the machines of the industrialised or motorised ensemble. Extremely significant here is that movement or kinetic energy does not form part of these machines. Instead, the experience is something that is perhaps more appropriately described as flow (Castells, 1996), or even smoothness.[7] It is in this context that we then need to consider how that might affect or effect the construction of subjectivity or sense of unicity. As Harvey has made clear

> [i]f spatial and temporal experiences are primary vehicles for the coding and reproduction of social relations (as Bourdieu suggests), then a change in the way the former get represented will almost certainly generate some kind of shift in the latter. (Harvey, 1989, p. 247)

It is precisely at the point where our connection to the machines of the digital ensemble occurs, the moment of interface, that we can begin to delineate the emergence of a new human–machine assemblage or, as Poster (2001b) terms it, a humachine.[8]

The Interface and the Internet

The key function of the interface is to regulate difference, whether that be differences in language (from analogue to digital and back again) or whether that be differences in speed. The key aim of the interface is to ensure such differences are smoothed out.[9] In that respect, the interface, as a key component, if not expression, of, for example, the internet, is both what enables the very connection of assemblages and allows those assemblages to function as components in one unit. In that respect, the interface eliminates both the user's awareness of the interface itself and the awareness of oneself as being an embodied entity (Bogard, 1996, p. 72; Stone, 2001, p. 193). At the moment of interface what is constituted is a new assemblage in which the body quite literally has no place, or at least, so it initially seems to some. In great part this is because there is no such thing as 'here' in the virtuality of digital machines. The consequence of that is that the body ceases to be a strong constitutive factor in the constitution of subjectivity (Poster, 2001a, p. 17), at least in moments of connection, because effectively what is eliminated in the moment of connection is the function of the body as a boundary that marks what is of the inside, that is, that which constitutes 'me', and what is of the outside, that is, that which constitutes 'not me' (Bogard, 1996, p. 37; Hayles, 1993, p. 72).

---

[7]For one thing, fluids do not move. By their very definition, they flow, that is, they have speed. It is a mistake, however, to think of the internet as a series of pipes through which a fluid flows. Instead, it is more useful to think of the internet as a whole as flow, in the same sense that the air we breathe occupies a room, and is both 'here' and 'there' at the same time. In other words, it does not move.

[8]From such a perspective any human being is always already a form of human–machine assemblage, even if it is only the use of a rock to crack a nut open with. In other words, from this perspective we have always been some form of cyborg, and the more interesting question instead is what sort of cyborgs we are. On this the work of Haraway and aspects of Guattari's (1992) work are very useful.

[9]When one has to work with a dirty mouse, for example, one can become acutely aware of how this interface is a smoothing device of sorts.

Indeed, when one connects there is no sense of mobility that is generated by the actual body. One does not move from one place to another but is potentially anywhere, or rather, anytime. It is perhaps more appropriate to ask not what sort of space you occupy and how you occupy that space but, rather, a question of when and how you are (Virilio, 1995, p. 155). Stated differently, in such a context one exists more as a temporal event than a spatial entity. Stated more simply, in the context of connecting and acting by way of the machines of the digital ensemble one exists as code.

Taking such a perspective, one has to understand that actions in the context of the digital ensemble are not performed by entities in space. Both the actor and the action are virtual and are, effectively, one and the same moment. The interface in effect eliminates the conceptual distinction between being and doing (Stone, 1995; Virilio, 1995, pp. 106–107). In many respects, in the context of the digital ensemble the actor only exists or occurs when an action is actually performed. Notably, any stream of code that is generated is an event in itself, and there need not be a specific unity to the multiplicity of code. In short, the body does not function in such a way that the multiplicity of code is necessarily attributable to it. The subject, in other words, 'is open to, even dispersed amongst, an endlessly proliferating number of information streams' (Mansfield, 2000, p. 155). The very idea of the subject as a form of experience or existence that has a coherent sense of unicity comes to be open to question at the moment of connection. Stated differently, it is a manner of existence that is both formless and indeterminate, and in that respect it makes sense to conceptualise it as being fluid, that is, as being flow. Significantly, if one takes seriously this idea then one cannot describe the actions of fluids by way of using the same language as one uses to describe the actions of solids. Consequently, in describing any politics of the internet one may well need to leave more Newtonian language, using words like 'mass', 'inertia', and 'force', behind.

It is this very manner of existence, this very manner of constituting oneself, that many describe as a negative experience. Virilio (2001) I think is most notable for this, as is Baudrillard. Indeed, Virilio (2001, p. 24) describes it as 'a total loss of the bearings of the individual'. This need not be a surprise. After all, in the wired world one's existence is not only characterised by an extreme degree of multiplicity (Turkle, 1995), a multiplicity that is dispersed in that it has no body anchoring it as such, but it is also characterised by the fact that it is momentary. In the context of the digital ensemble one only exists 'here and now', as Virilio emphasises (2001, p. 24). Identity, in other words, as the condition of being identical or the same over time, one's sense of being a unique self or individual, is in jeopardy from Virilio's perspective. However, rather than simply lamenting the disappearance of the individual, which in my view raises important questions concerning the politics of the digital, it is worth exploring what sense of unicity other than the one we know as individuality might be emerging – especially the moments or duration when one is connected, that is, of 'the network'.

First of all, it needs to be recognised that in the context of forming part of a digital machine assemblage one does not constitute oneself as a spatial entity. Rather, one constitutes oneself as flow, as a temporal event. In the context of connecting to the machines of the digital ensemble one does not move from one space to another space, connecting to different machinic components (class room, factory floor, hospital), in the process. In this context one constitutes, and is constituted as, flow. Indeed, one's existence may well be a combination of flows or flow lines. The moment one connects to the machines of the digital ensemble, which are all potentially of 'the network', one is always potentially at work, always potentially in education, irrespective of the geographical location one is in (Deleuze, 1992). Indeed, as Turkle (1995) points out, we may well have a presence by way of functioning through a variety of different windows on the one screen at the time.

In such a context, multiplicity is characterised by the fact that it is dispersed, simultaneous, instantaneous and continuous.[10] In some respects identity can be viewed as if in a potentially turbulent state. One can be constituted, and constitute oneself, as a number of different flows, each of which can be simultaneous and instantaneous and each of which is continuous. In that respect one does not connect to one assemblage, only to have to disconnect from it to move to another, but is always already potentially a component in a variety of assemblages at the same moment, which come to be increasingly difficult to distinguish, that is, turbulent. Interfaces play a crucial function in enabling and facilitating such connection. Anything that negatively affects this connection is immediately a threat to one's capacity to act and constitute an existence in the context of this ensemble. In the context of the machines of the industrialised ensemble, on the other hand, disconnection from the machine is more likely to be perceived as a release, since machines are often limited to a small number of actions.[11] In this respect, the form of unicity a person has is critical in their experience of both the digital and mechanical ensemble as it is essential to being able to act effectively within each technological ensemble.

The Superject

Already, however, a problem has emerged in attempting to describe the character of existence in the context of the digital ensemble. For one thing, to state that it is a multiplicity suggests that it is nonetheless a composition and that therefore it has a larger unity to it (Coyne, 1998), that is, that it is a subject of some form. Here I think that Deleuze's (1993) argument that just as we have a transformation in the status of the object to what he terms the objectile (Savat, 2009) so we have a transformation from the subject to what he terms the superject. The superject, and in this it is comparable to Leibniz's monad, exists temporally or virtually, has no

---

[10]It is important not to treat these flows in the manner that one treats sand as being capable of flowing, as this leads to a misunderstanding in terms of how the internet functions. Information does not 'flow' in the manner that an aggregate of solid bodies do (like particles of sand).

[11]This is not to suggest that all forms of work in the context of the digital ensemble are filled with creative joy. Far from it, but simply to suggest, just as one example, that both one's entertainment and one's work can come by way of the same machine, whereas with the machines of the industrial ensemble one has to disconnect from one machine and connect to another machine.

form and constitutes, indeed *is*, its own world. The superject is not an essence but an event (Deleuze, 1993). Significantly, Deleuze treats it as having a very different perception or sensibility from the subject, that is, the individual as we know it. Stated differently, it operates with a very different sense of perspective, as Deleuze explains in relation to Baroque's perspective:

> The point of view is not what varies with the subject, at least in the first instance; it is, to the contrary, the condition in which an eventual subject apprehends a variation (metamorphosis), or: something = X (anamorphosis)...It is not a variation of truth according to the subject, but the condition in which the truth of a variation appears to the subject. (Deleuze, 1993, p. 20)

To explain this further, in swapping from a spatial existence to a virtual existence one swaps 'the system of a window and a world outside [with] one of a computer screen in a closed room' (Deleuze, 1995, pp. 157–158). When one constitutes oneself spatially, one exists in a world with depth, and therefore one's point of view can be altered by way of altering one's position with respect to the object that one examines. In the context of constituting oneself virtually, one's existence is a projection. Any alteration of the point of view, which in any case is simulated, is done by changing the world, rather than changing one's position in that world.

More significantly, this virtual existence, this superject, does not relate to an object in the same manner that a subject does. Indeed, the very distinction between subject and object makes little sense in the context of the assemblage that enables the superject, and any simulation of such a distinction may well purely be a function of this superject. While some may argue that the virtual as such is not new, they ignore, as Poster points out, how the machines of the digital ensemble enable 'different capacities of reception' (Poster 2001b, p. 85). As Guattari states, these are technologies that open up a new universe of thought and action. Critical to this form of existence that is the superject is the interface. The more the distinction between the human assemblage and the machine assemblage can be eliminated, the more effective the superject, as the character of existence enabled by way of the digital ensemble, by way of 'the network', can be expressed.

From such a perspective disconnection is death for digital being because being connected is its very condition of existence. Anything that interrupts that existence is simply perceived as an interruption in its capacity to constitute itself as flow. Indeed, smoothness is precisely characterised by lack of interruption, and digital being strives for smoothness of flow above all. In that respect, what some refer to as internet addiction is an interesting phenomenon. At the very same time, '[n]o matter how virtual the subject may become, there is always a body attached' (Stone, 2001, p. 195). In that respect, to the extent that the superject can be said to have 'perspective', it can only, therefore, view the body, and being embodied, as an interruption to existence. In other words, at least for now perhaps, superjects have only a relatively short duration of flow. Indeed, prolonged manifestation of a superject may well result in death, as the experience of some gamers in South Korea has demonstrated (Simkin, 2003). Consciousness, in other words, is still very much 'rooted in the physical' (Stone, 2001, p. 195).

Nonetheless, in considering the more political and ethical question as to how to produce and maintain a sense of unicity despite the diversity of components that pass through a person or body, account must be taken of those components that form part of the digital ensemble, both components of objectification and subjectivation. It is precisely in the connection of the assemblages, in the interface, that a different construction of the political may be emerging, with both negative and positive manifestations; a construction of the political that may well not be associated with the figure of the individual so central to modern political thought. While for now much of this politics is couched in terms of 'internet access', we may see a whole new machine politics emerging because the machines of the digital ensemble, including the interface, are critical to how one constitutes oneself as flow, that is, how one is able to (dis)connect.

References

Baudrillard, J. (1994). *Simularcra & simulation* (S. F. Glaser, Trans.). Ann Arbor, MI: The University of Michigan Press.

Bogard, W. (1996). *The simulation of surveillance: Hypercontrol in telematic societies.* Cambridge: Cambridge University Press.

Buchanan, I. (2009). Deleuze and the internet. In M. Poster & D. Savat (Eds.), *Deleuze and new technology* (pp. 143–161). Edinburgh: Edinburgh University Press.

Carlyle, T. [1829] (1984). Signs of the times. In G. B. Tennyson (Ed.), *A Carlyle reader: Selections from the writings of Thomas Carlyle* (pp. 31–55). Cambridge: Cambridge University Press.

Castells, M. (1996). *The rise of the network society.* Oxford: Blackwell Publishers.

Chesher, C. (1997). The ontology of digital domains. In D. Holmes (Ed.), *Virtual politics: Identity and community in cyberspace* (pp. 79–93). London: Sage.

Coyne, R. (1998). Cyberspace and Heidegger's pragmatics. *Information Technology & People, 11*(4), 338.

De Landa, M. (1991). *War in the age of intelligent machines.* New York: Zone Books.

Deleuze, G. (1992). Postscript on the societies of control. *October, 59,* 3–7.

Deleuze, G. (1993). *The fold: Leibniz and the baroque* (T. Conley, Trans.). Minneapolis, MN: University of Minnesota Press.

Deleuze, G. (1995). *Negotiations* (M. Joughin, Trans.). New York: Columbia University Press.

Deleuze, G., & Guattari, F. (1977). *Anti-Oedipus* (R. Hurley, M. Seem., & H. Lane, Trans.). Minneapolis, MN: University of Minnesota Press.

Der Derian, J. (2001). *Virtuous war: Mapping the military-industrial-media-entertainment-network.* Boulder, CO: Westview Press.

Foucault, M. (1979). *Discipline and punish: The birth of the prison* (A. Sheridan, Trans.). Harmondsworth: Penguin Books.

Giese, M. (1998). Self without body: Textual self-representation in an electronic community. *First Monday, 3*(4). Retrieved from http://firstmonday.dk/issues/issue3_4/giese/index.html

Guattari, F. (1992). Regimes, pathways, subjects. In J. Crary & S. Kwinter (Eds.), *Incorporations* (pp. 16–35). New York: Zone Books.

Guattari, F. (1993). Machinic heterogenesis (J. Creech, Trans.). In V. A. Conley (Ed.). *Rethinking technologies* (pp. 13–27). Minneapolis, MN: University of Minnesota Press.

Guattari, F. (1995). *Chaosmosis: An ethico-aesthetic paradigm* (P. Bains, & J. Pefanis, Trans.). Sydney: Power Publications.

Haraway, D. J. (1991). *Simians, cyborgs, and women: The reinvention of nature.* London: Free Association Books.

Haraway, D. J. (1995). Cyborgs and symbionts: Living together in the new world order. In C. H. Gray (Ed.), *The cyborg handbook*. New York: Routledge.

Hardt, M., & A. Negri. (2001). *Empire*. London: Harvard University Press.

Harvey, D. (1989). *The condition of postmodernity: An enquiry into the origins of cultural change*. Oxford: Basil Blackwell.

Hayles, K. N. (1993). The seductions of cyberspace. In V. A. Conley (Ed.), *Rethinking technologies* (pp. 173–190). Minneapolis, MN: University of Minnesota Press.

Heidegger, M. (1993). *Martin Heidegger: Basic writings* (D. Lovitt, Trans., D. F. Krell, Ed.). New York: HarperCollins Publishers.

Jameson, F. (1991). *Postmodernism, or, the cultural logic of late capitalism*. London: Verso.

Kirby, K. M. (1996). *Indifferent boundaries: Spatial concepts of human subjectivity*. New York: The Guildford Press.

Levy, P. (1998). *Becoming virtual* (R. Bononno, Trans.). New York: Plenum Trade.

Lyotard, F. (1984). *The postmodern condition: A report on knowledge* (G. Bennington & B. Massumi, Trans.). Minneapolis, MN: University of Minnesota Press.

Mansfield, N. (2000). *Subjectivity: Theories of the self from Freud to Haraway*. St Leonards: Allen & Unwin.

Marx, K. [1857] (1973). *Grundrisse: Foundations of the critique of political economy (rough draft)*. London: Penguin Books.

Marx, K. [1867] (1990). *Capital*. London: Penguin Books.

Mihalache, A. (2002). The cyber space-time continuum: Meaning and metaphor. *The Information Society, 18*(Check Proquest), 293–301.

Mumford, L. (1995). *The Lewis Mumford reader*. D. L. Miller (Ed.). Athens: The University of Georgia Press.

Nunes, M. (1997). What space is cyberspace? The internet and virtuality. In D. Holmes (Ed.), *Virtual politics: Identity and community in cyberspace* (pp. 163–179). London: Sage.

Poster, M. (1995). *The second media age*. Cambridge: Polity Press.

Poster, M. (2001a). *The information subject*. Amsteldijk: G + B Arts International.

Poster, M. (2001b). *What's the matter with the internet*. Minneapolis, MN: University of Minnesota Press.

Poster, M. (2002). Everyday (virtual) life. *New Literary History, 33*(4), 743–760.

Romanyshyn, R. D. (1989). *Technology as symptom and dream*. New York: Routledge.

Savat (2009). Deleuze's objectile: From discipline to modulation. In M. Poster & D. Savat (Eds.), *Deleuze and New Technology* (pp. 45–63). Edinburgh: Edinburgh University Press.

Schivelbusch, W. (1986). *The railway journey: The industrialization of time and space in the 19th century*. Leamington Spa: Berg.

Simkin, M. (2003). South Korea – Computer games. *Foreign correspondent*. Canberra: ABC. Broadcast August 19, 2003 [Where ABC refers to the Australian Broadcasting Corporation].

Smith, A. (1986). Technology, identity and the information machine. *Daedalus, 115*(3), 155–169.

Soja, E. W. (1989). *Postmodern geographies: The reassertion of space in critical social theory*. London: Verso.

Stone, A. R. (1995). Split subjects, not atoms; or, how I fell in love with my prosthesis. In C. H. Gray (Ed.), *The cyborg handbook*. New York: Routledge.

Stone, A. R. (2001). Will the real body please stand up? Boundary stories about virtual cultures. In D. Trend (Ed.), *Reading digital culture* (pp. 185–198). Oxford: Blackwell Publishers.

Turkle, S. (1995). *Life on the screen: Identity in the age of the internet*. New York: Simon & Schuster.

Virilio, P. (1986). *Speed and politics: An essay on dromology* (M. Polizzoti, Trans.). New York: Semiotext(e).

Virilio, P. (1991). *The lost dimension* (D. Moshenberg, Trans.). New York: Semiotext(e).

Virilio, P. (1995). *The art of the motor* (J. Rose, Trans.). Minneapolis, MN: University of Minnesota Press.

Virilio, P. (2001). Speed and information: Cyberspace alarm! In D. Trend (Ed.), *Reading digital culture*. Oxford: Blackwell Publishers.

Language Deterioration Revisited: The Extent and Function of English Content in a Swedish Chat Room

Malin Sveningsson Elm

Introduction

Ever since the internet first became familiar to ordinary people and to popular media, it has been surrounded by conflicts and moral panics. Even if the technology has been praised for the advantages it may bring to its users, it has also been accused of influencing its users in a variety of negative ways. For example, in Scandinavian media during the late 1990s and early 2000s, the internet was accused of influencing people's language style, and teachers especially were concerned by the way it might affect children's language use as well as their knowledge of the vernacular language (Hård af Segerstad, 2002; Kasesniemi & Rautiainen, 2002).

English has been called the *lingua franca* of the internet (Danet & Herring, 2003; Hansson & van de Bunt-Kokhuis, 2004), even though at least two-thirds of internet users are not native English speakers (Danet & Herring, 2007), and in a large number of internet arenas around the world, interaction is consequently managed through various other languages, in non-native English or in a mixture of both. One characteristic that (at least at the time of the language deterioration debates) distinguished non-Anglophone from Anglophone computer-mediated discourse was the mixture of languages, where English words were sometimes mixed into sentences and phrases written in the vernacular language (Hård af Segerstad, 2002). Apart from the general linguistic deterioration discussed in the media, the Swedish language was thus also claimed to become too influenced by English. Such discussions had arisen before, due to the increased consumption of media content in English, but the broader population's adoption of the internet gave fuel to the discussions, and new communication technologies, such as the internet, were put forth as a main reason of the linguistic deterioration. Thus, not only were there fears that users would lose their knowledge of proper Swedish grammar and spelling, there were also fears that vernacular languages would be colonized by English, and eventually even disappear (cf. Herring, 2002).

M. Sveningsson Elm (✉)
Department of Media and Communication Studies, Karlstad University,
Karlstad, Sweden
e-mail: malin.sveningsson@kau.se

J. Hunsinger et al. (eds.), *International Handbook of Internet Research*,
DOI 10.1007/978-1-4020-9789-8_27, © Springer Science+Business Media B.V. 2010

Several years have passed since these debates took place. The moral panic concerning the linguistic decadence has given place to other fears. However, the public discussions on the English influence on Swedish (and other languages) were never really finished. With the distance that looking in the rear view mirror gives us, we now have the opportunity to revisit the debate and see which arguments still seem to hold. This article will examine a corpus of Swedish computer-mediated discourse collected in the late 1990s to see (1) to what extent English content really occurred, (2) what type of content users chose to write in English, and (3) what functions it may have filled – i.e. how much, what and why.

Approaches to Linguistic Studies of Computer-Mediated Communication

One of the subjects that attracted the interest of researchers during the 1990s and early 2000s was how computer-mediated communication was altering the way we shape texts and how we actually *use* written language in order to communicate (Ferrara, Brunner, & Whittemore, 1991; Lee, 1996). An important part of the linguistic research on computer-mediated communication consequently attempted to explain the distinctive character of computer-mediated discourse (see, for example, Collot & Belmore, 1996; Lee, 1996; Werry, 1996; Yates, 1996). In the following sections, three different clusters of explanations for the linguistic peculiarities of computer-mediated discourse will be presented.

The first cluster of explanations focuses on the medium's technical properties. These explanations generally build on theories belonging to the "cues-filtered-out perspective", according to which computer-mediated communication was seen as suffering from an absence of regulating feedback and a reduction of cues concerning the status and position of the interlocutors, as well as of the surrounding context (for an overview of such theories, see Baym, 2006). In its early years, computer-mediated communication was therefore characterized as unsuitable for personal communication (Kiesler, Seigel, & McGuire, 1984).[1] When it became clear that a good deal of the computer-mediated communication contrary to the predictions was very personal, researchers instead claimed computer-mediated communicative styles to be characterized by a desire to *compensate for cues that were missing* compared to conversations held face to face, due to the constraints of the medium in terms of time, space and information on social context. Thus, we still deal with the notion that something was missing – the communication was incomplete, and it was the specific (technological) conditions of the medium that shaped the characteristics of computer-mediated communication. As Herring (2003) notes, this kind of research also tended to be quite technologically deterministic.

---

[1] However, such claims were criticized by researchers such as Walther (1992).

The second cluster deals with more contextual explanations that look at computer-mediated communication as representing various communicative genres, or registers, register being defined as "a variety of a language appropriate for a particular situation" (Ferrara et al., 1991: 11, referring to Reid, 1956). Sometimes the reason why a certain communication looks in a certain way is not found in the technology, but rather in what genre or register it belongs to. For example, many researchers, myself included, have concluded that, in general, the *asynchronous* computer-mediated communication is more similar to written communication, while the *synchronous* one resembles spoken discourse (Collot & Belmore, 1996; Ferrara et al., 1991; Rintel & Pittam, 1997; Sveningsson, 2001b; Werry, 1996; Yates, 1996). However, according to the second cluster of explanations, we also need to consider factors such as whom one is addressing; if messages are directed to one or several persons; and what relationships they have to each other – personal or professional. Messages will likely be stricter and more carefully phrased in professional contexts, where the message will be stored, and when intended for many readers, especially if one is not previously acquainted with them. The asynchronous internet media that were most often studied and taken as example were BBSs and Newsgroups, which in most cases focused on discussing or debating a given subject. The synchronous media that were studied, on the other hand, were above all MUDs and chats, whose purpose was mostly easy social interaction with friends or potential friends. Aspects like these might very well have biased our understanding of what various types of computer-mediated communication are typically like, and this is what the explanations of this cluster try to justify (see, for example, Baym, 1995, 2006; Ferrara et al., 1991; Sveningsson, 2001b, 2002b).

Finally, a third cluster of explanations acknowledged the importance of the group to online language styles (see, for example, Cherny, 1999; Ferrara et al., 1991; Paolillo, 1999; Sveningsson, 2001b, 2002b). The principal thought of this perspective is that individuals who are members of the same social world tend to develop shared perspectives and values. By their participation they come to share experiences related to the activity around which the social world circle. These experiences are categorized in particular ways, and to refer to such meanings, a special vocabulary or jargon is developed, which may differ from the standard language (Shibutani, 1955). In short, individuals who gather in a specific environment or around a shared activity and communicate with each other on a regular basis will create their own norms and conventions for language use. The groups in question may be based on online or offline relationships. Whichever the case, language style or jargon is an important group marker, allowing the members to distinguish between those who belong from those who do not belong to the group. Showing that one masters the jargon is thus one way to demonstrate one's status as an insider (Cherny, 1999; Sveningsson, 2001b, 2002b).

In this article, the three clusters will be called the "technology", "genre", and "group perspective". In a previous research, there has been an overweight in favour of the technology perspective. A fourth purpose of this study is thus also to evaluate the three perspectives and see which of them is best suited to explain the occurrence of English content in chat conversations held in Swedish.

Method

As stated in the introduction, this article will examine a corpus of Swedish computer-mediated discourse collected in the late 1990s to see to what extent English content really occurred, what type of content users chose to write in English and what functions it may have filled. The corpus analysed consists of 7 hours of observations from an all-Swedish chat room, the Cloudberry chat.[2]

The Cloudberry chat was created and managed by a private Swedish enthusiast, and it was located in Sweden. Nearly all the users were Swedes, and the language spoken Swedish. The chat room was relatively small: 1 hour of observation would typically include between 15 and 50 active users. It had no explicit target group or assigned topic of discussion, and its activity was recreational and aimed at social interaction. The ages that users claimed to be ranged from 15 to 45, the majority being between 18 and 35. According to the nicknames used, the gender distribution was quite even.

The data that the article is based on were collected on seven occasions, each corresponding to 1 hour. It is part of a larger material collected during ethnographic fieldwork in the chat room during the years 1997 through 1999 (see Sveningsson, 2001b).

The analysis was done in two steps. First, in a quantitative analysis, an overview was made over to what extent English words and phrases occurred in the corpus. In the second step, in order to find out what *types* of words and phrases were written in English, the postings with English content were categorized in a thematic analysis. Finally, by looking at the function the English content may have filled, and why it was posted, we evaluate the three perspectives discussed above and see which of them holds as explanation for the English content.

The Extent of English Words and Phrases

The corpus in total contained 4116 messages. Of these, 155 postings contained words or phrases in English. After discussions that were held entirely in English, and involving at least one non-Swedish-speaking person, were removed, the number of remaining postings is 123. As can be seen in Table 1, the frequency of English content varied between the observations.

One hour of observation contained at the least 8 and at the most 29 postings that included English words or phrases. The average percentage of messages with English content was 2.9% (3.8% before the conversations held entirely in English were removed). The English content that occurred was sometimes whole phrases

---

[2]In order to render some of the local colour of the chat room, the users' nicknames have not been changed. Therefore, the choice was made to not reveal the real name of the chat room, even though it is unlikely that any of the users quoted in this article would still be there, almost 10 years after the data were collected. For an extended discussion on research ethics, see Sveningsson (2001b, 2003).

Table 1 The extent of English words and phrases

Observation number	Total number of messages	Number of postings that contained words or phrases in English	Percentage of postings that contained words or phrases in English
1	306	11	3.6
2	537	26	4.8
3	579	18	1.8
4	546	8	1.5
5	746	9	1.2
6	780	29	3.7
7	622	22	3.5
All	4116	123 (155)	2.9 (3.8)

and sentences, but in most cases, it consisted of single words. The distribution looks as follows:

Postings with more than one sentence in English	7
Postings with one sentence in English	17
Postings with more than one word but less than one sentence in English	21
Postings with only one word in English	30

As the figures show, not only were the postings that included English language few, but they also contained very few words. Thus, the answer to the first question posed in this article is that the media seem to have exaggerated the internet's threat to the Swedish language, because the habit of mixing English words and phrases into conversations held in Swedish appears to not have been so widespread after all. Let us now proceed to the other questions posed in the introduction and take a look at what kind of English language was posted, what function it may have filled and what reasons users might have had to include it.

Type of Content Written in English

The 123 postings with English content were classified into 11 categories (see Table 2). The following sections will take a closer look at what kind of English words and expressions were used within the various categories and what function they may have filled.

Song Lyrics

The most frequent English content was song lyrics, which occurred in 26 postings. Here, users typically wrote a message where they claimed to be singing or listening to a specific artist or song, and then went on to quote the lyrics. In the excerpt below, as in the other excerpts throughout the article, the left paragraphs show the excerpt

Table 2 Type of content written in English

Category	Number of postings	Total number of words	Average number of words/posting
Song lyrics	26	215	8.3
Sign-offs/sign-ons	25	51	2.0
Greetings/parting words	16	28	1.8
Technical/internet jargon	13	21	1.6
Emoticons/written actions	11	15	1.4
Flirtations/equivocalities	5	31	6.2
Irony/sarcasm	5	13	2.6
"Swenglish"	2	2	1.0
Miscellaneous	19	26	1.4

in original, with the mixture of Swedish and English content, while the paragraphs to the right show the excerpts translated. The content that was written in English in the original appear in italics in the translation.

Kirby*sjunger lite Sinatra*	**Kirby***singing some Sinatra*
Kirby"I DID IT MY WAY…!"	**Kirby**"*I DID IT MY WAY…!*"

Quoting songs lyrics in chat rooms can be one way of demonstrating shared knowledge, and it often leads to further conversations about music taste and favourite artists (Sveningsson, 2001b). Apart from that, quoting from songs can also be a way for users to express their feelings while hiding behind someone else's words. Thus, this type of English content functions as a means of expression that lets users show their feelings without exposing themselves too much. Should anyone blame them for being overly affectionate or melodramatic, they could always say that "sure, the lyrics are sugary, but I really like that song". The habit of using song lyrics as a communicative resource is not constrained to computer-mediated communication but can be found in offline contexts as well, especially among teenagers. The answer to why this type of English content is posted thus probably lies within language styles as related to group culture, and can thus be explained by the group perspective as referred to above.

Interestingly, in the studied data, there were no occurrences of Swedish song lyrics. Thus, the theme "song lyrics" may also be related to the theme "flirt and equivocalness" below, where the habit of writing potentially embarrassing content in another language than one's mother tongue is interpreted as a face-saving strategy.

Sign-Ons and Sign-Offs

The second most frequent English content, occurring in 25 postings, was sign-ons and sign-offs. In the chat room studied, the software automatically signalled when users logged on by displaying a message stating the name of the user, followed by

"Entering...". This let the logged on users see all arriving participants. However, many users also added a more personal sign-on to the automated message:

Bushman: Entering...

Bushman:...coming from the mountains...

In the chat room studied, the habit of writing sign-ons was widespread as a way to greet others and to call their attention. As researchers have noted (Pargman, 2000; Sveningsson, 2001b; Werry, 1996), chat users often had to compete for others' attention, making efforts necessary to catch and keep conversational partners. Herein was one important purpose of sign-ons, which were often creative, well worked out and consciously elaborated. Sometimes the sign-on consisted of an explicit call for specific friends and acquaintances. In most cases where it occurred in English, however, it was written to accompany personal entrances, to make an imaginative appearance and frame a performance in front of others. The framing effect was enhanced by the fact that the frame was separated by the regular discussion, not only being marked by asterisks or other punctuation marks but also written in another language. The sign-ons were ideally consistent with the nickname and enhanced the impression given by the performance of the online persona. Hence, the sign-on could sometimes be part of role playing, or read as "stage directions", giving information about actions, looks, moods and thoughts (cf. emoticons below).

In the studied chat room, the software would not announce when users logged off, meaning that there was no way to know for sure whether a user had left the room or if s/he was still there. This led the users into the habit of signalling their departure by writing a sign-off. Sign-offs were related and quite similar to sign-ons, although they were typically not as elaborate, probably because the need to catch others' attention was smaller. Since the users were anyway leaving the chat room, they were not interested in getting new conversational partners. The sign-off should rather be seen as a courtesy to other users, to tell them that one was leaving, and, of course, as part of the general impression management (Goffman, 1959/1990).

The data exhibited 20 postings with sign-offs written in English. In some of the cases, the function was similar to the sign-ons described above, i.e. as part of the performance of the online persona, or as in the example below, to create a snappy string of words:

Scream: Scream is closing the screen!

However, the most frequent sign-off written in English was the single word "Gone", which occurred 13 times in the material. Lee (1996) and Severinsson Eklundh (1986) acknowledge a similarity between computer-mediated communication and telephone calls in uncertainty and misunderstandings about whether conversations should be considered finished or not. Writing sign-offs as their last messages could function as a way for users to minimise such uncertainty. This is an example of habits invented in order to eliminate inconveniences caused by the disembodiment of the communication medium and the reduced social presence (Short, Williams, & Christie, 1976). Thus, we here deal with explanations from technology perspective as referred to above.

However, the fact that users felt a need to fill in the voids caused by the technology does not explain why the word "gone" was written in English, instead of in Swedish. One possible explanation could be that when writing "gone", users tried to create the impression that it was the (English-designed) software that signalled their leaving the room. This conjecture is supported by the following examples of sign-offs, where users imitate information given by the technology, either in the form of a system message or in imitating the sound of hanging up a telephone:

Gizmo & gwen: ~COnnection Terminated~
Evelina:*click*

When sign-ons and sign-offs were used in the impression management, they can be seen as part of general chat room jargon (genre perspective) or group cultures (group perspective). However, when they were used to call or attention when entering, or to give information about leaving, they should rather be seen as caused by the technology (even if there are of course overlaps and group cultures direct how sign-ons and sign-offs actually look).

Greetings and Parting Words

Sixteen postings (eight postings each) contained greetings and parting words where words such as "hi", "hello", "howdy", "bye", "got to go" or "see you" were used instead of the Swedish equivalents. The greeting words, as well as the parting words, sometimes stood alone, but more often were inserted within sentences in Swedish:

Ericsson/36:Hello på Er...	**Ericsson/36**:*Hello* Everybody...
.·°^~mobius~^°·. of ~ACD~ :	.·°^~mobius~^°·. of ~ACD~ : *greetings*
greetings folket...	*people...*
Calor: Yo gott folk!	**Calor:** *Yo* folks!
Stenros: SadBoy>> Hej	**Stenros:** SadBoy>> *Howdy..long time no*
hopp..long time no see...	*see...*
Gizmo & gwen: Felixa1.. Höres..	**Gizmo & gwen**: Felixa1.. *See you..*
Bye!.. Hälsa ALLA på mötet	*Bye!.. Say hi to ALL in the meeting*
från oss 2.. =) ~oM du törs!~	*from us 2.. =) ~iF you dare!~*
Oskar:Nä stänger av den här	**Oskar**:No, I'll turn this crap off! *bye*
skiten! *bye*	
Elin 22:Sergey>>gotta go, men	**Elin 22**:Sergey>>*gotta go*, but if you're
om du är här om ca 10 min så	here in about 10 min I'll see you again.
hörs vi säkert. *kram*	*hug*
StarDust*: nä, jag ska flyta vidare	**StarDust***: no, am floating on......*see ya*
nu......see ya all!	*all!*
SNOBB:3-2-1	**SNOBB**:3-2-1
.....Kaaaaaabbbooommmmm::::....Sorry	.....Kaaaaaabbbooommmmm::::....*Sorry*
Time's up. Vi ses.	*Time's up.* See you.

The choice of an English word instead of a Swedish one may be something that users do not reflect on much, but which was nevertheless a choice made among various possible alternatives. Do English words convey other information and carry other connotations than the Swedish equivalents? Probably. Do they stand out as more cool? Sometimes, yes. The expression "long time no see" does undeniably sound more cosmopolitan than the more provincial "det var länge sen sist". However, jargon using English words and phrases is far from always considered urbane or cool. Middle-aged people who lard their speech with English words and phrases in order to sound up to date with the latest jargon, may, for example, find themselves sneered at. The use of a certain language style or jargon is often not accepted by everybody, but requires the right subcultural affiliation.

There was little variation as to what words and phrases were used in the greetings and parting words. This suggests that it was certain words in English that had become conventionalized in the chat room register (genre perspective). Here, Hård af Segerstad (2002) offers a possible explanation by pointing out that chat users were not isolated in separate chat rooms, but were often regular users of several different internet arenas. In other words, it is likely that experienced users had also tried out international chat rooms, where they acquired a chat jargon including English words, phrases, abbreviations and acronyms, which were brought to the users' national chat rooms. The use of certain words or expressions may also be connected to the jargon of specific groups, within or outside of the internet, to which users belonged. Explanations are thus also found in the group perspective.

Computer- and Internet-Related Terms

In 13 postings, computer- and internet-related words occurred, for example, "message", "private message", "mess", "msg", "IRL", "In Real Life" and "Cyberlove". In contrast to citizens of other Scandinavian countries, such as Norway and Iceland, Swedes have often adopted computer- or internet-related terms in their original, English form. Through the work of "datatermgruppen" (the computer terminology group), authorities tried to limit this influence by inventing and recommending Swedish translations, but users often found the recommended forms ridiculous and continued to use the English words. So, for example, even though the word "e-post" (e-mail), with the corresponding verb "e-posta", was recommended, most people preferred "e-mail" or simply "mail" with the corresponding verb "maila" or "mejla", and it is also these forms that have survived and are used today. The only concession is that the inflected forms follow Swedish patterns. Like the previous category, the reason why these words and phrases were used is probably to be found in an international chat or internet jargon (genre perspective) and the users' group cultures (group perspective).

Emoticons and Written Actions

Eleven postings included so-called *emoticons* written in English. The word "emoticon" is a compound of "emotive" and "icon" and has been described as combinations of graphical symbols used to provide paralinguistic information. They could, for example, be used to show the mood of the writer, or give clues as to how to interpret the written sentence. The use of emoticons has been seen as a strategy to compensate for the lack of non-verbal information (Lee, 1996; Ma, 1996). The original emoticons, or *smileys*, as they were also called, formed images and were used as shortcuts for describing physical expressions, for example, the smiling face :-), the frown :-(or the ironic, blinking smile or flirt ;-). Emoticons could also consist of written descriptions of actions, typically (although not always) within asterisks. Hård af Segerstad calls the latter "poor man's smileys", which could be used also by those lacking knowledge of the shorthand of the "real", image-forming smileys. But the reason for using the "written actions" type of emoticons was not always a question of lacking knowledge – they had some advantages over the image-forming ones. Describing entire actions within asterisks left more freedom of expression than simply inserting a graphical symbol. The written actions could, for example, express physical information: *smile*; physical actions: *hug*; or emphasis: "No, I'm *not* leaving" (Ma, 1996). More importantly, they could also be used to create more elaborate and creative make-believe scenarios, similar to improvized theatre, which were often used as a means of interaction and a shared fun activity in its own right (see, for example, Danet, Ruedenberg, & Rosenbaum-Tamari, 1998; Sveningsson, 2001b).

Most of the written actions that occurred in the data were written in Swedish, and only 11 ones in English. Furthermore, the English written actions did not exhibit much variety: it was typically certain words and phrases that occurred, for example, *bored* and *boring*, or *smile*, sometimes being abbreviated to a single *s*. When written actions occurred in English, the content was typically emotional. Thus, although the overall function of emoticons is said to be to compensate for missing physical and contextual cues (technology perspective), the reason why Swedish users wrote emoticons in English was rather that they were part of the chat room register (genre perspective) and a shared in-group language style that users had acquired as a result of their internet use (group perspective).

Flirt and Equivocalness

As mentioned above, messages or parts of messages could sometimes be written in English when the content was emotional or affective. This also holds for messages with flirtatious or equivocal content. The corpus included six such occasions. The habit of writing sensitive content in another language than one's mother tongue can sometimes be a way to decrease embarrassment – words are not charged with the same meaning and do not evoke the same connotations. Four-letter words uttered in another language than one's own are generally not experienced as equally shocking (at least not by the speaker), and messages with sentimental content blend into the conversation in a more subtle way. This may be the explanation why postings with emotional and equivocal content were written in English, i.e. as a shield to hide behind, and a face-saving strategy. In neither case is it exclusive for computer-mediated communication, but occurs in offline contexts as well, especially in young people's language styles (group perspective). In some cases, however, there may be other explanations:

PinkFloyd:snuttis ja upp och ned in och
  ut *skratt* låter förträffligt
PinkFloyd:yeeeeeeees och vi står på
  stranden och tittar på

PinkFloyd:snuttis[3] yes up and down and
  in and out *laugh* sounds excellent
PinkFloyd:*yeeeeeeees* and we stand on
  the beach, watching

In the excerpt above, the choice of English in the single word "yes" is probably not used to avoid embarrassment. The conversation, of which only a small part is quoted above, gradually gets more and more sexually explicit, without any other English words being used than the "yes" above. In spoken Swedish, the use of "yes!" instead of "ja" is sometimes a way of emphasizing the word, or it can be used in the meaning "hooray". The single word "yes" is also (inspired by Meg Ryan's performance in the film "When Harry met Sally") a more or less conventionalized way of representing an orgasm, and it is in this sense we should interpret the excerpt above. In this way, the simple "yeeeeeeees" actually has a similar function as the emoticon (see above), i.e. to compensate for missing cues, for example, intonation and tone of voice that would, in this specific case, probably be the main communicative resource to rely on, had the conversation been spoken instead of written. Thus there are also explanations from the technology perspective at play here.

Irony and Sarcasm

Five postings had ironic or sarcastic content. The ironic postings typically consisted of assertions which were immediately contradicted in English:

In spoken conversation, Swedish words or phrases like "säkert" (sure), "jo visst" (certainly) or "jo, tjena" (hello!) would normally be used to mark irony. However, when these words are used, they are pronounced with a clear emphasis and ironic intonation, which is necessary for the content to be understood as ironic. The fact that in the analysed data, the contradicting words are written in a language other than Swedish can be seen as an alternative way of highlighting the contradiction and to make the ironic distance clear in a text-only medium, where there is no intonation to rely on. Thus, even though the use of English to mark irony may sometimes be part of the language style of specific groups (group perspective),[4] the function can mainly be explained by the technology perspective, that is, the technical limitations of the medium.

---

[3]Snuttis is the nickname of a female user. It is a Swedish word that is sometimes used as a word of affection, like "sweetie", denoting something small and cute ("snutt" also means "snippet")

[4]The words "not" and "sure" are sometimes used to convey ironic distance to an assertion just made in spoken Swedish too.

Nr-Gizer: JOhanna: Du skulle bara veta
hur dom flyger på än när man drar av
sig tröjan... HÖHÖHÖHÖ!! *e tyvärr
lite blek just nu men iaf... ;) *
Nr-Gizer: *noooooooooooooooooot*
Johanna: *skrattar*
Nr-Gizer:Johanna: SLUTA skratta!! ...
se på mig... se på mig! E jag inte
söööt?
Johanna: Nr-Gizer: *skrattar* du är
knäpp! men rolig!
Nr-Gizer: Johanna: Hahahaha... yeah
sure... :) Inte lika qL iRL! Jo,
ibland... :) Men inte alltid... o andra
sidan e jag ju inte alltid qL här inne
heller lilla du ;)

Nr-Gizer: JOhanna: You should only know
how they toss themselves on me when I take
off my shirt... HEHEHEHE!! *i'm a little
pale at the moment but anyway... ;) *
Nr-Gizer: *noooooooooooooooooot*
Johanna: *laughs*
Nr-Gizer:Johanna: STOP laughing!! ... look
at me... look at me! Ain't I cuuute?

Johanna: Nr-Gizer: *laughs* you're nuts! But
funny!
Nr-Gizer: Johanna: Hahahaha... *yeah sure...*
:) Not as fun iRL! Well sometimes... :) But
not always... on the other hand I'm not
always fun here either dear;)

"Swenglish"

In two postings, words formed a mixture of Swedish and English. Both examples concern verbs translated into English, although retaining the inflected forms from the Swedish. Instead of writing "vi rings" (we'll call each other), one user wrote "vi bells". In the second example, a more common "swenglish" word was used: "joinar". The word "joina" is sometimes used in spoken Swedish as well (group perspective), another explanation is that the verb "join" is more convenient than the Swedish equivalent "ansluta sig till" or "göra sällskap", which require more keyboard strokes (technology perspective) and also sound more old-fashioned.

Miscellaneous

Twenty-six words, distributed in 19 postings, did not fit into any of the categories and were categorized as "miscellaneous". Within this category, there were three recurring strands: affirmations, negations and excuses, to which 16 of the words belonged. The remaining words that could not be categorized were Good luck: 1, Well: 1, Please: 1, Soft: 1, Good looking: 1, Number: 1 and Home alone: 1.

Many of these words, especially the affirmations, negations and excuses, are often used in spoken Swedish too. The word OK, for example, was incorporated into spoken Swedish (as well as into many other languages) long ago, and the prolongation of OK, "okidoki", is quite common too, as are "peace", "sorry" and "oops". As for some of the other words, writing them in English may give them another colour. "Yep" and "nope", for example, sound more snappy and colloquial than "ja" (yes) and "nej" (no). The words "japp", "yup", "jäpp" and "yep" are basically the same words, although spelled in different ways. But why were they written in English instead of Swedish? As a matter of fact, the English spellings were not preferred to the Swedish ones. The Swedish spellings "japp", "jäpp" or "jepp" by far outnumber the English ones "yup" or "yep" (37 compared to 1), and the Swedish negations "nix" and "näpp" occurred more often than the English ones "no" and "nope" (12 compared to 4 times). As we see, the examples in this group of left-over phrasings had different functions, but mainly relate to the group culture perspective.

Discussion

As Herring (2003) notes, societies tend to be more sensitive to technological impacts in the early days of a new medium than at later stages of adoption and use. Thus, she continues, each new technology has been greeted with predictions of revolutionary changes in communication patterns. By the turn of the century, Swedish language, as well as the languages of many other small countries, was believed to become too influenced by English, largely due to the citizens' internet use. This article suggests that these fears may have been exaggerated, at least as concerns chat room conversations. When conversations involving non-Swedish-speaking persons were removed from the data, the proportion of English words used in Swedish conversations was in fact quite low: 123 out of 4116 postings, or 2.9%, contained one or more English words. If song lyrics were to be left out, this percentage would further diminish.

Moreover, the English words and phrases that occurred were of certain kinds and the use of English fulfilled certain functions:

- Some English words and expressions were used to refer to certain technical aspects of the medium or represented international internet jargon. As such, they would be more or less *conventionalized items* of chat room jargon.
- Messages with emotional or erotic content were sometimes written in English as a *face-saving strategy* – to decrease embarrassment while still expressing feelings or desires.
- Using English could serve as a way to draw attention to and *emphasize* irony and sarcasm, which would in offline contexts have been done by facial expression or intonation.
- Writing emoticons, sign-ons, sign-offs, greetings and parting words in English instead of Swedish was also a way *to frame messages*: to distinguish between messages coming from one's own online persona from meta-communication or to create messages that users felt should have been given by the system.
- The English content was also used in the *impression management* of users' online personas or to *support* the meaning of a message written in Swedish, rather than being part of regular conversation.

My conclusion is therefore that at least in the chat room studied, English words and phrases should not be seen as replacing or competing with Swedish vocabulary, but complementing it, being a communicative resource that in many ways filled the same function as emoticons did. In other words, the habit of blending English words into Swedish conversations was never a threat to the vernacular language, but a resource used to increase the means of expression.

While many attempts at explaining the characteristics of computer-mediated communication have focused on the technical properties of the medium, as this article has shown, explanations of why English content was mixed into Swedish conversations can be found in all three perspectives, albeit with an overweight in favour of the group perspective, which occurs twice as often as the other two (eight times compared to four each). Hence, to the extent language deterioration really took place, it seems to not have been the technology that caused it, but rather the group of people who used the technology.

The analysed data in this article were collected almost 10 years ago, and the internet landscape has changed quite a lot since then. The internet has been found to favour large languages, especially English (Paolillo, 2007), and in some internet genres, the use of English has accelerated throughout the years (Durham, 2007). In 2002, more than 70% of all web pages were found to be in English (Paolillo, 2007, referring to O'Neill, Lavoie, & Bennet, 2003).[5] However, in personal computer-mediated communication held in Swedish, the habit of inserting single words and phrases in English seems to have decreased or even disappeared. A quick and unsystematic survey of various Swedish internet arenas today indicates that not much English language content prevails, nor are smileys or emoticons used much. It should be noted that it is hard to prove that the genre has really changed, because of the lack of an equivalent contemporary corpus with which to compare it. Today, public chat rooms are hardly used at all except as part of dating sites, which have a clear agenda and target group, in contrast to the chat rooms that were popular in the mid-1990s, which were appreciated by their users just because of their ostensible lack of an explicit goal other than socializing (Sveningsson, 2001b, 2002a). If we seek for online arenas where the young people of today go in order to socialize, we will have to direct our attention to social network sites and community portals, where the content looks quite different for reasons related to technology, genre and group culture. Still, given the fact that I found the insertion of English content into Swedish conversations to be a communicative resource comparable to emoticons, I find the lack of it in contemporary internet arenas very interesting. It suggests that in the early days of the internet, there was a need for smileys and other strategies to clarify and enrich the communication, and this need has now decreased. One possible explanation of this is that today's internet arenas, with their increased bandwidth, allow for more social presence than could be given at that time. But this is likely not the whole truth, because even in those internet fora which look exactly the same as then (e.g. mailing lists), the use of emoticons and other strategies to compensate for missing cues seems to have decreased. This suggests that the shortcomings of the

---

[5]The reason why the figures are so high is probably that public web pages in smaller languages are translated into other languages that foreign interested parties would understand, in most cases English. Most universities, for example, have duplicates in English (Callahan & Herring, 2007). If one should only count independent web pages, which are not translations of other web pages, the figures would probably be less extreme.

technology were never really the only or even the most important reason why smileys and other contextualizing cues occurred in the first place, because there never *was* a real need of it. We are instead faced with two other possible explanations.

First, users may have *experienced* a need of contextualizing information, because the medium was still new and unfamiliar. As Baron (2008) notes, this is not unique for computer-mediated communication, and other media too (e.g. the telephone) were subject to similar uncertainties in their early days. As time went by and people got used to the medium, the number of strategies to deal with uncertainty became superfluous.

Second, users may just have wanted to adopt the specific language style or jargon of experienced internet users. Thereby, we are approaching the group perspective. Using internet jargon was one way of signalling that one belonged to the group of people that used and knew something about the internet. Throughout the 1990s, at least in Sweden, this was something that conveyed status. Knowledge about computers and the internet was associated with ideas of power and agency, which can be seen not only in popular media's representations of hackers at that time but also in ordinary people's representations of the internet and its users (Sveningsson, 2001a): the 1990s was the time when the "geek" unexpectedly became possible as part of a hegemonic masculinity. Moreover, the internet had an image of being cool and youthful, and some of this image was transferred to those who mastered the jargon. Finally, using jargon was a way to demonstrate one's group membership in specific online arenas. Cues that demonstrate knowledge about technology today are probably different and so is the type of technology that is seen as desirable to master. In the Western world of today, basic knowledge and use of the internet is so self-evident so it does not need to be demonstrated – this would rather instead give the user away as being a newbie. What was once seen as internet jargon has also become incorporated in mainstream language. Furthermore, the internet is no longer seen as a symbol of the youthful and modern, and other media, such as, for example, computer games, have taken this role.

Revisiting data in the way being done in this article gives an opportunity to re-evaluate previously given explanations and see which of them still seem to hold. In my opinion, there has often been a too marked focus on the technological conditions of internet media as explanations for linguistic peculiarities. At least for the data examined in this article, this explanation is not enough – had there been a real need to compensate for the limitations of the technology, the language style would have looked roughly the same today. Possibly, the early users may have *experienced* such a need. However, more important, although often overlooked, explanations deal with genres and with group identity. The habit of blending English words into Swedish conversations, as well as using emoticons and written actions, was part of the internet jargon, and using this jargon was one way to signal that one was part of the group of experienced internet users, who were in the know, cool and modern. The conditions upon which both these latter explanations build have changed: users no longer experience the same need to compensate for uncertainty in the medium, nor does internet jargon convey status. Which of the explanations is the most adequate is uncertain – probably both have their raison d'être.

References

Baron, N. (2008). *Always on: Language in an online and mobile world*. New York: Oxford University Press.

Baym, N. (1995). The emergence of community in computer-mediated communication. In S. Jones (Ed.), *Cybersociety: Computer-mediated communication and community* (pp. 138–163). Thousand Oaks, CA: Sage.

Baym, N. (2006). Interpersonal life online. In L. A. Lievrouw & S. Livingstone (Eds.), *The handbook of new media* (Updated Student Edition, pp. 35–54). London: Sage.

Callahan, E., & Herring, S. (2007). *Multilingual websites: Language choice, audience, and international identity*. Paper presented at the Internet Research 8.0: Let's Play. International and interdisciplinary conference of the Association of Internet Researchers.

Cherny, L. (1999). *Conversation and community. Chat in a virtual world*. Stanford, CA: CSLI Publications.

Collot, M., & Belmore, N. (1996). Electronic language: A new variety of English. In S. Herring (Ed.), *Computer-mediated communication. Linguistic, social and cross-cultural perspectives* (pp. 13–28). Amsterdam: John Benjamins Publishing Company.

Danet, B., & Herring, S. (2003). Introduction: The multilingual internet. *Journal of Computer-Mediated Communication, 9*(1). Retrieved from http://jcmc.indiana.edu/vol9/issue1/ho.html

Danet, B., & Herring, S. (2007). *The multilingual internet. Languages, cultures, and communication online*. Oxford: Oxford University Press.

Danet, B., Ruedenberg, L., & Rosenbaum-Tamari, Y. (1998). Hmmm ... where is that smoke coming from? Writing play and performance on internet relay chat. In F. Sudweeks, M. McLaughlin, & S. Rafaeli (Eds.), *Network and netplay. Virtual groups on the internet* (pp. 41–76). Menlo Park, CA: AAAI Press/The MIT Press.

Durham, M. (2007). Language choice on a Swiss mailing list. In B. Danet & S. Herring (Eds.), *The multilingual internet. Languages, cultures, and communication online*. Oxford: Oxford University Press.

Ferrara, K., Brunner, H., & Whittemore, G. (1991). Interactive written discourse as an emergent register. *Written Communication, 8*(1), 8–34.

Goffman, E. (1959/1990). *The presentation of self in everyday life*. London: Penguin Books.

Hansson, H., & van de Bunt-Kokhuis, S. (2004). E-learning and language change – Observations, tendencies and reflections. *First Monday, 9*(8). Retrieved from http://www.firstmonday.org/issues/issue9_8/hansson/index.html

Hård af Segerstad, Y. (2002). *Use and adaptation of written language to the conditions of computer-mediated communication*. Göteborg: Department of Linguistics, Göteborg University.

Herring, S. (2002). *The language of the internet: English dominance or heteroglossia? Keynote presentation*. Paper presented at the CATaC'02. Third international conference on cultural attitudes towards technology and communication.

Herring, S. (2003). Media and language change. *Journal of Historical Pragmatics, 4*(1), 1–17.

Kasesniemi, E.-L., & Rautiainen, P. (2002). Mobile culture of children and teenagers in Finland. In J. E. Kartz & M. Aakhus. (Ed.), *Perceptual contact – Mobile communication, private talk, public performance* (pp. 170–192). Cambridge: Cambridge University Press.

Kiesler, S., Seigel, J., & McGuire, T. W. (1984). Social and psychological aspects of computermediated communication. *American Psychologist, 39*(10), 1123–1134.

Lee, J. Y. (1996). Charting the codes of cyberspace: A rhetoric of electronic mail. In L. Strate, R. Jacobsen, & S. B. Gibson (Ed.), *Communication and cyberspace: Social interaction in an electronic environment*. Cresskill, NJ: Hampton Press.

Ma, R. (1996). Computer-mediated conversations as a new dimension of intercultural communication between East Asian and North American College Students. In S. Herring (Ed.), *Computer-mediated communication. Linguistic, social and cross-cultural perspectives* (pp. 173–185). Amsterdam: John Benjamins Publishing Company.

O'Neill, E. T., Lavoie, B. F., & Bennet, R. (2003). Trends in the evolution of the public web: 1998–2002. *D-Lib Magazine, 9*(4).

Paolillo, J. (1999). The virtual speech community: Social network and language variation on IRC [Electronic Version]. *Journal of Computer-Mediated Communication, 4,* from http://www.ascusc.org/jcmc/vol4/issue4/paolillo.html

Paolillo, J. (2007). How much multilingualism? Language diversity on the internet. In B. Danet & S. Herring (Eds.), *The multilingual internet. Languages, cultures and communication online* (pp. 408–430). Oxford: Oxford University Press.

Pargman, D. (2000). *Code begets community. On social and technical aspects of managing a virtual community* (p. 224). Linköping: Linköping Studies in Arts and Science.

Reid, T. B. W. (1956). Linguistics, structuralism and philology. *Archivum Linguisticum, 8,* 28–37.

Rintel, E. S., & Pittam, J. (1997). Strangers in a strange land. Interaction management on internet relay chat. *Human Communication Research, 23*(4).

Severinson Eklundh, K. (1986). *Dialogue processes in computer-mediated communication. A study of letters in the COM system* (p. 6). Linköping: Linköping Studies in Arts and Science.

Shibutani, T. (1955). Reference groups as perspectives. *American Journal of Sociology, 60*(6), 522–529.

Short, J. A., Williams, E., & Christie, B. (1976). *The social psychology of telecommunications.* New York: John Wiley & Sons.

Sveningsson, M. (2001a). An antisocial way to meet. Social representations of the internet. In M. Chaib (Ed.), *Perspectives on computer interactions – A multidisciplinary reader* (pp. 72–107). Lund: Studentlitteratur.

Sveningsson, M. (2001b). *Creating a sense of community. Experiences from a Swedish web chat.* Linköping: Linköping Studies in Art and Science.

Sveningsson, M. (2002a). Cyberlove. Creating romantic relationships on the net. In J. Fornäs, K. Klein, M. Ladendorf, J. Sundén, & M. Sveningsson (Eds.), *Digital borderlands: Cultural studies of identity and interactivity on the internet* (pp. 79–111). Amherst: Peter Lang.

Sveningsson, M. (2002b). Samtal och samtalsstilar på Internet. In P. Dahlgren (Ed.), *Internet, medier och kommunikation* (pp. 89–120). Lund: Studentlitteratur.

Sveningsson, M. (2003). Ethics in internet ethnography. In E. A. Buchanan (Ed.), *Virtual research ethics: Issues and controversies* (pp. 45–61). Hershey: Idea Group Publishing.

Walther, J. B. (1992). Interpersonal effects in computer-mediated communication: A relational perspective. *Communication Research, 19*(1), 52–90.

Werry, C. C. (1996). Linguistic and interactional features of internet relay chat. In S. Herring (Ed.), *Computer-mediated communication. linguistic, social and cross-cultural perspectives* (pp. 47–64). Amsterdam: John Benjamins Publishing Company.

Yates, S. J. (1996). Oral and written aspects of computer conferencing. In S. Herring (Ed.), *Computer-mediated communication. Linguistic, social and cross-cultural perspectives* (pp. 29–46). Amsterdam: John Benjamins Publishing Company.

Visual Communication in Web Design – Analyzing Visual Communication in Web Design

Lisbeth Thorlacius

Introduction

The model introduced in this article is based on Roman Jakobson's communication model *figure* 2. which focuses on the linguistic aspects of communication. Jakobson's model has been expanded and adapted so that it is applicable to visual communication in terms of the pictorial and graphical aspects of web design by drawing on insights from semiotics, art history, communication theory, and graphic design.

The practical use of the model will be demonstrated on two websites: Jakob Nielsen and Donald A. Norman's website www.nngroup.com and Walter Van Beirendonck's website www.waltervanbeirendonck.com.

Roman Jakobson's Model of Linguistic Communication

Jakobson's communication model consists of six communication factors, which cover the most important aspects of the communication situation: *addresser, addressee, context, message, contact,* and *code.* However, Roman Jakobson's main contribution with this model was to display the six language functions, which each relates to one of the communication factors: the *emotive,* the *conative,* the *referential,* the *poetic,* the *phatic,* and the *metalingual* functions. One of Jakobson's most important tasks with this model was to describe the poetic function, which is characteristic of poetic texts. The six factors and language functions are illustrated in Fig. 1 (Jakobson, 1960, pp. 353–357).[1]

L. Thorlacius (✉)
Institute of Communications, Business and Information Technologies,
Roskilde University, Roskilde, Denmark
e-mail: lisbetht@ruc.dk

[1]In this illustration I have combined the communication factors and the language functions, although it is not a direct copy of the model as it is presented in Jakobson's article "Linguistics and Poetics" from 1960, where Jakobson kept the factors and the language functions in separate illustrations.

J. Hunsinger et al. (eds.), *International Handbook of Internet Research,*
DOI 10.1007/978-1-4020-9789-8_28, © Springer Science+Business Media B.V. 2010

CONTEXT
(REFERENTIAL FUNCTION)

ADDRESSER   **MESSAGE**   **ADDRESSEE**
(EMOTIVE FUNCTION)   (POETIC FUNCTION)   (CONATIVE FUNCTION)

CONTACT
(PHATIC FUNCTION)

CODE
(METALINGUAL FUNCTION)

Fig. 1. Jakobson's communication model

Each of these six functions determines a different function of language. It is important to stress that the language functions, according to Jakobson, do not adhere to any order of precedence. Jakobson states that any linguistic message will contain more than one of the language functions, but one of the functions might be dominant and the remaining functions might play a minor role in the analysis of the linguistic message (Jakobson, 1960, p. 353). This principle also applies to the model of visual communication presented here.

A Model of Visual Communication Focusing on Web Design

Whereas Roman Jakobson was concerned with language functions, this model focuses on communication functions in regard to visual communication. Further-more, the model does not just cover the content that can be analyzed directly from the product itself (as Jakobson's model does). Since my model draws on pragmatic semiotics, I have also added the communication factor *addresser's intention*, which is an interview-based analysis of addresser that takes place outside of the product. The results of an analysis of addresser's intention might not match the results of an analysis of the expressive function, i.e., an analysis of addresser as he appears within the product. Likewise, I have added the communication factor, the *reception of the addressee*, which implies a reception analysis of the addressee's individual experi-ence with the product. This analysis is based on the addressee's actual perception and takes place outside the product. Such analyses could disclose whether the inten-tions of the addresser are in accordance with the actual reception of the addressee. In this article, however, I have chosen not to include guidelines for how to complete an examination of the addresser's intentions or the addressee's perception.

Furthermore, internet-specific aspects in terms of the navigational and the inter-active aspects that are relevant for websites have been taken into consideration in the model.

As is shown in Fig. 2, my model consists of the same six factors as Jakobson's model, although I have replaced the *emotive* function with the term *expressive* function and the factors *message* and *contact* with the terms *product* and *medium*,

CONTEXT
The referential
function and the
intertextual
function

THE ACTUAL ADDRESSER	THE IMPLICIT ADDRESSER	PRODUCT	THE IMPLICIT ADDRESSEE	THE ACTUAL ADDRESSEE
An analysis of the actual intentions of the addresser. The emotive function	The expressive function	The formal aesthetic function and the sublime aesthetic function	The conative function and the interactive function	An analysis of the reception of addressee. The emotive function

MEDIUM
The phatic
function and the
navigative
function

CODE
The
metacommunica
tive function
and the
intersemiotic
function

Fig. 2. A model of visual communication in web design

respectively. I have also replaced Jakobson's language functions with communication functions and I have added several communication functions that aid in analyzing the visual- and internet-specific aspects of a website. This article will focus on the communication functions within the structure of the model, that is, the communication functions that can be exposed by direct analysis of the product itself.

In the following, I will discuss each of the communication functions that are presented in the model.[2]

---

[2]For a more thorough insight into the model and the theoretical reflections behind the interpretation of Roman Jakobson's model, see my Ph.D. dissertation: *Model til analyse af lexi-visual, æstetisk kommunikation - med et særligt henblik på websites. (A model for the analysis of lexi-visual, aesthetic communication – focusing on Web sites). Part I and II, Roskilde University 2001.* This text is unfortunately not translated into English.

The Addresser

The first factor in the model is the *addresser*, i.e., the person or the persons who are responsible for what is being communicated on the website. The model distinguishes between the *implicit* and the *actual* addresser. The implicit addresser can be analyzed directly out of the website by focusing on the feelings, opinions, etc., that are expressed in the website through visible means. The actual addresser is the addresser outside the product, whom we would have to consult or interview in order to examine the real intentions behind the website. *The expressive function* is related to the implicit addresser. According to Jakobson, the emotive function or expressive function is focused on the addresser and aims at direct expression of the speaker's attitude toward what he is speaking about (Jakobson, 1960, p. 354). The expressive function covers the feelings, opinions, etc., that the addresser expresses in the product, and we can directly analyze this aspect in the product regardless of whether the addresser is conscious of these sentiments or not. This function is only related to the addresser, in other words we are only concerned with analyzing how the addresser appears in the product through the visual means of effect, such as colors, lighting effects, illustrations, typography, movements, etc. Jakobson did not distinguish between the emotive and expressive functions. I find, however, in accordance with Ogden and Richards that there is a difference between the two terms, because the emotive function concerns both the addresser and the addressee, which makes it difficult to apply it only to the addresser. According to Ogden and Richards, the emotive function includes the expression of emotions, attitudes, moods, intentions, etc., in the speaker as well as in the communication, i.e., the evocation in the listener (Ogden & Richards, 1969, pp. 149–150). In my model, *the emotive function* is connected to both the actual addresser and the actual addressee and can only be identified by carrying out an analysis of the addresser and the addressee.

The Expressive Function in www.nngroup.com and www.waltervanbeirendonck.com

In the following, I will present a comparative analysis of the expressive function of the website of Jakob Nielsen and Donald A. Norman and the website of Walter Van Beirendonck. I have chosen these two different sites in order to demonstrate all the functions of the model and how the dominance and relevance of the functions vary in different websites. Both sites are examples of representation sites, because the main purpose of each site is to introduce the addresser to the user (addressee). Websites within the genre of representation sites are supposed to represent and mirror the addresser and supply the interested users with relevant pieces of information. Visiting the site should be a pleasant experience for the user comparable to when we meet new people, where the visual, the verbal, and the nonverbal appearances play an important role in regard to the impression we get of each other.

In terms of style the two sites fall into very different categories. Www. nngroup.com combines two different styles: *the HTMinimaLism* and *the modernistic style.* The genre *HTMinimaLism* or *engineer-based hyper-functionalism* includes websites where the ideal is a simple design with traces back to the mid-1990s where Jakob Nielsen introduced the slogan "Less is More," a phrase that he borrowed from the modernist architect Mies van der Rohe (Engholm, 2003, p. 127). Engineer-based hyper-functionalism is a genre within Web design where the technical aspects, functionality, and user friendliness as well as content are in focus and the aesthetic dimension is subdued. The most important goal of the websites in this genre is that the user easily and quickly is able to find the desired pieces of information. The main task is an efficient, clear, and undisturbed communication with quick downloads (Engholm, 2003, p. 62).[3] However, www.nngroup.com also adheres to the modernistic style where the focus is on tight design, a layout with plenty of white space, subdued monochrome and controlled colors, sans serif print types, and well-planned aesthetical details.

Www.waltervanbeirendonck.com, on the other hand, is an *avant-garde site* or *designer site* where a series of stylistic experiments typically will be taking place. Www.waltervanbeirendonck.com also falls into the genre of *branding sites,* where aesthetic experiences are highly prioritized. For branding sites, the most important aspect is that the user has great experiences when visiting the site. The main goal of a branding site is to create an aura around the content by branding the addresser through stories and positive experiences, which the user will associate with the products. The aesthetic experiences are as important as the content.

The first impression one gets when entering www.nngroup.com, Illustration 1, is a tight design, open layout, subdued monochrome and controlled colors, the *Verdana* sans serif print type, and well-planned aesthetic details in accordance with the modernistic ideals within web design. The Verdana print type has been proclaimed to be the most easily read print type on the screen and is an example of a visual element that supports functionalism in www.nngroup.com. The bar on the top of the page is in a warm red color, which matches the red color in the logo and complements the light blue colors in the menu bar and data box. The links are accentuated in darker nuances of blue and purple. The white background and light blue color leave a fresh and clean impression, but on the other hand they also reflect coldness. However, the color blue contributes to establishing an *ethos* appeal, because the color blue conventionally refers to reliability, credibility, and authenticity. The red colors, however, and the picture at the bottom of the page depicting three smiling gentlemen accompanied by the text *Jakob, Don, Tog* counterbalance the cold and clinical aspects

---

[3]In terms of discussing genre and style in web design, I am indebted to the design researcher Ida Engholm and her Ph.D. dissertation from 2003. Her dissertation *WWW's designhistorie - website udviklingen i et genre- og stilteoretisk perspektiv* (*WWW's design history – the development of websites in a genre- and style theoretical perspective*) [my translation] is unfortunately not translated into English. Moreover, David Siegel's *Creating Killer Web Sites (1996),* and Curt Cloninger's *Fresh Styles for Web Designers* (2002) are inspirational reading in regard to style and genre in web design.

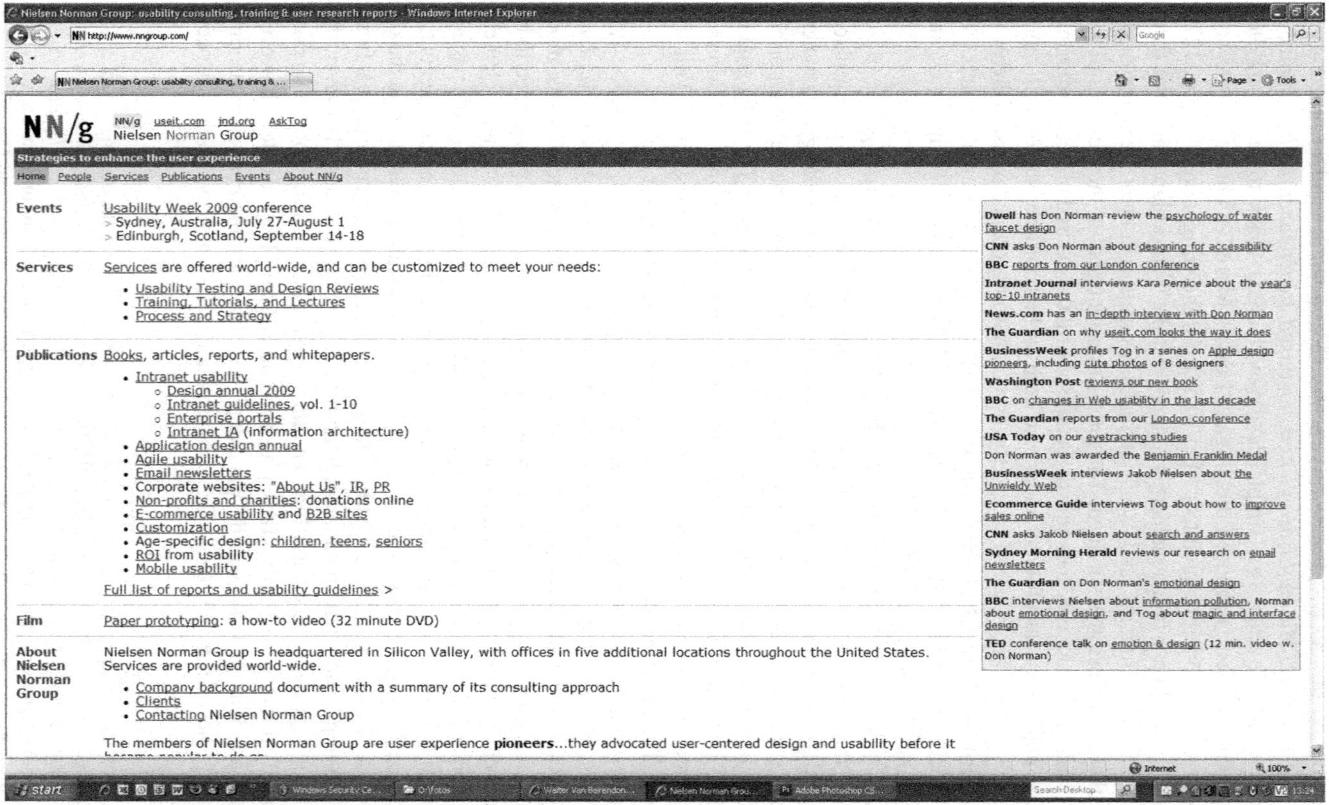

Illustration 1 Entrance page to www.nngroup.com

of the visual impression. As a whole the page appears well-organized reflecting professionalism and quality. The site appears fairly mainstream within the genre of modernistic web design and does not reflect a great deal of personality on the behalf of the addresser. However, it will appeal to the customer who wants quality and professional services primarily adhering to the modernistic taste where the experience-oriented aspects are inferior to the functional and user-friendly aspects. Considering that Nielsen Norman Group's main services are designing websites with the emphasis on human–computer interaction and usability testing, the site is very successful.

In contrast to http://www.nngroup.com, www.waltervanbeirendonck.com is an example of an experience-oriented site where the emphasis is on the aesthetic effects. The first thing that meets the eye when entering the site is an explosion of colors and we become aware, right away, that we have entered a site of an addresser with a strong and unique personality. The screen is filled with 24 pictogram-like men in bright colors and a bright red headline in large bold letters in the print type *Arial,* Illustration 2. Arial is not the most easily read print types on the screen, reflecting an addresser who prioritizes the aesthetic aspects to the functionalistic aspects in web design.

When you enter the page *projects,* Illustration 3, you are met with the car Nissan Micra, which is one of Walter Van Beirendonck's design projects. When you click on the car, which serves as a link, you enter a page where the car drives back and forth in unpredictable manners. When leaving Walter Van Beirendonck's website you feel you have been introduced into a new universe filled with stories and aesthetic experiences. To a young group of trendsetters and early adopters within clothing fashion, who share a lifestyle appreciating new and innovative aesthetic designs, a visit to www.waltervanbeirendonck.com will be a great source of inspiration. To this audience the site reflects a credible addresser who is orientated toward the avant-garde genres within web design.

The purpose of this analysis has been to uncover the addresser's personality, i.e., *the expressive function* as it appears on the website. The addresser's actual intentions would only be revealed by interviewing the addresser.

The Addressee

In every communication model there is an *addressee,* whom the addresser wishes to affect with his communication efforts. In this model there is a distinction between the implicit addressee and the actual addressee. The implicit addressee is the imagined addressee, who can be identified through an analysis of how the addressee appears on the website. However, the actual addressee is the addressee who actually experiences the product. Whether the addressee has been affected in any way by the addresser's sentiments (i.e., *the emotive function*) can only be determined by carrying out a reception analysis. However, in this article I have only focused on the implicit addressee; in other words I have not included a reception analysis that reveals how the actual addressee experiences the websites.

Illustration 2 Entrance page to www.waltervanbeirendonck.com

Illustration 3 Projects: sub page in www.waltervanbeirendonck.com

The communication functions that relate to the addressee and can be analyzed directly from the website are *the conative* and *the interactive functions*.[4] According to Jakobson, the conative function is an orientation toward the addressee and finds its purest grammatical expression in vocative and imperative sentence structures with the intent of affecting the behavior or the will of the addressee (Jakobson, 1960, p. 355). The conative function appears when the addresser uses a sentence such as "Fill out the form below and we will mail you a catalogue." An example of a visual conative communication function in web design is when appealing pictures are used as links in order to evoke the curiosity of the addressee to find out what the link reveals when clicking on it. In order to meet the specific needs of web design, I have included five communication designs in relation to the addressee: one non-interactive and four interactive designs. These communication designs are based on Jens F. Jensen's four communication patterns (Jensen, 1997, p. 41).[5] I have added a fifth design, *the transactive design,* to my model as I found it was lacking in Jensen's model (introduced further below). The model of the five communication designs is shown in Fig. 3.

(1) *The transmission design* is the only one of the five communication designs that is characterized by its non-interactive and one-way approach, such as, for example, when we watch a movie sequence on a website.
(2) *The conversation design* is encountered when e-mailing or chatting on the internet.
(3) *The consultation design* is taking place when a mutual exchange of information takes place. This is the case, for example, when the user types a request for

	Information/products Produced by the sender	Information produced by the user
The distribution controlled by the sender	1)**Transmission** *One-way communication* *Non-interactive design*	5)**Registration** *Two-way communication* *Interactive design*
The distribution controlled by the user	3)**Consultation** 4)**Transaction** *Two-way communication* *Interactive design*	2) **Conversation** *Two-way communication* *Interactive design*

Fig. 3. Five communication designs

---

[4]It is important to notice that the term *interaction* in this context refers to the physical interaction between the user and the machine and not to mental or interpersonal interaction, such as the addressee's personal construction of meaning when exposed to the media product.

[5]Jens F. Jensen's model is based on Jan L. Bordewijk and Ben van Kaam's matrix of the four communication patterns: allocution, conversation, consultation, and registration (Bordewijk & Kaam, 1986, p. 19). However, Jensen has updated the model by incorporating the interactivity aspect, which makes the model particularly suited to the analysis of visual communication on websites.

information into the computer and the computer responds with an answer to this request.

(4) *The transaction design* covers the interaction that takes place in connection with shopping on the internet. The transaction design differs from the consultation design because a mutual trade is taking place, i.e., the addresser and the web user both receive something. This is in contrast to the consultation design where it is exclusively the user who receives something.

(5) *The registration design* is employed when, for example, the web user fills out an application form which supplies the addresser with pieces of information from or about the web user.

The five communication designs will not be unfolded in regard to the two websites in this article. However, a more elaborate discussion of Bordewijk and Kaam's four communication patterns allocution, conversation, consultation, and registration can be found in the article "Towards a New Classification of Tele-information Services" (Bordewijk & Kaam, 1986, p. 19).

The Conative Function in www.nngroup.com and www.waltervanbeirendonck.com

On www.nngroup.com the conative function appears every time we encounter search buttons with linguistic invitations to click on the button. For example, on the front page of www.nngroup.com there is a link that says "Ask Tog," which is a direct invitation to act. There are very few examples of conative functions by the means of visual elements on www.nngroup.com. The textual links accentuated in blue are, however, examples of visual conative functions, because they are easily recognized and distinguishable from the rest of the text and invite to be clicked on. On www.waltervanbeirendonck.com we are, on the other hand, met with several examples of visual conative functions. For example on the page *Projects*, Illustration 3, all the illustrations serve as links and they, to a greater extent than the textual links, invite to be clicked on.

The Product

In Jakobson's model the poetic function is connected to the message. According to Jakobson, the poetic function is an orientation toward the message, where the focus is on the message for its own sake, i.e., the poetic function of the language (Jakobson, 1960, pp. 356–357). For example, the rhythm of a poem due to variation in line lengths or stress on syllables may create a poetic expression because we enjoy the form and rhythm of the poem for its own sake regardless of the content. I have replaced the term *message* with the term *product* in my model in order to make it more clear that it is both the content and the form of the entire product that is in focus and not only the message, which can be understood as an orientation only toward the content. I have also replaced Jakobson's term *poetic function* with the term *aesthetic function* in order to be able to apply this function to a wider spectrum of media in the communication situation besides the language. Moreover, I distinguish between two types of aesthetic functions: *The formal aesthetic function* and *the sublime aesthetic function* are the communication functions that relate to the product in the model.

The formal aesthetic function is the concept of visual symbols in terms of colors, typography, illustrations, and design in accordance with conventionally established criteria for how the visual aspects should appear in main stream websites. It adheres to the modernistic style where the focus is on tight design, a layout with plenty of white space, subdued monochrome and controlled colors, sans serif print types, and well-planned aesthetical details. Formal aesthetic experiences are the type of experiences that we are met with in the majority of websites. The formal aesthetic experiences are easy to describe because they are based on common, well-known ideals of beauty. They contribute with a "good look and feel" but not necessarily any extraordinary aesthetic experiences.

The sublime aesthetic function, however, is in question when using visual elements such as emotionally expressive photographs, flash elements, color combinations, or design elements in new and innovative ways. This aesthetic function is harder to describe, because it arises from "the space between the known and the unknown" which is not based on common, well-known ideals of beauty. This definition of the sublime is inspired by Jean Francois Lyotard's reflections on avant-garde art and the *sublime*. According to Lyotard, avant-garde art is a search for a dosage of the surprising and the well known. Formulas are reintroduced that have been confirmed in previous successes, and they are brought out of equilibrium by combining them with other incompatible formulas (Lyotard, 1994 (orig. 1984)). This definition of the aesthetic endeavors of avant-garde art can be directly applied to a description of the aesthetic expression that is created in the contemporary retro fashion, where for example clothing styles from different time periods are deliberately mixed in order to obtain new and personal expressions. In other words this eclectic expression that used flourish among subcultures has in the recent years become more and more mainstream especially among the youth cultures. In accordance to web design we encounter this definition of the sublime aesthetical expressions when different genres of styles are mixed in new and innovative ways which often is the case in branding sites for designers and architects as well as websites addressing the younger generations. In computer games the avatars and the peculiar dreamlike spaces and atmospheres in addition to surprising elements of the navigational structure may also create a sublime aesthetical experience that arise from the space between the known and the unknown. However, the sublime function may also to a smaller degree appear in more mainstream websites when an expressive photograph, a flash element, a color combination, or design element deviate from the more established design conventions. A relevant question to ask is the following: Is it the experience in the mind of the recipient that contains the sublime experience or is it inherent in the product? And the answer is both, because the sublime experience must be a visible function in the website but at the same time it will only be experienced as such by the visitors of the site who are susceptible or receptive to this type of aesthetical function.

The Formal and the Sublime Aesthetical Functions in www.nngroup.com and www.waltervanbeirendonck.com

Www.nngroup.com is designed in accordance to the formal aesthetic function. The style is modernistic and the focus is on a tight design, a layout with plenty of white space, subdued monochrome and controlled colors, sans serif print types, and well-planned aesthetical details. There are, in my opinion, not any distinct sublime aesthetic experiences on www.nngroup.com.

On www.waltervanbeirendonck.com there are, on the other hand, many sublime aesthetic experiences if you belong to a group of people who are oriented toward this specific avant-garde taste in regard to web design. The entrance page with the 24 brightly colored pictogram men winking at you is to some people a sublime experience for several reasons. First of all, the color combination in itself is unique and supplies the viewer with a new sensation of color experience. When you click on the links below the brightly colored men, they change to black, which affects the other colors on the screen. This aesthetical experience is both due to the effect of the color interaction and to the user experience of interacting with the website. The aesthetical means of effect on www.waltervanbeirendonck.com are examples of humorous, new, and innovative ways of combining colors with interactivity, which in its complexity is difficult to describe. The car on the link *projects* running across the screen is also an example of a sublime experience due to the humorous aspect combined with the surprising element. In this case it is largely the surprising aspect that entertains us the first time we meet it. The subsequent times we encounter this piece of entertainment we expect it, and the novelty gradually wears off. In other words it does not represent quite the same amount of aesthetical complexity as the entrance page.

The Context

The *context* refers in general to an abstract or real situation or environment in which a specific event takes place.

The referential and *the intertextual functions* are the communication functions that relate to the context in the model. The referential function is, according to Jakobson, evoked when focus is on the denotative task of the message. Thus, the referential function is a reference to the core of the content in the message, in contrast to the aesthetic function, where focus is on the form and the aesthetical expression of the message (Jakobson, 1960, p. 353). In order to fully understand the referential aspects of the model, it is useful to include Charles Sanders Peirce's three categories of signs: *symbols*, *icons,* and *indexes* (Peirce, 1955, p. 102). This sign theory opens up for interesting possibilities when analyzing visual communication. The iconic sign looks like the object it refers to. That is the case, for example, when a movie poster picturing Julia Roberts looks like the object it refers to, namely Julia Roberts. The definition of an index is a direct physical, causal connection between sign and object. For example, smoke coming out of a window is an index of fire. We imagine the fire even though we cannot actually see it. With the symbolic sign there is no direct connection between sign and object. A symbol is a sign whose connection with its object is a matter of convention, agreement, or rule within a certain culture. Words are, in general, symbols, because there is no reason why the shape of the word "horse" should refer to a horse. The symbolic sign does not look like the object it refers to, for example, a peace sign does not visually resemble "peace."

In the visual media, all the visual elements are either iconic, indexical, or symbolic signs that refer to content or meaning based on convention within a certain culture. However, these categories are not always separate and distinct. For example, the road sign picturing a deer is composed of iconic, indexical, and symbolic signs at the same time. The road sign is shaped as a red triangle and by the rule of the Highway Code it is a symbol which means "warning." The deer in the middle is an icon in that its form is determined partly by the shape of its object – a deer. And the road sign is an index in that it indicates that a deer might cross the road ahead of us.

The intertextual function is in play when a text is shaping meaning by referring to another text or when a graphical design is shaping meaning by referring to another graphical design. Intertextuality refers to something that takes place between the lines. I have added the intertextual function to the model, because in the visual media, the visual elements often in one way or another refer to other contexts. Colors, typographies, and graphic designs are signs that almost always refer to other time periods, trends, or products we have seen before. The intertextual elements in a website occur, for example, when the site is using print types, colors, or graphic elements that give associations to the psychedelic expressions of the 1960s.

The Referential and the Intertextual Functions in www.nngroup.com and www.waltervanbeirendonck.com

Nielsen and Norman Group's website is focusing on the content (the referential function) and not on the form (the aesthetic function). The content in www.nngroup.com primarily consists of symbolic signs in Peirce's sense. First and foremost the large amount of texts in the site is communicated by the means of symbolic signs. Www.nngroup.com is also composed of symbols in accordance with the conventional rules within interface design, that is, when you click on "X" in order to close down the page or when part of the text is accentuated in blue so that the experienced web user knows that it is a link. The only use of icons on www.nngroup.com is the portraits of the addressers, and without those visual icons the site would have been very monotonous and impersonal. The site uses indexical signs in the form of "breadcrumbs" when the blue links change into a purple color in order to indicate which links we have visited. However, this appears more confusing than supporting in terms of the usability because some of the links already are purple to begin with, which makes it hard to distinguish between the indexical signs and the symbolic signs.

The referential function performing as *icon, index,* and *symbol* can also be seen on www.waltervanbeirendonck.com. In this site, in contrast to www.nngroup.com, there are a large amount of visual elements that are based on the iconic signs in terms of portraits of Walter himself and pictures of his clothing collections and other design projects. In contrast to Nielsen and Norman Group, Walter Van Beirendonck is showing the content by the means of icons rather than symbols. There are also examples of indexical signs on www.waltervanbeirendonck.com, for example, when we run across a link with the mouse the link changes color indicating that it is active. There are not any indexes in the form of breadcrumbs, however.

In regard to www.nngroup.com the layout is an example of an intertextual reference. For an observer with insights in web design in a historical perspective the layout gives associations to the engineer-based functionalism, which is a genre that was introduced by, among others, Jakob Nielsen's website in the mid-1990s. The site was introduced with the declared goal of combating the multiplicity of home-made websites often pelted with graphics, which began to appear in the mid-1990s as private and commercial site builders gained access to the net. With his message about focus on content and functional graphics, Nielsen introduced the genre of engineer functionalism. (Engholm, 2004, p. 71). The graphic design in www.nngroup.com is clearly in accordance with the user-friendly and functional ideals of this genre. The graphic design is clear and well-organized and the links are accentuated by the color blue which refers back to this hyper-functionalistic style, which flourished among web designers in the mid-1990s.

The intertextual function is also present on www.nngroup.com in terms of the large amount of references to publications written by the founders of the Nielsen and Norman Group and the impressive list of references to clients who have received their web design services. These references serve as an element of ethos because they reflect back on the addressers as experienced professionals. However, these are a different type of intertextual references, because they refer more directly to concrete products in contrast to the more indirect intertextual reference where the content is "written between the lines."

In contrast to www.nngroup.com, Walter Van Beirendonck's website does not reflect just one specific era or trend within web design or other media designs. His website reflects a multitude of time periods and styles within the history of design. He is clearly mostly committed to the eclectic characteristics of the postmodern art and design principles. This is reflected in his design objects in terms of the mixture of references to several time periods: the 1950s, the 1960s, the 1970s and the 1980s, which are combined in a new and innovative way in order to achieve new aesthetic expressions. And the intertextual references to cartoons and animations serve as paramount elements in his unique clothing design.

The Medium

The *medium* is the connecting link between the addresser and the addressee. As Jakobson points out, in order for a communication act to take place, a medium or *contact* is necessary. *The phatic* and the *navigative functions* are the communication functions that are related to the medium in the model. I have added the navigative function to the model in order to include methods of analyzing the navigational aspects in web design.

The phatic function dominates, according to Jakobson[6], when the focus is on the establishment and the maintenance of the contact between addresser and addressee, rather than an actual exchange of information. The phatic function can also be described as *the connecting thread* that makes the product consistent and coherent. The phatic function occurs in the textual media, for example, when we send a Christmas card with the text *Merry Christmas and a Happy New Year*. The card is not supplying the addressee with any new pieces of information. The card is from the addresser's point of view intended as a ritual act with the purpose of maintaining contact with the addressee.

The navigative function is affiliated with the phatic function because the purpose of both functions is to maintain the contact between addresser and addressee. Maintaining the phatic function on a website requires a very well-structured navigation system. The links on a website also help maintain the contact with the user, if the links are consistent in their appearance. The links should be created as clear and consistent icons, graphic identification patterns and graphic or textual menus, which function as a connecting thread that gives the users a guideline for finding what they are looking for without wasting time in blind alleys. The model also includes the four most common navigational structures in web design: *The hierarchic structure, the sequence structure, the grid structure,* and *the hyper net structure* (Lynch & Horton, 1999). However, these navigational structures will not be unfolded in this article.

The Phatic Function in www.nngroup.com and www.waltervanbeirendonck.com

When we enter the entrance page in www.nngroup.com the layout principles in terms of the white background, the Verdana print type, the blue links, the logo, the red bar, and the light blue menu bar on top of the page serve as a phatic function in regard to the establishment of contact with the visitor. This establishment of contact in terms of visual elements is maintained throughout the website because

---

[6]Jakobson borrowed the term phatic function from Malinowski who established the term phatic communion in connection with his ethnographic fieldwork among some Melanesian tribes. Here he demonstrated that use of language in its most primitive form can be regarded as acts rather than a sharing of thoughts (Malinowski, 1969, pp. 312–315).

of the consistent use of the same recognizable visual elements on all the pages in www.nngroup.com. There are no variations in the design except when we click on the link to *about Bruce Tognazzini,* where the bar on the top changes into a green color. This works well, because the variation is aligned with the established design principles of the website, but it also serves the purpose of establishing that we have entered a new sub-page with different content.

Likewise, the consistent use of the red print on white background and the characteristic logo in bold red print type serve as a phatic function on www.waltervanbeirendonck.com. Each of the pages are, however, a little more varied in the layout, which breaks an otherwise monotonous experience, such as the experience of www.nngroup.com.

The Code

The *code* is a choice of signs that in a specific composition are given a meaning. That is, the code is a system of signs, where each sign is ascribed a meaning, which is presumed known to both the addresser and the addressee in order for the act of communication to succeed. The *metacommunicative* and the *intersemiotic* functions are the communication functions that relate to the code in the model.

I have replaced Jakobson's *metalingual function* with the *metacommunicative function* in the model in order to extend its usage to media other than the textual. According to Jakobson, the metalingual function applies whenever the addresser and the addressee need to check on whether they use the same code, or when they talk about the language with the language (Jakobson, 1960, p. 356). For example, when we discuss whether the word "color" is spelled with or without a "u," the speech performs a metalingual function. The concept of the metalingual language can be transferred to the concept of the metacommunicative function. Through the metacommunicative function, a media product reflects on another media product. When a genre speaks of itself it uses metacommunicative features, such as when a commercial speaks of, or reflects on, another commercial. The metacommunicative function or rather *metavisual* communication can be expressed through paraphrases. For example, Manet's *Dejeuner sur l'herbe* has been paraphrased innumerable times. Among others, Picasso has reflected on this painting in a painting.

The metacommunicative function should not be confused with the intertextual function even though they are closely related. The intertextual function is in play when a text is shaping a meaning by referring to another text or when a graphical design is shaping a meaning by referring to another graphical design. However, metacommunication is only in use when there is an act of interpretation taking place in connection with the intertextual function, which is the case when Picasso in his painting makes an interpretation of Manet's *Dejeuner sur l'herbe*. The intertextual function is per definition an implicit part of the metacommunicative function, but the metacommunicative function is not necessarily an integral part of the intertextual function.

I have chosen to combine *the intersemiotic function* with the code, since analysis of lexi-visual communication requires a function that covers the act whereby signs from one code system are used to explain signs from another code system. Thus, the intersemiotic function differs from Jakobson's metalinguistic function and the metacommunicative function. Within the metacommunicative function, the genre speaks of the genre, language speaks of language, etc., and this takes place within the same code system. In case of the intersemiotic function, on the other hand, signs from the language code explain signs from the visual sign code, or the other way around.

The intersemiotic function is operating, for example, in lexi-visual communication when an instruction manual explains how to operate a digital camera. The explanation might, for example, include an illustration that shows how we place the memory disk into the camera, accompanied by a text that translates what is shown in the drawing into words. Signs from one code system are used to explain signs from another code system. This kind of intersemiotic function that translates signs from one code system into another can be extended by including Roland Barthes' two terms *anchoring* and *relay* (Barthes, 1986, p. 28). Both of these terms *refer to* intersemiotic functions, but in different ways. The anchoring of a picture takes place when the text tells us what the picture represents. If we illustrate a text with a picture of Queen Elizabeth of the United Kingdom and the caption reads *Queen Elizabeth of the United Kingdom,* it is an anchoring of the picture. It helps the spectator to choose the right level of perception by anchoring one of several possible meanings of the object.

Relay occurs when the text and the image are in a complementary relation and together create a little narrative. An important part of the information is carried through the dialogue, but the crucial narrative is shown through the pictures. If we show a picture of Queen Elizabeth accompanied by a text informing us that she yesterday cut the ribbon to inaugurate a new bridge, then the text supplies an extra piece of information in addition to the picture. This is an example of relay.

The Metacommunicative and the Intersemiotic Function in www.nngroup.com and www.waltervanbeirendonck.com

The metacommunicative function is not represented on www.nngroup.com as there are no examples of elements on this site reflecting on itself. The layout in www.nngroup.com is an example of an intertextual reference, because it associates to the genre of engineer-based functionalism. However, it is not metacommunicative because Nielsen and Norman's group has not reflected on the original design in terms of a redesign or other interpretations of the original design elements.

The metacommunicative or rather metavisual function, however, is represented on the entrance page to www.waltervanbeirendonck.com, Illustration 2, in terms of the 12 differently colored pictogram-like men because they actually look like Walter Van Beirendonck himself. When we link to the page *Fact File,* Illustration 4

Illustration 4 People: Sub page in www.nngroup.com

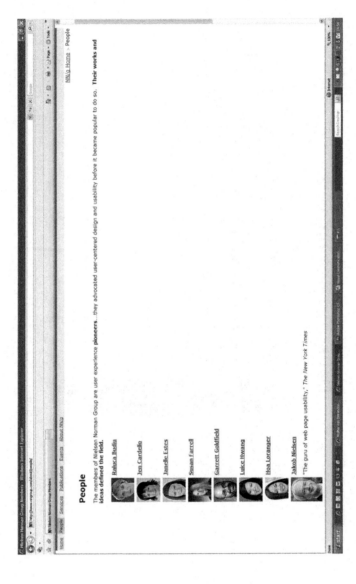

Illustration 5 Fact file: Sub page in www.waltervanbeirendonck.com

we find 19 different pictures of Walter Van Beirendonck and there is a clear resemblance between these pictures and the pictograms on the entrance page. The layout on Walter Van Beirendonck's website is full of intertextual references to other time periods and styles within the history of design. The layout is, however, also to a large extent metacommunicative in that he has interpretated these styles into his own personal design. Among other things because he has mixed design elements from the 1950s, the 1960s, the 1970s and the 1980s and combined them in new and innovative ways.

The intersemiotic function is found on www.nngroup.com on the sub page *people*, Illustration 5. On this page we are met with a series of portraits of the members of www.nngroup.com where the captions anchor the pictures by telling us who they are. The intersemiotic function in terms of a relay is also represented on this page in connection with both Jakob Nielsen and Donald A. Norman, when the captions supply the pictures with the texts "the guru of web page usability," The New York Times, and "the guru of workable technology," Newsweek. Walter Van Beirendonck also employs captions to anchor the majority of the pictures on his website. On the entrance page to www.waltervanbeirendonck.com there is, however, an interesting interpretation of a relay. Some of the pictogram men are acting as cartoon characters equipped with speech bobbles that inform us of some of the highlights on the site. This is a metacommunicative function with reference to the cartoon medium, but also an interesting way of supplying the picture with additional information.

Conclusion

The importance of each communication function varies from website to website, as I have illustrated with the comparative analysis of the website of the Nielsen Norman Group and the website of Walter Van Beirendonck. In terms of the expressive function, both websites reflect the addresser and leave an appropriate impression of these two addressers in regard to their different services and different target audiences. Www.waltervanbeirendonck.com. reflects, however, a greater amount of personality, which is also to be expected from a branding site addressing a target audience of sub-cultural trendsetters. Nielsen Norman Group is successful in terms of presenting and mirroring the professional services within usability and functionality in web design with its usage of formal aesthetical functions. However, we are missing a few more examples of visual elements to support the functionality and user friendliness on this site. Www.waltervanbeirendonck.com offers, on the other hand, lots of entertaining elements and sublime aesthetical experiences, which is appropriate considering the aim of this site, namely to mirror a creative and innovative designer.

The results of an analysis using the communications model presented in this article provide a general view of a website in terms of the site's strengths and weaknesses based on the use of – or the lack of – visual communication functions. The analysis should also take into account if the communication functions are used appropriately in regard to the image of the addresser, the functionality of the website, the website genre, and the target audience. The findings from this analysis should lead to some assumptions or "provisional hypotheses" regarding how the actual target audience might experience the site, which is a good starting point for an actual reception analysis. It is also recommended that the actual intentions of the addresser are examined and compared to the results of a reception analysis of the actual target audience.

References

Barthes, R. (1986). *The responsibility of forms: Critical essays on music, art and representation* (pp. 21–40). London: Blackwell. 1986.

Beaird, J. (2007). *The principles of beautiful web design.* Melbourne: Site Point.

Bordewijk, J. L., & Kaam, B. van (1986). Towards a new classification of Tele-information services. *Intermedia, 14*(1), 16–21.

Cloninger, C. (2002). *Fresh styles for web designers.* Indianapolis, IN: New Riders.

Engholm, I. (2002). Digital style history. The development of graphic design on the Internet. *Digital Creativity, 13*(4), 193–211.

Engholm, I. (2003). *WWW's designhistorie – website udviklingen i et genre- og stilteoretisk perspektiv.* Ph.D. dissertation. Copenhagen: The IT University.

Engholm, I. (2004). Webgenrer og Stilarter – om at analysere og kategorisere websites. In I. Engholm & L. Klastrup (Eds.), *Digitale Verdener.* Copenhagen: Gyldendal.

Jakobson, R. (1960). Linguistics and poetics. In: A. S. Thomas (red.), *Style in language* (pp. 350–377). Cambridge, MA: The MIT Press.

Jensen, J. F. (1997). "Interaktivitet" – på sporet af et nyt begreb i medie og kommunikationsvidenskaberne. *MedieKultur, 26,* 40–55.

Lynch, P. J., & Horton, S. (1999). *Web style guide: Basic design principles for creating web sites.* New Haven, CT and London: Yale University Press.

Lyotard, J. F. (1994) *Lessons on the analytic of the sublime. Kant's "critique of judgment".* Stanford, CA: Stanford University Press.

Malinowski, B. (1969). The problem of meaning in primitive languages. Supplement In C. K. Ogden & I. A. Richards (Eds.), *The meaning of meaning – A study of the influence of language upon thought and of the science of symbolism* (1923). London: Routledge & Keagan Paul Ltd.

Miller, D. (2000). The fame of trinis: Websites as traps. *Journal of Material Culture, 5*(1), 5–24.

Ogden, C. K., & Richards, I. A. (1969). *The meaning of meaning – A study of the influence of language upon thought and of the science of symbolism.* London: Routledge & Keagan Paul Ltd. (orig. 1923).

Peirce, C. S. (1955). Logic as semiotic: The theory of signs. In J. Buchler (red.), *Philosophical writings of Peirce* (pp. 98–115). New York: Dover Publishing.

Siegel, D. (1996). *Creating killer web sites* (2nd ed.). Indianapolis, IN: Hayden Books.

Thorlacius, L. (2001). *Model til analyse af lexi- visual, æstetisk kommunikation – med et særligt henblik på websites.* Del I og II. Roskilde University.

Thorlacius, L. (2002). A model of visual, aesthetic communication focusing on web sites. In J. Nielsen (red.), *Digital Creativity, 13*(2), 85–98. Holland: Swets & Zeitlinger.

Thorlacius, L. (2005). The role of aesthetics in web design. In: U. Carlsson, (red.), *Nordicom Review, 2,* 85–101.

Feral Hypertext: When Hypertext Literature Escapes Control

Jill Walker Rettberg

Hypertext is familiar to us as the basis of the world wide web, but its history extends considerably further back than 1990, when Tim Berners-Lee set up the first web server, website and web browser. Hypertext was first envisioned by Vannevar Bush just after the Second World War (Bush, 1945), although the word itself was coined by Ted Nelson in 1965 (Wardrip-Fruin, 2004). The first working hypertext systems were implemented a few years later on mainframe computers. In the 1980s hypertext became available on home computers, and the first works of hypertext fiction were created. In the 1990s, as we all know, the web took off, and today hypertext is such a fundamental part of our daily media that we barely consider how this way of organizing texts is different from the linear, non-hypertextual texts we used to take for granted.

Domestication

Feral (a): Of an animal: Wild, untamed. Of a plant, also (rarely), of ground: Uncultivated. Now often applied to animals or plants that have lapsed into a wild from a domesticated condition. (Oxford English Dictionary)

In the last decade there has been an increasing interest in the domestication of technology, that is, in how technology has become an integral part of our daily lives (Aune, 1996). One of the assumptions in this research is that computers and other technologies need to be "tamed" and made approachable and safe as part of the process of entering our homes and becoming part of our everyday lives. This domestication of technology is seen as a parallel to the domestication of animals, which has not only led to new forms of symbiosis between humans and other species – we love our pets, ride our horses and drink milk from our cows – but has also been accompanied by planned breeding and more or less planned selection of certain

J.W. Rettberg (✉)
Department of Linguistic, Literary and Aesthetic Studies,
University of Bergen, Bergen, Norway
e-mail: jill.walker.rettberg@uib.no

J. Hunsinger et al. (eds.), *International Handbook of Internet Research*,
DOI 10.1007/978-1-4020-9789-8_29, © Springer Science+Business Media B.V. 2010

traits that are useful or pleasing to humans. Modern day, domesticated dogs or pigs are very different from their pre-domesticated ancestors.

Computers are not, of course, newly domesticated wild animals, but neither were the first computers intended to be used by individuals in their homes. Early computers were seen as mathematical tools, business tools and military tools. In 1974, Ted Nelson's insistence that ordinary people need computers (Nelson, 1974) was radical, though only a few years later the first commercial personal computers were being sold. Today, of course, computers are used as toys, for writing love letters and high school essays, for storing family photos and for writing and reading hypertext. Children in industrialised nations only rarely learn how to ride a horse or milk a cow, but will begin to learn to use a computer before they can read and write.

Domestication is the process of taming and repurposing something to be useful in ways it was not developed or evolved for. "The Street finds its own uses for things", William Gibson wrote (1991), and those uses are often not the ones developers imagined. The telephone, for instance, was intended to allow voice communication between two points only: the factory and the factory owner's home. The inventors of the aerosol can did not plan the birth of graffiti and street art. The internet was developed by the military and by academic institutions with no intention of creating the social communication network of today.

Hypertext, on the other hand, was always intended to be a tool for individuals. Nelson insisted on the importance of *personal* computers ("You must understand computers NOW!" (Nelson, 1974) and Vannevar Bush's original vision was of an *intimate* technology, to be used by individuals at home:

> Consider a future device for individual use, which is a sort of mechanized private file and library. It needs a name, and to coin one at random, "memex" will do. A memex is a device in which an individual stores all his books, records, and communications, and which is mechanized so that it may be consulted with exceeding speed and flexibility. It is an enlarged intimate supplement to his memory. (Bush, 1945)

In the late 1960s, Andries van Dam built the first working hypertext system in collaboration with Nelson and with inspiration from Doug Engelbart. Van Dam and his collaborators built their system to run on mainframe computers in a research institution rather than in homes, and other early hypertext systems followed this pattern. Developers had little choice in this: there were no personal computers yet. Domestication as a general term is not limited to our homes, of course. Modern domestication of animals includes cattle ranches and battery-farmed hens as well as the more intimate companionship between humans and their pets. Hypertext on mainframe computers was a domesticated technology in the sense that it was tame: farmed and cultivated in a carefully controlled environment.

Although hypertext systems in the 1970s and 1980s were developed on mainframes rather than in homes, research often discussed individuals' uses of hypertext systems (Trigg & Irish, 1987). Despite the frequent references to large-scale hypertext systems such as the oft-cited aeroplane manual (van Dam, 1988), the actual focus on the varying and subjective ways in which individuals actually use hypertext is evident throughout the literature.

Though the first personal computers became available in the late 1970s, the first home hypertext systems were not available till the late 1980s. Peter Brown's GUIDE

(Brown, 1987) was followed by HyperCard, a hypertext authoring system that was packaged with Macintosh computers. Soon afterwards, Eastgate's Storyspace became available, first for the Macintosh and later for the PC. Tinderbox, released from Eastgate in 2001, is probably the tool that most closely follows in the footsteps of these systems, which were very much created in the spirit of Vannevar Bush and the desire for an intimate extension to memory. These hypertext authoring systems allow an individual to organise his or her personal notes and create his or her own self-contained hypertext which can be shared with others by copying it onto a diskette or CD or by emailing it as a single file. While Tinderbox and Hypercard were primarily intended as organisational tools, Storyspace was explicitly developed as a tool for fiction authors.

The advent of the web and the rapid spread of personal computers and internet connections in ordinary homes radically changed the ecosystem hypertext existed in. Hypertext, lovingly bred in captivity, was unleashed into the world wide web. Suddenly, anyone could publish a website and link and be linked at will.

The result? Hypertext went feral.

Spotting Feral Hypertexts

Feral hypertext has a tendency to move beneath the radar. It is easy to not identify feral hypertext as hypertext at all. Feral hypertexts are not as clearly delimited and disciplined as domesticated hypertexts are, and our language and culture are not designed to speak about things that lack boundaries.

What feral hypertexts have in common is that they have reverted to the wild, in one respect or another. They are no longer tame. They will not do what we expect and they refuse to stay put within boundaries we have defined. They do not follow standards – indeed, they appear to revel in the non-standard, while perhaps building new kinds of standards that we do not yet understand.

In a 2003 paper, Jim Rosenberg describes feral structure in hypertext authoring (Rosenberg, 2003), where nodes are placed loosely on the desktop, out of context. This is a typical way of using a hypertext authoring system that allows a spatial view of the nodes, such as Tinderbox. My use of feral is similar to Rosenberg's in that I am talking about unplanned structures, but I propose that it is the massive possibility for collaboration and emergence in the network that creates truly feral, uncontrollable hypertext. Collaboration and emergence are also key aspects of Web 2.0, a term put forward by Tim O'Reilly and associates (O'Reilly, 2005). The term is meant to characterise a second generation of websites. The first wave of web developers focused largely on publishing content. Web 2.0 sites, on the other hand, include services like the Wikipedia, YouTube, Flickr and Facebook, all of which allow users to share their own content and to use the web as a platform. These websites became valuable because they are being used. Rather than a carefully authored trail of connections between documents, such as Vannevar Bush envisioned, or a hypertext authored from scratch, as Ted Nelson imagined and as the early hypertext fictions were created, these websites are hard to predict and grow according to the way they are used. And yet, many of them are heavily structured. Facebook, for instance, has very clear structures within which users must fit their words, images and videos. However, with the introduction of third-party applications that plug in to your Facebook profile, the system becomes far less stable and predictable, and so even Facebook verges on the feral.

The clearest examples of feral hypertexts are large collaborative projects that generate patterns and meanings without any clear authors or editors controlling the linking. While the semantic web and other standards-oriented projects clearly follow the domesticated paradigm, attempting to retain control of hypertextual structures, these feral projects accept messiness, errors and ignorance and devise ways of making sense from vast numbers of varying contributions. The online version of the Encyclopædia Britannica is an example of a domesticated and carefully controlled hypertext, while the Wikipedia is an example of a feral hypertext. An online library catalogue, with its careful categorisation, is domesticated, while Google's interpretations of links, or Flickr, Del.icio.us and CiteULike's collaborative freeform tagging, are feral.[1] This does not mean there are no structures or rules. Quite the contrary: these systems work because they have simple but flexible ground conditions that establish environments that make emergent organisation instantly visible. These hypertexts are both "intimate extensions to memory" and complex representations of a collective narrative.

While the *folksonomy* or *ethnoclassification* of Flickr and its kin has been discussed online (Mathes, 2004), there is little awareness of how this affects literary hypertext. Are there equivalents to the emergent structures of collaborative, feral hypertexts in literature?

Spotting feral hypertext, and literary feral hypertext in particular, requires a willingness to accept structures that are neither pre-defined nor clearly boundaried. In discussing weblogs, one natural habitat for feral hypertexts, Steve Himmer wrote that weblogs' "absence of a discrete, 'completed' product makes the weblog as a form resistant to the commoditization either of itself, or of any one particular interpretation" (Himmer, 2004). Codework writer and net performance artist Mez Breeze has a similar explanation for the lack of visibility of her process-based writing:

> [I]t seems evident that various web/net/code artists are more likely to be accepted into an academic reification circuit/traditional art market if they produce works that reflect a traditional craft-worker positioning. This "craft" orientation (producing skilled/practically inclined output, rather than placing adequate emphasis on the conceptual or ephemeral aspects of a networked, or code/software-based, medium) is embraced and replicated by artists who create finished, marketable, tangible objects; read: work that slots nicely into a capitalistic framework where products/objects are commodified and hence equated with substantiated worth. (Breeze, 2003)

---

[1] Google interprets links from one website to another as peer endorsements of the linked-to website, so a website with more links pointing to it will rank higher in the search results. Tagging is the practice of assigning freeform keywords to an item, whether its a photo, a website, a video or something else. Tags are chosen by the user as he or she wishes, whereas conventional keywords, as in a library database, for instance, are usually part of a controlled vocabulary, so new keywords cannot be added at will.

It is simply far easier to see products and objects (say, a complete hypertext story on a diskette) than it is to spot feral hypertexts that have escaped from our grasp.

Before we can understand how hypertext went feral, we should examine ways in which hypertext and other literature have been kept disciplined.

Keeping Hypertext Under Control

It seems reasonable to assume that Nelson intended his definition of hypertext to be productive rather than restrictive. His first definitions are fairly concrete, listing possible kinds of hypertext and hypermedia and advocating for their realisation. His later definitions, written after many kinds of hypertext in fact existed, are far more open. In the 1987 edition of *Computer Lib/Dream Machine*, for instance, Nelson explicitly calls interactive fiction in the tradition of *Adventure* and *Zork* hypertexts, "since hypertext simply means nonsequential writing." (Nelson, 1987, 30)

While hypertext was being invented, and the process, as we know, took decades, it was necessary to be quite explicit in describing these newly imagined creations. Hypertext required boundaries in order to become a concept that we could talk about, let alone plan to develop. As Andries van Dam said in his keynote at the first ACM Hypertext conference, the founders of hypertext sought ways of disciplining the genre. Van Dam praised Ted Nelson for this disciplinary drive:

> Another thing we should thank Ted for is that he did not just say, "branch, link, make arbitrary associations." He tried very early to impose some discipline on linking. (1988)

The desire for discipline is evident in calls for systematically typed links (Trigg 1983), standardised metadata and a well-coordinated semantic web. Yet as sensible as these systems are, the web remains messy and unplanned. There are too many creators out there, and few bother to add metadata or follow standards. Even those who know the importance of metadata may fail to categorise their data for fear of failing to apply the taxonomy correctly. When value is given to metadata, spammers will abuse it. When other more implicit structures are given value, as with Google's interpretation of links, these structures are abused too (Walker, 2002). It is not easy to discipline hypertext.

One of the ways literary theorists have analysed our wish to impose discipline on texts is the idea of authorship. Nelson's concept of hypertext likewise deals with works that are *authored* by humans.

> Hyper-media are branching or performing presentations which respond to user actions, systems of prearranged words and pictures (for example) which may be explored freely or queried in stylized ways. They will not be "programmed," but rather designed, written, drawn and edited, by authors, artists, designers and editors. (Nelson, 1970, quoted in Wardrip-Fruin, 2004)

Interestingly, Nelson's idea of *authored* hypermedia was concurrent with an increasing trend in literary theory towards discounting the author, instead emphasising the potentially infinite associative connections between texts. Julia Kristeva introduced the concept of intertextuality in 1967, just 2 years after Nelson coined the term hypertext (Kristeva, 1967). Intertextuality refers to the idea that no text can exist alone, but is part of a network of explicit and implicit allusions to and citations of other texts. The similarities between hypertext's crafted and programmed links and the ubiquitous and implicit links between all texts posited by the concept of intertextuality are obvious and were often noted in the early stages of literary hypertext theory. Landow's statement that "hypertext creates an almost embarrassingly literal embodiment of a principle that had seemed particularly abstract and difficult when read from the vantage point of print" (Landow, 1992, p. 53) has been cited again and again, both in appreciation and to point out that (as Landow also expresses elsewhere) the relationship between hypertext and critical theory is not one to one.

What I would like to emphasise here is that the concept of intertextuality and much other late twentieth century critical theory expresses an idea of texts as *unruly* and fundamentally beyond discipline. Much hypertext research, on the other hand, attempts to find ways to discipline and tame our thoughts, at the same time as it admits that our mind works associatively and that there are multiple ways of viewing connections in texts.

Around the same time as Roland Barthes declared the death of the author (Barthes, 1977), Michel Foucault argued that our idea of authorship is the only thing that keeps fiction from enveloping our world:

> How can one reduce the great peril, the great danger with which fiction threatens our world? The answer is: One can reduce it with the author. The author allows a limitation of the cancerous and dangerous proliferation of significations within a world where one is thrifty not only with one's resources and riches, but also with one's discourses and their significations. The author is the principle of thrift in the proliferation of meaning. (Foucault, 1988)

Foucault argued that fiction is a potentially cancerous growth and that without limitations on its proliferation, it would spread without limit. We might well argue that this has in fact happened in today's world. Hoaxes, spams and scams abound on the internet, and often the reason that people get so upset by these cases is precisely that the author function has begun to slip. We can no longer trust that the person who claims to be the author of a text is its true author, as is evident from the Kaycee Nicole hoax and countless others (Rettberg, 2008, pp. 121–126).

Typed links, standards for metadata and a semantic web are ways of limiting the "cancerous and dangerous proliferation" of hypertext. They are ways of trying to keep this creature we have created domesticated, tame and controllable. In the following, we will particularly examine the ways in which metadata is used to attempt to keep hypertext in order.

Who Is in Charge?

There are three ways of creating metadata about information (Mathes, 2004). The metadata can be assigned by librarians or other skilled professionals who have been carefully trained in a taxonomy such as the Dewey decimal system or the Dublin

Core. Alternatively, metadata can be provided by the author or creator of the work. This does not always work, because authors are not skilled taxonomists, because they do not prioritise metadata and because some authors will abuse the system. This is the predominant system on the web. On a general level, metatags can be assigned to individual webpages using specific HTML tags, and XML provides a flexible yet potentially standardised framework for far more detailed metadata about any document. Finally, metadata can be provided by the users. This is the most chaotic system, because users will often have even less knowledge about the overall structure and nature of the information than an author, and because no single perspective will be shared by all users. A group you would classify as freedom fighters may well be classified as terrorists by somebody in a different situation than yours.

These three levels of organisation are evident in the traditional literary system as well as in the information we see on the web. Publishers and critics are the equivalents of the librarians, and in their different ways, these are the professionals who define a canon. Eastgate and other publishers of hypertext fiction like the series *The Electronic Literature Collection* and the journals *Drunken Boat, New River* and *The Iowa Review Web* declare the works they publish as being worthy of attention, as well as often giving them more specific metadata by describing works in catalogues, editorials and marketing. Awards given by organisations like AltX, trAce and the Electronic Literature Organization are also part of this system, as are the readings and performances held at conferences and festivals, and the critical readings of hypertext fiction published by various scholars and critics. These are all examples of how institutions, organisations and professional critics and publishers define what hypertext fiction is.

Authors of hypertext fiction can add explicit metadata to their works, but as with traditional fiction authors, this is not particularly common. Authors are more likely to provide implicit metadata about their work by submitting it to certain journals, presenting it in certain venues and so on.

User-provided metadata for hypertext exists a little, in comments on works in various readers' weblogs and on discussion lists. However, it has not yet reached the point where new usage and structure emerges. Traditional media objects such as books, movies and music have such systems, such as the popular Last.fm for music. When you sign up for last.fm, you can install a small application on your computer, a "scrobbler", that tells last.fm what music you listen to on your computer or mp3 player. You can note that you "love" a song, or you can "ban" a song so you never have to listen to it again. You can also tag songs as you like – love song, reggae, British, for instance. In this way, last.fm gathers explicit metadata from users – the tags – as well as implicit metadata from users – users who listen to this band tend to also listen to this band. Last.fm uses this information to recommend music to listeners, based on what other people who like the music they like also like listening to.

All of these ways of classifying objects assume that there is an object to classify, and that may be why classification systems like last.fm exist for music, but there is not yet an equivalent for hypertext, and certainly not for feral hypertext. For literary works, it is the author function, in Foucault's sense, that defines the extent of the work. Traditional literary works are also clearly bound by the way they are published: either as a separate book, as a clearly boundaried short story in a larger publication or as a series of episodes that are clearly marked as belonging together. Music is likewise easily seen in terms of individual works. This is also the case with the hypertext fiction that has become part of the canon. Hypercard and Storyspace works fit easily into this paradigm, limited not only by the author but by their format: the work includes whatever is on this disk. In rare cases extra material was provided. *Uncle Buddy's Funhouse* (McDaid, 1992) includes cassettes and a printout of the proofs of a manuscript for a short story by Uncle Buddy. When authors control their own publication, as they can on the web, there is no need for a work to be finished before it is published. For instance, *The Unknown*, a notoriously proliferate hypertext, was in the process of being written for 2 or 3 years (Gillespie, Rettberg, Stratton, & Marquardt, 1998). Yet even though this work grew and changed during that period, it could always be limited by the URL: anything on the domain http://unknownhypertext.com is a part of the work.

Folksonomies and Emergent Connections

Let me give you an example of a feral hypertext. Flickr is a photosharing website where individuals upload their photos and give them titles, descriptions and tags. Flickr supports a social network where you can choose to define other users as friends, family or contacts. Photos taken by your friends, family or contacts are displayed prominently for you, and you can mark each of your photos to be visible to anybody or only to friends or family.

The most interesting – and the most feral – aspect of Flickr is the tagging. Instead of providing a set list of possible keywords, Flickr allows users to type in any tag they like. Each photo can have as many tags as desired. If Jane clicks on one of the tags on a photo her friend Nina took, Jane is shown all Nina's photos that have that particular tag. From that page, she can continue by clicking the link titled "see all public photos tagged with [the tag]". This gives some very interesting results. Since there are no predefined rules for how to tag your photos, nobody has any control of the ways in which photos are presented, yet vast pools of photographs of specific places or events are gathered and made accessible. Different tags produce very different kinds of description, narrative or argument. Figure 1 shows a screenshot of the latest photos tagged with the word "Bush" on 27 March 2005.

As you can see, the page presents photos that refer to different senses of the word "Bush". Some photos are of plants, while others are of protests against George W. Bush's policies. No attempt is made to disambiguate the tag. To the left a list of related tags is shown: "protest, election, politics". These give a clear context to the most common use of the tag "bush" and give the user ample opportunity to follow the associative links made by other individuals using the system. These links are not paths cleared by the professional trail-blazers Vannevar Bush dreamed of, they are more like sheep paths in the mountains, paths that have formed over time as many animals and people just happened to use them. Once formed, it is easier to use such a path than to blaze a new trail.

Del.icio.us is a social bookmark system that uses tags similarly to Flickr and indeed was probably the inspiration for Flickr's use of tags. In Del.icio.us, users bookmark websites they are interested in and assign tags to them. Once tagged, you can see how many other people have bookmarked that page, and clicking through, you can see the tags they have chosen to describe the page. Often, their use of tags may inspire you to add a more commonly used tag to your description of the page, or you may follow the other tags used and find new, related sites that also interest you. CiteULike does exactly the same thing for academic papers and provides a fascinating way of surfing colleagues' reading interests and thereby finding research on topics related to the ones you're working on. Valuably, these systems allow you to find people who are interested in the same things as you but whom you did not already know about.

The example in Fig. 1 shows how the system in this case has enabled a collective argument to be made about relationships between a political person and various world events. Obviously the photos shown and the related tags depend on the pool of people sharing photos, and the connections might be different with a different group of people. Flickr's connections can express more poetic descriptions as well, as seen in Fig. 2, which shows recent photos tagged with the word "train".

Here the photos give the impression of a narrative. Perhaps it is because of the motif: trains mean journeys, and journeys form the quintessential narrative plot. Another reason why the images seem narrative may be the layout. We are used to reading a series of photographs as we read a comic book or a storyboard for a movie.

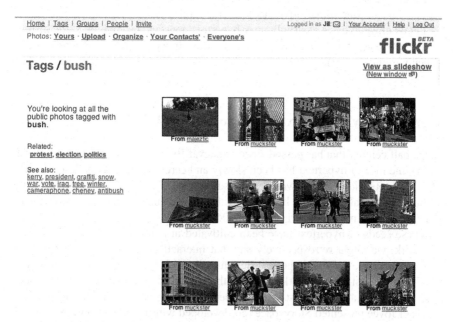

Fig. 1. The most recent photos uploaded to Flickr and tagged with "Bush". To the left you see related tags (http://flickr.com/photos/tags/bush)

Fig. 2. Photos tagged with the word "train". Flickr.com, 27 March 2005

If this can be seen as a form of narrative, it is a narrative that lacks both author and work. This is a kind of narrative that has gone feral.

Let us move to more clearly literary hypertext now, and take a look at the history of domesticated literary hypertext and at the ways in which literary hypertext today is beginning to go feral.

How Literary Hypertext Began to Go Feral

In the half century that has passed since Vannevar Bush described the memex (Bush 1945), the idea of hypertext has been slowly and carefully cultivated. Two decades after the initial idea was sown, Ted Nelson named it and described some of the forms it might take: discrete hypertext with nodes connected by links, stretchtext, hypergrams and more (Wardrip-Fruin, 2004).

These seeds of hypertext have been cultivated in many ways. In terms of literary work, we might retrospectively say that interactive fictions such as *Zork* and *Adventure* were a form of hypertext literature (Montfort, 2003). However, it was in 1987 that the first literary work explicitly thought of as hypertextual was presented. That was the year of the first ACM Hypertext conference, where Jay Bolter and Michael Joyce presented Storyspace (co-developed with John Smith) to the general public (Bolter & Joyce, 1987). Their paper at that conference included a footnote that offered interested persons a copy of Joyce's hypertext fiction, *afternoon, a story*, created in Storyspace. By 1990, both *afternoon* (Joyce, 1990) and Storyspace were being distributed by Eastgate Systems, and in the years since a number of hypertext fictions written in Storyspace and other platforms have been published and distributed by Eastgate.

These early hypertext fictions were sold as stand-alone applications on diskettes and later on CD-ROMs. The distribution mirrored that of traditional literary publishing. The format of the work itself was unfamiliar to readers, who for example found their expectations of closure to be challenged (Douglas, 2000; Walker, 1999). Yet many characteristics remained close to conventional literature, such as the mode of distribution, the relationship between author and work and the expectation of sustained reading of a self-contained work.

While it was in all cases easy to separate the literary work from other documents and applications running on the reader's computer, there were variations in how the works were presented. Some versions of *Patchwork Girl* (Jackson, 1995) distribute each node across the reader's screen, while *afternoon* is completely contained in a single window where each node "yields" to the next. The reader's interaction with these disk-based hyperfictions is limited to clicking on words and answering simple yes or no questions. Despite suggestions that this kind of hypertext fiction makes the reader a co-author of the work (Landow, 1992), authors may actually have more control over the work than in conventional fiction, where readers are free to read the end of the story first if they wish (Aarseth, 1997; Rettberg, 2003). In *afternoon* the only indication readers have that they have read the whole story is that nodes begin reappearing. It may be possible to trace a line from the earliest hypertext fictions, like *afternoon*, which gave little control of the story to the reader, and towards later works where the reader was given access to all the nodes, for instance through a map view or other overall representation of the work.

Authors were quick to start using the web for hypertext fiction. The early web was well suited to the node and link-based hypertext that had been developed in early hypertext fiction, although systems like Storyspace allowed conditional links, map views and other finesses that could make early HTML seem a simplistic form of hypertext. In her 1995 survey of hypertext fiction on the web, Carolyn Guyer noted of one of her favourite pieces that "In truth, this fiction begs for a fuller hypertextual form. I'd like to see it on disk." (Guyer, 1995). However, it soon became evident that the collaborative and open aspects of the web would allow hypertext fiction could evolve in ways that the diskette could not support.

Collaborative fiction was popular (Mills, 1995) as readers discovered how easy it was to *write* in the web instead of just reading. Many works used a tree structure or a sieve (Bernstein, 1998), rather like the Choose-your-own-adventure book series. At each plot point, readers could choose between two plot options. Tree fictions, like Gavin Inglis's *Same Day Test*, can be tightly structured. Since the reader selects one plot option at each step, each version of the story is itself completely linear and runs easily from a clear beginning to a clear end, allowing the author a great deal of control.

Collaborative fictions frequently used the same tree structure, but allowed readers to add their own storylines. Different structures allowed varying degrees of control to the initiators or lead authors of such works. Some such fictions allowed anybody to write anything. This kind of collaborative fiction also existed prior to the web, particularly in MUDs and MOOs like LambdaMOO or Hypertext Hotel and on listservs and discussion groups (Wittig, 1994; Rettberg, 2005).

This is where hypertext began to go feral. When readers can alter the text, the links and the structure of the text, the link begins to run wild. And yet even these hypertexts tended to remain reasonably predictable, perhaps largely because of the simplicity of the HTML on which they depended. The only possible structure for these works, at the time, was that of node-and-link hypertext.

Other collaborative fictions were more structured and had a clear format within which contributions were allowed. An example is *The Company Therapist* (Pipsqueak Productions 1996–1999), which told stories about individual characters and their relationships with each other by letting readers browse characters' diaries, transcripts of their sessions with their therapist and other material. Readers were invited to write a character of their own, but had to sign up and participate fully and within clear limits in order to do so.

In many ways the collaborative fictions of the early web days were a return to the collaborative hypertext systems that were developed in the 1970s and 1980s. Students using Intermedia at Brown University did not write fiction, but they developed collaborative hypertexts that were not under the control of a single author. Although it is possible for an author or a group of authors and editors to retain control (or repeatedly regain control) of a collaborative hypertext, as with *The Company Therapist*, these hypertexts are examples of how hypertext can escape from the orderly control of authors and/or editors and grow wild.

While early collaborative hypertexts expanded prolifically, they remained self-contained and did not spill out over their own borders. A website can grow almost infinitely and never become more visible from outside of itself. As long as all links in a work are internal to the work itself it remains self-contained and identifiable as a single entity or as a work.

In the late 1990s, web hypertext fiction began opening up and moving towards the feral. Authors like Deena Larsen and Noah Wardrip-Fruin started creating hypertext fictions that deliberately broke the boundaries between work and surroundings. In *The Impermanence Agent* (Wardrip-Fruin, Chapman, Moss, & Whitehurst, 2000) Wardrip-Fruin and his collaborators wrote a work that runs in the background as you browse the web, incorporating text and images from websites the reader encounters in the work itself. While this introduces an aspect of randomness in the work, the framework is still predetermined. Larsen used a less random technique that in some ways resulted in a greater abdication of power. In her work *Disappearing Rain* (1997) she included links out to other websites, fully aware that she could not guarantee that the websites she linked to would remain as they were when she linked to them. The reverse technique was used in *The Unknown*, where the authors encouraged inbound links, hoping that readers would arrive at a page of the labyrinthine hypertext while performing a pragmatic web search rather than looking for a literary experience (Gillespie, Rettberg, Stratton, & Marquardt, 1998; Rettberg, 2003).

While these works do not completely leave the domesticated paradigm where the work is bounded and kept under strict control, they do begin to challenge the idea of a tame, structured hypertext. They begin to work outside the borders.

Weblogs and Distributed Narrative

While literary hypertext presumably might go feral in many different ways, weblogs provide the clearest example of truly feral, literary hypertexts today. There are as yet no Flickrs for fiction, though there are fictional and literary projects within Flickr (see, for instance, the tag "flicktion").

Most individual weblogs are not feral at all. Quite the contrary, in fact, they are politely obedient and simply use the default templates, linking to other blogs or sites only if the blogging software makes linking very easy. Sometimes, however, systems or clusterings of weblogs escape and become something more than just a single website with occasional links and commentary.

Justin Hall's blog, closed since January 2005, is an example of a feral hypertext. Actually, I should not refer to this hypertext as Justin Hall's blog, because the hypertext I want to talk about spreads across many more sites than links.net, the website where Hall has narrated his life since 1994 (Wittig, 2003; Hall, 1994–present). Hall's narration of his life online began in January 1994, with a simple homepage, and extended into a detailed hypertextual version of his life told in traditional node and link HTML. When weblogging software began accessible, Hall started using it, and posted almost daily fragments in this decade-long autobiographical project until early 2005. At this point, Hall posted a video where he discussed the problems of publicly narrating one's life at the same time as relating to the people in one's life, and ceased his personal blogging.

Hall has been involved in many different projects, many of which have had an online component. Over the years, he has had relationships with women who themselves kept weblogs, he has written for various well-known online journals, he has kept a research weblog for his postgraduate studies and participated in other online fora. To look at the online *oeuvre* of Hall, then, it would be necessary to look beyond links.net and take note of the many connections between what he has written on his own sites and on other sites. In addition, one could look at what his friends have written about him and about their relationships with him as part of the story of his life during these years.

After ending his personal blogging, Hall has continued to write online. He posts photos to Flickr, many of them public, and he is a frequent contributor to the Wikipedia. Presumably he also participates in many online fora I am unaware of. In his personal user page at Wikipedia, he describes a current online writing goal as attempting to distribute his personal narrative across the web:

> Between 1994 and 2005, I wrote a few thousand web pages about my life. When Professor Peggy Weil proposed we compose an interactive media autobiographical piece for our Interactive Writing class, I initially thought to disperse that effort: to write on the web

itself, not on a web page. Disappear from any central location; instead, inhabit the web as a sort of spirit. My personality, commentary, reflections, stories, notions popping up on other websites. (Hall, 2005)

As a blogger and author of an autobiographical website, Hall has not defined the extent of his narrative, although he is one of the most self-aware, thoughtful and enduring of online diarists. It is up to me as the reader to decide what is part of this hypertext. I can choose to limit it by authorship, as Foucault suggests, in which case I would choose to look at everything Hall has written. Or I could choose to limit it by the main character in the narrative, Justin Hall, in which case I would look at his girlfriends' blogs and other writings about him as well.

In thinking thus, though, I am in a sense already trapped by an idea that boundaries are necessary. If I cannot control the hypertext that extends between weblogs by finding a clear object that I can point to and say look, that's the work, that's the literature, as I can point to Joyce's *afternoon*, then I try to find other ways of controlling the hypertext by limiting it by author or character. How might be we think about feral hypertexts without resorting to these feeble attempts to control them?

I think one way of thinking about hypertext non-structures such as those that ebb and flow in weblog clusters is that they are distributed narratives. Distributed narratives disregard the commodification of most literature, "opening up the formal and physical aspects of the work and spreading themselves across time, space and the network" (Walker, 2005). Distributed narratives and feral hypertexts are permeating our daily lives in a way that may be just as influential as traditional works, although they are harder to see.

Conclusion

There is no need to worry that hypertext is escaping from our domestic confines. If we lose the old ways of disciplining links and hypertext – authorship, metadata, clear structures – there is all the more need to research the ways in which feral hypertext can work. Hypertext will remain an intimate extension of our memory, but the focus will be on *our* in the collective rather than on the individual. Feral hypertext draws from our collective ideas and associations to create emergent structures and meanings. That is valuable, if only we can see it and appreciate it.

And remember, while van Dam praised Ted Nelson for reminding us that we must discipline our links, he also said of Nelson that

One of the most important things he taught me was that this is a new medium and you really can't be constrained to thinking about it in the old ways. Don't copy old bad habits; think about new organizations, new ways of doing things, and take advantage of this new medium. (Andries van, 1988)

Perhaps our greatest challenge, though, lies in recognising literary forms that do not adhere to our conventional forms of discipline: authors, works and commodities. I suspect that these forms of literature will be the most interesting in years to come.

References

Aarseth, E. (1997). *Cybertext: Perspectives on ergodic literature*. Baltimore and London: Johns Hopkins UP.

Aune, M. (1996). The computer in everyday life: Patterns of domestication of a new technology. In M. Lie & K. Sørensen (Eds.), *Making technology our own?* Oslo: Scandinavian University Press.

Barthes, R. (1977). The death of the author. In R. Barthes (Ed.), *Image, music, text*. New York, NY: Hill and Wang. Original edition, 1968.

Bernstein, M. (1998). *Patterns of hypertext*. Paper read at Hypertext 98, Pittsburgh.

Bolter, J. D., & Joyce, M. (1987). *Hypertext and creative writing*. Proceedings of the ACM conference on hypertext. Chapel Hill, NC.

Breeze, M. (2003). Inappropriate format][ing][: Craft-orientation vs. networked content[s]. *JoDI: Journal of Digital Information, 3*(3). Available from http://jodi.ecs.soton.ac.uk.

Brown, P. J. (1987). *Turning ideas into products: The guide system*. Paper read at Conference on Hypertext and Hypermedia, Chapel Hill, NC.

Bush, V. (1945). As we may think. *Atlantic Monthly, 176*(1), 85–110.

Douglas, J. Y. (2000). *The end of books or books without end? Reading interactive narratives*. Ann Arbor, MI: University of Michigan Press.

Foucault, M. (1988). What is an author? In D. Lodge (Ed.), *Modern criticism and theory: A reader*. London: Longman.

Gibson, W. (1991). Academy leader. In M. Benedikt (Ed.), *Cyberspace: First steps*. Cambridge, MA: MIT Press.

Gillespie, W., Rettberg, S., Stratton, D., & Marquardt, F. (1998). *The unknown*[Hypertext fiction]. Available from http://unknownhypertext.com.

Guyer, C. (1995). Web hyperfiction reading list. *Feed Magazine*. http://www.feedmag.com/95.09guyer/95.09guyer_sample1.html>(dead link: use archive.org).

Hall, J. (1994–2007). Links.net. http://links.net.

Hall, Justin User: JustinHall User: JustinHall.Wikipedia: The Free Encyclopedia, 2005. http://en.wikipedia.org/wiki/User:JustinHall.

Himmer, S. (2004). The labyrinth unbound: Weblogs as literature. In L. Gurak, S. Antonijevic, L. Johnson, C. Ratliff, & J. Reyman (Eds.), *Into the blogosphere*. Minneapolis, MN: University of Minnesota.

Jackson, S. (1995). *Patchwork girl*. Cambridge, MA: Eastgate Systems.

Joyce, M. (1990). *Afternoon, a story*. Watertown, MA: Eastgate Systems.

Kristeva, J. (1967). Bakhtine, le mot, le dialogue et le roman. *Critique, 239*, 438–465.

Landow, G. P. (1992). *Hypertext: The convergence of contemporary critical theory and technology*. Baltimore, MD: Johns Hopkins University Press.

Larsen, D. (1997). *Disappearing rain*. http://deenalarsen.net/rain.

Mathes, A. (2004). *Folksonomies – Cooperative classification and communication through shared metadata 2004*. http://www.adammathes.com/academic/computer-mediatedcommunication/folksonomies.html

McDaid, J. (1992). *Uncle buddy's phantom funhouse*. Watertown, MA: Eastgate Systems.

Mills, S. *Selected internet resources for writers*. trAce 1995 [cited]. Available from http://www.writersforthefuture.com/1995.

Montfort, N. (2003). *Twisty little passages: An approach to interactive fiction*. Cambridge, MA: MIT Press.

Nelson, T. (1970). No more teachers' dirty looks. *Computer Decisions, 9*(8), 16–23.

Nelson, T. (1974). *Computer lib/dream machines*. Self-published.

Nelson, T. (1987). *Computer lib/dream machine* (2nd ed.). Washington, DC: Microsoft Press.

O'Reilly, T. (2005). What is Web 2.0? Design patterns and business models for the next generation of software. *Oreilly.com*. Available from http://www.oreilly.com/pub/a/oreilly/tim/news/2005/09/30/what-is-Web-20.html.

Pipsqueak Productions. (2000). *The company therapist*[Web site] 1996–1999 [cited 3/1/2000]. Available from http://www.thetherapist.com.

Rettberg, J. W. (2008). *Blogging*. Cambridge, MA: Polity Press.

Rettberg, S. (2003). *Destination unknown: Experiments in the network novel*. Ph.D. thesis, Department of English and Comparative Literature, University of Cincinnati, Cincinnati. <http://loki.stockton.edu/□rettbers/PDFS/rettbergetd.pdf>

Rettberg, S. (2005). *All together now: Collective knowledge, collective narratives, and architectures of participation*. DAC 2005 conference proceedings. http://retts.net/documents/cnarrativeDAC.pdf.

Rosenberg, J. (2003). *Hypertext in the open air: A systemless approach to spatial hypertext*. Paper read at Third Workshop on Spatial Hypertext, Nottingham. http://www.csdl.tamu.edu/shipman/SpatialHypertext/SH3/rosenberg.pdf

Trigg, R. (1983). *A network-based approach to text handling for the online scientific community*. Ph.D. thesis, Department of Computer Science, Maryland, College Park, MD.

Trigg, R., & Irish, P. (1987). *Hypertext habitats: Experiences of writers in NoteCard*. Paper read at ACM Hypertext, Chapel Hill, NC.

van Dam, A. (1988).Hypertext '87: Keynote address. *Communications of the ACM, 31*(7), 887–895.

Walker, J. (1999). *Piecing together and tearing apart: Finding the story in 'afternoon'*. Paper read at Hypertext '99, Darmstadt, Germany. http://jilltxt.net/txt/afternoon.html.

Walker, J. (2002). *Links and power: The political economy of linking on the web*. Paper read at Hypertext 2002, Baltimore, MD. < http://jilltxt.net/txt/linksandpower.html>

Walker, J. (2005). Distributed narrative: Telling stories across networks. In M. Consalvo, J. Hunsinger, & N. Baym (Eds.), *Internet research annual*. New York, NY: Peter Lang.

Wardrip-Fruin, N. (2004). *What hypertext is*. Proceedings of the 15th ACM conference on hypertext & hypermedia. Santa Cruz, CA. http://doi.acm.org/10.1145/1012807.1012844.

Wardrip-Fruin, N., Chapman, A. C., Moss, B., & Whitehurst, D. (2000) *The impermanence agent*[Web narrative]. http://impermanenceagent.org.

Wittig, R. (1994). *Invisible rendezvous: Connection and collaboration in the new landscape of electronic writing*. Middletown, CT: Wesleyan UP.

Wittig, R. (2003). Justin hall and the birth of the 'blogs'. *Electronic Book Review*, http://www.electronicbookreview.com/thread/electropoetics/serial.

The Possibilities of Network Sociality

Michele Willson

The Possibilities of Network Sociality

> [T]he 'social' and the 'technical' are not separate spheres, but one and the same. New technologies reconfigure relationships between people and spaces they occupy, altering the basis of social interaction. The emergence of new media technologies, such as the mobile phone and the internet, creates new kinds of social relationships and a host of new activities and practices. (Wacjman, 2008: 66)

We live in a world where social practices are increasingly enacted through communication technologies. And while we have always been connected (or linked, to use the title of Barabási's 2002 book) not just to one another, though an essential and embedded sociality is taken for granted here, but at multiple levels of engagement with objects and environments, technology in many ways complicates the transmission and transparency of these engagements.

At one level, technological possibilities render social connections more visible. Technological interactions are often traceable and able to be archived, enabling evidence of social engagement to be recorded and analysis of this engagement to be undertaken. At another level, these connections are privatised and compartmentalised through technological means and within technological places, in many ways hidden from those outside of the interactions. On still another level, social practices and forms are constrained, shaped and enabled through the possibilities and limitations of the media and the ways in which these engagements are contextualised. What these possibilities mean for contemporary forms of sociality is a topic of ongoing enquiry.

Social software – software developed for the purposes of facilitating social interaction between individuals and groups using the internet – enables collaborative, communal and interpersonal engagements in a multitude of forums and formats. Blogs, wikis, social networking sites, MMORPGs; there are many different sites and applications for people to use for varying forms and experiences of sociality.

M. Willson (✉)
Department of Internet Studies, School of Media, Culture and Creative Arts,
Curtin University of Technology, Perth, Western Australia
e-mail: m.willson@curtin.edu.au

J. Hunsinger et al. (eds.), *International Handbook of Internet Research*,
DOI 10.1007/978-1-4020-9789-8_30, © Springer Science+Business Media B.V. 2010

As Maria Bakardjieva (2003) notes, users do different things for different reasons online. Individual self-presentation and identity construction, collective mobilisation, political persuasion, information collection and sharing, gaming, dating, to name just a few activities, all take place. Likewise, social activity that is sequestered within an online environment exists alongside practices that use the technology to connect and maintain 'offline' social relations/forms. The ramifications of using technologies in these ways are complex and deserving of further analysis.

This article focuses on *network sociality*: a term used here to describe a mode of sociality facilitated by and through technological means. According to Andreas Wittel (2001),

> Network sociality is a technological sociality insofar as it is deeply embedded in communication technology, transport technology and technologies to manage relationships. It is a sociality that is based on the use of cars, trains, buses and the underground, of airplanes, taxis and hotels, and it is based on phones, faxes, answering machines, voicemail, videoconferencing, mobiles, email, chat rooms, discussion forums, mailing lists and websites. Transportation and communication technologies provide the infrastructure for people and societies on the move. (Wittel, 2001: 69–70)[1]

Wittel uses the concept of network sociality to describe the networking social practices of new media industry practitioners. He is thus predominantly interested in examining the ways in which technology is used to manage mainly face-to-face, 'offline' relationships within a particular professional grouping and the ways in which this encourages particular forms of sociality (Wittel, 2001: 60). However, his hypothesis is that

> network sociality will become the paradigmatic social form of late capitalism and the new cultural economy.... it is a sociality based on individualization and deeply embedded in technology; it is informational, ephemeral but intense, and it is characterized by an assimilation of work and play. (Wittel, 2001: 71)

This article is not adopting the term network sociality strictly in accordance with the ways in which Wittel presents it. For Wittel (2001), network sociality is directly counterposed to community (applying a very specific understanding of community; one that I would argue is historically specific and of little use in contemporary circumstances), understanding community as stable and coherent and network sociality as ephemeral.

However, the concept offers us a useful starting point for discussions of sociality – understood as the various ways in which we relate as social beings – within an increasingly technologically mediated environment. Network sociality thus becomes a useful metaphor to describe the many directional, interconnected and rhizomatic features of social activity in contemporary techno-society.[2]

In western techno-society, the individual is simultaneously individuated and interconnected (Poster, 1995). Virtual community and social network literatures

---

[1]He also notes the centrality of databases in this process.

[2]'Network' is used while noting reservations about some of the normative claims associated with networks more generally (for example, see Barney, 2004).

offer partial contributions to understanding this phenomenon. Yet these analyses often fail to address questions about changing subjectivity: whether ways of being-together mediated though technologies (and frequently dispensing with presence as a primary mode of engagement) affect our understandings of ourselves and others. Instead technological connectivity and the growth in social software is uncritically celebrated as facilitating an enhanced form of sociality and for increasing individual opportunities, ignoring broader questions about the types of social forms and social relations that are practiced as a result.

While acknowledging the place of a range of technologies in enabling network sociality, this article will focus predominantly, though not exclusively, on internet technologies, recognising the multiple and expanding technological possibilities, applications and uses that this denotes. The article attempts to do several things: it raises questions about the types of sociality enacted in contemporary techno-society, critically explores the notion of the networked individual and the focus on the individual evident in much of the technology and sociality literature, and asks questions about the place of the social in these discussions. It argues for a more well-balanced and multilevelled approach to questions of sociality in networked societies. The article starts from the position that possibilities enabled/afforded by the technologies we have in place have an effect upon the ways in which we understand being in the world together and our possible actions and futures. These possibilities are more than simply supplementary; in many ways they are transformative. The ways in which we grapple with these questions reveals as much about our understandings of sociality as it does about the technologies themselves.

Social/Technology

Technologically networked social forms are broad, extensive and in demand. The rapid development and growth of web 2.0, or the social web, is evidence of the need and indeed hunger for social connectivity: people are searching for many and varied ways of enacting being-together. As Nancy Baym (2002) notes, one of the main attractions of computer-mediated communication (CMC) is the intensely social possibilities that it affords.

Social software is designed to facilitate interaction between groups of individuals. Indeed, some of this software is deliberately intended to 'make' communities. However, technology is rarely adopted, practiced or experienced exactly as its developers intended. And these uses and their consequences are often not singular, completely anticipated, nor are they always complementary (Wacjman, 2008: 70). For example, Ronald Rice (2002: 116) notes the 'contradictory' effects of a technology when he discusses the automobile:

> [D]uring the initial stages, the automobile increased sociability (especially for women and even more so for farm women), while the modern period associates the automobile with the rise of suburban sprawl and increased distances between homes (and thus female homemakers).

While the automobile increased the ability to transcend distance more easily and more 'individually', thus enabling the bringing together of people who were geographically distant from one another, it also facilitated material and social practices that meant that those who did not have access to this technology (the automobile) were less able to participate or at the very least were more constrained in their participation. New practices of sociability were enabled that accommodated both the possibilities and limitations of the technology, although as Fischer (1992) notes, these changes were not as dramatic as had been forecast by early commentators.

Various and contesting assertions were likewise made about internet technology and its possible effects on social forms. Some asserted an increase in communal possibilities and others posited increased alienation and anti-social outcomes. Thus, numerous studies have taken place investigating whether the internet has had a positive or negative effect on individuals' sociality (Kraut et al., 1998; Hampton, 2004; DiMaggio, Hargitti, Neuman, & Robinson, 2001). Claims and counterclaims have been made; however, there appears to be a growing general consensus that the internet (understood broadly) offers a wide range of affordances and may expand the possibilities of sociability (Hampton, 2004; Wellman & Haythornthwaite, 2002). It is asserted that once users are familiarised with the technology, and as it is increasingly ubiquitous, the internet is becoming simply another avenue for social practices (Hampton, 2004; Haythornthwaite, 2005). Also, there is growing recognition of the multitude of internet possibilities, practices and uses and therefore that it is necessary to 'disaggregate' many analyses and to focus instead on the specificity of practices and of social forms (Woolgar, 2004).

For example, Caroline Haythornthwaite (2005) has shown that people avail themselves of a portfolio of communicative media and apply their use of each specific technology according to purpose and on the basis of the communicative range of that mode of communication. This use takes into account the varying advantages and disadvantages of each particular medium. However, while Haythornthwaite, Fischer and others have noted the ways in which new communication technologies add range to the types, forms and practices of sociability, these types of analysis do not ask questions about the ways in which these engagements are understood by users or the intersubjective relations that these choices and acts denote. Nor do they account for the possibilities arising from the increased specialisation and demarcation involved in allocating and pursuing particular media and particular purposes in particular contexts.

As has often been noted, transport and communication technologies enable the possibility of sociality across temporal and spatial categories and through various modes of engagement (face to face, computer mediated, etc.). These technologies therefore enable the extension of relationships and acts of exchange. However, through their very extension, the manner, form and experience of this exchange are arguably affected. Network sociality requires the acquisition and application of specific material, technical and social skills. It engenders the possibility and, indeed, growing expectation of specific temporal and spatial enactments (a small example, student expectations of near-immediate access to lecturing staff are increasing, partly as a consequence of the technological and communicative possibilities of email). It both reflects and affects understandings of relationships, ways of being in the world and ways of accessing the world. Thus network sociality is experienced on a number of levels that are often not addressed in the studies mentioned above.

For example, these studies do not recognise or interrogate the ways in which technologies of connectivity are increasingly adopted into our sense of self. It is not unusual for people to talk of feeling naked, bereft or vulnerable if they leave behind or cannot access the technologies through which they connect with their social networks. As these technologies and uses become commonplace, practices are adopted by people who increasingly assume that everybody has a mobile (cell) phone or access to email and the internet. Social occasions are organised accommodating these possibilities: an invite is sent via email; a rendezvous organised 'on location' through a mobile phone while located in a crowd; social protest movements facilitated through updates via personal technologies.[3] And because 'everyone has one', these technologies are seen as increasingly essential for undertaking everyday life practices. Thus the relationship between the 'human' and the technical means by which we enact many of our social practices becomes increasingly complex.

Social activities are often not discrete activities; they can be mixed with other intents and purposes. When enacted through technology, these possibilities are accentuated further. For example, they are often intertwined with marketing, surveillance and data gathering, information sharing, and broader entertainment practices. MySpace™ may be a social networking site but it is also heavily implicated in the activities of consumer society. Activities on MySpace™ are of interest to marketers and music consumers, among others. Likewise recommender systems (such as those used with sites like Amazon) are useful for participants wishing to identify those with shared interests; but they are also of great interest to data miners in search of linked demographic product information. Such data gathering and associated surveillance activities are suggested as being constitutive of various forms of subjectivity (Poster, 1995; Willson, 1997). Thus the impact and experience of sociality is not able to be considered in isolation from these broader enframings and co-existent practices and their resultant effects.

Through the processes of networked sociality enabled by the internet, temporal and spatial configurations are both disrupted and constructed in numerous ways. Relations with others can be orchestrated, managed differently and often more efficiently and/or instrumentally through the introduction of a mediating interface (Wittel, 2001; Willson, 2006). New possibilities become available. While in some ways fashioned by the processes, possibilities and limitations of the technology, the ways in which the network/s relies on nodal points of contact offer the node (or individual) many opportunities for connectivity.

---

[3]There is a rapidly growing body of literature on the topic of mobile technologies and the possibilities they create for different social practices. See for example, Larsen, Urry, and Kay (2008).

Networked Individual

With the proclaimed change towards networks as the dominant organisational mode of practice, there is also claimed to be a corresponding rise in the networked individual (Castells, 2001): individuals who manage, co-ordinate and participate in various networks within which they are an important (if not central) nodal point.[4]

Manuel Castells and also Barry Wellman and his colleagues from Netlab in Toronto assert (though their focus of interest varies) that there has been an increase in the phenomenon of the so-called networked individual and personalised practices of sociality. Wellman (2001a, 2001b) utilises this notion to describe what he sees as a largely positive development whereby individuals are freed from many of the constraining and bounded qualities of more traditional homogenous social groupings. Instead, in societies where technologies are increasingly mobile and personal, social practices are enacted from person to person in ways that are not related to particular spatial restrictions,[5] a restriction attributed generally to many earlier social practices. Wellman also accedes that one of the 'negative' consequences of this type of social organisation is that there is a (heightened?) need for individuals to be cognisant and skilled in the acquisition of social capital; to know how to connect with others and with whom to connect (Wellman, 2001b).

Increased individuation takes place as nodal practices both interconnect and also demarcate. People (as nodes) are seen as able to access their social networks largely according to their own individual temporal, spatial and material needs and desires. These are constrained only by proximate and embodied demands and by the particular spatial and temporal rhythms of the various social networks in which they are involved. According to this understanding, the individual experiences her/himself as largely in control of her/his sociability through the possibilities of the technology: They access the technology when they wish to engage in social action. They are thus viewed and indeed are often theorised (Beck & Beck-Gernsheim, 1996) as compartmentalised or individuated persons who approach and engage in constitutive social practices in ways chosen by themselves.

There are a number of problems with this approach. The first is a tendency towards overstatement of the degree of choice available to the individual. It encourages the view of atomised and free-floating individuals without the constraints of environment, culture, social relations and so forth. Obviously, this is not the case and thus the degree of individual choice is more constrained than is indicated in these accounts. Another (related) problem is addressed in more detail below; however, it concerns the failure to recognise and engage with the importance of the social and of broader social and cultural frameworks within which individuals are situated.

---

[4] See Mascheroni (2007: 528) for a study of backpackers as a more extreme example.

[5] Other attributes are inferred with the lifting of spatial restrictions: increased freedom and choice for the individual from social constraints and pressures; more heterogeneity, etc.

A networked individual requires the existence of other individuals but also importantly the networks (hardware, software and relations) that connect them. Practices of sociality enacted through technologies such as web 2.0 or mobile telephones experientially reinforce such understandings but it is an understanding that places an emphasis on the individual as the originating point of or actor for that connection. Likewise much of the academic literature neglects consideration of broader social potentials outside of the existence of various networked configurations and of the possibilities of communication and connectivity availed to the individual. Social network analysis (SNA) does make some moves to correct this imbalance by placing consideration onto the *relationships* between individuals (Wasserman & Faust, 1994: 4); however, while it is able to describe shifting relationship configurations, density and structures, it is unable to deal with the broader social concerns (Howard, 2002; Monge & Contractor, 2003).

The notion of the networked individual is both useful and constraining. It is useful in encapsulating and representing many social practices that individuals engage in; as has been noted on numerous occasions, they are involved in multiple and overlapping individually negotiated social networks. It is also to some degree able to describe the seeming anomaly of increasingly interconnected but individuated persons, and the often proclaimed loneliness of such persons (Poster, 1995). However, it is also constraining: in terms of its largely uncritical and celebratory nature and, more importantly, in terms of its focus on the individual and an inability to interrogate questions of the social.

The Social Within Network Sociality?

> The 'someone' does not enter into a relation with other 'someones,' nor is there a 'community' that precedes interrelated individuals: the singular is not the particular, not a *part* of a group (species, gender, class, order). The relation is contemporaneous with the singularities. 'One' means: some ones *and* some other ones, or some ones *with* other one. (Nancy, 1997: 71)

By social, I am referring to something more complex than simply an aggregate of individuals, for there needs to be theoretical room to consider the individual, the relations between individuals and, also importantly, ways of being together (variously referred to as society, community or the public).[6] A failure to consider more than the individual and to make room for communal or social considerations is fraught on a number of levels. First, the validation of the centrality of the individual falls comfortably within the purview of common understandings of liberal individualism or even various celebrations of postmodern theory (Turkle, 1995) with all

---

[6]I recognize that each of these terms have their own specific conceptual meanings and inferences; however, there is something here that I am trying to suggest requires addressing that is larger than the individual, that is constitutive of shared horizons or understandings. These fall within the various discourses and interests of these terms.

the associated conceptual baggage that these understandings denote. Second is the associated inability to engage with questions of broader social frameworks.

Roger Silverstone (2003) in a critique of the promotion of personal networks, notes that

> [T]he idea of the personal community is possibly the ultimate step: an appropriately post-modern narcissistic move in which community becomes conceptually and empirically, and without irony or reflexivity, both a projection and an extension of the self. (Silverstone, 2003: 486)

More considered discussion is needed. Jean-Luc Nancy (1991: 3) notes that a solitary individual is a conceptual impossibility – an individual by definition requires the existence of other individuals. However, 'individual' also denotes a boundedness that writers like Nancy would like to avoid: he would prefer to write about being-together as being the relations, or incomplete sharing, between singularities as the quote at the beginning of this section indicates. He also writes that a focus on the subject or on the individual circumvents a thinking of community[7] and that instead one must focus more on the multiple yet singular relations between beings. While not wishing to engage in a debate about the intricacies of the use of the term individual (here it serves simply as useful and generically recognisable notion to denote persons), it is necessary to also conceptually and practically accommodate the importance of co-existence. It is also imperative – politically and ethically – to consider the ways in which co-existence is experienced and understood.

Elsewhere (Willson, 2006), I have noted the processes enacted when we use technologies to mediate and manage our social relations are more likely to lead to an instrumental approach being taken to these relations and for a more calculative understanding of relations as (potential) resources to be engaged. The other in these scenarios is approached as a social resource; indeed, the rhetoric of social capital popular at the moment in many ways confirms this instrumental and strategic approach to social forms. Wittel's discussion of network sociality and his analysis of new media industry attitudes and practices accords with this observation. In particular he notes the 'instrumentality and functionality of social relations' (Wittel, 2001: 60).

Some of the social networking sites such as MySpace™ or Friendster™ explicitly demonstrate this type of understanding of social relations inasmuch as they encourage the construction and representation of self as an available or desirable resource to be 'acquired'. As Gochenour (2006) notes, social software is focussed on assisting individuals to maintain and expand their individual social networks. This does not mean that these forms are unimportant to or not meaningful for participants, only that they represent particular social forms with particular (ego-centric, instrumental) intersubjective implications. Acts of sociality are increasingly 'specialised', one-dimensional or less multiplex and arguably thinner in their individual

---

[7]Here, 'community' is thought of more broadly than evidenced in many community studies. Instead, Nancy talks of community as an ontological relation that exists between singular beings, is always existent but is affected by social and political structures through which they are engaged.

enactment as a result of technological constraints than other forms of sociality may be. However, these individual enactments when performed in multiple arenas may form an overlapping, intersecting, dynamic montage or network of sociality. It is clear that the segmentation or compartmentalisation between these various groupings or communities is not rigid; the boundaries between and within are subject to contestation, conflict and ongoing negotiation (boyd, 2006). However, in the first instance, it is possible to identify these social networking acts as singular and largely purpose driven (e.g. a book reading 'community'; professional interest grouping; local neighbourhood grouping; intimate friend grouping). What this might mean for more sophisticated and nuanced understandings of sociality is unclear and as yet unable to be conceptually accommodated.

Related to the point above is that this individual focus and the (implicit) neglect of broader questions of the social mean that notions of shared social imaginaries (Taylor, 2004), notions of the public (Calhoun, 1998) and of shared horizons (Taylor, 1991) or of common cultural and social values (that in many ways make possible effective communication between persons possible) cannot be conceptually accommodated or discussed. If networked individuals interact within various, perhaps overlapping, personal networks, the question must be asked: how do we account for shared values, cultural understandings or other public goods that are larger than individual experiences and which the individual adopts in numerous ways in their everyday dealings? These questions point to the need for adequate analytical tools and languages able to interrogate the interrelationship between the individual and the social more broadly. Community and public sphere literatures do discuss shared understandings that are larger and more complex than utilitarian individualist approaches can account for though they often do not engage with network technologies; network literature talks of common protocols, clustering and weak and strong ties. However, there are problems here too.[8]

In some ways, recognition of being-together is in the network sociality literature but in an understated way and in a way that still needs further elaboration and refinement. As Taylor has noted (1991, 2004) there is an implicit conceptual requirement to accommodate the communal within these individualist understandings but that commonplace enactment and rhetoric fail to make this apparent or explicit. By default, therefore, the existence of others and of more communal associations is assumed even if represented as possible nodal connections. This is evident in the design and function of social software that sets out to facilitate interaction between groups of individuals. It is evident too in the practices of the open source movement and in the participation and types of relations enacted within online communities.

---

[8]For example, some community and public sphere literature is criticised for assumptions of homogenous memberships and an inability to deal with questions of difference. Totalising, reductive and determinist claims are made too about earlier community writings, but also potentially about some network literatures. Work is being undertaken in a number of spheres that seeks to reconcile the possibility of multiple pluralities and the possibility for solidarity (for example, Fenton, 2008).

However, the focus on the individual, and on multiple and fluid possibilities of association, in literature recounting social practices through technologies, and in the technologies themselves, largely fails to make space for consideration and discussion of broader commonalities, larger constitutive frameworks, and the co-existence and interrelationships of self and other.

Conclusion: Network Potentialities

Network sociality is practiced in ways that have certain implications that both represent and are constitutive of particular understandings of social engagement. In many ways, the increasing use of technology for practices and forms of sociality is suggestive more about our particular circumstances and our understandings of sociality itself than about the possibilities of the technology. By this I want to suggest that a reconfiguring of relationships is taking place, that the need or desire to conduct relationships through a variety of media and in a variety of forms that extend outside of the face to face is being driven by a range of factors, social, economic, cultural and political, including particular understandings of the individual and of community. These practices and understandings may be culturally specific, though the possibilities enabled by globalised technologies and practices must also be accorded some effect.[9] However, there is no doubt that our lives, practices and experiences of sociality have changed in some ways (and thus I reject outright the 'simply broadened media' forms of argument without consideration of broader subjective and intersubjective consequences).

Castells suggests,

> the study of sociability in/on/with the internet has to be situated within the context of the transformation of patterns of sociability. This is not to neglect the importance of the technological medium, but to insert its specific effects into the overall evolution of patterns of social interaction and into their relationship to the material supports of this interaction: space, organizations, and communication technologies. (Castells, 2001: 125)

I have suggested that the very transformation of patterns and the ways in which these patterns are practiced and experienced warrants closer examination. These patterns do accentuate the agency and nodal character of social participants (or networked individuals). But the research literature also obfuscates the importance of broader social patterns and co-existent (variously mediated) social forms. Network sociality is experienced in numerous ways that are not able to be accommodated by Castells' analysis. They also constitute specific subjective and intersubjective effects

---

[9]Castells, Tubella, Sancho, Diaz de Isla, and Wellman (2004) note that the Catalonians use the internet predominantly for information gathering and not social practices. While their article lacks an explanation as to how social practices are understood, this is still an interesting finding and suggests the need for further research into different social and cultural uses of the technology for sociality and what this means for intersubjective practices.

that, while culturally specific in terms of the ways sociality is practiced and thus the outcomes experienced, are insufficiently accommodated.

Simple measurement or mapping provides a part of the picture. But this is working within the language and presumptions of various paradigms that do not appear to recognise or engage with broader statements about ontological implications or new social configurations. I am not asserting a claim for or even the possibility of stepping outside of 'reality' or the present. However, I am asserting the need to reconsider the theoretical framing mechanisms and positions from which these undertakings are drawn.

An understanding enabled from the analogy of a network is an understanding of network as mesh seen as a complex interweaving of layers of connection and engagement. The many-layered engagements that are enacted within and across that mesh at all 'levels' merit more consideration. It may be possible, and useful, to extend the understanding of mesh to include multi-dimensional possibilities, i.e. to see the interstices and the interweaving to exist horizontally and vertically, in height and breadth (i.e. not an understanding that is flattened to a singular pane of understanding/practice or representation). This may then be able to accommodate consideration of the varying types, modes and forms of sociality practiced in techno-society.

At a phenomenological level, this might enable ways of conceptualising overlapping and concentric circles of sociality, affording the development of a more complete typology of different forms of sociality, an understanding of the types of intersubjective relations that dominate and what this means more broadly for acceptance of diversity and difference. More consideration of issues of power, ethics and of potentials, subject positions and the techno-human assemblages would form part of this reconsideration.

Such a re-conceptualisation allows for the recognition of different forms of sociality (according to different modes of organisation) co-existing at the same time. Thus it is able to incorporate some of the discussion about network sociality while also allowing space for consideration and discussion of the co-existence and influence of other modes of sociality. It would seek to understand the different ways in which relationships are practiced and experienced, the different forms of intersubjectivity and the types of power differentials evident in these forms. The question therefore is not whether sociality exists but about the ways in which it is experienced or manifested; as varying modes of being together, though these may present in different forms, through different media and in different practices.

There are broader questions too about ethics and consideration for the other – not only, though importantly for those who cannot enable themselves of this technological connectivity, whose lives are undeniably affected by broader social changes in some ways enabled or encouraged by these developments (remember the automobile example) but also for the ways in which we organise and understand our social relations, for the practices that are encouraged and the subjective experience that may result. The increasing prevalence of network social practices does result in a different subjectivity and encourage different forms and experiences of sociality. Rather than simply asserting the possibilities of the internet, we also need to consider what the ways in which we use it say about us and our understanding of social relations and what this might mean for future social forms of practices and directions. Is this the direction in which we want to go? What sorts of considerations do we need to take into account? How do we approach theorising these modes of sociality? And what are the questions we are not asking?

Acknowledgments The author would like to thank Robyn Mayes, Marta Celletti, Susan Leong, Teodor Mitew, and Jeremy Hunsinger for their helpful comments on various drafts. She would also like to acknowledge the support given by Curtin University's Research and Development strategic research grant scheme, enabling the time to write this article.

References

Bakardjieva, M. (2003). Virtual togetherness: an every-day life perspective. *Media, Culture & Society, 25,* 291–313.

Barabási, A.-L. (2002). *Linked: The new science of networks.* Cambridge, MA: Perseus Publishing.

Barney, D. (2004). *The Network Society. Key concepts series.* Cambridge, UK: Polity Press.

Baym, N. (2002). Interpersonal life online. In L. A. Lievrouw & S. Livingstone (Eds.), *Handbook of new media: Social shaping and consequences of ICTs* (pp. 62–76). London: Sage Publications.

Beck, U., & Beck-Gernsheim, E. (1996). Individualization and "Precious Freedoms": Perspectives and controversies of a subject-orientated sociology. In P. Heelas, S. Lash, & P. Morris (Eds.), *Detraditionalization: Critical reflections on authority and identity* (pp. 23–48). Cambridge, UK: Blackwell Publishers.

Boyd, D. (2006). Friends, friendsters, and top 8: Writing community into being on social network sites. *First Monday, 11*(12). Retrieved December 6, 2006, from http://www.firstmonday.org/issues/issue11_12/boyd/

Calhoun, C. (1998). The public good as a social and cultural project. In W. W. Powell & E. S. Clemens (Eds.), *Private action and the public good* (pp. 20–35). New Haven, CT: Yale University Press.

Castells, M. (2001). *The internet galaxy: Reflections on the internet, business, and society.* Oxford: Oxford University Press.

Castells, M., Tubella, I., Sancho, T., Diaz de Isla, M. I., & Wellman, B. (2004). Social structure, cultural identity and personal autonomy in the practice of the internet: The network society in Catalonia. In M. Castells (Ed.), *The network society: A cross-cultural perspective* (pp. 233–249). London: Edward Elgar.

DiMaggio, P., Hargitti, E., Neuman, W. R., & Robinson, J. P. (2001). Social implications of the internet. *Annual Review of Sociology, 27,* 307–336.

Fenton, N. (2008). Mediating solidarity. *Global Media and Communication, 4*(1), 37–57.

Fischer, C. S. (1992). *America calling: A social history of the telephone to 1940.* Berkeley, CA: University of California Press.

Gochenour, P. H. (2006). Distributed communities and nodal subjects. *New Media & Society, 8*(1), 33–51.

Hampton, K. (2004). Networked sociability online, off-line. In M. Castells (Ed.), *The network society: A cross-cultural perspective* (pp. 217–232). Cheltenham, UK: Edward Elgar.

Haythornthwaite, C. (2005). Social networks and internet connectivity effects. *Information, Communication and Society, 18*(2), 125–247.

Howard, P. N. (2002) Network ethnography and the hypermedia organization: new media, new organizations, new methods. *New Media & Society, 4*(4), 550–574.

Kraut, R., Lundmark, V., Patterson, M., Kiesler, S., Mukopadhyay, T., & Scherlis, W. (1998). Internet paradox: A social technology that reduces social involvement and psychological well-being? *American Psychologist, 53* (9), 1017–1031. Retrieved July 19, 2001, from http://www.apa.org/journals/amp/amp5391017.html

Larsen, J., Urry, J., & Kay, A. (2008). Coordinating fFace-to-face meetings in mobile network societies. *Information, Communication and Society, 11*(5), 640–658.

Mascheroni, G. (2007). Global nomads' network and mobile sociality: Exploring new media uses on the move. *Information, Communication and Society, 10*(4), 527–546.

Monge, P. R., & Contractor, N. S. (2003). *Theories of communication networks.* New York, NY: Oxford University Press.

Nancy, J.-L. (1991). *The inoperative community.* P. Connor (Ed.), P. Connor, W. Garbus, M. Holland, & S. Sawhney (Trans.). Minneapolis, MN: University of Minnesota Press.

Nancy, J.-L. (1997). *The sense of the world* (J. Librett, Trans.). Minneapolis, MN: University of Minnesota Press.

Poster, M. (1995). *The second media age.* Cambridge, UK: Polity Press.

Rice, R. E. (2002). Primary issues in internet use: Access, civic and community involvement, and social interaction and expression. In L. A. Lievrouw & S. Livingstone (Eds.), *Handbook of new media: Social shaping and consequences of ICTs* (pp. 105–135). London: Sage Publications.

Silverstone, R. (2003). Proper distance: Toward an ethics for cyberspace. In G. Liestol, A. Morrison, & T. Rasmussen (Eds.), *Digital media revisited: Theoretical and conceptual innovations in digital domains* (pp. 469–490). Cambridge, MA: MIT Press.

Taylor, C. (1991). *Ethics of authenticity.* Cambridge, MA: Harvard University Press.

Taylor, C. (2004). *Modern social imaginaries.* Durham, NC: Duke University Press.

Turkle, S. (1995). *Life on the screen: Identity in the age of the internet.* New York, NY: Simon & Schuster.

Wacjman, J. (2008). Life in the fast lane? Towards a sociology of technology and time. *The British Journal of Sociology, 59*(1), 59–77.

Wasserman, S., & Faust, K. (1994). *Social network analysis: Methods and applications.* Cambridge, MA: Cambridge University Press.

Wellman, B. (2001a). Computer networks as social networks. *Science, 293,* 2031–2034.

Wellman, B. (2001b). Physical place and cyberplace: The rise of personalized networking. *International Journal of Urban and Regional Research, 25*(2), 227–252.

Wellman, B., & Haythornthwaite, C. (2002). *The internet in everyday life.* Oxford: Blackwell.

Willson, M. (1997). Community in the abstract: A political and ethical dilemma? In D. Holmes (Ed.), *Virtual politics: Identity and community in cyberspace* (pp. 145–162). London: Sage Publications.

Willson, M. (2006). *Technically together: Rethinking community within techno-society.* New York, NY: Peter Lang.

Wittel, A. (2001). Toward a network sociality. *Theory Culture and Society, 18*(6), 51–76.

Woolgar, S. (2004). Reflexive internet? The british experience of new electronic technologies. In C. Manuel (Ed.), *The network society: A cross-cultural perspective* (pp. 125–142). Cheltenham, UK: Edward Elgar.

Web Search Studies: Multidisciplinary Perspectives on Web Search Engines

Michael Zimmer

Introduction

Perhaps the most significant tool of our internet age is the web search engine, providing a powerful interface for accessing the vast amounts of information available on the world wide web and beyond.[1] While the first web search engines focused on providing navigation to the various pages across the world wide web, search providers have steadily expanded their searchable indexes to include a wide array of online information, such as images, news feeds, Usenet archives, and video files. Additionally, search engines have begun digitizing the "material world," adding the contents of popular books, university libraries, maps, and satellite images to their growing indexes. Further, users can now search the files on their hard drives, send e-mail and instant messages, shop online, engage in social networking, organize photos, share videos, collaborate on projects, and publish blogs through various web search engine offerings. Consequently, users increasingly rely on a growing infrastructure of search-related services and tools to locate and access information online, as well as to communicate, collaborate, navigate, and organize their lives.

While still in its infancy compared to the knowledge tools that preceded it,[2] the impact of web search engines on society and culture has already received considerable attention from a variety of perspectives. Consistent with most other areas of internet research, interest in web search engines as a research topic crosses

M. Zimmer (✉)
School of Information Studies, University of Wisconsin-Milwaukee, Wisconsin, USA
e-mail: zimmerm@uwm.edu

[1] According to the Pew internet & American Life Project, 84% of American adult internet users have used a search engine to seek information online (Fallows, 2005: 1), making searching the web the second most popular online activity (behind using e-mail) (Rainie, 2005). In August 2007, over 750 million people worldwide over the age of 15 conducted a search, totaling more than 61 billion searches (Burns, 2007).

[2] The first full-text web search engine was WebCrawler, launched in 1994 (InfoSpace, 2007), making search engines relative "teenagers" compared to other tools and technologies for organizing and retrieving information. Encyclopedias, for example, date back to the first century AD.

J. Hunsinger et al. (eds.), *International Handbook of Internet Research*,
DOI 10.1007/978-1-4020-9789-8_31, © Springer Science+Business Media B.V. 2010

disciplines, ranging from the quite technical areas of computer and information sciences into the social sciences, law, and the humanities, providing a kaleidoscope of perspectives on the significance of these contemporary knowledge tools. This article aims to organize a meta-discipline of "web search studies," centered around a nucleus of major research on web search engines from five key perspectives: technical foundations and evaluations; transaction log analyses; user studies; political, ethical, and cultural critiques; and legal and policy analyses.[3]

Technical Foundations and Evaluations

Not surprisingly, some of the earliest research on web search engines was technical in nature. Numerous computer and information scientists have contributed not only valuable research on improving and enhancing the underlying web search engine technology but also technical analyses of the extent of coverage achieved by early search engine offerings and how well they met users' information-seeking needs. The former set includes early research that formed the technical foundation of various web search engines, some still in use today. For example, several papers focusing on crawling the web – an essential function for any web search engine – were presented at the first two world wide web conferences (Eichmann, 1994; McBryan, 1994; Pinkerton, 1994). These were followed by research describing more robust crawlers, such as Mercator (Heydon & Najork, 1999), one of the first scalable web crawlers supporting the AltaVista search engine, and the distributed crawler that fuels the search engine Google (Brin & Page, 1998).

Brin and Page's paper, "The Anatomy of a Large-Scale Hypertextual web Search Engine," introduced Google to the world and its unique "PageRank" method of using the link structure of the web to calculate a quality ranking for each page in its index (described in further detail at Page, Brin, Motwani, & Winograd, 1998).[4] Research into similar ranking schema was performed by Kleinberg (1999), who created the "Hypertext-Induced Topic Selection" (HITS) link analysis algorithm, and the similar "Stochastic Approach for Link-Structure Analysis" (SALSA) developed by Lempel and Moran (2000).[5] A large body of technical research continues to be produced related to all aspects of web search engine architecture and design,[6] including clustering (see Steinbach, Karypis, & Kumar, 2000), collaborative filtering (see Herlocker, Konstan, Terveen, & Riedl, 2004), personalization of results (see Khopkar, Spink, Giles, Shah, & Debnath, 2003; Keenoy & Levene, 2005; Teevan, Dumais, & Horvitz, 2005), understanding the structure of the web (see

---

[3]These categories are not necessarily mutually exclusive and are not put forth as airtight ontological divisions. They are meant simply to help organize this interdisciplinary collection of studies to aid discussion.

[4]Critical responses to PageRank, and Google overall, will be discussed below.

[5]For a comparison of web search engine ranking algorithms, see Borodin, Roberts, Rosenthal, and Tsaparas (2001).

[6]For a summary of literature on search engine design, see Arasu, Cho, Garcia-Molina, Paepcke, and Raghavan (2001).

Kleinberg, Kumar, Raghavan, Rajagopalan, & Tomkins, 1999; Broder et al., 2000; Kleinberg & Lawrence, 2001), and methods of crawling and indexing the hidden web (see Bergman, 2001; Raghavan & Garcia-Molina, 2001).

Efforts by Bergman or Raghavan and Garcia-Molina to help search engines crawl and index the hidden web – web content that might be dynamically created only after a user query, password-protected pages, unlinked pages, and so on – reveal a key challenge faced by web search engines: keeping up with the rapid growth and increased complexity of the world wide web. Early on, computer and informa-tion scientists understood the importance of evaluating the effectiveness of search engines in terms of their coverage: how much of the web has a particular search engine indexed. Lawrence and Giles (1998, 2000) were among the first to address this key evaluative dimension of web search engines, finding that any single search engine (at that time) had indexed only about one-third of the indexable web and only 16% of the entire world wide web. A recent attempt to update this research estimated that Google has indexed around 68% of the indexable web, with Yahoo!, MSN, and Ask following with 59%, 49%, and 43%, respectively (Gulli & Signorini, 2005).

Moving beyond statistical analyses of coverage attained by web search engines, other evaluative research has focused on measuring search engine stability and pre-cision (Vaughan, 2004), comparisons of results between different search engines (Bar-Ilan, Mat-Hassan, & Levene, 2006; Spink, Jansen, Blakely, & Koshman, 2006), and frequency with which search engines update their indexes (Lewandowski, Wahlig, & Meyer-Bautor, 2006). These studies are a subset within the larger area of information retrieval system evaluation,[7] which typically focuses on measuring the precision, recall, and reliability of a system to estimate its performance (see, for example, Sanderson, 2005). By their nature, such studies remain focused on the technical properties of an information retrieval system, measuring, for example, how precise a particular search engine's results are by comparing performance on a fixed set of queries and documents. The characteristics and considerations of the *users* of search engines remain absent from much of this research design, thereby overlooking the interactions between users and their search tools. To compensate, many web search engine researchers have turned to transaction log analysis to bring the user into the focus.

Transaction Log Analyses

Transaction log analysis takes advantage of the detailed server logs maintained by web search engines to learn about users interaction with the search engine, such as the structure of search queries, length of time spent on search tasks, selection of search results. Large-scale transaction log analyses typically rely on large data

---

[7] A library of research on information retrieval systems can be found at the website for the ACM Special Interest Group on Information Retrieval: http://www.sigir.org/proceedings/Proc-Browse.html.

sets provided by a particular web search engine; three of the largest studies involved data sets from AltaVista, Excite, and the German search engine Fireball. In his study of Fireball, Höelscher (1998) analyzed approximately 16 million queries processed in 1998, providing one of the first detailed examinations of search query structure. Höelscher discovered that the average search query length was 1.66 terms, with over 50% consisting of just one keyword, while less than 2% containing five or more keywords. The study also revealed that over 59% of users never went beyond the first page of search results, and 8 out of 10 users examined only 30 or fewer search results (Fireball presented 10 search results per page).

A similar transaction log analysis was performed by Silverstein, Henzinger, Marais, and Moricz (1999), this time taking advantage of a transaction log from AltaVista with almost 1 billion queries from a 42-day period of search activity. Along with a query structure analysis similar to the Fireball study (the average query length for the AltaVista data was 2.35 terms), Silverstein was also able to provide insights into user sessions with search engines, the series of queries made by a single user over a short period of time (in this study, the time cutoff was 5 minutes). The vast majority of sessions, over 77%, contained only one query, and for 85% of all queries, only the first screen of results was viewed. On average, users submitted just over two queries per session, seldom modified the original query, and only examined 1.39 screens of search results.

A third major transaction log study by Jansen, Spink, and Saracevic (2000) analyzed one day's worth of query data (over 51,000 queries from about 18,000 searchers) from the then popular Excite search engine. They reported on the number of queries per user, number of search terms per query, number of results clicked, query structure and modification, and the relative occurrence and distribution of particular search terms and subject areas. This research was expanded into a 6-year study, benefiting from additional search engine transaction logs, with updated results published a few years later (see Spink & Jansen, 2004). This longitudinal transaction log analysis provided new insights into various factors involving users search behaviors, including a growing diversity of search topics, increasing search query complexity, and an increase in the percentage of searchers viewing only the first page of results.

Complementing these large-scale transaction log analyses of users search behavior are various secondary studies that rely on smaller sets of user data or focus on narrower aspects of user search activity. A summary and comparison of these smaller-scale studies is provided by Jansen and Pooch (2001), while Jansen and Spink (2005) have consolidated results of nine separate transaction log analyses to provide a valuable insight into web searching trends. Yet, while transaction log analysis provides greater insight into users' actual experience with web search engines than formal technical analysis of search engine design, their ability to fully understand user behavior remains limited. Reliance on transaction logs to measure how many pages of results are viewed or how often search queries are modified or fails is unable to understand a user's actual motivations or reasoning behind such actions. User studies, whether in a laboratory setting or ethnographic in nature, help reveal these missing insights.

User Studies

Notwithstanding the value of transaction log data analysis, these types of studies offer limited insights into the behavior of web searchers beyond the decontextualized extraction of search queries and other session-based data that reside in the logs. Many researchers have turned to user studies, either in the form of controlled experiments, installation of tracking software, personal surveys, or qualitative ethnographies, in order to better understand usage of web search engines and whether the needs of users are being met. Choo, Detlor, and Turnbull (1998, 2000) combined three methods of data collection to better understand user search behavior: questionnaire survey, a software application that recorded web browser actions, and personal interviews with participants. They collected web search data from employees of seven different companies over the course of 2 weeks and provided insights into how a user's motivations (the strategies and reasons for viewing and searching) and moves (the tactics used to find and use information) are important factors when studying and evaluating web search activities. The work of Machill, Neuberger, Schweiger, and Wirth (2004) and Höelscher and Strube (2000) similarly combined surveys, interviews, and transaction log analysis to characterize a number of information-seeking behaviors of web search engine users.

Hargittai's (2002, 2004b) extensive use of surveys and in-person observation of search engine usage has provided insights into how people find information online in the context of their other media use, their general internet use patterns, and their social support networks. Broadening the analysis of user behavior beyond transaction logs also allowed Hargittai (2004a) to contextualize user search behavior, revealing the ways that factors such as age, gender, education level, and time spent online are relevant predictors of a user's web searching skills and chance of successfully finding the information they seek.

Other recent user studies include Wirth, Böcking, Karnowski, and von Pape (2007) whose experiments combined a client-oriented web content analysis, a think-aloud protocol, and an online questionnaire to determine how users make decisions concerning the results with which they are presented after performing a search; various experiments to measure how users view and interact with the results page of a search engine using eye-tracking technology (see, for example, Pan et al., 2004); Dennis, Bruza, and McArthur (2002) controlled experiment to compare search effectiveness between query-based internet search (via the Google search engine), directory-based search (via Yahoo), and phrase-based query reformulation-assisted search (via the Hyperindex browser), and Martey (2008) and Roy and Chi's (2003) examinations of gendered differences in web search engine use suggest that males and females demonstrate different web navigation patterns.

Thus far, the studies discussed in this section (as well as the previous one) sought to measure the particular *use and effectiveness* of web search engines. Another important area of user-based research has focused instead on measuring *user awareness* of how web search engines operate (such as whether users understand how sites are indexed and ranked by search engines) and how this awareness might impact their successful use of search tools.[8] For example, recognizing that users ability to benefit fully from web search engines (and mitigate any possible negative effects) is dependent on their understanding of how they function, Hendry and Efthimiadis (2008) examine the conceptual understandings that people have of search engines by performing a content analysis on the sketches that 200 undergraduate and graduate students drew when asked to draw a sketch of how a search engine works. Their user study reveals a diverse range of conceptual approaches, metaphors, representations, and misconceptions, calling attention to the importance of improving students' technical knowledge of how search engines work so they can be better equipped to fully utilize these important tools.

Political, Ethical, and Cultural Critiques

In their major research publication of longitudinal search engine transaction log analysis, Spink and Jansen (2004) note that the "overwhelming research focus in the scientific literature is on the technological aspects of Web search" and that when studies do venture beyond the technology itself, they are "generally focused on the individual level of analysis" (p. 181). This is evidenced above, where most user studies aim to construct the "typical user" in terms of their usage of web search engines or awareness of typical business practices within the search industry. While understanding these issues from the user perspective is crucial, implicit within the questions these studies ask ("are searchers finding the information they're looking for?"; "do searchers understand that some results might appear due to a business relationship with the search engine"?; "do searchers know their search activity might be tracked by the search provider?") are broader concerns, such as access to knowledge, bias, and privacy. In response, a wide array of political, ethical, and cultural critiques of web search engines have emerged.

Introna and Nissenbaum's (2000) seminal study, "Shaping the Web: Why the Politics of Search Engines Matter," was among the first to analyze search engines from such a critical perspective. They noted that while search engines have been heralded as a powerful source of access and accessibility, they "systematically exclude certain sites, and certain types of sites, in favor of others, systematically giving prominence to some at the expense of others" (p. 169), thereby undermining the potential of the world wide web – and search engines as the portal to the web – to be an inclusive democratic space. Expanding upon Introna and Nissenbaum's foundation, similar critiques have been applied to web search engines from a variety of standpoints. For example, Hargittai (2004b) has extended her user studies to include investigations of how financial and organizational considerations within the web search engine industry impact the way in which content is organized, presented, and distributed to users.

---

[8]These concerns relate to some of the cultural and social issues that will be discussed in more detail below.

Van Couvering (2004, 2008) has engaged in extensive research on the political economy of the search engine industry in terms of its ownership, its revenues, the products it sells, its geographic spread, and the politics and regulations that govern it. Drawing comparisons to concerns over market consolidations in the mass media industry, Van Couvering fears that the market concentration and business practices of the search engine industry might limit its ability to serve "the public interest in the information society" (Van Couvering, 2004, p. 25). Diaz (2008) arrives at a similar conclusion, noting that the inherent limitations of a commercialized, advertising-based search engine – Google, in this case – inevitably lead to a failure to support deliberative democratic ideals. Lev-On (2008), however, offers a different view, arguing that web search engines indirectly *contribute* to political organization and deliberative discourse by generating unintentional exposures to diverse and opposing views. In doing so, web search engines "cater to the concerns of both deliberative democrats aiming at enriching the deliberative qualities of democratic discussion, and pluralist democrats who are concerned about making the political marketplace more open, inclusive and competitive" (Lev-On, 2008). Additional contributions to this debate include Hindman, Tsioutsiouliklis, and Johnson (2003), Fortunato, Flammini, Menczer, and Vespignani (2005), and Menczer, Fortunato, Flammini, and Vespignani (2006).

Extending from these political critiques about their role in supporting deliberative discourse, web search engines have also been scrutinized from a broader moral and ethical perspective. A recent panel discussion at the Santa Clara University Markkula Center for Applied Ethics was one of the first to bring together ethicists, computer scientists, and social scientists for the express purpose of confronting some of the "unavoidable ethical questions about search engines," including concerns of search engine bias, transparency, censorship, trust, and privacy (Norvig, Winograd, & Bowker, 2006). A special issue of the *International Review of Information Ethics* on "The Ethics of Search Engines" (Nagenborg, 2005) brought into focus many of the ethical issues highlighted in the Santa Clara panel. For example, Rieder (2005) and Welp and Machill (2005) argue for more openness and transparency in web search engine practices, while Tavani (2005) expresses concern about the power of search engines to acquire information about persons online, narrowing the distinction between public and private information and threatening the privacy and liberty of individuals. Finally, Hinman (2005) provides a succinct summary of the persistent ethical issues in search engines, including the lack of transparency in ranking algorithms; concerns over the censorship of information by local authorities; and the problem of privacy with regard to the ability to track user search activity. Separately, Zimmer (2006) provides a brief introduction to how the practice of paid insertion and paid placement of search results presents challenges to a host of moral values, including freedom from bias, trust, and privacy.

Tavani, Hinman, and Zimmer all touch on key privacy issues surrounding web search: the routine practice of monitoring and archiving users' search activities. This threat to user privacy has drawn considerable attention, especially in the wake of recent news events where Google resisted a government request to turn over records of search activity (see Kopytoff, 2006) and AOL's release to the research community of over 20 million search queries from 658,000 of its users which were insufficiently anonymized and exposing user queries (see Hansell, 2006). For example, Chopra and White (2007) have criticized Google's defense of Gmail's "reading" of incoming e-mail messages in order to place relevant advertising – the claim that no human reads the message – by arguing that as natural language processing and semantic extraction used in artificial agents become increasingly sophisticated, the corporations that deploy those agents, such as Google, will be more likely to be attributed with knowledge of their users' personal information, thus triggering legitimate privacy concerns. Röhle (2007) expresses concern over how the push for the personalization of search results and related advertising results in the commercial exploitation of users' personal information. Zimmer (2008a, 2008b) shares Röhle's anxiety over the privacy implications of the drive for personalization of results and advertising, and elsewhere he utilizes the theory of privacy as "contextual integrity" to help clarify these privacy concerns, arguing that Google's widespread collection of user activity across all their products and services reflects a significant shift in the existing norms of personal information flows. Finally, Albrechtslund (2006) outlines the ethical problems and dilemmas that emerge as searching the web increasingly becomes a form of surveillance, both for purposes of control as well as social play.

Along with these political and ethical critiques, a number of scholars have studied and scrutinized web search engines from a broader cultural studies perspective, revealing, for example, how they impact notions of time, cognition, and the construction of knowledge. Iina Hellsten and her colleagues (Wouters, Hellsten, & Leydesdorff, 2004; Hellsten, Leydesdorff, & Wouters, 2006) have explored the ways in which search engines "re-write the past" due to the frequent updating of their indices, leading to both a loss of a historical record of content on the web and a disruption in the "temporal structure" of the web itself. Heintz (2006) explores the epistemological impact of web search engines, arguing that the distributed nature of the link structure of the web – and the related distributed assessment of web pages based on incoming links – leads to a new cognitive and epistemic processes that are, themselves, distributive. Various cultural and critical theorists build upon Deleuze and Guattari's (1987) notion of the rhizome when describing the potential of search engines to reflect the random interconnectedness of the internet and to foster non-hierarchical information spaces.

Legal and Policy Analyses

As the number of political, ethical, and cultural critiques of web search engines increases, so do calls for solutions to the dilemmas they present. A key avenue for such remedies is through law and policy. Scholarly contributions to this pursuit include two key articles establishing the area of "search engine law": Gasser's (2006) detailed outline of the legislation and litigation that has emerged in the US legal system alongside the rapid rise of web search engines, along with

Grimmelmann's (2007) systematic taxonomy of search engine law, broken down into the interests of the users, providers, third parties, and the search engines themselves. Together, these two articles provide the necessary legal backdrop to inform any attempt to regulate or legislate search engine practices.

Other legal scholars have focused their attention on particular issues related to web search engines, such as access control, bias, and manipulation of results. For example, Elkin-Koren (2001) focuses on the potential role of search engines as gate-keepers of information online, fearing that creating a right to exclude indexers opens up the door for increased control of access to content. Chandler (2008) argues that long-established free speech rights also extend to the right to reach an audience free from the discriminatory influence intermediaries, such as a search engine's decision as to how to rank a site (if at all). Like Elkin-Koren, Chandler proposes a mix of regulatory and legislative approaches to address her concerns and protect the flow of information mediated by web search engines. Goldman (2006), however, disagrees. In his view search engine bias is a beneficial consequence of search engines optimizing content for their users, and any attempt to regulate perceived biases would diminish search providers' ability to provide relevant results to their users. Adding to this debate, Pasquale and Bracha (2007) make perhaps the boldest call for regulating what they describe as the "manipulation" of search engine results. Comparing search engines to common carriers, such as phone companies or public utilities, the authors reject market- or technology-based solutions, and instead call for the creation of a regulatory framework that would balance secrecy with transparency and, in the end, prevent "improper behavior by search engines."

Additional legal and policy scholarship addressing web search engines continues to be generated, much of it focusing on copyright issues that emerge with the widespread indexing of online content, along with the expansion of web search services to include video and books. For example, O'Brien and Fitzgerald (2006; Fitzgerald, O'Brien, & Fitzgerald, 2008) examine search engine liability for possible copyright infringement and argue for changes in copyright law to better accommodate the unique value search engines offer society. Travis (2006) focuses on the particular copyright and fair use implications of Google's plan to scan and make searchable and viewable online the contents of up to 15 million library books, suggesting that the courts and policymakers should recognize that Google is making fair and permissible uses of copyrighted works when it enhances both their distribution and use. Vaidhyanathan (2007) provides a contrary view, criticizing Google's book project on three grounds: privacy (the fact that Google's interface can track what books users search and access), privatization (criticizing the shift from public libraries to a single, for-profit corporation), and property (criticizing Google's fair use claim for duplicating copyright-protected work). Vaidhyanathan concludes that Google's book scanning project threatens both the stability and utility currently provided by public libraries, as well as the fair use exception to copyright.

Along with this array of legal scholarship, recent workshops and symposia have been convened to focus and harness this array of attention in order to help arrive at workable legal or policy solutions to many of these search engine-related concerns.

For example, leading legal scholars, policy makers, and industry lawyers gathered in December 2005 at Yale Law School to discuss the possibility of regulating search engines and to map out the relevant legal and policy domains,[9] while a similar group convened a year later at the Haifa Center of Law and Technology to identify the role of the law and of regulators in governing the performance of search engines.[10] Outside of academia, the Federal Trade Commission recently held public meetings to examine the privacy issues that emerge with the growing practice of behaviorally targeting web advertising often performed by search engines based on keywords or other user profiling (Federal Trade Commission, 2007). Additionally, various legal journals are paying close attention to the ongoing debates, such as a special issue of the *Journal of Business and Technology Law* dedicated to the numerous legal issues surrounding Google.[11]

Directions for Future Research

While far from exhaustive, the preceding sections reveal the growing interest – and importance – of studying web search engines from a variety of disciplinary approaches. Along with the necessary technical design and evaluative research, significant contributions have been made to understand web search engines within the context of transaction log analysis and user studies, within political, ethical, and cultural perspectives, and to utilize legal and policy analysis to help understand where possible remedies to many search-related concerns might exist.

Future research must ensure continued progress in the multidisciplinary understanding of the design, use, and implications of web search engines. Four research areas can quickly be identified that deserve particular attention: search engine bias, search engines as gatekeepers of information, values and ethics of search engines, and framing the legal constraints and obligations.

(1) Search Engine Bias: Technical and evaluative studies must be undertaken to identify possible instances of bias in search engines, and additional user studies must attempt to measure its effects on users' experiences searching the web. Only when armed with such additional data can we begin to address the normative dimensions of the bias itself.
(2) Search Engines as Gatekeepers of Information: Future research must focus on reducing the opacity regarding how web search engines work, identifying whether any intentional gatekeeping functions exist. While we are aware of some gatekeeping functions of search engines, such as Google's complicity

---

[9]See "Regulating Search?: A Symposium on Search Engines, Law, and Public Policy" (http://isp.law.yale.edu/regulatingsearch/overview/).

[10]See "The Law of Search Engines" (http://law.haifa.ac.il/events/event_sites/se/).

[11]See http://www.law.umaryland.edu/journal/jbtl/index.asp.

with China's desire to censor certain search results, the extent to which gate-keeping might occur in versions of web search engines that exist in more open societies must be explored in more detail.

(3) Values and Ethics of Search Engines: Concerns over bias and gatekeeping point to the ways in which web search engines have particular value and ethical impli-cations for society. Additional work needs to take place to not only understand conceptually what values are at play with web searching, such as privacy, auton-omy and liberty, but also how users' search activities actually impact the values they experience in the real world.

(4) Framing the Legal Constraints and Obligations: It is clear from the sections above that law and policy can play a large role in mitigating many of the concerns expressed. For example, legal and regulatory frameworks could be constructed to ensure web search engines do not contain bias, for example, or to ensure the rights of copyright holders are protected, or that user privacy is protected. Yet, many argue against any attempt to regulate the search industry and instead insist that the marketplace will ensure users' needs are adequately fulfilled and rights are properly respected. Determining which approach is best requires further study and debate.

While web search studies appear to be out of its infancy, vast amounts of research remain to be undertaken for it to reach maturity as a discipline. I have provided only a few waypoints to guide that journey, and others will certainly take the reins and illuminate new perspectives, theories, and methodologies into understanding the design, uses, and wide-ranging impacts of web search engines on society, culture, politics, and law. As new scholarships into the implications of knowledge tools from our past continue to emerge, the field of web search studies has much room to grow.

References

Albrechtslund, A. (2006). *Surveillance in searching*. Paper presented at the EASST 2006, Lausanne.

Arasu, A., Cho, J., Garcia-Molina, H., Paepcke, A., & Raghavan, S. (2001). Searching the Web. *ACM Transactions on Internet Technology, 1*(1), 2–43.

Bar-Ilan, J., Mat-Hassan, M., & Levene, M. (2006). Methods for comparing rankings of search engine results. *Computer Networks, 50*(10), 1448–1463.

Bergman, M. (2001). The deep web: Surfacing hidden value. *Journal of Electronic Publishing, 7*(1). http://dx.doi.org/10.3998/3336451.0007.104.

Borodin, A., Roberts, G. O., Rosenthal, J. S., & Tsaparas, P. (2001). *Finding authorities and hubs from link structures on the world wide Web*. Proceedings of the 10th international conference on world wide web. Hong Kong (pp. 415–429).

Brin, S., & Page, L. (1998). The anatomy of a large-scale hypertextual Web search engine. *WWW7/Computer Networks, 30*(1–7), 107–117.

Broder, A., Kumar, R., Maghoul, F., Raghavan, P., Rajagopalan, S., Stata, R., et al. (2000). Graph structure in the Web. *Computer Networks, 33*(1–6), 309–320.

Burns, E. (2007). Worldwide internet: Now serving 61 billion searches per month. *SearchEngineWatch*. Retrieved November 2, 2007, from http://searchenginewatch.com/showPage.html?page=3627304

Chandler, J. (2008). A right to reach an audience: An approach to intermediary bias on the internet. *Hofstra Law Review, 35*(3), 1095–1138.

Choo, C. W., Detlor, B., & Turnbull, D. (1998). A behavioral model of information seeking on the Web: Preliminary results of a study of how managers and IT specialists use the Web. *Proceedings of the 61st Annual Meeting of the American Society for Information Science, 35,* 290–302.

Choo, C. W., Detlor, B., & Turnbull, D. (2000). Information seeking on the Web: An integrated model of browsing and searching. *First Monday, 5*(2), 2000.

Chopra, S., & White, L. (2007). *Privacy and artificial agents, or, is google reading my email?* Paper presented at the IJCAI 2007, Hyderabad, India.

Deleuze, G., & Guattari, F. (1987). *A thousand plateaus: Capitalism and schizophrenia* (B. Massumi, Trans.). Minneapolis, MN: University of Minnesota Press.

Dennis, S., Bruza, P., & McArthur, R. (2002). Web searching: A process-oriented experimental study of three interactive search paradigms. *Journal of the American Society for Information Science and Technology, 53*(2), 120–133.

Diaz, A. (2008). Through the Google goggles: Sociopolitical bias in search engine design. In A. Spink & M. Zimmer (Eds.), *Web searching: Multidisciplinary perspectives* (pp. 11–34). Dordrecht, The Netherlands: Springer.

Eichmann, D. (1994). *The rbse spider – balancing effective search against Web load.* Proceedings of the 1st international world wide web conference. Geneva (pp. 113–120).

Elkin-Koren, N. (2001). Let the crawlers crawl: On virtual gatekeepers and the right to exclude indexing. *University of Dayton Law Review, 26,* 180–209.

Fallows, D. (2005). Search engine users: Internet searchers are confident, satisfied and trusting – but they are also unaware and naïve. *Pew Internet & American Life Project.* Retrieved October 15, 2005, from http://www.pewinternet.org/pdfs/PIP_Searchengine_users.pdf

Federal Trade Commission. (2007). Ftc to host town hall to examine privacy issues and online behavioral advertising. Retrieved November 8, 2007, from http://ftc.gov/opa/2007/08/ehavioral.shtm

Fitzgerald, B., O'Brien, D., & Fitzgerald, A. (2008). Search engine liability for copyright infringement. In A. Spink & M. Zimmer (Eds.), *Web searching: Multidisciplinary perspectives* (pp. 103–120). Dordrecht, The Netherlands: Springer.

Fortunato, S., Flammini, A., Menczer, F., & Vespignani, A. (2005). The egalitarian effect of search engines. *Arxiv preprint cs.CY/0511005.* http://arxiv.org/pdf/cs.CY/0511005

Gasser, U. (2006). Regulating search engines: Taking stock and looking ahead. *Yale Journal of Law & Technology, 9,* 124–157.

Goldman, E. (2006).Search engine bias and the demise of search engine utopianism. *Yale Journal of Law & Technology, 8,* 188–200.

Grimmelmann, J. (2007). The structure of search engine law. *Iowa Law Review, 93*(1), 1–63.

Gulli, A., & Signorini, A. (2005). *The indexableWeb is more than 11.5 billion pages.* International World Wide Web Conference. Chiba: ACM Press (pp. 902–903).

Hansell, S. (2006). AOL removes search data on vast group of Web users. *The New York Times,* C4.

Hargittai, E. (2002). Beyond logs and surveys: In-depth measures of people's Web use skills. *Journal of the American Society for Information Science and Technology, 53*(14), 1239–1244.

Hargittai, E. (2004a). Informed Web surfing: The social context of user sophistication. In *Society Online: the Internet in Context* (pp. 257–274). Thousand Oaks: Sage Publications, Inc.

Hargittai, E. (2004b). *The changing online landscape: From free-for-all to commercial gatekeeping.* Retrieved October 14, 2006, from http://www.eszter.com/research/c03-onlinelandscape.html

Heintz, C. (2006). Web search engines and distributed assessment systems. *Pragmatics & Cognition, 14*(2), 387–409.

Hellsten, I., Leydesdorff, L., &Wouters, P. (2006). Multiple presents: How search engines re-write the past. *New Media & Society, 8*(6), 901–924.

Hendry, D., & Efthimiadis, E. (2008). Conceptual models for search engines. In A. Spink & M. Zimmer (Eds.), *Web searching: Multidisciplinary perspectives* (pp. 277–307). Dordrecht, The Netherlands: Springer.

Herlocker, J. L., Konstan, J. A., Terveen, L. G., & Riedl, J. T. (2004). Evaluating collaborative filtering recommender systems. *ACM Transactions on Information Systems (TOIS), 22*(1), 5–53.

Heydon, A., & Najork, M. (1999). Mercator: A scalable, extensible Web crawler. *world wide web, 2*(4), 219–229.

Hindman, M., Tsioutsiouliklis, K., & Johnson, J. A. (2003). *Googlearchy: How a few heavilylinked sites dominate politics on the Web.* Annual meeting of the Midwest Political Science Association. Chicago, IL.

Hinman, L. (2005). Esse est indicato in Google: Ethical and political issues in search engines. *International Review of Information Ethics, 3*, 19–25.

Höelscher, C. (1998). *How internet experts search for information on the Web.* World conference of the world wide web, Internet, and Intranet. Orlando, FL.

Höelscher, C., & Strube, G. (2000).Web search behavior of internet experts and newbies. *Computer Networks, 33*(1–6), 337–346.

InfoSpace. (2007). *About webcrawler.* Retrieved November 3, 2007, from http://www.webcrawler.com/webcrawler/ws/about/_iceUrlFlag=11?_IceUrl=true

Introna, L., & Nissenbaum, H. (2000). Shaping theWeb:Why the politics of search engines matters. *The Information Society, 16*(3), 169–185.

Jansen, B. J., & Pooch, U. (2001). A review of Web searching studies and a framework for future research. *Journal of the American Society for Information Science and Technology, 52*(3), 235–246.

Jansen, B. J., & Spink, A. (2005). How are we searching the world wide Web? A comparison of nine search engine transaction logs. *Information Processing & Management, 42*(1), 248–263.

Jansen, B. J., Spink, A., & Saracevic, T. (2000). Real life, real users, and real needs: A study and analysis of user queries on theWeb. *Information Processing and Management, 36*(2), 207–227.

Keenoy, K., & Levene, M. (2005). Personalisation of Web search. In *Intelligent Techniques for Web Personalization* (pp. 201–228). Berlin: Springer.

Khopkar, Y., Spink, A., Giles, C. L., Shah, P., & Debnath, S. (2003). Search engine personalization: An exploratory study. *FirstMonday.* Retrieved October 23, 2007, from http://www.firstmonday.org/issues/issue8_7/khopkar/

Kleinberg, J. (1999). Authoritative sources in a hyperlinked environment. *Journal of the ACM (JACM), 46*(5), 604–632.

Kleinberg, J., & Lawrence, S. (2001). The structure of the Web. *Science, 294*, 1849–1850.

Kleinberg, J. M., Kumar, R., Raghavan, P., Rajagopalan, S., & Tomkins, A. (1999). The Web as a graph: Measurements, models and methods. *Proceedings of the International Conference on Combinatorics and Computing, 6*(1), 1–18.

Kopytoff, V. (2006). Google says no to data demand. *San Francisco Chronicle*, A1.

Lawrence, S., & Giles, C. L. (1998). Searching the world wide Web. *Science, 280*(5360), 98–100.

Lawrence, S., & Giles, L. (2000). Accessibility of information on the Web. *Intelligence, 11*(1), 32–39.

Lempel, R., & Moran, S. (2000). The stochastic approach for link-structure analysis (salsa) and the tkc effect. *Computer Networks, 33*(1–6), 387–401.

Lev-On, A. (2008). The democratizing effects of search engine use: On chance exposures and organizational hubs. In A. Spink & M. Zimmer (Eds.), *Web searching: Multidisciplinary perspectives* (pp. 135–149). Dordrecht, The Netherlands: Springer.

Lewandowski, D., Wahlig, H., & Meyer-Bautor, G. (2006). The freshness of Web search engine databases. *Journal of Information Science, 32*(2), 131.

Machill, M., Neuberger, C., Schweiger,W., &Wirth,W. (2004). Navigating the internet. *European Journal of Communication, 19*(3), 321–347.

Martey, R. M. (2008). Exploring gendered notions: Gender, job hunting and Web search engines. In A. Spink & M. Zimmer (Eds.), *Web searching: Multidisciplinary perspectives* (pp. 51–65). Dordrecht, The Netherlands: Springer.

McBryan, O. A. (1994). *Genvl and wwww: Tools for taming the Web.* Proceedings of the 1st International world wide web conference. Geneva pp. 79–90).

Menczer, F., Fortunato, S., Flammini, A., & Vespignani, A. (2006). Googlearchy or googlocracy? *IEEE Spectrum, 43*(2). http://www. spectrum.ieee.org/feb06/2787.

Nagenborg, M. (2005). The ethics of search engines (special issue). *International Review of Information Ethics, 3.*

Norvig, P., Winograd, T., & Bowker, G. (2006). The ethics and politics of search engines. *Panel at Santa Clara University Markkula Center for Applied Ethics.* Retrieved March 1, 2006, from http://www.scu.edu/sts/Search-Engine-Event.cfm

O'Brien, D., & Fitzgerald, B. (2006). Digital copyright law in a YouTube world. *Internet Law Bulletin, 9*(6/7), 71, 73–74.

Page, L., Brin, S., Motwani, R., & Winograd, T. (1998). *The PageRank citation ranking: Bringing order to the Web.* Retrieved January 12, 2007, from http://dbpubs.stanford.edu/pub/1999-66

Pan, B., Hembrooke, H., Joachims, T., Lorigo, L., Gay, G., & Granka, L. (2004). In Google we trust: Users' decisions on rank, position, and relevance. *Journal of Computer-Mediated Communication, 12*(3), 801–823.

Pasquale, F., & Bracha, O. (2007). Federal search commission? Access, fairness and accountability in the law of search. *U of Texas Law, Public Law Research Paper No. 123.* Retrieved August 15, 2007, from http://papers.ssrn.com/sol3/papers.cfm?abstract_id=1002453

Pinkerton, B. (1994). *Finding what people want: Experiences with the webcrawler.* Proceedings of the 2nd International world wide web conference. Elsevier Science

Raghavan, S., & Garcia-Molina, H. (2001). *Crawling the hidden Web.* Proceedings of the 27th International conference on very large data bases. Rome (pp. 129–138).

Rainie, L. (2005). Search engine use shoots up in the past year and edges towards e-mail as the primary internet application. *Pew Internet and American Life Project.* Retrieved September 15, 2006, from http://www.pewinternet.org/pdfs/PIP_SearchData_1105.pdf

Rieder, B. (2005). Networked control: Search engines and the symmetry of confidence. *International Review of Information Ethics, 3,* 26–32.

Röhle, T. (2007). Desperately seeking the consumer: Personalized search engines and the commercial exploitation of user data. *First Monday.* Retrieved October 23, 2007, from http://www.firstmonday.org/issues/issue12_9/rohle/index.html

Roy, M., & Chi, M. T. C. (2003). Gender differences in patterns of searching the Web. *Journal of Educational Computing Research, 29*(3), 335–348.

Sanderson, M. (2005). *Information retrieval system evaluation: Effort, sensitivity, and reliability.* Proceedings of the 28th annual international ACM SIGIR conference on research and development in information retrieval. Salvador (pp. 162–169).

Silverstein, C., Henzinger, M. R., Marais, H., & Moricz, M. (1999). Analysis of a very large Web search engine query log. *SIGIR Forum, 33*(1), 6–12.

Spink, A., & Jansen, B. J. (2004). *Web search: Public searching of the web.* New York, NY: Kluwer Academic Publishers.

Spink, A., Jansen, B. J., Blakely, C., & Koshman, S. (2006). A study of results overlap and uniqueness among major Web search engines. *Information Processing & Management, 42*(5), 1379–1391.

Steinbach, M., Karypis, G., & Kumar, V. (2000). A comparison of document clustering techniques. *KDD Workshop on Text Mining, 34,* 35.

Tavani, H. T. (2005). Search engines, personal information and the problem of privacy in public. *International Review of Information Ethics, 3,* 39–45.

Teevan, J., Dumais, S. T., & Horvitz, E. (2005). *Personalizing search via automated analysis of interests and activities.* Proceedings of the 28th annual international ACM SIGIR conference on research and development in information retrieval. ACM Press (pp. 449–456).

Travis, H. (2006). Google Book search and fair use. *University of Miami Law Review, 61*, 601–681.

Vaidhyanathan, S. (2007). The googlization of everything and the future of copyright. *University of California Davis Law Review, 40*(3), 1207–1231.

Van Couvering, E. (2004). *New media? The political economy of internet search engines*. Annual conference of the International Association of Media & Communications Researchers. Porto Alegre, Brazil (pp. 7–14).

Van Couvering, E. (2008). The history of the internet search engine: Navigational media and the traffic commodity. In A. Spink & M. Zimmer (Eds.), *Web searching: Multidisciplinary perspectives* (pp. 77–206). Dordrecht, The Netherlands: Springer.

Vaughan, L. (2004). New measurements for search engine evaluation proposed and tested. *Information Processing and Management: An International Journal, 40*(4), 677–691.

Welp, C., & Machill, M. (2005). Code of conduct: Transparency in the net: Search engines. *International Review of Information Ethics, 3*, 18.

Wirth, W., Böcking, T., Karnowski, V., & von Pape, T. (2007). Heuristic and systematic use of search engines. *Journal of Computer-Mediated Communication, 12*(3), 778–800.

Wouters, P., Hellsten, I., & Leydesdorff, L. (2004). Internet time and the reliability of search engines. *FirstMonday*. Retrieved December 24, 2006, from http://www.firstmonday.org/issues/issue9_10/wouters/index.html

Zimmer, M. (2006). The value implications of the practice of paid search. *Bulletin of the American Society for Information Science and Technology*. Retrieved April 3, 2006, from http://www.asis.org/Bulletin/Dec-05/zimmer.html

Zimmer, M. (2008a). Privacy on planet Google: Using the theory of "contextual integrity" to clarify the privacy threats of Google's quest for the perfect search engine. *Journal of Business & Technology Law, 3*(1), 109–126.

Zimmer, M. (2008b). The gaze of the perfect search engine: Google as an infrastructure of dataveillance. In A. Spink & M. Zimmer (Eds.), *Web searching: Multidisciplinary perspectives* (pp. 77–99). Dordrecht, The Netherlands: Springer.

Appendix A: Degree Programs

Compiled by Rochelle Mazar, Collected by Jeremy

Digital Media and Design, IT University of Copenhagen
Rued Langgaardsvej 7, DK-2300 Copenhagen N, Denmark http://www.itu.dk

The BA degree programme in Digital Media and Design focuses on the study of how digital media influence our everyday lives and society as such; it aims at providing students with skills which will allow them to communicate professionally through digital media and enable them to design interesting experiences with and through digital platforms. It asks questions such as, What are the social consequences of our new ways of communicating? How do we communicate effectively using digital media? How do we design the interaction with digital media forms so they are easy and interesting to use? Cooperation is a key word in the education. Students will work closely with other students and in projects also with industry and organisations outside the university. Furthermore, the IT University collaborates with Georgia Institute of Technology (Georgia Tech) in the USA. All classes during the second year of study will therefore take place in English (first year and third year classes are mainly taught in Danish).

Furthermore, the IT University offers a MA programme in Media Technology and Games (MTG), taught in English only, and a MA programme in Digital Design and Communication, taught primarily in Danish. See more on the www.itu.dk website.

Degree Offered: BA, MA, Ph.D.

Contributing Faculty
   Rich Ling
   T.L. Taylor
   Gitte Stald
   Lisbeth Klastrup
   Susana Tosca
   John Paulin
   Lone Malmborg
   Anker Helms Jørgensen

J. Hunsinger et al. (eds.), *International Handbook of Internet Research*,
DOI 10.1007/978-1-4020-9789-8, © Springer Science+Business Media B.V. 2010

Tomas Sokoler
Irina Sklovski
Bjarki Valtysson

Analysis, Design and Management of Information Systems, London School of Economics

Information Systems and Innovation Group, Department of Management, London School of Economics, Tower One, Houghton St., London WC2A 2AE UK

ADMIS is a full-time, 1-year programme. It is one of the best established and most highly regarded courses in information systems in the United Kingdom. It regularly attracts over 120 students, typically from 30 to 40 different countries. The teaching on the course has been assessed by the Higher Education Funding Council for England as excellent and the group's research was rated 5 in the most recent RAE.

ADMIS is an advanced course based around the issues, approaches, and tools for information systems development and operation within organisations. ADMIS presents a balance between the management and technical themes that have an impact on the practice and theory of information systems. Rather than treating information systems solely as technical systems, the underlying premise is that information systems should be viewed as social systems operating within an organisational context.

The core curriculum focuses on information systems management, systems development, and the application of information technology in business. However, options within the course allow students to specialise in policy, economic, risk and security, or technological aspects.

The Science and Engineering Graduate Scheme (SEGS) run by the Home Office allows graduates of subjects such as ADMIS to stay and work in the UK for up to a year after they graduate. Employment prospects for our graduates are excellent and most are in permanent employment within 6 months of graduating. We have alumni in all the major consultancy companies, as well as in a wide range of other organisations throughout the world.

Degree Offered: M.Sc.

Contributing Faculty
    Ian Angell
    Chrisanthi Avgerou
    James Backhouse
    Antonio Cordella
    Tony Cornford
    Jannis Kallinikos
    Ela Klecun-Taylor
    Frank Land
    Jonathan Liebenau

Shirin Madon
Nathalie Mitev
Susan Scott
Steve Smithson
Carsten Sørensen
Will Venters
Edgar Whitley
Leslie Willcocks

Communication, University of Illinois at Chicago
1007 W. Harrison St. (m/c 132), Chicago, IL 60607 USA
http://www.uic.edu/depts/comm/

Doctoral study focuses on communication and technology. Students develop thorough understanding of the field, expertise in its theories, skills needed to conduct effective research, and experience teaching in a university setting. They also acquire a specialization from among those recognized in scholarly societies and reflected in the current research emphases among department faculty. Besides new technologies, current areas of faculty interest include political, diversity, visual, and health studies, among others.

Degree Offered: Ph.D.

Contributing Faculty
James Danowski
Steve Jones
Sharon Meraz
Rajiv Shah
James Sosnoski
Elaine Yuan

Communication, Information and Society, London School of Economics
Houghton Street, London WC2A 2AE UK
www.lse.ac.uk/collections/media@lse

This programme offers an intensive, year-long exploration of the changing relations among communication, information, and society providing the following:

- An interdisciplinary education in key social, institutional, and policy issues raised by the development, production and application of information, and communication technologies (ICTs).
- An opportunity to critically examine the theoretical and practical relationships between technological and social, political, and economic change, culminating in an independent research project.

- Career development for ICT practitioners and preparation for students entering high-level research and employment in the field of new media and information.
- An emphasis on business, civil society, and government applications of ICTs, so as to understand how policy nationally and globally is developed and implemented in an increasingly global society.
- The opportunity to take courses taught by the Information Systems Group in the Department of Management, as part of programme core and optional courses.
- A research track programme provides advanced methodological and statistical skills and is recognised by the UK Economic and Social Research Council and the Arts and Humanities Research Council.

Degree Offered: M.Sc.

Contributing Faculty
  Robin Mansell
  Sonia Livingstone
  Shani Orgad
  Damian Tambini
  Leslie Haddon

Communication Technology and Society, University of Washington
Box 353740, Seattle, WA 98195-3740 USA
http://www.com.washington.edu/Program/Grad/Areas/technology.html

Both new and old communication technologies have transformed modern culture. Graduate seminars in this program explore how media, particularly new digital media, shape and are shaped by the ways we build relationships, form communities, organize, exchange information, produce knowledge, govern ourselves, do business, and interpret the world. Graduate students have opportunities for collaborative research with departmental faculty and also benefit from courses and colloquia offered by faculty in the UW Information School, Department of Technical Communication, Computer Science, and other departments. Interdisciplinary research on the internet and digital media is supported by these UW centers: the Center for Communication and Civic Engagement, the Center for Digital Arts and Experimental Media, the Center for Information Studies, and the Simpson Center for the Humanities.

Degrees Offered: M.A., Ph.D.

Contributing Faculty
  Lance Bennett
  Kirsten Foot

Philip Howard
Malcolm Parks
Gina Neff
Crispin Thurlow

Design for Interactive Media, Middlesex University
Cat Hill, Barnet EN4 8HT UK

The programme takes a student-centred, project-based approach in which students can choose whether to concentrate on current technologies and practices or those of the future.

The context is one where media technologies, including the web, have often escaped the traditional desktop screen and are becoming ubiquitous, pervasive, physical, multimodal, and social.

Students investigate advanced forms of interaction supported by studies in information architecture, usability and accessibility assisted by the use of a three-camera usability lab, allowing them to balance inventive creation with rigorous evaluation. Graduates have influenced interactive media, and web design in particular, worldwide, working as freelancers and in every size of organisation from microbusinesses through SMEs to international corporations. They are senior designers, creative directors, project leaders, heads of interactive media or run their own businesses. They range from executives to acclaimed artists and have won many prestigious international prizes.

In common with our student-centred mission, suitably qualified students may complete their MA as a work-based degree. In this mode, students complete innovative projects in the context of their employed work and analyse these through a thesis. The Lansdown Centre has pioneered such approaches to combining immediate vocational relevance and academic depth. The staff represent a similar mix of industrial and academic expertise.

The centre provides a deeply stimulating environment with work at all levels from undergraduate courses to postdoctoral research. It is leader of a Skillset Academy, a UK government initiative in which only 17 institutions from 114 applications were honoured with academy status.

Degree Offered: M.A.

Contributing Faculty
Stephen Boyd Davis
Gordon Davies
Magnus Moar
Enrico Benco

Digital Communication and Culture, University of Sydney
www.arts.usyd.edu.au/digitalcultures

Digital Cultures is a transdisciplinary program in the School of Letters, Art and Media in Faculty of Arts. We are dedicated to social and cultural research into new media and the internet. Our interests include internet sociality, politics of standards, practice and criticism of new media and internet art, social software, computer games, FLOSS movement, online pedagogy, software criticism, web 2.0, digital identity and avatars.

Degrees Offered
    Masters in Digital Communication and Culture
    Master of Philosophy
    Master of Arts Research
    Doctor of Philosophy

Contributing Faculty
    Chris Chesher
    Kathy Cleland
    John Tonkin

Graduate School of Social Informatics, Yuan Ze University
135 Yuan-Tuang Rd., Chung-Li 320, Taiwan

Founded in 1997, the Graduate School of Social Informatics (GSSI) at Yuan Ze University is the very first graduate school focusing on the study of information and communication technologies (ICTs) and their implications from social sciences perspectives in Taiwan. The GSSI aims to bring about a greater understanding of the various social factors that are shaping, and being shaped by, the ICTs. This is an interdisciplinary program that integrates social science disciplines to examine the development of information society and to study the public policy and strategy for a better information society.

Degrees Offered: Ph.D.

Contributing Faculty
    Shu-Fen Tseng
    Yuntsai Chou
    Eric Y.K. Chiang
    Bing-Jynn Wang
    Chyi-In Wu
    C.S. Shih Stone
    Kai-Sheng Kao
    Roy Chun Lee

Human Centered Computing, Georgia Institute of Technology
College of Computing, Georgia Institute of Technology, Atlanta, Georgia 30332,
USA http://www.cc.gatech.edu/education/grad/phd-hcc

The Ph.D. in human-centered computing (HCC) brings together human–computer interaction (HCI), learning sciences and technology (LST), cognitive science, artificial intelligence (AI), and robotics. It draws on Georgia Tech's strengths in digital media, engineering psychology, assistive technologies, architecture, industrial and systems engineering, industrial design, music, and public policy. HCC students may have backgrounds in any of the above areas, as well as other related disciplines, such as anthropology, information science, and sociology.

HCC graduates are exceptionally well prepared for careers in both academia and industry. The cutting-edge Ph.D. program in human-centered computing (HCC) at the College of Computing meets industrial and societal needs for education and research in humanizing computer technology, while attracting the best and brightest from around the world.

The HCC Ph.D. program focus is not on computer technology, but rather on how computers affect lives in terms of advanced product development and human capabilities for many areas of research. The degree leverages Georgia Tech's strongest programs and concentrations, including multimedia and digital media studies, human factors, ergonomics, assistive technologies, industrial design, cognitive science, sociology, and public policy.

This interdisciplinary approach to computing that supports human needs allows possibilities for new discoveries in underlying issues of science, engineering, art, and design.

Degree Offered: Ph.D.

Contributing Faculty
Amy Bruckman
Irfan Essa
Rebecca E. Grinter
Blair MacIntyre
Elizabeth Mynatt
Ashwin Ram
Mark Riedl
Thad Starner
John Stasko

School of Information, University of California, Berkeley
102 South Hall, Berkeley, CA 94720-4600 USA
http://www.ischool.berkeley.edu/

The doctoral program at the UC Berkeley School of Information is a research-oriented program in which the student chooses specific fields of specialization, prepares sufficiently in the literature and the research of those fields to pass a qualifying examination, and completes original research culminating in the written dissertation. The degree of Doctor of Philosophy is conferred in recognition of a candidate's grasp of a broad field of learning and distinguished accomplishment in that field through contribution of an original piece of research revealing high critical ability and powers of imagination and synthesis.

Degree Offered: Ph.D.

Contributing Faculty
  Yale Braunstein
  Jenna Burrell
  Coye Cheshire
  John Chuang
  Paul Duguid
  Robert Glushko
  Marti Hearst
  Mitch Kapor
  Ray Larson
  Clifford Lynch
  Geoffrey Nunberg
  Tapan Parikh
  Kimiko Ryokai
  Pamela Samuelson
  AnnaLee Saxenian
  Doug Tygar
  Nancy Van House
  Hal Varian

School of Information, University of Michigan
304 West Hall, 1085 South University Avenue, Ann Arbor, MI 48109-1107 USA
http://www.si.umich.edu

The School of Information introduces you to the foundations or the information disciplines in an exciting and integrated way with its Master of Science in Information. Advanced courses prepare you for existing and emerging careers and challenge you to exercise your knowledge through practical engagement in the community. Choose to specialize in one or two areas within the MSI program or tailor your coursework toward your chosen career path; or choose from six dual-degree programs. Earn your MSI with a master's degree in law, nursing, business administrations, public policy, social work, or medicine.

The Doctor of Information degree involves working closely with faculty on projects of mutual interest, since mastery of research methods requires hands-on experience. The School of Information is an excellent environment for pursuing your doctoral studies. Faculty are active in research, pursuing projects in many different areas, using many different methods. The School has exceptional facilities and equipment, and through its faculty projects, has access to many off-campus research sites.

Degrees Offered: M.Sc., Ph.D.

Information and Knowledge Society, Internet Interdisciplinary Institute
Parc Meditarrani de la Tecnologia; Av. Canal Olimpic s/n, Edifici B3; 08860
Castelldefels (Bacelona), Spain

The rise and constant updating of information and communication technologies during the second half of the last century has seen them enter all spheres of human activity: culture, economy, education, media, business management, public services administration and the apparatus of the political system. Analysis of the uses of these technologies in the different spheres and of the profound transformations that accompany them is key for understanding today's society and developing professional activities therein. The links between the different social, economic, political and cultural systems mean that the traditional disciplinary barriers have to be overcome so as to be able to conduct a thorough and in-depth analysis. Thus, this Ph.D. programme is based on an interdisciplinary perspective that involves different theoretical standpoints and different methodological tools. Specifically, the Ph.D. on the Information and Knowledge Society, designed in line with the directives established by the Royal Decree regulating postgraduate courses (Royal Decree 56/2005, January 21 2005), bases this interdisciplinary perspective on the relationship between the Ph.D. programme and the research groups recognised by the UOC. Consequently, these groups offer a limited number of places, be they at a distance or in-house, on their research lines or projects. These places offer the students that join the conditions needed to carry out academic research that leads to the submission and defence of a Ph.D. thesis on any of the aspects that characterise the Information and Knowledge Society.

Degree Offered: Ph.D.

Contributing Faculty
    Eduard Aibar Puentes
    Anna Garcia Hom,
    Elena Barberà Gregori
    Eulàlia Hernández Encuentra
    Albert Batlle Rubio
    Joan Marquès Puig
    Laura Manuel Borràs Castanyer
    David Megías Jiménez
    Celilia Castaño Collado
    Julià Minguillón Alfonso
    Manuel Castells Olivan
    Josep M. Mominó de la Iglesia

Agustí Cerrillo Martínez
Adela Ros Híjar
Robert Clarisó Viladrosa
Teresa Sancho Vinuesa
Atanasi Daradoumis Harabalus
Imma Tubella Casadevall
Josep Maria Duart Montoliu
Jordi Vilaseca Requena
Rosa Fernández Palma
Raquel Xalabarder Plantada

Information, Communication and the Social Sciences, Oxford Internet Institute
1 St Giles, Oxford OX1 3JS UK
http://www.oii.ox.ac.uk/teaching/dphil/

The doctoral programme (D.Phil.) in 'Information, Communication and the Social Sciences' is open to high-achieving students wishing to undertake groundbreaking, detailed study of the internet and its social impact in a world-renowned multidisciplinary department. Students are encouraged to ask original, concrete questions and to adopt incisive methodologies for exploring them, in order to help shape the development of digital networked space and those whose lives are affected by it.

The D.Phil. programme is normally of 3 years duration. In their first year, students are expected to clearly define their research project and undertake preliminary literature reviews or run pilot studies. In addition, students receive tailored research methods training and an introduction to the main disciplinary and theoretical perspectives on key topics in the field. In their second and third years students will be expected to undertake any necessary fieldwork, experiments or data analysis before writing up their thesis. An open research culture places students at the heart of the OII's academic life and ensures that students enjoy a wide range of opportunities to engage with leading scholars, to work on important research projects and to participate in a stimulating programme of seminars and conferences.

Current doctoral research topics include the geography of social networks; the political and cultural framing of filtering in Iran; the future of copyright in the context of legitimate file-sharing networks; the meaning of fairness in online reputation systems and the role of nationalism in the development of Chinese Wikipedia.

Degree Offered: D.Phil.

Contributing Faculty
William Dutton
Helen Margetts
Jonathan Zittrain
Ian Brown

Paul David
Rebecca Eynon
Ellen Helsper
Eric T Meyer
Victoria Nash
Ralph Schroeder
Judy Wajcman
Yorick Wilks

Information Design and Technology, SUNY Institute of Technology
PO Box 3050, Utica, NY 13504 USA

Focus is on the effective use of internet technologies in education, business, politics, and society and the study of virtual cultures and the social impact of information technologies. The program faculty see its key constituents as new media professionals, instructional designers, public relations and information technologies managers, educators interested in using information technologies in the classroom, administrators interested in better use and integration of new information technologies, and technology managers.

Degree Offered: M.Sc.

Contributing Faculty
   Russell L. Kahn
   Kathryn Stam
   Steven Schneider
   Mona DeVestal
   Thomas Knauer

Information Management & Systems, University of California, Berkeley
School of Information, University of California, Berkeley, 102 South Hall,
Berkeley, CA 94720-4600 USA
http://www.ischool.berkeley.edu/

The Master of Information Management and Systems (MIMS) program at the UC Berkeley School of Information is a 48-unit, 2-year full-time program, designed to train students in the skills needed to succeed as information professionals. Such professionals must be familiar with the theory and practice of storing, organizing, retrieving, and analyzing information in a variety of settings in business, the public sector, and the academic world. Technical expertise alone is not sufficient for success; iSchool graduates will be expected to perform and manage a multiplicity of information-related tasks. In order to function effectively they will need to

- understand how to organize information;
- analyze user information needs;
- be able to design or evaluate information systems that allow an efficient and effective user interaction;
- be able to provide and assure the quality and value of information to decision makers;
- understand the economic and social environment in which their organization functions;
- be familiar with relevant issues in law, economics, ethics, and management.

Such a profession is inherently interdisciplinary, requiring aspects of computer science, cognitive science, psychology and sociology, economics, business, law, library/information studies, and communications.

Degree Offered: M.IMS.

Contributing Faculty
  Yale Braunstein
  Jenna Burrell
  Coye Cheshire
  John Chuang
  Paul Duguid
  Robert Glushko
  Marti Hearst
  Mitch Kapor
  Ray Larson
  Clifford Lynch
  Geoffrey Nunberg
  Tapan Parikh
  Kimiko Ryokai
  Pamela Samuelson
  AnnaLee Saxenian
  Doug Tygar
  Nancy Van House
  Hal Varian

Information Science and Language Technology, Heinrich-Heine-University
Heinrich-Heine-University Düsseldorf, Universitätsstraße 1, D-40225 Düsseldorf, Germany
http://www.informationswissenschaft-und-sprachtechnologie.de/bachelor_master/master.php

The Masters program of Information Science and Language Technology, taking 2 years, convey and delve professional and methodical acquirements regarding the two major fields of studies, information science and language technology on the one hand and accompanying fields such as computer science and linguistics on the other. The studies' profile is application oriented and contains six modules (each employing final examinations), a team project (with final examination), tutorial work, and a Master's thesis.

This includes central topics such as linguistics, language technology, applied computational linguistics as information extraction, automatic translation and abstracting, application of language technology in concrete implementations, database technology, knowledge management systems, and advanced methods and theories of information retrieval. Furthermore, students are to be qualified for structuring extensive problem areas as well as for autonomous application of theoretical and methodical knowledge.

Degree Offered: M.A.

Information Systems and Organizations (Research), The London School of Economics

Information Systems and Innovation Group, Department of Managementa, London School of Economics, Tower One, Houghton St., London WC2A 2AE UK

ISOR is a full-time, 12-month course. The course draws together the group's knowledge, experience, and skill base in Information Systems and Organisational studies into a teaching format.

The philosophy of the programme is to place concerns about epistemological issues alongside practical aspects of data collection and interpretation. This provides a basis for understanding how the use of evidence is related to wider epistemological positions, the status and nature of data sets, and the wider validity claims that can be built on different kinds of empirical material. Students will learn to recognise and critically evaluate both qualitative and quantitative research in Information Systems and Organisational studies. Graduates from this course will undertake a substantial research dissertation and be in a strong position to enter doctoral programmes. By providing a distinctive combination of modules with the LSE's Methodology Institute, we offer a uniquely focused course that leverages LSE's world class social science expertise in this area.

ISOR is designed to equip students with the necessary research skills for progression to Ph.D. programmes. It is also ideal as a basis for entry into high-level occupations, such as policy research, specialist journalism, and research-focused roles within corporations, international organizations or non-government organizations.

Degree(s) Offered: M.Sc.

Contributing Faculty
    Jannis Kallinikos
    Susan Scott
    Carsten Sørensen
    Edgar Whitley

Information Systems and Innovation Group, London School of Economics
Department of Management, London School of Economics, Tower One, Houghton
St., London WC2A 2AE UK

The M.Phil./Ph.D. programme in Information Systems is one of the largest programmes of its kind in the world. We have had over 20 years of success in
providing research training for over 100 scholars and we are building on this
expertise in research training with the launch of our new M.Sc. in Information
Systems and Organisations (Research) from October 2006. Former students are
currently at leading institutions in Britain, North America, or their home countries
throughout the world. Our students are well known as contributors to major international conferences and most publish in academic journals before they complete
their studies.

There are some 50 students from over 20 countries enrolled in the programme.
Each year 10–15 students join. Between 1997 and 2000, 22 students gained their
Ph.D.s. In the same period there were only 148 Ph.D.s in information systems in the
whole of North America.

The doctoral programme has been integral to the Information Systems and
Innovation Group since its origins in the 1970s. As part of the LSE, we have always
been closely allied to research in other parts of the School. Since 2006, we have
become part of the Department of Management (DoM) and collaboration takes
place with other academic groups both within DoM, such as Operational Research
Group, Employment Relations and Organisational Behaviour Group, Managerial
Economics and Strategy Group and outside, in particular with departments such as
accounting and finance, media and communications, economics, government, social
policy, development studies, and others.

Degrees Offered: M.Phil./Ph.D.

Contributing Faculty
   Ian Angell
   Chrisanthi Avgerou
   James Backhouse
   Antonio Cordella
   Tony Cornford
   Jannis Kallinikos
   Ela Klecun-Taylor
   Frank Land
   Jonathan Liebenau
   Shirin Madon
   Nathalie Mitev
   Susan Scott
   Steve Smithson
   Carsten Sørensen
   Will Venters
   Edgar Whitley
   Leslie Willcocks

Information Technology Law, University of Edinburgh
Old College, South Bridge, EH8 9YL, Edinburgh, UK
http://www.law.ed.ac.uk/ahrc/

The programme aims to promote advanced knowledge and understanding of information technology law, in its broadest sense, within international, European, and domestic settings. The programme encompasses regulatory approaches to information technology, jurisdiction, content liability, privacy and data protection, intellectual property, standards and competition, cybercrime, e-commerce, the digital divide, legal challenges in respect of new information and communications technologies (including the internet and virtual worlds), and using these technologies in investigation and dispute adjudication.

Having studied the programme, students will emerge with an understanding of information technology law not just in its legal but also in its social, ethical, cultural and commercial contexts. During study students will have access to the results of innovative cross-cutting research of the highest quality. The programme is suitable to prepare students for advanced research.

Degree Offered: L.L.M. (distance)

Contributing Faculty
Abbe Brown
Burkhard Schafer
Andres Guadamuz

Innovation Studies, University of East London
c/o Dr. Josephine Stein, Dockland Campus, University Way, London E16 2RD UK

The MA in Innovation Studies at UEL explores the complex, dynamic relations between social and technological forces shaping innovation processes in an international context. There is an emphasis on inequalities due to gender, socioeconomic status, and/or race; social distribution of responsibility, wealth, and risk; and ethical considerations related to the governance of innovation in both business and the public sphere. The MA can be taken as part of the European ESST Masters programme (European Society, Science and Technology), which is run by an association of universities from across the European Union, Norway, Switzerland and Turkey. The MA is closely linked to active research projects at UEL and with collaborators around the world.

Degree Offered: M.A.

Contributing Faculty
Josephine Stein
Graham Thomas

Kevin Carey
Geoffrey Oldham
Gavin Poynter
Tony Sampson
Charles Shoniregun
Eva Turner

Innovation, Technology and the Law, University of Edinburgh
Old College, South Bridge, EH8 9YL, Edinburgh, UK
http://www.law.ed.ac.uk/ahrc/

The programme aims to promote advanced knowledge and understanding of the relationship between law, technology, commerce, and society in the widest possible sense. It explores the role of the law in responding to, regulating, and promoting new and emerging technologies, and also emphasises the role of technology in supporting and guiding legal and judicial processes. The programme covers intellectual property law, information technology law, and medical law.

Distance learning reaches out to a body of students who may not otherwise have the opportunity to study the programme and creates opportunities for the programme organisers to disseminate results of cutting-edge research. Having studied the programme, students will emerge with an understanding of technology-related law and technology support for legal processes, not just in their legal but also in their social, ethical, cultural, and commercial contexts and will have access to the results of innovative cross-cutting research of the highest quality. The programme will be suitable to prepare students for advanced research.

Degree Offered: L.L.M.

Contributing Faculty
    Charlotte Waelde
    Graeme Laurie
    Burkhard Schafer
    Andres Guadamuz
    Abbe Brown
    Gerard Porter

Interdivisional Media Arts and Practice, University of Southern California
Institute for Multimedia Literacy Bldg., School of Cinematic Arts, 746 West Adams Boulevard, Los Angeles, CA 90089-7727 USA
http://cinema.usc.edu/programs/imap/

New to the School of Cinematic Arts in 2007, the interdivisional program in Media Arts and Practice (iMAP) situates technology and creative production alongside the historical and theoretical contexts of critical media studies. This practice-oriented Ph.D. program provides students with both practical experience and theoretical knowledge as they work to define new modes of research and production in the 21st century.

Media Arts and Practice was inspired by recent developments in media and technology that have altered the landscape of media production, analysis, distribution, and display. Our goal is to support a new generation of scholar-practitioners who are able to combine historical and theoretical knowledge with creative and critical design skills. Students who complete a Ph.D. in Media Arts and Practice will be uniquely prepared to shape the future of media and scholarship and to actively engage in the emerging cultural, technological, and political dynamics of a global media ecology.

Media Arts and Practice integrates the strengths of each program within the School of Cinematic Arts (production, critical studies, writing, interactive media, and animation and digital arts) by offering students the opportunity to substantially design their own course of study. The program seeks students who demonstrate their potential to succeed in a rigorous, hybrid, creative/critical environment and an interest in exploring new directions in scholarly research and creative practice.

Degree Offered: Ph.D.

Contributing Faculty
Steve Anderson
Anne Balsamo
Scott Fisher
Anne Friedberg
Kathy Smith

Internet Computing, University of Hull
School of Arts and New Media, University of Hull, Scarborough Campus, Filey Rd., Scarborough, YO11 3AZ

The rapid growth of the internet and its associated applications (notably the world wide web) has created a market for suitably qualified internet computing professionals. This innovative programme provides an industrially and commercially relevant knowledge that will allow you to design and develop effective internet applications, with a particular emphasis on the development of interactive websites. The aim of the programme is to equip students with the broad range of theoretical and practical skills required for developing interactive and creative internet applications, together with a specialised understanding of a chosen area of interest. It provides a unique opportunity for the future. Graduates from this M.Sc. programme gain exemption from British Computer Society professional examinations (Professional Graduate Diploma and PGD Project).

This full-time programme is 1 year in duration and comprises two semesters of six taught modules followed by a substantial individual dissertation project in the summer. Modules include dynamic web programming, website technology, research methods, web security, digital media management, and internet-based information systems. The summer is dedicated to an individual dissertation project, which allows students to specialise in a selected area of interest relating to the programme of study. Projects often include systems development, web design/implementation, multimedia systems, application of new technology or e-business studies. You will work closely with a project supervisor. In addition to the practical work you will also write a substantial dissertation. Students often select projects in areas related to their future employment goals.

Degree Offered: M.Sc.

Contributing Faculty
　　Darren Mundy
　　Tanko Ishaya
　　Toni Sant
　　John Whelan
　　Paul Warren
　　Linda Hockley
　　Robert Consoli
　　Christopher Newell

Social Science of the Internet, Oxford Internet Institute
1 St Giles, Oxford OX1 3JS UK

Recognising the lack of multi-disciplinary research training in this field, the OII will (subject to final institutional approval) launch a unique new M.Sc. programme titled 'Social Science of the Internet' for entry in October 2009.

Understanding the societal implications of the internet and related information and communication technologies requires the joining of multi-disciplinary perspectives. This proposed 1-year M.Sc. course at the OII will enable students to take courses in law, policy, and social sciences that are focused on the internet and web, even where students lack prior training in these areas.

The degree will be a 10-month taught Masters course, with a core syllabus designed to ensure that all students attain an in-depth understanding of the social science concepts, theories, and methods (including internet-specific research methods) required to undertake and assess rigorous empirical research or policy analysis of internet-related issues. The degree is designed for two types of students: students who wish to focus on internet studies in the further pursuit of a law degree or a doctoral degree in information, communication or any of the social sciences, or to move into professional careers in these fields or professionals who have done original, creative work on the internet, such as in their early career, and wish to gain a broader understanding of the societal aspects of its design or use.

Degree Offered: M.Sc.

Contributing Faculty
  William Dutton
  Helen Margetts
  Jonathan Zittrain
  Ian Brown
  Paul David
  Rebecca Eynon
  Ellen Helsper
  Eric T Meyer
  Victoria Nash
  Ralph Schroeder
  Judy Wajcman
  Yorick Wilks

Law and Technology, Tilburg Institute for Law, Technology, and Society
Tilbuirg University, P.O. Box 90153, 5000 LE Tilburg, The Netherlands
http://www.tilburguniversity.nl/faculties/law/research/tilt/education/master/

Emerging new technologies such as information technology, nanotechnology and biotechnology are pervasively transforming societies and turning them into dynamic, knowledge-based economies. Various national governments have put forward their visions for future knowledge and information management. National and international (non)governmental organizations have published policy documents, opinions and statements regarding the regulation of innovative technologies and the way in which society should deal with the influence these technologies have upon our day-to-day life. They are witness to the need for a careful assessment of the mutual shaping of technology and society. Research and development, as well as the introduction of new technologies into the market and into society as a whole, evoke all kinds of social and legal questions. The Master Law and Technology provides the cutting-edge, multidisciplinary knowledge on technology, law, and society needed for answering these questions. The program consists of four obligatory courses in the field of biotechnology, ethics, risk regulation, and intellectual property rights. Furthermore, students can choose three courses from a diverse spectrum of electives such as e-commerce, contracts and ICT, privacy, liability and the internet, government information law, and computer crime. The courses are given in small internationally composed groups focussed on the development of written and oral capabilities. Students are expressly invited to participate in discussions and challenged to think about interesting legal concepts and problems. There is a great demand for specialists in the field of law and technology. This provides graduates with a wide range of job opportunities.

Degree Offered: LLM

Media and Communications, London School of Economics
LSE, Houghton Street, London WC2A 2AE UK
www.lse.ac.uk/collections/media@lse

Media and communications research is developing rapidly, both theoretically and methodologically, in keeping with the vast expansion in the penetration, technological diversity, and social significance of the media globally. Media and communications research is essentially interdisciplinary, drawing on the theories and methods of a range of social science disciplines as they apply to the media, both old and new, and to communication networks of all kinds including the internet.

This programme offers the opportunity to undertake original interdisciplinary social science research in the field, emphasising in particular the relationships between media, communication, technology, and social change. The programme is based on a global centre of excellence in media and communications research. It is recognized by the UK Economic and Social Research Council and the Arts and Humanities Research Council.

Degree Offered: Ph.D.

Contributing Faculty
    Lilie Chouliaraki
    Robin Mansell
    Bart Cammaerts
    Sonia Livingstone
    Bingchun Meng
    Shani Orgad
    Raka Shome
    Terhi Rantanen
    Damian Tambini

Media, Technology, and Society, Purdue University
100 N. University Drive, West Lafayette, IN 47907 USA

Graduate work in Media, Technology, and Society is designed to aid the student in developing a systematic approach to understanding the processes and consequences of media and technology for a global society, including new and emerging information and communication technologies (ICTs). Current research being done in MTS at Purdue includes the impact of new technologies on media and society, spatial and location aware applications, cognitive and emotional reactions to media, children and video games, and health promotion in the media.

Degrees Offered : M.A., Ph.D.

Contributing Faculty
    Howard Sypher
    Sorin Adam Matei

Mohan Dutta
Glenn Sparks
Lorraine Kisselburgh
Seungyoon Lee
Josh Boyd
Gene Spafford
Erina McGeorge
Bart Collins

New Media and Digital Culture, University of Amsterdam
Turfdraagsterpad 9, 1012 XT Amsterdam, The Netherlands
http://mastersofmedia.hum.uva.nl/

The international MA in New Media and Digital Culture is for students interested in contributing to timely discourse surrounding critical media theory. It builds upon the pioneering new media scene that Amsterdam is known for, with an emphasis on the study of internet culture. Students gain an in-depth knowledge in new media theory, viewed from the perspectives of media archaeological, materialist, and other critical traditions and applied to such topics as blogging, locative media, networks, and protocol. Additionally students may be trained in the areas of info-aesthetics and visualization, with its emphasis on how to read, understand, and critique information graphics, interfaces as well as online interactivity. Among the expertise available to students is the emerging area of digital methods – internet research approaches and techniques that are specific to the new medium and the study of natively digital objects. Depending on interests and skills, students may participate in research projects that inform Amsterdam new media events, festivals, exhibitions, and installations as well as international new media issues, such as internet censorship.

The international MA in New Media and Digital Culture is a 1-year, full-time programme of study, made up of two semesters of university work, totaling 30 weeks. The New Media theories class runs for the entire first semester, 14 weeks. The New Media practicals course is in the first 7 weeks of the semester, and the New Media Research Seminar is held during the second half of the first semester, after the break week. A thesis workshop also takes place in the first semester, where students write a thesis proposal and choose a supervisor. First semester courses: New Media Theories, New Media Practices, New Media Research Seminar: Protocol. Second semester courses: Information Aesthetics and Visualization and a New Media thesis.

Degree Offered: MA

Contributing Faculty
Richard Rogers
Jan Simons
Geert Lovink
Yuri Engelhardt

Sociology, University of Surrey
Guildford, Surrey GU2 7XH UK

The Sociology Department has a thriving Ph.D. programme which places particular importance on methodologically rigorous sociological research training. The
programme has ESRC recognition and quota awards for postgraduate full-time and
part-time studentships, and students benefit from the department's top rating of 5∗ in
the last Research Assessment Exercise (RAE) receiving supervision from committed staff working at the forefront of their substantive area, the internet being a very
important research strand. This is evident in the formation, in 2008, of the centre
for Research in Media, Information, Communication and Society (ReMICS), which
conducts high-quality, substantively grounded research into the social and cultural
aspects of new media and digital technologies.

Focussing on the importance of information and communication technologies
in contemporary societies, ReMICS engages in critical, theoretically informed and
empirically focussed research into a wide range of socio-economic, technological,
political and cultural aspects of digital media and information and communication practices. The thematic topics of members' projects include new media and
everyday life, digital surveillance, the social contexts and impacts of social networking media and internet technologies, cyberscience, e-science and grid technology,
mobile communications, media and the arts, digital technologies and criminal
justice, and new media methods.

We have a significant critical mass of doctoral students researching the internet and digital technologies, and current and recent topics include online forums
and political participation, online gaming, affective properties of communication
technologies and the relation between online communication and travel.

Degree Offered: Ph.D.

Contributing Faculty
   Victoria Alexander
   Geoff Cooper
   Nigel Gilbert
   Nicola Green
   Christine Hine
   Paul Hodkinson
   Nigel Fielding
   Paul Johnson

Technology and Social Behavior, Northwestern University
Frances Searle Building, 2240 Campus Drive, 2-43dfdfd1, Evanston, IL 60208
USA

The study of Technology and Social Behavior involves many disciplines, but until
now it has been rare to find graduate training that prepares students to bridge several
of those disciplines in the way that is so demanded by both academic and industry
research jobs of today. The Northwestern TSB doctoral program recruits students

from a variety of backgrounds and gives them rigorous training in humanities, social sciences, human–computer interaction, and computer science methodologies to allow them to understand and participate in technological developments in their broadest possible contexts.

Degree Offered: Ph.D.

Contributing Faculty
 Larry Birnbaum
 Fabian Bustamante
 Noshir Contractor
 Jen Light
 Paul Leonardi
 Don Norman
 Barbara O'Keefe
 Bryan Pardo
 James Schwoch
 Jack Tumblin
 Michael Roloff

The Technology and Society Ph.D. Emphasis, University of California Santa Barbara

Center for Information Technology and Society, North Hall 2215, University of California Santa Barbara, CA 93106-2150 USA
http://www.technology-society.ucsb.edu

The optional Ph.D. emphasis in technology and society at UC Santa Barbara is a degree supplement that provides multi-disciplinary training for graduate students planning dissertations dealing with the societal implications of technology.

The emphasis is premised on the understanding that the study of technology and society is inherently multi-disciplinary. Most scholars in this area ground their investigations and claims in a home discipline and methodology, but find themselves of necessity exploring literatures and paradigms from others as well. In some cases, the tools necessary for understanding problems fully are spread across disciplines, and in others it is simply the case that many scholars have arrived at an examination of the same phenomenon from different directions.

For doctoral students preparing for dissertation work and in progress on dissertations dealing with information technology and society, a systematic introduction to the paradigms and literatures relevant to their interests from outside their home department is vital to cutting-edge scholarship. The doctoral emphasis in technology and society provides the curriculum for approaching these broader intellectual terrains.

Degrees Offered: Emphasis as part of an existing Ph.D. program

Contributing Faculty

Kevin Almeroth
Chuck Bazerman
Bruce Bimber
Dorothy Chun
Jon Cruz
Jenn Earl
Andrew Flanagin
James Frew
Lisa Jevbratt
Debra Lieberman
Alan Liu
Karen Lunsford
Patrick McCray
Miriam Metzger
Lisa Parks
Constance Penely
Rita Raley
Ron Rice
Rich Mayer
Dave Seibold
Eric Smith
Cynthia Stohl
Michael Stohl
Matthew Turk
Cristina Venegas
Bill Warner
John Woolley
Ben Zhao

Technology, Media and Society, ATLAS Institute University of Colorado at Boulder

1125 18th Street, 320 UCB, Boulder, CO 80309-0320 USA
www.colorado.edu/atlas/

The ATLAS Institute's technology, media, and society interdisciplinary Ph.D. program is designed to prepare students for productive research and professional careers working across traditional boundaries between information and communication technology and a wide variety of other areas, including media, telecommunications, business, law, and many of the social sciences, arts, and humanities.

It prepares students for university teaching and research careers, both in traditional departments (e.g., communications, computer science, or sociology) where the study of technology, media, and society is incorporated and in the growing range of interdisciplinary schools and colleges of information, informatics, computer and information science, and related areas, such as those mentioned above.

Upon completion of the Ph.D. in Technology, Media and Society, graduates will be scholars in their interdisciplinary field. Each will possess the intellectual tools to understand, critique, and conduct interdisciplinary research at the interface of technology, media, and society.

Degree Offered: Ph.D.

Web Design and Development, University of Hull
School of Arts and New Media, University of Hull, Scarborough Campus, Filey Rd. Scarborough, YO11 3AZ UK

An exciting programme providing students with the fundamental principles of internet computing and subsequently consolidating this with a creative approach to the design and management of digital media. Through an appreciation of internet computing, an understanding of human–computer interaction and web design and experience of the theory and practice of multimedia, you will be equipped with both the practical skills required by contemporary computing companies and the ability to adapt to future developments in digital industries. Example career paths include website designer, online media specialist, interactive designer, and mobile media developer. Graduates from this M.Sc. programme gain exemption from British Computer Society professional examinations (Professional Graduate Diploma and PGD Project).

This full-time programme is 1 year in duration and comprises two semesters of six taught modules followed by a substantial individual dissertation project in the summer. Modules include dynamic web programming, website technology, research methods, advanced interfaces, media design and interaction and internet-based information systems. The summer is dedicated to an individual dissertation project, which allows students to specialise in a selected area of interest relating to the programme of study. Projects often include systems development, web design/implementation, multimedia systems, application of new technology or e-business studies. You will work closely with a project supervisor. In addition to the practical work you will also write a substantial dissertation. Students often select projects in areas related to their future employment goals.

Degree Offered: M.Sc.

Contributing Faculty
Darren Mundy
Tanko Ishaya
Toni Sant
John Whelan
Paul Warren
Linda Hockley
Robert Consoli
Christopher Newell

Appendix B: Major Research Centers and Institutes

Compiled by Rochelle Mazar, Collected by Jeremy

Innovative Communication Research Group, Center for Computer Games Research, IT University of Copenhagen
Rued Langgaardsvej 7, DK-2300 Copenhagen N, Denmark
http://www.itu.dk

The IT University of Copenhagen is a small university dedicated completely to the digital world. The areas of study range from games and communication to business and software development.

In the Innovative Communication Faculty Group, we focus on advanced and innovative communication trends, theories and applications of new media, design and development of interactive technologies in the contexts of prior and emerging cultures of information, and networked culture and mobile media. Our research falls mainly into three areas: digital communication and culture, assistive technologies, and interaction design.

The Center for Games Research Group was formally established in 2003, building on ongoing work in the area at the ITU since its founding in 1999. Since its founding, the center has hosted a number of conferences, workshops, and seminars focusing on Games Research. We do basic and applied research, approaching games from a variety of perspectives. Areas of study are game aesthetics, game ontology, game culture, game play, player communities, game design theory, games and human computer interfaces/game testing, and game software development.

Keywords
networked culture, digital media, computer games, online games, social media, mobile media, mobile communication, mobile internet.

Leading Members
Rich Ling
T.L. Taylor
Espen Aarseth
Georgios Yannakakis

Gitte Stald
Lisbeth Klastrup
Susana Tosca
John Paulin
Lone Malmborg
Tomas Sokoler
Simeon Keates
Thomas Pederson
Dan Witzner Hansen
Anker Helms Jørgensen
Gordon Calleja

Recent Research Projects and Publications
> *Mobility. Development of a Social Network Mobile Platform for Danish Youth.* Partners: Danmarks Radio, Telia, Unwire, Innocept Consult. 2008–2009.
> *EU Kids Online II.* Enhancing knowledge regarding European children's use, risk and safety online. Various European partners. http:/www.eukidsonline.net. 2009.
> Serious Games on a Global Market Place. Partners: University of Århus, The Danish School of Education, University of Southern Denmark, Danish E-Learning Center, Kompan, Tricon, Serious Games Interactive, MovieStarPlanet Aps.
> *CEPEG (Capturing and Enhancing Player Entertainment in Games).* Partners: Maersk Mc-Kinney Moller Institute/University of Southern Denmark.
> *SPOPOS: In-door Location-Based Tracking and Service System.* Partners: Copenhagen Airport. 2006–2009.
> Sicart, M. (2009). *The Ethics of Computer Games.* Cambridge, MA: MIT Press.
> Haddon, L., & Stald, G. (2009). A comparative analysis of European press coverage of children and the internet". *Journal of Children and Media, 3* (4).
> Tosca, S., & Klastrup, L. (2009). Because it just looks cool! – Fashion as character performance: the case of WoW. *Journal of Virtual Worlds, 1* (3).
> Taylor, T. L. (2009). The assemblage of play. *Games and Culture, 4* (4).
> Paulin Hansen, J. Alapetite, A., Andersen, H. B., Malmborg, L., & Thommesen, J. (2009). Location-based services and privacy in airports. *Interact* (1) *1,* 68–181.
> Ling, R. (2008). *New Tech, New Ties – How Mobile Communication Is Reshaping Social Cohesion.* Cambridge, MA: MIT Press.
> Shklovski, I., Kraut, R., & Cummings, J. (2008). *Keeping in Touch by Technology: Maintaining Friendships after a Residential Move.* Proceedings of the Twenty-Sixth Annual SIGCHI Conference on Human Factors in Computing Systems.

AHRC/SCRIPT Centre for Research in Intellectual Property and Technology Law, University of Edinburgh
Old College, South Bridge, EH8 9YL Edinburgh, UK
http://www.law.ed.ac.uk/ahrc/

The centre's research themes explore the synergistic relationship between law, technologies, commerce, and society in the widest sense. In addition to intellectual property and information technology, the centre undertakes research in the adjunct areas of biotechnology, genetics and medical jurisprudence and ethics; law and artificial intelligence, including the distribution of legal knowledge via the web; forensic computing and electronic evidence; the regulation of media, electronic commerce, the internet, and the information society; as well as how law affects information management and cultural production and archiving. The Phase 2 centre moves beyond the project-driven approach of Phase 1 to embrace fully its role as an international research hub with clear thematic focus on the creation and development of new paradigms for the legal characterisation of, and response to, the demands and potentials of new technologies.

The centre also offers cutting-edge courses in its research fields. As of September 2008, the centre will offer three new LLM programmes: information technology law, intellectual property law, and medical law, which will be taught via a virtual learning environment (VLE) created specifically for the tuition of law via the internet; in addition to innovation, technology, and the law, which is taught both on-campus and via the VLE.

Research Topics
Intellectual property, Information technology, Medical law, Biotechnology, Forensic computing, Artificial intelligence, Electronic commerce, Internet, Regulation, Privacy

Leading Members
>Graeme Laurie
>Hector MacQueen
>Charlotte Waelde
>Rachael Craufurd-Smith
>Burkhard Schafer
>Andres Guadamuz
>Abbe Brown
>Gerard Porter

Recent and Forthcoming Publications
>Waelde, C., & Edwards, L. (Eds.). (2008). *Law and the Internet* (3rd ed.). Oxford: Hart Publishing.

Research Projects

    Networks architecture. This study explores the architecture of networks occasioned by the growth of the internet and reflected in the ways in which nodes, hubs and links interact. It will consider the regulation of networks and the legal implications of scale-free network architecture as present in P2P systems and other internet-based technological groupings.

    Deceptive computing. Decision-making relies increasingly on intelligent and autonomous advice given by computer systems that also deploy "deceptive computing," intentionally misleading the user into thinking that their interaction is with another human. This project will analyse how this affects fundamental legal conceptions such as the nature of responsibility, legal personality, and the limits of liability.

    MIA surveillance systems. This project focuses on "MIA" (mobile, intelligent, autonomous) surveillance systems and the law. Drawing on existing criminological theories of surveillance and legal doctrines on human rights and due process, this project will develop a theory of MIAs and their regulation.

Atlantic Centre for the Study of the Information Society, Mount Saint Vincent University
166 Bedford Highway, Halifax, Nova Scotia B3M 2J6

The Atlantic Centre for the Study of the Information Society (ACSIS) is a centre studying issues of equity, youth, and information-communication technology. The centre hosts and supports the research interests of Dr. Dianne Looker, Professor in Sociology and Anthropology and Tier 1 Canada Research Chair in Equity and Technology.

Part of Looker's research involves analysis of existing Statistics Canada data sets. Under contract with Statistics Canada, she has been granted access to the secure data sets from the Youth in Transition Survey, the Second International Survey of Technology in Education, and the Survey of Approaches to Educational Planning. She also has access to the General Social Survey, Cycle 14, which deals specifically with use of ICT. Once it becomes available she will also be examining the recent Aboriginal People's Survey, which includes several questions on use of ICT.

Looker is also in the process of completing a very successful research project that focuses on the ways in which a shift to more information- and knowledge-based society influences individuals' educational and occupational decisions. This study involved a cohort of youth, born in 1971, who were surveyed in 1989, 1992, 1994, and 2000–2002. She is working on a book based on the analysis of these data. The University of Toronto Press has expressed interest in the manuscript.

Keywords

    youth, information-communication technology, life-course, equity

Leading Members
Dianne Looker
Victor Thiessen
Ted D. Naylor

Recent Publications
Thiessen, V. (2008). Cultural centrality and the transformative potential of information and communication technology for Canadian youth. *Canadian Journal of Sociology* (forthcoming).
Thiessen, V. (2007). Cultural differences in information and communication technology access use, and skill development among high school students. In A. Pandian & M. Kell (Eds.), *Literacy: Diverse perspectives and pointers for practice*. Universiti Putra Malaysia Press.
Serdang: Thiessen, V. (2007). Digital divides and capital conversion. *Information, Communication and Society, 10*(2), 159–180.
Thiessen, V. (2003). Beyond the digital divide in canadian schools: From access to competency in the use of information technology. *Social Science Computer Review, 21*(4), 475–490.
Thiessen, V. (2002). *The digital divide in Canadian Schools: Factors affecting student access to and use of information technology*. Council of Ministers of Education, Canada.

City of Knowledge, University of São Paulo
Av. Professor Lúcio Martins Rodrigues, 443 – Bloco 04 – Sala 26 — Cidade Universitária — CEP 05508-900 — São Paulo – Brasil

The City of Knowledge is a research project designed in 1999 by economist, sociologist, and journalist Gilson Schwartzas, a visiting professor at the Institute of Advanced Studies of the University of São Paulo, Brazil. The digital city is built by "communities of practice" that develop new frameworks for the production of cultural identities and collective intelligence. The mission of the City of Knowledge is to promote research, development, and applications that foster public, community, or cooperative use of new digital information and communication technologies in Brazil. The networking program now operates with associated labs at the Department of Film, Radio and TV of the School of Communication and Arts, at the Faculty of Economics and Administrations' Technological Management and Policy Research Group and at the Production Engineering Department of the University of São Paulo. Participating groups in Brazil come also from the Catholic University of Sâo Paulo, Mackenzie University, University of Brasilia, and ESPM.

Research Topics
Economics, digital emancipation, internet governance, digital culture, netnography, media, local development

Leading Members
    Gilson Schwartz
    Guilherme Ary Plonski
    André Leme Fleury

Recent Research Projects
    development by design, MIT (2001–2). See http://www.thinkcycle.org/dyd/
        dydParticipants.htm
    OPEN AUDIENCE project (2003). Technological research and development
        project strongly oriented to scientific innovation and aimed to indus-
        trial innovation in the segments of hardware and software for audio-
        visual technologies. See http://openaudience.incubadora.fapesp.br/portal/
        how-to-participate/participant-institutions
    Liberating Voices (2005–8). Pattern Language for Social Change. See http://
        www.publicsphereproject.org/

The Communication Research Centre, Loughborough University
Department of Social Sciences, Loughborough University, Epinal Way,
Loughborough LE11 3TU UK

The internet and new communication technologies are increasingly central to
the centre's research agenda. The centre's new media research program has several focuses. The first concerns the digital divide. Graham Murdock and Peter
Golding have published widely in this area. Graham Murdock was jointly awarded
a £253,617 grant from the British *Economic and Social Research Council*'s
E-Society Programme for a project entitled *Navigating the E-Society: Dynamics
of Participation and Exclusion*.

The second focus relates to the way the internet is transforming aspects of
traditional political communication. As part of research on election communication, funded by the *UK Electoral Commission* and the *Guardian* newspaper, James
Stanyer and John Downey examined the use of the internet by British political parties during the 2005 campaign and the impact of blogging. Outside the
election periods, John Downey has conducted work on the way in which new
social movements use the internet. John Richardson and James Stanyer are currently
examining the impact of the internet on the news industry. Their research, funded
by the Department of Social Sciences, focuses on the relationship between online
newspapers and their readers.

The third area of focus is on new media policy. Both Graham Murdock and Jim
McGuigan have published on the national policy response to new technologies.

Research Topics
Internet and elections, internet and the news industry, counter public spheres, the digital divide, the social impact of new technology, new technology and media policy

Leading Members
Golding
Graham Murdock
Mike Pickering
Jim McGuigan
David Deacon
Dominic Wring
John Downey
James Stanyer
John Richardson
Sabina Mihelj
Emily Keightley
Thomas Koenig

Recent Publications
Downey, J., & Davidson, S. (2006). The internet and the 2005 UK General Election. In D. Wring, J. Green, R. Mortimore, & S. Atkinson (Eds.), *Political communications: The British General Election of 2005*. Basingstoke: Macmillan.

Downey, J. (2006). Counter public spheres. In L. Dahlberg & E. Siapera (Eds.), *Radical democracy and the Internet*. Basingstoke: Palgrave.

Golding, P. & Murdock, G. (2001). Digital divides: Communications policy and its contradictions. *New Economy, 8*(2), 110–115.

McGuigan, J. (2007). Technological determinism and mobile privatisation. In V. Nightingale, & T. Dwyer (Eds.), *New media worlds – challenges for convergence* (pp. 5–18). Melbourne: Oxford University Press.

Stanyer, J. (2008). Web 2.0 and the transformation of news and journalism: New possibilities and challenges in the internet age. In A. Chadwick & P. N. Howard (Eds.), *The handbook of internet politics*. New York, NY: Routledge.

Center for Contemporary and Digital Performance, Brunel University
School of Arts, Brunel University, West London, UB8 3PH UK
http://people.brunel.ac.uk/dap/condip.html

Performance research at Brunel University's School of Arts has undergone major transformational changes since 2000, having expanded to 12 staff members actively engaged in a wide range of research practices including virtual and mixed realities, intelligent space and augmented reality, telematic dance and interactive wearables, electronic and generative music synthesis, human–computer interaction, motion capture and distributed sensing, digital signal processing, wireless broadband, digital sculpture, and robotics. The Center for Contemporary and Digital Performance builds on the earlier Body, Space and Technology Research Group and its now internationally recognized online *Body, Space and Technology Journal.*

The common ground of the centre's research is performance, but units such as the DAP-Lab and the School's new MA Digital Performance have introduced trans-disciplinary investigations of digital creativity, virtual design, telematics, and wearable technologies. Postgraduate research in digital performance and game studies has been created in collaboration with the School of Engineering and Design, furthering integration of creative arts with science/technology to develop new modes of performance and real-time, distributed interaction. The DAP-Lab's cross-media research explores convergences between choreography, visual expression in dance/film/fashion and textile design, and real-time interactive data flow environments. Participants explore the relations between textiles and textures in motion and design fabrics and wearables in digital studios making the intelligent clothes usable for performance interaction with camera tracking and real-time data transformation (video, sound, motion graphics, motion capture, bio-physiological data, etc.). DAP-Lab involves research with telematic partner sites in the USA, Japan, Brasil, India, Italy and Germany.

Keywords
  augmented reality, telematic dance, interactive wearables, electronic and generative music synthesis, human–computer interaction, motion capture and distributed sensing, robotics, virtual and mixed realities, intelligent space

Leading Members
  Johannes Birringer
  Steve Dixon
  Stelarc
  Susan Boradhurst
  Kjell Yngve Petersen
  David Plans Casal
  Helen Paris
  Gretchen Schiller
  Fiona Templeton
  Jo Machon
  John Freeman
  Barry Edwards
  Fred Weimer

Recent Publications
  Birringer, J. (2008). *Performance, technology, and science.* New York, NY: PAJ Books.

Birringer, J. (2007). Transactivity in intimate transactions. In J. Hamilton (Ed.), *Art, exhibition and interaction within distributed networked environments* (pp. 106–15). Brisbane: ACID.

Dixon, S. (2007). *Digital performance: A history of new media in theater, dance, performance Art, and installation*. Cambridge: MIT Press.

Broadhurst, S., & Machon, J. (Eds.). (2006). *Performance and technology: Practices of virtual embodiment and interactivity*. Houndmills: Palgrave Macmillan.

Smith, M. (Ed.). (2005). *Stelarc: The monograph*. Cambridge, MA: MIT Press.

Affiliated Research Centres

Trans-Medien Akademie Hellerau-Dresden, Germany
Keio University, Japan
Attakkalari Centre for Movement Arts, Bangalore, India
Arizona State University, USA
Corpos Informaticos, Brasilia, Brasil
ViTe3 Studio, Rome, Italy

Center for Digital Discourse and Culture, Virginia Polytechnic Institute and State University (Virginia Tech)
531 Major Williams Hall 0130, Blacksburg, Virginia 24061 USA
http://www.cddc.vt.edu

The Center for Digital Discourse and Culture (CDDC) began as a college-level center at Virginia Polytechnic Institute and State University during 1998 in the College of Arts and Sciences, working with faculty in the Virginia Tech Cyberschool as well as the Institute for Distance and Distributed Learning (IDDL). Since 2003, the CDDC has continued its activities within the College of Liberal Arts and Human Sciences. The CDDC provides one of the world's first university-based digital points-of-publication for new forms of scholarly communication, academic research, and cultural analysis. At the same time, it supports the continuation of traditional research practices, including scholarly peer review, academic freedom, network formation, and intellectual experimentation as part of IDDL's support of the university's research mission.

Center for Digital Literacy, Syracuse University
School of Information Studies, 105 Hinds Hall, Syracuse University,
Syracuse, NY 13244 USA
http://digital-literacy.syr.edu/

The Center for Digital Literacy is an interdisciplinary, collaborative research and development center dedicated to understanding the impact of information, technology, and media literacies on children and adults in today's technology-intensive society.

Keywords
curiosity, perceived competence, impact of school libraries, motivation, innovative process, health literacy

Leading Members
Ruth V. Small
Marilyn P. Arnone
Tiffany Koszalka
Jian Qin
Megan Oakleaf
William Myhill

Recent Research Projects and Publications
Arnone, M. P., Small, R. V., & Hardy, T. (2007). From front-end analysis to evaluation: Developing an information literacy resource for educators. In *Educational media & technology yearbook*. Westport, CT Greenwood Publishing Group.

Chew, F., & Sushma, P. (2005). Establishing an Internet-based tobacco-control network for Czech health professionals. *Health Promotion Practice, 6*(1), 109–116.

Koszalka, T., Grabowski, B., & Darling, N. (2005). Predictive relationships between web and human resource use and middle school students' interest in science careers: An exploratory analysis. *Journal of Career Development, 31*(3), 169–182.

Small, R. V. (2008). Surviving in the information age. *Threshold: The Magazine of Cable in the Classroom* (This article describes the digital literacy skills required by citizens of the 21st century).

Small, R. V. (2005). Building collaboration through technology. *Journal of Informatics Education Research* (International Academy for Information Management).

Center for Emerging Network Technologies, Syracuse University
School of Information Studies, 205 Hinds Hall, Syracuse University, Syracuse, NY 13244 USA
http://cent.syr.edu/

The Center for Emerging Network Technologies (CENT) is an applied research laboratory that provides testing and analysis of emerging enterprise information technologies. Its predecessor, the Network Computing Real World Lab, was established in 1993. Over the past 14 years, CENT has developed core competencies in delivering repeatable, reliable measurements that map effectively to real-world implementations. In addition to CENT's applied research, the lab provides educational outreach through Syracuse University's School of Information Studies (iSchool). CENT's student staff members, all of whom are actively involved in research within the lab, regularly consult with faculty and staff on integrating lab experiences into classes and assist students with technology projects throughout the curricula. These efforts are coordinated through the iSchool's Information Technology Experiential Learning Lab as well as through the development of in-house learning testbeds designed to deliver practical interaction with leading edge enterprise information technologies. In addition, CENT coordinates industry certification courses like Cisco's CCNA and CompTIA's Security+.

CENT is also engaged with the community at large. Leveraging its relationships with major enterprise technology companies, CENT routinely brings in speakers to participate in the CASE Center's Technology Roundtable and lends both equipment and expertise toward community-based projects such as the Salina Electronic Village project and the Connective Corridor.

Keywords
emerging technologies, testing, evaluation, enterprise, IT, wireless, VoIP, Wi-Fi, testbed

Leading Members
David Molta
William Gibbons
Michael Fratto

Recent Research Project and Publications
Molta, D. (2007). 802.11n wireless: Is now the time to deploy? *InformationWeek,* 29 Oct 2007.

Blandford, J. (2007). WLANs: One size does not fit all. *InformationWeek,* 03 Nov 2007.

Ginevan, S. (2007). Mobile e-mail for business: How five platforms compare. *InformationWeek,* 08 Oct 2007.

Ginevan, S. (2007). Analysis – fixed wireless: So near and yet so expensive. *Network Computing,* 28 May 2007.

Molta, D. (2007). 802.11r: Wireless LAN fast roaming. *Network Computing,* 16 Apr 2007.

Center for Human-Computer Interaction, Virginia Polytechnic Institute and State University
2202 Kraft Drive Blacksburg, VA 24060 USA

Research Topics
social computing, personal information management, mobile communication, ubiquitous computing, education

Leading Members
  Francis Quek
  Steve Harrison
  Deborah Tatar
  Manuel A. Perez-Quiñones
  Andrea Kavanaugh
  Scott McCrickard

Recent Publications
  Turow, J., & Kavanaugh, A. (Eds.). (2003). *The wired homestead: An MIT Press Sourcebook on the Internet and the family.* Cambridge, MA: MIT Press.
  Cohill, A., & Kavanaugh, A. (Eds.). (1997/2000). *Community networks: Lessons from Blacksburg, Virginia* (Revised ed.). Norwood, MA: Artech House.
  Tauro, C., Ahuja, S., Pérez-Quiñones, M., Kavanaugh, A., & Isenhour, P. (2008, in press). Deliberation in the wild: A visualization tool for blog discovery and citizen-to-citizen participation. In *Proceedings of the 2008 Digital Government Research Conference* (Montreal, Canada, May 18–21). New York, NY: ACM Press.
  Kavanaugh, A., Kim, B. J., Schmitz, J., & Pérez-Quiñones, M. (2008, in press). Net Gains in political participation: Secondary effects of the Internet on community. *Information, Communication and Society, 11*(7).
  Kavanaugh, A., Zin, T. T., Rosson, M. B., Carroll, J. M., Schmitz, J., & Kim, B. J. (2007, September). Local Groups Online: Political learning and participation. *Journal of Computer Supported Cooperative Work. 16*, 375–395.

Communications and New Media Programme, National University of Singapore
Blk AS6 Level 3, 11 Law Link, Singapore 117589

Communications and New Media (CNM) is the only academic programme in Singapore and Southeast Asia that offers an *integrated* approach to the study of communications and new media studies within a single department. The undergraduate programme, leading to the degrees of B.A. or B.Soc.Sci. (Hons), is very flexible and students are encouraged to take any of the modules offered in CNM as well as modules from other departments in the Faculty of Arts and Social Sciences, the School of Computing and the School of Business. CNM also offers graduate programmes leading to M.A. and Ph.D. degrees – mainly by research.

The core of the CNM programme is new media studies, which focus on the societal impact of new technologies on our social, cultural, political and economic landscape. Students can choose from a wide range of courses covering subjects like computer-mediated communication; human–computer interaction; culture industries; media policy and regulation; and game; visual and interactive media design. The communication management area provides an overview of the theory, principles and application of communication research, planning and management in organizations. Students interested in careers in communication management in the age of interactive and new media have the unique opportunity to combine learning about interactive media with designing content for new media and doing research for communication management.

With this multi-faceted understanding of new media and communications, CNM graduates will be able to work in a wide spectrum of private corporations, public agencies, non-profit organizations, and media-related industries in policy formulation, public relations, corporate communication, media relations, journalism, and research and information management positions, among others.

Contributing Faculty
   Milagros Rivera
   Lonce Wyse
   Hichang Cho
   Peichi Chung
   Ingrid Hoofd
   Sun Sun Lin
   Timothy Marsh
   Kevin McGee
   Byungho Park
   Sreekumar TT Pillal
   Leanne Chang

The Creative Technology Research Group, Adelphi Research Institute for Creative Arts and Science
Research Centre for Art & Design, The University of Salford, Centenary Building, Peru Street, Salford M3 6EQ UK
http://www.adelphi.salford.ac.uk/adelphi/p/?s=25&pid=40

Formed in 2000, the Creative Technology research group emerged from a wide array of new media research activities taking place across the University. The core emphasis of this group centres on redefining and developing digital and electronic technologies and concepts for creative arts, applications and solutions that will enhance our human interaction and cultural engagement. Ranging from interactive media arts and performance to virtual environments and artificial life experiments, this research group locates itself at the forefront of its specific fields. Current research activities in the areas of telematics, telepresence, interactive arts, new media narratives, digital performance, and sonic arts have secured research and development funding from sources such as The Arts Council of England, The Arts and Humanities Research Board, The Leverhulme Trust and The National Lottery Fund, supporting projects that have been disseminated through participation in international exhibitions, symposiums, theatre productions, and publications – including The Ars Electronica Centre Linz, The MIT Press, Siggraph USA, The International Symposium of Electronic Arts – ISEA, The ZKM Centre for Arts and Media Karlsruhe, and The InterCommunication Centre Tokyo.

The broad range of creative technology research group members ensures a high level of inquiry and debate that creates both research synergies and interdisciplinary collaboration across the university. Projects resulting from these links have included an Arts Council England-funded symposium and Artist-in-Residence programme at the Salford Centre for Virtual Environments in collaboration with Prof. David Roberts and a Leverhulme Trust-funded Fellowship programme "Robotic Performance" in partnership with Prof. Darwin Caldwell from the Centre for Robotics. Further external collaborations include the Futuresonic 04/05/06 international festival of electronic media arts and membership of the D-Ring consortium of European Media Arts.

Leading Members
  Paul Sermon
  Mathias Fuchs

e-Learning Lab: Center for User Driven Innovation, Learning and Design, Aalborg University
roghstraede 1, DK-9220 Aalborg OE, Denmark

The center aims to create a dynamic environment for research that contributes to the development of knowledge within Computer Supported Collaborative Learning, networked learning, participatory design, and user driven innovation. In particular the center conducts research within the areas of Health Informatics, Human Computer Interaction, internet culture, youth and new media, ICT for sustainable ICT, and e-government. The center engages in experimental collaborations and projects, and participates in international, national and regional networks and research projects.

The center draws on theory and methods from educational research, social studies of technology, philosophy of technology, systems development, human–computer interaction, cultural studies, ethics, and design. It works with concrete IT implementations, interventions and developmental activities within a variety of well-established domains, such as education, health care, and e-government. Simultaneously, the center has a strong focus on exploring emerging practices by studying technology in more informal domains, such as user creativity in relation to games, virtual 3D worlds, mobile media, use of social software and youth's creative use of social media.

The center is characterized by a social-experimental approach and contributes to the development of knowledge and solutions in collaboration with users from the various research domains. The research is grounded in the concept of user-driven innovation through using, and developing tools, standards and methods derived from observation of user inventions and practice. Research is motivated by the principle of inclusiveness, where the smallest unit of research includes both the researcher, the user, and their needs and situations. The vision is to develop ways of giving a voice to those not heard in design and innovation processes.

Keywords
networked learning, e-learning, user driven innovation, human–computer inter-action, participatory design, philosophy of technology, ethics, youth and new media, ICT for development

Leading Members
Lone Dirckinck-Holmfeld
Ellen Christiansen
Ann Bygholm
Anne Marie Kanstrup

Listing of Recent Publications
Ryberg, T., & Larsen, M. C. (2008). Networked identities: Understanding rela-tionships between strong and weak ties in networked environments. *Journal of Computer Assisted Learning, 24*(2), 103–115.
Wentzer, H., & Bygholm, A. (2007). Attending unintended transformations of health care infrastructure. *International Journal of Integrated Care, 7*, e41.
Albrechtslund, A. (2007). Ethics and technology design. *Ethics and Information Technology, 9*(1), 63–72.
Jones, C., Dirckinck-Holmfeld, L., & Lindström, B. (2006). A relational, indi-rect, meso-level approach to CSCL design in the next decade. *International Journal of Computer-Supported Collaborative Learning, 1*(1), 35–56.
Christiansen, E., & Nyvang, T. (2006). Understanding the adoption of TELEs: The importance of management. *European Journal of Education, 41*(3–4), 509–519.

Affiliated Research Centers
Open University – Institute of Educational Technology, Milton Keynes, United Kingdom
Bergen University – InterMedia, Bergen, Norway
Umeå University – Department of Informatics, Umeå, Sweden
University of Birmingham – School of Education, Birmingham, United Kingdom
University of Oslo – InterMedia, Oslo, Norway
The University of Southern Denmark – Humanistic information science, Kolding, Denmark
Lancaster University – CSALT, Department of Educational Research, Lancaster, UK
Göteborg University – Department of Education, Göteborg, Sweden
Italian National Research Council – Institute for Educational Technologies, Palermo, Italy
Members of *DEMO-net* from 2006 to 2010. DEMO-net is a Network of Excellence project funded under the European Commission's sixth frame-work programme: Information Society Technologies IST (FP6-2004-27219).

Members of the *Kaleidoscope Research Network* from 2004 to 2007 –
Kaleidoscope is a Network of Excellence, supported by the European
Community under the Information Society and Media Directorate-General,
Content Directorate, Learning and Cultural Heritage Unit.

The Imagining the Internet Center at Elon University, Elon University
100 Campus Drive, Elon, NC 27244 USA
http://www.imaginingtheinternet.org

The Imagining the Internet Center's mission is to explore and provide insights
into emerging network innovations, global development, dynamics, diffusion, and
governance. Its research holds a mirror to humanity's use of communications technologies, informs policy development, exposes potential futures and provides a
historic record. It strives to illuminate emerging issues in order to serve the greater
good, making its work public, free, and open. The ITIC at Elon University is a network of faculty, students, staff, alumni, advisers, and friends working to identify,
explore, and engage with the challenges and opportunities of developing communications forms and issues. It investigates the tangible and potential pros and
cons of new-media channels through active research. It engages a spectrum of
issues including politics, power, privacy, property, augmented reality, synthetic and
mirror worlds, control, commerce, and the challenges presented by accelerating
technology. It works to expose and help develop best practices for international
development efforts in distribution and use of ICTs. It builds its work into an
open online platform incorporating audio, video, archived content, research studies, quotable internet predictions, and other resources, all available to the public for
free. It sponsors work that brings people together to share their visions for the future
of communications and the future of the world.

Contributing Faculty
    Janna Quitney Anderson
    Connie Book
    Ken Calhoun
    Byung Lee
    Harlen Makemson
    Glenn Scott

Center for Information Policy Research, University of Wisconsin-Milwaukee
PO Box 413, Milwaukee, WI 53202 USA

With information infrastructures and technologies and the globalization of information evolving at a faster pace than our social, legal, and educational systems, it is
imperative that information policy issues be examined systematically in an interdisciplinary environment. The CIPR's research agenda revolves around social, ethical,
economic, legal, and technical aspects of information and information technologies with a focus on such key information policy issues as intellectual property

(copyright, patents, etc.), privacy, equity of access to information, ethics of information use and service, censorship, cyberlaw, and government, corporate, and international information policies.

Keywords
> information policy, information ethics, research ethics, intercultural ethics

Leading Members
> Elizabeth A. Buchanan
> Johannes Britz
> Dick Kawooya
> Tomas Lipinski

Center for Information & Society, University of Washington
Box 352840, Mary Gates Hall, Ste 370, Seattle, WA 98195-2840 USA
http://www.cis.washington.edu/

The Center for Information & Society (CIS) conducts independent, high impact research on the internet, technology, and information and their interrelations with societies and their government, business, and non-profit institutions.

CIS collaborates university-wide to promote and conduct multidisciplinary and interdisciplinary research, identifying and analyzing challenges posed by and in the context of information and society and constructively addressing these challenges in systemic and transformative ways. We envision the CIS as a leader in a global network whose work empowers people, communities, institutions and governments.

CIS research focuses on four main research pillars:

> *Information Policy* focuses on the articulation and enforcement of state regulation and self-regulation, with particular interest in examining the how and why of cyberspace regulation and the concept of basic information rights.

> *Cultural Dynamics and Diversity* influences outcomes in sustainable development, knowledge exchange, connectivity, and the ways ICT impacts generational values.

> *Digital Inclusion* search examines the social and economic impact of ICT on developing countries and underrepresented populations. Research is concentrated on questions of usage, access, e-literacy and skills, and communal/governmental support that promote inclusion.

> *Practical Implications.* CIS research builds understanding of how to increase the effectiveness and usefulness of ICT in electronic government, business, healthcare, education, and in individual lives.

Research Topics
> information policy, digital inclusion, cultural implications, ICT and development, e-government and e-business, quality of life, civic engagement, accessibility, usability

Leading Members
   Karine Barzilai-Nahon
   Robert M. Mason
   Christopher T. Coward

Recent Research Projects
   e-Government and e-Commerce research identifies and evaluates similarities
   and differences in the adaptation of internet-based information technologies
   and the resulting process and policy changes in the public and private sectors.
   The research examines the impacts of those technologies on information policy, information politics of decision makers, process redesign and technology
   diffusion approaches.
   Public Access to Information and Communication Venues. This program
   focuses on public access to information and communication landscapes in
   24 countries, with specific focus on the information needs of underserved
   communities and the role of ICT in supporting human development.
   *Empowering Users: Making Information Accessible to People with Disabilities
   Today.* Most web content (e.g., web pages, multimedia content or blogs) is
   produced by non-professionals. The goal of the project is to enhance information accessibility for people with disabilities by identifying the constraints
   and incentives for producing accessible information.
   *ICT and Public Access: Investigating the Social and Economic Impact of Public
   Access to Information and Communication Technologies.* The program is
   undertaking longitudinal and comparative research on the impacts of different models of public access to ICT. Research will look at both positive and
   negative downstream impacts in areas like employment and income; educational levels; civic engagement; government transparency and democracy;
   cultural and language preservation; and improved health.
   Cultured Technology: Internet and Religious Fundamentalism. This project
   investigates the relationship between religious fundamentalist communities
   and the internet. Investigators are analyzing the ways communities reshape
   technology and make it part of their culture, while also allowing this technology to make changes in their customary way of life and in unwritten
   laws.

Information Science, Heinrich-Heine-University
Heinrich-Heine-University Düsseldorf, Universitätsstraße 1, D-40225 Düsseldorf,
Germany
http://www.phil-fak.uni-duesseldorf.de/infowiss/

The Department of Information Science at the Heinrich-Heine-University in
Düsseldorf works on several internet-related research projects referring to information retrieval, knowledge representation, infometrics, information market, and
knowledge management. Special research fields in knowledge representation are
ontologies and folksonomies as well as semantic relations in general. Information

retrieval projects include Dark Web research, new output formats (e.g., the table view), ontology-based crawlers, topic detection and tracking, recommender systems and relevance ranking. Research in the information market is mainly concerned with Deep Web databases (e.g., commercial information suppliers). Foci in knowledge management are evidence-based practices, the application of Web 2.0 services in corporate intranets, and information need analyses in companies.

Research Topics
web information retrieval, knowledge representation, Web 2.0 – blogs, wikis, folksonomies, information need analyses, Deep Web (commercial web information suppliers), semantic relations, knowledge management

Leading Members
Wolfgang G. Stock
Sonja Gust von Loh
Isabella Peters
Katrin Weller

Recent Publications and Research Projects
Ontoverse. Mainz, I., Weller, K., Paulsen, I., Mainz, D., Kohl, J., & von Haeseler, A. (2008). Ontoverse: Collaborative ontology engineering for the life sciences. *Information – Wissenschaft und Praxis, 59*(2), 91–99.
We introduce ontologies as a new method for detailed and formalized knowledge representation, with particular focus on their use for the life sciences. Furthermore, we demonstrate the need for collaborative approaches in constructing elaborated scientific ontologies. The Ontoverse ontology wiki is presented as one tool to support all phases of collaborative ontology engineering.
Folksonomies. Peters, I., & Stock, W. G. (2007). Folksonomy and information retrieval. In *Joining Research and Practice: Social Computing and Information Science. Proceedings of the 70th ASIS&T Annual Meeting, 44,* 1510–1542. CD-ROM.
We present criteria for tagged documents to create a ranking by relevance (tag distribution, collaboration, and actor-based aspects). Furthermore, we show the necessity of handling tags by means of natural language processing.
Semantic Relations. Peters, I., & Weller, K. (2008). Paradigmatic and syntagmatic relations in knowledge organization systems. *Information – Wissenschaft und Praxis, 59*(2), 100–107.
Classical knowledge representation methods have been successfully working for years with established – but in a way restricted and vague – relations such as synonymy, hierarchy (meronymy, hyponymy), and unspecified associations. Recent developments like ontologies and folksonomies show new forms of collaboration, indexing, and knowledge representation and encourage the reconsideration of standard knowledge relationships for practical use.

Retrieval of Dark Web Information. Heesemann, S., & Nellißen, H.-D. (2008).
Facettierte Wissensordnungen und dynamisches Klassieren als Hilfsmittel
der Erforschung des Dark Web. *Information – Wissenschaft und Praxis,*
59(2), 108–117.

The identification and observation of terrorist and/or extremist activities and
plans on the internet, especially on the Dark Web, are moving more and more
into the centre of inquiry. The amount of relevant information requires focus
on a specific jargon, with the help of which suspicious developments can be
detected and an analysis system can be built up.

Commercial Information Suppliers in Intellectual Property. Stock, M., & Stock,
W. G. (2006). Intellectual property information: A comparative analysis of
main information providers. *Journal of the American Society for Information*
Science and Technology, 57(13), 1794–1803.

After modeling expert user needs with regard to intellectual property
information (especially patents and trademarks), we analyze and compare the main providers in this specific information area (Thomson
DIALOG, Esp@cenet by the European Patent Office, Questel-Orbit, and
STN International) in terms of system content and system functionality.

The Information Society Project, Yale Law School
127 Wall Street, New Haven, CT 06511 USA

The Information Society Project at Yale Law School is an intellectual center
addressing the implications of the internet and new information technologies for
law and society, guided by the values of democracy, human development, and social
justice.

Much of the Information Society Project's focus has been on memes, genes, and
bits, the building blocks of our knowledge, our technologies, and ourselves. Memes
are the fundamental units of the knowledge within a culture, propagating from one
mind to another, flowing from one society to the next. Genes are the hereditary units
that determine the makeup of organisms; they define who and what we are. And bits
are the basic units of digital computing, fueling the rise of powerful information and
communication technologies.

The Information Society Project brings together students, scholars, activists, and
policymakers to define the problems and identify the solutions on topics stemming
from the interplay between memes, genes, and bits in our contemporary information
society. The ISP produces scholarship, teaches, engages in activism, and develops and spreads ideas addressing four key research areas: access to knowledge,
preserving democratic values in the digital age, digital education, and law and
genomics.

Keywords

Internet, information society, law, access to knowledge, digital rights, privacy,
technological standards, digital education, genomics, search engines

Leading Members
Jack Balkin
Laura DeNardis

Recent Research Projects

Access to Knowledge, Research project protecting and expanding access to knowledge to secure broader participation in cultural, civic, and educational affairs helps realize the benefits of scientific and technological advancement and inspire innovation, human development, and social progress across the globe. The 3rd annual Access to Knowledge conference is planned for Fall 2008 in Geneva, Switzerland.

Reputation Economies in Cyberspace, Reputation economies in cyberspace have a broad effect on the ways in which we study, conduct business, shop, communicate, create, and socialize. This research project addresses questions of the norms for cyber-reputations and how they differ from offline models, issues of anonymity and privacy, quality assurance, "ownership" of online reputations and transportability of reputations from one system to another.

Dynamic Coalition on Digital Education (DCoDE), The Yale ISP has joined with more than a dozen institutions and individuals from around the world to create a coalition dedicated to providing teachers and students with better access to digital information. DCoDE will develop norms, policies, and regulations that promote the best use of technological resources in education – giving educators the access they need to digital information while at the same time protecting content producers.

Open Technological Standards, Research project addressing issues relating to open technological standards, including the controversial and value-laden concepts of openness, interoperability, democratic participation, and competitiveness in the context of standards; and creating a theoretical framework exploring the concepts of open standards in the larger context of technology, markets, politics, and law.

Law and Genomics, Research project addressing the complex ethical, legal, social, and policy impacts of the genomic revolution, including outlining the benefits and harms created by intellectual property and patent claims on biological entities, and ethical issues related to the digitization of the human genome.

Affiliated Research Centers

The Information Society Project enjoys informal relationships with Yale University's Technology and Ethics Working Group, the Berkman Center for Internet & Society at Harvard Law School, and the Information Law Institute at New York University.

Information Systems and Innovation Group

Dept. of Management, London School of Economics, Tower One, Houghton St., London WC2A 2AE UK

Within LSE's Department of Management, we form the leading European university-based Group focusing on Information Systems and Innovation and are recognised widely as amongst the top 10 such groups in the world. We have 16 full-time academics and also benefit from the contributions of our Centennial and Visiting Professors, all of whom are scholars of international repute and leaders in the field; from Visiting Fellows who are experts in their respective fields; and from project researchers. There are also over 45 Ph.D. students undertaking research in any one year.

The Group is international in its reputation, its activity, its staff and its students. Members are active in the International Federation of Information Processing (IFIP), the Association for Information Systems (AIS), the UK Academy for Information Systems (UKAIS), the British Computer Society (BCS), and other national and international organisations including United Nations and European Union bodies. Academic staff are Editors-in-Chief of four major journals (JIT, ITP, JSIS, JISS) and variously serve as Senior and Associate Editors on most high-quality refereed journals in the IS field (e.g. MISQ, MISQE, ISR, EJIS, ISJ plus over 20 others). Our students also produce a journal – *ISChannel* (*available electronically from our website*).

The Group's teaching has been rated as excellent by the UK's Quality Assurance Agency and its research is recognised as internationally excellent by the Higher Education Funding Council for England.

The Group has received from funding bodies and industry more than £2 million in research income in the last 4 years. Staff have made over 60 keynote addresses at major academic and practitioner conferences in the last 5 years, and have been very active in advisory and representational roles on panels and committees for governments, major corporations, and institutions. Members have made major policy interventions in recent years, notably in the UK governments, National Identity Card scheme 2005–2007. Awards and recognition are extensive and include Frank Land's Leo award of the AIS for Lifetime Exceptional Achievement, Ciborra's AIS Distinguished Member award, and Willcocks's Price Waterhouse Coopers/Corbett Associates World Outsourcing Achievement award for academic contribution to this field.

The Group runs several high profile seminar programmes. These include the annual *Social Study of ICTs* seminar run over 2 days in March each year. This attracts over 200 international participants and has a related 2-day Ph.D. workshop. We also host throughout the year a trans-disciplinary seminar series entitled *ICTS in the Contemporary World*. All such events are open to external participants, including doctoral students, and are advertised on our website.

Research Topics
    Information Systems Security
    Health Informatics
    ICT in Financial Markets
    Mobile Technologies
    ICT Policy and e-Government

ICT and Socio-Economic Development
Technical and Organizational Innovation
Knowledge and IS
Global and Open Sourcing

Leading Members
Ian Angell
Chrisanthi Avgerou
James Backhouse
Antonio Cordella
Tony Cornford
Jannis Kallinikos
Ela Klecun-Taylor
Frank Land
Jonathan Liebenau
Shirin Madon
Nathalie Mitev
Susan Scott
Steve Smithson
Carsten Sørensen
Will Venters
Edgar Whitley
Leslie Willcocks

Recent Publications
Avgerou, C. (2003). *Information systems and global diversity.* Oxford: Oxford
    University Press
Cornford, T., & Smithson, S. (2005). *Project research in information systems:
    A Student fs Guide* (2nd ed.). Basingstoke: Palgrave Macmillan.
Kallinikos, J. (2007). *The consequences of information: Institutional implica-
    tions of technological change.* London: Edward Elgar.
Willcocks, L., & Lacity, M. (2006). *Global sourcing of business and IT services.*
    London: Palgrave.
Wynn, E., Whitley, E. H., Myers, M. D., & De Gross, J. I. (Eds.). (2003). *Global
    and organizational discourse about information technology.* Boston, MA:
    Kluwer.

Center for Information Technology Policy, Princeton University
C231A Equad, Princeton University, Princeton NJ 98542 USA

In 1981, there were fewer than 300 computers on the internet. Since that time, dramatic improvements in the power and usefulness of information technology have
earned it a central place in our lives. We rely on it to reach new levels of economic productivity, keep in touch with each other, optimize our medical care, learn
about world events, and even to vote. Major changes in each of these areas, brought

about by information technology, are forcing leaders in government, industry, and the academy to adapt old rules to a new environment. The stakes are high: Wise leadership could permit dramatic improvements in almost every area of life, and poor choices could threaten not only innovation and wealth but also privacy, safety, and trust in government.

The Center for Information Technology Policy uses Princeton's unique strengths to help leaders react to new technology with thoughtfulness and confidence. Combining faculty expertise in public policy, technology and engineering, and the humanities with a strong University tradition of service, the Center's workshops, speakers and other programs seek to be a valuable resource for those who bring information technology into our lives.

Center participants come from Princeton departments including Computer Science, Economics, Electrical Engineering, Operations Research and Financial Engineering, and Sociology, and the University's Woodrow Wilson School of Public and International Affairs.

Keywords
> internet policy, voting machines, copyright, digital technology, net neutrality, open government, digital culture

Leading Members
> Ed Felten
> Vince Poor
> Andrew Appel
> Paul DiMaggio
> Michael Oppenheimer
> Stan Katz
> Matt Salgnik
> Markus Prior

The Center for Information Technology and Society, University of California Santa Barbara

North Hall 2215, University of California, Santa Barbara, CA 93106-2150 USA
http://www.cits.ucsb.edu

CITS is dedicated to research and education about the cultural transitions and social innovations associated with technology. The Center comprises a diverse team of more than a dozen scholars in the social sciences, engineering, and the humanities. We conduct research, organize public forums, provide multi-disciplinary doctoral education on technology and society, and facilitate partnerships with industry and the public sector. Our research examines many aspects of the social and cultural transitions under way at present around the globe, but we have a particular focus on technological change and three topics: Social Collaboration and Dynamic Communities; Global Cultures in Transition; and Technology in Education.

Leading Members
Kevin Almeroth
Bruce Bimber
Jennifer Earl
Andrew Flanagin
James Frew
Lisa Parks
Rita Raley
Ronald Rice
Richard Mayer
Matthew Turk

Recent Publications
Flanagin, A. J., Stohl, C., & Bimber, B. (2006). Modeling the structure of collective action. *Communication Monographs, 73,* 29–54.

Bimber, B., Flanagin, A. J., & Stohl, C. (2005). Reconceptualizing collective action in the contemporary media environment. *Communication Theory, 15,* 365–388.

Bimber, B. (2004, October 24–26). *The internet and political fragmentation.* Paper prepared for presentation at the *Democracy in the 21st Century* conference, University of Illinois, Urbana-Champaign; revised for forthcoming publication.

Bulger, M., Mayer, R., & Almeroth, K. (2006). Engaged by design: Using simulations to promote active learning. In E. Pearson & P. Bohman (Eds.), *Proceedings of world conference on educational multimedia, hypermedia and telecommunications 2006* (pp. 1770–1777). Chesapeake, VA: AACE.

Mayer, R., Almeroth, K., Bimber, B., Chun, D., Knight, A., & Campbell, A. (2006, March–April). Technology comes to college: Understanding the cognitive consequences of infusing technology in college classrooms. *Educational Technology, 46*(2), 48–53.

The Infoscape Research Lab, Ryerson University
350 Victoria Street, Toronto, Ontario, Canada M5B 2K3

The Infoscape Research Lab hosts research projects that focus on the cultural impact of digital code. The lab engages in software and other new media tool development, code mapping, interface design, and new media content analysis. The lab is funded in part with grants from the Social Science and Humanities Research Council of Canada and the Canadian Media Research Consortium.

Research Topics
Canadian Media, Digital Humanities, Informational Politics, New Media Studies.

Leading Members
Greg Elmer

Ken Werbin
Zach Devereaux
Ganaele Langlois
Peter Malachy Ryan
Elley M. Prior
Fenwich McKelvey
Andres Zelman

Recent Publications

Elmer, G., Ryan, P. M., Devereaux, Z., Langlois, G., Redden, J., & McKelvey, F. (2007). Election bloggers: Methods for determining political influence. *First Monday, 12*(4).

Elmer, G., & Opel, A. (2006). Pre-empting panoptic surveillance: Surviving the inevitable war on terror. In D. Lyon (Ed.), *Theorizing surveillance: The panopticon and beyond.* Cullompton: Willan Publishers.

Elmer, G., (2006). The vertical Net. In D. Silver et al. (Eds.), *Critical cyberculture studies: New directions.* New York, NY: NYU Press.

Elmer, G., & Opel, A. (2006). Surviving the inevitable future: Preemption in an age of faulty intelligence. *Cultural Studies 20*(3), 447–492.

Elmer, G., Devereaux, Z., & Skinner, D. (2006). Disaggregating Online News. *Scan: Journal of Media Arts Culture.*

The Center for the Study of the Information Society, University of Haifa
Mount Carmel, Haifa 31905

The Center is a unique, interdisciplinary forum of researchers and advanced gradu-ate scholars. It is a home to academics from various disciplines (computer science, history, communications, business, law, psychology, sociology, etc.). We meet to discuss various aspects of the information society, the technology that makes it hap-pen, and the interactions between society, information and technology. The center's activities include regular meetings, conventions, simulation development and a large variety of research.

Keywords

computer-mediated communication, internet, online behavior, virtual commu-nities, interactivity

Leading Members
Sheizaf Rafaeli
Azy Barak
Niva Elkin-Koren
Aharon Kellerman
Gad M. Landau
Sara Lev
Yael Maschler
Daphne Raban

Gilad Ravid
Rivka Ribak
Yael Steinhart
David Bodoff

Recent Research Projects/Publications
Israel Science Foundation Study of Government Information Provisions
Israeli Internet Association Study of Wiki structures

Rafaeli, S., & Ariel, Y. (2007). Assessing interactivity in computer-mediated research. In A. N. Joinson, K. Y. A. McKenna, T. Postmes, & U. D. Rieps (Eds.), *The Oxford handbook of internet psychology* (Chapter 6, pp. 71–88). Oxford: Oxford University Press.

Rafaeli, S., Raban, D. R., & Ravid, G. (2007). How social motivation enhances economic activity and incentives in the Google Answers knowledge sharing market. *International Journal of Knowledge and Learning (IJKL), 3*(1), 1–11.

Raban, D.R., & Rafaeli, S. (2007). Investigating ownership and the willingness to share information online, *Computers in Human Behavior, 23*, 2367–2382.

Ravid, G. Bar-Ilan, J. Baruchson-Arbib, S., & Rafaeli, S. (2007). Popularity and findability through log analysis of search terms and queries: The case of a multilingual public service website. *Journal of Information Science, 33*, 567.

Kalman, Y. M., Ravid, G., Raban, D. R., and Rafaeli, S. (2006). Pauses and response latencies: A chronemic analysis of asynchronous CMC. *Journal of Computer-Mediated Communication (JCMC), 12*(1), article 1.

Affiliated Centers
Center for Applied Computer Science, Center for Technology and Law, the Center for the Study of Organizations.

The Internet Governance Project, Syracuse University
School of Information Studies, 217 Hinds Hall, Syracuse University, Syracuse,
NY 13244 USA
http://www.internetgovernance.org

The Internet Governance Project (IGP) is a consortium of academics with scholarly and practical expertise in international governance, internet policy, and information and communication technology. The Project conducts research on and publishes analysis of global internet governance. The work is intended to contribute to policy discussions in the Internet Governance Forum, ICANN, WIPO, and related debates at the global, international, regional and national levels.

Keywords
Internet governance, global governance, public policy, institutions, freedom of expression, regulation, domain names, ICANN

Leading Members
  Milton Mueller
  John Mathiason
  Lee McKnight
  Derrick Cogburn
  Brenden Kuerbis
  Jeanette Hofmann
  Michel van Eeten

Recent Publications
  Mueller, M., et al. (2007). *Net neutrality as global principle for internet governance* (November 5). Internet Governance Project. Paper IGP07-003. Available from http://internetgovernance.org/pdf/ NetNeutralityGlobalPrinciple.pdf

  Network neutrality can serve as a globally applicable principle that can guide internet governance. The paper defines network neutrality as the right of internet users to access content, services and applications on the internet without interference from network operators or overbearing governments. It also encompasses the right of network operators to be reasonably free of liability for transmitting content and applications deemed illegal or undesirable by third parties.

  Kuerbis, B., & Mueller, M. (2007). *Securing the root: A proposal for distributing signing authority* (May 17). Internet Governance Project. Paper IGP07-002. Available from http://internetgovernance.org/pdf/ SecuringTheRoot.pdf

  A newly standardized protocol, DNS Security Extensions (DNSSEC), would make the internet's infrastructure more secure. In order to fully implement DNSSEC, the procedures for managing the DNS root must be revised. Therein lies an opportunity. In revising the root zone management procedures, we can develop a new solution that diminishes the impact of the legacy monopoly held by the U.S. government and avoids another contentious debate over unilateral U.S. control.

Affiliated Research Center
  The Convergence Center

Internet Interdisciplinary Institute, Universitat Oberta de Catalunya
Parc Mediterrani de la Tecnologia; Av canal Olimpic s/n, Edifici B3; 08860
CASTELLDEFELS (Barcelona) SPAIN

The Fundació per a la Universitat Oberta de Catalunya (FUOC, Foundation for the Open University of Catalonia) is the legal entity that encompasses the Universitat Oberta de Catalunya (UOC, Open University of Catalonia) and the IN3. Research is, alongside teaching, knowledge spread, and dissemination, one of the characteristics that defines, demarcates, and sets a university apart. The essence of the Universitat

Oberta de Catalunya, characterised for its intensive use of the full potential of information and communication technology (ICT), also sets the focus for research: the study of the effects of ICT on people, organisations and society in general, and its influence on the changes seen as we move from the industrial society to the information and knowledge society. The IN3, as a tool to catalyse research and innovation at the University, offers institutional and administrative support to all UOC researchers and teaching staff who take part in research projects. This support includes both academic and scientific aspects of the research, and aspects involving its management, monitoring, or promotion.

Keywords

research, information society, e-learning, e-governance, digital culture, e-law, new economy, networking technologies

Leading Members

Manuel Castells Olivan
Eduard Aibar Rubio
Julià Minguillón Alfonso
Albert Batlle Rubio

Recent Research Projects/Publications

Project Internet Catalonia. The Project Internet Catalonia is an interdisciplinary research programme on the information society in Catalonia that has been conducted by faculty and researchers at the Universitat Oberta de Catalunya's (UOC, Open University of Catalonia) Internet Interdisciplinary Institute (IN3). The first study focused on the transition to the network society in Catalonia, and it took place between 2001 and 2003. Between 2002 and 2007 six additional studies were carried out. These studies focused on the effects of ICT on the competitiveness and productivity of business firms, the use of the internet and computers in primary and secondary schools in Catalonia, the use of ICT in the Catalan university system, the e-administration and e-governance in Catalonia, the interaction between internet and Television in Catalonia, and the uses of internet in the health system of Catalonia. The results of the research have been made public and distributed over the internet, via the UOC's portal (www.uoc.edu), as well as published in books, articles in scientific journals and papers at academic meetings and professional seminars.

Castells, M. (2007). Communication, power and counter-power in the network society. *International Journal of Communication, 1*, 238–266.

Caballé, S. (2007). A Service-oriented platform for the enhancement and effectiveness of the collaborative learning process in distributed environments. *Lecture Notes in Computer Science, 4804*, 1.280–1.287. ISSN: 03029743.

Aibar, E., & Waksberg, A. (2007). Towards a network government? A critical analysis of current assessment methods for e-government. *Lecture Notes in Computer Science, 4656*, 330–331. ISSN: 03029743.

Marquès, J. M., Daradoumis, A., & Navarro, L. (2007). Middleware for self-sufficient online collaboration. *IEEE Internet Computing, 11*(2), 56–64. ISSN: 10897801.

Vilaseca, J., Jimenez, A. I., & Torrent, J. (2007). ICT use in marketing as innovation success factor: Enhancing cooperation in new product development process. *European Journal of Innovation Management, 10*(2), 268–288. ISSN: 14601060.

The Centre for Internet Research, University of Aarhus
Helsingforsgade 14, DK-8200 Aarhus N, Denmark
www.cfi.au.dk

The Centre for Internet Research was established on September 18, 2000, in order to promote research into the social and cultural implications and functions of the internet. The Centre for Internet Research is located at the Department of Information and Media Studies, University of Aarhus, Denmark.

The Centre for Internet Research encourages research in its field through a range of activities:

- serving as a meeting place and forum for local and international researchers who work with internet-related research within the humanities and social sciences;
- organising internal and external research seminars, conferences and other fora working for the endowment of Ph.D. stipends within the field of internet research;
- presenting research in the field through publications, lectures, teaching and other media;
- serving as a centre for knowledge about internet research through such activities as a documentation centre and a net portal;
- creating a network for the exchange of knowledge about the centre's research;
- collaborating on research projects with other research institutions;
- hosting national and international visiting scholars.

The Centre for Internet Research has taken part in several major national and international research projects, it has recently hosted Distinguished Professor Charles Ess from Drury University, Missouri, as a visiting Professor, and has organized seminars and conferences with the participation of, among others, Jay D. Bolter, Kevin Crowston, Sharon Strover, David Kolb, Lev Manovich and James Slevin. The Centre participated in the development of the National Danish Internet Archive, Netarkivet.dk, in collaboration with The Royal Library, Copenhagen, and The State, and University Library, Aarhus (2000–2005).

Research Topics

cross media studies, internet strategies, internet and the mass media, internet and cultural diversity, internet discourses and genres, internet archivation, internet history, theories of media, website analysis, organizational theory

Leading Members
Niels Brügger
Christian Dalsgaard
Vidar Falkenberg
Bo Fibiger
Niels Ole Finnemann
Ejvind Hansen
Per Jauert
Constance Kampf
Jakob Linaa Jensen
Anja Bechmann Petersen
Signe Herbers Poulsen
Jesper Tække

Recent Publications
Brügger, N. (2005). Archiving websites. *General Considerations and Strategies*. Aarhus: The Centre for Internet Research.
Finnemann, N. O. (2006). Public space and the co-evolution of digital and digitized media. *Media and Politics*. Joint Edition of *Tidsskriftet Politik, Vol. 9 no. 2, & Mediekultur No. 40*. Copenhagen.
Hansen, E. (2008). Det digitale spøgelse. In D. Kreutzfeldt, I. Sylvestersen, & E. Hansen (Eds.), *Digitale mellemværender* (108–130). Sweden: Forlaget Philosophia.
Dalsgaard, C. (2006). Social software: E-learning beyond learning management systems. *European Journal of Open, Distance and E-learning, 2006/II*.
Tække, J. (2005). Media sociography: On Usenet newsgroups. *Cybernetics And Human Knowing, 12*(4), 71–96.

Research Projects
The history of www.dr.dk, 1996–2006. Funded by The National Danish Research Council for Communication & Culture, 2007–2010.
Analysis of the Internet Mediated Public Sphere in Denmark. Supported by "The Knowledge Society" project, The Faculty of the Humanities, Aarhus University, 2007–2008.
Changing Borderlines in the Public Sphere: Mediatization & Citizenship. Funded by The National Danish Research Council for Communication & Culture, 2008–2011.
Deconstructive readings of the digital media. Funded by the Carlsberg Foundation.

Knowledge Media Design Institute, University of Toronto
40 St. George St. rm 7222, Toronto, ON M5S 2E4 Canada
http://kmdi.utoronto.ca

The Collaborative Program in Knowledge Media Design provides a specialization for graduate students from a variety of academic backgrounds to engage in the design, prototyping, evaluation, and use of media intended to enable individuals and groups to think, communicate, learn, and create knowledge. Since knowledge media are emergent and complex socio-technical phenomena, they do not fit neatly into any existing academic discipline. We seek to expose students from a wide range of backgrounds to new ways of understanding and developing knowledge media.

Students engage with KMDI's human-centered approach to design, an approach that puts people at the heart of its practice. Students are involved in the design and use of new media in the context of real world practices of individuals and communities. Access to our collaborative and cross-disciplinary faculty encourages students to take a broader view of technological and social change and to be constructively critical of both technological utopians and dystopians. Students to take into account heritage and history to understand the realities of today and to design for tomorrow. Students have access to a community of scholars and the network of relationships coordinated by the Institute; they gain first-hand experience of a living network of innovation and an environment in which the resources are people and knowledge and the social capital and value that are generated through collaboration.

Leading Members
Jim Slotta, Ontario Institute for Studies in Education
Gale Moore, Sociology
Andrew Clement, Faculty of Information Studies
Mark Chignell, Mechanical and Industrial Engineering
Joan Danahy, Architecture, Landscape and Design
Gerald Penn, Computer Science
Lisa Steele, History of Art/Visual Studies

Lansdown Centre for Electronic Arts, Middlesex University
Cat Hill, Barnet EN4 8HT UK
http://www.cea.mdx.ac.uk/

The Lansdown Centre leads research in areas where technology combines with creative activity. We investigate how technology transforms expression and interaction. The context is one where media technologies, including the web, are escaping the traditional desktop screen and becoming ubiquitous, pervasive, physical, multimodal, and social.

Research takes place at all levels: MA, M.Phil., Ph.D. and post-doctoral. Staff research feeds into the teaching of the Media Arts programmes. Staff and students exhibit, perform, publish and present work internationally.

Particular themes of the work are space and place, with several projects in locative media and spatialised sound, including the use of ambisonics; multidisciplinary work with health scientists, psychologist and computer scientists; several aspects of digital games; and DARE, a project-based analysis of how the internet may be used to introduce learners to new aspects of visual arts. Current PhD research includes eye-tracker analysis of screen-viewing and older people's access to communication technologies.

The Centre also hosts the Lansdown Lectures which deal with a wide range of issues arising from the relationship between technology and creative work. Speakers include Bill Gaver, Professor of Interaction Research at Goldsmiths London University; Scanner, independent artist; Prof. Harold Thimbleby, Professor of Computer Science at Swansea University; Per Mollerup, Professor at the Oslo National Academy of the Arts; Jennifer Sheridan, digital live artist and computer scientist; Paul Brown, Visiting Professor at the Centre for Computational Neuroscience and Robotics and Department of Informatics, University of Sussex; Mikael Wiberg, Associate Professor at the Department of Informatics, Umeå University, Sweden.

Research Topics
creative design, multimodality, HCI, advanced interaction, locative media, sonic arts, interactive media

Recent Research Projects/Publications
Locative Artwork

A world-first locative artwork used GPS and heart-rate to create a distributed experience in both single and multiplayer modes, the latter using GPRS for intercommunication with a web server. (see 'Ere be Dragons: Heartfelt Gaming 2006 in *Digital Creativity, 17*(3), 157–162. ISSN 1462-6268).

Locative Audio

This ongoing project is a series of locative audio works with the BBC, premiered at the Freethinking Festival in Liverpool in November 2007 (http://www.bbc.co.uk/radio3/freethinking/2007/festival-events/#).
"Can virtual environments enhance the learning of historical chronology?" Foreman, Boyd Davis, Moar, Korallo and Chappell. *Instructional Science.* Vol. 36, No. 2 (March 2008).

Learning Initiatives on Reforms for Network Economies, Communica Foundation
Dr. Pablo de Maria 1036, Montevideo, Uruguay

The LIRNE.NET mission is to facilitate telecom reform and infrastructure development throughout the world – through research, training, dialogue, policy, and regulatory advice; and to build human capital in the area as the foundation for effective regulation and governance for new network economies. LIRNE.NET is a global network with affiliates in Africa, Asia, the Americas and Europe.

Keywords
regulation, internet, policy, ICTs, access, pro-poor, networks, infrastructure

Leading Members
W.H. Melody
Amy Mahan
Bruce Girard
Alison Gillwald
Hernan Galperin
Rohan Samarajiva
Anders Henten

Recent Research Projects and Publications

Mahan, A. K., & Melody, W. H. (2007). *Diversifying participation in network development.* LIRNE.NET, IDRC and infoDev (World Bank). http://www.regulateonline.org/content/view/1044/63/
This report assesses different approaches to regulation in a rapidly changing telecom environment. With the advent of privatisation, competition, and converging infrastructure sectors, the role of the regulator is in a transitional phase. This report comprises research which considers these issues from the perspectives of: Affordability and Use, Models to Extend Participation in Network Development, and Regulatory and Information Practices.

Mahan, A. K., & Melody, W. H. (2005). *Stimulating investment in network development: Roles for regulators.* World Dialogue on Regulation (WDR), IDRC and infoDev (World Bank). http://www.regulateonline.org/content/view/435/65/
Traditionally, neither regulators, policymakers, industry players or analysts have considered that stimulating investment in network development is a priority goal of regulation. This report assesses different approaches to regulation in a rapidly changing telecom environment.

Henten, A., Samarajiva, R., & Melody, W. H. (2002). *Designing next generation telecom reform: ICT convergence or multisector utility? Research Cycle 1 Report.* http://www.regulateonline.org/content/view/215/64/
This report provides an assessment of evidence and a framework for analysis that will assist countries in examining the issues, options and implications, as they establish the policy objectives and design the structure of their particular next generation telecom regulation.

Affiliated Research Centers

DIRSI (Regional Dialogue on the Information Society for Latin America and the Caribbean – www.dirsi.net)
LINK Centre, Wits University, South Africa (http://link.wits.ac.za/)
Research ICT Africa (RIA! http://link.wits.ac.za/)
LIRNEasia (http://www.lirneasia.net)

Center for Information and Communication Technologies (CICT), at the Technical University of Denmark (http://www.cict.dtu.dk/)

Economics of Infrastructures Section, at Delft University of Technology (http://www.ei.tbm.tudelft.nl/)

Media@LSE Programme at the London School of Economics (http://www.lse.ac.uk/collections/medialse/)

Media@LSE, London School of Economics
Houghton Street, London WC2A 2AE UK
fd

Media@lse undertakes research and teaching at the interface between media, technology, and social change. We critically address key issues in the emerging digital world under five themes:

Innovation, Governance and Policy: Consequences of the uneven spread of technologies in the context of changing relationships among states, governments and the law, including 'digital divide' policies, international governance of new media/ICT and the dynamics of innovation, intellectual property rights, public service regulation, policy in changing media markets; financial market regulation and governance.

Democracy, Politics, and Journalism Ethics: Significance of media in the information environments of democratic societies, including participation in global social movements, mediation of suffering and journalism ethics, professionalisation and marketing of politics, and citizens' engagement in the changing public sphere.

Globalisation and Comparative Studies: Historical and current nature of mainstream and alternative media in national and comparative perspective, including cross-national contexts of mediated childhoods, television and film industries in India and China, global trends in media representations, transnational shifts in mediations of ethnicity, gender, human rights in India and USA, and global media, global news, post-communist, media, media history, and history of media studies.

Media and New Media Literacies: Potentially new literacies and identities associated with changing expressions of identity, including the aesthetics of mediation processes, adult and youthful responses to mediated risks and opportunities, ICT-related capabilities in low income countries, and the nature of story telling online.

Communication and Difference: Culture and everyday life, the politics of otherness, and the production of exclusion, drawing on traditions in post-colonial studies and innovation studies to critique contemporary communicative practices that give rise to perceptions of difference.

Keywords

innovation, governance, democracy, politics, globalisation, new media, literacy, journalism ethics, difference

Leading Members
  Robin Mansell
  Bart Cammaerts
  Lilie Chouliaraki
  Sonia Livingstone
  Bingchun Meng
  Shani Orgad
  Raka Shome
  Terhi Rantanen
  Damian Tambini

Recent Publications
  Couldry, N, Livingstone, S., & Markham, T. (2007). *Media consumption and public engagement: Beyond the presumption of attention.* Houndmills: Palgrave McMillan.
  Lievrouw, L., & Livingstone, S. (Eds.). (2006). *Handbook of new media: Social shaping and social consequences* (Fully revised student edition). London: Sage.
  Mansell, R., Avgerou, C., Quah, D., & Silverstone, R. (Eds.). (2007). *The Oxford handbook of information and communication technologies.* Oxford: Oxford University Press.
  Livingstone, S., & Magdalena Bober, M. (2005, April 28). *UK children go online: Final report of key project findings.* http://www.children-go-online.net/

Projects
  EU Kids Online (June 2006–June 2009). Sonia Livingstone and Leslie Haddon. http://www.eukidsonline.net/
  The project addresses European research on cultural, contextual, and risk issues in children's safe use of the internet and new media in 18 member states. Funded by the European Commission.
  Open Philosophies for Associative Autopoietic Digital Ecosystems (OPAALS) Network. (June 2006–May 2010). Paolo Dini and Robin Mansell. http://oks.opaals.org/website/
  Two overarching aims are to build an interdisciplinary research community in the emerging area of Digital Ecosystems (DE), and to develop an integrated theoretical foundation for Digital Ecosystems research spanning three different disciplinary domains: social science, computer science, and natural science. Funded by the European Commission.
  Mediation perspectives on digital storytelling among youth. (2006–2009). Sonia Livingstone. Funded by the Research Council of Norway. One of 20 networked researchers from Nordic countries, UK and USA.

Affiliated Research Centers
  POLIS

Center for Natural Language Processing, Syracuse University
School of Information Studies, 245 Hinds Hall, Syracuse University, Syracuse NY
13244
http://www.cnlp.org

The mission of the Center for Natural Language Processing is to advance the development of software capabilities with human-like language understanding of electronic text such as email, blogs, news text, and trouble tickets, for research, government, commercial, and consumer applications.

Keywords
natural language processing; information retrieval; information extraction; metadata generation; machine learning; text categorization

Leading Members
Anne R. Diekema
Ozgur Yilmazel

Recent Publications
DHB: Investigating the Dynamics of Free/Libre Open Source Software Development Teams – The team is investigating the dynamics through which Free/Libre Open Source Software (FLOSS) teams develop shared mental models, the norms and rules for interaction and work processes, and the ability to automatically code text using an NLP-based system.

Understanding the Connotative Meaning of Text – In this Aquaint project, the goal was to develop and test Natural Language Processing capabilities that can recognize, interpret, and characterize implicit levels of meaning in text without requiring human intervention.

Enhanced Access to Digital Humanities Monographs – this project aims to extend traditional indexing and retrieval methods to better research and discovery in e-books. NLP techniques are applied to utilize the rich, intellectually-viable information contained in tables of contents and back-of-the-book indexes, capitalizing on the internal structure of the book.

Improving Public Health Grey Literature Access for the Public Health Workforce – the broad, long-term objective of this NLM-funded project is to provide the public health workforce with improved access to high quality, highly relevant public health grey literature reports, and to positively impact the quality, effectiveness, and efficiency of planning, conducting, and evaluating public health interventions.

Computer-Assisted Content Standard Assignment & Alignment (CASAA) – The result of this NSF-funded project are two tools which (1) automatically suggest relevant educational standards for educational content and (2) automatically align state and national standards.

NEXA Research Center for Internet and Society, Politecnico di Torino
Corso Duca degli Abruzzi 24, 10129 Torino Italy
http://nexa.polito.it

Internet is a powerful technology, disruptive and generative at the same time. Founded in November 2006, the NEXA Research Center for Internet and Society of the Politecnico of Torino is an independent research center, focusing on quantitative and multidisciplinary analysis of the nature and possible directions of the versors of disruptiveness and generativeness that characterize the strength, a strength that can produce radical changes in the way reality is lived, perceived, organized, as well as trigger extraordinary opportunities for development.

As usual when facing new phenomena, the novelty and complexity of these changes, of their dynamics and of their interactions with development opportunities require significant efforts to revise concepts and research methodologies. Understanding the internet, its limitations and potentialities not only deserves such effort, but is indispensable to ensure economic, technical, scientific, cultural and political development for the years to come.

NEXA is born from the activities of a multidisciplinary group – with expertise in technology, law and economics – that grew up in Torino from 2003 and that has conceived, designed and implemented several initiatives, including Creative Commons Italy (2003–now), Harvard's Internet Law Program Torino 2005, SeLiLi (2006–now) and COMMUNIA, the European Commission-funded thematic network on the digital public domain (2007–2010).

NEXA aims to become one of the main center devoted to multidisciplinary internet research. In particular, NEXA wants to become a most relevant point of reference in Europe, interacting with the European Commission, regulators, local and national governments, as well as with business and other institutions.

Research Topics
Creative commons, network neutrality, digital archives, distributed creativity, intellectual property, commons-based peer production, law, economics, computer science, public domain.

Leading Members
Juan Carlos De Martin
Marco Ricolfi

Recent Research Projects
COMMUNIA (http://www.communia-project.eu/): coordination of the European Thematic Network on the public domain, funded by the European Union.
SeLiLi (http://selili.polito.it/): free legal and technological advice for creators and programmers want to use free software and free content licenses.

Creative Commons Italy Working Group (http://www.creativecommons.it/): the official team that translates and maintains the Italian version of Creative Commons licenses.

OpenNet Initiative (http://www.opennet.net/): the Italian analysis of the international project.

Oxford Internet Institute, University of Oxford
St Giles, Oxford, OX1 3JS, UK
www.oii.ox.ac.uk

The Oxford Internet Institute was founded as a department of the University of Oxford in 2001, as an academic centre of excellence for the study of the societal implications of the internet. Our research faculty, academic visitors and students are engaged in a variety of research projects covering social, economic, political, legal, industrial, technical and ethical issues of the internet in everyday life, governance and democracy, science and learning and shaping the internet.

We offer a Doctoral degree (DPhil) in Information, Communication and the Social Sciences and hope to offer an MSc in Social Science of the internet for entry in 2009. Around thirty top doctoral students from around the world congregate every year to attend our Summer Doctoral Programme,

We run a wide variety of academic and policy-oriented lectures, seminars, forums and conferences, involving leading figures in academia and other sectors, many of which are webcast.

Research Topics
The internet in everyday life, Governance and democracy, Science and learning, Shaping the internet.

Leading Members
William Dutton
Helen Margetts
Jonathan Zittrain
Ian Brown
Paul David
Rebecca Eynon
Ellen Helsper
Eric T. Meyer
Victoria Nash
Ralph Schroeder
Judy Wajcman
Yorick Wilks

Recent Research Projects
Companions (http://www.companions-project.org/): Companions aims to change the way we think about the relationships of people to computers and

the internet by developing a virtual conversational 'Companion'. The project is led by Professor Yorick Wilks and consists of a consortium of 14 partners from across Europe and the US.

Oxford Internet Surveys (http://www.oii.ox.ac.uk/microsites/oxis/): Internet Survey (OxIS) research is designed to offer detailed insights into the influence of the internet on everyday life in Britain. OxIS is an authoritative source of information about internet access, use and attitudes.

Networks for Web Science (http://www.oii.ox.ac.uk/research/project.cfm?id= 4): Web Science brings together computer scientists and engineers, social scientists and policy makers to study complex information systems as personified by the web. The aim of this proposal is to establish networks of researchers from different technical and social science research disciplines to begin to develop a Web Science research agenda.

OpenNet Initiative (http://opennet.net): The OpenNet Initiative is a collaborative partnership of four leading academic institutions. The aim is to investigate, expose and analyze internet filtering and surveillance practices in a credible and non-partisan fashion.

Breaking Barriers to eGovernment (http://www.egovbarriers.org): The European Commission funded a three year project to investigate the legal, organisational, technological and other barriers to expanding effective eGovernment services using the internet and to define possible solutions at a European level to overcome such obstacles.

POLIS, London School of Economics
Houghton Street, London WC2A 2AE
www.lse.ac.uk/collections/media@lse

A joint initiative established in 2006 with the University of the Arts London/London College of Communication, POLIS is a public forum to debate the present and future of journalism, to work on policy, to undertake research and to deliver short courses to mid-career journalists. The origin of the word POLIS is the idea of the 'city-state'. The Greek Polis was the site of debate, discussion of current affairs and political judgement. It was where private individuals became citizens. The name POLIS refers to the continuing centrality of public debate for national and global citizenship and the continuing centrality of the news media for its 21st century manifestation. POLIS is aimed at working journalists, people in public life and students in the UK and around the world. It is the place where journalists and the wider world can examine and discuss the media and its impact on society.

Keywords
Journalism, News Media, New Media, Ethics

Leading Members
Charlie Beckett
Lilie Chouliaraki

Recent Research Projects/Publications
> Beckett, C., & Kyrke-Smith, L. (Eds.). (2007). *Development, governance and the media: The role of the media in building African society.* London: POLIS.

Affiliated Research Centers
> Media@LSE

Center for Research on Collaboratories and Technology Enhanced Learning Communities, Syracuse University
School of Information Studies, 339 Hinds Hall, Syracuse University,
Syracuse NY 13244
http://cotelco.syr.edu/

The Center for Research on Collaboratories and Technology Enhanced Learning Communities (Cotelco) is a social science research center in the School of Information Studies (http://ischool.syr.edu) at Syracuse University (http://cotelco.syr.edu). Cotelco is also an affiliated center of the Burton Blatt Institute: Centers of Innovation on Disability (http://bbi.syr.edu). Our broad research agenda uses mixed-methods approaches to investigate three inter-related themes. The first theme takes an interdisciplinary social science approach to explore the institutional mechanisms for global governance and international regime formation for the internet and information and communication technology, with a particular focus on epistemic communities and transnational policy networks. Applied, use-inspired research drives the second theme, which focuses on designing, implementing, and evaluating accessible cyberinfrastructure, collaboratories and virtual organizations to support geographically distributed collaboration at national and international levels. Finally, the third theme integrates lessons learned from these streams into an exploration of geographically distributed collaborative learning environments. The Cotelco research agenda has been supported by diverse public, private, and international sources, including: National Science Foundation, National Institute for Disability and Rehabilitation Research, W.K. Kellogg Foundation, Markle Foundation, World Bank, UNESCO, European Union, Danish International Development Agency, Microsoft Research, Cisco Systems, and Hewlett-Packard. In 2002, John Chambers, CEO of Cisco Systems, nominated Cotelco for a Computerworld Honors Award (also known as the Smithsonian Innovation Award) for its contribution to building the Information Society. A case study on Cotelco is on deposit in the Smithsonian Institution in Washington, DC and in museums and archives around the world (http://www.cwheroes.org).

Keywords
> Global internet governance; Transnational civil society policy networks; Multistakeholder participation in global governance; Cyberinfrastructure and virtual organizations; Computer-mediated communication in knowledge work;

Development of trust in virtual organizations; Geographically distributed collaborative learning communities; Cross-cultural collaboration in virtual teams

Leading Members
Derrick L. Cogburn
Benjamin Kwasi Addom
David James
Dr. Norhayati Zakaria
Fatima Espinoza
Andrew Bennett
Sara Frewen
Jane Finnerup Johnsen
Charles Lewis

Centre for Research in Media, Information, Communication and Society (ReMICS)
Department of Sociology, University of Surrey, Guildford, Surrey GU2 7XH UK
www.soc.surrey.ac.uk/

Launched in 2008, and located within the Department of Sociology, University of Surrey, the ReMICS centre for Research in Media, Information, Communication and Society conducts high quality, international scholarship and substantively grounded research into the social and cultural aspects of new media and digital technologies.

Focusing on the importance of information and communication technologies in contemporary societies, the centre engages in critical, theoretically informed, and empirically focused research into a wide range of socio-economic, technological, political and cultural aspects of digital media, and information and communication practices. ReMICS members are involved in a diverse range of projects, including interdisciplinary research in collaboration with academic, commercial and regulatory partners, as well as projects funded by the EU, ESRC, and DTI. The thematic focus of members' projects ranges from new media and everyday life, to digital surveillance, the social contexts and impacts of social networking media and internet technologies, e-science and grid technology, cyberscience, mobile communications, media and the arts, digital technologies and criminal justice, and new media methods. Their shared intention is to bring a range of disciplinary traditions to the critical understanding of contemporary digital media, information and communication technologies, and their conception, design, dissemination, contexts and uses.

Research Topics
Virtual methods, digital surveillance, social networking, mobile communications, new media and the arts, cyberscience, E-science and grid technology, digital technologies and criminal justice, new media and everyday life, new media and popular culture.

Leading Members
   Victoria Alexander
   Geoff Cooper
   Nigel Gilbert
   Nicola Green
   Christine Hine
   Paul Hodkinson
   Nigel Fielding
   Paul Johnson

Recent Publications/Projects
   Brown, B., Green, N. & Harper, R. (Eds.). (2002). *Wireless world: Social, cultural and interactional issues in mobile communications and computing.* London: Springer-Verlag.
   Hine, C. (2000). *Virtual ethnography.* London: Sage.
   Hine, C. (2008). *Systematic as cyberscience.* Cambridge, MA: MIT Press.
   Hodkinson, P. (2007). Interactive online journals and individualisation. *New Media and Society, 9*(4), 625–650.

European Indicators, Cyberspace and the Science-Technology-Economy System (EICSTES), an EU funded research project led by Nigel Gilbert, to develop indicators of how the Science-Technology-Economy system is being affected by the growth of the internet.

Affiliated Centres
Digital World Research Centre

Convergence Center, Syracuse University
School of Information Studies, Newhouse School of Public Communications, 217 Hinds Hall, Syracuse University, Syracuse NY, 13244
http://dcc.syr.edu/index.htm

The Convergence Center supports research on and experimentation with media convergence. The Center is a joint effort of the Syracuse University School of Information Studies and the Newhouse School of Public Communications . Its mission is to understand the future of digital media and to engage students and faculty in defining and shaping that future.

Keywords
   Digital convergence, internet economy, telecommunication industry, public policy, mobile handset

Leading Members
   Milton Mueller
   Steve Masiclat

Derrick Cogburn
Lee McKnight
Martha Garcia-Murillo
David Molta

Recent Research Projects and Publications

Broadcast-Telecommunications Convergence and its Impact on U.S. Regulation and Market Structure, January 31, 2008. Project sponsor: Electronics and Telecommunications Research Institute, Republic of Korea. Principal Investigators: Milton Mueller, Martha Garcia-Murillo, Dave Molta. Research Assistants: Hesham Sayed, Manish Dhyani, M.S. candidates, School of Information Studies. How broadcast content is moving to the internet.

Digital Cameras and Expanding Mobile Handset Functions : Competing Value Chains in the Consumer Imaging Industry

The Role of Camera-Bundled Image Management Software (IMS) in the Consumer Digital Imaging Value Chain. Milton Mueller, Anu Mundkur, Ashok Balasubramanian, Virat Chirania, August 2004

Reinventing Media Activism: Public Interest Advocacy in the Making of U.S. Communication-Information Policy, 1960-2002. Milton Mueller, Brenden Kuerbis, and Christiane Page. July 2004.

Research Institute for Media, Art and Design, University of Bedfordshire
School of Media, Art & Design, University of Bedfordshire, Park Square,
Luton LU1 3JU, IK
www.beds.ac.uk/research/rimad

The Research Institute for Media, Art and Design (RIMAD) supports research initiatives in media art and design within the University of Bedfordshire, UK. The editorial office of the international refereed journal, *Convergence: The International Journal of Research into New Media Technologies* is partially based within the Institute. Convergence has an international editorial board, with members drawn from Europe, Australia, USA, Canada, Hong Kong and Japan, and it has subscribers world-wide. The journal acts as a bridge between the research work of the staff and postgraduate students of the Institute and the wider community of scholars.

RIMAD has research specialisations in new media, cross-media integration, political communication, journalism, sport and the media, post-Jungian psychology and screen-based media, community media and new media writing.

Research Topics
Aesthetics, publishing, journalism, gaming

Leading Members
Alexis Weedon
Garry Whannel
Ivor Gaber

Jon Silverman
Luke Hockley
Gavin Stewart

Center for Technology and Social Behavior, Northwestern University
Frances Searle Building, 2240 Campus Drive, 2-431, Evanston, IL USA 60208
http://ctsb.northwestern.edu

The Center for Technology and Social Behavior gathers researchers from across Northwestern University and beyond to study and participate in technological developments in their broadest possible contexts. It is a central goal of the center to support researchers in their quest to understand the role that technology plays in our everyday social interactions, and to facilitate the development of the next generation of technologies that will work towards supporting positive social ends.

To address these goals, the center brings together an interdisciplinary mix of researchers from disciplines as diverse as communication, computer science, engineering, history, interaction design, learning sciences, visual arts, psychology and sociology. The center hosts a monthly speaker seminar series that brings internationally renowned speakers to Northwestern, provides support to graduate students and post-docs studying at the intersection of technology and social behavior, oversees shared facilities to support research studies and technology development, provides physical space for meetings, funds interdisciplinary undergraduate research opportunities, and in general aims to nurture connections between researchers from complementary disciplines. A number of the researchers and students also participate in a new joint Ph.D program in Technology and Social Behavior prepares students for a wide range of academic and industrial research jobs.

Research Topics
Online communities, trust in mediated communication, CMC, culturally-sensitive software development, innovative technologies for autism, human–computer interaction, multimodal communication, computer supported cooperative work, digital divide, interpersonal perception.

Leading Members
Justine Cassell

Recent Publications
Cassell, J., & Cramer, M. (2007). "Hi tech or high risk? Moral panics about girls online". In T. MacPherson (Ed.), *Digital youth, innovation, and the unexpected: The MacArthur Foundation Series on Digital Media and Learning* (pp. 53–75). Cambridge, MA: MIT Press.

Pardo, B. (2006). Music information retrieval. *Communications of the ACM, 49*(8), 29–31. Horswill, Ian (2007).

Magerko, B. & Riedl, M. O. (Eds.). *Psychopathology, narrative, and cognitive architecture (or: why NPCs should be just as screwed up as we are)*. Proceedings of the AAAI Fall Symposium on Intelligent Narrative Technologies.

Hollingshead, A. B. & Contractor, N. S. (2006).

New Media and Small Group Organizing. In S. Livingstone & L. Lievrouw (Eds.), *Handbook of new media: Student edition* (pp. 114–133). London: Sage.

Gergle, D., Rosé, C. P., & Kraut, R. E. (2007). "Modeling the impact of shared visual information on collaborative reference," In *Proceedings of CHI 2007* (pp. 1543–1552). New York, NY: ACM Press.

School of Information, The University of California, Berkeley
102 South Hall, Berkeley, CA USA 94720-4600
www.ischool.berkeley.edu

Research by faculty members and doctoral students keeps the iSchool on the vanguard of contemporary information needs and solutions. To facilitate the transformation of information into knowledge, our research incorporates insights into the social, aesthetic, and technical design of information systems.

Current faculty projects include developing user-friendly interfaces, new approaches to security and privacy, economically informed design of peer-to-peer networks, and context-aware mobile media technology. Meanwhile, our Ph.D. candidates – often in collaboration with faculty members —are conducting research to advance the fields of information search, retrieval, organization, use, and policy. Both faculty and Ph.D. research projects demonstrate the iSchool's hallmark interdisciplinary perspective.

Research Topics
Human–computer interaction, Information security, Information privacy, Information economics, User interface design, Search and retrieval, Information policy and regulation, Technology in developing areas, Document engineering.

Leading Members
  Yale Braunstein
  Jenna Burrell
  Coye Cheshire
  John Chuang
  Paul Duguid
  Robert Glushko
  Marti Hearst
  Mitch Kapor
  Ray Larson
  Clifford Lynch
  Geoffrey Nunberg
  Tapan Parikh
  Kimiko Ryokai

Pamela Samuelson
AnnaLee Saxenian
Doug Tygar
Nancy Van House
Hal Varian

Information Institute of Syracuse, Syracuse University
School of Information Studies, Syracuse University, 211 Hinds Hall,
Syracuse University, Syracuse, NY 13244
http://iis.syr.edu

The Information Institute of Syracuse (IIS) is a library science think tank. It both constructs and funds its own research agenda as well as serving as an umbrella organization for a number of highly visible and widely successful digital education information services. The agenda of the Institute is one of science, to better understand how information can enrich the lives of people, as well as an activist agenda to improve libraries and their positions in society.

Keywords
digital libraries, librarianship, participatory networks, gaming

Leading Members
R. David Lankes
Scott Nicholson

Recent Research Projects and Publications

Exploring the Social Internet – Funded by the American Library Association, the project will research and create a detailed technology brief on the topic of the social internet, with emphasis on interactive and social web applications such as blogs, social networks, and include a survey of the "Web 2.0" and "Library 2.0 " development world.

"Participatory Networks: The Library as Conversation." Lankes, R. David, Silverstein, J. L., Nicholson, S. (forthcoming). *Information Technology and Libraries.*

Credibility Commons (MacArthur Foundation) – an experimental environment enabling individuals the opportunity to try out different approaches to improving access to credible information on the world wide web. The Commons can be viewed as a collaborative space in which to share ideas, data sets, results and innovations.

"Trusting the Internet: New Approaches to Credibility Tools". Lankes, R. David (Forthcoming). In MacArthur Digital Media Series, *Digital Media, Youth, and Credibility.* MIT Press.

Nicholson, S. (2007). *The Role of Gaming in Libraries: Taking the Pulse*. White paper available at http://librarygamelab.org/pulse2007.pdf

Tilburg Institute for Law, Technology, and Society, Tilburg University
P.O.box 90153, 50000 LE Tilburg, Netherlands
www.tilburguniversity.nl/faculties/law/research/tilt

TILT's research programme is entitled: 'Regulation in the Information Society: The Interaction of Law, Technology (in Particular ICT and Biotechnology), and Social Structures'. It focuses on re-orienting legal systems, regulatory structures, and enforcement mechanisms in light of technological developments. Attention is given to various dilemmas to balance societal interests, for example, security versus privacy and freedom versus ownership of information. By using the research results from the perspectives of law, technology, and social values and relationships as building blocks, TILT aims at creating a normative framework for the regulation of technology. Professors Bert-Jaap Koops, Han Somsen, and Corien Prins are the programme managers.

Research Topics
Privacy, security, e-commerce, e-government, e-health, identity management, cyber crime, intellectual property, genetics regulation, propertization and regulation.

Leading Members
    B.J. (Bert-Jaap) Koops
    J.E.J. (Corien) Prins
    H. (Han) Somsen
    C. (Kees) Stuurman

Recent Research Projects and Publications
    Koops, B. J., Lips, A. M. B., Prins, J. E. J., & Schellekens, M. H. M. (2006). *Starting points for ICT regulation; Deconstructing prevalent policy one-liners*. The Hague: TMC Asser Press (IT & Law, 9).
    Leenes, R. E., & Fischer-Hubner, S. (2006). *PRIME framework V2. EU: PRIME; privacy and identity management for Europe*. For more information: http://www.prime-project.eu
    Prins, J. E. J., & Schellekens, M. H. M. (2006). *Unreliable information on the internet: a challenging dilemma for the law. ICES, Journal for Information, Communication and Ethics in Society*, 4(1), 45–59.
    Koops, B. J., & Brenner, S. (2006). *Cybercrime and Jurisdiction; A global survey*. Den Haag: TMC Asser Press (IT & Law, 11).
    Vedder, A. et al. (2007) "NGO Involvement in International Governance and Policy: Sources of Legitimacy." Leiden: Brill/Martinus Nijhoff, 2007. (Nijhoff Law Specials 72; Paperback, 245pp, ISBN 978 90 04 15846 7)

The Internet Governance Project
School of Information Studies, 217 Hinds Hall, Syracuse University, Syracuse, NY 13244
www.internetgovernance.org

The Internet Governance Project (IGP) is a consortium of academics with scholarly and practical expertise in international governance, internet policy, and information and communication technology. The Project conducts research on and publishes analysis of global internet governance. The work is intended to contribute to policy discussions in the Internet Governance Forum, ICANN, WIPO, and related debates at the global, international, regional and national levels.

Keywords
Internet governance, global governance, public policy, institutions, freedom of expression, regulation, domain names, ICANN

Leading Members
  Milton Mueller
  John Mathiason
  Lee McKnight
  Derrick Cogburn
  Brenden Kuerbis
  Jeanette Hofmann
  Michel van Eeten

Recent Research Projects and Publications
  Mueller, M. et al. (2007). *Net neutrality as global principle for internet governance* (November 5). Internet Governance Project. Paper IGP07-003. Available from http://internetgovernance.org/pdf/NetNeutralityGlobal Principle.pdf
  Kuerbis, B. & Mueller, M. (2007). *Securing the root: A proposal for distributing signing authority* (May 17). Internet Governance Project. Paper IGP07-002. Available from http://internetgovernance.org/pdf/ SecuringTheRoot.pdf

Affiliated Research Centers
  The Convergence Center

Centre for Material Digital Culture, University of Sussex
Department of Media and Film, Education Development Building, University of Sussex, Falmer, Brighton, BN1 9RG UK
www.sussex.ac.uk/rcmdc

The Centre aims to provide an organizing context within which depth studies can be conducted while also acting as a framework for collaboration and cross-fertilization for the study of new media forms within and beyond the boundaries of media studies. With this goal in mind we have an ongoing programme of speakers and events designed to provoke connection, investigate developments in the field, encourage the development of shared research programmes on a local, national and international level. We house a community of researchers, PhD work, post-doctoral research, and the Masters Programme in Digital Media. We welcome offers of collaboration, indications of interest in shared projects, and suggestions for the sustained exchange of ideas.

The Centre is multi-disciplinary but it also has a core concern and a disciplinary home. We feel that there is something valuable about maintaining at the heart of a project concerning new media a tradition and an insistence on exploring processes of mediation, which we take to be at once material and symbolic. So our initial aim is to re-connect media studies – and film studies – with forms of thinking that have traditionally been marginal to the discipline, but which have been more centrally concerned with thinking through early techno-culture: in particular medium theory, cultural geography, and science and technology studies (STS). We would also like to critically engage with developing and established forms of technocultural theory.

Keywords
> Materiality
> Sense perception
> Narrative
> Sexualities
> New Media Ethnographies
> Networked Culture
> Convergence
> Media theory
> Digital humanities

Leading Members
> Michael Bull
> Kate Lacey
> Kate O'Riordan
> Dolores Tierney
> Andrew Duff
> Mary Agnes Krell
> Sharif Mowlabocus
> Martin Spinelli
> Lizzie Thynne
> Sue Thornham
> Ben Highmore
> Jerome Hansen
> Cate Thomas
> Alison Bambridge
> Iqbal Akhtar

Trine Bjørkmann Berry
Beth Granter
Alan D-Aiello
Giota Aleviziou
Paolo Oprandi
Jinnie Chae
Frauke Behrendt
Nikki Strange

Listing of Recent Research Projects/Publications

Bassett, C. (2007). *The arc and the machine: Narrative and new media.* Manchester: MUP.

Bassett, C., Hartmann, M. & O'Riordan, K. (Eds.). (2008). After convergence what connects. Fibreculture. 13, 2008.

Bull, M. (2007). *Sound moves. iPod culture and urban experience.* New York, NY: Routledge.

O'Riordan, K. & Phillips, D. (Eds.). (2007). *Queer online: Media technology and sexuality.* New York, NY: Peter Lang.

Digital Media: European Perspectives. Ongoing network project in collaboration with the European Communication Research and Education Association.

Center for Research in Computing and the Arts, University of California, San Diego
9500 Gilman Drive, Malicode 0037, La Jolla, CA 92093-0037
http://crca.uscd.edu

CRCA is an Organized Research Unit of the University of California. Our mission is to foster the invention of new art forms that arise out of the developments of digital technologies. Founded originally as the Center for Music Experiment in 1972, it has expanded to include work in virtual reality, computer games, digital cinema, spatialized audio, networked multimedia, interactive performance, live performance techniques for computer music and graphics, and other media forms.

CRCA researchers include artists, engineers and scientists at UCSD as well as industry partners and collaborators at other institutions. We cultivate work by UCSD faculty, visiting artists, staff, graduate students, and undergraduate students by developing partnerships and through use of our specialized facilities, which include 3D Fabrication, Experimental Gaming, Spatialized Audio, Virtual Environments, Motion Capture, Digital Cinema and Performative Computing. Our researchers work together to research and develop innovative methodologies, engage the field of critical discourse, and explore cultural forms transformed by the diverse field of computing and the arts.

Keywords
New Media Art

Multimedia
Virtual Reality
Spatialized Audio
Computer Games
Interactive Performance
Digital Cinema
Computer Music

Leading Members of the Center

Miller Puckette
Adriene Jenik
Lev Manovich
Roger Reynolds
Noah Wardrip-Fruin
Philippe Manoury
Shahrokh Yadegari
Harold Cohen
F. Richard Moore
Amy Alexander

The Scalable City by Sheldon Brown.
A virtual urban environment created via a data visualization pipeline. Each step
builds upon the previous, amplifying exaggerations, artifacts and the patterns of algorithmic process. This results in multiple artworks such as prints,
video installations, interactive multi-user games and virtual environments.
http://www.sheldon-brown.net/scalable/
The Theory and Technique of Electronic Music by Miller Puckette.
The first book to develop both the theory and the practice of synthesizing musical sounds using computers. Each article starts with a theoretical description
of a technique or problem and ends with a series of working examples
which cover a wide range of applications. http://www.worldscibooks.com/
compsci/6277.html
Software Studies Initiative by Lev Manovich and Noah Wardrip-Fruin.
Software Studies is a new initiative shaping the research field for intellectual
inquiry and projects surrounding how to effectively study "software society," bringing the software layer to the forefront in discussions of IT and its
cultural and social effects by examining the programs and social cultures that
produce technological artifacts. http://softwarestudies.com
SPECFLIC by Adriene Jenik.
SPECFLIC is an ongoing creative research project in a new storytelling form
called Distributed Social Cinema which seeks to integrate communication
gadgets (cell phones, laptops, etc.) with live telematic performance, pre-
recorded media elements, street performers and the audience's own social
activity to create a multi-modal story event. http://www.specflic.net/

Affiliated Research Centers
California Institute for Telecommunications and Information Technology

Centre for Research in Learning and Change, University of Technology, Sydney
Building 10, Jones Street, Ultimo NSW 2007, Australia
www.research.uts.edu/strenghts/rlc/overview.html

This program seeks to understand the educational worth of diverse kinds of engagement with emerging digital cultures. It is concerned with understanding changes in learning through authentic use of technologies. The research is underpinned by, socio-cultural and generative learning theories. The program addresses the increasing dissonance between formal and informal learning environments with a view to making a significant contribution to enhancing the learning of students and teachers, individuals, schools and communities, locally and globally, in our era and beyond.

Research in the *Learning and Teaching in a Digital Age* program explores the implications of online social networking for teaching and learning at all levels – primary, secondary, tertiary and adult education. The program is focused on understanding internet use from the perspective of both educators and learners. Our research also explores the authentic use of the internet outside formal education settings to uncover the impact of the internet on cognition, socialisation and cultural development.

The scope of our projects is broad to reflect the multiple applications for the internet in education. The research methodologies employed by the Program's researchers are varied to reflect traditional research approaches while integrating new online research methods. The integration of online and offline ethnography is key to our work. Specific online methods of data collection such as online surveys, eJournals and content analysis of online materials are carefully integrated into our research designs. With this, comes a new range of ethical issues and the research team is particularly interested in the development of ethical guidelines for researching online communities.

Keywords
designs for learning with new media, ICT in education, online social networking, e-learning, teacher education, pedagogy using digital tools, young digital learners, professional development of teachers using digital tools, e-mentoring, ethical online research

Leading Members
Sandy Schuck
Lynette Schaverien
Peter Aubusson
Matthew Kearney
Kirsty Young

Recent Research Projects/Publications

> Young, K. (2008). Toward a model for the study of children's informal internet use. *Computers in Human Behavior. Special Edition, 24*, 173–184.
>
> Schuck, S., & Kearney, M. (2006). Using digital video as a research tool: Ethical issues for researchers. *Journal of Educational Multimedia and Hypermedia, 15*(4), 447–463.
>
> Schuck, S., (2003). Help wanted, please! Supporting beginning teachers through an electronic mentoring community. In D. Lassner & C. McNaught (Eds.), *Proceedings of Ed-media 2003 world conference on educational multimedia, hypermedia and telecommunications* (pp. 1904–1911). Norfolk, VA: Association for the Advancement of Computing in Education.

StudyResponse Center for Online Research, Syracuse University

School of Information Studies, 315 Hinds Hall, Syracuse University, Syracuse NY 13244

http://studyresponse.syr.edu/studyresponse/

The StudyResponse project in the School of Information Studies at Syracuse University facilitates online social science research by distributing research participation requests to adult research participants. To date, StudyResponse has facilitated more than 250 studies for researchers at more than 50 universities in the U.S., Canada, U.K., Australia, and New Zealand. Project researchers have generated an annual workshop, seven technical reports, and three conference papers specifically about the project as well as dozens of substantive research articles published in social science journals.

Keywords

> Surveys, Online research, Nonresponse

Leading Members

> Jeffrey Stanton
> Alecia Santuzzi
> Agnieszka Kwiatkowska

Recent Research Projects and Publications

> Rogelberg, S. G., & Stanton, J. M. (2007). Understanding and dealing with organizational survey nonresponse. *Organizational Research Methods, 10*, 195–209.
>
> Stanton, J. M., & Rogelberg, S. G. (2002). Beyond online surveys: Internet research opportunities for industrial-organizational psychology. In S. G. Rogelberg (Ed.), *Handbook of research methods in industrial and organizational psychology* . Oxford: Blackwell.

Rogelberg, S. G., Church, A. H., Waclawski, J., & Stanton, J. M. (2002). Organizational survey research: Overview, the internet/intranet and present practices of concern. In S. G. Rogelberg (Ed.), *Handbook of research methods in industrial and organizational psychology.* Oxford: Blackwell.

Stanton, J. M., & Rogelberg, S. G. (2001). Using internet/intranet web pages to collect organizational research data. *Organizational Research Methods, 4,* 199–216.

Stanton, J. M. (1998). An empirical assessment of data collection using the Internet. *Personnel Psychology, 51,* 709–725.

Author Index

Subject Index